PUBLISHED ON BEHALF OF
THE INTERNATIONAL SOCIETY OF FAMILY LAW

THE INTERNATIONAL SURVEY OF FAMILY LAW

2002 EDITION

General Editor

Andrew Bainham

Fellow of Christ's College, Cambridge
Lecturer in Law, University of Cambridge, UK

Associate Editor (Africa)
Bart Rwezaura
Associate Professor of Law
University of Hong Kong
Hong Kong

Associate Editor (Asia)
Savitri Goonesekere
Vice-Chancellor
University of Colombo
Sri Lanka

Family Law

Published by Family Law
a publishing imprint of
Jordan Publishing Limited
21 St Thomas Street
Bristol
BS1 6JS

British Library Cataloguing-in-Publication Data

A catalogue record for this book is available from the British Library.

ISBN 0 85308 767 9

This volume is produced in-house by Jordans.
Printed in Great Britain by MPG Books Ltd, Bodmin, Cornwall

THE INTERNATIONAL SURVEY OF FAMILY LAW

PUBLISHED ON BEHALF OF
THE INTERNATIONAL SOCIETY OF FAMILY LAW

PRESIDENT
Professor Lynn D Wardle
School of Law, 518 JRCB
Brigham Young University
Provo, UT 84602
USA
Tel: +1(801) 378-2617
Fax: +1(801) 378-5893
e-mail: Wardlel@lawgate.byu.edu

SECRETARY-GENERAL
Professor Gillian Douglas
Cardiff Law School
PO Box 427
Cardiff CF10 3XJ
Wales, UK
Tel: +44 (0)29 2087 4704
Fax: +44 (0)29 2087 4097
e-mail: DouglasG@cardiff.ac.uk

TREASURER
Professor Paul Vlaardingerbroek
Tilburg University
Postbus 90153
5000 LE Tilburg
The Netherlands
Tel: +31-13-466 2032/466 2281
Fax: +31-13-466 2323
e-mail: P.Vlaardingerbroek@kub.nl

EDITOR OF THE INTERNATIONAL SURVEY
Dr Andrew Bainham
Christ's College
Cambridge University
Cambridge CB2 3BU
England
Tel: +44 (0)1223 33 4978
Fax: +44 (0)1223 33 4967
e-mail: ab10030@cam.ac.uk

IMMEDIATE PAST PRESIDENT: Professor Petar Sarcevic, Croatia

VICE PRESIDENTS

Professor Michael Freeman, UK
Professor Peter Lodrup, Norway
Professor Bea Verschraegen, Austria/Germany

Professor Olivier Guillod, Switzerland
Professor Nigel Lowe, UK

EXECUTIVE COUNCIL 2000–2002

Margaret Brinig (USA), Ruth Deech (UK), John Dewar (Australia), William Duncan (Ireland and the Netherlands), Olga Dyuzheva (Russia), John Eekelaar (UK), Rainer Frank (Germany), Marsha Garrison (USA), Dominique Goubau (Canada), Maarit Jantera-Jareborg (Sweden), Sanford Katz (USA), Miroslava Gec-Korosec (Slovenia), Eduardo de Oliviera Leite (Brazil), Miguel Martin Casals (Spain), Marygold Melli (USA), Marie-Thérèse Meulders (Belgium), Thandabantu Nhlapo (South Africa), Linda Nielsen (Denmark), Koji Ono (Japan), Maria Donata Panforti (Italy), Stephen Parker (Australia), Patrick Parkinson (Australia), Bart Rwezaura (Hong Kong and China), Jacqueline Rubellin-Devichi (France), June Sinclair (South Africa), Barbara Bennett Woodhouse (USA)

Bank Account: Postbank, Amsterdam, The Netherlands 63.18.019

A   THE HISTORY OF THE SOCIETY

On the initiative of Professor Zeev Falk, the Society was launched at the University of Birmingham, UK in April 1973. The Society's first international conference was held in West Berlin in April 1975 on the theme *The Child and the Law*. There were over 200 participants, including representatives of governments and international organisations. The second international conference was held in Montreal in June 1977 on the subject *Violence in the Family*. There were over 300 participants from over 20 countries. A third world conference on the theme *Family Living in a Changing Society* was held in Uppsala, Sweden in June 1979. There were over 270 participants from 26 countries. The fourth world conference was held in June 1982 at Harvard Law School, USA. There were over 180 participants from 23 countries. The fifth world conference was held in July 1985 in Brussels, Belgium on the theme *The Family, The State and Individual Security*, under the patronage of Her Majesty Queen Fabiola of Belgium, the Director-General of UNESCO, the Secretary-General of the Council of Europe and the President of the Commission of the European Communities. The sixth world conference on *Issues of the Ageing in Modern Society* was held in 1988 in Tokyo, Japan, under the patronage of HIH Takahito Mikasa. There were over 450 participants. The seventh world conference was held in May 1991 in Croatia on the theme, *Parenthood: The Legal Significance of Motherhood and Fatherhood in a Changing Society*. There were 187 participants from 37 countries. The eighth world conference took place in Cardiff, Wales in June/July 1994 on the theme *Families Across Frontiers*. The ninth world conference of the Society was held in July 1997 in Durban, South Africa on the theme *Changing Family Forms: World Themes and African Issues*. The Society's tenth world conference was held in July 2000 in Queensland, Australia on the theme *Family Law: Processes, Practices and Pressures*. The eleventh world conference will be held in August 2002 in Copenhagen and Oslo on the theme *Family Life and Human Rights*. The Society has also increasingly held regional conferences including those in Lyon, France (1995); Quebec City, Canada (1996); Seoul, South Korea (1996); Prague, Czech Republic (1998); Albuquerque, New Mexico, USA (June 1999); Oxford, UK (August 1999); and Kingston, Ontario (2001).

B   ITS NATURE AND OBJECTIVES

The following principles were adopted at the first Annual General Meeting of the Society held in the Kongresshalle of West Berlin on the afternoon of Saturday 12 April 1975.

(1)   The Society's objectives are the study and discussion of problems of family law. To this end the Society sponsors and promotes:

    (a)   International co-operation in research on family law subjects of world-wide interest.

    (b)   Periodic international conferences on family law subjects of world-wide interest.

    (c)   Collection and dissemination of information in the field of family law by the publication of a survey concerning developments in family law throughout the world, and by publication of relevant materials in family law, including papers presented at conferences of the Society.

(d) Co-operation with other international, regional or national associations having the same or similar objectives.

(e) Interdisciplinary contact and research.

(f) The advancement of legal education in family law by all practical means including furtherance of exchanges of teachers, students, judges and practising lawyers.

(g) Other objectives in furtherance of or connected with the above objectives.

C   MEMBERSHIP AND DUES

In 2000 the Society had approximately 550 members in some 60 countries.

(a) Membership:

- Ordinary Membership, which is open to any member of the legal or a related profession. The Council may defer or decline any application for membership.
- Institutional Membership, which is open to interested organisations at the discretion of, and on terms approved by, the Council.
- Student Membership, which is open to interested students of law and related disciplines at the discretion of, and on terms approved by, the Council.
- Honorary Membership, which may be offered to distinguished persons by decision of the Executive Council.

(b) Each member shall pay such annual dues as may be established from time to time by the Council. At present, dues for ordinary membership are 41 USD (or equivalent) for one year, 100 USD (or equivalent) for three years and 155 USD (or equivalent) for five years, plus 7 USD (or equivalent) if cheque is in another currency.

D   DIRECTORY OF MEMBERS

A Directory of Members of the Society is available to all members.

E   BOOKS

The proceedings of the first world conference were published as *The Child and the Law* (F Bates, ed, Oceana, 1976); the proceedings of the second as *Family Violence* (J Eekelaar and S Katz, eds, Butterworths, Canada, 1978); the proceedings of the third as *Marriage and Cohabitation* (J Eekelaar and S Katz, eds, Butterworths, Canada, 1980); the fourth, *The Resolution of Family Conflict* (J Eekelaar and S Katz, eds, Butterworths, Canada, 1984); the fifth, *Family, State and Individual Economic Security (Vols I & II)* (MT Meulders-Klein and J Eekelaar, eds, Story Scientia and Kluwer, 1988); the sixth, *An Ageing World: Dilemmas and Challenges for Law and Social Policy* (J Eekelaar and D Pearl, eds, Clarendon Press, 1989); the seventh *Parenthood in Modern Society* (J Eekelaar and P Sarcevic, eds., Martinus Nijhoff, 1993); the eighth *Families Across*

Frontiers (N Lowe and G Douglas, eds, Martinus Nijhoff, 1996) and the ninth *The Changing Family: Family Forms and Family Law* (J Eekelaar and T Nhlapo, eds, Hart Publishing, 1998). These are commercially marketed but are available to Society members at reduced prices.

F   THE SOCIETY'S PUBLICATIONS

The Society regularly publishes a newsletter, *The Family Letter*, which appears twice a year and which is circulated to the members of the Society and reports on its activities and other matters of interest. *The International Survey of Family Law* provides information on current developments in family law throughout the world and is received free of charge by members of the Society. The editor is currently Andrew Bainham, Christ's College, Cambridge, CB2 3BU, UK. The Survey is circulated to members or may be obtained on application to the Editor.

PREFACE

The International Survey of Family Law (2002 Edition) contains 29 articles from around the world and, as usual, every continent is represented. Ethiopia and Uganda are appearing for the first time in the *Survey* and the contribution on Pakistan is the first for many years.

Again this year I have received the indispensable support of a number of people. First, I would like to express my gratitude to Bart Rwezaura and Savitri Goonesekere who, as Associate Editors, have provided invaluable assistance with the commissioning process in Africa and Asia respectively. As in previous years I owe a considerable debt to Peter Schofield for his translation work. On this occasion I would like to thank him for translating the Spanish version of the article from Argentina and for his assistance with the Portuguese version of the contribution from Brazil. For the first time this year I have received the secretarial support of Ed Carter of Jordans. I would like to welcome her to the team and thank her for her patience in transforming my editorial scribbles into an intelligible manuscript. I also want to acknowledge with thanks the work of Jo Morton, also of Jordans, at proof stage. Last but not least, I am grateful as always to all those who have contributed to this year's *Survey*.

ANDREW BAINHAM
Christ's College Cambridge
May 2002

INTERNATIONAL SOCIETY OF FAMILY LAW
SUBSCRIPTION FORM

☐ I prefer to communicate in ☐ English ☐ French

☐ Please charge my credit card ☐ **MASTERCARD or EUROCARD** ☐ **VISA or JCB**

☐ Subscription for 1 year $41/$37 USD

☐ Subscription for 3 years $100/$89 USD

☐ Subscription for 5 years $155/$138 USD

Name of Card Holder: _____

Card no. ☐☐☐☐ ☐☐☐☐ ☐☐☐☐ ☐☐☐☐

CVC-code (three figures at the back of your card behind the 16 figures): ☐☐☐

Expiry date: ____/____

Address of Card Holder: _____

_____

☐ I pay by *postgiro* to **63.18.019** $155[1] for 5 years, $100 for 3 years or $41 for one year, plus $7 if cheque in another currency (from)

The International Society of Family Law,
Den Hooiberg 17
4891 NM Rijsbergen
The Netherlands

(We have a bank account at the Postbank, Amsterdam, The Netherlands.)

☐ Payment enclosed *by cheque* to the amount of $155[1] for 5 years, $100 for 3 years or $41 for one year, plus $7 if cheque in another currency

Date: _____ Signature: _____

☐ *New member, or*

☐ *(Change of) name/address:* _____

_____

Tel: _____

Fax: _____

e-mail: _____

Comments: _____

_____

To be sent to the treasurer of the ISFL:
Prof. Paul Vlaardingerbroek
International Society of Family Law
Den Hooiberg 17
4891 NM Rijsbergen
THE NETHERLANDS (or by fax: +31-13-466 2323;
e-mail address P.Vlaardingerbroek@kub.nl)

[1] Or its *counter*value in US dollars.

ASSOCIATION INTERNATIONALE DE DROIT DE LA FAMILLE FORMULAIRE DE COTISATION

☐ Je désire de communiquer ☐ en français ☐ en anglais

☐ Je vous prie de charger ma carte de crédit: ☐ **MASTERCARD/EUROCARD** ☐ **VISA/JCB**

☐ Souscription pour une année $41/$37 USD

☐ Souscription pour trois années $100/$89 USD

☐ Souscription pour cinq années $155/$138 USD

Le nom du possesseur de la carte de crédit: _____

Card no. ☐☐☐☐☐ ☐☐☐☐☐ ☐☐☐☐☐ ☐☐☐☐☐

CVC-code (trois numéros sur l'arrière-coté de votre carte) ☐☐☐☐

Date d'expiration: _____ / _____

L'adresse du possesseur de la carte de crédit: _____

_____

☐ Je payerai par postgiro à **63.18.019** $155[1] pour 5 ans ou $100 pour 3 ans ou $41 pour 1 an, *plus* $7 surcharge si paiement est un autre cours,

(du) International Society of Family Law
Den Hooiberg 17
4891 NM Rijsbergen
Les Pays-Bas
(Nous avons un crédit au Postbank, Amsterdam, les Pays-Bas)

☐ Paiement est inclus avec un chèque de $155[1] pour 5 ans ou $100 pour 3 ans ou $41 pour 1 an, *plus* $7 surcharge si paiement est un autre cours.

La date: _____ Souscription: _____

☐ *Nouveau membre, ou*

☐ *(Changement de) nom/adresse:* _____

_____

Tel: _____

Fax: _____

e-mail: _____

Remarques: _____

_____

Veuillez envoyer ce formulaire au trésorier de l'Association:
Prof. Paul Vlaardingerbroek
International Society of Family Law
Den Hooiberg 17
4891 NM Rijsbergen
LES PAYS BAS (ou par fax: +31-13-466 2323; e-mail address
P.Vlaardingerbroek@kub.nl)

[1] Ou la contrevaleur en francs français ou US dollars.

CONTENTS

page

ANNUAL REVIEW OF INTERNATIONAL FAMILY LAW

*Gillian Douglas and Nigel Lowe**

In this Survey we will necessarily be selective. We begin by briefly reviewing developments on the great troika of Hague Conventions affecting children, namely the Hague Convention on the Civil Aspects of International Child Abduction 1980 (the Abduction Convention), the Hague Convention on the Protection of Children and Co-operation in respect of Intercountry Adoption 1993 (the Intercountry Adoption Convention) and the Hague Convention on Jurisdiction, Applicable Law, Recognition, Enforcement and Co-operation in respect of Parental Responsibility and Measures for the Protection of Children 1996 (the Protection of Children Convention). We then discuss the so-called 'Brussels II Regulation' and conclude with a review of the jurisprudence of the European Court of Human Rights (ECtHR) for 2000.

I   THE THREE HAGUE CONVENTIONS

A   The Abduction Convention

In terms of ratifications and accessions[1] the Abduction Convention continues to go from strength to strength, with Turkey ratifying and Brazil, Malta, Trinidad and Tobago, and Uruguay all acceding during 2000. As of 31 December 2000 there were 63 Contracting States.

The main international activity on the Convention was preparing for the Fourth Review to be held in The Hague in March 2001. To this end there were three international conferences of note: the Judicial Seminar on the International Protection of Children held at De Ruwenberg in June 2000, the Common Law Judicial Conference on International Child Custody (hosted by the US State Department) held in Washington, USA in September 2000 and the 2nd International Child Abduction Forum (organised by the International Center for Missing and Exploited Children) held in Alexandria, USA in November 2000.

The Common Law Conference supported all the conclusions from De Ruwenberg including in particular the recognition that 'in cases involving the international abduction of children considerable advantages are to be given from a concentration of jurisdiction in a limited number of courts/tribunals'. In addition it concluded that prompt decision-making under the Abduction Convention serves the best interests of children and that, similarly, Central Authorities have a

---

[*]   Professors of Law at Cardiff Law School.

[1]   Under Art 37 only States which were Members of the Hague Conference on Private International Law at the time of its 14th Session can ratify, but any other State can, under Art 38, accede. The difference between ratifications and accessions is that all Contracting States must accept a ratification but (see Art 38) they can choose whether to accept an accession.

responsibility to process applications quickly. Interestingly and importantly, it also concluded:

> 'Left-behind parents who seek a child's return under the Hague Child Abduction Convention need speedy and effective access to the courts. Lack of legal representation is a significant obstacle to invoking the Convention's remedies. To overcome this obstacle, left-behind parents should be provided promptly with experienced legal representation, where possible at the expense of the requested State.'

Among its other recommendations was that State parties should ensure that there are simple and effective mechanisms to enforce orders for the return of children.

The key recommendation of the 2nd International Forum was that the Abduction Conference 'produce and promote Practice Guides to assist in the implementation and operation of the Convention'.

In addition, Contracting States have been asked to respond to a detailed questionnaire about law and practice under the Convention prepared by the Permanent Bureau of the Hague Conference and to a statistical questionnaire about all 1999 applications, prepared jointly by the Bureau and Cardiff Law School. The outcome of the Fourth Review will be discussed in next year's edition of the Survey.

B   The Intercountry Adoption Convention

As with the Abduction Convention, the number of Contracting States to the Intercountry Adoption Convention continues to expand, with Panama, Italy, the Czech Republic and Albania[2] each ratifying and Iceland and Mongolia acceding to the Convention.[3] As of 31 December 2000 there were 41 Contracting States. Significantly, the USA passed legislation, the Intercountry Adoption Act 2000 (HR 2909), paving the way for eventual ratification within 24–36 months.

The first Special Commission to review the practical operation of the Intercountry Adoption Convention[4] was held at The Hague, 28 November– 1 December 2000.[5] Among the Commission's Conclusions and Recommendations were that each Contracting State should provide 'a description of the manner in which the various responsibilities and tasks under the Convention are divided ... so that the entities responsible to act under the particular Articles of the Convention are clearly identified, as well as the mechanisms by which they interact with one another. The Permanent Bureau should develop a model chart which would assist States in providing this information'. There were also a number of detailed recommendations designed both to improve communication

---

[2]   Albania's ratification came into force on 1 January 2001.

[3]   Under Art 43 of this Convention, States who were Members of the Hague Conference at its 17th Session can ratify, but others can accede (see Art 44). As with the Abduction Convention, all Contracting States must accept ratifications, but can choose whether or not to accept an accession. However, unlike the Abduction Convention, Contracting States must *positively* object to an accession, see Art 44(3).

[4]   Although a Special Commission on the Implementation of the Convention had been held in 1994.

[5]   The International Society of Family Law (represented by Carolyn Hamilton) attended as an observer.

under the Convention and the understanding of how the Convention operates in different States. There was much discussion about accredited bodies and accreditation. It was agreed that:

(a)   accreditation criteria should be explicit and the outcome of a general policy on intercountry adoption;
(b)   accredited bodies should report annually and be subject to periodic review; and
(c)   accreditation requirements should include evidence of the body's sound financial basis and of a system of financial control coupled with a requirement to maintain itemised accounts.

It was agreed that prospective adopters should be provided in advance with an itemised list of costs and expenses likely to arise from the adoption process itself. Emphasis was also placed on the need for thoroughness and objectivity by the authorities in the receiving country in their assessment and preparation of the prospective adopters and in their consequent drawing up of the report on the applicants in accordance with Art 15.

The importance both of the 'Model Forum for the Statement of Council' and the 'Model Forum for the Certificate of Conformity of Intercountry Adoption' (both approved by the 1994 Special Commission) was re-emphasised. A full report of the Conclusions of the Special Commission can be found on the Hague Website: *http://www.net/e/conventions/adospec_e.html*.

C   The Protection of Children Convention

Although one outcome of the Common Law Judicial Conference on International Child Custody[6] was to urge States to give 'prompt consideration' to the ratification of the Protection of Children Convention, progress towards even the Convention coming into force has been disappointingly slow.

As of 31 December 2000 only two States had ratified (Monaco and the Czech Republic) with three others having signed (Morocco, the Netherlands and Poland). In fact, as will be discussed below,[7] there is a problem about the individual competence of Member States of the European Union to ratify the Protection of Children Convention. Given the undoubted usefulness of the Convention it can only be hoped that progress is made in States committing themselves to it.[8]

---

6   Referred to in **I.A** above. A not dissimilar declaration was made by the UK–German Judicial Conference on Family Law held in Edinburgh in September 2000.
7   See **II.F** below.
8   In fact, at the time of writing, Slovakia having ratified in September 2001, the Convention will at last come into force on 1 January 2002.

II   THE BRUSSELS II REGULATION

A   The background to the Regulation

The overall inspiration for Brussels II or, to give it its full title, Council Regulation (EC) No 1347/2000 of 28 May 2000 on Jurisdiction and the Recognition and Enforcement of Judgments in Matrimonial Matters and in Matters of Parental Responsibility for children of both spouses[9], was the Brussels Convention on Jurisdiction and Enforcement of Judgments in Civil and Commercial Matters 1968 ('Brussels I'). This provides a general framework for recognition and enforcement of judgments but expressly excludes status and rights of property arising from marriage, although it does include maintenance. This exclusion of matters of status in Brussels I was revisited following a formal proposal to do so made by Germany in 1992.

Germany was specifically concerned with problems of recognition and enforcement of divorce and legal separation particularly in regard to France. Although these issues had been addressed (quite adequately in the British view) by the Hague Convention on Recognition of Divorces and Legal Separation 1970, neither Germany nor France had felt able to ratify that Convention and both felt that a Brussels initiative would be a good solution. The German proposal was confined to divorce, separation and annulment, but in 1995 Spain and France proposed that questions relating to the children should also be included and, notwithstanding arguments that such a proposal would complicate and therefore delay matters and anyway overlapped with the proposed revision of the Hague Protection Convention 1961, the Council of Ministers, in September 1995, instructed work to go ahead on this basis.

The Convention was finally presented to the Council of Ministers for signing in May 1998. Even then it was not expected to be implemented for some time. But following the Treaty of Amsterdam, which inter alia conferred upon the Commission a right of initiative under what is now Title IV of the new Treaty of the European Community, the Commission presented a proposal for a Regulation based on the text of the Convention which was adopted by the Council on 29 May 2000 thereby effectively converting a Convention into a directly applicable Regulation.[10] Furthermore, under the terms of the Regulation, Member States party to it (that is, all Member States *except* Denmark,[11] Ireland and the UK having opted in) were given a mere nine months' notice of its coming into force, namely on 1 March 2001.

---

[9]   OJ No L160, 30.6.2000, p 19.

[10]   But note that it has been argued that the Regulation might be invalid upon the basis that it is discriminatory insofar as it provides for jurisdiction (see below) to be taken upon nationality, see Wolfgang Hau 'Das System der internationalen Entscheidungszuständigkeit in europäischen Eheverfahrenrecht' Fam RZ 2000, Heft 21, 1333.

[11]   See Art 1(3).

B   The scope of the Regulation

When considering the scope of the Regulation it is worth bearing in mind both that it is modelled as far as possible on Brussels I (one commentary put it well,[12] saying that Brussels I is 'now seen as a general Convention' and Brussels II 'as a "lex specialis", which follows the principles of the earlier Convention as far as possible') and, as the Borras Report (the Explanatory Report on the 'former' Brussels Convention)[13] explains, identical terms in this Regulation and Brussels I must be given the same meaning with the European Court of Justice case-law having to be taken into account.

Under Art 1, the Regulation applies to:

'(a) civil proceedings relating to divorce, legal separation or marriage annulment; and
(b) civil proceedings relating to parental responsibility for the children of both spouses on the occasion of the matrimonial proceedings referred to in (a).'

By referring to 'civil' proceedings the Regulation excludes religious proceedings.[14] On the other hand, proceedings officially recognised in a Member State are to be regarded as the equivalent to judicial proceedings while the term 'court' extends to all authorities having jurisdiction in these matters.[15] 'Member State' specifically excludes Denmark.[16]

Unlike its unlimited application to proceedings relating to divorce, separation and annulment (hereafter referred to as 'matrimonial proceedings') in relation to the parties' status,[17] the scope of Art 1(1)(b) is limited to issues relating to the parental responsibility for the children of *both* spouses arising in those proceedings. Accordingly, the Regulation has no application to issues arising in 'non-matrimonial proceedings'[18] nor to issues arising in matrimonial proceedings unless the children concerned are those of *both* spouses. In other words, it has no application to step-children or to non-marital children.

The phrase 'children of both spouses' is not unproblematic, for while it seems clear that it refers to both the biological and adopted children of the couple[19] it is less clear whether it covers *all* children regarded by any individual Member State as the legal children of both spouses, for example, those conceived as a result of donor insemination or embryo transplants or even, as in the case of English law, parental orders made under s 30 of the Human Fertilisation and Embryology Act

---

12   Shannon with Kennedy, 'Jurisdictional and Recognition and Enforcement Issues in Proceedings Concerning Parental Responsibility under the Brussels II Convention' [2000] IFL 111.
13   (1998) OJ C221/27, at para 6.
14   See the Borras Report, op cit, at para 20B.
15   Article 1(2) which was drafted bearing in mind (ironically in view of Art 1(3)) the position in Denmark and in Finland; see the Borras Report, op cit, at para 20A.
16   Article 1(3).
17   But note that, it does not extend to matters *beyond* status. In particular, the Regulation has no direct application to matrimonial property, although of course by determining the forum for the matrimonial proceedings, the Regulation will in practice also determine the forum for hearing ancillary relief proceedings.
18   Ie to 'freestanding applications' concerning children, and note that jurisdiction under the Regulation continues only until the making of a 'final' order: see Art 3(3), discussed below.
19   See the Borras Report at para 25.

1990. Similarly, there may be difficulty in determining what is meant by 'parental responsibility' (which is not defined in the Regulation)[20] and in particular to how it extends to issues ancillary to determining with whom the child is to live and with whom the child can have contact.[21] According to Shannon and Kennedy[22] it is for each State to decide what falls within the definition of parental responsibility but, in matters of doubt, a domestic court can and in some circumstances must, make a reference to the European Court of Justice in Luxembourg, although the ensuing delay is hardly likely to be conducive to the child's welfare.[23]

C   Jurisdiction

Chapter II deals with jurisdiction with Arts 2 and 3 setting out *exclusive*[24] rules of direct jurisdiction that determine the competency of a Member State court to rule upon status and related matters concerning parental responsibility.[25] So far as matrimonial proceedings are concerned, Art 2(1)(a) vests jurisdiction in the court in whose territory:

> 'the spouses are habitually resident; or
>
> the spouses were last habitually resident, insofar as one of them still resides there; or
>
> the respondent is habitually resident; or
>
> in the case of a joint application either of the spouses is habitually resident; or
>
> the applicant is habitually resident provided he or she resided there for at least a year immediately before the application was made; or
>
> the applicant is habitually resident if he or she resided there for six months provided he or she is either a national of the Member State in question or, in the case of the UK and Ireland, has his "domicile"[26] there.'

In addition, jurisdiction can also be taken on the nationality[27] or, in the case of the UK and Ireland, domicile of both spouses.[28]

---

[20]   Such difficulties are hinted at in the Borras Report, at para 23.

[21]   These issues are known as residence and contact issues in the UK but may be more widely referred to as custody and access issues.

[22]   Op cit, at p 113.

[23]   Cf Shannon, op cit, at 112, who comments: 'The notion that custody cases should be stayed while the matter is referred to the ECJ for a preliminary ruling is absurd'. References to the European Court of Justice are made under Art 234 of the EC Treaty.

[24]   See Art 7 which provides that a spouse who is either habitually resident in or a national of or, in the case of the UK and Ireland, has his domicile in, a Member State 'may be sued in another Member State *only* in accordance with the Regulation'. But note that if Arts 2 to 6 do not apply then jurisdiction is to be determined in each Member State, by the laws of that State – Art 8(1), extensively discussed in the Borras Report at paras 46 ff.

[25]   As Shannon, op cit, points out, this establishment of direct jurisdiction is a major departure from Brussels I.

[26]   Under Art 2(2) 'domicile' has the same meaning as it has under the UK and Irish legal systems.

[27]   The Regulation is silent on the consequences of dual nationality. According to the Borras Report, op cit, at para 33, judicial bodies must apply their 'national rules within the framework of general Community rules on the matter'.

[28]   Article 2(1)(b).

Under Art 3(1) whenever courts have jurisdiction over matrimonial matters according to Art 2, they also have jurisdiction over matters relating to parental responsibility for a child of both spouses provided that the child is habitually resident in that Member State. If the child is not so habitually resident then a court still has jurisdiction provided the child is habitually resident in one of the Member States *and* at least one of the spouses has parental responsibility for the child *and* the court's jurisdiction has been accepted by the spouses and is in the child's best interests.[29] In other words, jurisdiction is *not* automatic simply because there is jurisdiction to hear matrimonial proceedings. Accordingly, where a couple have more than one child, the court might not necessarily have jurisdiction over all of them.[30]

The jurisdiction conferred by Art 3 only lasts pending a final determination in the matrimonial proceedings or, if at that stage a determination on parental responsibility is pending, upon a final judgment on that issue.[31] Furthermore, jurisdiction will be lost upon the cessation of the aforementioned proceedings for other reasons, for example, because they have been withdrawn or one of the parties has died.[32]

As one commentator has well said,[33] it is a great paradox of Brussels II that in a quest for an arrangement which will avoid if possible parallel proceedings we have ended up with the Regulation providing a multiple choice of jurisdictional connecting factors with no hierarchy, thereby extending substantially the potential for parallel actions. To solve this problem, Art 11 provides[34] that:

'1.   Where proceedings involving the same cause of action,[35] and between the same parties are brought before the courts of different Member States, the court second seised shall of its own motion stay its proceedings until such time as the jurisdiction of the court first seised is established.'

Under Art 11(3) where jurisdiction of the court first seized is established, the court second seized has to decline jurisdiction in favour of that court. For these purposes Art 11(4) states that a court shall be deemed to be 'seized' either when the document instituting proceedings or an equivalent document is lodged with the court, or if the document has to be served before being lodged with the court at the

---

29   This formulation is in line with that provided by Art 10(1) of the 1996 Hague Convention on the Protection of Children, save that the Regulation does not require one of the parents to be habitually resident in the State in question. See the Borras Report, op cit, at para 38.

30   Eg where one child is habitually resident in a non-Member State. In practice, however, children will commonly be habitually resident in the State where the court has jurisdiction to hear matrimonial proceedings.

31   Article 3(3), which again is in line with Art 10(2) of the 1996 Hague Convention on the Protection of Children: see the Borras Report, op cit, at para 39.

32   Article 3(3)(c): see the Borras Report, op cit, at para 39(c).

33   Peter Beaton, 'The Brussels II Regulation' – a paper given at the UK–German Conference on Family Law held in Edinburgh, September 2000.

34   As the Borras Report says, ibid at para 52, Art 11 is based on Art 21 of Brussels I.

35   The phrase 'same cause of action' must be given an 'independent European meaning'; see the ECJ decision in *Gubisch Maschinenfabrik v Palumbo* (Case 144/86) [1987] ECR 4861, discussed by Shannon with Kennedy, op cit, at 113. Note that, in the case of matrimonial proceedings, this enjoinder to stay is extended in cases involving the same parties even where they do not involve the same cause of action. See the Borras Report, ibid, at para 54.

time when it is received by the authority responsible for service. It will be noted that under this scheme no provision is made for declining jurisdiction in favour of a more appropriate forum. Nor is there an equivalent of Art 17 of Brussels I permitting prorogating of jurisdiction by agreement.

Notwithstanding these foregoing jurisdictional provisions, Art 12 provides[36] that in urgent cases nothing in the Regulation will prevent courts of a Member State from taking 'such provisional, including protective, measures in respect of persons or assets in that State, even if, under this Regulation, the court of another Member State has jurisdiction as to the substance of the matter'.

D   Recognition

Recognition and enforcement are covered by Chapter III. Art 14(1) obliges Member States to recognise judgments (even those not involving cross-border issues)[37] given in other Member States party to the Regulation 'without any special procedure being required'. In other words, recognition is automatic by operation of law. Nevertheless under Art 14(3) any interested party[38] may apply 'for a decision that the judgment be or not be recognised', although recognition proceedings may be stayed if the judgment in question is subject to an appeal.[39]

The *sole* grounds for non-recognition are set out by Art 15 (courts are forbidden to review the jurisdiction of the court of origin (Art 17) or to review a judgment as to its substance (Art 19)).

So far as matrimonial proceedings are concerned there are just four grounds provided by Art 15(1), namely:

(1)   recognition is manifestly contrary to the public policy of the Member State;[40] or
(2)   a decree was given in default of appearance and the person in default was not served; or
(3)   the judgment is irreconcilable with a judgment given in proceedings between the same parties in the Member State in which recognition is sought; or
(4)   the judgment is irreconcilable with an earlier judgment given in another Member State or a non-Member State.

---

[36]   This is similar to Art 24 of Brussels I, but see the discussion in the Borras Report, op cit, at paras 58 ff and by Shannon, op cit, at 114.

[37]   See the arguments of Rolf Wagner in 'Recognition and Enforcement of Judgments under the Brussels II Regulation', a paper given at the UK–German Conference on Family Law held in Edinburgh, September 2000, based on the interpretations of the parallel provision, Art 25(4) of Brussels I.

[38]   According to Borras Report, op cit, at para 65, the concept of an 'interested party' should be interpreted in a broad sense and 'may include the public prosecutor or other similar bodies where permitted in the State in which the judgment is to be recognised or contested'.

[39]   Article 20(1).

[40]   As Shannon, op cit, at 115, points out, under the analogous provision in Brussels I, the public policy defence has been very narrowly construed by the ECJ, according to which even fraud is not sufficient, see *Société d'Information Service Réalisation v Ampersand Software BV* (1993) *The Times*, 29 July.

So far as judgments relating to parental responsibility[41] are concerned the grounds of non-recognition are set out by Art 15(2), namely that:

(1)   the judgment is manifestly contrary to the public policy of the Member State in which recognition is sought; or
(2)   taking into account the best interests of the child, it was given (except in the case of urgency) without the child being given an opportunity to be heard, in violation of the fundamental principles of procedure in that Member State; or
(3)   it is irreconcilable with a later judgment given in that State or another Member State or the State of the child's habitual residence; or
(4)   it was given in default of appearance and the person in default was not served or without giving an opportunity for a holder of parental responsibility to be heard.

The grounds for non-recognition provided by Art 15(2) essentially replicate those provided by Art 23(2) of the Hague Convention on the Protection of Children 1996 but they are not exactly the same, not least because whereas under the Regulation they are mandatory, under the 1996 Convention recognition may be, but does not have to be, refused.[42] Nevertheless, it is worth making the point that, unlike the Hague Convention or indeed those of the Council of Europe where interpretation is left to the discretion of domestic courts, overall interpretation of the Regulation will be subject to the European Court of Justice, which might not necessarily apply established domestic jurisprudence under the other Conventions.

E   Enforcement

Unlike matrimonial judgments where, being matters of status, recognition is sufficient, special provision is made for the enforcement of judgments relating to parental responsibility. As Shannon points out,[43] the procedure for enforcement is analogous to that under Brussels I but less complex. Under Art 21(1) an enforceable judgment on the exercise of parental responsibility made in one Member State can be declared enforceable in another Member State on the application of any interested party, although within the UK, under Art 21(2) judgments only become enforceable when, upon application, they have been registered for enforcement. Under Art 29 there can be partial enforcement, so it will be no objection that only parts of a judgment (for example, those relating to a child of both spouses) are enforceable under the terms of the Regulation. For these purposes 'interested party' covers not only spouses or children but also in some

---

41   It should be noted that, whereas it is accepted that recognition applies only to so-called 'positive decisions' in relation to divorce, nullity or separation, under the terms of Art 13(1) it would appear that recognition should *prima facie* be accorded to *all* decisions relating to parental responsibility.

42   These differences are important in relation to Member States' competence to ratify the 1996 Convention – see further below.

43   Op cit, at 117. See the Borras Report, op cit, at para 82 ff.

States a relevant public authority.[44] The applicant does not have to be resident in the jurisdiction.

The Regulation only governs the procedure necessary to obtain declarations of enforceability – actual enforcement is left to the national law of the enforcing State. It is expected that enforcement of foreign judgments will be almost automatic,[45] and in any event refusals will only be justified on the grounds set out in Art 15[46] with an absolute prohibition against reviewing a judgment as to its substance.[47]

F   Commentary

Brussels II is the first EU instrument directly affecting child law, but from the family lawyer's point of view, this first taste of EU legislation is not a happy one. It is surely a matter of regret that a choice of jurisdictional rules is laid down without a hierarchy. This is bound to lead to unnecessary complication, which in itself is contrary to the goal of improving and simplifying recognition and enforcement procedures set out by Art 65 of the Treaty of the European Communities. Furthermore, the so-called solution under Art 11 to give absolute priority to the first jurisdiction seized is both crude and, by effectively providing for a race to gain jurisdiction, *not* in keeping with modern family thinking to encourage mediation.[48] The rules themselves are at least questionable insofar as they refer to nationality as a connecting factor.[49] So far as its scope is concerned, it is most unfortunate that the Regulation applies only to children of both spouses since divorces increasingly involve step-children as well, yet for these children quite different rules will have to be applied. This makes for surely unnecessary complication and might also make enforcement decisions problematic.

Quite apart from these criticisms, the Regulation complicates the application of existing international instruments. Although under Art 4, the Hague Abduction Convention 1980 takes precedence over the Regulation, the Regulation in turn takes precedence (see Art 37) over the European (or Luxembourg) Convention on the Recognition and Enforcement of Decisions Concerning Custody of Children 1980. This means that where it is sought to enforce a custody or access decision in respect of children of both spouses made in matrimonial proceedings (but not in free-standing proceedings) in another Member State, the Regulation must be used. Consequently, the applicant will not be entitled, as he would be in the UK under the European Convention, to free legal aid regardless of means or merit,[50] nor will

---

[44]   See the Borras Report, op cit, at para 80.

[45]   At any rate this is Shannon's view, see op cit at 117.

[46]   Article 24(2).

[47]   Article 24(3), which repeats the provision in Art 19.

[48]   See the Council of Europe's Recommendation No R(98) 1 on Family Mediation.

[49]   This was one of the principal objections to common law countries ratifying the Hague Convention on the Protection of Children 1961 and one which was sought to be addressed in the revised 1996 Convention.

[50]   Article 30 only makes provision for legal aid according to domestic law provisions. Article 30 provides that an applicant who has benefited in the Member State of origin from complete or partial legal aid is entitled 'to benefit from the most favourable legal aid or the most extensive exemption from costs and expenses provided for by the law of the Member State addressed'.

the court have any power to modify the access order as it can under Art 11(2) of the European Convention. These differences become all the more exaggerated where step-children are concerned, for the application must be made, if at all, under the European Convention. In these circumstances it might also be pointed out that the grounds for refusing recognition and enforcement under Arts 9 and 10 are not the same as under the Regulation.

Although under Art 37 the Regulation will take precedence over the 1996 Convention with regard to children habitually resident in a Member State, the Regulation will not prevent use being made of the Convention insofar as it does not overlap with Brussels II (although insofar as it sought to use the Convention as well as the Regulation it makes for a complicated inter-relationship). Ironically, however, although each instrument was drafted with the other in mind,[51] those Member States that are party to the Regulation might well have lost their independent competence to ratify at any rate in part the 1996 Convention. The argument centres on the impact of the *AETR* case-law[52] under which the European Court of Justice has ruled that each time the Community exercises its internal competence by adopting provisions laying down common rules, it acquires *exclusive* external competence to undertake obligations with third countries which affect those under rules or alter their scope. It is argued that, since the 1996 Convention rather than the Regulation would apply to children habitually resident outside the EU but in a Contracting State, it would alter the scope of the Regulation (albeit without creating a clash), and the *AETR* ruling therefore applies. Furthermore, it is thought that both the UK and Ireland are bound notwithstanding that, unlike other Member States (except Denmark), they opted into the adoption and application of Brussels II and, in the case of the UK, had sought expressly to preserve its freedom to ratify the 1996 Convention.

Assuming the argument holds good[53] then it seems that further legislation would be required to allow EU Member States to ratify the Convention as regards those parts lying within the Community's competence.[54] Although this adds a further complication, it by no means forecloses future ratification and indeed the EU Commission itself is in favour of ratification. How this issue will eventually be resolved remains to be seen.

---

[51] See eg the Borras Report, op cit, at para 9.

[52] See Case 22/70, [1971] ECR 263, para 17; Opinion 2/91, [1993] ECR 1-1061, para 26; Opinion 1/94, [1994] ECR 1-5267, para 77, and Opinion 2/92, [1995] ECR 1-521, para 31.

[53] It is understood that Ireland, having embarked upon ratifying legislation, has now accepted that it has no unilateral power to do so.

[54] There is no provision in the 1996 Convention permitting ratification or accession by an international organisation. Accordingly, this means either a Protocol would have to be negotiated or, as would seem preferable, Member States can in some way be permitted to ratify.

III　JURISPRUDENCE OF THE EUROPEAN COURT OF HUMAN RIGHTS

A　The welfare of the child

During 2000, the court dealt with a variety of cases raising family matters. As is usual, however, these were complaints overwhelmingly raised by parents – or adults – and not on behalf of (still less by) children themselves. The European Convention remains adult-focused, at least in its application by the European Court. Nonetheless, it is clear that the court attaches considerable weight to the interests of children, and will uphold domestic decisions where these are shown to have been taken in the child's best interests. It has become used, in the context especially of complaints brought under Art 8 (the right to respect for family life), to asserting the primacy of the child's welfare. This appears to be the case even where it would appear that the exercise required in balancing out different family members' rights might result in a different outcome.[55] Thus, Art 8(2) provides that an interference with the right may be justified where, inter alia, it is 'for the protection of health or morals, or for the protection of the rights and freedoms of others'. It is common for the European Court to justify an interference with a parental right, eg to contact with the child, because this is deemed necessary to protect the child's own competing interest. For example, in *Graeme v UK*,[56] the applicant and his wife had three children. The English High Court made a residence order in the mother's favour and ordered that the father should have only indirect contact with the children. Having found that the applicant had created 'an aura of harassment and intimidation', the court also directed[57] that he could not make further applications for orders relating to the children without leave of the court for the next two years. He complained to Strasbourg. The court ruled his complaint inadmissible on the basis that the restrictions imposed, both as to indirect contact only and preventing him seeking further orders, pursued the legitimate aim of protecting the rights and freedoms of the mother and children.

B　The State's obligation to uphold the right to respect for family life

Perhaps one of the most pressing problems facing States wishing to uphold family rights is the difficulty of enforcing orders. Particularly intractable disputes can arise, of course, in relation to enforcing contact arrangements. It is a difficult line to draw for the domestic authorities between rigorous enforcement and harmful coercion or, at the other extreme, between a 'softly softly' approach and inaction. It is unsurprising that non-resident parents, faced with a continuing failure, as they would see it, to live up to the terms of a binding court order, should seek a remedy – albeit one that will usually come too late – in Strasbourg.

---

[55]　The argument put forward by some commentators, eg H Swindells et al, *Family Law and the Human Rights Act 1998*, (Family Law, 1999) paras 3.156, 6.26, that the welfare principle, as enshrined in English law, is incompatible with the Convention, appears to have been rejected by the European Court. See further below.

[56]　9 March 2000, App 41519/98.

[57]　Under Children Act 1989, s 91(14).

But it is hard to discern a clear approach emanating from the European Court as to how such cases will be evaluated. In *Glaser v UK*,[58] the applicant and his wife had three children. After they separated and divorced, the mother stopped all contact saying that the children did not want to see the applicant, alleging sexual abuse (which was unsubstantiated). Court orders for contact were made but the mother ignored them. She then moved to Scotland with the children and disappeared. The applicant sought to enforce the orders in Scotland but had difficulty in tracing the family. Eventually, he accepted that only indirect contact with the children was possible. He enjoyed no direct contact with them for seven years. He complained that his right to respect for family life under Art 8 had been infringed because the courts in Scotland and England had not enforced the contact orders. Although the European Court held that where a contact dispute arises between parents, Art 8 includes a right for the parent to have measures taken with a view to being reunited with his child, the obligation on the national authorities is not absolute. It considered that any obligation to enforce the order through the application of coercion must be limited since the interests as well as the rights and freedoms of all concerned must be taken into account. These especially include the best interests of the child and *his* rights under Art 8. The court concluded that where contact might appear to threaten those interests or interfere with those rights, it is for the national authorities to strike a fair balance between them. In assessing this, the key consideration is whether all necessary steps have been taken to facilitate contact as can reasonably be demanded in the circumstances. The court found no fundamental defect in the structure applying in England and Scotland to enforce the applicant's rights. Given the complex nature of the proceedings, and the importance of the work that had to be done to rebuild the children's confidence and trust in the applicant, the length of time which had elapsed throughout the whole process was not unreasonable.

By contrast, in *Ignaccolo-Zenide v Romania*,[59] the applicant, a French national, had two children with her husband, who had dual French/Romanian nationality. A French court ruled on their divorce that the children should live with her and stay with the father during the summer holidays. At the end of the holiday he refused to hand the children back and took them to Romania. In 1994, a court in Bucharest issued an injunction requiring him to return the children but this was not enforced. Since then, the applicant had seen the children only once. The Strasbourg court this time stressed that Art 8 imposes positive obligations which are inherent in an effective 'respect' for family life. There had, in the court's view, been delay and inaction by the Romanian authorities; they had failed to take coercive action against the father, and they had not arranged to prepare the children for return to the mother, eg by arranging meetings with child psychologists or social workers. Thus, on this occasion, the court found that the domestic authorities had failed to take adequate and sufficient steps to comply with the applicant's right to the return of her children and had therefore infringed Art 8.[60] Here, the emphasis appears to have been on the authorities' failure to act with any vigour, while the English and Scottish courts in *Glaser* appear to have

---

[58]   19 September 2000, App 32346/96.

[59]   25 January 2000, App 31679/96.

[60]   Cf the similar conclusion reached by the court in *Hokkanen v Finland* (1995) 19 EHRR 139.

been regarded as having done as much as they could given the hostility between the parents. But it is, in reality, difficult to discern much real difference between the two cases.

C   Discrimination and family life

Article 14 of the Convention provides that the enjoyment of the rights and freedoms set out therein shall be secured without discrimination 'on any ground such as sex, race, colour, language, religion, political or other opinion, national or social origin, association with a national minority, property, birth or other status'. Article 14 cannot be relied upon in its own right but must be allied to one of the substantive rights.[61] Its broad terms clearly include discrimination on the basis of birth outside marriage,[62] and anomalies regarding the position of children born outside marriage are now very likely to be struck down by the European Court. For example, in *Mazurek v France*,[63] the court held that a provision in the French Civil Code[64] limiting the share of an estate that could be taken by a child born of an adulterous union was a disproportionate response to the legitimate aim of upholding the 'traditional' family. There had therefore been a breach of Protocol 1, Art 1 (which protects the peaceful enjoyment of one's possessions) taken with Art 14. The case was striking given that the applicant's half-sibling, who inherited a larger share, did so only because he had been legitimated. The court emphasised that it was wrong to penalise a child for actions that were not his fault. It noted that legislation to ameliorate the position of such children had been introduced into France, but not enacted, in 1991, thus suggesting that the French authorities themselves recognised that the position was unsatisfactory.

The 'child' in *Mazurek* was in fact an adult at the time of his complaint. In *Camp and Bourimi v The Netherlands*,[65] a complaint was made on behalf of a minor, born in 1992. Ms Camp's partner, Mr Bourimi, died when she was pregnant with his child. They were cohabiting and had planned to marry. His parents refused to accept that the child was his. They took over his property and inherited his estate. Ms Camp complained on the child's behalf that there was no legally recognised family relationship between the child and the dead father and his relatives. The European Court held that this was not enough by itself for breach of Art 8, but when taken with Art 14, a breach had occurred, because the child was treated differently in being unable to inherit, when compared with legitimate children. The child was entitled to compensation equal to the value of the estate and the mother entitled to non-pecuniary damages for distress.

Discrimination based on homosexuality is another aspect of different treatment that has been the subject of complaints to Strasbourg, but here, the

---

[61]   Protocol 12 to the Convention, which was opened for signature on 4 November 2000, elevates Art 14 into a substantive provision as regards 'the enjoyment of any right set forth by law'. The Protocol is not yet in force, having been signed (as of September 2001) by 26 States but ratified by only one.

[62]   See the leading case of *Marckx v Belgium* (1979) Series A, No 31.

[63]   1 February 2000, App 34406/97.

[64]   Article 760.

[65]   3 October 2000, App 28369/95.

court's approach is proving to be less consistent. It seemed that it was taking a more liberal stance in *Salgueiro da Silva Mouta v Portugal*.[66] In that case, the Lisbon Court of Appeal had given an unmarried mother custody of a child because, inter alia, the father was homosexual and living with another man. The father complained under Arts 8 and 14. It was held that the Lisbon Court's judgment had interfered with his right to respect for family life in having regard to his homosexuality in determining what should happen to the child. The court stated that there had therefore been a difference in treatment by the domestic court of the mother and the father based on their respective sexual orientations, and that such difference had been discriminatory because it had no objective or reasonable justification. The court in particular objected to the Lisbon Court's categorisation of homosexuality as 'an abnormality and children must not grow up in the shadow of abnormal situations'. It is not uncommon in some jurisdictions for homosexual parents to give undertakings that they will not 'expose' their children to their 'unconventional' way of life. The court's decision in the present case appears to cast doubt on the legitimacy of requiring such an undertaking.

Yet, in *Craig v United Kingdom*,[67] the court upheld this very requirement. The applicant was a lesbian, whose partner had four children. The partner had a shared care arrangement with her former husband and had reached an agreement with the husband that she would not let the children come into contact with anyone she knew was a lesbian. The agreement was embodied in an order of the High Court, and the court accepted her undertaking that she would not let the applicant call at her home during contact visits. The applicant complained under Art 8 that this precluded her from having contact with the partner's children and thus amounted to a violation of her private and family life with her partner. The complaint was held inadmissible. The European Court considered that the High Court's order did not constitute a disproportionate interference with the right under Art 8. In particular, it found it significant that the applicant's partner had *agreed* to the limitations on their relationship. But the reality may be that, in the absence of such undertakings, a homosexual parent may find it difficult to obtain either care of, or contact with, her child. It may be that the true point of distinction between this case and *Salgueiro da Silva Mouta* is that in the former, the applicant was himself the child's parent, while in the latter, she was merely a partner of the children's parent. Perhaps the court was really finding that her 'family life' with the children was less deserving of protection.

The other group of applicants who have attempted to use Art 14 in conjunction with Art 8 are unmarried fathers. Here, the court has made it clear that States are entitled to treat unmarried fathers differently from unmarried mothers, or married fathers. This is because:

'the relationship between unmarried fathers and their children varies from ignorance and indifference to a close stable relationship indistinguishable from the conventional family-based unit. For this reason the court has held that there exists an objective and

---

66 21 December 1999, App 33290/96.
67 7 March 2000, App 45396/99.

reasonable justification for the difference in treatment between married and unmarried fathers with regard to the automatic acquisition of parental rights.'[68]

Thus, in *Balbontin v United Kingdom*,[69] the court ruled inadmissible a complaint by an unmarried father that there had been a breach of his rights under Arts 8 and 14 when the mother took the child out of the jurisdiction before he had been able to obtain an order granting him parental responsibility. He had no rights over the child at the time of the removal, and this was because of the policy of English law requiring unmarried fathers to take positive steps to acquire such rights. Although he had been enjoying contact with the child, the court refused to treat this as sufficient to place him on an equal footing with those who have a child in their care, because of the different responsibilities involved in the two situations. The difficulty for the father in this case was that his institution of legal proceedings to obtain such rights had itself probably prompted the mother's removal of the child from the country. Such a father therefore finds himself in a 'Catch 22' situation. If he takes proceedings which are interpreted by the mother as 'hostile', she may pre-empt him by taking the child away, and if he does not do so, he has no legally enforceable right to prevent such removal in any case.[70]

Another unmarried father fared better in *Elsholz v Germany* [71] but not because of his reliance upon Art 14. He had lived with the family for 18 months after the child's birth, and subsequently had three years of regular contact with the child, which the mother then terminated. The district court found that further contact would negatively affect the child. In so finding, it took account of the child's wishes, but did not obtain an expert psychological opinion of the family relationships. The father's appeal was dismissed without an oral hearing. The European Court found that the domestic courts' handling of the case amounted to a breach of Art 8, and of the father's Art 6 right to a fair trial. It held that the courts should have ordered an independent report, and should have allowed an oral appeal hearing. Their failure to do either had meant that the father was insufficiently involved in the decision-making process. But they rejected his argument based on discrimination, finding that the courts would have treated a divorced father in the same way.

D   Involvement in family proceedings

The European Court's stress on the importance of parental involvement in the decision-making process as an aspect of both Art 6 and Art 8 rights is apparent in other decisions too. In *Ciliz v The Netherlands*,[72] for example, the applicant was a Turkish national who had a right to reside in the Netherlands, based on his

---

[68]   *Balbontin v United Kingdom*, 14 September 1999, App 39067/97.

[69]   Ibid.

[70]   In fact, the English courts have recognised the difficulty in which this places unmarried fathers and have held that, so long as the court is actively seized of the issue, then the court itself will be regarded as having 'rights of custody' within the Hague Convention on International Child Abduction, such as to enable the father to invoke the protection of the Convention to try to obtain the child's return to the jurisdiction: *Re H (Abduction: Rights of Custody)* [2000] 1 FLR 201, CA.

[71]   13 July 2000, App 25735/94.

[72]   11 July 2000, App 29192/95.

marriage to a Dutch woman. Their child was born in 1990. The following year, the parents separated and the applicant lost his right of residence, although he was given a work permit for one year. He did not seek contact with the child for some time. When he later did so, the domestic court did not approve a formal contact arrangement with the child, and refused to grant him residence. Later, he began having weekly contact but was still refused residence. He appealed and the court ordered an evaluation of his relationship with the child, involving a number of trial meetings. But during a delay in arranging these, he was deported by the authorities. The Dutch court then ruled that since he had not had contact for a number of years and the child was now hostile to the idea, a formal arrangement would not be in the child's interests. The applicant argued that the authorities' failure to extend his residence permit was a breach of Art 8. The European Court upheld his complaint, ruling that the deportation was an unnecessary interference with his right to respect for family life. There had been no urgent need to remove the father before the trial meetings had taken place, and the effect had been to deprive him of any meaningful further involvement in the proceedings. The failure of the authorities to co-ordinate their decision-making about contact and deportation had resulted in him being unable to develop his family ties with his child.

Provided a parent is given sufficient opportunity to involve herself in proceedings, however, the court is unlikely to find a breach. In *Scott v United Kingdom*,[73] the applicant mother was an alcoholic whose child was placed with foster carers when about 18 months old. There followed a long series of planning meetings to determine the child's future. The local authority's original plan was for rehabilitation with the mother, but there was conflicting expert evidence on her ability to control her drinking and care adequately for the child. A year later, she relapsed and the local authority obtained a full care order over the child, granting the authority parental responsibility. The mother attended a residential clinic at the local authority's expense. She failed to attend a child protection conference[74] to discuss the child's future although she had been invited. At the next conference, she was not invited although she sent her written views. She was unable to attend the following conference. There, it was decided to place the child for adoption. Court proceedings were held to free the child for adoption against the mother's wishes. The court found that adoption was in the child's best interests and dispensed with her consent. She then complained to Strasbourg under Art 8 and Art 13 (which provides that there must be an effective remedy before a national authority for breach of the rights set out in the Convention). The European Court held her complaint inadmissible. It found that she had had a proper opportunity to make her views known to those at the child protection conferences and had been legally aided and represented in the court proceedings which were the only measure formally affecting her rights. The domestic court could not be criticised for reaching the conclusion that its only option was to free the child for adoption. The case is a disappointing one for those seeking to uphold parental procedural rights, since it stops short of requiring that a parent has a *right* to attend the child

---

[73] 8 February 2000, App 34745/97.

[74] A multi-disciplinary meeting at which future plans for the child are discussed by all the relevant professionals involved.

protection conference even though this is often a key step in the decision-making process over a child in the public care system. The court considered that the mother could have sought a discharge of the care order, but this is, with respect, unrealistic given her situation at the time.

E Removing children from the birth family

Scott appears out of step with the prevailing tenor of earlier judgments which have generally held that, while an initial decision to remove a child into care may be justified, very strict scrutiny will be required to uphold a decision to curtail family relationships, such as through the ending of contact, or the placement for adoption.[75] Indeed, in *Scozzari and Giunta v Italy*,[76] the court adopted this more usual approach. The parents had two children. The father absconded from a Belgian prison, where he was serving a life sentence. The parents returned to Italy. The father was violent, and a social worker began looking after the elder child but was himself convicted of child abuse. The family was then investigated and both children were placed in a children's home even though there were known abusers working there. The parents' parental rights were suspended and they had no contact with the children for nearly two years. The mother and maternal grandmother complained under the Convention. The court held that there had been no breach of Art 8 in the authorities' original taking of the children into care or suspending the parents' rights. However, a breach had occurred because of the delays and limited contact that had resulted once the children had been removed, which was compounded by the children's placement in a home where a risk of danger was known. The authorities had acted to the detriment of both the mother's rights and of the superior rights of the children because, by their actions, they had driven them apart.

It is interesting to note that the children's grandmother was an applicant in the *Scozzari and Giunta* case. Generally, grandparents have not fared well under the Convention, because the European Court and Commission have regarded them as having a less important 'family life' with the child. This view was apparent in *GHB v United Kingdom*.[77] Grandparents had agreed[78] to the grandchild's adoption, on the understanding that they would continue to have contact with her. However, the child was nearly 12 by the time of the adoption and had wanted to break off contact herself. The European Court found that, in light of the child's age and the fact that the adoption order did not *prevent* contact if the child wanted it in the future, the decision of the domestic court to give weight to her views was justified. To have required her to have direct contact against her wishes would

---

[75] See, eg, *Johansen v Norway* (1996) 23 EHRR 33; *K and T v Finland* 27 April 2000, App 25702/94, discussed by Geraldine Van Bueren and Randini Wanduragala, in 'Annual Review of International Family Law' in *The International Survey of Family Law (2001 Edition)*, ed A Bainham, at p 3. (Note that this case was referred to the Grand Chamber at the request of the Finnish Government. The Grand Chamber upheld the earlier decision, although it differed on some of its conclusions: *K and T v Finland* 12 July 2001, App 25702/94.)

[76] 13 July 2000, Apps 39221/98 and 41963/98.

[77] 4 May 2000, App 42455/98.

[78] This is not a legal requirement of adoption under English law, but was simply part of the factual background to the case.

have been a failure to respect the child's own rights under Art 8, and the relationship between grandparents and grandchildren generally calls for a lesser degree of protection than that between parent and child.

F   The position of children themselves

This reference and emphasis placed upon the wishes of the child is an important aspect of the European Court's greater willingness in recent years to view the child as a person in his or her own right, whose voice must be heard with care. Yet in an important case concerning the liberty of a child, and in the only case reviewed here which actually involved a direct application by a young person herself, the court ruled the complaint inadmissible. In *Koniarska v United Kingdom*[79] an order was made in respect of a 17-year-old girl under s 25 of the Children Act 1989 to keep her in secure accommodation until she reached the age of 18. She had access to 'studies' and attended these regularly until a disturbance with another young person. Thereafter, she had chosen not to go to these 'studies'. She complained of a breach of her rights under Art 5, which only permits the detention of a minor for educational supervision. She argued that since she was beyond school leaving age and had not attended classes, her detention was not for this purpose. Moreover, she claimed a breach of Art 3 on the basis that her detention had led to intense mental suffering, and of Art 8 on the basis that her continuing detention was in breach of her right to respect for family life.

The court held that 'educational supervision' is not to be equated rigidly with notions of classroom teaching. It considered that secure accommodation orders could constitute part of 'educational supervision' of the child. Within the specialist facility where she was detained, 'life and social skills' programmes were held and the fact that she chose not to attend many classes did not affect the underlying position which was that extensive educational provision was made and she benefited from it to a certain extent. Although the court accepted that she was unhappy to be placed in a secure unit, there was no evidence to indicate that the minimum level of severity had been reached at which Art 3 applied. Nor was there a breach of Art 8, as her detention was for the protection of her own health.

The rather paternalistic approach taken by the European Court in this case is disappointing. It suggests that there is still some way to go before the court truly takes on board the increasing international recognition of the child's developing autonomy rights. Although the court has reference to the United Nations Convention on the Rights of the Child when interpreting the European Convention, it has perhaps had few good opportunities to face squarely what is the most important question confronting authorities dealing with family matters at present. This is how to balance out the competing interests – and, in the Convention context – rights, of different family members. It has been able, as noted above, to 'trump' adults' asserted rights by reliance on the welfare of the child or, very occasionally, by noting the child's own strongly held wishes and feelings. But it has not had to deal in any very sophisticated way with the arguments presented by parents in conflict, still less where parents and children

---

[79]   12 October 2000, App 33670/96.

are in conflict with each other. This is perhaps not surprising. The Convention is primarily concerned with controlling State action and protecting the individual in his or her dealings with State authorities. The issues arising from private disputes between individuals only indirectly engage the Convention once the parties themselves have in some way invoked the State's assistance or intervention. The court's focus remains, correctly, on scrutinising the actions, or inaction, of the State authorities. Thus, the true nature and essence of the dispute between family members becomes hidden from view and is not amenable to Strasbourg control. This may help to underscore how far the notion of 'rights' may have rather limited scope in defining and regulating inter-familial relationships.

ARGENTINA

PROBLEMS OF BIOETHICS AFFECTING FAMILY LAW

Cecilia P Grosman and *Delia B Iñigo*

A number of bioethical questions have considerable impact on family law and affect the personal rights of its subjects. What we shall comment on here will be three aspects which have come recently before the courts: (a) voluntary sterilisation, which involves both the right to procreate and the right not to procreate; (b) change of sex; and (c) the rights of children and adolescents in relation to their reproductive welfare in connection with parental authority.

I   VOLUNTARY STERILISATION

A   The legal prohibition

Voluntary sterilisation of human beings is forbidden in Argentina and, in consequence, consent to the carrying out of this medical procedure by a professional has no legal effect whatever. Only in exceptional cases is it permitted, provided that therapeutic indications are clearly present and that there is no way in which the reproductive system could be saved (Art 20, sub para 18 of National Law 17.132).[1]

Further, the Code of Medical Ethics of the Argentine Medical Confederation lays down that 'the doctor shall not sterilise a man or woman in the absence of clearly established therapeutic indications' (Art 19). Therapeutic indication is to be interpreted widely, not restricted to cases where there is a specific danger to the person's physical or mental health. It includes problems arising from having a large number of children, the socio-economic situation of the couple, and the existence of reasons why contraception should not be used.[2]

---

[*]   Titular Consultant Professor of Family Law and Succession, Faculty of Law, University of Buenos Aires.

[**]   Professor of Family Law in the Faculty of Legal and Social Sciences of the Universidad Nacional del Litoral. Translated by Peter Schofield.

[1]   This rule applies in the federal law, but as the Provincial Legislatures have acceded to, or replicated this legislation, it applies more or less uniformly across the country.

[2]   This broad interpretation is rejected by Roberto Adorno in a case note 'Qué debe entenderse por "indicación terapéutica" para una esterilización?', *La Ley*, Buenos Aires 1997, p 659. This author considers as permissible only a sterilisation which arises as a secondary consequence of a surgical procedure undertaken to cure some condition – for example, ligation of Fallopian tubes where a woman suffers from breast cancer.

B   Development of the test applied by the courts

The cases on voluntary sterilisation have varied. At first, a person who wanted such treatment had to have recourse to a judge for authorisation of the operation and, generally, judges refused it, even if both spouses appeared and relied on the fact that a further pregnancy could damage the woman's physical or mental health.

In recent years, judges have authorised bilateral tubal ligation,[3] when the circumstances indicate this. What is more, a judgment has struck down, as unconstitutional, Art 20, sub para 18 of National Law 17.132, which forbids the sterilisation of human beings. The judgment considered that rule inapplicable to ligation of Fallopian tubes decided on freely in the context of personal privacy and, hence, exempt from judicial authority. A request for ligation of Fallopian tubes is protected by Art 19 of the National Constitution,[4] since this is an act referring only to one's self, within the intimate ambit of personal privacy and does not compromise third party interests, which renders it a matter of personal morality free from sanction on the part of the State and exempt from any prohibition.[5]

We shall review certain judicial decisions related to the question of voluntary sterilisation, distinguishing them according to whether those involved have legal capacity or not.

1   PERSONS HAVING LEGAL CAPACITY

In one case a woman had produced seven children. Facing a further pregnancy, she applied, with her husband's consent, for court authorisation for tubal ligation. Doctors recommended the treatment, because the numerous pregnancies had caused bleeding outside her menstrual periods, and of the risk of (spontaneous) abortion. This called for strict rest and prevented her working, with consequent loss of earnings and reduction of assets which, in turn, made it impossible to keep a suitable home for children.

The judge held that, despite the general prohibition on sterilisation in Art 23 of the Code of Medical Ethics of the Province of Buenos Aires and in Art 20, sub para 18 of Law 17.132, 'Where there are well-founded therapeutic indications, there is no illegality on grounds of bodily harm or mutilation to detract from the justification on grounds of necessity'.[6]

Doctrinal writers strongly maintain that sterilisation is a matter that should be left to the conscience and to the privacy of those concerned – the woman and her husband – without the need for a prior judicial decision. 'The treatment chosen by

---

[3] Bilateral tubal ligation is a surgical procedure which sterilises a woman, temporarily or permanently; while in place it prevents her from becoming pregnant.

[4] Article 19 of the National Constitution says that: 'Private acts of individual persons which in no way offend public order or morality, nor prejudice the interests of a third party, are subject only to God and exempt from judicial authority'.

[5] Juzgado Correccional de General Roca, 21 September 2000, Ch J Del C, *Supplemento de Derecho Constitucional, Revista La Ley*, 15 December 2000, pp 37–41. It was there held that, as third parties have no power to prevent a person's sterilisation, since it does not affect them, such conduct is clearly unobjectionable on moral grounds.

[6] Juzgado Criminal y Correccional No 3, Mar de Plata, Provincia de Buenos Aires, causa MLA de A, 12 August 1991.

the doctor and accepted by the patient cannot be interfered with by the State by way of arbitrary interventions.'[7] Iñigo, one of the signatories to this article, took a similar position in saying that 'it is left to the personal decision of the patient whether or not to submit herself to such treatment, once she has received the advice of her doctor who, obviously, bases his decision on scientific grounds and on the ethical principles derived from his Hippocratic oath. It is not necessary to secure the consent of any other authority'.[8] It has been held that the right to health guaranteed by a number of Human Rights treaties (Art II of the American Declaration of Human Rights and Duties, Art 25 of the Universal Declaration of Human Rights, Art 112 of the International Treaty on Economic Social and Cultural Rights), gives expression to a wider notion: the right to a better quality of life, and takes in the people's right of access to appropriate medical services to ensure the protection and preservation of health.[9]

Also, in certain cases we find judicial decisions to the effect that this is not a matter for courts to determine; it is for the medical practitioner to advise on appropriate treatment and for those concerned, in the context of personal privacy, to decide whether to consent in the exercise of the most personal of human rights.[10]

One judgment held that judicial intervention was called for only if the medical centre denied the possibility of obtaining a sterilisation. The judge argued that, faced with adequate clinical indications, the Public Hospital ought to proceed in accordance with the requirements of medical science, and have the facilities for carrying out sterilisations. Such operations, the judgment held, are not illegal, but, on the contrary, are a measure of respect for the rights of the patient who has asked for this treatment. As a result, said the judge, judicial authority is not required before performing a tubal ligation if there are sufficient therapeutic indications; rather, medical practitioners can act on the written consent of the woman and her husband. Where the health service authorities deny the patient appropriate medical attention, despite the existence of clinical indications, those concerned have the right to have recourse to judicial remedies.[11]

In another case, a woman asked for sterilisation on the grounds that she had had eight children, two spontaneous abortions and a Caesarean section to deliver a dead child. At the time she presented, she was in the 29th week of another pregnancy and in a depressed emotional state. It was established that she was

---

[7] Bidart Campos Germán, 'La tutela médica del estado providente y la privacidad matrimonial' *ED* 145-440.

[8] Delia B Iñigo, 'Esterilización en caso de personas incapaces por causa de enfermedad o deficiencia mental', *ED T* 139, p 839, punto III A.

[9] Cf Eduardo Luis Tinant, 'El derecho a la salud y la omisión inconstitutional del Juez. La tutela de la 'Persona Vulnerable' en sentido bioético', *La Ley* 2000-C-545 ff.

[10] Juzgado Nacional de Primera Instancia en lo Civil N 1 de la Capital Federal. L de G, ME, *ED* 130-532 y Juzgado Nacional de Primera Instancia en lo Civil N 26 GME Y MLS/autorización de ligadura de trompas, 1 March 1998, *ED* 138-364, Cámara Nacional de Apelaciones en lo Civil de la Capital Federal, Sala B, 1 September 1985, *ED* 115-282 y Juzgado Civil y Comercial N 5, de Lomas de Zamora, Provincia de Buenos Aires, R de G, G, *ED* 161-204; idem Juzgado Correccional N 18 de General Roca, 9 September 2000, *Supplemento de Derecho Constitutional, Revista La Ley*, 15 December 2000, pp 37–41.

[11] Juzgado Civil y Comercial N, Trenque Lauquen, 31 July 1997, YGE c/Municipalidad de Tres Lomas, LL Buenos Aires, 1998 – 1139.

socially at risk to a high degree, since her home situation was insecure and evidenced extreme poverty and overcrowding, so that at times the family group depended on public charity. The judge decided to authorise the operation, arguing that the reference, in Law 17.132, to a 'therapeutic purpose' as an exceptional ground for authorising tubal ligation '... should be construed in a broad sense, inclusive of anything which might affect the case directly or indirectly, on the positive or the negative side, in relation to the patient's health, which is not just a matter of absence of illness, but of his or her physical and emotional balance'. The judgment held that respect had to be shown to the freedom of conscience of those directly involved and, in the instant case, both husband and wife expressed their free decision to use this method of contraception. Even if it could be argued that this was a detriment to physical health, it would not violate the 'principle of non-maleficence' (not aggravating already existing psychosocial damage), because it prevented the greater harm which would result from a further pregnancy, which would affect psychological health and put at risk the growth and development of the child, because of the unfavourable family environment.[12]

An interesting question was resolved on the petition of a woman who had cohabited for five years with a man, by whom she had borne two daughters. She asked for termination of a pregnancy in its 27th week and for bilateral tubal ligation. She set out that she suffered from severe insulin dependent diabetes, that this caused malformation of the foetus (both cardiac and a significant microcephaly resulting in mental disability). This meant that the judge had two fundamental issues to resolve: that of tubal ligation – not permitted, as we have already noted – and abortion of the foetus – also prohibited unless required to save the life of the mother, in which case it is considered to be 'therapeutic' (Art 86, sub para 1 of the Penal Code). The facts having been proved, the question was whether what was applied for fell within the exceptions cited. The judge held that it was a matter of an autonomous decision of the mother, within the scope of her private life, and that her cohabitant had consented to the petition as father of the unborn child. Thus he held that the mother's constitutional right to health must be protected, refusal could make her condition worsen and might even be life-threatening, which would affect not only her, but also the other two little girls in her care. As the termination was to be performed in a public health centre, the judgment left open the right of any of the professionals not to take part in the operation on grounds of conscience. Consequently he decided that the birth could be induced prematurely and the tubal ligation be carried out, since the case was shown '... as a means of protecting values and rights rooted in the constitution in face of the proven and serious danger that a future possible pregnancy could mean for the petitioner's health and even her life'.[13]

Another case concerned a woman who had three children of her marriage, had a further child in a de facto union and, at the time of the petition for sterilisation, was expecting a fifth. She suffered from blood pressure causing kidney disease

---

[12]   Juzgado Criminal y Correccional N 3 de Mar de Plata, Provincia de Buenos Aires, Case N, MH, 23 August 1996, *Jurisprudencia Argentina* 10 December 1997, commentary by Walter F Carnota, 'El dictamen biologico'.

[13]   Juzgado Criminal y Correccional N 3 de Mar de Plata, Provincia de Buenos Aires, Case AK, 5 September 1997, *Jurisprudencia Argentina* 28 October 1998, noted by José A Mainetti and María M Mainetti, 'El amparo de la bioética cuando ser madre resulta un drama'.

and serious convulsions. Contraception was inadvisable and she had had a number of spontaneous abortions. The judge authorised tubal ligation, on the grounds that the constitutionally protected right to health and life was in issue. The judgment affirmed that '… the right to procreation was to be seen in the frame of responsible procreation in the context of a responsibility ethic and appealing to the freedom of conscience of those directly involved, taking account of what has been referred to as respect for the human conditions of procreation, whereby, in certain circumstances, the right to have children is transformed into a duty not to have them'.[14]

In a further case, a mother of four children, was pregnant a fifth time and the doctors had decided to deliver by Caesarean section. The petitioner, aged 38, had been recently widowed. She had already had one spontaneous abortion and had been unable to cope with other methods of contraception. The judge, relying on a psychological expert, found that she had given her free and informed consent to the operation and to its consequences. He considered it was a decision to be taken within the scope of her private life. Medical prognosis was that a further pregnancy would entail psychological danger, and would contravene the duty of the State to ensure the life and health of citizens, laid out in the National Constitution and in treaties and conventions of constitutional rank. Bearing this in mind, he granted the petition, authorising the doctors to carry out ligation of the tubes at the time of the Caesarean section.[15]

Likewise, the Superior Tribunal de Justicia of Entre Rios Province gave authorisation for tubal ligation for a 35-year-old married woman with five children and problems of hypertension who was unable to use other methods of contraception.

2   PERSONS UNDER INCAPACITY

People under incapacity are in a different position, because it is not they themselves who petition, but a representative on their behalf. This being so, judges examine the background of the case in detail, which concerns what is to happen to the body of someone who cannot give informed consent in person.

We cite as an example the case of an insane person, whose representative applied to the court for her to be sterilised. The judge rejected the petition, because '… representation by a curator does not extend to actions affecting the person of one under incapacity' and, further, because such intervention was not justified on any medical grounds.[16]

A judge came to the contrary decision in the case of a woman who had been declared insane by the court and was detained in a psychiatric establishment. Her curator had applied for her to have her tubes tied. Four children of her marriage

---

[14]   Juzgado Criminal y Correccional de Transición N 1 de Mar del Plata, Provincia de Buenos Aires, Case AZ, CN, 3 February 1999, *Jurisprudencia Argentina* 21 July 1999, noted by Marcelo Tinant 'Salud, privacidad y acceso a la jurisdicción'.

[15]   Juzgado Criminal y Correccional N 1 de Mar del Plata, Provincia de Buenos Aires, Case G, LM, 2 March 1999, in *Jurisprudencia Argentina* 10 May 2000, p 75, with commentary by Elsa B Benitez and Carlos A Ghersi, 'Los conflictos entre derechos personalisimos: Derecho a la salud o la procreación y el Derecho de la mujer a decidir su proprio projecto'.

[16]   Juzgado Nacional de Primera Instancia en lo Civil N 1 de la Capital Federal, Case ING, 5 November 1987, *ED* 130-525.

were living with their father. Another three children born of a de facto union had been placed for adoption. Her last two daughters were in an institution for minors. Her state of health prevented her from caring for her children. Contraception was not advisable as she could not cope with it. She had no family support, failed to continue with psychiatric treatment when not in hospital, and there was no means of stabilising her mental condition. The court found that sterilisation would be therapeutic, since the medical evidence was that it would avoid a worsening of her psychiatric condition, that is to say it would be preventive in character. By the operation 'the benefit principle' would be achieved (to secure the fuller well-being of the person) in favour of the patient and with regard to her potential future children, for whom '… situations of deprivation and social danger' would be avoided. In essence, the decision maintains the full force of the bioethical justice principle, in that it preserves the health, quality of life and well-being, in its widest sense, both of the person directly concerned – the mother – and her existing and potential children, and also of society in general.[17] Iñigo has pointed out that this is a situation which involves preventing a woman '… continuing a pregnancy without fully understanding her own reproductive functions and the responsibility of parenthood, the possible physical and emotional consequences and, most grievous of all, the separation of mother and baby soon after birth, because of her inability to give responsible care'.[18]

3   WOMEN APPLY TO BE STERILISED, NEVER MEN

In our view, whether between partners in a married or a de facto relationship, it is reasonable for the choice of methods of sterilisation (tubal ligation or vasectomy) to be made by the agreement of the couple themselves.

What we find is that, in the judicial precedents we have set out, petitions before the Argentine courts have been presented exclusively by women who seek sterilisation. There is no record of a man applying for a vasectomy, whether in marriage or in a stable irregular union. It is also noteworthy that judges, rather than proceeding to deal with the surgical procedure on the basis of the woman's decision alone, also cite the man with whom she is in a stable relationship, whether they are married or not, and require his consent. Apparently this is necessary since the operation has effects for both, even if the operation only affects the woman's body.

All we can see from the cases is that for the woman to be sterilised requires the consent of the man; there are no cases in which the possibility that the man should have a vasectomy was considered. This failure to weigh up both possibilities amounts to a subtle and accepted form of discrimination against women. After bilateral tubal ligation, if the couple splits up and new relationships are entered upon, the woman's fertility, unless the operation can be reversed, will have been lost, while the man keeps his intact. Obviously, using sterilisation as a means of birth control impacts on one or other of the couple. What is alarming is that in Argentina the cases show it is always the woman who is affected.

---

[17]   Juzgado Criminal y Correccional N 3, Mar del Plata, Provincia de Buenos Aires, Case C, JL, judgment of 6 December 1996, *Jurisprudencia Argentina* 6 August 1997, note by Morello Augusto Mario, 'Esterilización de incapaces, derechos fundamentales y garantías procesales'.

[18]   Delia B Iñigo, op cit at fn 8 above, p 843.

In our view, programmes need to be developed to inform women of the basic workings of reproductive health and to harmonise the rights of men and women in relation to sterilisation. It is a matter of protecting health and physical integrity, rights recognised in international documents having constitutional rank in Argentina.[19] So long as the present regime, whereby a person asking to be sterilised is compelled to seek judicial approval, is in force, judges ought to make sure such a person knows all the choices available to the couple. Indeed, to ensure informed consent to the treatment, medical professionals undertaking it ought to provide that information themselves.

II CHANGE OF SEX

Another no less interesting question the courts now have to face embraces two issues: (a) the possibility of sanctioning surgery directed at changing – so far as possible – the genitalia of a person to conform to that person's sense of sexual identity; and (b) giving legal recognition, once such an operation has been performed, to the person's new sexual identity. In either case, the person concerned will ask for a change of name, and hence the amendment of the birth record, national identity documents and educational qualification certificates.

In one case, the petitioner was now 59 years old, registered as male, but had always exhibited 'feminine' behaviour. For years she suffered the jokes of fellow students, her biological mother abandoned her and she was asked to leave home by her adopted mother when her husband died. Then she took up residence where nobody knew her and dressed as a woman. She stated that her whole life was a constant and inescapable breach of her human rights, since she worked without being registered, so as not to be forced to provide explanations relating to intimate personal matters. As a result she had no pension contributions or medical insurance. She completed Red Cross training as a geriatric nurse but could not receive certification for want of national identity papers. Finally, she stated that there was a severe discrepancy between her 'legal' (masculine) sex and her inclinations, emotions and life experiences (which were feminine).

We must note that Law 17.132, Art 19(4) includes, in the list of prohibited surgery, operations 'which modify a patient's sex', save '*where they have been judicially authorised*', but it does not set out criteria justifying such a decision.

In that case, the judge held '… such legislative silence does not prevent the courts from giving effect to the law, so as to protect constitutional rights, values and principles, linked in the actual situation to the right to "*personal identity*" in general and "*sexual identity*" in particular'. He added that '… the right to what is called "personal identity", in which category the "right to sexual identity" forms a subset, presents a gap in the ever-growing assemblage of rights of the person ("personalísimos"), which is now a notion both richer and deeper than the old concept linked to mere "identification"'. The judge pointed out that the

---

19   Inter alia, Art 1 of the Declaración Humana de los Derechos y Deberes del Hombre (Bogotá, Colombia, 1948), Art 3 of the Universal Declaration of Human Rights, Arts 4 and 5 of the American Convention on Human Rights (San José de Costa Rica), Arts 6 and 7 of the International Pact on Civil and Political Rights, Arts 1, 12 and 16 of the Convention on the Elimination of all forms of Discrimination against Women.

incompatibility between sex determined on the basis of external characteristics and psychological or psychosocial sex creates various problems in the solving of which, so far as possible, the judge must avoid all rigidity.

The judicial decision distinguishes *transsexuality* (a conflict between the rejected biological sex and psychological sex), *homosexuality* (the individual, whose biological sex is not denied, is sexually attracted to persons of the same sex), *transvestism* (while biological sex is not denied, the person wants to wear opposite-sex clothing) and *hermaphroditism* (an individual with internal and/or external organs of both sexes, or with ambiguous organs – pseudo-hermaphroditism). A *transsexual* is convinced of belonging to the opposite sex to that indicated by the external sexual organs – 'a woman imprisoned in a man's body' (or vice versa) – and hence has the feelings, attitudes, desires and interests of the opposite sex. The judge found that the petition was within the frame of self-directed conduct, supported by the National Constitution (Art 19), not affecting public order or causing harm to third parties, since it was a case of a single, childless person. In the result, the judgment was that it would be appropriate to authorise surgery, to harmonise the legal sex with the psychosocial, and to amend the birth registration, in order to harmonise principles, concepts and values such as human dignity, freedom – and the right to self-realisation – the right of personal identity, the right not to be discriminated against and the right to health, all rooted in the Constitution.[20]

Recently, in Córdoba city, the petition was granted of a person whose sexual organs had been surgically altered in three operations in Chile. The life history was like the preceding case but the other way round. The person always dressed as a male, and, at a Catholic girls' school, wore boys' underclothes under the school uniform. This also incurred the mockery of fellow pupils. In 1996 a first operation removed the breasts. On a second visit to Chile in 1999, the female reproductive organs were removed and prosthetic silicon testicles implanted. In 2000 a prosthetic penis formed from the skin of the abdomen was implanted, conserving the greater part of the clitoris to permit sexual enjoyment. A fourth operation directed the urinary tract through the prosthesis. The judge granted the petition to annul partially and absolutely the former birth registration, and ordering that the new entry retain the details of filiation, parentage, date and place of birth, but changing the name and sex.[21] The judgment affirms that this 'assimilates, as far as possible, the person to the sex he feels and in which he wishes to be established'. It is this right to personal and sexual identity that must be recognised, bringing the courts and their application of the law into line with other disciplines, which give support and practical solutions to the human realities that confront them. The decision adds that not recognising the force of the petitioner's claim 'would

---

[20]   Juzgado Criminal y Correccional de Transición N 1, Mar del Plata, Provincia de Buenos Aires, Case n 7/60, 19 July 2001 (unreported).

[21]   Juzgado en lo Civil y Comercial de Decimonovena Nominación de la Ciudad de Córdoba a cargo de Dr Mario Raúl Lescano, Provincia de Córdoba, judgment N 753, 18 September 2001, *La Nación daily*, 21 September 2001, p 17.

clearly and completely violate and ignore rights established in the International Law of Human Rights'.[22]

The judge added that the current identity documents of the petitioner contained an error – an obvious reference to the sex and name – which, he held, justified annulment. Consequently, he found it necessary to take measures, both administrative and in relation to registration, to ensure that, should marriage be contemplated in the future, the prospective spouse would have the opportunity of knowing the real identity of the person with whom the union was to be formed. Also, as the operations resulted in sterilising the patient, should an adoption be proposed, it would be necessary that the judge be given the relevant information. For these reasons and to protect the rights and freedoms of third parties, the judge ordered that, in the new birth record, an annotation be inserted stating explicitly: 'In case of marriage or adoption, he must, in good faith and in advance, inform the future spouse and the competent authorities or the adoption judge of the terms of this judgment ...'. This annotation permits interested parties, and only them (because it is their right) to know what they need to know about the situation of the proposed spouse or adopter to make a free and informed decision. The individual's right to privacy is protected, while at the same time preventive measures are taken to protect the right of others to information so as to avoid subsequent actions for annulment.

III THE RIGHTS OF CHILDREN AND ADOLESCENTS IN RELATION TO REPRODUCTIVE HEALTH

The rights of children and adolescents to the protection of their reproductive health forms part of the broader issue of their autonomy, in line with the development of the ability to understand the situations which affect them personally. The logic of growing towards adulthood, 'preparing for an independent life in society' (Preamble to the Convention on the Rights of the Child), comes up against the fear that children's independence may endanger the legitimate exercise of the parents' role.

In our country, in spite of various legislative measures on childhood and adolescence, based not only on their protection, but also on their advancement, we still have not created a system that adequately guarantees the right of children or adolescents to the control of their own bodies.

Under our Civil Code, minors over 14 years of age have capacity to give informed consent as they have discretion (Art 921, CC). This allows them to perform a number of actions, inter alia to recognise children, to be parties to criminal proceedings, to work, to administer their income, to take proceedings in relation to the employment contract, to work in a profession, to give evidence, etc. Still, there is no law giving them the necessary autonomy to decide on the care of their own bodies.

---

[22] The Pact of San José de Costa Rica (Art 5), Universal Declaration of Human Rights, International Treaty on Civil and Political Rights, treaties ranking with the Constitution (Art 75 sub para 22 of the National Constitution), and Antidiscrimination Law N 23.592.

Currently, in our country, the consent of parents or legal representatives is needed for any medical treatment of a minor up to the age of 21 (Law 17.132, Art 19, sub para 3). Some laws exist allowing the consent of persons below that age. For example the law on blood donation (N 22.990), establishes that donations can be made over the age of 16, but those under 18 must obtain consent of parents or legal representatives (Art 44, a and b); the law on organ and tissue donation (N 24.193) requires that a donor must be over 18. In the case of bone marrow transplants, those under 18 can be donors with prior consent of their legal representative (Art 15).

On the other hand, the Code of Ethics of the Medical Confederation of the Argentine Republic establishes that no operation on minors should be performed without the consent of the patient's parents or guardians. For minor adults (over the age of 14) their own consent is enough for urgent and essential operations if there is no time to contact their family (Art 18).

Within this broad picture, it is important to single out the laws on reproductive health and responsible paternity passed in the City of Buenos Aires and in some provinces. These laws give special priority to adolescents, as they are a sector of the population in which we see most dramatically the need for policies for the prevention of unwanted pregnancies. This situation is seen particularly in poor homes, where more than six million children and young persons under 18 live, that is 53% of the children and adolescents in the country.

One objective of these laws on reproductive health has been to reduce the death rate of mother and child, which, in the case of adolescents is alarmingly high. In the face of an unwanted pregnancy, abortion is one of the alternatives for a young woman who lacks resources, if she has the support neither of a partner nor of her family. As abortion is not permitted in our country, it is carried out clandestinely, in primitive and deficient conditions, which endanger the life of the pregnant woman. It is hard to establish the figures, but it is thought that more than half a million abortions are performed each year, many of them on women under 20. Complications resulting from these form the primary cause of admissions in public hospitals and the third most frequent cause of death among women of childbearing age. In Argentina, according to the 1998 data relating maternal death to the mother's age, this was 45.1 per thousand for under-15s, 22 per thousand for 15-to-19-year-olds, and came down to 12.4 among 19-to-25-year-olds. It is even more marked in poor provinces. Many adolescent mothers have one or two children already. Births to girls between 12 and 14 years old have risen in recent years. One in every two hundred babies in the country is born to a woman younger than 15, and in the City of Buenos Aires, 18% of births in 1992 were to adolescents.

This social background shows that conceiving a child is not a matter of choice, but results from ignorance and poor conditions, for a girl lacking basic necessities, and without parental support.

The reproductive health laws that have been passed have been directed at giving effect to international agreements, especially the Convention on the Elimination of all forms of Discrimination against Women, which has constitutional ranking (Art 75, sub para 22), and obliges signatory States to take measures to ensure access to medical attention, including information, advice, and services in relation to family planning (Arts 12, 14.2.b and 16.1.e).

The law in force in Buenos Aires covers 'providing access to information and to the benefits in kind, methods and services necessary for the responsible exercise of their reproductive and sexual rights' (Art 3). Similar laws apply in other provinces. The law is directed at persons of 'fertile age'. This means that it is the adolescents and young persons themselves who have access to the services, at any age, if they have reproductive capacity, and who give informed consent to the services on offer. It envisages personalised advice, that is the right use of the services in each individual case (Art 7).

There is no doubt that the moment at which one wants to have a child is a highly personal decision, which cannot be replaced by the wishes of one's parents who, even if they have the right and duty to advise, bring up and educate their children according to their convictions, can never prevent them from determining such a personal and private matter, in line with their own possibilities, life plan and beliefs. When it is a question of the care of health it is necessary to distinguish between the bioethical concept of 'competence' and that of 'legal capacity'. From the moment when the adolescent is physically capable of procreation, the law allows him or her to take care of this aspect of health and to decide whether he or she wants to become a parent. It is sufficient to have the ability to receive the information and to understand the details of provisions for contraception, to be able to come to a decision.

We wish to point out that there has been a complaint that some parts of the 'Law of Reproductive Health and Responsible Paternity' of the City of Buenos Aires are unconstitutional, because they give minors the right of access to the services described in the law, without the consent of parents or legal representatives. The complainants maintain that this violates the right to exercise parental authority (patria potestas). The case is still pending.

In our view, not only does the law on reproductive health in question respect the freedom of parents to educate their children according to their values and beliefs, but also it furthers their active participation in 'everything pertaining to the reproductive health of their children' (Art 7.e) and promotes joint discussion of the matter between parents and children (Art 4.n). Further, the information provided in these reproductive health services is also offered to parents or other adults, in compliance with Art 18.2 of the Convention on the Rights of the Child, to ensure their proper orientation in the matter.

If it is primarily the responsibility of parents to rear and bring up their children (Art 18 of the Convention on the Rights of the Child), the State, in the role of guarantor of those rights, must protect children if parents are absent, or are not in a position to advise them as they come to puberty, on account of their economic and cultural situation. We must not forget that many children and adolescents, with fragile or non-existent family networks and lacking support, daily use various survival strategies which lead to indiscriminate sexual practices and to consequent early pregnancies. It is also well known that, all too often, children do not talk to their parents about sexual matters, nor do the parents know how to tackle these problems. From the moment when the adolescent is physically able to procreate, it is his or her right to take care of this aspect of health and decide whether he or she really wants to become a father or mother since, whatever their age, adolescents have the right to protect their life, biopsychosocial integrity, health and development. Certainly many young people who live with their parents have good communication with them and receive, at this crucial stage, essential information, guidance and adequate support, including where necessary consulting professionals. On the other hand there are a large number of adolescents and young people who lack family backup and resources and who require action by the community and by the State to take care of their health and mature sexuality.

However, it is also necessary to remember the right to confidentiality arising from the highly personal right to one's private life recognised in Art 16 of the Convention on the Rights of the Child and other treaties on human rights. We must realise that many adolescents will neither seek information nor call on the reproductive health services, if in so doing they must get parental consent. While involvement of parents in this has to be encouraged and promoted, still confidentiality is a crucial aspect of any preventive strategy. It must be noted that children's right to health, which parents have to support, as defined by the World Health Organisation, implies their total welfare, physical, mental and social, not just the absence of disease.

We must also consider the prevention of AIDS and other sexually transmitted diseases. If parents oppose a child's recourse to the services and receipt of the established benefits, this conduct also adversely affects the adolescent's essential human rights (right to life, to psychophysical integrity, to development and to health).

The orientation, control and educational patterns of parents and other adults, aimed at creating a responsible, mature sexual culture in adolescence, does not mean the negation of their right to privacy in their lives, including the possibility of establishing relationships of their choice in the external world,[23] especially in its emotional aspects.

Naturally, it is for parents and guardians to intervene if the child or adolescent becomes the victim of abuse or is exposed to danger. Necessarily, the reproductive health services open the way to circumstances in which dangerous situations arise, which could affect children and adolescents. The doctor must assess in the consultation, in each actual case, not only the appropriate prescription, given the age of the adolescent,[24] but also strategies to be followed in which, within the context of advice tailored to personal situations and circumstances, participation of parents or guardians can be recommended, so as to encourage their involvement to resolve any underlying problems that may be uncovered in the course of professional intervention.

---

[23] From the interpretation given by the European Human Rights Commission to Art 8 of the European Convention on Human Rights.

[24] Programme of Action approved by the International Conference on Population and Development, 1994, para 7.44.

AUSTRALIA

WHAT CHANGE IS FOR THE BETTER? AUSTRALIAN FAMILY LAW IN 2000

Frank Bates[*]

I   INTRODUCTORY

There can be little doubt that Australian family law in the year 2000 has been something of a strange mixture. There have been statutory reforms which, arguably at the very least, have done something to make the administration of family law rather more difficult than need have been the case, including one which this writer urged against when it was first canvassed.[1] Other changes appear largely to be unworkable. At the same time, there have been some interesting and worthwhile developments in case-law, especially as they relate to the amendments to child law as effected in 1995.[2]

II   STATUTORY CHANGES

A   Financial agreements

The Family Law Amendment Act 2000 introduces a new Part VIIIA into the Act which deals with financial agreements whensoever they were made.[3] Thus, s 90B provides that such agreements may be made before marriage; s 90C provides that they may be made during marriage and s 90D provides that they may be made after a decree absolute.[4] There are no real differences regarding the procedures governing these kinds of agreement. This presents an immediate problem: prenuptial agreements are treated no differently from those which are entered into as part of a divorce settlement. This, it is submitted, is absurd in that a prenuptial agreement cannot meaningfully anticipate a marital breakdown, say, 25 years[5] before the event when the parties' financial circumstances normally cannot be known. In the divorce situation, of course, usually all the relevant circumstances which are necessary for a proper determination will be known.

---

[*]   LLM Professor of Law, The University of Newcastle.

[1]   See F Bates, 'Reforming Australian Matrimonial Property Law' (1989) 17 Anglo-Am LR 46.

[2]   For comment, see, P E Nygh, 'The New Part VII – An Overview' (1996) 10 Aust J Fam L 4.

[3]   The new Part VIIIA takes the place of the pre-existing ss 86 and 87 of the Family Law Act 1975.

[4]   Section 71A of the Act provides that Part VIII, which deals with the discretionary aspects of family property law, does not apply to property which is the object of an agreement.

[5]   The period is wholly coincidental – it is based on the length of the author's marriage, at least at the time of writing … !

Given all of that, it will readily be apparent that the kind of legal advice which parties are obliged to receive is likely to be a central issue. In particular, this is of especial importance given the rather limited grounds on which these agreements can be set aside.[6] Section 90G of the Family Law Act 1975 now sets out the kind of advice which practitioners are required to provide. The agreement must, in relation to each party, contain a statement to the effect that the relevant party has had independent legal advice from a legal practitioner, prior to signing the agreement, relating to: first, the legal effect of the agreement; secondly, whether or not the agreement was to the advantage of the party; thirdly, whether or not it was prudent for the party to enter into the agreement and, finally, whether or not the provisions of the agreement were fair and reasonable in the light of such circumstances as were reasonably foreseeable. An annexure to the agreement must contain appropriate certificates signed by the person who has provided the advice which state that the advice has been provided. Once again, a problem arises: the legislation merely requires that there must be a *statement*[7] to the effect that the advice has been received, not that the parties have actually received the advice. The question thus arises as to whether the courts may look behind the certificate to see whether appropriate advice was given.[8] Whatever the strict legalities, evidentiary problems are likely to be considerable and there may be significant reluctance on the part of legal practitioners to sign s 90G(1) certificates.[9]

The grounds on which agreements can be set aside are set out in s 90K. There are five of these, largely derived[10] from previous legislation: a court may make an order setting aside a relevant agreement:

(1)   if the agreement was obtained by fraud, including non-disclosure of a material matter;
(2)   if the agreement is void, voidable or unenforceable;
(3)   if in the circumstances which have arisen since the agreement was made, it is impracticable for the agreement or part of the agreement to be carried out;
(4)   if since the making of the agreement, a material change has occurred, being circumstances which relate to the care, welfare and development of a child of the marriage, and, as a result of the change, the child or, if the applicant has caring responsibility for the child, a party to the agreement will suffer hardship if the court does not set aside the agreement; or
(5)   if, in respect of the making of such an agreement, a party to an agreement has engaged in conduct which was, in all the circumstances, unconscionable.

---

[6]   Text at note 10 below.

[7]   Author's emphasis.

[8]   There is conflicting authority: in cases involving family companies, there is a reluctance to look behind the corporate veil, see *Ascot Investments v Harper* (1981) 148 CLR 337. On the other hand, in procedural matters there may be a greater willingness so to do, see *In the Marriage of Garlick* (1993) FLC 92-428.

[9]   The writer has considerable anecdotal evidence that that might be the case.

[10] The first two paragraphs are derived from s 87(8) of the Act which concerned the setting aside of s 87 agreements. The third could have been found in both s 87(8) and s 79A, which deals with the setting aside of property orders. The fourth is substantially derived from s 79A, although the change of circumstances which relates to the welfare of the child does not have to be exceptional, as is the case in s 79A. The last paragraph is new.

Although a detailed analysis of these provisions is beyond the scope of a commentary of this nature, some general points must be made. First, in family law proceedings, Australia has not been happy in matters relating to fraud – in particular in relation to entry into marriage itself.[11] As regards the second ground, the relevance of unilateral mistake and estoppel is unclear and many of the same considerations are likely to be applicable to the last ground. *In fine* it may be quite some time before the problems attaching to these agreements are even remotely resolved. During that time, members of the legal profession in Australia and who practice in the area (and were taught by this writer) might reap some relatively rich rewards!

B   Parenting order compliance

If the new provisions relating to financial agreements are likely to be productive of litigation, the complexity of the amendments relating to compliance with orders affecting children is still more so. First of all, failure to comply with orders affecting children is to be dealt with separately from failure to comply with other orders – compliance with orders affecting children being contained in a new Division 13A of Part VIII of the Family Law Act 1975.[12] In essence, the new Division contains a three-stage 'parenting compliance regime' in respect of contravention of orders affecting children. This involves *prevention*,[13] *remediation*,[14] and *sanctions*.[15]

Under Stage 1 of this regime, parents entering into parenting plans and persons who are affected by parenting orders must be provided with information regarding the obligations which the parenting plan or order creates and the possible implications of failure to comply with them. Thus, people entering into parenting plans must be given information about the availability of programmes to help those who experience problems with parenting plans. Likewise, people affected by parenting orders must be given information regarding the availability of programmes to assist them in understanding their responsibilities under parenting orders, as well as the way in which location and recovery orders are used to ensure that parenting orders are enforced.

Although that aim might, *prima facie*, be both desirable and straightforward, it would be wrong to suggest that problems do not exist.

First, the explanatory information required by the new legislation[16] to be included in a parenting order must be in a language which is likely readily to be understood by the person to whom the order is directed. It goes without saying that Australia is an immigrant community[17] and it is very far from unlikely that an

---

[11]   See *In the Marriage of Deniz* (1977) 31 FLR 114; *In the Marriage of Otway* (1987) FLC 91-807; *In the Marriage of El Soukmani and Al Soukmani* (1990) FLC 92-107; *In the Marriage of Osman and Mourrali* (1990) FLC 92-111; *Najjarin v Houlayce* (1991) FLC 92-246.

[12]   Failure to comply with other orders is contained in Part XIIIA, and provisions relating to contempt will now be contained in a new Part XIIIB.

[13]   Family Law Act 1975, ss 63DA and 65DA, as introduced in 2000.

[14]   Ibid, Division 13A, Subdivision B.

[15]   Ibid, Division 13A, Subdivision C.

[16]   Ibid, s 65D.

[17]   See, for example, R Hartley (ed) *Families and Cultural Diversity in Australia* (1995).

order might be directed to someone who does not read English. It is far from clear whether the provision means that the order itself will be in English and the explanatory memorandum which accompanies it will be in a language that the person can read, or whether the whole order should be translated into the appropriate language. In turn, that raises the issue of the costs of the translation and the possibility (or likelihood) of delay in obtaining a translation of an urgent order.

Furthermore, when the court makes a parenting order, the court must include in the order particulars of the obligations created by the order[18] and the consequences which may follow if the order is contravened.[19] However, it is further provided[20] that the court is enabled to request that parties' legal representatives assist in explaining the latter provision to their clients. Strangely, the section does not require the court to explain these matters to anyone, as they are required to be contained in the order.[21] Even more peculiar is the power in the same provision which enables the court to request that legal representatives explain to clients the availability of programmes which seek to help people understand their responsibilities under parenting orders and the availability of location and recovery orders aimed at ensuring that parenting orders are complied with.[22] That provision only applies to unrepresented parties!

Section 63DA seems almost to be as greatly disorganised as s 65DA: it first requires counsellors, mediators and legal practitioners who give assistance to people in relation to the making of a parenting plan to explain the obligations which such a plan creates. Unfortunately, parenting plans do not appear to create any legal obligations (as opposed to moral obligations, with which the legislation is, presumably, not concerned).[23] It is also unclear as to the effect of a failure to comply with the provisions of s 63DA on the validity of a parenting plan. Although s 65DA provides that failure to comply with those provisions will not affect a plan's validity, there is no equivalent provision in s 63DA.

As regards Stage 2 of the process: s 70NF(1) provides generally that if a contravention of an order affecting children has occurred to the satisfaction of the court and the person does not prove that he or she had a reasonable excuse for the contravention and no previous order has been made, or if the court determines that it is more appropriate that, notwithstanding the existence of a prior order, that contravention be dealt with under Stage 2, various orders may be made. One provision of particular note[24] is that Stage 2 will not apply if the court dealing with the *current contravention*[25] is satisfied that the person who contravened the

---

[18]   Family Law Act 1975, s 65DA(1).

[19]   Ibid, s 65DA(2).

[20]   Ibid, s 65DA(5).

[21]   Ibid, s 65DA(2).

[22]   Ibid, s 65DA(30).

[23]   If a parenting plan is registered under s 63E, particular consequences may arise under ss 63FF and 63G from the fact of registration, but s 63DA is silent on any obligations arising from registration.

[24]   Family Law Act 1975, s 70NF(2).

[25]   So described at ibid, s 70NF(1)(b).

primary order[26] had behaved in a way which demonstrated a serious disregard for his or her obligations under the Act.

There are a wide variety of orders available under the amendments.[27] The court may do all, or any, of the following: first, the court may order the person who has contravened the order (or another specified person) to attend before the provider of a specified, appropriate post-separation parenting programme. The purpose of this is that the provider can make an initial assessment of the suitability of the person to attend such a programme; if the person is assessed as being suitable and the provider nominates a particular programme (or part of any such programme), the court may direct the person to attend. Secondly, the court may make a further parenting order which compensates for contact which has been forgone as the result of the current contravention. Additionally, the court is empowered to adjourn the proceedings to permit either party to apply for a further parenting order which discharges, varies or suspends the primary order or revives some or all of an earlier parenting order.[28] In deciding whether to adjourn the proceedings, courts must have regard to four matters:[29]

(1)   whether the primary order was made by consent;
(2)   whether either or both of the parties in which the primary order was made were legally represented in those proceedings;
(3)   the length of the period between the making of the primary order and the occurrence of the current contravention; and
(4)   other matters which the court thinks relevant.

Further, courts must not order[30] a person other than the person who contravened the order to attend a post-separation parenting programme[31] unless that person is the applicant or otherwise a party to the proceedings. Courts must also be satisfied that it is appropriate to make the order because of the current contravention and the carrying out by the person of his or her parental responsibilities in relation to any children to which the primary order relates. It is provided[32] that where a person attends a programme for assessment or the programme itself, the provider must advise courts of three matters. These are: first, whether the person who attends for assessment is considered unsuitable to attend any such programme;[33] secondly, if a person fails to attend a programme or part of a programme which that person was required to attend;[34] or thirdly, if the provider considers that the person is unsuitable to take any further part in the

---

[26]   So described at ibid, s 70NF(1)(a).

[27]   Ibid, s 70NG(1).

[28]   Ibid, Part VII, Division 6.

[29]   Ibid, s 70NG(1A).

[30]   Ibid, s 70NG(2).

[31]   A post-separation programme is described, in ibid, s 70NB, as a programme which is designed (including by providing counselling services or by teaching techniques to resolve disputes) to help people resolve problems that adversely affect the carrying into effect of their parenting responsibilities and is included in a list of such programmes compiled by the Federal Attorney-General. It consists of lectures, discussions, (including group discussions) and other activities.

[32]   Ibid, s 70NHI.

[33]   Ibid, s 70NH(1).

[34]   Ibid, s 70NH(2)(a).

programme or part of the programme.[35] If it appears to the court that a person has not attended a programme or part of a programme which he or she was ordered to attend, the court may make further directions with respect to that person's attending the programme.[36]

There are very serious difficulties with this part of the legislation. Most obviously, the legislation makes no provision regarding what is to be done if a person ordered to attend a post-separation programme is assessed as being unsuitable to attend that programme or continue to attend the programme. Why then is the provider required to inform the court? In turn, there is no provision[37] with respect to the manner in which the provider is to inform the court. In turn, it is unclear as to whether any such information will be admissible and, if so, under what conditions. Again, it will be remembered that[38] courts are empowered to make a compensatory contact order at Stage 2, but there is no provision for compensatory residence orders. Hence, matters may turn solely on the manner in which a particular order is described. Finally, the position of a person who has contravened a previous order without reasonable excuse is generally uncertain.

Stage 3 of the parenting compliance regime[39] applies in the same circumstances as Stage 2[40] unless courts are satisfied that it is more appropriate for the matters to be dealt with under Stage 2[41] and, if Stage 3 does apply, courts *must*[42] make an order under the relevant subdivision.[43] Thus, courts must make[44] one or more of the following orders: a community service order; an order requiring the respondent to enter into a bond; if the order is a parenting order, then an order varying that order may be made;[45] an order imposing a fine of not more than 60 penalty units;[46] or an order imposing a sentence of imprisonment not exceeding 12 months. When making any of those orders, courts may make any other order which is considered necessary to ensure compliance with the order which was contravened.

Despite the apparent simplicity of Stage 3 provisions, there are, inevitably, problems which arise. Thus, for instance, despite the apparently mandatory nature of that stage,[47] courts retain the power to find that a particular case is more appropriately dealt with under Stage 2.[48] Again, it is unclear whether breach of a different order will bring Stage 3 into operation: thus, if the current contravention is of a contact order and the prior contravention is of a specific issue order, then

---

[35]   Ibid, s 70NH(2)(b).

[36]   Ibid, s 70NHIA.

[37]   Presumably, the Rules of Court will ultimately make such provision.

[38]   Text at note 27 above.

[39]   Family Law Act 1975, Division 13A, Subdivision C.

[40]   Text at note 24 above.

[41]   Family Law Act 1975, s 70NJ(1), (2).

[42]   Author's emphasis.

[43]   Note 39 above.

[44]   Family Law Act 1975, s 70NJ(3), (8).

[45]   If the order is an order affecting children which is not a parenting order, it cannot be varied.

[46]   'Penalty unit' is defined in s 4AA of the Crimes Act 1914 (Cth) as meaning $110. Thus the maximum fine would be $6,600.

[47]   Text at note 42 above.

[48]   Family Law Act 1975, s 70NJ(2).

Stage 3 may very well not be able to be utilised. Likewise, it does not appear that Stage 3, unlike Stage 2, permits courts to make compensatory contact orders.[49] It may be that it was considered that, once Stage 3 had been reached, compensatory orders were not of any real value. However, the contradictory nature of this part of the legislation will readily be apparent.

As regards the practical application of the parenting compliance regime, there are evidential issues which arise. At the hearing of the contravention application, courts will be initially required to decide whether it is satisfied that the applicant has, in fact, contravened the order – the burden of proof resting on the applicant. The standard of proof will be on the balance of probabilities, having regard to the gravity of the issue.[50] Courts will then be required to determine whether the respondent had a reasonable excuse for the contravention; again, the standard of proof will be the balance of probabilities[51] and the onus of proof will be on the respondent. If courts are satisfied that the contravention has taken place and there is no reasonable excuse, they must then decide whether the respondent has been found to have contravened the same order without reasonable excuse, or that the respondent's behaviour showed a serious disregard for his or her obligations under the relevant order. It would seem likely (though not certain) that the onus would rest on the applicant, to the civil standard of proof. Courts which are satisfied of those matters *must*[52] make an order under Stage 3, unless they are satisfied that it is more appropriate to make an order under Stage 2.

It will be readily apparent that the legislation in this area is far from satisfactory and seems to have been put together in some haste, possibly with political motivation. Journalistic comment suggests[53] that it has come about through years of political lobbying by lone fathers' support groups. One such commentator, a Mr Andrew Thomson, is quoted[54] as saying that the legislation would, '... make women a bit more accountable for their actions'. At the same time, he doubted whether the penalties specified in the amendments[55] would be carried out. It is, of course, possible to view the legislation in a different light. Hence, a family law specialist quoted in the same account[56] stated that there was no history of mothers instituting court proceedings to force fathers to have time with their children. 'This whole legislation', he stated, 'is termed a parenting compliance regime, but nothing in the legislation is going to force those recalcitrant fathers, who don't want to see their children, from [*sic*] being proper parents.'

---

49 Text at note 27 above.

50 See Evidence Act 1995 (Cth), s 140. At common law, *Briginshaw v Briginshaw* (1938) 60 CLR 336.

51 Family Law Act 1975, s 70NEA.

52 Author's emphasis.

53 E Connolley, 'Jail New Weapon in Custody Fights', *Sydney Morning Herald* No 50, 976 (December 28, 2000) at 1.

54 Ibid.

55 Text at note 44 above.

56 Mr Duncan Holmes, op cit, note 53 above.

In fine, when taken together with the legislation on financial agreements,[57] it is suggested that the Family Law Amendment Act 2000 may very well represent a genuine disaster in family law reform!

III   CASE-LAW

A   Child law

First, the issue of children's wishes and the use of family reports was considered by the full court of the Family Court of Australia in *R and R: Children's Wishes*.[58] There, the parties had been married for approximately ten years before their separation, when the husband left the matrimonial home. At the time of the hearing at first instance, the two male children of the marriage were aged 12 and ten. Since the separation, the children had lived in the matrimonial home with their mother. During the marriage, the husband's occupation[59] required him to spend considerable periods of time in other parts of Australia and in Asia. The wife and the children usually joined him for all or part of these postings during the marriage. For the two years following the separation, it appeared that there were flexible and sensible arrangements between the parties regarding contact. These arrangements included very frequent visits to the home, camping holidays and a visit to Japan, when the wife accompanied the children.

This pattern was disrupted when the husband was required to live in Thailand, for reasons connected with his employment, for over two years. This greatly distressed the children, even though contact was maintained by telephone, holiday visits to Thailand and visits by the husband to Sydney. On these last occasions, he moved into the matrimonial home with the acquiescence of the wife. Following these various visits, it was clear that the children were distressed on separation from their father.[60]

The trial judge had received and, apparently, accepted a Family Report: the Report indicated that the boys both wished to live with their father, but it also raised concerns about his interactions with the children and his commitment to facilitating contact with their mother. The trial judge had also expressed some reservations regarding the husband's attitude towards his wife and her point of view. In reaching her decision, the trial judge had balanced the children's wishes against factors which favoured the children's remaining in the care of their mother, having regard to the father's attitudes. Although she accepted that the children's views were a weighty consideration, and she viewed them in the light of the fact that they missed their father during his absences, the trial judge nevertheless made a residence order in favour of the wife in respect of both children and ordered that she have responsibility for their day-to-day care, welfare and development. Further orders were made for contact between the children and the husband.

---

[57]   Text at note 33 ff above.

[58]   (2000) FLC 93-000.

[59]   He was an airline engineer.

[60]   That was not disputed by the wife and appeared to have been accepted by the trial judge.

The only issue pursued at the appeal involved the trial judge's treatment of the children's wishes. There were two arguments which were principally advanced: first, that the wishes of children were important and ought not to be departed from where they were soundly based, expressed without influence from either parent and were expressed against a background of particular facts and circumstances; and secondly, that the trial judge was mistaken in fact, in that the expressed wishes of the children were not that they should spend more time with their father but that they should live with him. The Full Court[61] unanimously dismissed the husband's appeal.

First, the court concluded[62] that the trial judge had not misapplied the law and had taken appropriate account of earlier decisions, especially *H v W*[63] and commented that the trial judge, '... was obviously conscious of factors such as the age and degree of maturity of the children and she gave very real and appropriate consideration to their wishes. However it is not the law that those wishes are determinative of the outcome which may be overridden by other factors relevant to the determination of the child's best interests'. In that context, the court referred[64] to a submission made on behalf of the husband that the trial judge had not attempted to determine that the wishes of the children were unsound, or founded on improper considerations or influenced by others. The court, however, took the view that, whilst those considerations would be relevant in many cases, they were not the only issues which a trial judge ought to take into account when considering a child's best interests. '[T]here are many factors,' the court stated, 'that may go to the weight that should be given to the wishes of children and these will vary from case to case and it is undesirable and indeed impossible to catalogue or confine them ... Ultimately it is a process of intuitive synthesis on the part of any trial judge weighing up all the evidence relevant to the wishes of the children and applying it in a common sense way as one of the factors in the overall assessment of the children's best interests.'

This part of the decision does help to clarify the relationship between the best interests of the children and their expressed wishes. However, there are parts of the last quoted passage which are of concern to the present writer: 'intuitive synthesis' is a term which is unlikely to commend itself to critics of the discretionary process to be found in s 68F(2) of the Family Law Act 1975. Although the discretion is altogether more structured after the 1995 amendments than it was when the Act came into force initially, when it was effectively entirely unstructured,[65] criticism of the discretionary process still exists, to the degree that it does not need documentation. Similarly, the use of the platitude 'common sense' does not advance the issue much further at all. As I have written elsewhere,[66] one person's common sense is another's idiocy!

---

[61]   Nicholson DJ, Finn and Guest JJ.

[62]   (2000) FLC 93-000 at 87,073.

[63]   (1995) FLC 92-598; *Doyle and Doyle* (1992) FLC 92-286; *Re P (A Minor) (Education)* [1992] 1 FLR 316.

[64]   (2000) FLC 92-598 at 87, 072.

[65]   Family Law Act 1975, s 64.

[66]   See F Bates, 'Psychiatric Evidence of Character' (1976) 5 Anglo-Am LR 99 at 103.

In respect of family reports, the court commented[67] that the counsellor who had prepared the report had done so on the basis of her professional expertise, rather than on the basis of specific statements made by the children. She had, however, and most properly in the view of the court, when asking the children where they would like to live, told each of them that they did not have to answer the question if they found it uncomfortable so to do. However, it did not appear that a question in similar terms was asked as to how each child would feel if the court did not reach the same conclusion. In the court's view, it was generally desirable that such a question be asked when children did feel comfortable in expressing a preference. The court were of the opinion that the inclusion of such information, as well as the counsellors' assessment of it, was an aid to the better understanding of children's wishes and the process of giving weight to them. The same considerations, the court stated, were applicable to child representatives.[68] These comments seem, likewise, relevant and useful.

One other area which, to this commentator's surprise,[69] has not caused more curial activity in Australian child law is that of education. This did arise in 2000 in the Full Court's decision in *Re G: Children's Schooling*.[70] The case involved an appeal against orders made at first instance which permitted the wife to enrol the two sons of the parties[71] at a particular private school as day students. The parental situation was that, pursuant to consent orders made in 1997, the parties were jointly responsible for the long-term care, welfare and development of the children; the wife was solely responsible for the daily care, welfare and development of the children who resided with her, with the husband having contact. The children had been educated at another private school since pre-school but the wife had always wanted the children to attend the other school. The parents had agreed on the school at which they had hitherto been educated as a compromise. The trial judge had made up her mind as to which school the children attended on the basis of the opinion expressed by the parents.

In reaching the conclusion which she did, the trial judge had taken into account various matters. These were: first, that the children had lived constantly with their mother; secondly, that the wife had undertaken thorough research into the relative merits of the two schools; thirdly, the children's wishes that they remain at their present school; fourthly, the fact that the younger child had a physical disability; fifthly, the fact that the travel time to the school proposed was much shorter than the travel time to and from the school which the children presently attended; sixthly, in view of that fact, that the wife's intention to undertake retraining or employment might be hindered; last, a family report which had been prepared for the proceedings which was consistent with the wife's opinion that the children would be able to cope with a change of school.

The husband's appeal raised four grounds: first, that the trial judge was wrong in law in deciding that the parent with whom the children lived had the right to decide the school which the children should attend; secondly, that the trial judge

---

[67]   (2000) FLC 93-000 at 87, 073.

[68]   See Family Law Act 1975, s 68L; also *P and P* (1995) FLC 92-615; *A v J* FLC 92-619.

[69]   See F Bates, 'Maintenance and Private School Fees' [1988] 2 Aust J Fam L 125.

[70]   (2000) FLC 93-025.

[71]   Who were aged eight and ten at the time of the trial.

had wrongly applied the earlier decision in *Newbery and Newbery*[72] regardless of the 1995 amendments to the Family Law Act 1975; thirdly, that the trial judge had erred either in law or fact by holding that a change of education was appropriate without any cogent evidence that such a change would benefit the children; and fourthly, that the trial judge was in error in not treating the best interests of the children as the paramount consideration. The Full Court[73] dismissed the appeal, although they were far from satisfied with the processes by which the trial judge had arrived at her decision.

First, the court were of the view[74] that the trial judge's reliance on the decision in *Newbery* cast a shadow over the process by which she had reached her decision, as that case did not represent the law either before or after the 1995 amendments to the Act. In particular, the court referred[75] to comments of the Full Court in the central case of *B and B: Family Law Reform Act*[76] that, 'Residence is not custody by another name. It has a more constrained meaning, being limited to identifying the person or persons with whom a child is to live'. It followed, the court considered, that, at the time *Newbery* was decided, the responsibility conferred upon a custodial parent was greater than that which existed, certainly after 1995.

The court also applied the decision of the Full Court in *R and R: Children's Wishes*[77] and concluded[78] that, '... proper regard must be had to the expressed wishes of the children and reasons for decision must reflect their importance. However, there is no presumption that decisions should accord with expressed wishes and it is not to be expected that lengthy reasons for departing from expressed wishes is the equivalent to showing "good reason" for doing so'. That being the case, the trial judge had not misdirected herself in any regard concerning the facts of the instant case.

After having examined the detailed provisions of s 68F(2) of the Family Law Act 1975, as amended in 1995, the court took the view[79] that the wife's greater understanding of the children tempered concerns regarding the consequences of change upon them and increased the weight which should be placed on her assessment of the benefit of change of schools. Likewise, considerable weight should be given to the wife's views on transport and, in that context, the court noted[80] that the considerations to which they had referred were not confined to the interests of the residential caregiver. They were of the view that there were obvious benefits to the best interests of the children (which were the paramount, although not the only, consideration in their being able to participate readily in activities outside school hours without the necessity for extensive travel).

---

[72] (1977) FLC 90-205.

[73] Nicholson CJ, Kay and Brown JJ.

[74] (2000) FLC 93-025 at 87, 409.

[75] Ibid at 87, 410.

[76] (1997) FLC 92-755 at 84, 218 per Nicholson CJ, Fogarty and Lindenmayer JJ.

[77] Text at note 58 ff above.

[78] (2000) FLC 93-025 at 87, 415.

[79] Ibid at 87, 419.

[80] Ibid at 87, 420.

Re G: Children's Schooling, although an interesting case and one which reinforces the view to be found in *R and R* regarding the importance to be attached to children's wishes, does not really resolve any fundamental dilemmas relating to education. In part, that is because the dispute involved attendance at separate private schools, so that ideology was not involved and, hence, despite the rejection of *Newbery*, the court has failed to resolve the issue raised by the Full Court of the Family Court of Australia in *Mee and Ferguson*.[81] There, the court stated that, 'The development of the dual school system in Australia is an interesting aspect of Australian history, but courts have always avoided being drawn into the issue of preference between them as a generality'. How long it will be before the courts in Australia have to come to grips with the public/private school dichotomy is hard to predict, but the fact that *Re G* was litigated at all suggests that it may be sooner rather than later.

In view of the importance and the factual situation in *B and B: Family Law Reform Act 1995*,[82] which was the first major decision of the Full Court after the 1995 amendments, it would have been surprising had there not been decisions on parental relocations. A particularly interesting instance is the decision of the Full Court in *A v A: Relocation Approach*.[83] In that case, the parties had married in 1990 and had separated in 1994; there was one child of the marriage who, at the time of trial, was nine years of age. The wife also had another child from a previous marriage who presently lived with her father in Portugal. In 1995, Nicholson CJ made orders, using the terminology of the Family Law Act 1975, as it then stood, that the parents be joint *guardians* of the child, that the mother have *custody* and that the father have *access* as specified. In 1999, the mother sought, and the father opposed, an order enabling her to relocate, together with the child, to Portugal. About the same time, contact between the child and the father ceased and, at the time of the appeal, there were orders suspending contact until further order.

The mother had terminated contact on the basis of 'inappropriate' behaviour on the part of the husband. However, the trial judge was of the view that steps ought to be taken as quickly as possible to re-establish contact between the father and daughter. The mother appealed against orders which provided that the father have specified contact with the child. The Full Court[84] allowed the appeal and ordered an expedited re-trial.

In reaching that conclusion, the court regarded[85] earlier case-law[86] as being authority for the following propositions: first, in determining a parenting case which includes a proposal to relocate the residence of a child, the best interests of the child remain the paramount, although not the sole, consideration. Secondly, in determining such a case, courts cannot require the applicant for the child's

[81]   (1968) FLC 91-716 at 75, 200 per Asche ACJ, Fogarty and Cook JJ. For comment, see F Bates, 'Maintenance and Private School Fees' (1988) 2 Aust J Fam L 125.

[82]   (1997) FLC 92-755. For comment, see F Bates, 'Something Old, Something New ... – Australian Family Law in 1997' in A Bainham (ed) *The International Survey of Family Law* (Family Law, 1999) 23.

[83]   (2000) FLC 93-035.

[84]   Nicholson CJ, Ellis and Coleman JJ.

[85]   (2000) FLC 93-035 at 87, 544.

[86]   In particular, the decision of the High Court of Australia in *AMS v AIF* (1999) 73 ALJR 927.

relocation to demonstrate compelling reasons for the relocation contrary to the proposition that the welfare of the child would be better promoted by the continuance of the existing circumstances.

In addition to those basic premises, the court was of the view[87] that it was necessary for courts to evaluate each of the proposals advanced by the parties. Taking the earlier case-law[88] and the structure of the legislation into account, the court concluded[89] that three stages of analysis were required: first, the identification of the relevant competing proposals. Secondly, the court must take into account every factor set out in the legislation which the courts are required to consider in deciding what are the child's best interests.[90] In so doing, courts must set out the relevant evidence and the respective submissions with particular attention being given as to how each proposal might be said to have advantages or disadvantages for that factor and make findings as to how each factor affects the best interests of the child.[91] Thirdly, on the basis of that analysis, courts must determine and explain why certain of the proposals is to be preferred, having regard to the principle that the child's best interests are the paramount, but not the sole, consideration.

In turn, in evaluating the proposals, courts must have regard[92] to three particular factors: first, that none of the parties bore an onus; secondly, the importance of a party's right to freedom of movement and, thirdly, that matters of evidentiary weight should be explained.

The primary error of the trial judge, the Full Court considered,[93] was his failure to carry out the necessary process of evaluating each of the proposals which had been placed before him. In addition, the trial judge was in error in treating the issue of the father's contact with the child as being effectively decisive of the issue without taking account of other relevant factors.[94] Finally, the trial judge erred in requiring the mother to justify relocation of the child's residence.

The principles set out in *A v A* were reiterated by the same judges in the Full Court's coterminous decision in *H and L*,[95] where, although the mother's appeal was dismissed, the orders at first instance had given residence of the children to the mother with liberal contact to the father.[96] The orders also restrained the mother from moving the children's residence from the Sydney metropolitan area without either the written consent of the father or the court. The wife had proposed to relocate with the children from Sydney to the north of the State of New South Wales.

---

[87]　(2000) FLC 93-035 at 87, 545.

[88]　*AMS v AIF*, above, note 86; *Paskandy v Paskandy* (1999) FLC 92-878; *Martin v Matinglio* (1999) FLC 92-876.

[89]　(2000) FLC 93-035 at 87, 851 ff.

[90]　Family Law Act 1975, s 68F(2).

[91]　Ibid, s 60B.

[92]　(2000) FLC 93-035 at 87, 549.

[93]　Ibid at 87, 553.

[94]　Ibid at 87, 554.

[95]　(2000) FLC 93-036.

[96]　The parties had begun cohabitation in 1983, married in 1989 and divorced in 1997. There were two children of the marriage aged eight and six.

In *H and L*, the trial judge had undertaken an extensive analysis of the parties' respective circumstances and proposals, the mother's reasons for wishing to relocate, the distance and costs associated with the relocation proposal, the wishes of the children and the effect of the proposed changes on the children's circumstances and the parents' relationship with the children. In rejecting the appeal, the Full Court stated[97] that, 'It is not the law that a legal presumption in favour of relocation is enjoyed by the parent with unchallenged residence of the children. In each case the focus of the evidence and submissions must remain upon how the proposals are said to impact upon the children'.

These two cases will, it is hoped, go some way towards alleviating the fears of some of the critics of *B and B*[98] which was, inaccurately, interpreted by some as meaning that mothers with residence orders could relocate whensoever they wished and for whatever reason. They also provide a systematic basis for courts in further dealings with the issue of relocation, which is unlikely to dissipate in the foreseeable future in a jurisdiction of Australia's geographical and demographical nature.

A particular matter which was given considerable emphasis in the 1995 amendments to the Family Law Act 1975[99] is that of family violence. This issue was involved in the decision of Mullane J in *M v M*,[100] where the parents involved had cohabited between late 1992 and early 1997. There were two children of the relationship aged three and four who, since the separation, had remained with their father. In addition, the mother, who had since formed a new relationship, had a seven-year-old son from an earlier relationship. In February 1997, interim orders were made which provided that the mother had contact with the children of the relationship from each Monday morning until Wednesday afternoon. In July of that year, the father, who had alleged that the mother's son had sexually abused the elder of the children of the relationship, succeeded in having contact varied.

Mullane J found[101] that, 'The father suffers a serious handicap in that he cannot deal with people without resorting to abuse. He is aggressive, violent and intimidating'. Further, the judge was of the view[102] that the father refused to accept responsibility for his behaviour, blaming others for provoking him. In consequence, the judge took the view that the father's abusive behaviour presented a '... multi-faceted danger for the children. There is a risk of violence to them personally and injury. There is a risk that violence poses when it involves living with fear, insecurity and vigilance. There is the danger of ongoing fear that the father will emotionally or physically abuse the mother they love. There is the danger that [the younger child] will learn from the father's abusive behaviour that abuse is part of life for females and become even more accepting of such behaviour. There is a danger that both children will come to believe from the father's abuse of the mother, that women are lesser beings'.

---

[97]   (2000) FLC 93-036 at 87, 575.

[98]   Note 82 above.

[99]   Family Law Act 1975, s 43(ca), s 68FZ(g) (i), (j).

[100]   (2000) FLC 93-006.

[101]   Ibid at 87, 157.

[102]   Ibid at 87, 159.

Not wholly surprisingly, the judge concluded[103] that, in all but the short term, the children's best interests required that they had no contact with their father except to the extent necessary to avoid the distress of immediate separation. Mullane J was of the view that the children should have a sequence of supervised contact of reducing frequency aimed at facilitating a separation. That supervision, he considered, ought to be by a professional person in order to ensure the children's safety.[104] The only available option was the Family Court's counselling service and, because of its finite staff and resources, contact would necessarily be limited. The judge also took the view[105] that, despite the discharge of the interim contact orders, a recognizance of good behaviour given by the father should continue. In addition, he was of the view that there was no reason why the mother's new partner ought not, despite the considerable hostility which existed between him and the father, to be permitted to stay overnight or otherwise have contact with the children.

Mullane J further ordered[106] that, with the assistance of the Department of Community Services, the children should attend pre-school for as many days each week as possible in order that they learn how to relate to other children in a normal environment. The mother, his Honour also decided, should be restrained from moving beyond the general area where she and the children were presently living. Finally, the judge ordered that the father not be permitted to institute proceedings for contact for the next three years without the leave of the court.[107]

It is suggested that *M* represents a rather excessively cautious judicial approach: there can be no doubt that the father's behaviour, objectively viewed, was quite appalling and would almost certainly continue in the same vein. It is hard to escape the conclusion that the children's best interests required that their father be removed from their lives, and the quicker the better. It may, in the end, be that Mullane J's orders will have that effect, but there is a level of equivocation which some, at least, might find exceptionable.

B   Family property

In the area of family property, an especially important case is the decision of the Full Court of the Family Court of Australia in *Tomasetti and Tomasetti*,[108] which involved an appeal against an order at first instance which had, in effect, divided the parties' property 80/20 in favour of the wife. The husband, aged 51, and the wife, aged 39, began living together in 1982 and were married in the following year. There were four children of the marriage aged between eight and 15. The husband had initially left the matrimonial home in May 1997, but had returned in the December of that year. The parties attempted a reconciliation, but separated

---

[103]   Ibid at 87, 159.

[104]   Mullane J did not consider the paternal grandmother to be an appropriate person to supervise contact as she did not accept that the father had a problem and could not be relied on to protect the children.

[105]   (2000) FLC 93-006 at 87, 160.

[106]   Ibid at 87, 161.

[107]   See Family Law Act 1975, s 118(1)(c).

[108]   (2000) FLC 93-023.

under the one roof in the following January, the husband finally leaving in August 1998. Since the separation, all of the children continued to live with their mother in the former matrimonial home.

The parties' history regarding their respective contributions was as follows: in late 1967, the husband had completed his commercial pilot cadetship and was employed by Qantas, Australia's national airline. Since that time, he had undertaken a number of additional training courses and had achieved various promotions and, in 1998, had attained his present position as Captain, flying 747 400 aircraft. The nature of his employment with the airline enabled him, during the period between 1976 to 1996, to work as a builder and he obtained his builder's licence in 1989. At the time of the marriage, the husband had assets of approximately $237,000, which included a house and two townhouses in Sydney. At the same time, the wife was studying to be a teacher and had relatively little in the way of personal assets.

Throughout the marriage, the wife was the children's primary caregiver and homemaker, although the husband's limited working periods afforded him time to spend with the children during the six months of the year when he was in Australia.[109] The former matrimonial home was bought in the husband's sole name in 1983. Over half of the purchase price was funded from the sale of one of the townhouses and a loan from a building society. The parties carried out extensive renovations on the home between 1983 and 1994. The mortgage was finally paid off in mid-1993 after the husband had borrowed $45,000 from the Qantas Staff Credit Union. In 1994, the husband bought, again in his sole name, a property in northern Queensland. The purchase price had again been obtained by means of a loan from the credit union as well as an unsecured loan. At the time of the hearing, that property was being let to a friend of the husband's at less than market rate. In 1997, the husband bought a flat in Sydney and to enable him to buy that property and to discharge his loans from the credit union he obtained a loan from Citibank of $680,000. At the time of the hearing, the husband was required to pay $4,108 per month in respect of that last loan. After the separation, the husband put that property on the market but, at the time of the hearing at first instance, it remained unsold.

Since 1996, the husband had experienced problems with his knees and, in late 1997, underwent orthopaedic surgery and, in consequence, he anticipated that he would be forced to resign from Qantas if he were to fail the airline's annual medical examination. The trial judge found that the parties had net assets of $1,800,937. Despite her finding that the husband's direct financial contributions were greater than those of the wife, when that was compared with the wife's significant contribution as homemaker and parent, the trial judge concluded that a 60/40 initial division in favour of the husband was applicable. The trial judge then turned her attention to the considerations to be found in s 75(2) of the Family Law Act 1975. She concluded that, given the respective ages and state of health of the parties, the husband's greater earning capacity together with the fact that the wife had care of four young children (including one with learning difficulties), an adjustment of 40% in favour of the wife was appropriate, which gave rise to the

---

[109] From about 1994, the parties also employed domestic help.

division which was the subject of the appeal. The appeal in essence claimed that the trial judge was in error at every stage[110] of the adjudicative process.

The Full Court[111] allowed the appeal, holding,[112] first, that the trial judge had been in error in treating the husband's leave entitlements as property by including their notional value in the calculation of the net pool of property available for division. The court were of the view that, '... an inability to enforce payment in lieu of the accrued leave (except in case of retirement) would invalidate against a conclusion that such an entitlement, held by a person who has not reached retirement age, could constitute "property" ...'. Secondly, the court found[113] that it was not open, on the facts of the case, to disregard the husband's debt against the Queensland unit, when determining property division between the parties.

Thirdly, turning to the issue of financial resources, the court held[114] that it was open to the trial judge to find that the husband's income indemnity insurance, in connection with his loss of income, would provide him with security in the event that he became ill before his superannuation entitlement became available. Fourthly, the Full Court considered[115] that the trial judge had been acting within the range of reasonable financial assessment, not only in determining that the parties' non-financial contributions were equal, but also in determining that their overall contributions were 60/40 in favour of the husband.

Finally, the court held the trial judge to be in error in failing to give any weight to identified factors to be found in s 75(2) of the Family Law Act which favoured the husband, but only to those which favoured the wife. Further,[116] the approach of the trial judge in separately evaluating each s 75(2) factor in favour of the wife, determining an appropriate percentage, and then adding those together to reach the ultimate adjustment, was wrong in principle. In the *ipsissima verba* of the court: '[T]he whole is not necessarily the sum of its component parts, and at the very least one has to stand back, at the end, and look at the final result, to ensure that the cumulative process has not produced a manifestly unjust result'. The trial judge, the court considered had not done that.

In the event, the court were of the opinion[117] that a 40% adjustment in favour of the wife, having regard to the matters set out in s 75(2), was outside the range of a reasonable exercise of discretion and that a 30% adjustment was more appropriate. Thus, *Tomasetti* is an interesting case which strongly suggests that an appraisal of what the court described as the 'overall picture' is as at least as important as any mechanistic process.

An instance involving a related issue concerning the nature of property is provided by the decision of Moss J in *B and B*.[118] The central issue was whether the husband's partnership share in a well-known firm of solicitors was 'property'.

---

110   See *In the Marriage of Pastrikos* (1980) FLC 90-897; *In the Marriage of Whiteley* (1996) FLC 92-684.

111   Lindenmayer, Finn and Brown JJ.

112   (2000) FLC 93-023 at 87, 381.

113   Ibid at 87, 384.

114   Ibid at 87, 385.

115   Ibid at 87, 387; 87, 390.

116   Ibid at 87, 391.

117   Ibid at 87, 393.

118   (2000) FLC 93-002.

Evidence as to the nature of the partnership interest was given that it was inalienable in the sense that the partners were not permitted to sell or otherwise trade their interest in the partnership and goodwill was not accounted for by the partnership. Each of the parties' valuers proceeded on that basis and also on the basis that the interest in the partnership was 'property'. Moss J held that the partnership interest be classified as a non-assignable chose in action and, hence, was a personal right vested in the husband rather than a right of a proprietary nature.

In reaching that decision, Moss J was forced to confront the decision of the Full Court of the Family Court of Australia in *Best and Best*.[119] That case also involved a partnership interest in a firm of solicitors; however, in *Best*, the partnership interest was assignable, even though the partnership agreement required particular approvals from the other partners and a permitted assignment was subject to restrictions. The Full Court[120] held that the interest was capable of assignment and, hence, could be regarded as property. After a consideration of various decisions of the High Court of Australia,[121] Moss J concluded[122] that: '[T]he reason why such interests are held to be property notwithstanding the unassignability has been imposed by statute, or in the document creating and evidencing the property, or by taking into account reasons of public policy'.

Moss J had also noted that the court in *Best* had discussed what the situation might have been had the interest in that case not been assignable.[123] The court in *Best* did go a deal further than Moss J seemed to suggest: after a consideration of authority from the nineteenth century onward,[124] they stated[125] that '... alienability is not an essential quality of property'. The situation is, thus, unclear, at any rate in the abstract. A definitive statement is yet to be made, although, in the present writer's view, there is much to be said for the opinion expressed by Lord Langdale MR in *Jones v Skinner* [126] that '... the word "property" is the most comprehensive of all terms which can be used inasmuch as it is indicative and descriptive of every possible interest which the party can have'.

In *B*, reference had been made to the views of valuers,[127] and the related issues of valuation and disclosure were discussed by Chisholm J in *Anderson v Anderson*.[128] In that case, consent orders had been made in late 1997 whereby the parties agreed that the assets of a family company and a family trust would be

---

[119]   (1993) FLC 92-418.

[120]   Fogarty, Lindenmayer and McGovern JJ.

[121]   *R v Toohey: Ex parte Meneling Station Pty Ltd* (1982) 158 CLR 327; *Cummings v Claremont Petroleum* (1996) 185 CLR 124; *Georgiadis v Australian and Overseas Telecommunications Corporation* (1994) 179 CLR 297.

[122]   (2000) FLC 93-002 at 87, 089.

[123]   Moss J, ibid, seemed critical of their doing so when he said: 'Given that the Full Court was dealing with an interest which was assignable, it is not clear why it was thought relevant to give consideration to the situation of an unassignable partnership interest'.

[124]   *Jones v Skinner* (1835) 5 LJ Ch 87; *Duff and Duff* (1977) FLC 90-217; *FCT v Everett* (1980) 143 CLR 440; *FCT v Gallard* (1986) 162 CLR 408; *Reynolds v Commissioner of State Taxation (WA)* (1986) 86 ATC 4528.

[125]   (1993) FLC 92-418 at 80, 289.

[126]   (1835) F LJ Ch 87 at 90.

[127]   (2000) FLC 93-002 at 87, 083.

[128]   (2000) FLC 93-016.

realised and the net proceeds divided between them. The sole asset of the trust, of which the company was the trustee, was an undivided half share in a particular block of land. At the time of entering into these orders, the husband had not had the property valued, but believed that the trust's entitlement would be in the order of $200,000. Valuers employed by the wife assessed the property's value at $165,000 but, since it was based on comparisons with land which was not so highly regarded as that which was in issue, the wife instructed her solicitors not to rely on the valuation and she did not disclose the valuation to her husband. In September 1998, the property was passed in at auction for $100,000. The husband argued that he had suffered detriment because the wife had failed to disclose her valuation and he argued that he would not have settled had he known that the trust's share was so limited.

Accordingly, the husband argued that the orders be set aside[129] on the grounds that the wife had an obligation to make a full and frank disclosure of the valuation and that her failure so to do amounted to a miscarriage of justice. Conversely, the wife applied to have the husband's application summarily dismissed, an application which the judge accepted.

The first issue related to the nature of the notion of miscarriage of justice: Chisholm J, relying on strong earlier authority,[130] concluded[131] that the phrase 'miscarriage of justice' referred to the integrity of the judicial process and that it might arise where there was a unilateral mistake by one party which was known to the other. This statement of principle was, of course, connected with the wife's failure to disclose the valuation. The judge was of the opinion[132] that the wife was under no obligation to disclose the valuation and her decision not to inform the husband did not amount to suppression of evidence. Chisholm J was of the view[133] that the valuation report was privileged under both the principles of common law and relevant legislation.[134] It followed that failure to produce a privileged document did not constitute 'suppression of evidence' under the Family Law Act 1975,[135] so as to justify the orders being set aside. In addition, the judge found that the husband had not relied on any statement made by the wife regarding the value of the property and, hence, it could not be said that the wife had either induced a belief as to the value of the property or knew of his mistake. Furthermore, the husband had not elected to value his own property and the fact that he had negotiated on a false view of its value did not indicate any improper behaviour on the part of the wife or her solicitors. The wife was not responsible for her husband having formed an inaccurate view, the more so as she had no obligation to disclose her valuation to the husband.[136] Whether the factual situation in *Anderson* really illuminates or obfuscates the situation remains to be seen.

---

[129] Family Law Act 1975, s 79A.
[130] See *Bigg v Suzi* (1998) FLC 92-799; *Lowe v Harrington* (1997) FLC 92-747.
[131] (2000) FLC 93-016 at 87, 307.
[132] Ibid at 87, 309.
[133] Ibid at 87, 310.
[134] Evidence Act (1995) (NSW), s 126B.
[135] Family Law Act 1975, s 79A(1)(a).
[136] (2000) FLC 93-016 at 87, 311.

Another issue which has been productive of difficulty in recent years in Australian family property law has been the matter of transactions to defeat claims. An interesting example of that process occurred in the decision of Lindenmayer J in *Ivanovic v Ivanovic*.[137] There, the wife brought an application to vary a lump sum child support order made in 1995, together with an application to set aside a transaction[138] under which the husband had transferred his remainder interest in a particular property to his brother, who had intervened in the action.[139] In July 1990, the husband's mother had executed a will which provided for the husband's stepfather to have a life interest in the particular property and, upon his death, the husband and his brother were to take in equal shares. The husband had failed to disclose his remainder interest in any of the proceedings prior to 1995.

In 1995, the husband was ordered to pay the wife $20,240 as a lump sum payment for child support. In facilitating this order, the judge[140] ordered the husband to transfer to the wife two other properties which the wife would then sell for not less than $14,000 each. In 1997, the wife caused an enforcement summons to be issued against the husband in respect of those orders, in consequence of which the husband assigned his remainder interest in the first property to his brother for a cash payment of $45,000, which the husband subsequently spent on the payment of debts and on gambling.

In 1998, the enforcement summons came for hearing before yet another judge,[141] who dismissed it.[142]

Before Lindenmayer J, the husband submitted that, if any act had defeated or was likely to defeat any order, it was his later dissipation of the proceeds of sale of the first property, rather than the disposition to his brother. He also argued that a reasonable disposer, in 1997, would not have considered the disposition as being likely to defeat the original order since that order had provided its own method of enforcement through the sale of the other two properties. As regards the variation application, the wife relied on s 129(3)(e) of the Child Support (Assessment) Act 1989, which enabled a court to vary an order if satisfied that '... material facts were withheld from the court that made the order ... or that material evidence previously given before such a court was false'. Lindenmayer J allowed both of the wife's applications.

First, Lindenmayer J held[143] that, at the time of the assignment of his interest in the first property, the husband had intended to defeat any order which might be made in the enforcement proceedings. However, irrespective of any intention, the disposition was likely to defeat an existing or anticipated order.[144] The judge also

---

[137]   (2000) FLC 93-003.

[138]   Family Law Act 1975, s 85.

[139]   Ibid, s 92.

[140]   Warnick J.

[141]   Jordan J.

[142]   The judge took the view that, although it appeared not to be a commercially viable exercise to sell the latter properties to enforce payment of the lump sum, the husband had not been in breach of the orders as he had executed transfers of them in favour of the wife. Jordan J suggested that an order for variation might be more appropriate.

[143]   (2000) FLC 93-003 at 87, 103.

[144]   Ibid at 87, 104.

found[145] that it was the disposition of the remainder interest in the first property, rather than the latter dissipation of the proceeds, which was likely to defeat orders made in the earlier proceedings. Although the husband's interest in the first property was not, in the judge's words, 'the very property' against which the wife was seeking an order at the time of the disposition, it was the only property available to be made the subject of further orders. The disposition could not be separated from any order which might be anticipated in the proceedings.[146]

Lindenmayer J also rejected[147] the argument that a reasonable disposer would not have considered the disposition likely to defeat the original order because of the machinery provisions stipulated in relation to the sale of the latter properties. Any reasonable disposer, the judge considered, ought readily to have foreseen that it was unlikely that, once the wife had knowledge of the husband's remainder interest, she would not seek to have resort to that interest in order to satisfy the order. The husband could not reasonably have believed, at the time of the sale of the latter properties, that it would generate sufficient funds to satisfy the financial obligation to the wife.

As regards the child support order, the judge was of the view[148] that, since the husband had failed to disclose his financial interest in two financial statements filed in the original proceedings, not only had he withheld a material fact, but also given material evidence which was false. It was irrelevant, for the purposes of the legislation, whether the evidence which had previously been given was false by reason of an innocent oversight or not.[149]

Thus, *Ivanovic* seems to suggest that, properly, courts are taking transactions to defeat claims seriously and are interpreting the statutory provisions strictly. This is to be welcomed.

C   International issues

In other areas, there have been interesting developments. Thus, in *Hooshmand and Ghasmezadegan*[150] the issue of the validity of a foreign marriage was involved: the parties, who were both born in Iran, took part in a marriage ceremony in Iran in accordance with the Baha'I religion in 1987. Shortly after, they left Iran and arrived in Australia in 1988. According to the Constitution of Iran, the Baha'I religion was not capable of legally performing religious rites and ceremonies, including marriage. Hence, the parties' marriage was invalid under Iranian law. After arriving in Australia the wife sought a declaration that the marriage was valid. Her application was not opposed by the husband. Penny J of the Family Court of Western Australia granted the declaration sought by the wife.

In essence, the judge found that, even though the marriage was not valid under Iranian law, it could still be recognised as valid under Australian law[151] by

---

[145]   Ibid at 87, 107.
[146]   Ibid at 87, 108.
[147]   Ibid at 87, 104.
[148]   Ibid at 87, 110.
[149]   See *Taylor v Taylor* (1979) FLC 90-674.
[150]   (2000) FLC 93-044.
[151]   Ibid at 87, 680.

reason of s 88E of the Marriage Act 1961 which provides that a marriage which is not valid under the *lex loci celebrationis* may be recognised in Australia if it satisfies the common law rules of private international law. Penny J was of the view[152] that those rules began with the proposition that a marriage will not be regarded as a marriage anywhere if it is not a marriage in the place where it took place. However, there was an exception to that rule if it was impossible to comply with the *lex loci celebrationis*.[153] In *Hooshmand* it was impossible for the parties, as people of the Baha'I faith, to undertake a valid marriage ceremony in Iran as there was no civil marriage available[154] and their own religion was not appropriately recognised.

The next step was to determine whether the parties' marriage complied with the common law requirement for a valid marriage. Those requirements were that the parties take one another as husband and wife and do so in the presence of an episcopally ordained minister.[155] In the instant case, there was no evidence of the presence of the minister, although the other formalities had been complied with. However, the judge noted[156] that that principle had been limited where the presence of the minister had been difficult or impossible under local circumstances.[157] Penny J was of the opinion[158] that that '... line of authority represents a logical development to the common law requirements for a valid marriage. Any other approach would necessarily involve the artificial requirement for the presence of an episcopally ordained Minister at marriage ceremonies where neither party is a Christian or where such a Minister is difficult to locate'.

Hooshmand is redolent of the earlier decision of the Full Court of the Family Court of Australia in *W v T*[159] to the effect that all that an authorised celebrant has to do in relation to a marriage is be present. The present writer has expressed the view[160] that that view is not wholly borne out by the authorities. However, given the different factual circumstances, it is hard to disagree with the adjudication in *Hooshmand*.

In *Ferrier-Watson v McElrath*,[161] the Full Court of the Family Court held that the Commonwealth Domicile Act 1982 was not a code and, hence, the common law continued to be applicable, as modified by the Act, to issues of domicile. As further regards international issues, in *Anisis v Anisis*,[162] Mullane J held that, despite the fact that particular international conventions had not been incorporated

[152] Ibid at 87, 681.
[153] See *Savenis v Savenis* [1950] SASR 309.
[154] Expert evidence had been given that only marriages solemnised in accordance with the rites of Christianity, Judaism and Islam were regarded as valid in Iran.
[155] See *R v Millis* (1844) 8 ER 844.
[156] (2000) FLC 93-044 at 87, 683.
[157] See *Kuklycz v Kuklycz* [1972] VR 50; *Catterall v Catterall* (1847) 1 Rob Ecc 580; *Wolfenden v Wolfenden* [1946] 2 All ER 539; *Isaac Penhas v Tan Soo Eng* [1953] AC 304; *Preston v Preston* [1963] 2 All ER 405; *Quick v Quick* [1953] VLR 225; *Persian v Persian* [1970] 2 NSWLR 538.
[158] (2000) FLC 93-004 at 87, 684.
[159] (1998) FLC 92-808. Fogarty, Baker and Lindenmayer JJ.
[160] F Bates, 'The History of Marriage and Modern Law' (2000) 74 Aust LJ 844.
[161] (2000) FLC 93-002. Finn, Holden and Jerrard JJ.
[162] (2000) FLC 93-013.

into Australian municipal law,[163] they gave rise, by reason of their ratification by Australia, to a legitimate expectation that courts will act in accordance with such conventions.[164] Accordingly, Mullane J granted an application for the return of a husband's Australian and British passports and the discharge of an order restraining him from leaving Australia where his circumstances did not disclose an intention to leave Australia for anything other than a temporary purpose.

IV THE ADMINISTRATION OF THE LAW

A major change to the administration of family law in Australia is represented by the Federal Magistrates Act 1999. This legislation, which came into effect in June 2000, creates a new court. The court will be constituted by a single Magistrate and its process, judgments and orders will have effect throughout Australia.[165] The new court must proceed without undue formality and must endeavour to ensure that proceedings are not protracted.[166] The Federal Magistrates Court has jurisdiction under the Child Support Assessment Act 1988 as well as the Family Law Act 1975. It appears that advantage is already being taken of the new procedures instituted by the legislation. At the same time, however, supporters of the Family Court of Australia regret that Federal government money is not being spent on that court rather than on what is perceived as a cheaper alternative.

In addition to this innovation, the Family Law Act 1975 has been amended by the Family Law Amendment Act 2000 to facilitate the use of arbitration. Hence, the Family Court of Australia may make an order referring proceedings to an arbitrator in accordance with applicable Rules of Court.[167] The court may make such orders as facilitate the effective use of private arbitration,[168] although an arbitrator may refer proceedings to the Family Court or any State Family Court on any question of law[169] or to the Federal Magistrates Court.[170] Awards or agreements may be set aside if they have been obtained by fraud (including non-disclosure of a material matter); the award or agreement is void, voidable or unenforceable; in the circumstances that have arisen since the award or agreement was made, it is impracticable for it to be carried out; and, finally, if the arbitration was affected by bias or there was a lack of procedural fairness. In such circumstances, the award or agreement may be set aside either by the Family Court of Australia or any State Family Court[171] or by a Federal Magistrates

---

[163]   International Covenant on Civil and Human Rights; International Covenant on Civil and Political Rights. Mullane J, ibid at 87, 249, noted that the former had been adopted to a limited extent in s 47 of the Human Rights and Equal Opportunity Act 1986.

[164]   See *Minister for Ethnic Affairs v Teoh* (1995) 183 DLR 273.

[165]   Federal Magistrates Act 1999, s 10(3).

[166]   Ibid, s 42.

[167]   Family Law Act 1975, s 19D(1).

[168]   Ibid, s 19E(1).

[169]   Ibid, s 19EA(1).

[170]   Ibid, s FA(1).

[171]   Ibid, s 19G.

Court.[172] It is far from easy to predict, at this stage, how much these provisions will be utilised.

V   CONCLUSIONS

The various changes in Australian family law which have been wrought in 2000 have certainly been a rather odd mixture. Whilst the developments in case-law might have been predictable and largely desirable, the statutory reforms are, it is submitted, less so. One really can only wait to see whether any of the aims (if, indeed, there are any) of the legislation are brought about or eventuate.

---

[172]   Ibid, s 19GA.

AUSTRIA

THE NEW AUSTRIAN CHILD LAW 2001

*Bea Verschraegen**

I   INTRODUCTION

The new Child Law 2001[1] was adopted by the Austrian National Council on 22 November 2000. The main part of the Child Law 2001 came into force on 1 July 2001.[2] The most important incentive[3] for this far-reaching reform was the existing human rights instruments, ie the European Convention on Human Rights and the UN Convention on the Rights of the Child.[4] Basically, the new law tries to respond to the principle of the best interests of the child, the right of self-determination, and the principle of family autonomy and parental responsibility[5] and pursues the following aims: to strengthen the position of persons below the age of majority, to increase the rights of parents and their children in the event of divorce,[6] to adapt the law on the recognition of paternity to modern standards by allowing a 'fathers' switch'[7] and, finally, to introduce a modern curatorship.[8]

---

[*]   Full professor at the Law Faculty of the University of Vienna, Présidente de la Commission Internationale de l'État Civil.

[1]   *Kindschaftsrechts-Änderungsgesetz* 2001 (KindRÄG), Law amending the child law (Child Law 2001), *Bundesgesetzblatt* (BGBl, Federal Gazette) I 135/2000.

[2]   The provisions dealing with the recognition of foreign judgments in matrimonial matters and in matters of parental responsibility for children of both spouses have been in force since 1 March 2001. They are based on the Brussels II Regulation, Council Regulation (EC) No 1347/2000.

[3]   See G Hopf and J Weitzenböck, 'Schwerpunkte des Kindschaftsrechts-Änderungsgesetzes 2001', in: *ÖJZ (Österreichische Juristen-Zeitung)* 2001, 485–494, 530–542 (486).

[4]   B Verschraegen, *Die Kinderrechtekonvention* (Vienna, 1996).

[5]   Hopf and Weitzenböck, op cit, 487f.

[6]   For a critical assessment of the original Bill see eg B Gründler, 'Die Neuregelung einer Teilnahme an der Obsorge nach Trennung und Scheidung der Eltern durch den Entwurf des KindRÄG 1999', in *ÖJZ* 2000, 332–343.

[7]   This expression is used by M Stormann, Director of the Department of Family Law at the Austrian Ministry of Justice. See eg in: *Das Kindschaftsrechtsänderungsgesetz* 2001 (Typoscript 2000) p 23ff.

[8]   See the Report of the Judicial Committee on the Bill (JAB), in: 366 der Beilagen zu den Stenographischen Protokollen des Nationalrates XXI. GP, 1, as well as the Government Bill (RV), in: 296 der Beilagen zu den Stenographischen Protokollen des Nationalrates XXI. GP, 25ff.

II   STRENGTHENING THE LEGAL POSITION OF MINORS

A   Majority at 18 years of age

The age of full capacity was lowered from 19 to 18 years of age.[9] The reasons for this amendment were threefold. First of all, it was considered that persons close to the age of majority are now much more experienced and mature in business affairs than persons of the same age a couple of years ago. Secondly, consumer law sufficiently protects persons who are economically inexperienced and, thirdly, none of the other Member States of the Council of Europe had an age of majority above 18 years of age. The change, then, was due.[10]

B   Marriageable age

Marriageable age, which was 19 for men and 16 for women, is now 18 years of age for both men and women, in line with the age of full capacity.[11] This equal treatment was especially urged by the civil registrars, who indicated that women seem no more inclined than men to enter into marriage at an early age and the pregnancy of, for example, a 15-year-old girl would not justify a premature marriage.[12] However, a 16-year-old person can be declared capable of entering into marriage, if he/she seems mature enough and his/her partner has reached the age of majority.[13]

C   Procedural independence of minors

Minors between 14 and 18 years of age can, in important matters concerning themselves (eg in procedures concerning their care and upbringing, custody as far as care and upbringing are concerned, and contact rights), act in court in their own name.[14]

D   Personal wishes of the child

Parents are obliged to take into account the wishes of the child when it comes to care and education, unless those wishes are disadvantageous to his/her interests or to the welfare of the family. The impact of the child's wishes increases according to the degree to which the child is able to understand the reason for, and the importance of, a measure and to act accordingly.[15]

---

[9]   Article 21 ABGB (Allgemeines Bürgerliches Gesetzbuch, Austrian Civil Code).

[10] See also W Teschner, 'Das Kindschaftsrechts-Änderungsgesetz 2001 (KindRÄG 2001) und seine Auswirkungen auf die Tätigkeit der Standesämter (Personenstandsbehörden)' in: *Österreiches Standesamt* (ÖstA) 4/2001, 37–44 (37f).

[11] Article 1 para 1 EheG (Ehegesetz, Marriage Law).

[12] Teschner, op cit, 39f.

[13] Article 1 para 2 EheG.

[14] Article 182a para 1 AußStrG (Außerstreitgesetz, Procedural Code on non-adversary proceedings).

[15] Article 146 para 3 ABGB.

E   Personal consent to medical treatment

Any child, who is able to understand and to judge (age of discernment) the impact of an impending medical treatment can consent to such treatment only himself/herself. With minors between 14 and 18 years of age such ability to understand and discern will be presumed.[16] This presumption can be rebutted in court proceedings, in which case the consent of the legal representative (in matters of care and education) is required. The court proceedings may be initiated ex officio or upon application of a person with custody rights.[17] In cases where the medical treatment envisaged usually leads to severe or enduring impairment of the body or the personality of the minor patient, his or her consent to such treatment must be accompanied by the consent of the legal representative (in matters of care and education), unless any postponement would endanger the patient's life or severely harm his or her health or life.[18] Article 146c ABGB also applies to piercing or tattooing.[19] An abortion does not fall within the scope of application of Article 146c para 3 ABGB, because pregnancy and the termination of pregnancy answer to criteria that are different from those which apply to cases directly involving a person's integrity.[20] Pregnancy and its termination merely depend on the capacity to judge and act accordingly on the part of the person concerned. In this case, the legal representative does not have the right to consent or object.

Under the former law, sterilisation of persons lacking legal capacity upon official instruction had been considered to be in their interest, especially in order to protect female incompetents from undesired pregnancy. However, not only the separation of mother and child, but also sterilisation of women lacking legal capacity may severely interfere with their mental health and may appear to protect the offender rather than the victim.[21] Therefore, the new law distinguishes as follows: sterilisation of minors upon official instruction is – under civil law – now basically forbidden, ie no one can consent to such an intervention, if the medical treatment is merely for the purpose of sterilisation. If, however, the main purpose is to treat a serious illness, eg testicular cancer, and sterility is or may be an effect of that treatment, necessary medical treatment is not forbidden. So what the new Child Law 2001 prohibits is the sterilisation of a minor. Sterilisation upon official instruction of adults lacking legal capacity is, under very specific conditions, allowed (eg when pregnancy at an advanced age would definitely endanger the life of that person).

---

[16]   Article 146c para 1 ABGB.
[17]   Article 154b ABGB.
[18]   Article 146c paras 2 and 3 ABGB.
[19]   See Stormann, op cit, 12; Hopf and Weitzenböck, op cit, 533.
[20]   RV 54.
[21]   See Stormann, op cit, 13.

III RIGHTS OF PARENTS AND CHILDREN ON DIVORCE

A Custody of both parents[22]

According to Austrian law, both parents have custody rights during marriage, ie they can act separately even if – inter partes – there is no internal consensus, eg each of them can apply for a passport, each of them can consent to a training contract or admission to another school, whereas more far-reaching steps by each parent separately are no longer covered by their custody rights (eg change of the name, religion or nationality). Such steps require joint acts of the child's parents.[23]

The child's parents can, upon divorce, agree that one of them will have custody, that they should both exercise the same custody rights as during marriage, or that one parent will have full custody and the other parent will have custody rights with regard to specific matters, eg property administration, school matters or medical treatment. In the absence of an agreement, custody as it was during marriage basically remains unchanged upon divorce.[24] This is, however, only half true, because in each (shared) custody model the parents are obliged to submit to the court an agreement on the main residence of the child. In the absence of such an agreement the parents cannot both have custody upon divorce. The residence of the child must always be that of the parent who has full custody.[25] The court must approve the agreement when it is in the best interests of the child.[26] Therefore, the child's parents have the same[27] custody rights upon divorce as during marriage, if they draw up an agreement stating with which parent the child will mainly reside and if the court approves the agreement. If the parents do not come to an agreement, the court will decide on the custody and this means that one parent will have sole custody over the child.[28] Upon application of a parent, custody of both parents can be altered into sole custody of one parent.[29] The court will decide according to the principle of the best interests of the child; the law provides for mediation in this matter.[30] The law does not define the notion of 'main residence'. One may assume that it is the place where the child habitually resides, ie the household in which the child is mainly raised.[31]

---

[22] Articles 177–177b, 167 ABGB.

[23] Article 144 ABGB deals with the principle of common agreement between the parents (inter partes); Article 154 para 1 ABGB deals with the right (and the duty) of each parent to represent the child vis-à-vis third parties. Internally the parents should try to come to an agreement, externally only specific matters require the common agreement of both parents (Article 154 paras 2 and 3 ABGB).

[24] Article 177 para 1 ABGB.

[25] Article 177 para 2 ABGB.

[26] Article 177 para 3 ABGB.

[27] With one important exception: the non-custodian cannot determine the place where the child resides or habitually will reside.

[28] Article 177a para 1 ABGB.

[29] Article 177a para 2 ABGB.

[30] Article 177a ABGB.

[31] Hopf and Weitzenböck, op cit, 489.

B Boycott-clause

Parents exercising custody or access rights are obliged to refrain from doing anything which could render more difficult the relationship of the child with persons having such rights.[32] This provision is a reaction to the daily experience in which people try to influence the child against the former partner. The court can make special orders to ensure that this obligation is met. Such orders will not be made if access to the child is reduced or forbidden anyway[33] or if custody rights are withdrawn.[34]

C Right to be informed and freedom of expression

The parent having no custody but access rights enjoys more rights to be informed than used to be the case. The parent who has no custody rights has the right to be informed on all important matters,[35] eg how the child is doing in school, whether the child is healthy or ill, etc. If regular contact rights cannot be exercised by the other parent, the latter still has the right to be informed of major matters and to express his/her opinion on them. This parent may apply for ex officio measures to be taken by the court,[36] eg amendment of the custody agreement (or order). The right to be informed and to express freely an opinion may be withdrawn, if it is abused.[37]

D Contact rights

The parent with whom the child does not share his/her main residence enjoys the right to have personal contact with his/her child. Custody and contact rights are conditional rights in that they must serve the best interests of the child. The right of contact has been regarded as a right of one parent to visit his/her child. The new law introduced an important change in that the right of contact is now a right of the child to have contact with his/her parent.[38] This right is also ensured on a procedural level.[39] In addition, if a parent unreasonably refuses to have contact with the child, he/she will lose not only the right to be informed and to express his/her opinions[40] but also the right to reduce the minimum hereditary portion of the child, even if all other legal conditions were fulfilled.[41]

---

[32] Article 145b ABGB.
[33] Article 148 para 2 ABGB.
[34] Article 253 ABGB.
[35] Article 178 para 1 ABGB. This now also applies to parents of an illegitimate child.
[36] Article 178 para 2 ABGB.
[37] Article 178 para 3 ABGB.
[38] RV 33ff.
[39] Article 145b AußStrG.
[40] Article 178 para 3 ABGB.
[41] Article 773a ABGB; RV 34, 82.

E   'Family-sitter'

The law also provides for the possibility of exercising contact rights in the company of a person who, with the consent of both parents, is willing and able to accompany the parties.[42] In practice, one of the parents or even both often act in such a way that future contact would be of no benefit to any of the parties, the child included. The presence of a third person may, as is hoped by the legislator, reduce possible (emotional) conflict.[43]

F   Mediation

Finally, the new Child Law introduces mediation in all child-related matters, notably access and custody rights.[44] It is very much hoped that this form of dispute settlement will reduce hostility between the parties in order to give the child and the parties the possibility of exercising custody and access rights in a reasonable way.

IV   ABOUT REAL AND PRESUMED FATHERS

A   'Fathers' switch'

At present, most of the illegitimate children born in Austria are recognised by their father, ie over 95%. Most of the children born after the dissolution of marriage through divorce or annulment are from a legal point of view legitimate, but in reality illegitimate.[45] Under the law in force, contesting legitimacy on the one hand and determination of illegitimate paternity on the other require different procedures. It is proposed that these procedures will be joined in the future. Until then, another solution applies:[46] acknowledgement of paternity with the effect of destroying legitimacy.[47] This means that a man can acknowledge his paternity even though another man is legally regarded as the father, eg on the ground of the presumption of legitimacy. The 'switch' is allowed on the condition that the mother acknowledges the man who wishes to recognise his paternity as the father of her child and, further, that the child agrees. Minor children are represented by the youth welfare board. The man who was presumed to be the father of the child, until the acknowledgement of paternity by the third party, can file an objection. The acknowledgement is then declared to have no effect and, the former father remains father of the child.[48]

---

[42]   Article 185c AußStrG.
[43]   See also RV 35, 91ff.
[44]   Article 182e AußStrG, Article XVI Child Law.
[45]   Teschner, op cit, 38.
[46]   See Stormann, op cit, 23ff.
[47]   Article 163e ABGB.
[48]   RV 61f.

B Presumption of legitimacy

The legal period of presumption of legitimacy has been reduced from 302 to 300 days.[49] A child will be considered as legitimate if, when the ex-spouse of his/her mother dies, he/she is born within 300 days after dissolution of the marriage, whereas the time limit expires in the case of divorce or annulment of the marriage when the judgment has become absolute. If the child turns out to be the legitimate child of the mother's husband, he/she must claim for a judicial declaration of legitimacy.[50]

V SOCIAL PARENTHOOD

A Foster parents

The notion of foster parents is now defined as 'persons, who are entirely or partly responsible for the care and upbringing of a child and who have a relationship with the child which comes or will come close to that of natural parents and a child'. They have the right to file petitions in proceedings concerning the child.[51] Foster parents may, therefore, be step-parents or cohabitees, whereas childminders, for example, are not.[52]

VI MODERN CURATORSHIP

The terminology in the General Civil Code concerning the legal representation of a minor was difficult to understand. The new Child Law[53] drastically simplifies the concepts concerning the various forms of legal representation of a minor. 'Legal guardianship'[54] has been removed. Instead 'custody exercised through other persons' has been introduced. The same applies to 'legal assistance' for minors,[55] eg on the ground of mental disorder. 'Legal assistance' is now confined to adults, mentally handicapped or mentally ill persons. Minors can only have a custodian or, in specific cases (where there is conflict of interest between the parent exercising custody of rights and the child), a curator.

Upon application the court will decide with effect *erga omnes* that a minor lacks the necessary capacity to judge and to act accordingly or even lacks full capacity – as the case may be – and that he or she is not able to look after all or specific affairs himself or herself.[56]

---

[49] Article 138 ABGB.
[50] Article 155 sentence 2 ABGB.
[51] Article 186 ABGB.
[52] RV 69f.
[53] Articles 187–189 ABGB.
[54] So-called 'Vormundschaft'.
[55] So-called 'Sachwalterschaft'.
[56] Article 154b ABGB.

In curatorship procedures, data protection has been improved in that parties who gain knowledge of certain aspects of private and family life in the course of such proceedings, must treat such information confidentially. Any breach of this duty will lead to penal sanctions.[57] The court can, in addition, specify data which must be treated confidentially.

VII PROPERTY MATTERS

A   Guardian of property

Until the introduction of the new child law, the basic philosophy was one of all-embracing judicial duties to care for and supervise the property of a minor. These duties have been reduced to a mere duty to supervise.[58] This means that the court will in the future just supervise the economic administration of the property by the legal representative.

B   Investment of ward's money

The new law takes into account the freedom of services and of capital within the European Union and acknowledges that investments must not necessarily be restricted to the Austrian territory, but may well be held in a foreign country. To this extent the Federal Minister of Finances and the Federal Minister of Justice will specify in regulations which foreign forms of investment offer adequate security.[59]

C   Accounting

The law on the statement of account provides for more detailed provisions than hitherto and now expressly defines the duties of the legal representative and of the court as well as the effect of the statement of account.[60] The court can for example order a specific time-limit by which a statement of account must be rendered; this limit may provide for three-year periods. Basically every legal representative – except the social welfare service – must submit an initial as well as a final account.[61] There is essentially no obligation to submit regular accounts if there is no immovable property or if the income does not exceed □10,000, but even in such a case the court can limit the obligation to accounting, if disadvantages for the minor are not expected. Every three years the account must be submitted to the court. The court can demand additional information or corrections of the account if it deems this necessary. The account will only be accepted if the court is satisfied with it. If necessary, special security measures may be issued.

---

[57]   Articles 182d, 209 AußStrG.

[58]   Articles 193 AußStrG.

[59]   Article XVII Child Law.

[60]   See Articles 150 and 229 ABGB; Articles 194, 204–209 AußStrG.

[61]   Article 229 ABGB.

D   Reward

Provisions dealing with the reward have also been modified.[62] Instead of a reward, compensation will be given. The compensation amounts to 5% of the net income. If the value of the property exceeds ☐10,000 the court can, in addition, grant another 2% per year of the amount exceeding this value. This additional compensation will be granted when the custodian has taken a lot of trouble to preserve the property or to use it for special needs of the child. In exceptional cases the compensation can amount to 10% per annum.

E   Liability of the legal representative

The liability of the legal representative is now dealt with expressly in the context of curatorship.[63] The judge may reduce the liability of the legal representative, whereas such a possibility is not provided for in the case of professional assistants of welfare. Parents, grandparents and foster parents are – as was the case under former law – liable *quam in suis*.[64]

F   'Mini-legal assistance of handicapped persons'

There was some confusion with regard to the extent of duties of the legal assistants of handicapped persons, more precisely with regard to the question of whether such assistance also relates to the care for the person in question. The new law[65] provides that care for the person is only included in legal assistance if the court says so. However, the legal assistant must personally keep in touch with the handicapped person and must make every effort to ensure that that person receives the necessary medical and social assistance.[66]

---

[62]   Articles 266, 267 ABGB.
[63]   Articles 264, 265 ABGB.
[64]   Article 149 para 1 ABGB.
[65]   Article 282 para 1 ABGB.
[66]   Article 282 para 2 ABGB.

BOTSWANA

OVERVIEW OF RECENT DEVELOPMENTS IN THE LAW OF MARRIAGE IN BOTSWANA

Siamisang Morolong[*]

I   INTRODUCTION

The previous review, which was the first contribution on Botswana to the *International Survey*, lamented the limited legal reforms that had taken place in the area of family law in Botswana over the past two decades. The review further noted that often these reforms were 'piecemeal amendments of specific statutes, which tended to be ad hoc, reactive, rather than proactive ...'.[1] The situation noted has not changed. No holistic review of family law has been undertaken in Botswana. Instead parliament and the courts continue to amend the law in an ad hoc manner. Not withstanding the aforesaid, there has been some activity in the area of marriage law. This paper therefore presents an overview of the recent developments in the marriage law of Botswana. In particular, the paper diarises the changes to be made to the Marriage Act [Cap 29:01]. The paper further presents a commentary on a recent High Court decision on dissolution of customary marriages. Lastly, the paper addresses the developments in the area of matrimonial property.

II   THE LAW OF MARRIAGE IN BOTSWANA

A   Background

Botswana law recognizes two systems of marriage, marriage under Customary Law and marriage under the General Law which is marriage under the Marriage Act [Cap 29:03] of Botswana.

A customary marriage is one contracted in terms of the rules and traditions of a particular ethnic group.[2] The essentials for a customary marriage will vary from one tribe to another. However, two essential elements which seem to characterize customary marriage are that there be, first, agreement between the families of the

---

[*]   Lecturer, University of Botswana.

[1]   A Molokomme, 'Overview of Family Law in Botswana' in *The International Survey of Family Law (2000 Edition)*, ed A Bainham (Family Law, 2000), p 43.

[2]   U Dow and P Kidd, 'Women, Marriage and Inheritance', National Institute of Research, University of Botswana, Gaborone, *Women and Law in Southern Africa* (1994), p 17.

prospective spouses and, secondly, the transfer of bogadi or bride wealth.[3] A customary marriage is seen as essentially a contract between families and not one between individuals. As long as the two families agree and other formalities are complied with, a valid customary marriage will be concluded.

A marriage under the Marriage Act is a contract between two consenting and competent persons of opposite sexes wherein the parties undertake to live together and afford each other sexual privileges exclusively. Marriage under the Marriage Act requires that banns are published three weeks before the intended marriage, or a special license is obtained.[4] The marriage must be solemnized by a marriage officer or a minister of religion both of whom the minister must appoint and whose appointment must have appeared in the *Government Gazette*.[5] The Marriage Act is augmented by various pieces of legislation relating to the proprietary consequences of marriages,[6] dissolution of marriages,[7] and common law rules on marriage.

Grounds for divorce under customary law are different for men and women. A wife cannot divorce her husband on the grounds of infidelity and cruelty unless his behaviour is excessive.[8] The husband may divorce his wife on the grounds of infidelity, barrenness, repeated adultery, sorcery, refusal to perform household chores, or acts of insubordination.[9]

An action for divorce in the case of a marriage under the Marriage Act must be brought in terms of the provisions of the Matrimonial Causes Act. This Act exclusively applies to dissolution of marriages under statute.[10] The sole ground on which an action for divorce may be presented to the court, under the Matrimonial Causes Act, is that the marriage has broken down irretrievably.[11] The Matrimonial Causes Act provides four factors that a plaintiff may invoke to prove an irretrievable breakdown of marriage. These factors are the adultery of the defendant resulting in the plaintiff finding joint life intolerable; the behaviour of the defendant which is such that the plaintiff cannot reasonably be expected to live with the defendant; desertion by the defendant for at least two years immediately preceding the action; and that the parties have lived apart for two years before the action and the defendant consents to the decree being granted.[12]

The grounds for divorce which apply to customary and statutory marriages are not interchangeable between the two systems.[13]

---

[3]   A Molokomme, 'Women's Law in Botswana: Laws and Research Needs', in *The Legal Situation of Women in Southern Africa*, eds J Stewart and A Armstrong, *Women and Law in Southern Africa* (1990), p 15.

[4]   Ibid, p 16.

[5]   Ibid, p 16.

[6]   Married Persons Property Act [Cap 29:03].

[7]   Matrimonial Causes Act [Cap 29:06].

[8]   Schapera, *A Handbook of Tswana Law and Custom*, pp 159–163.

[9]   Ibid.

[10]   Section 3 Matrimonial Causes Act.

[11]   Section 14 Matrimonial Causes Act.

[12]   Section 15 Matrimonial Causes Act.

[13]   A Molokomme, supra, p 21.

B   Amendments to the Marriage Act [Cap 29:01]

One of the most significant developments in the area of marriage is the passing of the Marriage Bill 2000.[14] The Marriage Bill will become an Act of Parliament after presidential assent and will be cited as the Marriage Act 2000.[15] Effectively the Marriage Act 2000 will repeal the subsisting Marriage Act [Cap 29:01] (hereinafter referred to as the old law).[16]

The objects of the Marriage Bill, as stated in its Memorandum, are 'to re-enact the Marriage Act, with amendments so as to make it obligatory for customary, Muslim, Hindu, and other religious marriages to be registered under the Act; to raise the marriageable age for both males and females to 18 years; to allow a minor to apply to court for consent to marry where the consent of one parent is given but that of the other parent is refused; and to substitute the stigmatising word "illegitimate" with the relatively neutral words "born out of wedlock".'[17] The Bill further repeals special provisions in the old law regarding publication of banns when the intended marriage is between British subjects, one of whom is residing in the United Kingdom and one of whom is residing in Botswana.[18]

The Marriage Bill is divided into three Parts. Part I contains provisions pertaining to civil marriages. Part I does not apply to customary, Muslim, Hindu and other religious marriages.[19] Part II makes provision for the registration of customary, Muslim, Hindu and other religious marriages, and Part III contains general provisions pertaining to keeping of registers, appeals to the minister, transitional provisions and provisions on regulations governing the operation of the Act.

By and large the Bill retains the provisions of the old law. Provisions on publication of banns, marriage by special licence, solemnization of marriage, impediments to marriage and other provisions are re-enacted on the same terms in the Marriage Bill.

The first major change introduced by the Marriage Bill relates to the minimum legal age of marriage. Section 16 of the old law provided that '... no male person below the age of 16 years or female person below the age of 14 years may marry'. This section was criticised as being contrary to Botswana's obligations under Art 2 of the Convention on the Rights of the Child, which proscribes discrimination between children, *inter alia*, on the basis of sex.[20] Section 16, by applying different rules for males and females on marriage, was

---

[14]   Bill No 16 of 2000, *Botswana Government Gazette* dated 29 December 2000.

[15]   Section 1 Marriage Bill 2000.

[16]   Section 31 Marriage Bill 2000.

[17]   *Government Gazette*, 29 December 2000.

[18]   Ibid.

[19]   Section 2 Marriage Bill provides that Part I shall apply to all marriages solemnized in Botswana except marriages contracted in accordance with any customary law of Botswana or Muslim, Hindu or other religious rites.

[20]   Article 2 provides that States parties shall respect and ensure the rights set forth in the present Convention to each child within their jurisdiction without discrimination of any kind, irrespective of the child's or his or her parent's or legal guardian's race, colour, sex, language, religion, political or other opinion, national, ethnic, or social origin, property, disability, birth or other status.

seen to be discriminatory. The Marriage Bill addresses this age differential by providing a uniform minimum legal age of marriage for both males and females. The Bill provides that the minimum legal age for marriage for all persons will be 18 years.[21] This not only takes care of the problem of discrimination but will in my view also help to guard against early child marriages, especially in the case of girls. Thus, persons below the age of 18 are restricted from contracting marriage absolutely. Those who have attained the age of 18 may marry but must obtain the consent of their parents, or guardian or the court.

The Bill re-enacts, in s 15, the provision that no person below the age of 21 may marry without the consent in writing of his parents or guardians. This is because the age of majority is 21 in Botswana. This provision is consonant with Art 16 of the Universal Declaration of Human Rights which enshrines the right to marry and accords this right only to men and women of full age.

Section 15 of the Marriage Bill further enacts a new proviso which allows a minor to apply to a magistrates' court or to the High Court for consent to the marriage where consent has been given by one parent and refused by the other.[22] For the purposes of such an application the minor does not require the legal assistance of his/her guardian.[23] This provision will protect the minor where one guardian or parent unreasonably withholds his consent as the courts will now be able to assess whether the marriage is in the best interests of the minor and may grant consent where the refusal to give consent by one parent is unjustified.

The old law made provision for solemnizing marriages intended between British subjects one of whom was residing in the United Kingdom. Section 9 of the old law provides that where a marriage is to be solemnized in Botswana between British subjects, one residing in Botswana and the other in the United Kingdom, a certificate issued for marriage in the United Kingdom will have the same effect, in Botswana, as the publication of banns.[24] Where a marriage was to be solemnized in the United Kingdom, between British subjects one of whom was resident in Botswana, the banns of such intended marriage in respect of the party residing in Botswana might be published as if such a marriage were intended to be solemnized in Botswana.[25] These two provisions have been repealed under the Marriage Bill.[26] The logical effect of this repeal is that if the marriage is to be solemnized in Botswana, the provisions of the Marriage Act of Botswana should be followed; if it is to be solemnized in the United Kingdom, the relevant provisions of the law in the United Kingdom should be adhered to.

The old law provided that where a minor is illegitimate he/she must obtain consent to marry from his/her mother or other legal guardian.[27] Under the Bill the word 'illegitimate' is replaced with the words 'born out of wedlock'.[28] This is a bid to try and remove the stigma invoked by the word 'illegitimate'.

---

[21] Section 14 Marriage Bill 2000.

[22] Section 15(i) Marriage Bill 2000.

[23] Ibid.

[24] Section 9 Marriage Act [Cap 29:01].

[25] Section 10 Marriage Act [Cap 29:03].

[26] See the Memorandum to the Marriage Bill 2000, *Government Gazette* of 29 December 2000.

[27] Section 17(ii) Marriage Bill.

[28] Section 15(ii) Marriage Bill.

Part II of the Bill, as mentioned previously, makes provision for the registration of customary and religious marriages. The Marriage Act 2000, under this part, will apply to customary, Muslim, Hindu and other religious marriages. This will be a deviation from the practice in the old law where no provision was made whatsoever for customary, Muslim, Hindu or other religious marriages. Under the Marriage Bill, parties to a customary, Muslim, Hindu or other religious marriage are required to register their marriage within two months of contracting such a marriage with the Registrar of Marriages.[29] The application to register such a marriage can be made by either spouse, who is required to furnish the Registrar of Marriages with all information pertaining to the marriage in order to satisfy the latter of the existence of the marriage. Once the Registrar is satisfied that a valid customary, Muslim, Hindu or other religious marriage was concluded he is required to register the marriage. Registration is achieved by recording the identity of the spouses, the date of the marriage and property in cash or kind, which a prospective spouse undertakes to give to the other prospective spouse's family in consideration of the marriage. The Registrar must also issue a certificate of registration, which will be prima facie evidence of the existence of a customary or other religious marriage.[30]

If the Registrar is not satisfied that a valid customary, Muslim, Hindu or other religious marriage has taken place he shall not register such a marriage.[31]

Customary, Muslim, Hindu or other religious marriages contracted before the coming into operation of the Marriage Act 2000 may be registered upon application, by any of the spouses to such marriage.[32]

Spouses who fail to register their customary, Muslim, Hindu or other religious marriage will be deemed guilty of an offence punishable by a fine or a term of imprisonment not exceeding one year or both.

The requirement of registration of customary, Muslim, Hindu and other religious marriages is very important as it provides publicity of the marriage. Often there is doubt as to the subsistence of such marriages as no record is kept and this requirement for registration will alleviate this problem.

III DISSOLUTION OF CUSTOMARY MARRIAGES BY THE HIGH COURT IN BOTSWANA

On 29 November 2000, the High Court of Botswana delivered a decision relating to dissolution of customary marriages. The dispute revolved around the interpretation of s 95 of the Constitution. The issue before the court was whether in terms of that section the High Court has the jurisdiction to hear and to dissolve customary marriages.

In the case of *Jane Nutah Mafokate v Isaac Tsholofelo Mafokate*,[33] the plaintiff brought an action for divorce before the High Court in Lobatse. The

---

[29] Section 23 Marriage Bill 2000.
[30] Section 26 Marriage Bill 2000.
[31] Section 24(2) Marriage Bill 2000.
[32] Section 24(2) Marriage Bill 2000.
[33] Matrimonial Cause No 166/2000 (High Court, unreported).

marriage between the parties was contracted under Customary Law at Mochudi on 7 April 1993. After the marriage of the parties, as aforesaid, the parties lived together. They had two children born in 1990 and in 1995. The plaintiff believed the marriage had broken down and wanted a divorce from the defendant. She issued a writ of summons under Order 6 Rule 5 of the Rules of the High Court; her declaration was fashioned on the same lines as a declaration prepared and issued under the Matrimonial Causes Act, both in terms of form and the legal ground upon which the plaintiff relied for divorce.

The court reviewed the provisions of s 95(1) of the Constitution of Botswana and the provisions of s 3 of the Matrimonial Causes Act, and referred also to the provisions of the Customary Courts Act and the Common Law and Customary Law Act [Cap 16:09].

Section 95(1) of the Constitution provides that:

> 'There shall be for Botswana a High Court which shall have unlimited original jurisdiction to hear and determine any civil or criminal proceedings under any law and such other jurisdiction and powers as may be conferred on it by this constitution or any other law.'

Section 3 of the Matrimonial Causes Act [Cap 29:06] provides:

> 'This Act shall not apply to any marriage contracted in accordance with customary law.'

In interpreting the provisions of s 95(1) of the Constitution the court held that the provision meant that the jurisdiction of the court was 'without limit ie it is full and without a ceiling or boundaries and is unconstrained', both in relation to civil and criminal matters brought to it otherwise than under its appellate jurisdiction.[34] The court held that it has power to hear and determine any proceeding without any constraint on the issue of its jurisdiction.[35] This necessarily meant that the court had power to hear a divorce relating to a customary marriage.

The court further averred that the phrase 'under any law' which appears in the provision of s 95(1), should be interpreted to mean that the High Court has power, in the sense of its jurisdiction, to hear and determine under, by virtue of, or in accordance with any law operating in Botswana whether written law, common law, or customary law, any matter.[36] The court further stipulated that except where there is a written law validly limiting its power, its jurisdiction is uncurtailed.[37]

The court stated that in addition to the jurisdiction conferred upon it by s 95 of the Constitution the court had additional powers and jurisdiction as conferred upon it by other provisions of constitution and any other law. This is also a reference to such jurisdiction and powers that the Constitution or any other law may in the future confer on the High Court.

In interpreting s 3 of the Matrimonial Causes Act the court stated emphatically that the provisions of the Matrimonial Causes Act could not be used to hear and

---

[34] Ibid, p 2.
[35] Ibid, p 5.
[36] Ibid.
[37] Ibid, p 6.

determine customary law marriages.[38] In particular what it states as the grounds for divorce in a civil marriage does not affect the grounds of divorce for a customary marriage under Customary Law.[39] Such divorces must be heard and determined under another appropriate law.

The court stated that s 3 of the Matrimonial Causes Act does not preclude the High Court from hearing and determining matters relating to customary law marriages under appropriate law. Section 3, therefore, is not an impediment to the High Court exercising jurisdiction over customary law marriages, which it has by virtue of s 95(1) of the Constitution.

The High Court further reviewed the provisions of s 5 of the Common Law and Customary Law Act. The section enjoins the courts of Botswana to apply Customary Law in all cases where Customary Law is the proper law applicable; that in any proceeding before any court in Botswana in relation to customary marriage, customary law must be applied unless the law specifically authorizes or enjoins otherwise. The court on the basis of the foregoing held that the law applicable to the dissolution of a customary marriage is Customary Law and the customary law applicable is the customary law of the tribe or tribal community to which the couple belongs.[40]

The principle of law therefore that can be derived from this case is that a party bringing a divorce in relation to a marriage contracted under Customary Law before any court must therefore base that divorce solidly on Customary Law.[41] The court held that it is erroneous for a plaintiff who wants to dissolve a customary law marriage to seek to base his grounds on legal grounds provided under the Matrimonial Causes Act as these do not apply to customary marriages.[42]

The court held that the plaintiff's declaration was based on the provisions of the Matrimonial Causes Act and was therefore not justiciable before the court as the marriage ought to be dissolved by virtue of legal grounds based on Customary Law.

The High Court stated *obiter* that, although it is bound to hear any party that properly comes before it, the dissolution of customary marriages and other matters ancillary thereto are matters eminently suited to be brought before Customary Courts rather than the High Court.[43] Customary Courts would have a special advantage of being in a position for ascertaining the proper grounds for divorce in the tribal community of the couple;[44] the matter would be heard faster and less expensively than at the High Court and necessary witnesses would not have to travel far.[45]

---

[38]   Ibid, p 6.

[39]   Ibid, p 7.

[40]   Section 4 Common Law and Customary Law Act [Cap 16:01].

[41]   Ibid, p 10.

[42]   Ibid, p 11.

[43]   Ibid.

[44]   Ibid, pp 14–15.

[45]   Ibid, p 15.

IV   MATRIMONIAL PROPERTY: AMENDMENTS TO THE DEEDS
REGISTRY ACT

In 1996 s 18 of the Deeds Registry Act was amended by the Deeds Registry
Amendment Act 1996.[46] The Amendment introduced new subss (3), (4) and (5)
into s 18 of the Deeds Registry Act. Under the Act as amended it is possible for
immovable property to be transferred or ceded to a woman married in community
of property as if she were married out of community of property and the marital
power did not apply.[47] It is also now possible for immovable property to be
bequeathed to a woman married in community of property and such property will
not form part of the joint estate.[48] The amendment further introduced a provision
which stipulates that neither spouse can alone deal with immovable property of
the joint estate unless the consent of the other spouse is obtained or unless
authorised so to do by the courts.[49] This latter provision was seen to be protection
for wives who had previously complained that the law allows husbands literally to
sell the roof over their families' heads without consulting them.

In the recent case of *Cynthia Obolokile Sekga v Ernest Pule and Others*,[50] the
High Court had an opportunity to pronounce on the provisions of s 18(5) of the
Deeds Registry Act, as amended. The issue before the court was whether the wife
had given consent to the sale of the immovable property of the joint estate as
required by s 18(5) of the Deeds Registry Act.

The facts of the case are that the applicant (as purchaser) had entered into a
written contract of sale of a plot with the first respondent (as seller). After the
agreement was signed the first respondent took additional steps to have the
transfer registered. He wrote a letter to the conveyancers requesting the release of
the title deed from the mortgagee to enable transfer to be passed. This letter was
signed by the first respondent and countersigned by his wife, the second
respondent. The first respondent signed a power of attorney authorising the
conveyancers to transfer to the applicant. All conveyancing documents were
lodged with the Deeds Registry office save for the consent to the transaction by
the respondent's wife which was required in terms of the Deeds Registry Act as
the respondent and his wife were married in community of property. The second
respondent steadfastly refused to sign the consent necessary for the purposes of
completing the transaction. The court found that the second respondent was
involved in the transaction and found that, by appending her signature to the letter
written to the applicant's conveyancers, she had consented to the sale of the
property to the applicant. The court held that for the second respondent now to
withhold her formal written consent in order to comply with the terms of s 18(5)
of the Deeds Registry Act was an attempt to avoid the contract, and could not be
allowed.

---

[46]   The background to the amendments was dealt with in the previous review and will therefore not
       be dealt with here.

[47]   Section 18(3) Deeds Registry Act as amended.

[48]   Section 18 (4) Deeds Registry Act as amended.

[49]   Section 18(5) Deeds Registry Act as amended.

[50]   Misca no 285/99 (unreported) (High Court).

The court then ordered that the first respondent be authorised to deal with the plot – in particular to transfer it to the applicant without any formal consent by the second respondent which would otherwise be required in terms of s 18(5).

In my view, with all due respect, the decision of the court here was erroneous because the Deeds Registry Act requires a written consent to be given by the spouse before the transfer can be registered. The court interpreted the letter signed by the respondents as consent to the transfer by the wife. This to me is erroneous as consents under the Deeds Registry Act are made to the Deeds Registrar. In my view the court seems to erode the protection given by s 18(5) of the Deeds Registry Act because it allows the requirement of formal written consent to be dispensed with. Although the respondent had signed the letter, it is my view that she had not formally consented within the meaning of s 18(5) of the Deeds Registry Act and she was within her rights to refuse to consent to the transaction.

V   CONCLUSION

This overview of marriage law shows that there have been some significant developments, both legislative and judicial, in the marriage law of Botswana, the most significant development being the enactment of the Marriage Bill, which in particular will help to alleviate problems relating to questions on the existence of customary and other religious marriages in Botswana. The register will now provide prima facie evidence of the existence of such marriages. Another significant change brought in by the Marriage Bill is the raising of the minimum legal age of marriage from 16 for males, and 14 for females, to the higher age of 18. This not only takes care of the discriminatory provision that existed in the old law, it will also help to guard against early childhood marriages which may be detrimental to the child's well-being. The case of *Jane Nutah Mafokate and Isaac Mafokate* clearly establishes the principle that customary marriages can be dissolved by the High Court but can only be dissolved in accordance with the Customary Law principles. The provisions of the Matrimonial Causes Act are inapplicable to customary marriages. This is a welcome decision as it puts the matter beyond any doubt. The bone of contention, insofar as this review is concerned, is with respect to the interpretation of the High Court of s 18(5) of the Deeds Registry Act. The decision of the court seems to erode the protection given to spouses as it allows transfer of immovable property even where the formal written consent of the spouse has not been given. The case implies that consent need not be formal but can be inferred from the circumstances of the case.

It is hoped that future developments in family law will take place in the context of a properly planned law reform programme, which will be able to identify all the gaps and to address them accordingly.

BRAZIL

BRAZILIAN FAMILY LAW IN THE TWENTY-FIRST CENTURY AND PSYCHOANALYSIS

*Rodrigo da Cunha Pereira**

I   INTRODUCTION

Family law has undergone great changes in Brazil, especially in the second half of the twentieth century. We have never seen such great changes in family legislation in such a short time.

For the reason behind these changes we must look to the times in which we live, and the way family legislation is being developed at the turn of the millennium.

The Brazilian historical perspective is certainly similar to that of other legal systems in the Western hemisphere; the decline of a patriarchal society, globalization, sexual and customary revolution, evolution of scientific knowledge, etc. All of this is related to and has originated from the ideas of freedom and equality that have imposed the watchword of our times: 'citizenship'.

It is in this context of citizenship that Brazilian law has sought to meet the needs of society. And it is precisely through the ideal of justice that we have tried to understand the various forms of social representation of families, to include them in the social fabric, recognising that the legal system is also a relevant instrument of ideology, which may include or exclude people from the social circle, and make them legitimate or illegitimate.

Family law in Brazil, and supposedly in all other Western States, is currently faced with two major questions:

(i)   the borderline between public and private, that is, to what extent the State may interfere in the private issues of citizens, for example, to establish if one of the spouses is to blame for the end of their marriage, or to regulate the relations of concubinage etc; and

(ii)   the consideration of subjectivity in objective legal actions and facts. In other words, after Freud's revelation about the existence of the unconscious, we can no longer ignore that persons subject to law, who practise legal actions, who do and undo businesses, are also guided by *desire*, that is, by the *unconscious person*.

*   President of IBDFAM – the Brazilian Institute of Family Law. Attorney-at-law in Belo Horizonte/MG/Brazil. Professor at PUC/MG – The Pontifical Catholic University in Minas Gerais. Master of Civil Law, author of several books, among which: *Sexuality viewed from the courts* (2000) and *Family Law – a psychoanalytic approach* (2nd edn, 1999). These publications are available in Portuguese. E-mail: *rodrigocp@br.inter.net*. The editor wishes to acknowledge the assistance of Peter Schofield with the editing of this contribution.

II THE BRAZILIAN LEGAL FRAMEWORK IN A HISTORICAL AND CONSTITUTIONAL PERSPECTIVE

From the discovery of Brazil in 1500 until 1822, when the colony of Brazil became an independent State, everything was directed by Portugal. After independence, a few acts were passed in an attempt to organise families legally, but nothing very significant.

In the second half of the nineteenth century, however, by influence of European thinking, especially French ideas, a Civil Code started to be framed and, obviously, it contained a whole chapter on family law. In fact, this Civil Code regulated families constituted by marriage, or 'matrimonial families', to use the canon law term.

While the Civil Code was being written, submitted and approved, several decades elapsed. Finally, it was enacted in 1916 and it is still in force. Thus, the Brazilian legal order adopted the French system of codification, as did most Western countries. In fact, the Brazilian Civil Code is almost identical to the French Civil Code of 1804. Naturally, during this long period of time, the Brazilian Civil Code has undergone changes and adaptations, just as the French Code. But the point to understand is that this Code is a reflection of the moral concept of the family at the time when it was written, that is, at the end of the nineteenth century. At that time Catholicism was the established religion in Brazil. The State and the ecclesiastical power were separated only in 1891. Several phrases in our Civil Code were taken directly from the Canonic Code, which used to regulate the Catholic Church all over the world, and still does.

In a short synthesis, and just in order for us to have a general overview of Brazilian family law, let us mention the two main Acts that changed the Brazilian Civil Code. In 1962, Act 4,121, also known as the Statute of Married Women, conferred legal capacity on women, removing them from their previous relative incapacity. In 1977, after various failed attempts and intense debate with the Catholic Church, Act 6,515 was finally approved and enacted, and it became known as the Divorce Act. Under this law, a marriage could be dissolved after five years of de facto separation. With the Republican Constitution enacted in 1988, the waiting period was reduced to two years. We continued to have the so-called 'desquite' (now 'judicial separation'), that works as a 'pre divorce' and may be converted into a divorce after one year.

Parallel to the Brazilian Civil Code, we have had quite a few Brazilian Constitutions. Some were imposed and others were voted, depending on the political and historical time of framing and approval. The first one was imposed two years after independence from Portugal, by Emperor D Pedro I, in 1824, bringing in an imperial regime. The second Constitution came in 1891, adopting a republican regime. From then on, we had new Constitutions in 1934, 1937, 1946, 1967 and 1969.

The above-mentioned Constitutions co-existed peacefully with the Brazilian Civil Code and no important changes were made in family law.

The Republican Constitution was enacted in October 1988 and it is still in force. As opposed to the previous Constitutions, it made deep changes in Brazilian family law and modified about one hundred articles of the Civil Code, which were completely outdated. Of all Brazilian Constitutions, this is the most democratic and it speaks of collaboration and influence from different segments of society. It became known as 'The Citizen Constitution' as it reflects and expresses contemporary thinking and the ideas of freedom and equality.

Therefore, we can say that, by absorbing the changes of the contemporary world, the Brazilian Constitution of 1988 brought about a true revolution in family law, based on three primary pillars: it conferred equality between men and women; changed the legal filiation system; and legitimized several other forms of family, in addition to that established by marriage.

By introducing the constitutional principle of equality[1] between spouses, the Republican Constitution automatically revoked dozens of Articles in the Brazilian Civil Code, which established a supposed male superiority and dictated, for example, that the husband was the head of the conjugal society; that the marriage could be annulled where the wife was not a virgin; that the male line enjoyed preference in the choice of trustees or curators, etc. We know that the principle of equality between genders is not simple, because men and women are different. As we establish this equality in general terms, it may become abstract and thus even cause injustice. Perhaps, the next step to approach the ideal of justice is to replace the general discourse of equality by a particular discourse of difference.

The second pillar of the constitutional revolution is included in Article 227, § 6°,[2] which prohibits any discriminatory designation of children. No longer can we refer to legitimate or illegitimate children. Children must be treated equally, and all children are recognized as legitimate by the State. Since then, it became 'politically correct' to refer to children as being born inside or outside a marriage. This regulation translated into a relevant intervention in the Brazilian legal filiation system, including the fact that it eliminated a hypocritical institution that prohibited children born outside marriage to have their father's name in their birth certificate. Eliminating this hypocritical attitude and recognizing the equality of all children in face of the law also meant a step towards the recognition of true paternity, which may lie far beyond biological bonds, that is, social-affective paternity. Based on deeper considerations about the meaning of a father–child relationship, we can go beyond biological bonds and even state that true paternity must necessarily include social responsibility, that is, if a father does not accept social responsibility for his child, even if it is his own biological child, there will be no paternity. I attribute the expression 'social-affective paternity' to Luis Edson Fachin, a major Brazilian civil lawyer, author of a book on *Paternity – a biological and affective relationship.*[3]

---

[1]   Art 5°: 'All persons are equal in the face of the law, without distinctions of any nature, assuring to Brazilians and foreigners resident in the country, full protection of the rights to life, freedom, equality, safety and property, according to the following terms. I – men and women are equal in rights and duties, according to the terms of this Constitution.'

    Art 226, § 5°: 'All rights and duties in relation to a conjugal society shall be equally exercised by men and women.'

[2]   § 6°: 'The children, born from a marriage relationship or not, or by adoption, will have the same rights and qualifications, thereby prohibiting any discriminatory designations in relation to filiation.'

[3]   Luis Edson Fachin, *Paternidade: relação biológica e afetiva* (Belo Horizonte: Del Rey, 1996).

The third pillar of the constitutional revolution is contained in another simple Article[4], which says that the State will provide protection to various forms of families: those established by marriage, those established by a stable union and single-parent families. Families established by marriage have been, and will seemingly continue to be, the paradigm in Western culture. But it does not mean that, for this reason, they are superior to other families established in different ways, or that other families may be considered second-rate.

Single-parent families or, according to the words in the legislation, 'any one of the parents living with his/her descendants' have become a growing reality. Estranged parents, widows and widowers, single parents, brothers and sisters who live without their parents and other compositions represent a factual reality, which may no longer be ignored by the legal system, and the Brazilian State has already recognized those as 'legitimate'.

III POST-CONSTITUTIONAL REGULATIONS AND NEW FORMS OF FAMILY STRUCTURE

As a result of the Constitution enacted in October 1988, several regulations became outdated, obsolete, including a few dozen Articles of the Civil Code. Then, we began to see the elaboration of ordinary regulations, which represented an attempt to provide adequate answers, in line with the new constitutional framework. But they were not many and still much work remains to be done to meet the new family demands.

A gap remains in that no law has been passed at the ordinary level to give effect to what we have referred to as the first pillar of the revolution at the constitutional level: namely equality between the spouses. On the other hand, our court decisions, as well as the doctrine have tried to adapt to the Constitution.

In relation to the filiation system – the second pillar – we have had two important enactments. The first one was enacted in 1990, under Act 8,069, more widely known as the Statute of Children and Adolescents – ECA, probably one of the most advanced regulations on this topic in the world, which became a reference for over ten other countries in Latin America. The second was enacted in 1992, under Act 8,560, and it is, in short, an attempt by the State to find a father for those citizens who do not have one in their birth certificates, thus establishing that the State itself must promote paternity investigations. As regards the father–child relationship, our judges have moved towards recognising and considering social-affective paternity or, according to Brazilian lawyer João Baptista Villela, towards a 'non-biological' concept of paternity.[5]

In relation to the third pillar of the constitutional revolution, that is, the new understanding about various forms of social representation of families, we have seen two new acts that aim to regulate concubinage, which is referred to as a

---

[4]   Art 226: 'As the basis of our society, families enjoy special protection from the State. ... § 3°: For the purpose of protection, the State recognizes a stable union between man and woman as a family unit and the law must facilitate the conversion of such family unit into a marriage. § 4°: Also considered as a family unit is a community formed by any one of the parents and his/her descendants.'

[5]   João Baptista Villela, 'A desbiologização da paternidade' in *Revista da Faculdade de Direito da UFMG*, Belo Horizonte, ano XXVII, n 21, 1979.

'stable union' by the Constitution. This legislation was enacted on 29 December 1994 and 13 May 1996, respectively under Act 8,971 and Act 9,278.

Even before the 1988 Constitution, concubinage was already recognized as a relationship that generated rights. However, such rights were established in the field of contract law, rather than family law. Therefore, the great change in 1988 was to establish the discussion of these relations in the family realm.

The new designation of concubinage has made the doctrine evolve, differentiating between an adulterous and a non-adulterous relationship, the latter being referred to as a stable union, considering that the entire Brazilian legal framework is based upon the principle of monogamy. From a non-adulterous relationship that has a certain durability and stability, three rights will originate, according to the above mentioned legislation: alimony, inheritance and partition of all property acquired for value during the course of the relationship.

IV A 'NEW' CIVIL CODE AGAINST THE TREND OF HISTORY: A FAMILY CODE?

The two regulations about concubinage mentioned above are the most recent pieces of significant legislation for Brazilian family law. After that, several bills of law were submitted to Congress, but they were not voted upon because of a more recent initiative to approve a whole new Civil Code.

The turn of a century always brings with it the idea of great change, renewal and hope. The law, which portrays and reflects social changes, thereby becomes a source of hope for a more just social organisation. Right now, a promise has been made in Congress to vote this bill of law and approve a new Civil Code for the Brazilian legal order, as one might announce an item of 'good news'.

At this time, when it is no longer appropriate to speak about totalitarian and totalizing ideals, advocates of the 'new' Brazilian Civil Code insist on an old recipe, framing a system of generalising codes. However, the trend of legal systems worldwide seems to be headed in a different direction, that is, towards micro-systems: Consumer Protection Code, Traffic Code, Statute of Children and Adolescents, Telecommunications Code, so why not a Family Code?

However, even the approval of this 'new-old' Civil Code will not bring great advances. This Civil Code draft was written nearly half a century ago, and it is supposed to regulate civil and family relations in the twenty-first century. In particular, the book on the legal organisation of families is outdated and erroneous, because it is based on moral concepts of the last century, when the current Code was conceived. All of us know that the current Civil Code is outdated in many respects, but its substitution by another one will not necessarily bring answers to our reality. On the contrary, it may be an even greater error. The original draft has undergone changes and modifications and an attempt was even made to adapt it to the Republican Constitution (1988). All in vain. Despite Herculean well-intended efforts by its advocates, the Civil Code draft, and especially its family book still remain old, archaic and absurdly incompatible with the new forms of family structure and the evolution of scientific and technological knowledge.

In October 1999, lawyers, judges, prosecutors, psychologists, social workers, major thinkers and theoreticians of family law from all regions of Brazil gathered in Belo Horizonte, at the 2nd Brazilian Congress of Family Law, promoted by the Brazilian Institute of Family Law (IBDFAM) and the Brazilian Bar Association – Minas Gerais Chapter (OAB/MG). The Congress discussed the difficulties of creating a legal framework to organize family relations at the turn of the millennium, in the face of globalization, a new discourse on sexuality and the new forms of social representation of families. The participants of the meeting unanimously concluded that the Civil Code Bill is inadequate, but it remains on the verge of being approved. Concurrently, a group of renowned lawyers, most of whom are associated with IBDFAM and ISL, have joined efforts to write a new Brazilian Family Code.

While we wait for the approval of a 'new' Civil Code, or even a Family Code, current Brazilian family law still remains basically the same: the Civil Code of 1916, in addition to the Divorce Act of 1977, the Statute of Children and Adolescents (Act 8,069/90) and a few regulations on stable unions, herein mentioned, which must be interpreted at all times in accordance with the principles contained in the 1988 Constitution.

V   FAMILY LAW AND PSYCHOANALYSIS

Much more important than the regulatory text is to understand the new concepts and the reasons behind such changes in family law. The legal science, on its own, might not be able to provide all the answers, which we persistently seek, all of us who are interested in thinking about our lives and how to improve the quality of our relationships.

Legal science has always drawn on other fields of knowledge, such as sociology, anthropology, history, psychology, etc. As psychoanalysis came about at the end of the last century, Freud (1856–1939) introduced the world to the *unconscious*. After this 'discovery', the world is not the same and contemporary thinking has taken a different direction. The unconscious produces effects and, based on these effects, we can recognize it (Freudian slips, lapses, etc). Although unconscious, such effects produce an impact on the law.

The language of psychoanalysis is of more recent origin than that of the law. From the beginning of his studies, Freud made reference to legal questions. In 1906, he wrote *Psycho-analysis and the Establishment of the Facts in Legal Proceedings*. In this and other writings of his, we find elements, which lead readers into deeper reflections and concepts about law, such as *Totem and Taboo* (1913), *Psycho-Analytic Notes on an Autobiographical Account of a Case of Paranoia (Dementia Paranoides)* (1911), *Civilization and its Discontents* (1930), *Moses and Monotheism* (1939), etc.

It is not easy to promote a dialogue between law and psychoanalysis, especially because it requires the re-examination of some long-standing legal concepts. However, at this time, it has become necessary to rethink our paradigms and the concept of the legal person, based on the revolutionary contribution of psychoanalysis to legal science, with the 'discovery' of the unconscious person.

But after all, what does law have to do with psychoanalysis, or what is the contribution provided by psychoanalytic science to law?

At the beginning of last century, a Russian-Polish lawyer, Leon Petrazycki[6] proposed a theory of legal psychology demonstrating that the law, as an intuitively intelligible aspect of human mental processes, is, basically, composed of individual feelings of moral obligation and responsibility. At that time, psychoanalytic theories were beginning to produce a small impact on European and American jurisprudential reasoning. During the Thirties, this impact became more significant with the ideas of Thurmam Arnold and Jerome Frank about the nature of legal reasoning and the role of judges and lawyers, which were clearly based on the notions and concepts of psychoanalysis. Also inspired by psychoanalysis, Albert Ehrenzweig conducted studies about the liability for crime and damage, which became widely known. Many other lawyers wrote their own ideas about how to apply psychoanalytic techniques to modern criminology.

Despite his early papers about the distinction between pure theory of law and psycho-sociological speculation, later in his career, Hans Kelsen (1881–1973) conceived the sovereignty of a State in terms of Freudian psychoanalysis. In fact, Freud and Kelsen were contemporary European thinkers. In his text, *The Concept of State and Social Psychology,* Kelsen made reference to Freud's work, especially *Totem and Taboo* and *Group Psychology and the Analysis of the Ego.* Also in his last book, in which he reviewed some of his concepts, *General Theory of Norms,* Kelsen made a relevant contribution to approach law and psychoanalysis. While investigating the origin of our laws, he takes us into a *regressum infinitum,* reminding us that all regulations are determined by a higher standard, *fictio,* until we come to the first norm. Coincidently, psychoanalysis also refers to a first norm, *norm du père.* Could it possibly be that Freud and Kelsen were talking about the same original norm, so that the legal law and the 'psychoanalytic' law would cross each other, or share the same origin?

The concept of fiction adopted by Kelsen was further elaborated by Jacques Lacan (1901–1981), who took, as his point of departure, Jeremy Bentham's theories. Lacan constructed his thinking saying that the *unconscious* is structured as language. He did not consider legal theories in his reasoning. In his *Seminar,* book 20 (1972–1973), he explained the connection between law and psychoanalysis:[7]

'... I did not feel uncomfortable having to lecture in a Law School, because there the existence of codes makes language manifest ...

... and I remind lawyers that deep inside, the Law speaks about what I want to speak about – happiness.

... I will clarify in one word the relationship between law and happiness. Usufruct – it is a notion of law, is it not? – gathers in one word what I have mentioned in my seminar about ethics, that is, the difference that exists between usefulness and

---

6   Leon Petrazycki, *Law and morality,* Twentieth Century Legal Philosophy series, vol VII (Cambridge (Mass), 1955).

7   Jacques Lacan, *The Seminar* Book 20. Translated into Portuguese by MD Magno (Rio de Janeiro: Jorge Zahar, 1985).

happiness. Useful for what? It has never been well-defined, because of a prodigious respect that speaking beings feel for the language, which is only a means after all. Usufruct means we can enjoy our resources, but we must not spoil them. When we have the usufruct of an inheritance, we can enjoy it, provided that we do not waste it. Is this not the essence of law – partition, distribution, retribution of whatever is related to happiness.'

Influenced by Lacan, lawyer, psychoanalyst and professor of Roman Law in France, Pierre Legendre said that the tradition of civil law can be explained in terms of a specific ideology, which is particularly permeable to a psychoanalytic interpretation. We may say that lawyers Pierre Legendre and Peter Goodrich from England are pioneers of the explicit connection between law and psychoanalysis. In September 1993, they promoted a seminar in New York on Law and Psychoanalysis, which can be considered the cornerstone of the relationship between these two fields of knowledge. They have published extensive materials, but we wish to highlight some of Legendre's work, such as *L'amour du Censeur, L'Inestimable Objet de la Transmission, Le Crime du Caporal Lortie, L'Empire de la Vérité*, etc.

In Brazil, the first record of a dialogue between law and psychoanalysis came from the Minas Gerais Federal University Law School, in 1976, in an article called 'Direito e Psicoanálise', written by psychoanalyst and professor at the Minas Gerais Federal University, Célio Garcia, published in the Law School magazine.[8]

Now, we could dive into epistemological research in these two fields of knowledge, and point out a few agreements and disagreements, such as, for example:

(1) A legal person is someone who behaves *conscious* of his/her rights and obligations, who is subject to the regulations established by a given legal framework; for psychoanalysis, individuals are subject to laws established by the *unconscious*. After all, can we say that conscious manifestations and regulations, which so highly interest legal science, are not previously determined by the unconscious?

(2) In penal law, crimes of a sexual nature are typified and investigated in terms of their material characteristics. For this reason, for legal purposes, sexuality has always been considered in its genital aspects, as expressed in the Brazilian Penal Code (Arts 213, 215, 216, 217, 218, etc), which adopts the expression 'carnal connection'; for psychoanalysis, sexuality belongs in the realm of *desire*. Can the law regulate desire, or is it that desire rules over the law? After all, if there is a regulation, its purpose is to oppose a desire. The Ten Commandments were written because of ten pre-existing desires. Or even, *the Law exists only because wrong exists* (Giorgio Del Vecchio).[9]

---

[8]   Célio Garcia, 'Direito e Psicanálise' in *Revista da Faculdade de Direito de UFMG*, vol 24, n 17, October 1976.

[9]   Giorgio del Vecchio, *Justice: An Historical and Philosophical Essay*. Translated into Portuguese by Antônio José Brandão (Coimbra: Arménio, 1959), vol I.

VI NEW FAMILY CONCEPTS

Sex, marriage and reproduction have always been the foundations that support family law. In other words, all family legal frameworks, starting from the principle of monogamy, have historically been organized around these three elements. With the evolution of scientific knowledge and the appearance of psychoanalysis, which presents a new way of talking about sexuality, these three elements were 'separated out'. Sex is no longer needed for reproduction, and marriage is no longer the only way to legitimize sexual relations.

With the separation of these three elements, the family ceased to be primarily an economic unit for reproduction and, today, it is the place and space of companionship and affection. These ideas tend to coincide precisely with the concept of family developed by Jacques Lacan,[10] when he said that a family is a 'psychic structure', where each member plays a role. With these concepts in mind, we can think about a family unit consisting of any group of people, in any space. With this new concept, we must necessarily review the ideas and paradigms that have traditionally supported family law.[11]

VII FAMILY LAW, SEXUALITY AND THE DESIRING SUBJECT

The very first law in any social organization is a family norm: the prohibition of incest. This is the basic law, adopted to structure social relations. Only where this prohibition is respected can one be a legal person. This primary interdiction makes it possible to cross over from a state of nature to one of culture and, as a consequence, social relations are established, and then a legal framework to regulate them.

If family law originated in a sexual prohibition, the entire legal family framework will be built around sexuality. Therefore, talking about family law means talking about sexuality, affection and consequences of wealth partition that may arise. This branch of legal science is basically an attempt to regulate these relationships, so as to permit a greater social organisation, that is, the State.[12]

In the theoretical construction of family law, the core issue has always been related to an attempt to organize and regulate affective relationships and to establish some minimum parameters for what Freud called the strongest source of satisfaction for human beings: sexuality. And the law will regulate it, establishing what is legitimate and what is not, in terms of sexuality.

We must understand sexuality in a broader and deeper sense, rather than limit its meaning to the genitalia only, which would be a very poor understanding of human relations. The dimension of sexuality, as Freud so rightly revealed, is present in every aspect of human existence. Libidinal energy provides life to life. It pushes us to work, produce, create and rest; love and suffer; feel joy, pleasure

---

10   Jacques Lacan, *Os Complexos Familiares*. Translated into Portuguese by Marco Antônio
      Coutinho Jorge and Potiguara Mendes da Silveira Júnior (Rio de Janeiro: Jorge Zahar, 1990),
      p 13.
11   Rodrigo da Cunha Pereira, *Family Law: a psychoanalytic approach* (Belo Horizonte: Del
      Rey, 1999). Available in Portuguese.
12   Rodrigo da Cunha Pereira, *Sexuality viewed from the courts* (Belo Horizonte: Del Rey, 2000),
      passim. Available in Portuguese.

and pain. It is *desire*. It starts with birth, ends with death and sustains us throughout our lives. As life starts, so is desire installed. When desire ends, so does life. It keeps alive the promise of the rainbow.

Aligned with this attempt to organize legally affective relationships, we can find an ideological element, which presents itself through a certain sexual morality that determines the relations of power and reveals the subjective positions of legal operators. The civilized sexual morality has adopted a male paradigm, whereby most restrictions apply to women.

If sexuality belongs in the realm of desire, then we cannot ignore the existence of a *desiring subject*. And desiring subjects practise legal actions, they make and unmake transactions, get married, separate, have children, suffer, feel joy, and use their libidinal energy in various forms of living. This new notion of sexuality, coupled with the consequences of the industrial revolution and the decline of a patriarchal society have redesigned male and female roles and, together with the evolution of scientific knowledge, have revolutionized family law. Sex, marriage and reproduction are no longer necessarily interconnected. It is possible to have reproduction without sex, and marriage is no longer the only form of legitimate, or healthy sexual relationship. When we consider sexuality in the realm of desire, we can conceive it as an expression of desire. Thus, legitimate sex is no longer just a means for reproduction, now we can have sex for pleasure. And again, the law, the legal framework must intervene to avoid excess. Otherwise, we may have chaos as a result of unrestrained joy.

Therefore, a new discourse about sexuality has led to dramatic changes in families and, consequently, in their legal framework. For this reason, the Brazilian State has legitimized other forms of social representation of families, in addition to marriage, as clearly stated in Art 226 of the Republican Constitution: stable unions and single-parent families.

VIII   THE SUBJECTIVITY OF JUDGES

Freud's great achievement was to show the world that the *unconscious* manifests itself, and how it does so. Since then, contemporary thinking took a new direction.

All legal actions and facts that we deal with, as operators of the law, are determined, or at least influenced by the unconscious. These reasons are unknown to our own reasoning, but we can no longer ignore the unconscious 'reason' that permeates all legal actions and facts.

Subjectivity is also present in the behavior of judges. A judge's most important action is judgment, which is not exempt from subjectivity. In this sense, we may say that neutrality is a myth. Two recent trials at the Minas Gerais State Justice Court, both dealing with sexuality, can help us understand how this subjectivity can determine the result of objective trials and the law.

On 21 September 1993, the First Panel of Judges from the Minas Gerais State Justice Court denied a request to annul the marriage of a man who had found out that the woman he had married was not a virgin (Appeal 1,078/4). Although it is against Art 219, paragraph IV of the Civil Code, the argument that prevailed in the trial was correct; the legal system is dynamic and cannot be tied to the letter of the law. In view of the principle of equality between men and women, the same right would have to be granted also to women. Now, considering the impossibility of proving male virginity, then Brazilian law can no longer annul a marriage because the woman was not a virgin. And this is stated in the judgment.

On 11 April 1994, the Fifth Panel of Judges from the same court, despite the prohibition in Art 183, paragraph XII of the Civil Code, authorized the marriage of a 17-year-old young man to a 21-year-old woman he had 'deflowered'.

The assumption underlying the legal argument, equally against the law, is the same as in the previous case, that the legal system cannot remain static. Since the young man had deflowered the young woman, they had better become married 'to avoid her going into prostitution' (Appeal 3,764/89).

These two cases seem to come from a remote past, but they illustrate very well how trials are permeated by the subjectivity of judges, and therefore, how their own moral values and concepts about sexuality can be determining factors. Both adopt the same objective assumption, that the legal system must be dynamic and translate the social reality, rather than be tied to the letter of the law. However, the arguments entirely belong in the realm of subjectivity.

With his/her own moral values and concepts, each judge is responsible for issuing legal judgments. The examples mentioned here simply demonstrate the presence of subjectivity in the law and in jurisdictional actions.

But this is not remarkable, not new or old. Trials have always been like this and will remain as such. The news is that now we can recognize the subjectivity that exists in objective reality. In other words, if the law can stop denying that objective actions and facts are permeated by the unconscious and recognize the legal role of subjectivity, then we may come closer to the ideal of justice.

IX UNDERSTANDING THE END OF A CONJUGAL UNION UNDER NEW CONCEPTS OF FAMILY LAW: THE REMAINDERS OF LOVE

The psychoanalytic discourse has changed the way we view works of art, literature and movies about affective relationships. By considering and further understanding affective relationships, and that a legal person is also a desiring subject, we can view the end of a conjugal union in a whole new way.

According to Freud, the genesis of being enamoured is essentially narcissistic. This is because love means to project your ideal self in the other. Thus, you create the ideal image of the person you have selected as your loving object, who has come to you precisely to complete what is missing in you, so you can achieve the ideal of your dreams. That is why it is often said that you love in the other person what you lack within yourself. In love, you promise to give your beloved what he/she lacks and by doing so, you become the object of his/her desire.

The natural path of love includes dating, feeling passion and, nearly always, mating. The 'last' stage of this enamoring cycle is a conjugal union, which often transforms the dream into a nightmare. In marriage, when you have to face the routine, the veil of passion can no longer hide the other person's defects. That is when you are faced with a reality, completely different from the ideal of your dreams. Then you may say you made a mistake when you chose your spouse, or companion: 'I was betrayed', 'fooled', 'framed', 'my marriage was a lie', etc.

Phrases and complaints of this nature are often heard by lawyers who deal with family law. That is when we have conjugal litigation. Because they are not capable of solving their own disputes, the parties transfer this responsibility to a judge. And their love, who would have guessed ... has ended in court.

A court of justice is the place where people dispose of their remains. Remnants of love and a conjugal uinon that left behind a feeling of being fooled, betrayed. As passion cools down and love fades away, 'your beloved' turns into 'your belongings'. It is amazing how two versions of the same marriage story can be so different, depending on who is telling the story. At the end of a marriage, who was right and who was wrong? Is there a truth to be revealed in conjugal litigation, or are there simply two different versions that generate aversion? The law still insists on establishing who is guilty. In general, the one who has had extramarital relations is considered guilty. But often, the party considered guilty of the separation was somehow 'pushed' to doing something by the absence of affection and tenderness, so that he/she did it because the conjugal relationship had ended already. This is an old story: which came first, the chicken or the egg? In other words, who betrayed first, the one who did not give tenderness and affection, and thus opened space and emptied the relationship, or the other, who engaged in extramarital relations? What the law considers the cause of a separation may well be a consequence.

When a conjugal union comes to an end, when love and desire no longer exist and there are no more common interests to provide continuity to a relationship, the separation will be painful, but it might not lead to hatred or a fight. However, a feeling of loss will remain. Once again, the human being is faced with that inexorable emptiness. But there is no remedy for this. We are 'lacking' beings, we always lack something.

Conjugal litigation is not only the symptom of something still pending to be solved by the couple, but also an attempt not to lose. Most clients tell their lawyers: 'I just want what is rightfully mine'. But they all have the feeling that they are losing something, and they project and transfer their loss to the discussion about alimony, who keeps custody of the children, who takes the assets, etc. So litigation starts, to establish a winner and a loser. Both want to gain as much as possible, as if to mitigate the inevitable loss of a separation. But you cannot have it all. Some things you win, others you lose. In fights between couples, there is no winner. When a separation is inevitable as a responsible action and, sometimes to protect a couple's health, it must be seen as medication and also as a process to gain freedom. After all, in the words of a Brazilian song, 'if that ring you gave me was glass and got broken ...'.

X   CONCLUSION: ALL DEMAND IS FOR LOVE

Most of the legal suits we deal with as practitioners of family law have a component of sexual nature. For example, in paternity investigations, we end up digging into the mother's sexual life; nearly all marriage annulments are related to issues of sexual nature and content, such as impotence, homosexuality, frigidity, sexual behavior deviations from 'normal' standards, etc; discussions about the custody of children always bring to the fore prohibitions or restrictions connected to sexual morality; the long-lasting processes of litigious separation commonly end up as a desperate effort by both parties to degrade the other party, so that he or she will be declared guilty, and these are often connected to adultery or dishonorable conduct, often mixed with a moral and sexual content.

Family law has always been, and will continue to remain the same. However, we must be aware that all of these demands, presented in a certain form and with a sexual content, which represents desire, are simply trying to deal with the parties' feeling of helplessness. Deep down, all of these legal demands and litigation simply represent an attempt to avoid the feeling of helplessness and lack of love. A legal or judicial demand usually reveals other aspects. Behind a legal demand, we often find a repetition of the original demand for love. For this reason, we can invoke Lacan, when he said: *'all demand is for love'*. The issues of family law are always related to the eternal challenge and essence of life: to give and receive love. Therefore, we can say that family law is sustained by, and aims to organize legally, affective relations; and the resulting consequences in terms of property. According to João Baptista Villela: 'Love stands for Family Law just as the Will stands for Contract Law'.

BIBLIOGRAPHY:

BEVILAQUA, Clovis. *Direito de Família* (Rio de Janeiro: Editora Rio, 1976).

DEL VECCHIO, Giorgio. *Justice: an historical and philosophical essay.* Translated into Portuguese by Antônio José Brandão (Coimbra: Arménio, 1959), vol I.

FACHIN, Luís Edson. *Da paternidade: relação biológica e afetiva* (Belo Horizonte: Del Rey, 1996).

FREUD, Sigmund. *The Unconscious.* Translated into Portuguese by Thenira de Oliveira e outros (Rio de Janeiro: Imago, 1974), vol XIV.

GARCIA, Célio. 'Direito e Psicanálise' in *Revista da Faculdade de Direito de UFMG*, vol 24, n 17, October 1976.

KELSEN, Hans. *General Theory of Norms.* Translated into Portuguese by José Florentino Duarte (Porto Alegre: Fabris, 1986).

LACAN, Jacques. *The Seminar.* Book 20. Translated into Portuguese by MD Magno (Rio de Janeiro: Jorge Zahar, 1985).

LACAN, Jacques. *Os complexos familiares.* Translated into Portuguese by Marco Antônio Coutinho Jorge e Potiguara Mendes da Silveira Júnior (Rio de Janeiro: Jorge Zahar, 1990), p 13.

LEGENDRE, Pierre. *L'amour du Censuer – Essai sur l'ordre dogmatique* (Paris: Seiul, 1974).

PEREIRA, Caio Mário da Silva. *Instituições de direito civil.* Direito de Família (Rio de Janeiro: Forense, 1979), vol V.

PEREIRA, Rodrigo da Cunha. *Family Law – a psychoanalytic approach* (Belo Horizonte: Del Rey, 1999). Available in Portuguese.

PEREIRA, Rodrigo da Cunha. *Sexuality seen from the courts* (Belo Horizonte: Del Rey, 2000). Available in Portuguese.

PETRAZYCKI, Leon. *Law and morality.* Twentieth Century Legal Philosophy series, vol VII (Cambridge (Mass), 1955).

VILLELA, João Baptista. 'A desbiologização da paternidade' in *Revista da Faculdade de Direito da UFMG*, Belo Horizonte, ano XXVII, n 21, 1979.

VILLELA, João Baptista. *Liberdade e Família* (Belo Horizonte: Faculdade de Direito da UFMG, 1980).

VOULET, Jacques. *Le divorce et la séparation de corps* (Paris: Delmas, 1991).

BULGARIA

THE BULGARIAN CHILD PROTECTION ACT: THE START OF CHILD WELFARE REFORM?

Velina Todorova[*]

I   INTRODUCTION

Bulgaria ratified the United Nations Convention on the Rights of the Child (CRC) in 1991. It is only ten years later that the State can be said to have conceptualised its reform in children's policies by making a cautious start. At the end of 1997, we saw intensified law-making activity in the area of social support and child care. Several female MPs started the legislative initiative by bringing before Parliament five Draft Acts on the Protection of the Child.[1] Although these drafts were focused on the public protection of children, the debate on the relevant issues inspired legislative action and expanded the scope of the reform. The Ministry of Justice and the Ministry of Labour and Social Policy respectively drew up a Draft Family Code, which was brought before Parliament by the Council of Ministers in 1999, and a Social Support and Children Benefits Draft (brought before Parliament by the Council of Ministers in 1998). Of all these Draft Bills only the Child Protection Act (CPA) was passed (31 May 2000). The remaining two Drafts will have to await the final decision of the forthcoming parliament. The Act itself, although a manifestation of positive political intentions, is far from perfect. It is also unfamiliar to the broader public, irrespective of the fact that it is the focal point of high social expectations. The adoption of the CPA was the catalyst for the highlighting of children's policy as one of the priorities of the Bulgarian government. December 2000 saw the adoption of the 2000–2003 National Strategy and Action Plan for the Protection of Children's Rights in Bulgaria.

II   SCOPE AND EFFECT OF THE CHILD PROTECTION ACT

The Child Protection Act is the first legislative act in Bulgaria which makes an attempt to regulate, on an overall basis, the issue of public care of children and in this respect it regulates the relations between the State and children, and the State and parents where the necessity arises for granting protection to children. The Act elaborates on the constitutional principle of children being placed under the special protection of the State and society (Art 14 of the Constitution) and of the provision by the State and society of special protection for children left without

---

[*]   Institute for State and Law, University of Sofia.

[1]   See V Todorova (2000) 'The Bulgarian Children Act: A Battlefield for Adult Policies or a Genuine Commitment to Children' in Mavis Maclean (ed) *Making Law for Families*. Hart Publishing.

the care of their family/relatives (Art 47, para 4 of the Constitution). The CPA pertains mainly to the area of procedural law, but also contains substantive legal provisions regulating rights of the child.

The innovative character of the Act is manifested in several aspects. In the first place, it provides for the setting-up of an institutional infrastructure focused on the protection of children and a new system of services to be offered to children at risk or to such children who demonstrate a special talent. New bodies are to be established at both central and local levels, and provision is made for their functions and interaction. In the second place, a list of children's rights is included, some of which are new to the Bulgarian tradition, such as special protection, protection against violence, receiving information, participation, etc. Finally, the Act sets up a legislative basis for forms of public care unprecedented so far, such as placing a child with a foster family.

The Act has been in effect since the beginning of 2001, having to be implemented in a social environment which was not quite ready for it. There is no tradition or practice in the area of social work. The culture of treatment for children at risk is lacking. Resources are insufficient. The implementation of the Act started contemporaneously with both the establishment of the supporting state and social structures (the State Agency for Child Protection (SACP) and the Child Protection Departments (CPD) and the setting up of links between them. Currently, the professionals in the area – social workers, lawyers and policemen – are undergoing their training. In this context, the implementation of the Act can be viewed as a kind of social experiment. It will be an interesting experience to apply modern practices to a relatively poor country which endeavours to maintain low social expenditure. It will also be interesting to observe the application of the law in an environment dominated by a patriarchal attitude to children and the resultant changes in parental attitudes to the public protection of children.

The contradictions between the political decision and the social environment, however, are not the only factor which might compromise the reform concerning the welfare of children. The current emerging practices make it clear that the Act is far from being precise in terms of the legal solutions it offers. Some of its mechanisms, for instance for the hearing of the child, for the participation of social services in court procedures, for the placement of the child outside the family, etc, are not yet clearly defined. The new legal agents created are not only unfit for the procedural regulations currently in effect, but also, which is even worse, they have not been backed up by regulations fulfilling the demands of practice. All this poses the question: should this law be the leading element in the reform and what course will such reform take?

Against the backdrop of satisfaction with the very fact of adoption of the Child Protection Act, following three years of parliamentary debate, these are the questions that trouble the minds of researchers of the law and of its social effectiveness. The presentation below will describe, from a critical perspective, some of the major provisions of the Act and will outline some emerging ideas for change.

III   THE PHILOSOPHY OF THE ACT

The Act introduces a philosophy new to Bulgarian society concerning the situation of the child and the provision for public care which is contained in eight explicit principles (Art 3 CPA). The new concept can be perceived in the new terminology and especially the new legal terms of 'family environment', 'a child at risk' and 'foster family'.

The first governing principle is the recognition and respect for the child's personality. The very articulation of this principle can by itself be termed an achievement: it has no precedent in our country's legislation. This underlines the new standpoint of legislators: the respect for the child and for his or her autonomous personality. It also elaborates a new approach to the legal treatment of children as persons. Their rights are no longer expressed in a negative manner: by assigning obligations to other persons (most often, the parents). This was the traditional approach thus far. The Child Protection Act articulates rights in a positive manner, but those rights mostly concern the public domain. These are: the right to protection (Art 10 CPA), protection against violence (Art 11 CPA), protection of religious beliefs (Art 14 CPA); the right to expression (Art 12 CPA); information and consultation (Art 13 CPA); and the procedural rights of the child set out in Art 15, which deals with their participation in judicial and administrative proceedings. Thus, the child is turned into a subject rather than an object of the Act. The Act also tackles special hypotheses for considering the opinion of the child: for the eventualities of placing the child outside the family of origin or the termination of such placement (Art 30, para 11 CPA).

Another principle is the upbringing of the child in a family environment. The introduction of the legal concept of 'family environment' is the cue for the reconsideration of the public care philosophy. In recent years, the institutionalisation of children in need of care was identified as the major disadvantage of the old concept. The focus on the 'family environment' must mean the highlighting of family care as a priority. Therefore, services addressing biological families are introduced for the purpose of protecting the child (Art 23 CPA), together with family alternatives of placement in public care. In the meaning of the Act, a 'family environment' is not only the family of origin or the adoptive family, but also the family of relatives of the child or the foster family (sub para 1, §1 of the Supplementary Provisions, CPA). The Act deliberately specifies that a placement with an institution may be undertaken only where it is impossible for the child to remain within the family environment (Art 35, para 2 CPA). This principle is also capable of a second interpretation: it functions as a criterion for grading the intervention in implementing the special protection of the child (Art 4 CPA).

Further, the Act formulates the principle of 'ensuring the interests of the child in the best possible manner'. This is the only principle, which, in debating the Draft, underwent a corrective revision. The wording of the Draft read: 'ensuring the best interests of the child' whereas the Act reads: 'ensuring the interests of the child in the best possible manner'. When analysing this text, we can generalise that it consists of a clumsy interpretation of Art 3 of the CRC, indeed a contradiction of the Convention. This principle could be interpreted as addressing, not the complex interests within which the interest of the child is being taken into account, but rather the resources available for the protection of children. The idea is that the interests of the child need to be ensured with the highest possible quality of available care. Unfortunately, the Act does not reproduce the principle of making 'the best interests of the child a primary consideration' (Art 3 of the Convention). However, in a number of places in the text the interests of the child are referred to as a criterion for taking a decision. This applies, for instance, for situations of placement, change of placement or termination of placement (Art 28, paras 3 and 5 CPA), the maintenance of relations with the parents when a child is placed with a foster family (Art 33, para 1 CPA), etc.

The principle of providing special protection for children at risk or for children demonstrating special talents is the cornerstone of the Act. It encapsulates the 'special protection' concept. This is a fundamental concept for the law together with the right to protection (Art 10 CPA), which applies to every child and to all children. Special protection means additional services by which the State can intervene in the private domain for the purpose of protecting a child or preventing a certain risk. The term 'child at risk' is being introduced. The meaning of this term is explained in §1, sub para 5 of the Supplementary Provisions of the Act:

'"A child at risk" is a child:

    (a) who does not have parents or has been permanently deprived of their care;

    (b) who has become the victim of abuse, violence, exploitation or any other inhuman or degrading treatment or punishment either in or out of his or her family;

    (c) for whom there is a danger of causing damage to his or her physical, mental, moral, intellectual and social development;

    (d) who is afflicted with mental or physical disabilities and difficult-to-treat illnesses.'

The principle of non-discrimination is categorically stated (Art 10, para 2 CPA).

The encouragement of voluntary participation in the activities aimed at child protection is another principle of the Act. As early as Art 1, the Act states that it is to regulate the participation of non-profit making legal entities and natural persons in such activities (the protection of children). These organisations participate on an equal basis with ministries in the work of the National Council on Child Protection, which is a body with consultative functions at the State Agency for Child Protection (Art 18 CPA). On a local level, NGOs can co-operate with the municipal Child Protection departments (Art 21, para 7 CPA). Beyond this, however, the participation of non-profit making legal entities and that of physical persons in the activities of child protection is not really well defined and needs additional elaboration. The future prospects are that such organisations will co-ordinate their efforts with competent municipal departments for providing services to children and families.

Further the Act stipulates that '… restrictive measures shall be of temporary nature' and that '… the effectiveness of measures undertaken shall be controlled'. The idea behind this is that guarantees should be provided for the right of the child to be brought up in a family environment. The latter clause is meant to provide for external and independent control over public care measures such as foster placement and placement with an institution. For the first time, the Act sets up services relating to social work and providing counselling to children and families. To this end, social workers are granted a number of powers, including the right to carry out inspections in response to calls and complaints in relation to violations of children's rights and giving obligatory prescriptions to parents (Art 21, para 3 CPA). However, the mechanisms of administrative control over the decisions of social workers are not precisely elaborated. There is no express opportunity for appealing against the prescriptions to parents. Special provisions are included for appealing against a municipal department's decision on the temporary placement of children outside the family of origin (Art 27, para 4 CPA). A court decree ruling in favour of placement or termination of placement is subject to appeal, but only before the District Court (Art 28, para 4 CPA). Special control must be kept over the implementation of a special measure: police protection (Art 38 CPA). Where the police undertake protective action (which is provided for in the case of risk, where the child might become the victim of a crime or where the child's life is endangered), they shall immediately notify the prosecutor and the Municipal Social Assistance Service. The head of the Municipal Social Assistance Service must exercise current control on the effectiveness of measures undertaken including the placement of a child with an institution.

IV   HEARING THE CHILD

The Child Protection Act introduces a new regulation for hearing the child. According to Art 15, para 1, 'all cases of administrative or judicial proceedings affecting the rights and interests of a child should provide for an obligatory hearing of the child, provided he or she has reached the age of 10, unless that proves harmful to his or her interests'. This means that the capacity of children to act is being broadened not only within the family, but is extended to all other areas: education, health care, social support and care, etc. It is also worth noting that, for the first time, as a rule, the participation of the child in judicial proceedings is not dependent upon the opinion of the court (the administrative body). The Act does not provide any clues as to the weight to be attributed to the opinion of the child. The hearing is meant to inform the respective bodies of the opinion of the child and it is those bodies which will determine the weight of such opinion.

A necessary condition for the right to be heard to take effect is that the child has reached a certain *degree of maturity*. Legislators tend to stick to the Bulgarian tradition in this respect: the maturity of the child is related to reaching a certain *age*.[2] The new trend here is that the CPA accepts, as a rule, a lower age (10 years) at which the attainment of maturity is presumed. As far as the hearing is concerned, the Act even takes a further step (although providing for the 10-year

---

[2]   Age is also a criterion for the limited or full civil capacity of persons pursuant to the Act on Persons and the Family. Limited civil capacity is enjoyed at the age of 14. At this age, the hearing of the child is provided for in a number of legislative acts such as the Family Code, the Civil Registration Act, the Public Health Act, and the Public Education Act.

age criteria as the bottom limit) by not excluding such opportunity for younger children too. The lower age groups also share in this right: 'In cases where the child has not reached the age of 10, he or she may be given a hearing depending on the level of his or her development'. (Art 15, para 2, 1st sentence).

Therefore, those not affected by the 'maturity presumption' will necessarily have to take a maturity test in order for the hearing provision to take effect. The test is obligatory. This follows directly from the provision stating that the 'hearing decision shall necessarily be substantiated' (Art 15, para 2, 2nd sentence). The Act, however, does not give an express answer regarding the persons, bodies or agencies entitled to carry out the test of maturity on the child. It is necessary that persons having the respective training and competence perform such testing. Such teams or expert groups may be established at the Child Protection Departments of the Municipal Social Assistance Service (MSAS) and the MSAS representatives in their statements may report their conclusions on the proceedings (Art 15, para 5 in reference to Art 21, para 14 CPA).

The Act stipulates that 'the court may', whereby the court has the power but is not obliged to (rule for any certain action). The ruling of the court will, therefore, be necessarily based on the results of the 'maturity' test of the child, and not on any other circumstances in the case, such as the necessity for the hearing, degree of certainty involved, etc. Here we do not refer to the so-called 'optional' or non-obligatory hearing following the revisions of Art 106, para 3 of the Family Code (the court shall hear children aged between 10 and 14 'where appropriate') and of Art 72 of the Family Code (the child shall be given a hearing 'if necessary'). Such interpretation would be contradictory to the inner logic and the spirit of the provision in question, and its application, therefore, is inappropriate.

It is well known that the Convention on the Rights of the Child does not affix any lower age limit for hearing the child and does not support this type of approach by national legislative standards. The expression 'capable of forming his or her own views' (Art 12, para 1 of the Convention) can be interpreted in a very broad sense implying that even the smallest children are formally entitled to a hearing.[3] In conformity with this provision, national legislatures in Europe predominantly settle maturity as the governing criterion for the hearing of the child rather than age. The States using age as a criterion have adopted a higher age limit. The assessment of the child in relation to each particular case seems to be the fairest criterion for the attainment of maturity. This approach, however, requires the availability of better resources in terms of time, facilities and competent professionals. On the other hand, it might be thought that the particular assessment is dependent on specific circumstances, which might not necessarily bring about a result coinciding with the political intention to expand the special capacity of children. Therefore, against the background of relevant European national legislations, Bulgarian legislators seem to have adopted a regulation which legitimises the opportunity of a court hearing for a broad range of children, even from the lowest age group. This provision is, of course, in accordance with dominant tradition and with the necessity for financial prudence.

---

[3] See *Implementation Handbook for the CRC*. UNICEF, 1998, p 150. CRC *Guidelines for Periodic Reports*.

Within the context of the history of Bulgarian family legislation, this standard seems to be a natural step in the development of the approach to children. The implications of this step, however, seem to be quite peculiar.[4] With the appropriate application of the law, it can bring forth a change in the treatment of children, which has been traditionally paternalistic. It is possible that this relatively liberal regulation might, with the current state of social attitudes, remain either little understood or – as regards the settling of particular cases – face resistance from public opinion which is stubbornly conservative on the subject.

V   COURT HEARING AND THE INTERESTS OF THE CHILD

The literal interpretation of the text in Art 1, para 15 demonstrates that the active party in the hearing of the child is the court (the administration). No action is required from the child as regards the initiation and the realisation of the hearing. The Act implies only direct and personal contact between the child and the respective authorised body, which cannot be replaced by any 'representation of the child's point of view' by third parties.

The CPA provides only for the personal participation of the child. Therefore, it introduces the 'interests' criterion. This, however, could be seen as not being in harmony with the spirit of the Convention. The CRC does not require the personal appearance of the child before the respective body, but provides an opportunity for the various legislatures to create appropriate participation mechanisms so that the viewpoint of the child is necessarily presented to the authority taking the decision. In the case of the CPA, Bulgarian legislators failed to draw up special rules for the hearing of the child by departing from the scheme of general civil proceedings and their formalism. Debate is still continuing on the introduction of special terms, the venue and the guarantees of hearing, and, for some categories of cases, the introduction of a 'guardian ad litem' to express the viewpoint of the child, especially for younger children, the setting up of a specialised family court, etc.[5]

Although not quite consistently, the CPA sets up a standard in this respect. For instance, para 3 stipulates that:

'Before the hearing of the child, the court or the administrative body shall:

1.   provide the child with the necessary information, which would help them form their opinion; inform the child on the possible consequences of their desires, of the maintenance of their opinion as well as on any decision of the judicial or the administrative body involved.'

---

[4]   It should be noted that Bulgaria ratified the Convention without reservations. However, it has taken 9 years for the national legislation to settle the child's right to a hearing. The situation in Bulgaria can still be viewed as having certain advantages when compared to that in Poland, which, as a State-Party to the Convention, makes the following declaration upon ratification: '... the rights of the child set forth by the Convention, and those provided for under Art 12 in particular, ... shall be exercised with respect to parental authority and in conformity with Polish customs and tradition as regards the status of the child within or without the family' (CRC/C/2/Rev 5, p 29).

[5]   This is also a matter which has long been the subject of discussion. See T Tzankova, *The Enrichment of Family Legislation Standards as Regards Parent–Children Relations*, p 24.

Several questions can be raised at this point. Is the court (the administrative body) presumed to perform such actions on its own? Would it not be better for the child if they were to be informed at an earlier stage by persons with special qualifications, such as social workers or psychologists from the MSAS? Here the matter concerns professional assistance for the child bearing in mind that Bulgarian judges are not really quite trained for the new role they are being given in the hearing procedure.

Further on, the Act reads: 'In all cases the hearing and the consulting of the child shall be performed in appropriate settings and in the presence of a social worker or another appropriate specialist' (para 4). It is not made clear what the meaning of 'appropriate settings' is or whether this is meant to be the venue for the court proceedings or any other premises.[6] The MSAS are also to play an assisting role in the child's appearance in the legal domain: 'where any proceedings are instituted, the court or the administrative body shall notify the Municipal Social Assistance Service located at the child's place of residence, which shall send their representative' (para 5). It is not clear what are the exact functions of the MSAS representative. They have no special procedural functions except for those provided for under Art 21, paras 13 and 14 of the CPA:

- '... to participate in cases concerning the restriction or the termination of parental rights' and
- 'upon request ... to draw reports and opinions on the situation of children'.

It could be appropriate that such representatives are assigned with the assessment of the maturity of children younger than 10, as well as with the presentation of such reports on all cases and not only 'upon request'. This matter is relevant to the setting-up of an individual procedural right and obligation for the MSAS to draw on independent expertise in the interests of the child, which would be used as evidence in taking the decision.

The omission to provide for a hearing compromises the decision and can constitute a basis for appeal under the provisions of the Civil Procedural Code or the Administrative Proceedings Act. Paragraph 7 of Art 15 of the CPA stipulates that: 'a child shall have the right to appeal in any proceedings affecting their rights or interests'. This wording provides for the child a new extension of his or her procedural capacity. The general revision of this regulation, however, poses the question as to the subject of the appeal – the omission or rejection of a hearing, or the decision affecting the child's interests in the respective proceedings.

The logical interpretation of the regulation determines that the right to appeal must be expressly recognised only with reference to the hearing. The right to appeal is associated with the procedural status of a litigant. Whereas a hearing does not automatically make a child as such party to a lawsuit. Therefore, outside the situation where the child is a party acting in a personal capacity or through a representative, the right to appeal is hard to substantiate.

---

[6] For instance, it is pointed out that courts and other places where children are to be given a hearing will need some readjustment to such function. For court venues this might mean changes in the layout, which would render it less formal and more friendly to children, such as redecoration of premises or the allocation of special rooms where children can wait, providing some occupational facilities, etc. See *Implementation Handbook for the CRC*. UNICEF, 1998, p 151.

The right to allow a hearing is a procedural obligation of the court and its violation generates the right to appeal. In its practice, as early as the period when the 1968 Family Code applied, which did not contain a provision for an obligatory hearing, the Supreme Court made a pronouncement that: 'the non-observance of the obligation to give a hearing shall constitute a violation of a judicial proceedings rule'.[7] In this sense the omission or the tacit rejection of a hearing may be appealed against and this is done through appealing against the decision. The rejection of a hearing can also be challenged by filing an appeal. In this case, the appeal is filed against the very ruling of the court rejecting the hearing. At this point we can refer to the hypothesis of Art 213, sub para 'b' of the Civil Procedural Code: the right to a private appeal is provided for in the special CPA. The child also has a right to appeal against the ruling of a court regulating the regime of their personal relations with their parents when the child is placed with a foster family (Art 33, para 2).

In all these situations, however, the question remains whether a child could carry out independently all actions relevant to filing an appeal or whether he or she would need to act through a representative. The matter concerns technical difficulties which might not provide a problem for older children, but which could prove insurmountable for younger ones. It is not necessary that, in all cases, a child should file an appeal in person. In many cases this action might be undertaken by the child's legal representative. This, however, cannot be expected where there are conflicts of interests in the case. In such circumstances, the appeal could be filed by the special representative or by the representative of the Municipal Social Assistance Service where they represent the child under the provisions of Art 15, para 6 of the CPA. A hearing should also necessarily be allowed at the instance of appeal (second instance), where such an appeal reviews the substance of the case.[8]

VI GUARDIAN AD LITEM

Unfortunately, the Act does not elaborate on the figure of special guardian of the child – such as a guardian ad litem. Such guardian need not always be appointed according to para 6 of Art 15, but only where the law provides expressly for such appointment. For the time being, no such express provision exists. According to Art 16, para 6 of the Civil Procedural Code, a child must have a lawyer appointed as his or her special guardian in the case of instituted legal proceedings where the court finds a conflict between the interests of the child and those of his or her parents or legal guardians.

---

[7]   See the Procedural Rules of the Supreme Court (PRSC)-1-74, vol 4 in N Mladenov, P Bratanova, *The Family Code, the Text, the Judicial Practice, Bibliography, Regulation Acts*. Sofia, 1996, p 315.

[8]   Art 208, para 1 of the Civil Procedural Code and the High Court Decision-1-74, sub para 4 and Decision-1202-73-High Court – II Civil Division.

A certain protection can be given to the child by the representative of the MSAS, who, by virtue of the regulations of Art 15, para 5 of the CPA, might take part in the lawsuit, but not represent the child. However, the unclear procedural capacity of such representative poses another problem in practice. A representative is neither a party to the litigation, nor an expert, nor a witness in the case. The latter's status is very similar to that of a prosecutor who can take part in civil proceedings only in those cases expressly set forth by the law. A prosecutor can enter the proceedings as a representative and defender of the public interest. Defence of the interests of a child constitutes an aspect of such public interest.

In conclusion, it should be noted that the Act's elaboration on the procedural participation and representation of the child is not up to the required standard. The same applies to the new figure of social worker introduced into the litigation process. Only the first steps have been taken as yet, however, leaving social workers without clear-cut rights and obligations to guarantee their effective participation in procedural action.

VII MEASURES TO PROTECT THE CHILD

According to Art 4 of the Act, the measures to protect the child are:

(1)   assistance, support and services rendered in the child's family environment;
(2)   placement of the child with relatives or close family;
(3)   placement of the child with a foster family;
(4)   placement of the child in a specialised institution;
(5)   police protection.

These measures can be classified according to whether they are undertaken within the child's own family or outside the family. The first measure from the list above is in the first category whereas the others pertain to the second.

A   Assistance, support and services within a family environment

The Child Protection Act endeavours to prioritise the expansion of the relatively under-developed specialised services to children, which are currently offered in Bulgaria. Such services include day care, fostering, counselling families at risk, special mediation services for disadvantaged individuals, etc. The super-institutionalisation of children whose parents face difficulty in their upbringing is considered as one of the most grievous problems in the public protection of children. The measures for the protection of children will be drafted and presented to the Child Protection Departments of the MSAS.[9]

---

[9]   The development of services as an alternative to institutions and of measures for the prevention of child abandonment is initiated under the Child Welfare Reform Project, which is financed by a loan from the World Bank and donations by the European Union, Japan, the United Kingdom, Sweden, etc.

B Rights and obligations of parents

The relations between the State and parents can be projected on two planes: according to Art 8, paras 1 and 2, parents are entitled to:

– *receive assistance* from State bodies where protection is needed for the child. This right covers protection measures applicable within the family environment: counselling, assistance, mediation (Art 21, paras 4 and 5 and Art 23, paras 1, 4–6);
– *receive information and counselling* for all measures and action undertaken by the law except for the cases covered under Art 13. The text reads: 'Every child has a right to be informed and consulted by the child protection body even without the knowledge thereof of his or her parents or of the persons who take care of his or her rearing and upbringing, should that be deemed necessary in view of protecting his or her interests in the best possible way and where informing the said persons might harm the child's interests';
– *require a change in the measures undertaken* where there is a change of circumstances;

Paragraph 3 of Art 8, however, reads:

'parents shall *necessarily perform the measures* undertaken under of this Act and provide assistance in the implementation of the action aimed to protect the child.'

It seems that the Act constitutes a new obligation for parents, which is of public character and addresses the fulfilment of parental function. The measures with which parents are obliged to co-operate are the actions of the Child Protection Departments (CPD) undertaken where there has been the violation of any interest or right of the child. The specific measures depend on the CPD social workers' assessment of the violation and the particular protective action taken in view of the best interests of the child. The measures may be consensual, but may also go against parents. In that case, the social worker may issue an obligatory prescription, directed to another body or person or to the parents themselves (Art 21, para 3). On the other hand, if there are grounds for such intervention, a child can be placed temporarily outside his or her family at the order of the MSAS head official (Art 26, para 2, and Art 27). The statutory grounds for placement allow for wide interpretation (Art 25, paras 2–3):

'A child may be placed to live out of his or her family in cases where his or her parents: ... without valid reason permanently fail to provide care for their child; are in a position of permanent inability to rear their child.'

With such hypotheses it is possible that tension may arise between the measures recommended or undertaken by the social worker and the intended actions of the parents. What is the opportunity provided for the parents to defend their legal domain? On the other hand, however, this wording of the Act does not explicitly give the ground for intervention when the child has been abused which raises the question of the need for the Act to be amended.

There is no general provision for refusal to comply with the obligatory prescriptions of social workers. Such a defence would be possible under the general principle of appeal against administrative acts pursuant to the Administrative Proceedings Act where the prescription in question is deemed to be as such an act. As far as the CPA has articulated no express procedure for appeal, it could be assumed that the prescription does not fall within the category of such acts. The explanation could be that the Act does not intend to create new rights and obligations for parents, but rather to regulate the termination of violations of children's rights. It also emphasises general statutory parental obligations, for instance those provided for under other Acts, such as assuring the rights of the child in relation to education, health examination, regular care and support, etc. All these are obligations of the parents that constitute a component of the rights-and-obligations complex. The meaning of the prescription is to warn about their fulfilment regardless of the parents' consent. A prescription can be the opening step for a range of measures pertaining to more serious public intervention in relation to parental rights and obligations. A parent, for instance, may be compelled to provide their child access to a social worker or a child psychologist, or to observe a temporary regime of contact with their child until the pronouncement of the court.

As far as an order of the head official of the MSAS regarding the placement of the child outside the family is concerned, the Act (Art 27, para 4) provides an opportunity for defence by the appeal of such order before a higher administrative body and, only after that, before the court, pursuant to provisions of the Administrative Proceedings Act. A serious imperfection, however, is the lack of any legal procedure enabling the parents to challenge the placement of the child before the court, where such placement has not been requested by them. This drawback could be viewed as a violation of the parents' right to respect for family life, which is guaranteed by the Bulgarian Constitution (Art 32) and by the European Convention for the Protection of Human Rights and Fundamental Freedoms 1950. The reason for overlooking this kind of imperfection is most probably rooted in the very situation relevant to the adoption of the CPA and especially in the fact that the detail on the subject matter was based directly on the Draft Family Code. The enactment of the CPA became subject to a more pressing deadline than that of the Family Code, whereupon the latter was completely removed from the Parliament's legislative agenda. Thus, the relevance between the provisions of the family legislation for intervening in parent–child relations and the corresponding measures of the CPA was lost. Moreover, the placement regulations had to be moved from the Draft Family Code to the CPA, which resulted in additional omissions. For instance, according to the Draft Family Code, Art 86, the protection measures, such as placement outside the family of origin, may be initiated at the court's discretion where parental rights have been restricted or terminated, whereas Art 96, para 2 of the Draft Family Code contains an express provision that parents may appeal against the placement of the child with a foster family.

C   Placement outside the family of origin

Until the CPA came into effect, there was no legal standard regulating the general regime of placement. Currently, according to Art 26, para 1 of the Act, a placement can be effected by the court on the request of the MSAS, a prosecutor or a parent. A considerable drawback of the law is the exclusion of a parent or guardian from the legal proceedings if the request is not filed by the parent(s). Article 27 provides for a temporary placement executed on the order of the MSAS head official.

In choosing the placement, the court must follow the sequence set forth by the same text and by Art 35, para 2: '... with a family of relatives or friends, as well as placement of a child to be reared by a foster family or a specialised institution ...'. The child can be placed with an institution only where the opportunities for placing him or her within a family environment have been exhausted. This is an important rule, bearing in mind the principle of prioritising family placement. However, consideration needs to be given to the effective secondary legislation, which is in contradiction with the CPA. Moreover, the Act itself stipulates that placement with a specialised institution must be executed by the requirements and by the order set forth in the effective legislation.

According to that legislation, namely the Rules for the Medical and Social Care Establishments and for the Establishments for Children Left Without Parental Care, which were adopted in the year 2000, the placement of a child in a public care children's establishment is effected by an administrative procedure. The initiative is undertaken by the parent(s), whereas the placement is carried out on the approval of the establishment's head official (for the medical and social care establishments) or by the decision of a collective body such as a placement commission elected by the teachers' board of the establishments for children.

It is of absolute certainty that any placement of the child outside the family is necessarily effected by a court: the only body authorised to assess the best interests of the child and the need for them to be placed outside the family. Therefore, every such placement needs to be initiated, not before the head official of the respective establishment, but before the Child Protection Department (CPD). The philosophy is that the CPD needs to examine the effectiveness of the suggested measures within the family environment or institute a court procedure for placement. In this sense, the regulations in the two sets of Rules regarding the placement have been overruled by the CPA. In practice, however, placements initiated on the request of the parent(s) are still performed freely by head officials of children's establishments. The Child Protection Departments do not yet entertain the capacity to control such placements.

D   Foster care

For the first time in contemporary legislation, the CPA settles the institution of foster care. Placement with a foster family is one of the measures for protecting the child within a family environment. The placement is authorised by the regional court's decision or, temporarily, until such decision becomes effective, on the order of the head official of the MSAS. The foster parents and the MSAS sign a contract, which settles the terms and conditions of the placement: the duration, payment of foster parents and their rights and obligations in relation to the MSAS. There are also provisions regulating the relationship with the parents of origin where such relations are in the interest of the child. This matter is determined by the ruling of the regional court.

The law deals with the foster family at a very broad level of generality and does not elaborate in sufficient detail on two very important questions. In the first place, what are the rights and the obligations of the foster parents as regards the child? The text is quite laconic in stating only that they are not the bearers of any parental rights and obligations. The legislators' answer is awaited and it is expected to clarify the exact responsibilities of foster parents and whether they coincide with those of the child's guardian or trustee. If the answer is no, then we have quite a complex picture of three categories of caretaker persons: the child's parents (with whom the child does not share a common home), a guardian/trustee, who is legally assigned to take care of the rights and the property of the child, and a foster parent who is supposed to provide the day-to-day care for the child. This situation, however, is charged with the potential to limit excessively the opportunities of the foster parents to fulfil, adequately and urgently, the daily needs and interests of the child. Secondly, it is not clear how the interests of the child could be guaranteed in situations of emergency. Should the foster carers consult the CPD or the parents or not?

E   Protection against child abuse

A child can be placed outside his or her family of origin only on one of the following grounds as set forth in Art 25 of the Act:

'... the parents: have passed away, are unknown or have had their parents' rights terminated or limited; without valid reason permanently fail to provide care for their child; are in a position of permanent inability to rear their child.'

The Act does not envisage abuse itself as a ground for administrative intervention. Local authorities can initiate placement of the child only on the grounds of prolonged deprivation from parental care as a form of abuse.

It is an undoubted merit of the CPA that it establishes the right of the child to be protected against any type of violence:

'Every child has a right to protection against involvement in activities that are harmful to his or her physical, mental, moral and educational development; ... against all methods of upbringing that undermine his or her dignity; against physical, psychological or other types of abuse; against all forms of influence which go against his or her interests; ... use of children for purposes of begging, prostitution, dissemination of pornographic material, receipt of unlawful pecuniary income, as well as protection against sexual abuse; ... forcible involvement in political, religious and trade union activities' (Art 11).

In order to have this right protected a child can approach law enforcement bodies such as the Child Protection Departments and require assistance, support and services.

The very adoption of these legal definitions and norms has to be regarded as a positive step in the recognition and the articulation of the child abuse phenomenon in Bulgaria. It is also the first attempt to provide special protection to child victims of abuse. At the same time, the Act seems to be lacking in terms of consistency. The broad scope of Art 11 seems to recognise violence outside the family rather than taking account of incidence within it. This formula can be regarded as a political move intended to answer public expectations in this respect: the protection of children against new forms of violence: luring into prostitution, use of drugs, pornography, etc. Paragraph 2 of Art 11, however, reaffirms the intention of legislators to cover all forms of abuse happening at home also, starting from emotional and physical abuse and extending to sexual abuse against the child.

On the other hand, in attempting to identify the children at risk, the Act categorises them alongside child victims of abuse.

'A child at risk' is a child: ... who has become victim of abuse, violence, exploitation or any other inhuman or degrading treatment or punishment either in or out of his or her family; ... for whom there is a danger of causing damage to his or her physical, mental, moral, intellectual and social development' (§1, para 5, Supplementary Provisions).

Where abuse arises, the child should be registered in the local services special register (Art 21, para 6) as needing protection. In the case of an emergency, the police have the power to place the child in a safe place for 24 hours. The grounds for such placement are very limited and cover instances where the child has become the victim of a crime or where the child's life or health is under immediate threat; where the child is in danger of being involved in a crime; where the child has been lost and is in a helpless condition; where the child is left without supervision (Art 38). At this point it should be emphasised that the involvement of the police in emergency protection has a historical background which, however, does not derive from their previous power, but from the absence (until recently) of professional social workers in the area of children and families. It was only 10 years ago that the concept of individual social work was introduced as an alternative to centralised state care in Bulgaria. Developments are seen in both the area of social work education and within the profession itself, but the recognition of social workers and raising the awareness of the demand for their services will take longer.

In order to facilitate the identification of cases of abuse, the Act introduces a special obligation for reporting abuse. According to Art 7, persons aware of a child in need of protection will be obliged to report to the CPD. This obligation also applies to persons who come to know of such children in the course of practising their profession or occupation, regardless of the fact that they might be bound by professional privilege. The provision does not imply sanctions. Its logic is to make those who witness child abuse, especially the professionals, more responsible for protecting the rights of children.

F   Bodies assigned with child protection

The Act places an emphasis on the interaction between the State, local authorities and civil society in carrying out the activities for the protection of the child (Art 1). The attainment of co-operation in the activities aimed to protect the child is one of the goals which the Act sets for itself and proclaims. However, very few guarantees are provided for the attainment of this goal. On the one hand, there is no tradition of co-operation and coordination, whereas on the other the structure of bodies which is being set up represents a risk to the aspirations of the Act in this respect.[10] It must also be noted that, to a great extent, the very genesis of the Act was inspired by serious widespread criticisms of the incoherent and even contradictory government policy towards children. Previously, policy on children was assigned to five different ministries and remained ever on the periphery of their functions and policies were formulated leaving the interests of the child out of account. As far as the providers of other types of service are concerned (in the face of the MSAS), children were just another customer together with other vulnerable and marginalised groups.

According to the CPA, the rights of, and the obligations for, the protection of the child are assigned to the bodies of the State, the municipalities, civil (volunteer) organisations and physical persons. The CPA sets up the administrative structure of the state and municipal bodies. A central authority is being established: the State Agency to the Council of Ministers, together with local bodies: the Child Protection Departments. However, local departments are not subordinate to the State Agency, but to the existing municipal social services departments, which are the local bodies of the Ministry of Labour and Social Policy. Even this fact in itself creates an opportunity for conflict and for the overlapping of activity and influence.

The State Agency for Child Protection and the municipal service departments are assigned the rights and obligations in the implementation of all measures for the protection of the child together with safeguarding the exercise of their rights under Chapter Two of the CPA.

Voluntary organisations and individuals are also entitled to participate in child protection activities. With voluntary organisations this right has been limited to providing social services. Such organisations may set up establishments within the meaning of the Social Assistance Act and apply for a licence if they want to apply for finance from the Social Assistance Fund. Voluntary organisations and individuals can co-operate with the Municipal Social Assistance Services in providing co-operation, assistance and services within the family environment, as well as upon placement with a foster family. This action is based on the provisions of Art 9, para 2 of the CPA. Physical persons participate in the placement of children with foster families or with the families of relations and close friends whereby they are vested with the respective rights and obligations.

The Child Protection Act serves as a basis for reform of child care policies in Bulgaria. It could be viewed as an achievement in the context of the current national realities. In the context of the needs that have arisen in practice, however,

---

[10]   In the Government Strategy and Action Plan, the lack of coordination is emphasised as one of the reasons for carrying out the reform in relation to the welfare of children.

it is clear that the Act should be further amended and improved. This means that the reform itself is expected to establish the norms which should be given effect in the future.

CANADA

NON-MARITAL UNIONS, FINALITY OF SEPARATION AGREEMENTS AND CHILDREN'S ISSUES

Nicholas Bala[*] *and Rebecca Jaremko*[**]

I INTRODUCTION

Canadian family law continues to undergo a process of slow but significant reform. Recently, the most significant changes have been made by the judiciary, but there has also been some legislative reform, often in response to judicial activism.

Invoking the Charter of Rights, the courts have been expanding the definition of 'spouse'. The courts have ruled that it is discriminatory to deny long-term conjugal same-sex and opposite-sex partners the same rights as the married are afforded. This may ultimately lead to the recognition of 'same-sex marriage' by the Canadian courts, although this has not yet occurred. There has been some legislative response to this judicial activism, with one province enacting a law to allow a limited form of same-sex or opposite-sex non-marital registered domestic partnership.

Canadian courts have been taking a more expansive approach towards spousal support issues, although spousal support is only awarded in a minority of cases of spousal separation. There is significant controversy over the weight to be given to provisions of a separation agreement dealing with spousal support issues. Recent jurisprudence reveals a judicial willingness to vary spousal support provisions in agreements that, in the light of subsequent developments, do not deal fairly with this issue. This usually means that the courts are intervening to provide equitable relief to women.

The courts are struggling with a range of child-related issues. Recent decisions have revealed a significant judicial reluctance to award grandparents visitation rights when children are living with their parents. One highly publicised Canadian case deals with a custody dispute between parents of different races. The courts have also been interpreting Canada's Child Support Guidelines, which were introduced in 1997. While the Guidelines have produced greater certainty and more settlements, they have also resulted in a considerable amount of litigation. Judges have tended to take interpretive approaches that favour larger amounts of child support being paid. There is the prospect that in 2002 Canada's Parliament will embark on a more ambitious project of reforming the child-related provisions of the Divorce Act.

---

[*]   Professor of Law, Queen's University, Canada.
[**]   LLM Candidate, Queen's University, Canada.

Courts have dealt with Charter-based challenges to child welfare statutes, with recent decisions favouring State intervention to promote the welfare of children over protection of legal rights. A Supreme Court of Canada decision upheld legislation that allows for apprehension of children believed to be at risk of harm without prior judicial authorization, even if the situation is not an emergency. A lower court ruling upheld the validity of Alberta legislation allowing for apprehension and detention of adolescents believed to be engaging in juvenile prostitution, and a number of other provinces are considering enacting similar statutes.

In this paper, we summarize the major developments of 2000–2001 in Canadian family law. Concerns about protection of the vulnerable and ending discriminatory treatment are dominant themes.

II   AN INCREASINGLY INCLUSIVE DEFINITION OF 'SPOUSE': SAME-SEX AND UNMARRIED PARTNERS

Historically, heterosexual marriage was the only type of conjugal relationship to have social acceptability and legal recognition in Canada. Over the past three decades, there has been a growing acceptance of non-traditional conjugal relationships, with some of the most dramatic social and legal changes occurring in the past few years.

At the time of the last census in Canada in 1996, 14% of all Canadian opposite-sex couples residing together were unmarried, up from 6% in 1981.[1] Starting in 1974 Canadian legislatures slowly began to give legal recognition to unmarried opposite-sex conjugal partners (often called 'common law relationships'[2] in Canada). In a number of provinces, legislation was amended to give limited 'spousal rights' to those cohabiting in a conjugal relationship in which a child was born or cohabiting for specified time periods (in the range of one to five years).[3] However, in the mid 1990s some important differences between legal marriage and common law marriage remained. Quebec and Alberta did not join the other provinces in enacting legislation to recognize private support rights or obligations for common law spouses. Although in many cases the courts would use the constructive trust to recognize property claims at the end of long-

---

[1]   Statistics Canada, 1996 Census. See 'More People are Giving Marriage a Try' *National Post* (22 May 2000). A census was conducted in May 2001, which for the first time includes questions about same-sex common law relationships. It will take some time before the results of the 2001 census are known.

[2]   Historically the term 'common law marriage' was used to refer to a situation in which a man and a woman lived together and held themselves out as husband and wife, as distinguished from a marriage effected under statute, which required a ceremony and registration. While some American States still recognize 'common law marriage' as a way of entering into a legally valid marriage, modern Canadian courts have rejected this as a legally valid marriage: *Dutch v Dutch* (1977) 1 RFL (2d) 177 (Ont Co Ct). Today in Canada, in everyday parlance and some legislation, the term 'common law marriage' refers to unmarried opposite-sex conjugal cohabitation. In some statutory definitions, the term 'common law relationship' now includes same-sex partners living in a conjugal relationship.

[3]   There is a considerable body of jurisprudence that helps to define whether a relationship is 'conjugal', or merely intimate but without conjugal rights and obligations; see eg *Molodowich v Penttinen* (1980), 17 RFL (2d) 376 (Ont Dist Ct); *Thauvette v Malyon* (1996), 23 RFL (4th) 217 (Ont Gen Div), and *M v H* [1999] 2 SCR 3.

term relationships,[4] no province enacted legislation to recognize property rights for common law partners.

In the last few years, Canadian courts have invoked the Canadian Charter of Rights and Freedoms virtually to eliminate the legal differences between marriage and long-term opposite-sex cohabitation.[5] In 1995 in *Miron v Trudel*[6] the Supreme Court of Canada held that the exclusion of long-term common law partners from the definition of 'spouse' for the purposes of automobile insurance legislation violated the provisions of the Charter prohibiting discrimination. In 1998, the Alberta Court of Appeal held that the failure of Alberta, one of Canada's most conservative provinces, to include common law opposite-sex partners in the definition of 'spouse' for purposes of support law also violated the Charter, and allowed a woman to make a spousal support claim at the end of a long-term relationship.[7]

While no province has legislation recognizing property rights for non-marital partners,[8] in April 2000, the Nova Scotia Court of Appeal in *Walsh v Bona*[9] ruled that the provisions of that province's matrimonial property statute which limited property rights to married partners were discriminatory and unconstitutional for excluding those in common law opposite-sex relationships. The Supreme Court of Canada has granted the Nova Scotia government leave to appeal.[10]

If the Supreme Court of Canada upholds the decision of the lower courts in *Walsh v Bona*, it will be difficult to defend any Canadian legislation that distinguishes between the married and partners in long-term opposite-sex conjugal relationships.[11] Although it is difficult to predict the outcome of any significant constitutional case in the Supreme Court of Canada, the general trend of litigation and legislation has clearly been to equate long-term opposite-sex conjugal relationships to marriage. This recognizes that, from an economic, social and psychological perspective, these informal relationships are often functionally identical to marriage. Perhaps most significantly, failing to recognize legally these

---

4   See eg *Peter v Beblow* [1993] 1 SCR 980, 44 RFL (3d) 329 where the Supreme Court of Canada held that this constructive trust claim could be based on purely domestic contributions. The Supreme Court of Canada has a free website with access to the Supreme Court Reports (SCR) as well as postings of recent decisions online at *http://www.scc–csc.gc.ca.*

5   See eg Winifred Holland, 'Intimate Relationships in the New Millennium: The Assimilation of Marriage and Cohabitation?' (2000) 17 Can J Fam L 114–168.

6   [1995] 2 SCC 418.

7   *Taylor v Rossu* (1998), 39 RFL (4th) 242 (Alta CA). Quebec still has not enacted legislation to recognize unmarried partners for support law purposes. However, for a range of public and private law purposes, Quebec law extended rights and obligations to two persons of either sex 'who live together in a de facto [marital] union': SQ 1999, c 14.

8   For example, 'spouse' is defined for property law purposes in Ontario's Family Law Act, section 1 to apply only to the legally married, while, in Part III of the Act, which addresses spousal support, 'spouse' applies also to non-marital cohabitants. Only the sparsely populated jurisdictions of the Northwest Territories and Nunavut have property statutes that include in the definition of 'spouse' a person of the opposite sex who has cohabited outside of marriage for two years or in a relationship in which the couple are the natural or adoptive parents of a child. See Family Law Act, SNWT 1997, c 18, s 1.

9   [2000] NSJ 117,186 DLR (4th) 50 (NSCA).

10 [2000] SCCA 517, leave to appeal granted 15 February 2001.

11 For a fuller discussion of the constitutional issues raised by same-sex and opposite-sex conjugal partners seeking marital rights, see N Bala, 'The *Charter of Rights* and Family Law in Canada', (2001), 18 Can Fam LQ 373–428.

informal relationships may impose unfair burdens on those who are most vulnerable or who have contributed more to the relationship. This would usually impact upon the female partner disproportionately. Failing to recognize these relationships may also result in inappropriate shifting of responsibilities from private individuals to the State.

While unmarried opposite-sex partners began to receive legal recognition in Canada more than a quarter of a century ago, it is only in the past few years that there have been significant changes in legal approaches to the rights and obligations of same-sex partners. However, in the past few years there have been quite dramatic changes in law and social attitudes to homosexuality. According to public opinion polls, a majority of Canadians now believe gay and lesbian couples should be allowed to marry, and the number of Canadians who 'approve' of homosexuality has doubled in the past five years.[12]

In the mid-1990s the Supreme Court of Canada had ruled that discrimination on the basis of sexual orientation is a violation of the Charter of Rights, and a prohibited ground of discrimination for such purposes as employment law.[13] In 1999, the Supreme Court of Canada held in *M v H* that provincial family law legislation which granted 'spousal support' rights to opposite-sex conjugal partners but excluded same-sex conjugal partners violated the Charter of Rights.[14] The failure to recognize same-sex relationships was found to violate fundamental principles of 'human dignity'. While the Court did not equate same-sex partners to those who are married, it effectively required that all legislation recognizing opposite-sex conjugal relationships (or 'common law marriage') must grant the same rights to same-sex partners.

Most governments in Canada have responded to *M v H* by amending statutes to afford the same rights and obligations to same-sex partners as are afforded to opposite-sex unmarried partners. After a period of 'conjugal cohabitation' (usually one to five years), the partners are afforded many of the rights and obligations of marriage. This is called granting of partial spousal status by 'ascription'. Nova Scotia has gone further than other Canadian legislatures. That province amended a number of statutes in 2001 to broaden the definition of 'common law partner' to give same-sex partners who 'cohabit ... in a conjugal relationship' for a prescribed period, one or two years depending on the statute, the same rights and obligations as opposite-sex unmarried cohabitants. The Nova Scotia law also permits any two individuals who 'are cohabiting or intend to cohabit in a conjugal relationship' to enter into a 'registered domestic partnership'.[15] This allows a 'registered domestic partner' to have the status of a 'spouse' for the purposes of a

---

[12]   Findings of survey by the Environics Research Group in April 2001; see '55% Back Same-Sex Marriage, Survey Says' *National Post* (10 May 2001).

[13]   Salient cases establishing this right are *Egan v Canada* [1995] 2 SCR 513, where homosexuality was conceded as an analogous prohibited ground of discrimination under s 15 of the Charter; and *Vriend v Alberta* [1998] 1 SCR 493, where the Supreme Court of Canada held that the failure of Alberta's human rights code to prohibit discrimination on the basis of sexual orientation violated the Charter.

[14]   [1999] 2 SCR 3. For a fuller discussion of issues related to same-sex marriage and alternatives for legislative reform in Canada, see generally vol 17(1) of the *Canadian Journal of Family Law*, and Kathleen Lahey, *Are We 'Persons' Yet? Law and Sexuality in Canada* (Toronto: University of Toronto Press, 1999).

[15]   Law Reform Act, SNS 2000, Chap 29.

dozen provincial statutes, including matrimonial property and support laws. While this new law does not give full spousal status to same-sex partners for purposes of provincial law, and has no direct effect on matters within the federal area of jurisdiction, it is the first Canadian statute to give same-sex partners the ability to establish a relationship based on registration, and a number of same-sex couples in Nova Scotia registered their partnerships after the new legislation came into effect on 1 June 2001.[16]

In addition to making significant strides towards attaining the functional legal equivalent of marital status, in the past year, same-sex partners in Canada have intensified an ongoing legal battle to gain access to full legal marriage.

Notwithstanding growing social acceptance of homosexuality and same-sex partnerships, they remain highly contentious. Same-sex marriage, in particular, remains very controversial. About one-quarter of Canadians still 'strongly' disapprove of homosexuality.[17] While Canadian courts have held that it is unconstitutional to prohibit adoption by same-sex partners, this also remains a contentious subject, and such adoptions are still quite rare.[18]

The strongest organized opposition to recognition of same-sex marriage is from some religious groups. For example, the religion with the most adherents in Canada is Roman Catholicism,[19] and the Vatican has issued a document attacking homosexual unions as 'much more grave' than the heterosexual common law equivalent. It calls homosexual unions a 'deplorable distortion', and attacks attempts to allow same-sex partners to adopt children. The Vatican sees same-sex partnerships as detrimental to society and leading to the breakdown of the family. According to the document, legalization of same-sex marriage 'would be an arbitrary use of power which does not contribute to the common good because the original nature of marriage precedes and exceeds, in an absolute and radical way, the power of the state'.[20]

Recent Canadian cases faced the challenge of balancing legal prohibitions against discrimination on the basis of sexual orientation with the freedom to hold and espouse religious beliefs that disapprove of homosexuality.

In *Chamberlain v Surrey School Board*,[21] the British Columbia Court of Appeal upheld the right of a school board to prevent three children's books depicting same-sex couples from being used in the grade one curriculum. In setting this policy, the school board members clearly indicated that they were influenced by their religious belief that homosexual behaviour is a sin. The policy was challenged by a teacher, supported by civil liberties and homosexual rights groups, arguing that such religious beliefs should not determine policy in the public, secular school system. The court noted that this was really a confrontation

---

16 'Nova Scotia Same-Sex Couples Celebrate Legal Recognition' *http://www.cbc.ca* (webposted 4 June 2001).

17 Findings of survey by the Environics Research Group in April 2001 as published in T Arnold '55% Back Same-Sex Marriage, Survey Says', *National Post* (10 May 2001).

18 See M Philip, 'Gay adoption breaks new ground: Court rulings have forced most provinces to allow same sex couples to adopt children', *The Globe and Mail*, 9 July 2001.

19 46% of Canadians are Roman Catholics, with various Protestant denominations making the second largest group, at 36%: *http://www.statcan.ca/english/freepub/92-125-GIE/html/rel.htm*.

20 'Vatican Attacks Homosexual Unions', *National Post* (22 November 2000).

21 *Chamberlain v Surrey School District No 36* [2000] BCJ 1875 (CA).

between adults over values, and whatever the motivation of the litigants, they all 'appear to agree that issues of sexual orientation do not belong in the [grade one] curriculum'. Under the ruling, the books are still available as library resources to which students have access and which teachers can use 'incidentally'. In his judgment, Mackenzie JA acknowledged that 'homosexuality and same sex relationships remain morally controversial'.[22] He concluded that the constitutional protection of freedom of religion includes the right to believe that homosexuality is immoral, holding that[23] a religiously informed conscience should not be accorded privilege but neither should it be placed under a disability ... Secularism cannot make religious unbelief a condition in participation in the setting of the moral agenda.

Accordingly, the fact that members of the school board were religiously motivated did not invalidate an otherwise educationally acceptable policy.

In *Trinity Western University v College of Teachers*[24] the Supreme Court of Canada considered the decision of the British Columbia College of Teachers to refuse to recognize certification for graduates of the education program of a small Evangelical Christian university. The College considered the certification of these graduates unacceptable on the basis that as students they were required to adhere to a code of conduct which prohibited 'practices that are Biblically condemned' including 'sexual sins', and of particular concern, 'homosexual behaviour'. The College considered this code of conduct discriminatory.

The Supreme Court held that the decision of the College of Teachers could not be upheld as it violated the constitutionally protected freedom of religion of the students in this program, ruling that while teachers are entitled to hold 'sexist, racist or homophobic beliefs ... acting on those beliefs, however, is a very different matter'.[25] The court recognized that some students are themselves gay or lesbian, or are members of families with gay or lesbian parents. Any discriminatory conduct or disparaging remark made based on sexual orientation by teachers in a secular, public school would be unacceptable. Individual teachers, however, are not precluded from holding discriminatory religiously based beliefs and may act on those beliefs to govern their private conduct.[26]

In 1993 a Canadian court rejected a Charter-based claim by two same-sex partners who wanted to marry one another.[27] However, in the light of subsequent Supreme Court of Canada jurisprudence, especially in *M v H*, it is understandable that advocates for gays and lesbians are again challenging the constitutional validity of the common law and legislative requirement that two persons of the

---

[22] At para 20.

[23] At paras 28 and 31.

[24] *Trinity Western University v College of Teachers* [2001] SCJ No 32.

[25] At paras 36 and 37.

[26] In some provinces there are publicly funded Catholic schools which have rules governing teacher belief and conduct. Such regulation has withstood Charter scrutiny. For example, in *NTA v Newfoundland (Treasury Board)* [1988] NJ 287 (Nfld CA) the Court upheld the right of a school system founded upon denominational instruction, and held that school boards in that system have the right to require that teachers who were adherents to that denomination continue to respect and abide by the basic precepts of that faith, including rules that govern sexual conduct, such as prohibitions on adultery.

[27] *Layland v Ontario (Minister of Consumer and Commercial Relations)* (1993), 14 OR (3d) 658, 104 DLR (4th) 214 (Div Ct).

opposite sex can marry another. Challenges have been launched in British Columbia, Ontario and Quebec.

The Ontario case has gained the most public attention. It was initially based on an application by six same-sex couples to the Government to issue marriage licences, with supporting intervenors including a gay and lesbian rights group,[28] and opposing intervenors including a coalition of Catholic, Sikh and Muslim religious groups, joined together as the 'Interfaith Coalition on Marriage and Family'.[29]

In January 2001, gay rights activists used what has been termed a legislative 'loophole'[30] to attempt to subvert governmental refusals to issue marriage licences to same-sex couples. Most marriages in Canada are solemnized after a couple receives a marriage licence from the municipal government, and then has a religious or civil celebrant perform and register their marriage. However, in most jurisdictions in Canada it is also possible to have a valid marriage performed without a licence, according to the Christian tradition of 'publication of banns' of marriage. For example, under the Ontario Marriage Act,[31] a couple may request that their local church parish 'publish banns', with the minister announcing the names of the intended couple during religious services on three successive Sundays preceding the intended marriage and asking for any person with a 'lawful objection' to come forward (eg if anyone is aware that a party is already married to another person). The minister is then authorized to perform the ceremony without a licence, although he or she is obliged to register the marriage with the Government after it is performed. Section 5 of the Act provides that any 'person who is of the age of majority may obtain a licence or be married under the authority of the publication of banns, provided no lawful cause exists to hinder the solemnization'.

The Metropolitan Community Church of Toronto, a Christian church with a largely gay and lesbian membership, went through a process of publication of banns and then performed a double same-sex wedding in Toronto, Ontario on 14 January 2001. The ceremony has been hailed as marking the first legal Christian marriage between two persons of the same sex since medieval times.[32] The event attracted global media attention and was followed by political and legal controversy.

Although the Ontario Marriage Act does not specify that only two individuals of the opposite sex can marry, the Ontario Government has taken the position that it will not register these same-sex marriage ceremonies, and the same-sex partners who took part in these ceremonies have joined the ongoing litigation. As a matter of common law and legislation, the Ontario government is correct that a marriage

---

[28]   The high profile lobby group, EGALE ('Equality for Gays and Lesbians Everywhere'); *Halpern v Toronto* [2000] OJ 4514 (SC).

[29]   'Interfaith Coalition on Marriage and Family Granted Intervenor Status', *Catholic Civil Rights League Press Release* (23 January 2001).

[30]   S Roberts, 'Loophole May Allow World's First Gay Marriage', *National Post* (5 December 2000).

[31]   Ontario Marriage Act, RSO 1990, c M3, section 5.

[32]   A Humphreys, 'First Gay Marriage Legal, For Now', *National Post* (15 January 2001). The Netherlands has since then brought into force legislation to allow same-sex partners to marry.

in Canada requires one man and one woman.[33] However, the real issue which the courts are being called upon to decide is whether this legal rule is a violation of the Charter and hence invalid.

The Supreme Court of Canada in *M v H* was careful to point out that it was not ruling that same-sex partners are entitled to marry, but only holding that same-sex partners who cohabit for a prescribed period (three years in the relevant statute) are entitled to the same rights as opposite-sex partners who cohabit for the same period. While the rhetoric of *M v H* recognizes that same-sex partnerships perform many of the same social, emotional and economic functions as marriage, and that same-sex partners are entitled to be treated with the same 'human dignity' as opposite-sex partners, the issue of same-sex marriage remains contentious. The outcome when the case gets to the Supreme Court is thus far from certain.[34] In a controversial interview, Justice Bastarche, who joined the Supreme Court of Canada after *M v H* was decided, disparaged the majority judgment in that case as:[35]

> 'the most obvious example of result-oriented reasoning … it was absolutely clear what the purpose of that [spousal support] legislation is in all of this … and I don't think it was a consistent application of the principles of statutory interpretation that would have brought the court to define the purpose of that legislation as it did.'

It is apparent that for the foreseeable future in Canada, the prospect of same-sex marriage will remain contentious in Canada. Politicians are very unlikely to take the lead in dealing with such a controversial question. It seems certain that the present challenges to the prohibition on same-sex marriage will end up in the Supreme Court for resolution. It is interesting to observe that, as the Supreme Court has gradually changed the law, and has incrementally given greater rights to same-sex partners, it has also had a role in changing social attitudes. While same-sex marriage remains controversial, there is much greater acceptance of this idea by the Canadian public now than there was a decade ago.

---

[33] In 2000, in response to *M v H*, the federal government extended to same-sex conjugal partners the same statutory rights and obligations which it already afforded to opposite-sex 'common law' partners who cohabit for one year. However, in the same law, the federal Parliament codified the common law of capacity to marry, defining 'marriage' as 'the union of one man and one woman'. See Modernization of Benefits and Obligations Act, SC 2000, c 12.

[34] The majority of the Court emphasized the social importance of recognizing same-sex relationships, with Cory J writing: 'the human dignity of individuals in same-sex relationships is violated by the impugned legislation'(at paras 73–74). This type of rhetoric would suggest that the Court may be sympathetic in future cases to an argument that the failure to allow same-sex partners to marry is an affront to their 'human dignity'.

[35] C Schmitz, 'The Bastarche Interview: Reasoning to Results as SCC', *The Lawyer's Weekly*, 26 January 2001.

III   DIVORCE , SPOUSAL SUPPORT AND SEPARATION AGREEMENTS

While it is possible to obtain a divorce on the fault-based grounds of adultery or cruelty, the vast majority of divorces in Canada are now granted on the no-fault ground of one year living 'separate and apart' under the federal Divorce Act.[36]

Canada's divorce rate remains high. After rising in the 1980s, it peaked in 1993 and declined slowly in the mid-1990s. However, the Canadian divorce rate climbed 2.5% from 1997 to 1998, the most recent year for which data are available. Based on 1996 rates, 36% of marriages in Canada can be expected to end in divorce within 30 years and 39% within 50 years.[37]

Divorces today generally take place after a longer duration of marriage than in the past. The average age of divorce was 39.4 years for women and 42 years for men in 1998. These average ages have increased about 3 years since 1989. A possible explanation for the increase in age at divorce and the increase in the duration of marriages pre-divorce is demographic. As the post-World War II 'Baby Boom' generation starts to reach an age when their children are reaching adulthood, some of them are ready to divorce. As Jessie Tzeng, a sociologist at McGill University in Montreal speculates, the increase in the divorce rate may be increasing the number of 'empty nesters' who want to 'start over' once their children have left home. Robert Glossop, of Canada's Vanier Institute for the Family suggested that the prosperous economy in the mid-1990s may also explain the increase in the divorce rate, pointing out that 'divorce is expensive'.[38]

While judges decide the most contentious cases, the majority of Canadians who divorce resolve their disputes by negotiating an agreement, either on their own, or commonly with the assistance of lawyers or a mediator.[39] These separation agreements are typically incorporated into a court order made 'on consent', at the time of granting the divorce. The vast majority of divorces are obtained without the parties appearing in court, by a judge simply reviewing papers filed with the court.

Judges have a statutory responsibility at the time that a divorce is sought to ensure that the provisions for child support are 'reasonable'. Typically, this assessment is made with reference to the Child Support Guidelines.[40] In some cases, a judge will refuse to grant a divorce if the amount of child support appears inadequate. Although in practice the level of judicial scrutiny of child support provisions in separation agreements varies, most child support orders made 'on

---

[36]   Divorce Act, RSC 1985, c 3 (2nd Supp), s 8(2).

[37]   S Nolen, 'Divorce Rate Bucks Declining Trend', *The Globe and Mail*, 29 September 2000. For further statistical information on Canadian divorce rates, see *Statistics Canada* online (18 May 1999) *http://www.statcan.ca/Daily/English/990518/d990518b.htm*.

[38]   S Nolen, 'Divorce Rate Bucks Declining Trend', *The Globe and Mail*, 29 September 2000.

[39]   See L Bertrand, J Hornick, J Paetsch and N Bala, 'The Survey of Child Support Awards: Interim Analysis of Phase II Data (October 1998–March 2000)' (Canadian Research Institute for Law & Family for Department of Justice Canada, September 2000) – a report on a study of divorce files and orders in cases where children of marriage identified in divorce petition *http://canada.justice.gc.ca/en/ps/sup/pub/rap/phase2.html*. Over 85% were obtained on an 'uncontested' or 'consent'basis, and a significant portion of the remaining 15% were settled before trial.

[40]   Divorce Act, s 11(1)(b).

consent' provide for at least the Guidelines amount.[41] Bertrand et al[42] report that most awards were the same as the amounts in the Federal Child Support Guidelines (59.4%), or greater (34.2%). Only 6.4% of cases reported award amounts less than those in the Guidelines, and some of these may have involved non-monetary benefits being provided for the child, such as exclusive possession of the matrimonial home to the custodial parent. If circumstances change after an agreement is made, the courts have clearly indicated that they are not bound by the child support provisions of an agreement or prior order, and will vary child support to accord with the new circumstances.[43]

Unlike with regard to child support, there is no judicial responsibility to examine the amount of spousal support in a separation agreement at the time that a divorce is granted.[44] While there is an order for child support in about three-quarters of all divorces, at present a spousal support order is made in only about one-tenth of all divorce cases.[45] As discussed below, reported spousal support jurisprudence offers broad bases for obtaining support. However, spousal support is unlikely to be ordered in cases where the spouses' income is roughly equal, the marriage is of relatively short duration, there are no children, or the potential recipient has a new partner. Also, legislation makes clear that if there are limited resources, there is a priority for an order for the full amount of child support under the Guidelines before any order is made for spousal support,[46] and in many cases a payor can only reasonably be expected to pay child support. Further, some spouses, who may in fact have sacrificed much for the marriage, are nevertheless psychologically reluctant to ask for spousal support. As a result, generally there is only provision for spousal support at the end of relatively long-term relationships with children and middle or upper income payors.

If an agreement is made about spousal support, most frequently both parties are prepared to live with it, or lack the financial and emotional energy to apply for variation. However, there are a significant number of cases in which one party will apply to a court to vary or override a support provision in a separation agreement that was incorporated 'on consent' into a court order at the time of granting the divorce.

An application to vary a support order can be made by either the payor or the recipient. In practice, however, most of the applications are made by women who made agreements that provided them with a limited term or amount of support, or waived support altogether. Typically the applications are made by a woman who entered into the agreement in the emotionally difficult period following separation in the hope that she would become fully self-supporting, but who later found that she still needed financial support from her former spouse.

Canadian courts have long accepted that if the separation agreement was the product of 'duress' or 'unconscionability', provisions regarding spousal support or

---

[41] See eg *Orellana v Merino* (1998), 40 RFL (4th) 129 (Ont Gen Div); *Reid v Reid* (1995), 11 RFL (4th) 85 (BCCA); and *Geddart v Geddart* (1993), 50 RFL (3d) 102 (Man CA).

[42] See footnote 40 above.

[43] See eg *Fung-Sunter v Fabian* (1999), 48 RFL (4th) 95 (BCCA).

[44] *Colletta v Colletta* (1992), 42 RFL (3d) 277 (Ont CA).

[45] Bertrand et al, supra.

[46] Divorce Act, s 15.3.

property might be set aside. In deciding whether to set aside an agreement on these grounds, the courts focus on the circumstances at the time that the agreement was signed, including whether each party had independent legal advice, whether there were threats, and the adequacy of the disclosure of financial information.[47]

There is controversy about the nature of the jurisdiction that courts have to override or vary provisions for spousal support in a separation agreement that is not 'unconscionable' or otherwise invalid when entered into.

There is a provision in the Divorce Act to allow for variation of spousal support. If a spousal support order was made after a contested hearing, the courts have accepted that this order may be varied if there has been a 'material change in circumstances'. This is a relatively low threshold.[48] However, until recently, judges were of the view that if the spousal support order was based on a separation agreement, then the jurisdiction to vary a support provision of a separation agreement should be exercised very narrowly. The dominant judicial attitude has been that the courts should respect and enforce the agreement of the parties.

The attitude of judicial conservatism towards variation of spousal support provisions of valid separation agreements was established by the Supreme Court of Canada in a 'Trilogy' of cases[49] decided in 1987 pursuant to the Divorce Act of 1968.[50] In one of these cases, *Pelech v Pelech,* Madame Justice Wilson wrote:[51]

'It seems to me that where the parties have negotiated their own agreement, freely and on the advice of independent legal counsel, as to how their financial affairs should be settled on the breakdown of their marriage, and the agreement is not unconscionable in the substantive law sense, it should be respected. People should be encouraged to take responsibility for their own lives and their own decisions. This should be the overriding policy consideration ...

Absent some causal connection between the changed circumstances and the marriage, it seems to me that parties who have declared their relationship at an end should be taken at their word. They made the decision to marry and they made the decision to terminate their marriage ... The causal connection between the severe hardship being experienced by the former spouse and the marriage provides, in my view, the necessary legal criterion for determining when a case falls within the 'narrow range of cases ... where an applicant seeking maintenance or an increase in the existing level of maintenance establishes that he or she has suffered a *radical change in circumstances flowing from an economic pattern of dependency engendered by the marriage,* the court may exercise its relieving power. Otherwise, the obligation to support the former spouse should be, as in the case of any other citizen, the communal responsibility of the state.'

Pelech and the other 1987 Supreme Court decisions dealt expressly with the judicial authority to override the effect of the spousal support provisions of a separation agreement. Initially these decisions had a narrowing effect on all

---

[47]   See eg *Mundinger v Mundinger* [1969] 1 OR 606 (Ont CA); and *B (JF) v B (MA)* (1999), 1 RFL (5th) 339 (Ont SCJ), aff'd (2001), 14 RFL (5th) 1 (Ont CA).

[48]   Divorce Act, s 17.

[49]   *Pelech v Pelech* [1987] 1 SCR 801, 7 RFL (3d) 225; *Richardson v Richardson* [1987] 1 SCR 857; *Caron v Caron* [1987] 1 SCR 892.

[50]   Divorce Act, RSC 1970, c D-8.

[51]   (1987), 7 RFL (3d) 225, at 269–270. Emphasis added.

spousal support decisions. In the late 1980s, formal gender equality was a dominant political sentiment in family law in Canada. Many commentators, lawyers and the judges subscribed to a 'clean break' model of divorce, with the Supreme Court Trilogy being taken as authority for the proposition that spousal support should only be awarded if an applicant could establish a need 'causally connected' to the marriage. The decisions emphasized the desirability of mutual spousal independence as soon as possible post-divorce. Marital ties were to be severable relatively easily, completely and with finality.

By the early 1990s this narrow approach to spousal support was under attack by many scholars and advocates for women, who argued that it was an unrealistic approach to long-term marriages, especially those involving children and significant career sacrifices.[52] In 1992 the decision of the Supreme Court of Canada in *Moge v Moge*[53] reversed the trend towards narrowing of spousal support. Madame Justice L'Heureux-Dubé, writing for the court in *Moge*, acknowledged that in many cases one spouse, usually the woman, will have suffered lifelong economic consequences as a result of her contributions and role in the marriage:[54]

'in the proper exercise of their discretion, courts must be alert to a wide variety of factors and decisions made in the family interest during the marriage which have the effect of disadvantaging one spouse or benefiting the other upon its dissolution.'

The *Moge* decision expressly recognized the reality that for many women (and their children), separation resulted in impoverishment. After *Moge*, there was an increase in the number of women receiving spousal support, often on an indefinite basis.[55] The judgment, however, left questions unanswered.

Over the past few years, case-law continued to define and clarify the obligations of parties upon the breakdown of marriage. Important cases, however, remained frustratingly vague. In particular, the decision of the Supreme Court of Canada in *Bracklow v Bracklow*[56] in 2000 held that need alone might justify an award of support for a sick or disabled spouse, but the case did not give a clear indication of how long such support should continue for a marriage of medium duration, such as the seven-year relationship in *Bracklow*.

---

[52] See eg Kirstie MacLise, 'Causal Connection and Spousal Support: Variation of Maintenance' (1990) 6 Can Fam LQ 371–379; and Carol Rogerson, 'The Causal Connection Test in Spousal Support Law' (1989) 8 Can J Fam L 95–132.

[53] [1992] 3 SCR 813, 43 RFL (3d) 345.

[54] At para 91.

[55] See eg Nicholas Bala, 'Spousal Support Law Transformed: Fairer Treatment For Women' (1994) 11 Can Fam LQ 13–56; and Carol Rogerson, 'Spousal Support After *Moge*' (1996–97) 14 Can Fam LQ 281. See Marie Gordon, 'What Me Biased?: Women and Gender Bias in Family Law' (2001) 19 Can Fam LQ 53 for a discussion of the many difficulties that women still face in obtaining spousal support.

[56] [1999] 1 SCR 420, 44 RFL (4th) 1. See critical commentaries in Julien Payne, 'An Overview of Theory and Reality in the Judicial Disposition of Spousal Support Claims Under the Canadian Divorce Act' (2000) 63(2) Sask L Rev 403–443; Christine Davies, 'Spousal Support under the Divorce Act: From *Moge* to *Bracklow*' (1999), 44 RFL (4th) 61–73; and Dominique Goubau, 'The Clear and Clouded World of Spousal Support in Canada' (2001) 18 Can Fam LQ 333–355. See also N Bala, 'Court Decisions on Same-Sex and Unmarried Partners, Spousal Rights and Children', *International Survey of Family Law (2001 Edition)*, ed Andrew Bainham (Family Law, 2001).

At least in theory, however, the Supreme Court has articulated a vision of spousal support, in the absence of an agreement. Support must be assessed in the light of all of the circumstances of the case, and may be intended to compensate for gains or losses arising out of the marriage, or on the basis of need alone. However, despite a number of opportunities, a majority of the Supreme Court of Canada declined to indicate whether its 1987 Trilogy is still binding in situations where there is a separation agreement.[57]

Some judgments and commentators have continued to advocate an approach that emphasizes the sanctity of a separation agreement as a binding contract, at least absent the 'radical change in circumstances causally connected to the marriage' required by the 1987 Trilogy.[58]

There has, however, recently been a line of lower court decisions that have recognized that a separation agreement is not an ordinary commercial contract, and that there is a legitimate role for judicial override of agreements. The Ontario Court of Appeal in its 2001 decision in *Miglin v Miglin*[59] adopted this broader judicial approach, ruling that a former wife could claim spousal support, despite her earlier waiver of support rights in a separation agreement.

In *Miglin* the spouses were married in 1979 and had four children. The wife was the primary caregiver of the children, although she spent some time working in the family business. Acting with independent legal advice, the parties signed parenting and separation agreements in 1994, pursuant to which the children were to reside primarily with the mother and she was to receive child support; she was also to receive payments for herself for five years from the family business, but waived any further right to seek spousal support. The parties were divorced in 1997, and in 1998 the woman brought an application under the Divorce Act seeking sole custody of the children, spousal support and child support.

The Ontario Court of Appeal in *Miglin* affirmed the decision of the trial judge to award the woman spousal support for an indefinite period despite the earlier waiver. The court held that the 1987 Supreme Court decisions no longer applied, since they were decided under the Divorce Act 1968, and this case was decided under the Divorce Act 1985. While it is true that there is a different Divorce Act in effect, the most significant changes from the 1968 Act to the 1985 Act related to the grounds for divorce. Arguably the Court of Appeal was using the fact that there was a different Act in force to justify using the more equitable approach to spousal support in general by the Supreme Court in 1992 in *Moge*, rather than follow the much narrower approach that the Supreme Court articulated in 1987 in the Trilogy to deal explicitly with the effect of separation agreements on spousal support.

Writing for the Court of Appeal in *Miglin*, Madame Justice Abella stated:[60]

---

[57]   See eg *B (G) v G (L)* (1995), 15 RFL (4th) 201 (SCC) and *Willick v Willick* (1994), 6 RFL (4th) 161; and M Shaffer and Daniel Melamed, 'Separation Agreements Post-*Moge*, *Willick* and *LG v GB*: A New Trilogy?' (1999), 16 Can J Fam L 51.

[58]   See eg Stephen Grant, 'Family Law: Where Have We Been and Where Do We Go From Here? Spousal Support – Will There Ever Be an End to It?' (Apr 1998) 13 Money & Fam L 25–28; and *Santuosso v Santuosso* (1997), 27 RFL (4th) 234 (Ont Div Ct).

[59]   *Miglin v Miglin* [2001] OJ No 1510; see also *Scheel v Henckelman*, [2001] OJ No 55 (CA).

[60]   *Miglin v Miglin*, [2001] OJ No 1510, at paras 77 and 79.

'The philosoph[y] of support in *Moge* reinforces an interpretation of the 1985 Divorce Act which is inconsistent with the Trilogy principles or, at the very least, undermine the conceptual support pillars underlying the Trilogy, leaving standing only the finality objective which, it seems to me, must therefore be reassessed in light of the new support pillars created by the 1985 Act ... Under the new Divorce Act ... self-sufficiency, the primary support objective prevailing at the time of the Trilogy, is only one of four objectives of spousal support. The others, the recognition of economic advantage or disadvantage resulting from the marriage, the apportionment of financial consequences resulting from the care of children, and the amelioration of economic hardship are given equal weight with the promotion of self-sufficiency.'

The Court of Appeal held that judges have discretion to override final divorce settlements if circumstances change 'materially'[61] after divorce, reasoning that 'the terms of a valid agreement, while clearly not determinative, ought to be given significant weight'.[62] A material change in circumstances was found in this case by reason of the fact that the woman continued to bear the major responsibility for the care of the children. The implication of this ruling for domestic contracts is very significant: separation agreements will always be subject to judicial scrutiny.

Some practitioners have expressed concerns about the approach of *Miglin*. Stephen Grant, a lawyer for a husband involved in one of these cases, commented that these decisions are opening 'a Pandora's box, [it is] an invitation for judges to undo private contracts'.[63] An editorial in the conservative newspaper, *The National Post*, under the banner headline 'A Deal is a Deal', offered incensed commentary, complete with an unflattering cartoon portrait of Justice Abella, on purported inconsistencies between a decision in which she upheld the finality of an agreement made settling a civil litigation suit and her ruling in *Miglin* that separation agreements are never final.[64]

Some are concerned that the decision will lead to an increase in expensive, stressful family law litigation and will increase conflict between estranged spouses, which will be detrimental for children. Philip Epstein, lawyer for Ms Miglin, commented on the decision:[65]

'It means a lot of litigation in the family law arena, and it ultimately means that the most common way of settling a family law dispute doesn't mean that it's settled ... this is a clear message to mostly husbands and their lawyers that too good of a deal will come back to haunt them ... for some women who signed agreements at a time when courts emphasized their self-reliance, the doors are potentially re-opened.'

Others have criticized the protective reasoning employed in *Miglin*. In acknowledging the dependent status of women in these 'traditional' type of marriages, the decision may serve to encourage women to enter into relationships of dependency and so perpetuate their marginalization. Karen Selick, an Ontario

---

[61]   At para 96.

[62]   At para 96.

[63]   Quoted in S Delacourt, 'The Death of Divorce', *Elm Street* (October 2000) at 81.

[64]   'A Deal is a Deal', *National Post* (11 June 2001).

[65]   C Schmitz 'Divorce Settlements Never Final: Court', *National Post* (11 June 2001).

family lawyer with a libertarian perspective, wrote that she is 'revolted by [this type of] case ... women are seen as perpetual incompetents and victims'.[66]

While courts should not be quick to vary domestic contracts, they are a unique type of contract. There are probably no contracts that can have as profound an effect on the psychological and economic integrity of the parties as a domestic contract. Even with independent legal advice, in the emotionally difficult period following separation, it may be very difficult for an individual to appreciate fully what his or her future circumstances will be like.[67] The difficulty in assessing future prospects realistically may be especially strong for an emotionally vulnerable woman who has sacrificed a great deal for a relationship in the expectation that it will be permanent, only to be told that the relationship is 'over'. A woman in this position is likely to have deep anxiety, doubts about her self-worth and feel profoundly reluctant to litigate. She may well accept her husband's 'hard bargain' – a settlement offer that is less advantageous than a litigated resolution but not unconscionable – in the hopes that 'things will work out'. Not infrequently, a woman in this position may be able to secure her economic future, either by employment or remarriage, but in other cases it may be unfair to hold her to this bargain.

It is argued by some lawyers that if courts override agreements, separated spouses will be reluctant to enter into agreements and will be more likely to litigate. However, by overriding agreements that, with hindsight, may seem unfair or unfortunate, the courts are not discouraging spouses from entering into agreements. Rather the courts are encouraging spouses to be fair in negotiations. Spouses are encouraged to recognize that they are not simply entering a commercial contract, but rather making an agreement to live separately, even though their lives may never be truly disentangled.

Further, the fact that child support and custody arrangements are never final and always subject to judicial variation does not prevent most parties from making agreements about theses matters. And in most cases, these agreements are honoured, or at least not subject to applications for judicial variation.

For the moment, the equitable reasoning of the Ontario Court of Appeal in *Miglin* seems to be prevailing over the traditional contractual approach of the 1987 Supreme Court Trilogy. Doubtless, however, the issue of the finality of contractual provisions in separation agreements will be revisited by the Supreme Court of Canada.

IV CHILD-RELATED DISPUTES: CUSTODY, GRANDPARENT ACCESS AND CHILD SUPPORT

Canada is going through a contentious process of reforming the child-related provisions of the federal Divorce Act. In 1997, after almost a decade of study and debate, Canada introduced the Child Support Guidelines. In 1998 a Parliamentary Committee issued a controversial report proposing major changes to the

---

[66] Quoted in S Delacourt, 'The Death of Divorce', *Elm Street* (October 2000) at 88.

[67] I Ellman, 'Contract Thinking Was *Marvin*'s Fatal Flaw' (2001): see *http://papers.ssrn.com/sol3/papers.cfm?cfid=746797&cftoken=2590556&abstract_id=265067.*

provisions of the Act that deal with custody and access, and significant changes to the Guidelines.[68] Since the release of that Parliamentary Report, the federal government has consulted with professional groups, advocacy groups for women and men, and members of the public.[69] The federal and provincial governments have a Joint Committee working on law reform in the family law area and the federal task force Minister of Justice has promised to submit a detailed plan for reform in this area in 2002.[70]

The process of law reform has brought to the fore disagreements between feminist and fathers' rights groups over such issues as shared parenting, child support, enforcement of access and domestic violence.[71]

Professionals' organizations, like the Canadian Bar Association, have also submitted briefs advocating reform, albeit from a less partisan perspective than some other groups.[72] The level of hostility between these groups is such that women's organizations are no longer prepared to attend government-sponsored law reform consultation sessions together with men's groups.[73]

Pending statutory reforms that may come out of this process, the courts have continued to struggle with the child-related issues that arise in the context of family breakdown and divorce.

Disputes about the care of children – custody and access in Canadian legal terminology – are decided on the basis of the 'best interests' test. Judges have significant discretion in how to interpret and apply this test. The scope and potentially controversial nature of judicial discretion in this area is illustrated by a highly publicized and controversial custody dispute, *Van de Perre v Edwards*, that has ended up in the Supreme Court of Canada. The case involves a child born as a result of an affair between a highly paid black American married man who was

---

[68]　Canada, 36th Parliament, 1st Session, *For the Sake of the Children: Report of the Special Joint Committee on Custody and Access,* 10 December 1998. See Parliamentary website: *http://www.parl.gc.ca/InfiCom/CommitteeDocument*. For a commentary on this report and the law reform process, see Bala, 'A Report from Canada's Gender War Zone: Reforming the Child Related Provisions of the Divorce Act' (1999), 16 Can J Fam L 163–227; and Cohen and Gershbain, 'For the Sake of the Fathers?: Custody Reform and the Perils of Maximum Contact' (2001), 19 Can Fam LQ 121.

[69]　'Putting Children's Interests First: Custody, Access and Support in Canada' *Federal-Provincial-Territorial Consultation Paper* (March 2001) *http://canada.justice.gc.ca/en/cons/ancien.html*. There are a number of useful research reports about the child related provisions of the Divorce Act which are also available on the Department of Justice website: *http://canada.justice.gc.ca/en/ps/cca/index.html*.

[70]　In Canada, family law is an area of complex overlapping federal and provincial responsibility. Significant law reform, such as the 1997 Child Support Guidelines, is most likely to be effective if there is federal–provincial co-operation and co-ordination. Under the Constitution Act 1867 the federal government is responsible for the Divorce Act, including 'corollary relief' issues like custody, access and support. The provinces have jurisdiction over property issues, and over legislation dealing with custody, access, and support if there is no divorce (either because the parties did not marry or because they are not seeking a divorce), as well as for issues related to the enforcement of orders and the administration of justice.

[71]　For a feminist analysis of reform of the child-related provisions of the Divorce Act, see Ontario Women's Network on Custody and Access, *Brief to the Federal, Provincial, Territorial Family Law Committee on Custody, Access and Child Support*, 6 June 2001: *http://www.owjn.org/custody/brief-e.htm*. For fathers' rights perspective, see eg the website of DADS Canada: *http://www.dadscanada.com*.

[72]　See eg 'Force parents to take courses: lawyers', *National Post* (9 July 2001).

[73]　C Cobb, 'Women's Groups Balk at Sitting With Father's Rights Advocates', *National Post* (7 June 2001).

playing professional basketball in Vancouver at the time, and a poorly paid but very attractive Caucasian woman (who was characterized as a 'sports groupie'). The woman told a friend that she was having a 'profit pregnancy'. After the child was born, the woman pursued the man for very substantial amounts of child support. The man, who is married and has two daughters with his black American wife, initially denied paternity, although this was established through blood tests. The father then applied for custody. After a 26-day trial, the judge awarded custody to the mother, rejecting the views of the court-appointed psychologist, who had recommended that the child should live with the father and his family and who characterized the mother as 'histrionic, narcissistic ... and self-preoccupied'.[74] In significant measure, the trial judge's decision reflected his concerns about the future of the father's marriage, because of his sexual affairs, although both the father and his wife testified about the stability of their relationship.

The British Columbia Court of Appeal reversed the trial judge, and ordered that the father and his wife should jointly have custody of the boy, who by that time was almost three years old, with the mother having access rights. By the time of the appeal, the father and his family were living in the southern United States. While the Court of Appeal focused on the psychological evidence about the parenting capacity of the three adults, concluding that the step-mother was the most stable and child-focused of them, Newbury JA also considered race as a factor in the decision to award custody of a mixed-race child to his Afro-American father and step-mother, citing:[75]

'consideration of issues of race and inter-racial problems as they relate to [the boy], who is the product of a Caucasian mother and an Afro-American father. As much as one might wish it were otherwise, the existence of inter-racial problems in Canadian (and indeed North American) society cannot be ignored.'

The Court of Appeal concluded that the boy would grow up being 'seen by the world as "being black" and that it would "obviously" be in his best interests to live with a 'person of that colour ... who can appreciate and understand the day-to-day realities that black people face in North America'.[76] The Appeal Court dismissed the trial judge's concern that as a child of mixed race the boy should also be exposed to his Caucasian Canadian heritage, questioning 'whether there is a "Caucasian Canadian culture"'.[77] This decision has caused a furore in Canada, where the comments about race and culture outraged race relations organizations and cultural nationalists, and the comments about the superiority of a two-parent family over the home of a single mother of limited means angered anti-poverty groups.[78] The Supreme Court of Canada decision, when rendered, will likely deal

---

[74] 2000 BCCA 167, 184 DLR (4th) 486, (2000) 4 RFL (5th) 436, [2000] BCJ No 491.

[75] 4 RFL (5th) 436, at 449 (para 9) (BCCA).

[76] 4 RFL (5th) 436, at 467 (para 50) (BCCA).

[77] 4 RFL (5th) 436, at 462 (para 38) (BCCA).

[78] 'Appeal Court Ruling on Race in Custody Battle Causes Furor', *The Lawyer's Weekly* (24 March 2000). See also 'Ex-NBA Player's Custody Case Reaches High Court', *National Post* (30 June 2001); and 'His Rock of a Wife Swayed Judges', *National Post* (10 March 2001).

with the race issue, as well as the bonding between mother and son, and the weight to be given to the relative financial circumstances of the parents.[79]

For more than a quarter of a century the Canadian courts have recognized the importance of 'psychological parents' and been prepared to award legal custody to a person who has had long-term care of a child custody in preference to a biological parent.[80] In recent years, grandparents have begun to pursue claims to access to their grandchildren in the courts.

Grandparents lobbied politicians successfully to ensure the 1998 Parliamentary Report on child-related provisions of the Divorce Act contained a recommendation that 'the relationships of grandparents … with children should be recognized as significant and provisions for maintaining and fostering such relationships, where they are in the best interests of … children, should be included' in the parenting plans reflected in court orders and agreements.[81]

In Quebec and Alberta, legislation specifically provides that grandparents can apply for access.[82] Even in jurisdictions without specific mention of grandparents in legislation, grandparents may have a claim for custody or access. This claim will be particularly strong in situations where grandparents have had responsibility for the care of a child for a significant period, effectively becoming the child's psychological parents. Where the grandparents' own adult child has died, or their adult child has ceased to play a meaningful role in the grandchild's life, grandparents may also be in a good position to seek access.[83]

In *Chapman v Chapman*, the Ontario Court of Appeal was asked to determine whether a grandparent's access should be imposed against the wishes of both of the children's parents. The children's paternal grandmother sought monthly access and weekly telephone access. The parents did not oppose access in principle, but argued that its frequency and timing should be their decision. The grandmother brought an application for access under Ontario's Children's Law Reform Act,[84] which provides that 'a parent of a child or any other person may apply to a court for an order respecting custody of, or access to, the child'. The grandmother was successful at trial and the parents appealed.

Madame Justice Abella, writing for a unanimous court, allowed the appeal, dismissing the grandmother's claim for access, and ruling that the nature and frequency of any access should be at the discretion of the parents. In her judgment, Abella JA stressed that determination of access is to be made in the 'best interests' of the child, and considered from the child's perspective, not the perspective of the grandparent.[85] She concluded that ordinarily:[86]

---

[79] Argument heard by Supreme Court of Canada, 14 June 2001. See *KV v TE* [2000] SCCA No 232.

[80] See eg *King v Low* [1986] 1 SCR 31, 44 RFL (2d) 113.

[81] Canada, 36th Parliament, 1st Session, *For the Sake of the Children: Report of the Special Joint Committee on Custody and Access*, 10 December 1998, Recommendation 12, p 32.

[82] Provincial Court Act, RSA 1980, c P-20 s 32.1. The Quebec Civil Code, Article 611 provides that parents should not 'without grave reason interfere with personal relations between the child and his grandparents'.

[83] Examples include *Adams v Martin* 1992 Carswell Ont 1679 (Ont Prov Ct) and *V(G) v S(L)* (1997) 35 RFL (4th) 122 (Ont Prov Ct).

[84] RSO 1990, c C12, s 21.

[85] *Chapman v Chapman* [2001] OJ 705 (CA), at para 15.

[86] *Chapman v Chapman* [2001] OJ 705 (CA), at para 21.

'parents have the right to protect the children's best interests and determine how their needs are best met ... their right to make decisions and judgments on their children's behalf should be respected, including decisions about whom they see, how often and under what circumstances they see them.'

This decision and other judgments[87] demonstrate a reluctance of judges to intrude in intact families. The courts are reluctant to give grandparents the legal right to make claims against their own adult children in situations where the child's biological natural parents continue to reside together with the child.

After almost a decade of study and controversy, in 1997, Canada adopted the Child Support Guidelines.[88] While there is significant complexity to the Guidelines, in a majority of cases parents use them to establish the amount of child support fairly simply, establishing the amount of support as a percentage of the payor's income. On the whole, the Guidelines have resulted in an easier process for establishing the amount of support, and resulted in somewhat larger amounts being paid to custodial parents. There is, however, a great deal of reported litigation concerning the interpretation of some of the provisions of the Guidelines.

A highly publicized (although not typical[89]) type of case involves high income parents. Section 4 of the Guidelines allows that where the payor's income exceeds $150,000 a year, a court has a discretion to award the amount considered 'appropriate' if the Guidelines amount is regarded as 'inappropriate' by the court. In 1999 in *Francis v Baker*, the Supreme Court of Canada confirmed that the table amount could be reduced in high income cases, but emphasized that there is be a 'strong presumption' in favour of the table amount.[90]

The courts have begun to clarify how this discretion to award less than the Guidelines amount in the case of high income payors is to be exercised, indicating that this is quite a narrow jurisdiction.[91] In *Tauber v Tauber*[92] the parties were married for only one year, during which they had one child. The wife sought $17,000 monthly child support for the then three-year-old child, which represented the amount under s 4 of the Guidelines. Justice Rosenburg, for a unanimous Ontario Court of Appeal, accepted that there is a presumption in favour of the Guidelines percentage of payor's income as the amount of child support, but also noted that child support is intended to meet the child's 'reasonable needs' and not simply to be a wealth transfer. While the payor's income is clearly relevant for establishing 'reasonable needs', these needs should

---

[87] *Chapman v Chapman* [2001] OJ 705 (CA). See also *F (N) v S (HL)* (1999), 49 RFL (4th) 250 (BCCA); and *Droit de la Famille - 291*, [1986] RJQ 1763 (CA)

[88] *http://canada.justice.gc.ca/en/ps/sup/index.html.*

[89] While this is an important legal issue, this type of wealth is not the norm for Canadian children. The child support awards in these cases, and the income levels of the children's parents, are far from ordinary. Alarming numbers of Canadian children grow up in poverty. More than half of single parents in Canada live in poverty; lone mothers constitute the largest share of the welfare rolls; 15.5% of Canada's children are considered poor under a recent UNICEF survey. See eg M Philp, 'Canada Does Poorly on Child Poverty', *The Globe and Mail*, 13 June 2000.

[90] [1999] 3 SCR 250.

[91] In one highly publicized lower court interim ruling, a multi-millionaire father was ordered to pay $59,500 per month in child support; see 'BC children awarded record $59,500 monthly support', *The Lawyer's Weekly*, 22 June 2001, p 3.

[92] (2000), 48 OR 3d 577 (CA).

not be viewed as unlimited. The Appeal Court ruled that the Guidelines percentage of income was 'out of proportion' with the needs of the child and remitted the case for a new hearing.

An issue that is frequently litigated in applying the Guidelines is determining the income of the payor, especially if the payor is self-employed, owns his own business or has non-employment income. There is a general trend of the courts to scrutinize the self-reported income of payors. For example, in appropriate cases, the courts may impute income for purposes of child support on the basis that the payor has ordered his financial affairs to have a low taxable income by deducting personal expenses. Such deductions may be legal for tax purposes, but should not be used to reduce the amounts of child support otherwise payable. [93]

An interesting issue has arisen concerning payors involved in high-tech companies who receive significant stock options, the values of which may be difficult to determine. In *Arnold v Washburn*,[94] Rutherford J of the Ontario Superior Court ruled that $3.5 million in taxable income that the payor received from the sale of stock options in 1993 and 1999 was a 'non-recurring amount' and should not be included when making a fair determination of annual income under the Guidelines.

A number of other issues related to the Guidelines remain contentious. In cases of 'shared custody', if each parent has physical custody or access of a child more than 40% of the time, there is significant judicial discretion in setting the amount of child support. The determination of whether the 40% threshold has been reached can be very difficult. Some fathers argue that there should be discretion to vary (ie reduce) the amounts of child support to take account of access costs at a much lower threshold than 40% of the time, while advocates for women argue that the 40% threshold is too low and encourages fathers to seek (but not necessarily exercise) very extensive access in order to pay lower child support.

The Federal Minister of Justice, as part of the legislation that made the Child Support Guidelines law, is obliged to report to Parliament in 2002, and is likely to recommend some changes to them. Canada will not, however, abandon guidelines in favour of a return to individualized assessment, and is unlikely to change the fundamental nature of its guideline-model, with child support based on a percentage of payor's income.

V   CHILD WELFARE LAW – PROTECTION CONCERNS LIMIT CONSTITUTIONAL RIGHTS

In 1999, the Supreme Court of Canada rendered an important judgment in *New Brunswick (Minister of Health and Community Services) v G (J)*[95] in which the court recognized that parents and children have constitutionally protected interests that are at stake in child protection proceedings. The court accepted that s 7 of the

---

[93]   C Schmitz, 'Judge Imputes Income, Quadruples Child Support Award', *The Lawyer's Weekly*, 18 August 2000; *Sarafinchin v Sarafinchin* [2000] OJ 2855, 189 DLR (4th) 741 (Sup Ct).

[94]   [2000] OJ 3653 (Sup Ct). See also '$3.5m in Stock Option Profits Don't Count For Child Support', *The Lawyer's Weekly*, 6 October 2000.

[95]   [1999] 3 SCR 46.

Charter of Rights, which provides that no person shall be deprived of 'liberty or security of the person except in accordance with the principles of fundamental justice' requires that indigent parents generally have the right to counsel paid by the State in child protection proceedings. This decision was viewed as establishing the right to procedural protections in cases where the State, through a local child welfare agency, seeks to intervene compulsorily to protect a child in situations of alleged abuse or neglect. More recently, however, two important decisions indicate that the courts will be reluctant to extend further constitutional rights to parents or children in child protection proceedings. These decisions continue to recognize a core of constitutionally protected interests. However, they also suggest judicial deference to agency claims that recognition of constitutional protections *might* harm children, although in neither case was there any proof that there would be actual harm from the extension of fairly modest procedural rights.

In *Winnipeg Child and Family Services v KLW*,[96] a one-day-old child was apprehended by child protection workers at the hospital where she was born, based on concerns about the mother's parenting ability as a result of neglect of previously born children. Since the child was in the hospital at the time of apprehension, this was not an emergency situation, and in a number of Canadian provinces the agency workers would have had to establish grounds for the issuing of a warrant for apprehension of a child from a Justice of the Peace (lower level judicial official). However, under s 21 of Manitoba's Child and Family Services Act,[97] even in situations where there is *not* 'immediate danger', agency workers are permitted to search for and apprehend a child whom they believe is 'in need of protection', without any prior judicial authorization, although they must take the case before a judge within four days of the apprehension. The mother challenged the apprehension on various grounds, and eventually secured the return of this child.

The issue before the Supreme Court of Canada was the constitutional validity of the Manitoba statute that allows for apprehension of a child without prior judicial authorization in non-emergency situations. The majority of the Supreme Court held that there is no violation of the Charter when legislation allows a child to be apprehended without prior judicial authorization if there is 'a risk of serious harm' to the child, whether or not the situation is an emergency. Madame Justice L'Heureux-Dubé, writing for a majority of the court, reasoned that the underlying philosophy of child protection legislation must be considered when assessing its constitutionality, stating that:[98]

'child protection legislation is about protecting children from harm; it is a child welfare statute and not a parent's rights statute ... parent's and children's rights and responsibilities must be balanced together with children's right to life and health ... the underlying philosophy must be kept in mind when interpreting it and determining constitutional validity.'

---

[96] [2000] 2 SCR 519,10 RFL (5th) 221 (SCC). For a more detailed discussion of this case and its context, see A Harvison Young, 'The Changing Family, Rights Discourse and the Supreme Court of Canada' (2001) 80 *Canadian Bar Review* 749; and N Bala, 'The Charter of Rights and Family Law in Canada' (2001), 18 Can Fam LQ 373.

[97] SM 1985-86, c 8, s 21(1).

[98] At para 80.

The majority of the court worried that a requirement for prior judicial authorization, even in situations of non-imminent danger, might make workers more reluctant to apprehend children and might increase the risk of harm to children. The court did, however, reiterate that the entire protection process must accord with the principles of fundamental justice, and that apprehensions are to be a 'last resort' used only in situations where there is a 'risk of serious harm'. Further, the court held that the constitution requires a 'fair and prompt' resolution of the entire proceedings, suggesting that agency delay in bringing a case to trial might give rise to a claim for relief.[99]

There was a strong dissent in *KLW* by Arbour J (with McLachlin CJC concurring). In the dissent, Arbour J emphasized that there are vital privacy rights at stake in a child protection proceeding, and that prior judicial authorization of non-emergency apprehensions does not pose a direct risk of harm to children. The trial and appellate decisions in a recent Alberta case mirrored the deep split in *KLW* in the Supreme Court of Canada. The case of *Alberta v KB*[100] considered the constitutional validity of the Protection of Children Involved in Prostitution Act (PCHIP),[101] a statute enacted in 1999 in Alberta to allow a rapid response to situations where adolescents are found engaging in juvenile prostitution. Juvenile prostitution is a serious social problem in Canada, especially in urban centres, where adolescent 'street kids' often resort to prostitution as a means of support.[102]

Alberta was the first province in Canada to enact legislation specifically to deal with juvenile prostitution, with PCHIP allowing for the apprehension without a warrant by police or a child protection worker of a youth (under 18) believed to be engaging in juvenile prostitution, with a judicial review within three days. Apprehended youths are detained in 'safe houses,' where they receive counselling and support.

In *Alberta v KB* two 17-year-old girls challenged the constitutionality of their apprehension and detention, pointing out that if they had been arrested as suspected young offenders (which sometimes happens to juvenile prostitutes who are charged with public solicitation or other offences), they would have had broader rights, including the right to a court hearing within 24 hours of initial apprehension.

The trial decision in *KB*, rendered before the Supreme Court decision in *KLW*, concluded that by failing to provide for a prompt post-apprehension hearing, the protective legislation violated the Charter rights of adolescents.[103] The lower court decision was reversed by the Alberta Court of Queen's Bench, with Rooke J relying heavily on the Supreme Court judgment in *KLW*, which was released before his decision. While the legislation restricts the freedom of adolescents, Rooke J concluded that it 'effectively balances the rights of children with the

---

[99]   For a further discussion of the implications of the decision, see DAR Thompson, 'Case Comment: *Winnipeg Child and Family Services v W (KL)*' (2000), 10 RFL (5th) 221 (SCC).

[100]   [2000] AJ No 1570 (QB), revg [2000] AJ 867 (Prov Ct).

[101]   SA c P – 19.3.

[102]   The judgments in this case offer a useful review of literature on juvenile prostitution in Canada.

[103]   *Alberta v KB* [2000] AJ No 876 (Prov Ct). In response to the lower court ruling, the government amended the legislation: Protection of Children Involved in Prostitution Amendment Act 2000, SA 2000, c 22, s 2. The amendments require an appearance before a judge, within one day of a youth requesting a judicial review of her detention.

responsibility of the State to protect these children' with three days' detention not considered to 'constitute a major impairment of the child's rights'.[104] The court emphasized the need to consider the child protection context of the legislation. Since the intent of the legislative scheme is the promotion of the welfare of children, the court held that denial of rights that are afforded youths charged with criminal offences is constitutionally justified.

The conflicting judicial opinions in *KLW* and *KB* reveal a judicial debate about how to balance State interests in protecting children with the protection of civil rights. At present, the dominant approach is that the State's claim to be acting in the interests of children will justify a curtailment of rights, even if it turns out later that involuntary intervention was not justified, or did not actually help the child.

There are some problematic aspects to the involuntary State intervention permitted by the juvenile prostitution legislation in Alberta. Introduction of the legislation coincided with dramatic decreases in social funding for welfare and preventative strategies; concerns have been raised that apprehension is not an appropriate substitute for more financially intensive preventative strategies.[105] In Alberta, as of August 2000, more than one-third of the teens apprehended under the PCHIP Act had been 'forced through the program more than once'.[106]

A troubling aspect of the juvenile prostitution legislation is likely to affect disproportionately aboriginal youth, many of whom are victims of violence and abuse in their homes, and may resort to prostitution as a result of poverty and a lack of support from their families and society as a whole.[107] Canada has a distressing history of intervening in the lives of children and youth in a way that is intrusive and often unsuccessful in promoting the welfare of aboriginal children or their communities.

While juvenile prostitution is a very serious problem in Canada which affects children as young as 12 years of age, there is a need for research to determine the effectiveness of this type of intrusive legislative response. Many advocates for children question the effectiveness of this type of intrusive, legislative approach to juvenile prostitution.[108] There is no doubt that many of those who favour this type of legislative response are motivated by a genuine desire to help vulnerable youth, but some of the support for this type of law comes from those who simply want to give the police another tool to 'clean the streets'. Whether or not it is the best

---

[104]   [2000] AJ No 1570 (QB), at para 109.

[105]   The leader of the opposition social democratic party in Alberta commented: 'While I support the thrust of the Bill, more needs to be done to address underlying causes that often lead children to fall under the control of pimps. Children growing up in poor families are the most at risk of ending up on the street. I urge the government to focus more on prevention by adjusting social assistance rates and by supporting the development of safe secure housing for poor families' (Alberta New Democratic Party Leader Raj Pannu, quoted in 'Bill 1 Recognizes that Child Prostitutes Need Protection; More Needs to Be Done to Address Underlying Causes Like Poverty', Alberta New Democratic Party Opposition Press Release (1 February 1999)).

[106]   Editorial, 'You Must Be Helped', *The Globe and Mail*, 21 December 2000.

[107]   A study 'Save the Children Canada' reports that poverty and racism have driven native youngsters into prostitution in cities across the country: Cherry Kingsley and Melanie Mark, *Sacred Lives: Canadian Aboriginal Children and Youth Speak Out About Sexual Exploitation* (Toronto, Save the Children, Canada: November 2000); see *http://www.savethechildren.ca.*

[108]   See eg *Canadian Press*, 11 July 2001: 'Law criminalizes kids: Critics', and 15 May 2001, 'Social workers sceptical about funding to fight child prostitution in Ontario'.

approach to dealing with juvenile prostitution, the Alberta juvenile prostitution legislation is being replicated elsewhere in Canada, with Ontario already proposing similar legislation, and other provinces expressing an interest in this type of approach.[109]

VI   CONCLUSION

The general trend of Canadian family law jurisprudence in 2000–2001 has been to promote more equitable or protective treatment of those who are vulnerable. There was more equitable treatment for those who have contributed to, or relied upon, non-marital conjugal relationships, and greater protection for those women who made separation agreements that were unfavourable. There was also a greater emphasis on the protection of children in situations of abuse or neglect, including those subject to sexual exploitation through juvenile prostitution. Many of the most significant legal changes were judicially led, with politicians reluctant to deal with controversial issues. Public opinion polls suggest that while Canadians may disagree with individual judicial decisions, they have a higher degree of confidence in the judiciary than in politicians.[110]

Canadian politicians are starting to respond to some of the pressures for change, with a few provinces enacting legislation to allow for registered domestic partnerships and allow for apprehension of juvenile prostitutes. It is likely that in the near future there will be further efforts at legislative reform, in particular in the contentious area of child-related issues in the context of parental separation and divorce.

---

[109]   Ontario, Bill 86, 37th Legislature, 2nd Session, First Reading, 21 June 2001. The Ontario law, however, requires an initial review hearing 'within 24 hours or as soon afterwards as practical'. British Columbia, Manitoba and Saskatchewan are considering similar statutes: see 'Detaining Child Hookers OK, Judge Says', *The Globe and Mail*, 22 December 2000.

110   See 'Canadians feel Supreme Court tainted by partisan politics', *The Globe and Mail*, 3 July 2001, p A1, reporting on public opinion survey results. While 69% of Canadians believe that partisan politics may influence the Supreme Court, 91% of Canadians have 'a great deal or a fair amount of respect' for the judiciary (compared to 85% in the United States).

ENGLAND AND WALES

EXPLORING THE BOUNDARIES OF FAMILY LAW IN ENGLAND IN 2000

Michael Freeman[*]

For an account of English family law in 2000 to be conventional it would have to focus on decisions which, with a few exceptions, did not attract, and do not warrant, great attention. With the implementation of the Family Law Act 1996 now permanently shelved,[1] there was not much discussion of divorce[2] nor much on its economic or psychological consequences.[3] The most interesting divorce cases reported concerned conflict of laws issues.[4] The only significant case dealing with property and financial matters is *White v White*.[5] There was only one important case on residence orders (*Re H (Residence Order: Child's Application for Leave)*),[6] and the centre of gravity in contact applications has now shifted almost entirely to the interface between contact and domestic violence (as broadly interpreted to include also sexual abuse).[7] The law on parental responsibility, tested so often in recent years,[8] seems to have settled, at least temporarily.[9] Whether it will survive the Human Rights Act 1998 (implemented in October 2000) is dubious.[10] In the meanwhile, its limits were examined in the context of medical decision-making,[11] most famously in 2000's highest profile case, that of the conjoined twins (*Re A (Conjoined Twins: Medical Treatment)*).[12]

An examination of the *Family Law Reports* reveals that family law in England today is about human rights, reproductive rights, religious minority practices, medical decision-making within the family, mental health questions, the family

---

[*] Professor of English Law, University College London.

[1] *The Guardian*, 2 September 2000.

[2] Human rights arguments were raised for the first time in a divorce case in *Dennis v Dennis* [2000] 2 FLR 231 ('A right to divorce could not be derived from Art 12' *per* Wall J at p 246).

[3] On financial provision see *Purba v Purba* [2000] 1 FLR 444 (an interesting application by a 12-year-old boy).

[4] *El Fadl v El Fadl* [2000] 1 FLR 175; *Kellman v Kellman* [2000] 1 FLR 785; *B v B (Divorce: Northern Cyprus)* [2000] 2 FLR 707.

[5] [2000] 2 FLR 981.

[6] [2000] 1 FLR 780.

[7] *Re L (Contact: Domestic Violence, Re V (Contact: Domestic Violence), Re M (Contact: Domestic Violence), Re H (Contact: Domestic Violence)* [2000] 2 FLR 334. See also *Re S (Violent Parent: Indirect Contact)* [2000] 1 FLR 481 and *Re Z and A (Contact: Supervision Order)* [2000] 2 FLR 406.

[8] A novel point was raised in 2001 in *Re D (Parental Responsibility: IVF Baby)* (2001) EWCA Civ 230 [2001] 1 FLR 972 in relation to IVF treatment.

[9] And see S Sheldon (2001) 9 *Feminist Studies* 93.

[10] But it withstood initial attacks: see *Re H; Re G (Adoption: Consultation of Unmarried Fathers)* [2001] 1 FLR 646.

[11] *Re J (Specific Issue Orders: Child's Religious Upbringing and Circumcision)* [2000] 1 FLR 571.

[12] [2001] 1 FLR 1.

rights of the gay, abuse and (I am tempted to say interminably) international child abduction. If I discussed abduction, there would be room for nothing else. It is therefore, with the exception of one case, omitted from this survey which, after a brief discussion of *White v White* and its implications, concentrates on some of the controversies of 2000 in family law's newer terrain. I doubt if any of the issues in this survey (*White v White* apart) was discussed by family lawyers (or in some cases at all) when I first encountered family law 35 years ago.

I   THE *WHITE* REVOLUTION

How significant *White v White*[13] will prove only time will tell. The House of Lords decided that, instead of emphasising 'reasonable requirements'[14] in the discretionary exercise of the court's powers when making financial provision awards on divorce, the court should use equality as a 'yardstick',[15] as 'a form of check',[16] 'guideline'[17] or 'starting point'.[18] The court should only depart from this if there are good reasons to do so. That the Lords were only prepared to tread cautiously into what for them was bold new terrain is evident from their reluctance to elevate this new emphasis on equality into a presumption of equal division.[19] They said that this would go 'beyond the permissible bounds of interpretation of s 25',[20] and drew a distinction with comparable Scottish legislation[21] which specifically provides for equal sharing. Not a lot is said about what equality involves but 'there is no place for discrimination between husband and wife and their respective roles',[22] and 'there should be no bias in favour of the money-earner and against the home-maker and the childcarer'.[23]

White v White was a 'big money'[24] case (although this litigation had dissipated more than one-ninth of the total assets).[25] The House of Lords upheld the Court of Appeal's award of £1.5 million to Mrs White. The trial judge, looking to her 'reasonable requirements', had concluded £800,000 was the appropriate sum. Mr White was thus left with approximately £2.5 million or about 62 per cent of the total assets.[26] This was a clean break case and the children were adults. Despite the rhetoric about equality, Mr White emerges almost twice as well off as

---

[13]   [2000] 2 FLR 981.

[14]   As courts have done since *O'D v O'D* [1976] Fam 83.

[15]   [2000] 2 FLR 981 at p 989 *per* Lord Nicholls of Birkenhead.

[16]   *Ibid*, at p 990 *per* Lord Nicholls of Birkenhead.

[17]   *Ibid*, at p 999 *per* Lord Cooke of Thorndon.

[18]   *Ibid*. For Thorpe LJ in *Dharamshi v Dharamshi* [2001] 1 FLR 736, the yardstick is a 'principle'.

[19]   *Ibid*, at p 989 *per* Lord Nicholls of Birkenhead.

[20]   *Ibid*, at p 990 *per* Lord Nicholls of Birkenhead.

[21]   Family Law (Scotland) Act 1985, s 10.

[22]   [2000] 2 FLR 981 at p 989 *per* Lord Nicholls of Birkenhead.

[23]   *Ibid*.

[24]   In *Cowan v Cowan* [2001] EWCA Civ 679, [2001] 2 FLR 192 it was stressed that *White v White* was directed at the 'big money case'.

[25]   Lord Nicholls of Birkenhead thought this 'appalling' ([2000] 2 FLR 981 at p 996).

[26]   In the later case of *Cowan v Cowan* [2001] EWCA Civ 679, [2001] FLR 192, these were the exact percentages.

Mrs White, a result not all that dissimilar from what the discredited 'one-third' rule achieved.

White v White has in general been welcomed. But it raises more questions than it answers. Eekelaar is surely right to observe that the 'proclamation of equality as a guide takes us little further'.[27] Certainly the Lords offer little by way of a normative framework. *White v White* is judicial legislation but it lacks many of the hallmarks of legislation. Does it apply to income as well or only to property? If it does apply to income, it will make clean breaks particularly difficult. If it only applies to property, does it apply to all property (for example to pension funds or intellectual property) and does it apply only to existing property and not future property? It presumably applies only to marriage (Bailey-Harris recommends its extension to cohabitants.[28]) Will it then deter some (presumably rich men) from getting married? Or will they turn to the pre-nuptial agreement? If they do, how will the courts react to this? In one pre-*White* decision, *Dart v Dart*,[29] the court ordered the husband, worth £400 million, to provide the wife with £9 million. She would, of course, get considerably more now, although *White* gives us little guidance as to how much more or by what process of reasoning the court would depart form the yardstick of equality, as it surely would. But suppose the Darts had agreed – either before marriage or before divorce – that she would on divorce receive £9 million, would a post-*White* court hold her to her pre-nuptial agreement or *Edgar*[30] agreement or *Xydhias*[31] agreement? Or would it allow her to resile from it? And will the courts allow women the opportunity to reopen consent orders which held them to sums of money far short of a *White* award – is *White v White*, in other words, a *Barder* event[32] – and if so, how many such orders are open to such an attack? Equality is to be the yardstick and the assumption is that it will often be departed from. Judges, still predominantly male, will find it difficult to extirpate the gender bias for which Peter Singer[33] (as he then was) castigates them, and will find reasons for awarding sums lower than 50 per cent. This is certainly the evidence emerging from the early *post-White v White* case-law.[34] But if equality is a yardstick only, is there any reason why awards of more than 50 per cent should not also be made? Certainly, Australian courts have found a way towards doing this.[35]

A fundamental question is whether the equality principle is limited to 'big money' cases. Lord Nicholls in *White v White* says it is 'of universal application'.[36] Connell J in *D v D (Lump Sum: Adjournment of Application)*[37]

---

27 'Back to Basics and Forward to the Unknown' [2001] Fam Law 30 at p 32.
28 'Dividing the Assets on Family Breakdown: The Content of Fairness' (2001) 54 *Current Legal Problems* 533 at pp 550–551.
29 [1996] 2 FLR 286.
30 [1980] 3 All ER 887. In relation to which, see *G v G (Financial Provision: Separation Agreement)* [2000] 2 FLR 18.
31 *Xydhias v Xydhias* [1999] 1 FLR 683.
32 See *Barder v Caluori* [1988] 1 AC 20, and E Hamilton [2001] Fam Law 135.
33 See [2001] Fam Law 115 (a paper presented in 1992).
34 The only case thus far in which a wife has been awarded 50% is under inheritance provisions, and not matrimonial legislation (*Adams v Adams* [2001] WLTR 493).
35 See, for example, *In the Marriage of Waters and Jurek* (1995) 20 Fam L R 190.
36 *White v White* [2000] 2 FLR 981 at p 989.

found it unnecessary to decide this (but he anyway characterised the case as a 'big money' one). There is no reason why the ex-wives of rich men should profit from this new principle and other women lose out. Indeed, there would be considerable irony if this were the conclusion reached by the courts: the rich are not the most prominent believers in equality! Of course, in many divorce cases there is nothing to divide: *White v White* can be of no assistance to the poor. But for many there will be property to divide, even if the sum involved would be 'loose change' to the Darts or the Conrans. And these sums might be greater if the division can be deferred. We may therefore anticipate more postponements of final orders[38] and perhaps also a revival of *Mesher*[39] orders to facilitate fairer division of assets of middle income groups.

White v White raises many more questions. For example, how significant will Lord Nicholls' reference to 'available'[40] assets be? Does this mean the yardstick of equality will only begin to bite where assets are realisable? How will the courts confront the problem of illiquidity?[41] And what of deliberately planned illiquidity?[42] What impact will *White v White* have on pension-sharing?[43] If it ushers in, what one judge has called, 'a changing climate',[44] it may lead to more pension-sharing. Perhaps, most importantly, can we anticipate the situations in which courts are likely to deviate from the yardstick of equality? Will the length of the marriage make any difference? In principle, the fact that the marriage is short should make no difference. However, I suspect it will.[45] The derivation of the assets, perhaps also the time when they were acquired, is likely to have an impact. The courts may well feel their way to something approaching a continental acquests doctrine.[46] There may too be a resurgence of conduct allegations: conduct may be taken into account where it would be inequitable to disregard it.[47] It would be unfortunate if the threshold of conduct were lowered as ex-husbands try to frustrate entitlement.

If equality were to become the norm – I take this to be a most unlikely scenario – the judges may have constructed a sort of community of property

---

[37]   [2001] 1 FLR 633.

[38]   See *Davies v Davies* [1986] 1 FLR 497. *Cf Burgess v Burgess* [1996] 2 FLR 34. See also *MT v MT (Financial Provision: Lump Sum)* [1992] 1 FLR 362.

[39]   Particularly in small money cases where the ex-wife's priority is accommodation for herself and the children. The *Mesher v Mesher* ruling is at [1980] 1 All ER 126.

[40]   *White v White* [2000] 2 FLR 981 at p 989.

[41]   A problem especially with family companies. P Duckworth and D Hodson in a very valuable article ([2001] Fam Law 24) draw attention to *Fisher v Fisher* 1997 ND 176 (a decision of the North Dakota Court of Appeals which confronted this issue).

[42]   *Cf Martin v Martin* [1976] Fam 335. And see especially *Beach v Beach* [1995] 2 FLR 160 and *H v H (Financial Relief: Conduct)* [1998] 1 FLR 971.

[43]   In *S v S (Financial Provision: Departing from Equality)* [2001] 2 FLR 247, Mr S sought to exclude his pension from the matrimonial assets, but was not allowed to do so. In the light of the ideology of the Welfare Reform and Pensions Act 1999, this must be right.

[44]   See *A v A (Maintenance Pending Suit: Provision for Legal Fees)* [2001] 1 FLR 377 at p 387.

[45]   E Cooke [2001] CFLQ 81 at pp 87–88 does see its relevance.

[46]   See H Lücke in R Bailey-Harris (ed), *Dividing the Assets on Family Breakdown* (Family Law, 1998).

[47]   Matrimonial Causes Act 1973, s 25(2). But see *S v S* (above) (conduct peremptorily disregarded).

regime by the back door.[48] Whether community of property is desirable or not, its introduction is not suitable terrain for judicial creativity. It would require a properly considered statutory framework and what the Lords offered us in *White v White* is far from this. And, if ultimately *White v White* was confined to 'big money' cases (whatever this means), it would be rather odd if the only persons to whom community of property applied were the divorced rich.

White v White will undoubtedly have an impact on litigation strategy.[49] It will make England a more attractive forum for some litigants, and a less attractive one for others. Within the context of Europe – particularly with Brussels II[50] having come into operation some seven months before the Lords ruled in *White v White*[51] – everything will depend upon which spouse initiates litigation first, and where. The wealthy German marrying the Englishwoman may ensure that any future matrimonial litigation takes place in Germany by inserting a jurisdiction agreement into a pre-nuptial agreement.[52] Short of this, if his wife initiates divorce in England (assuming he is domiciled[53] in England or Art 5(2) of Brussels I[54] can be satisfied)[55] there is no longer any scope for staying her action on *forum non conveniens* grounds.[56] Another question with an international dimension that the courts (including the European Court of Justice) will have to decide is whether a *White v White* award is 'maintenance'. If it is for support then it will be, with the consequence that an action to recover it in another Brussels I/Lugano[57] Contracting State will fall within these Conventions.[58] If, on the other hand, it is to count as equitable redistribution of property, an award will come outside the scope of Brussels I altogether,[59] and enforcement questions will fall to the common law. There is no indication in *White v White* as to how a *White* award should be characterised. I believe the better view is that Mrs White got what she was entitled to, not what she needed, so that such an award does fall outside Brussels I. These could become major problems, and too little attention has thus far been given to them.

---

[48] And see *Report to the Lord Chancellor of the Advisory Group on Ancillary Relief* (Lord Chancellor's Department, 1998). This opposed a presumption of equal shares of matrimonial property on divorce.

[49] See David Truex [2001] IFL 7.

[50] Brussels Convention on Jurisdiction and the Recognition and Enforcement of Judgments in Matrimonial Matters and in Matters of Parental Responsibility for children of both spouses 1998.

[51] See David Truex [2001] IFL 7.

[52] This will need to satisfy Art 17 of Brussels II and will not govern rights in property arising out of a matrimonial relationship. On pre-nuptial agreements following *White,* see S Bruce [2001] Fam Law 304.

[53] 'Domiciled' in its Brussels meaning, not according to common law concepts.

[54] Brussels Convention on Jurisdiction and Enforcement of Judgments in Civil and Commercial Matters 1968.

[55] This has been interpreted expansively in *Farrell v Long* [1997] QB 842.

[56] I cannot imagine *Re Harrods (Buenos Aires) Ltd* [1992] Ch 72 being dragged into matrimonial litigation.

[57] Lugano Convention on Jurisdiction and the Enforcement of Judgments in Civil and Commercial Matters 1988.

[58] *De Cavel v De Cavel* [1979] ECR 1055.

[59] *Van Den Boogaard v Laumen* [1997] QB 759.

II SOLOMON'S JUDGMENT

When the Bible wished to teach us the meaning of wisdom it chose a dispute over a child.[60] The true mother was identified by King Solomon because she did not wish her child to be cut in half – a solution which the other woman was prepared to countenance.

England's 'conjoined twins' case (*Re A (Conjoined Twins: Medical Treatment)*)[61] comes close to an actualisation of the Solomon story. The Court of Appeal declared that doctors could separate conjoined twins, even though the weaker one would inevitably die as a result. The parents, who are Catholics from Gozo, an island off Malta, did not wish the separation to take place. In their eyes the twins were equal, and God's will should be allowed to prevail. The Court of Appeal recognised the importance of the parents' views. They were, said the court, devoted and responsible parents with 'sincerely held religious views' which were 'not obviously contrary to any view generally accepted by our society'. Further, it was not suggested that it was 'selfish or unreasonable that they should have concerns about their ability, either financially or personally, to care for [the surviving twin] at home'.[62] This was a case of sincerely held religious views, not one where opposition was 'promoted by scruple or dogma'.[63]

As is well known, a court's decision in any case such as this is governed by the paramountcy principle.[64] Whilst it is generally accepted that surgery was in the best interests of Jodie, the stronger twin, it was known that Mary, the weaker twin, could not survive the operation to separate her from her sister. The Court of Appeal concluded (by a majority) that the operation could not be justified as in the best interests of Mary, since it was not in her best interests to die. It was, however, in the best interests of Jodie. How was the court to resolve this conflict? The House of Lords in *Birmingham City Council v H*,[65] confronted with a conflict of interests between a mother, who was a child, and her baby, neatly avoided a solution. The majority in *Re A* accordingly fell back on the Court of Appeal's resolution of the dilemma in the *Birmingham* case:[66] as Evans LJ put it in that case, the paramountcy requirement 'must be regarded as qualified, in the cases where the welfare of more than one child is involved, by the need to have regard to potential detriment for one in the light of potential benefit for the other'.[67] So, for Ward LJ in *Re A* it was necessary to choose the 'lesser of the two evils'[68] and find 'the least detrimental alternative'[69] (a conscious or an unconscious adoption of Goldstein, Freud and Solnit's hallowed phrase).[70] It was not then difficult to

---

[60]   1 Kings.

[61]   [2001] 1 FLR 1. A special issue of the *Medical Law Review* ((2001) 9 *Medical Law Review* 201–298) focuses on the case.

[62]   *Re A (Conjoined Twins: Medical Treatment)* [2001] 1 FLR 1 at p 104 *per* Robert Walker LJ.

[63]   *Ibid*, at p 52.

[64]   Children Act 1989, s 1(1).

[65]   [1994] 2 AC 212.

[66]   *Birmingham City Council v H (No 2)* [1993] 1 FLR 883.

[67]   *Ibid*, at p 899.

[68]   *Re A (Conjoined Twins: Medical Treatment)* [2001] 1 FLR 1 at p 49.

[69]   *Ibid*.

[70]   *The Best Interests of the Child* (Free Press, New York, 1996), at p 50.

conclude – I pass over the lawfulness of the operation[71] – that since the weaker twin had only a few months to live, and the stronger one had the prospect of a relatively normal life if the operation took place, that the operation should be performed.

However, Robert Walker LJ (agreeing with Johnson J at first instance) was of the opinion that the proposed operation was in the best interests of both twins. As far as Mary was concerned, to prolong her life for a few months 'would confer no benefit on her but would be to her disadvantage'.[72] He argues that if she had been born separated from Jodie but with the defective brain and heart and lungs which she had and if her life were being supported not by her sister but by mechanical means 'it would be right to withdraw that artificial life-support system and allow [her] to die'.[73]

I find Robert Walker LJ's analysis – thus far – the more realistic and the more convincing. Ward LJ conceded that if Mary had been a singleton she would not have been viable and resuscitation would have been abandoned. He also admitted that it was hard to see any benefit flowing from her continued life and that she existed 'pathetically on borrowed time'.[74] Mary was unquestionably 'alive', and I believe had the right to life although she could not exercise it. She also had the right to die with dignity, a right which sometimes, as I think here, trumps the more obvious and fundamental right to life.[75] She was not 'living' and could never do so. Had she been a singleton, it would not have been worthwhile to treat her. This is not because she was a parasite[76] (Ward LJ's use of this term is to be deprecated). Nor is it because she was 'not innocent' (I think comparing her, as Ward LJ did, to a 6-year-old with a gun is morally blind).[77] It is because treatment would have achieved nothing for her beyond prolonging her 'aliveness' for a short period of time. Her body could not sustain life. She was, as Ward LJ acknowledged, 'lost to her parents anyway'.[78] But to say she was 'designated'[79] for death merely obfuscates. It is meaningless – all medical intervention is directed to persons who will die – and/or a nod in the direction of religion (Calvinism perhaps, which seems an odd ideology to inflict on parents whose own Catholicism was not allowed to dictate the decision).

---

[71] The Coroner stated that the 'purpose and the reason for the separation was not to kill Mary even though her death arose from it' (*The Guardian*, 15 December 2000).

[72] *Re A (Conjoined Twins: Medical Treatment)* [2001] 1 FLR 1 at p 105.

[73] *Ibid.*

[74] *Ibid*, at p 38.

[75] And see Raphael Cohen-Almagor, *The Right To Die with Dignity: An Argument In Ethics, Medicine, and Law* (Piscataway, NJ, Rutgers University Press, 2001).

[76] *Re A (Conjoined Twins: Medical Treatment)* [2001] 1 FLR 1 at p 54.

[77] *Ibid*, at p 61.

[78] *Ibid*, at p 53.

[79] *Ibid*, at p 54. John Harris (2001) 9 *Medical Law Review* 221, at pp 230–232 is especially scathing on this.

III THE RELIGION OF MINORITIES

Re A was not the only case in 2000 where religion was of central importance. Perhaps the other most interesting case concerned male circumcision.[80] A lot of attention has focused on this recently. The *British Journal of Urology* devoted a special issue to the subject[81] and Sweden is about to become the first country since Nazi Germany to regulate it (its legislation came into operation in October 2001). In England, in *Re J* the courts were given their first opportunity to pronounce on the legality of a male circumcision. A Turkish Muslim father sought specific issue orders in relation to his 5-year-old son, one requiring the nominally Christian mother to raise the child as a Muslim, and another requiring her to have the boy circumcised. The mother and the guardian ad litem opposed both applications. The father was not a devout Muslim.

The court refused to make either order. As far as upbringing was concerned, it was not practical to make an order that a child whose home is with a mother who is a non-practising Christian should be brought up as a Muslim. The judge saw this as an application of the principle in the Act that the court should not make an order unless making the order was better for the child than not making an order.[82] He held that male circumcision was lawful – the first authority to this effect in England – but that to circumcise a son was not a decision that could be taken by a parent alone, despite the fact that the Children Act 1989 provides that each person with parental responsibility (and both parents in this case had it) 'may act alone and without the other (or others) in meeting that responsibility'.[83] This judicial gloss on a clear legislative provision was justified by the judge because circumcision is 'an irrevocable step'.[84] The only other issue relating to parental responsibility upon which the parents were at odds concerned the eating of pork, a matter on which the judge thought there was room for compromise and agreement. But, in any case, it was not in J's welfare interests, ruled the judge, to make a specific issue order in relation to it. Of course, if the circumstances had been such that such an order was appropriate, the court would have had to decide whether the eating of pork was in this child's best interests. Whether this is a justiciable issue may be doubted.

The Court of Appeal, in upholding this decision, paid especial attention to the meaning of religion in the context of child care.[85] The correct focus, said Thorpe LJ, was religious upbringing rather than religion, because no matter what religion the child belonged to by birth, the child's own perception of his religion would derive from inculcation in worship and teaching within the family. A newborn 'does not share the perception of his parents or of the religious community to which the parents belong'.[86] This ruling is of greater significance to the Muslim community, where the age for circumcision is commonly between

---

80   *Re J (Specific Issue Orders: Muslim Upbringing and Circumcision)* [1999] 2 FLR 678.
81   (1999) 83 *British Journal of Urology International Supplement* 1.
82   Children Act 1989, s 1(5).
83   *Ibid*, s 2(7).
84   *Re J (Specific Issue Orders: Muslim Upbringing and Circumcision)* [1999] 2 FLR 678 at p 702.
85   *Re J (Specific Issue Orders: Child's Religious Upbringing and Circumcision)* [2000] 1 FLR 571.
86   *Ibid*, at p 575.

5 and 7 years old, than the Jewish community, where it is invariably performed on the eighth day of a boy's life. And this is conceded by Thorpe LJ who felt 'conflict' that where it is the practice to carry out circumcision within days of birth 'there is much less likelihood of forensic dispute'.[87]

The Court of Appeal agreed with the first instance judge that, despite the clear language of the Children Act 1989, there was a small group of important decisions (Dame Elizabeth Butler-Sloss P mentioned sterilisation and name change as well as circumcision)[88] which ought not to be carried out or arranged by one parent carer with parental responsibility.

In *Chief Adjudication Officer v Bath*[89] the Court of Appeal smiled benignly on an irregular marriage entered into by two young Sikhs in a Sikh temple in England in 1956. The Sikh population of Britain in the mid-1950s would have been very small, and it is hardly surprising that Sikh temples (or the one in question) were not registered buildings for the purpose of marriage. It is no less surprising that a 16-year-old Sikh girl marrying a 19-year-old Sikh man should have been unaware that their ceremony was failing to comply with English law. He died in 1994 and she was denied a widow's pension on the grounds that she was not a widow because there was no evidence of a valid marriage ceremony in accordance with the Marriage Act 1949. Since there is no principle more firmly established in private international law than *locus regit actum*, this conclusion seems right, if unjust.[90] The Baths had failed to comply with the *lex loci celebrationis* and other considerations, their domiciliary law for example, were irrelevant.

The Commissioner, to whom the appeal initially went, held that the marriage was validated by the common law presumption from long cohabitation pursuant to the law's policy that marriages entered into in good faith should be upheld wherever possible.[91] The Chief Adjudication Officer appealed this, submitting that the presumption of marriage arising from cohabitation was rebutted by the appeal tribunal's finding that the temple in which the marriage was held was not registered to hold such ceremonies in 1956. Rarely, thought Evans LJ in the Court of Appeal, could there have been such an 'unattractive case' to argue.

> 'For 39 years two departments of government, the Inland Revenue and the Department of Social Security, treated Mr Bath as a married man and claimed taxes and contributions accordingly. When Mrs Bath after his death claimed the pension to which his widow is entitled, for the first time, the agency said that he was never married and that their children are illegitimate.'[92]

The Court of Appeal accordingly held the ceremony to constitute a valid marriage. It would only be void if the parties had knowingly and wilfully failed to comply with the Marriage Act 1949, and this clearly was not the case. This decision is

---

[87]   *Ibid*, at p 576.

[88]   *Ibid*, at p 577. Gillian Douglas, *An Introduction to Family Law* (Oxford University Press, 2001) at p 82 has questioned whether the court gave sufficient weight to the cultural significance attached by Muslims (and Jews) to male circumcision.

[89]   [2000] 1 FLR 8.

[90]   It goes back to the eighteenth century.

[91]   See *Commissioner's Decision R(G) 2/70*.

[92]   *Chief Adjudication Officer v Bath* [2000] 1 FLR 8 at p 11.

doubtless just, but I am doubtful whether it is correct. That a couple think they are going through a marriage ceremony does not endow the process with such a legal consequence. The question is not whether the marriage is valid or void: rather whether it is a marriage at all. True, if there had been no ceremony at all, the law may well have presumed marriage from lengthy cohabitation. And it would seem odd to make such a presumption where there was no ceremony and not do so where there was one of sorts (and this one certainly had all the trappings of a wedding). The Court of Appeal may have created a troublesome precedent.

This tolerance of religious minority practices is reflected in a number of other cases. *Re S* concerned an abduction of children from Israel.[93] The father and mother were orthodox Jews. They married in Israel and two of their children were born and raised there. When the mother was 8 months pregnant with her third child, she left Israel and came to England with the two older children. The mother resisted the father's demand to return the children. She pleaded consent to removal and acquiescence – and neither of these arguments was really tenable. In addition, she raised the defence under Art 13B of the Hague Convention that return would place the children in an intolerable situation, creating a risk of psychological harm. She argued that because the father came from a Polish family with a 'status almost equivalent to royalty',[94] she would not get justice from the religious court in Israel (the *Beth Din*). She also argued that in any proceedings in Israel she would not get a fair hearing, but also because she could not obtain a divorce in Israel (a *get*) without the positive assistance and consent of the father.[95]

The children were returned to Israel. Connell J was not convinced that there was a grave risk of psychological harm to them if they were returned. He emphasised the family background in Israel and concluded that it was appropriate and in the children's best interests to have the matter decided by the Israeli courts. The mother was an orthodox Jew, raising the children as orthodox Jews. Accordingly, it was by her own choice that she was to be judged by the religious courts in Israel, rather than by the civil courts. Nor could she claim that the application of the religious rules by the religious courts breached her human rights – although I do not see why not – or her children's human rights – an argument that I view as even more unsustainable. The court seemed impressed that Israel was a Hague Convention signatory – it could not be treated as a separate case because of the dual system of justice in Israel – and by the fact that the father had agreed to certain undertakings including one to assist the mother to obtain a *get* if she sought one. It never ceases to amaze me how willing courts are to accept undertakings. Surely Connell J must realise that men like the father in this case have no respect whatsoever for secular courts. The undertaking was not worth the paper on which it was written.

In *El Fadl v El Fadl*[96] it was an Islamic divorce, a *talaq*, that was in issue. This had been pronounced by a Lebanese national and domiciliary eight months after the husband entered into a valid polygamous marriage with the wife. The *talaq* had been registered with a Sharia court in Lebanon. Now, 18 years later, the

---

[93]   *Re S (Abduction: Intolerable Situation: Beth Din)* [2000] 1 FLR 454.
[94]   *Ibid*, at p 459.
[95]   *Ibid*, at p 459.
[96]   [2000] 1 FLR 175.

wife, by now domiciled in England, was seeking to divorce the husband. She could, of course, only do so if there was a subsisting marriage to dissolve. English law has long recognised the *talaq*.[97] The latest legislation (the Family Law Act 1986) distinguishes those by means of proceedings from 'bare' *talaqs*.[98] The jurisdictional grounds for recognition are wider in the former and the grounds for refusal to recognise in the latter one narrower. Hughes J considered the *talaq* in this case to be by means of proceedings. Readers of the case might consider this to be little more than a veneer, but I will let that pass. Of greater concern is whether an English court should have exercised its discretion to refuse recognition. Not only was the wife given no advance notice of the *talaq* but no notice after the event either. Hughes J's reasons for not refusing recognition on this ground were:

(i) notice 'could avail the wife nothing';[99]

(ii) 'this was the prescribed form of divorce in the country in which both parties were domiciled'[100] and married;

(iii) the divorce was 'accomplished' in the 'natural forum' for both parties;[101]

(iv) '[the wife] has known of the divorce for many years'.[102]

The judge peremptorily disposed of another ground (failure to give the wife an opportunity to participate) by saying that if this were a non-proceedings *talaq* (which he has held that it was not) questions of participation would not arise. This 'confirms' his decision that 'recognition should not be refused on the basis of an English-imposed requirement for notice or participation which is wholly foreign to the law of the domicile of both parties'.[103] This seems to me to be an extraordinarily generous application of comity, and makes me wonder whether we have any standard by which to judge a foreign institution. Not surprisingly, the judge also found that this divorce was not manifestly contrary to public policy. He was satisfied that 'however much a unilateral divorce without notice may offend English sensibilities comity between nations and belief systems requires ... that one country should accept the conscientiously held but very different standards of another where they are applied to those who are domiciled in it'.[104] This husband not only did not inform his wife of the divorce but carried on for a number of years as if they were still married.[105] If ever a case cried out for a refusal of recognition this was it.

---

[97] Even *talaqs* pronounced in England were recognised 30 years ago (although not now).

[98] Family Law Act 1986, s 46(1) and (2).

[99] *El Fadl v El Fadl* [2000] 1 FLR 175 at p 189.

[100] *Ibid.*

[101] *Ibid.*

[102] *Ibid.*

[103] *Ibid.*

[104] *Ibid*, at p 190.

[105] See the account at pp 180–181.

IV   HUMAN RIGHTS

The Human Rights Act 1998, embodying the European Convention on the Protection of Human Rights and Fundamental Freedoms 1950 into English law, came into operation in October 2000. For United Kingdom lawyers it was unquestionably the event of the year. Not surprisingly, it was used to challenge a variety of decisions in family law matters. The 2001 law reports are replete with human rights cases – doubtless, next year's *Survey* article will address these.

Human rights issues had a strong profile in 2000. Two decisions of the European Court of Human Rights on matters of English law are especially significant.

In *B v UK*,[106] an unmarried father, whose children were taken to Italy by the mother after he applied for a parental responsibility order and a contact order, and who failed to recover them using the Hague Convention on the Civil Aspects of International Child Abduction 1980, because he lacked custody rights, also failed to sustain a complaint under the European Convention on Human Rights. His complaint was ruled inadmissible because there was an objective and reasonable justification for the difference in treatment between married and unmarried fathers with regard to the automatic acquisition of parental rights. This related to the range of possible relationships between unmarried fathers and their children.[107]

In *Scott v UK*[108] an alcoholic mother challenged an order freeing her child (who had foetal alcohol syndrome) for adoption. Her consent had been dispensed with: there was no assurance that she would ever be alcohol-free and it was unacceptable to expose the child to further uncertainty and the risk of suffering serious harm. The court had held that no reasonable parent in the circumstances would withhold consent. The mother claimed a violation of Arts 8 and 13 of the European Convention on Human Rights. The European Court held against her. The mother contended that the interference with her family life was not 'necessary in a democratic society'. The court noted that 'what is in the best interests of the child is always of crucial importance'[109] and that the authorities 'enjoy a wide margin of appreciation in asserting the necessity of taking a child into care.'[110] Having analysed the decision-making process, the court did not consider it to be unfair. The court concluded that the interference with the mother's family life was necessary in a democratic society 'being proportionate to the aim of protecting the rights of the daughter'.[111] There will clearly be difficult cases where the balance tilts the other way. I for one am certainly uncomfortable about a child's welfare being tied to a 50-year-old Convention drafted when attitudes to children were very different from what they are now.

In *Re A (Permission to Remove Child from Jurisdiction: Human Rights)*[112] the father challenged the mother's right to remove the child permanently from the

---

[106]   [2000] 1 FLR 1.

[107]   And see now *Re M (Adoption: Rights of Natural Father)* [2001] 1 FLR 745.

[108]   [2000] 1 FLR 958.

[109]   *Ibid*, at p 968.

[110]   *Ibid*, at p 969.

[111]   *Ibid*, at p 971.

[112]   [2000] 2 FLR 225.

jurisdiction. The court had given her permission to do so,[113] her job prospects being much better in New York. Clearly the father and the child had a right to a family life – it is gratifying that the Court of Appeal recognised the baby's right too – and the mother had a right to a private life. Again, resort to Art 8(2) became necessary. The Court of Appeal refused to interfere with the way in which the balancing had been done. It saw the existing English law as consistent with the Convention. This challenge was inevitable: the court's response equally inevitable – and, I am sure, right. In the early days of the Human Rights Act 1998 we can expect, indeed are finding, challenges to perceived injustices, and perhaps frustration when it is found that the code does not offer the quick solution.

I doubt if the father expected to succeed. Nor can Mr Mellor, in the most intriguing of the human rights challenges to date (*R v Secretary of State for the Home Department ex parte Mellor*[114]). He is a prisoner serving a life sentence for murder. He met and married a member of the prison staff and asked to be allowed to inseminate her artificially. The request was refused on the basis of concern about the stability of the marriage (it had not been tested under normal circumstances). He failed in his challenge. He had a right to respect for his family life under Art 8 but this did not include the right (in Hohfeld's terms more accurately a 'privilege'[115]) to create a family. There was no basic right of access to artificial insemination facilities. And even if he did, 'the present restriction on that "right" is an inevitable consequence of his imprisonment, because he has lost the right to freedom of association with his wife (including cohabitation and the artificial equivalent for making her pregnant) in consequence of that lawful imprisonment'.[116] If conjugal visits can be denied,[117] then so can access to artificial insemination. This case, of course, fell outside the Human Fertilisation and Embryology Act 1990. But this did not stop the judge taking principles from that legislation[118] – and, it may be said, expanding them. He thought it appropriate for States to apply regulating standards, 'taking into account the interests of the child and moral and ethical considerations, where medical intervention is required for the conception of a child and the assistance of the Secretary of State is sought to enable that to take place'.[119] Mellor's appeal failed. Somewhat controversially, the Court of Appeal read into Art 12 the exceptions to Art 8(1), which of course, are not in Art 12, where an absolute right is formulated.[120]

---

113 Following a line of authorities going back to *Poel v Poel* [1970] 1 WLR 1469.
114 [2000] 2 FLR 951.
115 *Fundamental Legal Conceptions As Applied in Judicial Reasoning*, ed WW Cook (Yale University Press, 1923).
116 [2000] 2 FLR 951 at pp 971–972.
117 *ELH and PBH v UK* (1997) A D & D 61.
118 In particular using s 13(5) – probably the most controversial provision in the Act.
119 [2000] 2 FLR 951 at p 975.
120 *R v Secretary of State for the Home Office Department ex parte Mellor* [2001] EWCA Civ 472, [2001] 2 FLR 1158.

V   REPRODUCTIVE RIGHTS

Mellor's case concerns the right to reproduce. A number of other cases in 2000 also raised this most fundamental of rights. There was the first involving an involuntary sterilisation of a learning disabled young man.[121] It is almost a quarter of century since sterilisation of the learning disabled was first litigated[122] and twelve years since it was (controversially) upheld in Jeanette's case (*Re B (A Minor) (Wardship: Sterilisation)*).[123] Unlike many other countries, the United Kingdom has never had sterilisation legislation.[124] This, it may be thought, makes it somewhat worse: a practice covertly went on, seemingly unchallenged, until the chance intervention of an educational psychologist in the mid-1970s.[125] Sterilisations were often carried out to facilitate mixed-living arrangements in institutions whilst protecting female residents from exposure to pregnancy. But not until 1999 was the attention of a court ever drawn to a proposed case of male sterilisation.

A was 28, had Down's Syndrome, and lived with his mother (aged 63) who was concerned that as her health declined she would become unable to supervise him and he might make a woman pregnant. The mother's application for a declaration that sterilisation was in A's best interests was refused. The reported decision upholds this refusal. The President of the Family Division distinguishes applications in respect of men and women.

> 'It is not a matter of equality of the sexes but a balancing exercise on a case-by-case basis. There are obvious biological differences and sexual intercourse for a woman carries the risk of pregnancy which patently it does not for a man. Indeed there is no direct consequence for a man of sexual intercourse other than the possibility of sexually transmitted diseases [against which a vasectomy does not protect]. There may be psychological consequences for him in pregnancy or in the birth of his child. He may be required to take responsibility for the child … and may … attract disapproval and criticism … His freedom of movement might … be restricted and consequently his quality of life might be diminished.'[126]

But sterilisation would not save A from the possibility of exploitation (although there is less chance of this in the case of a male) nor help him cope with the emotional implications of a relationship. Nor apparently was the level of supervision in the day centre he attended related to fertility. The court was clear that best interests encompassed 'medical, emotional, and all other welfare issues',[127] that it was 'the judge, not the doctor, who makes the decision that it is

---

[121]   *Re A (Male Sterilisation)* [2000] 1 FLR 549.

[122]   *Re D (A Minor) (Wardship: Sterilisation)* [1976] Fam 185.

[123]   [1988] AC 199.

[124]   But see – if you can, because the book was suppressed before publication – Stephen Trombley, *The Right To Reproduce* (London, Weidenfeld and Nicolson).

[125]   In *Re D* (above). Fortunately, the National Council for Civil Liberties (now 'Liberty') was prepared to finance the litigation.

[126]   *Re A (Male Sterilisation)* [2000] 1 FLR 549 at p 557.

[127]   *Ibid*, at p 555, following the forced Caesarean case of *Re MB (Medical Treatment)* [1997] 2 FLR 426 at p 439.

in the best interests of the patient that the operation be performed'[128] (not, it has to be said, the opinion of the House of Lords, so that the authority of this must be questioned),[129] and that it is the patient's interests and not third party interests, for example the protection of vulnerable women, which must be looked to (although the question whether third party interests should ever be considered was left open). Although this decision was always going to be open to the criticism – not well-founded in my view – that the court protected a young man when it failed to protect many young women, it is welcome in a number of respects, not least in the recognition that medical paternalism cannot be allowed to ride roughshod over the rights of the vulnerable. In the end, however, it must be asked what was being protected here. Was it really A's right to reproduce or his right to physical integrity? The proposed vasectomy in A's case would have required a general anaesthetic and was therefore somewhat more invasive than the run-of-the-mill case.

Two other sterilisation cases may be briefly noted. Both *Re ZM and OS (Sterilisation: Patient's Best Interests)*[130] and *Re S (Sterilisation: Patient's Best Interests)*[131] raised alternatives to subtotal hysterectomy. In *Re S* the Court of Appeal decided that sterilisation and hysterectomy were not in the best interests of a 29-year-old woman with severe learning difficulties. The expert evidence was unanimous that non-surgical alternatives (the less invasive Mirena coil treatment) were more appropriate. Subtotal hysterectomy was out of proportion to the problem to be solved. The President of the Family Division said:

> 'The patient has the right, if she cannot herself choose, not to have drastic surgery imposed upon her unless or until it has been demonstrated that it is in her best interests.'[132]

Wall J was in error 'in offering the alternatives of the hysterectomy or the insertion of the Mirena coil ... To offer ... the alternatives was not to decide which treatment was the better for S'.[133] In *Re ZM and OS* Bennett J decided that sterilisation of a 19-year-old with Down's Syndrome was in her best interests. It was in her interests for her heavy periods to end, and to remove the real risk of pregnancy (she had already had physical contact with her boyfriend who also had Down's Syndrome, but had not yet had sexual intercourse). The alternative of a Mirena coil, although involving less of a risk to her, would not completely prevent menstruation and thus offer an improved quality of life, which would result from the end of her periods.

---

[128] *Ibid*, at p 555. See also *Re S (Sterilisation: Patient's Best Interests)* [2000] 2 FLR 389, at pp 401 and 402.

[129] *Re F (Mental Patient: Sterilisation)* [1990] 2 AC 1.

[130] [2000] 1 FLR 523.

[131] [2000] 2 FLR 389, overruling Wall J at [2000] 1 FLR 465.

[132] *Ibid*, at p 398.

[133] *Ibid*, at p 401.

VI PARENTS, CHILDREN AND DOCTORS

In a number of cases, conflict between parents and doctors about the medical care and treatment of a child were raised. The 'conjoined twins' case, already considered, is only the most dramatic of these cases. Conflict arose in other situations too. The parents' views were overridden in *Royal Wolverhampton Hospitals NHS Trust v B.*[134] Bodey J held that where parents and experts disagreed, and in the absence of trust (the parents had lost confidence in the medical practitioners), the best interests of the child dictated that she had a firm and confident medical team doing all that could be done. The court was also prepared to override the parents in *Re MM (Medical Treatment)*[135] (it was not necessary to do so because they agreed an order). They were Russians in England for a fixed period (the father had an academic post) and they disagreed with the programme of therapy supported by the doctors. This was partly because they were unhappy with the approach of the English doctors, partly because the Russian approach seemed to have been working, partly because they felt their concerns and arguments were not being listened to by the English doctors, and partly because they were concerned about the dangers of using blood products, particularly when they returned to Russia. The court found the parents' objections to be rational, but it was still prepared to override their refusal to agree to a particular form of treatment. The parents were also overruled in *A National Health Service Trust v D.*[136] Doctors told committed parents that their child of 19 months was dying. The parents wanted him admitted to paediatric intensive care but medical opinion was unanimous that mechanical ventilation and the processes of intensive care were not in the child's best interests. The NHS Trust sought a declaration that the child be treated as advised by his paediatrician, including non-resuscitation in the event of respiratory or cardiac failure or arrest but with palliative care to ease his suffering and permit his life to end peacefully and with dignity. The parents opposed the declaration, but this was granted. The argument that the right to life Article in the European Convention on Human Rights was breached was rejected by the court. Following *D v United Kingdom*[137] it was held that Art 3 of the Convention, which requires that a person is not subjected to inhuman or degrading treatment includes 'the right to die with dignity'.

VII SOME MENTAL HEALTH QUESTIONS

Mental health questions can emerge in conventional areas of family law: the capacity to marry,[138] the meaning of 'behaviour' in the context of divorce,[139] the use of an anti-molestation injunction, etc.[140] They can also arise more marginally.

---

[134]   [2000] 1 FLR 953.
[135]   [2000] 1 FLR 224.
[136]   [2000] 2 FLR 677.
[137]   (1997) 24 EHRR 423.
[138]   *Re Park's Estate* [1954] P 89; *Bennett v Bennett* [1969] 1 All ER 539.
[139]   *Thurlow v Thurlow* [1976] Fam 32.
[140]   *Wookey v Wookey; Re S (A Minor)* [1991] 2 FLR 319.

Re F (Mental Health Act: Guardianship)[141] is one such case. The question which confronted the local authority and then the court was how to protect a 17-year-old with a mental age of between 5 and 8, the eldest of eight children chronically neglected and prone to sexual exploitation. Too old for interim care, she was accommodated under s 20 of the Children Act 1989 but, as proved the case here when the parents withdrew their consents, this offers fragile protection. Pre-Children Act 1989 there is no question but that wardship would have been used, although it would give no more than one year's breathing space. The authority instead sought and was granted a guardianship order under the Mental Health Act 1983[142] (on the basis that the young woman suffered from mental impairment).[143] She wanted to return home: severe mental impairment is, inter alia, associated with 'seriously irresponsible conduct',[144] and the desire to return home was so labelled.[145] The Court of Appeal thought this wrong. Quoting research on care orders,[146] Thorpe LJ noted 'the urge to return is almost universal'.[147] The Court of Appeal thought wardship (inherent jurisdiction under s 100(3) of the Children Act 1989) more appropriate, but, as clearly indicated, this is a temporary expedient, and the *parens patriae* jurisdiction does not extend to adults. Not surprisingly therefore, Thorpe LJ called for Family Division judges to be given wider powers to deal with the welfare of adult patients where that cannot be fully achieved under the Mental Health Act 1983.[148] It is clear that the law is inadequate to protect vulnerable young adults from abuse and neglect. *Re F* exposes a gaping hole in the law's protective net.

Not surprisingly, this case returned to the courts and is reported once again as *Re F (Adult: Court's Jurisdiction)*.[149] The girl was now 18 and the local authority sought a declaration from the court that it would be in her best interests to remain in local authority accommodation and for it to supervise contact with her mother. There is no statutory foundation for this (the mental health legislation does not cover the day-to-day affairs of mentally incapable adults). Wardship, of course, could not be used. Justification was therefore sought in the doctrine of necessity. This has previously been used to justify jurisdiction to sterilise a mentally handicapped woman in her best interests,[150] and to detain a mentally disordered patient without recourse to the powers in the Mental Health Act 1983.[151] Here it was invoked to allow a local authority to keep this young woman in local authority accommodation against the wishes of her mother (her father had died since the first case), and also to restrict her mother's access to her even though this was tantamount to the guardianship power which was removed by Parliament by

---

[141]   [2000] 1 FLR 192.

[142]   Section 7.

[143]   See s 7(2) (a) and s 1(2).

[144]   See the definition in s 1(2).

[145]   This is to adopt an over-broad definition: as to which see Brenda Hoggett (Hale LJ) in *Mental Health Law* (Sweet & Maxwell, 4th edn, 1996).

[146]   Roger Bullock *et al*, *Children Going Home* (Ashgate, 1998).

[147]   *Re F (Mental Health Act: Guardianship)* [2000] 1 FLR 192 at p 198.

[148]   *Ibid*, at p 200.

[149]   [2000] 2 FLR 512.

[150]   *Re F (Mental Patient: Sterilisation)* [1990] 2 AC 1.

[151]   *R v Bournewood Community and Mental Health NHS Trust ex parte L* [1999] AC 458.

the Mental Health (Amendment) Act 1982.[152] This may concern those with a sense of constitutional propriety who may remember that Parliament is (or was) sovereign (Sedley LJ was so concerned).[153] The Human Rights Act 1998 was not then in operation. Sedley LJ thought the decision did comply with the Convention and he may be right, but room for a challenge remains. The State can restrict the personal freedom of persons of unsound mind, provided it is in accordance with a procedure prescribed by law[154] and that this law accords respect due under Art 8 to private and family life. Sedley LJ's conclusions that 'The family life for which Art 8 requires respect is not a proprietary right vested in either parent or child: it is as much an interest of society as of individual family members, and its principal purpose, at least where there are children, must be for the safety and welfare of the child ... The purpose ... is to assure within proper limits the entitlement of individuals to the benefit of what is benign and positive in family life. It is not to allow other individuals, however closely related and well-intentioned, to create or perpetuate situations which jeopardise their welfare'[155] are some of the most important statements made by a judge on the human rights legislation. However, *Re F* remains a troubling saga. The problems it uncovers cry out for legislative intervention. At the same time it demonstrates the power of the common law. It would be interesting to know how civilian systems would respond to this dilemma.

Two cases in 2000 explored the meaning of 'nearest relative'[156] in the Mental Health Act 1983. *JT v UK*[157] will lead to a change in the law. JT challenged the designation of her mother as 'nearest relative'. She had had a difficult relationship with her and alleged abuse by her stepfather. She wanted to replace her mother with a named social worker and alleged that her inability to do so was a violation of her right to respect for private life. The case was settled upon agreement that the UK would amend the Act. As a result there is no judgment that the system does breach the Convention. It is a pity that no precedent as such is created. In *Re D (Mental Patient: Habeas Corpus)*[158] the meaning of 'cared for' was tested. A patient was detained after the younger of his two children was consulted. The legal requirement is to consult with the person 'appearing to be the nearest relative'.[159] Under s 26 of the Mental Health Act 1983 this was the elder of his two children. However, the younger had undertaken several caring duties. The Court of Appeal had to decide what 'care for' meant. These, it said, were 'clear and everyday words set in a context where the approved social worker has to act in a pragmatic and common sense manner'.[160] They were to be given their 'common and everyday meaning'.[161] The younger child could thus qualify as a

---

[152]   Now in the Mental Health Act 1983.
[153]   [2000] 2 FLR 512 at pp 530–531.
[154]   European Convention on Human Rights, Art 5(c), and see *Winterwerp v The Netherlands* (1979) 2 EHHR 387.
[155]   [2000] 2 FLR 512 at pp 531–532.
[156]   Mental Health Act 1983, s 26.
[157]   [2000] 1 FLR 909.
[158]   [2000] 2 FLR 848.
[159]   Mental Health Act 1983, s 11(4).
[160]   *Re D (Mental Patient: Habeas Corpus)* [2000] 2 FLR 848 at p 852.
[161]   *Ibid.*

carer provided her services were 'more than minimal'.[162] They did not have to be long term. It also had to decide whether the social worker could consult the younger child if the elder child were the legally correct 'nearest relative'. It held that she could: the duty was to consult the person who 'appeared' to be that relative (there was no suggestion that the social worker had acted dishonestly).

VIII   GAY RIGHTS

English law, in contrast to Continental European developments,[163] has done little to promote gay rights. 2002 will see the first promotion of a Civil Partnerships Bill,[164] but this cannot be expected to do more than air a proposal to recognise gay unions. The gay themselves have not pressed for gay marriages to be recognised, partly because many (lesbians in particular) do not want to buy into what they see as a discredited institution, but also because they see the attack on discriminatory legislation as more urgent.[165] Gillian Douglas discussed *Fitzpatrick v Sterling Housing Association Ltd*[166] in the 2001 *Survey*.[167] She noted that the House of Lords went beyond European jurisprudence in recognising that homosexuals had the right to 'family' life. In 2000 their right to respect for 'private' life was recognised again by the European Court of Human Rights.[168] The court impugned the Sexual Offences Act 1956, s 13 insofar as this criminalised homosexual acts between more than two men in private. It held that in the absence of any public health considerations and given the purely private nature of the behaviour, the reasons submitted for the maintenance of the legislation were not sufficient to justify it (or, of course, the prosecution). Without root-and-branch reform to remove discriminatory laws, there are going to be further challenges to English laws regulating the sexual behaviour of homosexual men.

This applies also to transsexuals. At the end of 2000 Johnson J decided that he could not grant a declaration that a 'marriage' between a man and a woman (who had been born male and had undergone gender reassignment surgery) was valid.[169] The Court of Appeal – although it thought the law profoundly unsatisfactory – agreed.[170] Discussion of this case properly belongs to the next *Survey*. But in the light of the general tenor of this year's article, Thorpe LJ's remarks in his

---

162   *Ibid*, at p 853.

163   In France ,the law of 15 November 1999 (PACS) (C civ, art 515-1–515-8); in the Netherlands, the law of 5 July 1997 (C civ, art 1: 180a–180e); in Belgium, the law of 23 November 1998 (see *Moniteur Belge*, 1 December 1999).

164   Lord Lester is introducing the Bill into the House of Lords in January 2002.

165   I discussed these in J Basedow, KJ Hopt, H Kötz and P Dopffel (eds), *Die Rechtsstellung gleichgeschlechtlicher Lebensgemeinschaften* (Mohr Siebeck, 2000), at pp 173, 174–178.

166   [2000] 1 FLR 271.

167   'Balancing Rights' in *The International Survey of Family Law (2001 Edition)*, ed A Bainham (Family Law, 2001).

168   *ADT v United Kingdom (Case 35765/97)* [2000] 2 FLR 697.

169   *B v B (Validity of Marriage: Transsexual)* [2001] 1 FLR 389. And see A Barlow (2001) 13 CFLQ 225.

170   *Bellinger v Bellinger* [2001] EWCA Civ 1140, [2001] 2 FLR 1048. By the time of the next *Survey*, an appeal to the House of Lords is likely to have been heard (see *The Independent*, 22 January 2002).

dissenting judgment ought to be recorded, for they capture what all family lawyers should undoubtedly feel:

> 'The family justice system ... must always be sufficiently flexible to accommodate social change. It must also be humane and swift to recognise the right to human dignity and to freedom of choice in the individual's private life.'[171]

This reflects the experience of recent years – but it also offers a philosophy for the future. One that we must grasp if, as a profession, we are not to sink into insignificance.

---

[171]   *Ibid*, at p 1092.

ETHIOPIA

REFLECTIONS ON THE REVISED FAMILY CODE OF 2000[*]

Tilahun Teshome[**]

I   INTRODUCTION

The 1960 Civil Code of Ethiopia, which encompasses all the major areas of the civil law, is the first comprehensive legal instrument in the history of the hitherto traditional society of Ethiopia. Of the different options that were suggested for legal reform at the time, it was the codification approach that was preferred by the man who was entrusted with this daunting task, Professor René David of the University of Paris, one of the most distinguished civil lawyers of the twentieth century. Reflecting on the very difficult choice he had to make, he once had this to say:

> 'Ethiopia cannot wait 500 years to construct in an empirical fashion a system of law which is unique in itself, as was done in two historical eras by the Romans and the English. The development and modernization of Ethiopia necessitate the adoption of a ready-made system ... in such a manner as to ensure as quickly as possible a minimal security in legal relations ...'[1]

The Code, many aspects of which are held to be fairly modern, is still in force save for some areas of the law of property dealing with immovables.[2] In as much as the main features of the law are concerned, it may well be argued that even the new family law in Ethiopia is as old as the Civil Code itself. Despite the fact that

---

[*]   Unless the context demands otherwise, expressions set out in this article in the masculine gender also apply to the feminine gender.

[**]   Associate Professor of Law, Addis Ababa University; former judge of the Supreme Court of Ethiopia. I am grateful to Professor Dr Ulrich Spellenberg, Chair for Civil Law, Private International Law and Comparative Law at the University of Bayreuth (Germany), for his valuable suggestions and constructive comments on this article. My thanks also to Ms Kirstin Freitag who took the trouble of typing and formatting the manuscript.

[1]   René David, 'A Civil Code for Ethiopia: Consideration on the Codification of Civil Law in African Countries', *Tulane Law Review*, 37, 1960. See also George Krzeczunowicz, 'The Ethiopian Civil Code: Its Usefulness, Relations to Custom and Applicability', *Journal of African Law*, 7, 1963. In his preface to the Civil Code, Emperor Haile Selassie I also reiterated this view by saying '... it is important that a law which embraces a varied and diverse subject, as in the case with the Civil Code, form a consistent and justified whole ...'.

[2]   Following the Revolution in 1974, all rural and urban lands as well as urban extra houses were nationalized. See *Proclamation No. 31/1975 and No. 47/1975, Negarit Gazetta 34th Year.* (Incidentally the *Negarit Gazetta* is the official law gazette in Ethiopia.) For accounts on these developments, see also Harrison C Dunnings, 'Rural Land Reform in Socialist Ethiopia', *Verfassung und Recht in Übersee*, 10, 1977; and Heinrich H Scholler, 'Ethiopia: Revolution, Law and Politics', *Verfassung und Recht in Übersee*, 11, 1978.

some provisions of the Code were coined to bring the family under the patria potesta of the man, provisions which are now regarded by the progressive sector of the society as being anachronistic, it would rather be a disservice to the genius of Professor David to fail to give credit to the liberal content of many ideas that found their ways into the Code. Most of the provisions on the conditions of marriage, incorporation of rules on the matrimonial property regime, recognition of marriage as a monogamous and lasting social institution, the abolition of traditional sources of inequality such as the privileges of primogeniture, legitimacy and masculinity, may only be paralleled by the standards of the most developed legal systems.

As for the timely amendment of those rules that deserved the effort, the first move was made in the mid-1980s by the military government.[3] For reasons that were not made public, however, work on the revision of basic laws of the country, including, of course, the law of family and succession, was discontinued.

But development since the change of government in 1991 revitalized the move towards family law reform. The struggle for equal rights of women brought demands for reconsideration of marital relationships to the forefront, ideas that had long been germinating in Ethiopian society during the preceding two decades. The political forces that took control of state power following the fall of the military regime also came up with a Charter that was designed to serve as the supreme law of the land during the subsequent years, officially designated as the Transitional Period of Governance. In this Charter, it was stated that the rights of the individual as expounded in the 1948 Universal Declaration of Human Rights were respected.[4] A few years later, the Government took further steps in this direction by ratifying the rest of the International Bill of Human Rights, the United Nations Convention on the Rights of the Child and the United Nations Convention on the Elimination of all Forms of Discrimination Against Women. Then followed the 1995 Constitution of the Federal Democratic Republic of Ethiopia (hereafter the Constitution) which gave serious consideration to equality of women with men, to the institution of marriage and to the right of the child, so much so that it devoted several of its Articles to the subject.[5]

Blessed with this constitutional and political background, the continued efforts of a number of pressure groups and civil society organizations[6] culminated

---

[3] Law revision committees were set up by the Ministry of Justice, one of which was the committee responsible for revision of family law. After a few years' work it came up with a draft for consideration by the relevant organs.

[4] Article 2, *Transitional Period Charter of Ethiopia, Negarit Gazetta 50th Year No 1*, 1991.

[5] Among other things, Art 35, for example, provides that women shall have equal rights with men in the enjoyment of the rights contained in the Constitution and further entitles them to affirmative measures. Article 34 affirms the equal rights of women in marriage while entering into it, during its continuance and upon its dissolution. Article 36 lays down principles contained in the United Nations Convention on the Rights of the Child. See also Fasil Nahum, *Constitution for a Nation of Nations: The Ethiopian Prospect* (The Red Sea Press Inc, 1997), pp 136–50. Also Heinrich H Scholler, *The New Ethiopian Constitution and the Ethiopian Legal Order* (unpublished) (University of Munich, 1999).

[6] In this connection, The Ethiopian Women Lawyers Association deserves more credit than any other organization. Relentless efforts have been exerted over the last decade or so through this Association for promotion of programmes on gender equality. It has also been quite active in advocacy and lobbying works. For obvious reasons, in a society like that of Ethiopia, it is not uncommon for this activism to come into confrontation with different social forces and even, at times, with government cadres.

in the enactment of the Revised Family Code (RFC) of 2000. This law, which came into force as of 4 July 2000, has, in its preamble, outlined the following principles as its policy premises:

(1)   To make rules of the Civil Code on family relations consistent with the overall economic reality and with the Constitution.
(2)   To amend existing laws in such a way that they give priority to the well-being, upbringing and protection of children.
(3)   To provide an efficient machinery for a fair and speedy resolution of marital and other familial disputes.[7]

II   SCOPE OF APPLICATION

On account of its ethnic, linguistic and religious diversities, Ethiopia is regarded as a mosaic of peoples and cultures. But much as it is treasured by many, the diversity has, more often than not, been a source of conflicts and civil strife for decades now. A socio-political structure tailored to the principles of a democratic federal arrangement is widely thought would prove to be a panacea to this age-old problem. That is why this idea has now found its place in the current Constitution and Ethiopia has become a Federal State.[8]

By operation of the residual powers provision of the Constitution, 'all powers not given expressly to the Federal Government alone, or concurrently to the Federal Government and the States are reserved to the States'.[9] On the basis of this principle, family law matters are in the domain of state powers and it is in pursuance of these powers that one of the states that make up the Ethiopian Federation enacted its regional Family Code in November 1998.[10] There are also reports that similar works are well underway in some of the other national States.

This being so, why then did the Federal Government have to proclaim on an area that is the exclusive domain of its state members? This is certainly the immediate question that springs to mind. But noting these legal limitations, the preamble to the RFC specifies that its provisions are 'to be applicable in administrations that are directly accountable to the Federal Government'. The repeals provision of the RFC also states that provisions of the Civil Code regulating matters contained in the RFC shall not be applicable in the administrations where it is to be applied.[11] The RFC goes on further and empowers the Council of Ministers of the Federal Government and the administrations in which it is to be enforced to issue directives and rules of procedure that are necessary for its implementation.[12]

---

[7]   Preamble to the Revised Family Code, Proclamation No 213/2000, *Federal Negarit Gazetta* Extraordinary Issue No 1/2000.
[8]   The Constitution provides that Ethiopia is a Federal Democratic State with nine member States and the city of Addis Ababa as an independent administrative unit with a full measure of self-government – Arts 1, 47 and 49.
[9]   The Constitution, Art 52(I).
[10] 'Family Code of the National State of Tigrai', *Negarit Gazetta of Tigrai*, November 1998, 7th Year No 33, published only in Tigrigna and in Amhariq.
[11] RFC, Art 319.
[12] RFC, Art 323.

But the new law speaks of administrations accountable to the Federal Government in the plural, while the Constitution provides for Addis Ababa, the capital, as the only territorial administration directly responsible to the centre.[13] The city of Dire Dawa in the eastern part of the country has for several years now been subjected to the jurisdiction of the Federal Government. But the legal basis for this state of affairs is obscure, to say the least.

Be that as it may, however, it is these two metropolitan areas that are now the beneficiaries of the new legal regime. In all but one of the national States, the provisions of the Civil Code of 1960 are still active. But it is expected that the RFC will serve as a model for their forthcoming family codes.

III   BASIC FEATURES OF THE LAW

With 13 chapters and 323 Articles, the RFC contains detailed substantive and procedural rules. Provisions in the first eight chapters are primarily devoted to the regulation of the various facets of marital relations and, though to a lesser degree, matters pertaining to problems of cohabitation without marriage to which both the RFC and the Civil Code refer as an 'irregular union'. The remaining chapters deal with a host of other issues such as filiation, adoption, the obligation to supply maintenance, rights of minors and the guardianship authority.

The following may be taken as some of the major departures of the new law in the light of the 1960 Civil Code.

(1)   Although not in express terms, the RFC recognizes relationships by consanguinity, by affinity and by adoption as sources of familial ties with a number of legal effects. But it has deliberately omitted to incorporate the old rules of the Civil Code[14] describing these relations and the extent, as well as the modalities, of calculating degrees of relationships. The reason forwarded by the committee in charge of drafting the law is that these provisions would serve no substantive purpose apart from complicating issues of consanguinity and affinity.[15]

(2)   The institution of betrothal[16] is not to be found in the law. The reason advanced by the drafters was that in view of Ethiopia's cultural diversities,

---

[13]   The Constitution, Art 49 (3).

[14]   The Civil Code of 1960 (hereafter 'Civ C' in this article), Arts 550–554. According to these provisions, relationship by consanguinity exists between ascendants and descendants and, on the collateral line, between persons who descend from one or more common ancestors to the seventh degree. Relationship by affinity exists between a person and the ascendants and descendants of his spouse as well as with the collateral relatives of his spouse to the third degree. The law also provides for a bond of double affinity between a person and the spouse of the person to whom he is related by affinity.

[15]   *Explanatory Notes on the Draft Family Code of Ethiopia*, prepared by the Ethiopian Institute of Justice and Legal System Research, March 2000 (Amharic).

[16]   Under the Civil Code, betrothal is regarded as a contract in which representatives of the families of future spouses agree on their future marriage. It is, of course, considered superior to a simple promise of marriage and has a number of effects. See Arts 560–576, Civ C.

the wisdom of retaining betrothal in the law as a uniform practice would not serve any meaningful purpose.[17]

(3) The marriageable age is raised from 15 to 18 in accordance with the prevailing policies stated in the Constitution and to make the law compatible with the UN Convention on the Rights of the Child.[18]

(4) Provisions in the Civil Code, particularly in the areas of the personal and pecuniary effects of marriage, which clearly place women in a position of subordination in their marital relations,[19] have all been repealed and replaced by new ones.

(5) New rules on compulsory registration of marriages were included. Foreign marriages were recognized so long as they do not contravene public morality,[20] the proviso being an apparent reference to same sex marriages and similar such relationships.

(6) The powers of family arbitration councils have been reduced to a considerable degree with compulsory arbitration no longer a requirement.[21]

(7) Emphasis on fault-based divorce no longer exists and provisions on unilateral divorce as well as divorce by mutual consent are better clarified.[22]

(8) Cohabitation without marriage is accorded better legal protection.[23]

(9) Notable amendments to the rules of adoption have been made.[24]

(10) Rules on the rights of minors and on guardianship authority have changed places from the area of the Civil Code dealing with persons and status in general and have become part of the new law.[25]

IV MARRIAGE

A Introductory considerations

As one of the most important legal and social institutions, the family is accorded constitutional protection in Ethiopia. The emphasis on marriage more as an institution than as a contract, characteristic of both the RFC and the Civil Code,

---

[17] See note 15 *supra*. There were, of course, many people who argued in favour of retaining betrothal during the nationwide discussions that were made on an earlier draft by the Federal Ministry of Justice which led the committee of experts to submit draft rules to the Parliament. These rules were not, however, incorporated into the law by the latter.

[18] RFC, Art 6; Civ C, Art 581.

[19] The husband is the head of the family, Art 635(1); the wife owes obedience to the husband, Art 635(2); the husband is the manager of the family, Art 637(1); common residence shall be chosen by the husband, Art 641(1), the husband may watch over the relations of the wife and guide her in her conduct, Art 644(2); the wife is bound to attend to household duties, Art 646; common property other than the earnings and income of the spouse shall be administered by the husband, Art 656.

[20] RFC, Arts 5, 28–30 and 321.

[21] On the powers of family arbitration councils, see Civ C, Arts 666, 668, 674–682, 692–695, 724–729, 732–737 and the discussion below at IV(D).

[22] RFC, Arts 74–84; Civ C, Arts 664, 665, 669–673 and 692–695.

[23] RFC, Arts 98–107; Civ C, Arts 708–718.

[24] RFC, Arts 180–196; Civ C, Arts 796–806.

[25] Provisions on minors and the guardianship authority were not part of the law of family. See the structure of the Code.

stems from this reality. Although the element of consent in the formation of marriage is still as important as it was in 1960, Ethiopian marriage laws give more weight to its social attributes than to the patrimonial obligations of the spouses. That is mainly the reason why essential marriage obligations are governed by mandatory provisions of the law that cannot be easily derogated from at the wishes of the spouses.[26] Neither is the influence of customary law as strong as one would think it is. The Civil Code reduced the significance of custom to its bare minimum by its repeals provision. This categorically stated that all rules whether written or customary previously in force concerning matters provided for in the Code were repealed.[27] It is, of course, possible to celebrate marriage according to custom. In fact, both the RFC and the Civil Code recognize customary marriages as valid, the other two forms of marriage being civil and religious marriages.[28] But whatever the form of celebration, the law requires essential conditions relating to age, consent, relationship and bigamy to be fully observed.[29] All three forms of marriage do also have identical effects as the law does not draw any distinction between marriages on the basis of the manner in which they are celebrated.[30]

In some of the areas which might be regulated by a contract of marriage, too, spouses cannot simply make an agreement on matters of common concern by mere reference to custom. The practice in the custom which has been agreed upon needs to be clearly identified.[31] Upon dissolution as well, customary practices do not have much significance save for attempts by close acquaintances to reconcile the spouses. Again, the grounds for and effects of dissolution of marriage are the same whatever the form of celebration.[32] It has been argued that this radical departure from custom can be justified by the uncertainty of what constitutes custom in a given area and, even more so, by the variations of custom not only from one locality to another but also by the multitude of interpretations to which it is susceptible.[33]

This being what the law has to say about customary and religious marriages, Art 34(4) of the Constitution, on the other hand, provides that laws giving recognition to marriages concluded under systems of customary and religious laws may be enacted. But, since most of the religious and customary laws in the country fall short of upholding the equality principles enshrined in the other provisions of the Constitution, this particular sub-Article has turned out to be a bone of contention for many. Although the provision has not been tested by case-

---

[26] For a concise description of the nature of marriage in the Civil Code, see George Krzeczunowicz, 'The Nature of Marriage Under the Ethiopian Civil Code', *Journal of African Law,* 1.3, 1967.

[27] Civ C, Art 3347(1).

[28] Customary marriage is defined under Art 4 of the RFC as marriage that takes place 'when a man and a woman have performed such rights as deemed to constitute a valid marriage by the custom of the community in which they live or by the custom of the community to which they belong or to which one of them belongs'. See also Civ C, Arts 577 and 580. The customary form of marriage is in fact the most widely practised form mainly due to the fact that there is no system of compulsory civil registration. On religious marriages, see RFC, Arts 3, 26, 40 and 74, and Civ C, Arts 579, 605(2), 623, 625 and 662.

[29] RFC, Art 27(2); Civ C, Art 606(2).

[30] RFC, Art 40; Civ C, Art 625.

[31] RFC, Art 46(2); Civ C, Art. 631(2).

[32] RFC, Art 74; Civ C, Art 662.

[33] See the discussion in Krzeczunowicz, *supra* note 26.

law or in any other manner, it may be argued that the deficiency can be remedied through rules of positive contextual interpretation. As a constitution is supposed to be the supreme instrument for expression of the public will, it has an inner unity and, in the event of conflicts, a single provision should only be given effect to in the context of the whole. The argument laid down by the German Constitutional Court in the *Südweststaatenentscheidung* (*South West Case*) in 1951 is worth quoting here:

> 'Taken as a unit, a constitution reflects certain overreaching principles and fundamental decisions to which individual provisions are subordinate ... that a constitutional provision itself may be null and void is not conceptually impossible just because it is part of the constitution. There are constitutional principles that are so fundamental and so much an expression of the law that have precedence even over the Constitution that they also bind the framers of the Constitution, and other constitutional provisions that do not rank so high may be null and void because they contravene these principles.'[34]

B   Essential conditions

Essential conditions for validity of marriage pertain to biological (sex, age and state of health), psychological (freedom of will) and sociological (bigamy, marriage between persons related by consanguinity and, to a certain degree, by affinity as well as by adoption) factors. On attaching weight to the validity or otherwise of marriages, the Ethiopian legal regime does not draw much of a distinction between void and voidable marriages. Marriages that do not fulfil any one, or some, of the essential conditions for their validity are only deprived of effect for the future but hold good for the past. Some of the prohibitions are even superficial in the sense that their non-observance alone does not bring about nullity.[35] Compliance with what the law refers to as the 'period of widowhood' is one such example. Inspired by the rule *turbatio sanguinis on patris,* the draftsman introduced this concept according to which a woman is prohibited from remarrying within the next one hundred and eighty days following the dissolution of her marriage.[36] But if she does so, the marriage cannot be nullified solely on this ground.[37]

---

[34]   DP Kommers, *The Constitutional Jurisprudence of the Federal Republic of Germany*, 2nd edn, (Duke University Press, 1997), p 63.

[35]   See, for example, Katherine O'Donovan, 'Void and Voidable Marriages Under Ethiopian Law', *Journal of Ethiopian Law*, 8.1, 1972; William Buhagiar, 'Marriage under the Civil Code of Ethiopia', *Journal of Ethiopian Law*, 1.1, 1964.

[36]   It may sound awkward why the legislator inserted such a requirement in the midst of modern advances in medical science in which pregnancy tests are not at all issues to worry about. But, even then, to many women access to facilities providing such services is not as easy in Ethiopia as one would take it to be. The RFC, of course, provides exceptions to this rule – where a woman gives birth after the dissolution of her marriage, where she remarries the same husband she has divorced, where it is medically proved that she is not pregnant or where a court dispenses her from observing the period of widowhood for any other valid reason, she may marry without this restriction.

[37]   RFC, Art 37.

The other group of conditions for validity relate to age, mental capacity, consent and bigamy. Marriages that suffer from any one or some of these deficiencies are voidable but not void. The *ex-post facto* removal of the facts that gave rise to their invalidation or the passage of time may result in their validity.[38] A marriage contracted with a minor, for example, may no longer be annulled after the age required by the law is satisfied,[39] and the dissolution of a bigamous marriage may not be ordered after the death of the former spouse of the bigamous spouse.[40] Even in the case of duress, dissolution may not be sought where the spouses have continued to live together as husband and wife for more than six months after the cessation of violence or, in any case, two years after the marriage took place.[41]

The last category of conditions embraces obstacles that are deemed to be so grave that they can never be cured. Prohibitions of marriage on the grounds of relationships by consanguinity, by affinity and, *mutatis mutandis*, by adoption fall in this group. On the blood line, marriages between ascendants and descendants, between brothers and sisters, between an uncle and a niece as well as between an aunt and a nephew are not possible.[42] In the case of affinity, a person cannot get married to someone related to him by affinity on the direct line. Nor can he or she conclude marriage with his sisters-in-law or her brothers-in-law.[43] In all cases, dissolution may be ordered at any time upon the application of any interested person or the public prosecutor.[44]

Another notable difference between the RFC and the Civil Code is in their approach to the issue of an error in the contracting of marriage. While the Civil Code is restrictive and enumerates the grounds of error, the RFC has adopted a relatively flexible position. By making use of the phase 'without prejudice to the provisions of sub-article 2 of this Article' it is possible for the court, by operation of Art 13 of the RFC, to come up with grounds based on fundamental error other than the ones enumerated. As regards the specified grounds, on the other hand, error of identity and error 'on the bodily confirmation of the spouse who does not have the requisite organs for consummation of the marriage' give rise to nullity under both laws.[45] Concerning the state of health of the spouses, while the Civil Code mentions only leprosy as a ground, the RFC speaks of it in genetic terms by stating 'a disease that does not heal or that can be genetically transmitted to descendants'. Error concerning the religion of the spouse, considered by the Civil

---

[38] O'Donovan, *supra* at note 35.

[39] RFC, Art 31; Civ C, Art 608(2). Note also that a minor who has concluded marriage before the required age does not need to ratify it afterwards.

[40] RFC, Art 33; Civ C, Arts 612(2), 613.

[41] RFC, Art 35; Civ C, Art 617(2).

[42] In the Civil Code, the prohibition extends to the seventh degree between collateral relatives and to the third degree between those related by affinity. But these prohibitions were not always adhered to in many parts of the country because in some areas they were in clear conflict with societal values. The law only targeted part of Ethiopian society where it considered that it was a taboo to allow marriage between persons related in these degrees. This may be said to be one of the areas of the Code which, to use Emperor Haile Selassie's words in the preface of the Code 'has failed to reach the heart of those to whom it was intended to apply'.

[43] RFC, Art 9.

[44] RFC, Art 32.

[45] RFC, Art 36; Civ C, Art 591.

Code, does not have a place in the new law, while the latter has introduced error concerning 'the behaviour of the spouse who has the habit of performing sexual acts with a person of the same sex'[46] as a new ground.

C   Effects of marriage

Gender equality is the ideological foundation on which the provisions of the RFC stand. Rules of the Civil Code which are close to the old Roman maxims of *manus* and *patria potestas*, in which marriage is presumed to subsume the identity of the wife in the person of the husband, are giving way to new values in the relationship between the sexes. But simply because the RFC says so does not mean that it is the final word. In view of the realities on the ground, Ethiopian society has a long and arduous way to go to make its dream of gender equality come true. It is in fact the provisions of the Civil Code in this area that were persistently criticised by many as being grossly unfair to women, thus igniting the nationwide movement for law reform.[47]

The underlying principles of the RFC regarding personal effects of marriage are therefore mutual respect and equality of the spouses. These principles are expressed in the provisions dealing with cohabitation and choice of residence, with the sharing of life in common, with support and assistance to one another and with the duty of fidelity.[48] Rules of the RFC in this connection provide for joint management of the family, and for co-operation in all matters affecting the spouses' common life, particularly in child upbringing, in the determination of their residence and administration of common property. The law also speaks of separation by agreement, but such an agreement may be revoked by either of the spouses unless this move itself is found to be arbitrary.

In much the same way as does the Civil Code, the RFC provides for the regulation of financial matters by means of the contract of marriage or through the legal regime. Spouses may conclude the contract before, upon or after marriage and agree on the financial effects of their union and even on some aspects of their personal relations.[49]

In the absence of a contract of marriage or on matters not covered by it, the legal regime does, of course, apply. As in many other legal systems, the legal regime in the RFC consists of separate property of the spouses and community of property. According to Art 57, property acquired before marriage and acquired during marriage by way of donation or succession remain personal.[50] A more

---

[46]   Incidentally, the 1957 Penal Code which is still in force provides that a person who performs an act corresponding to the sexual act is punishable. The penalty may range from simple imprisonment of 10 days to rigorous imprisonment of 10 years depending on the gravity of the case and the degree of state of helplessness of the victim, if it is forced on another person against his will. Penal Code, Arts 600–601.

[47]   See, for example, the chapter on the regulation of personal and pecuniary effects of marriage. For contents of individual provisions, see note 19 *supra*.

[48]   RFC, Arts 46–56, 66(I) and 210.

[49]   RFC, Arts 42–48 and 73. The new law employs the term 'agreement of marriage' for 'contract of marriage' to distinguish it from contracts proper, the obligations of which are solely proprietary in nature. See the comments of Committee of Experts, note 15 *supra*.

[50]   See also Civ C, Art 647.

complex institution of personal property is, however, the form envisaged under Art 58. It specifies that property acquired during marriage through exchange of other personal property, by monies owned personally, or by monies derived from alienation of personal property shall also constitute personal property on the proviso that there is earlier court approval recognising such property as personal.[51] In reality, however, most people do not seek such approval as they are unaware of the existence of such a requirement. The law does not address the fate of property acquired through chance winnings, intellectual property rights, pension benefits and entitlements to compensation for injury to health or body. All property that is not personal constitutes community property even if registered in the name of one of the spouses. Individual contributions of the spouses are not taken into account in the determination of community property.[52] Right up to the moment of division, which may not always be equal,[53] community property remains *differentia specifica* and neither of the spouses has any greater or lesser rights over it. Thus Art 62 provides that property acquired by the joint efforts of the spouses during marriage, and all income derived either by personal efforts or generated through personal or common property make up community property. So does property donated or bequeathed to both of the spouses.[54]

Concerning management and administration of community property, while each spouse has the right to receive his earnings and may deposit it in his bank account or in a joint account with the other, as a rule community property is managed and administered jointly. This rule may, however, be derogated from where it is agreed in the contract of marriage that one of the spouses is to receive the income of the other and/or administer all or part of the community property, or where one of the spouses is an agent of the other in accordance with provisions in the law of agency, or where one of the spouses is declared incapable, is deprived of his right of property management or is unable to exercise his right over it for any other valid reason.[55] In all cases, the spouse in charge of performing such acts of management[56] is duty bound to render accounts to the other upon request.[57] Where a piece of property constituting community property is to be alienated, another provision governs the transaction. All actions for disposition, mortgage, or rent of immovable property for a duration of more than three years, require the agreement of both spouses even if one of them alone administers it. The same holds true for similar actions in relation to movable property the value of which exceeds 500 Ethiopian Birr (some 55 US$). They cannot either borrow or lend money exceeding the above sum or stand surety for a debt short of common consent. Non-compliance with these rules entitles the other party to bring an

---

[51] See also Civ C, Art 648.

[52] RFC, Art 63(I); Civ C, Art 653.

[53] It is possible for one of the spouses to be entitled to a greater share upon partition when the other is condemned to pay damages on account of his responsibility for the divorce. RFC, Art 84.

[54] RFC, Art 62; Civ C, Art 652.

[55] RFC, Arts 64–66; Civ C, Art 654.

[56] Civ C, Art 2204: 'Acts done for the preservation and maintenance of property, leases for terms not exceeding three years, the collection of debts, the investment of income and the discharge of debts, … the sale of crops, goods intended to be sold or perishable commodities shall be deemed to be acts of management'.

[57] RFC, Art 61; Civ C, Art 651.

action for nullity within six-months after he became aware of this fact or, in any case, within two years after such obligation has been entered.[58] The rule does not, however, become operative with regard to business activities where one of the spouses is a trader within the meaning of the Commercial Code of 1960.[59]

With respect to debts, the RFC classifies them as debts owed by one spouse and debts incurred in the interest of the household. In the ordinary course of events, debts owed by one spouse are those that arise from dealings of the spouse with his personal property or those that existed prior to the conclusion of marriage. But it may also be contended that debts emanating from delicts and torts for which one of the spouses alone is responsible also fall into the realm of separate debts. Whatever the controversy over the source, the RFC provides that debts owed by one spouse may be recovered from the personal property of the spouse and, in the absence of such property, from the community property.[60] On the other hand, debts incurred to fulfil the livelihood of the spouses and their children, those incurred to meet an obligation of maintenance which either of them or both of them are bound to meet, or any other debt so acknowledged by a court are deemed as debts incurred in the interest of the household within the meaning of the law and thus common.[61] Creditors therefore have recourse against one or both spouses by operation of the rules of obligations of solidarity.[62]

D   Dissolution of marriage

Dissolution either by death, or on account of nullity, or by divorce results in the breaking apart of the conjugal bond and the cessation of most of the effects[63] of marriage. But for obvious reasons, the most complex one of the three is divorce. As the phenomenon of divorce assumes a valid marriage, the RFC requires divorce to be pronounced only by a court of law. The petition may be made by mutual consent or on an application by either of the parties. Of course, the Civil Code does not prohibit divorce per se but it strongly discourages moves towards divorce by laying down a number of obstacles the most notable ones being the following:[64]

(1)   Unilateral repudiation is prohibited.

---

[58]   RFC, Arts 68 and 69; Civ C, Art 658.

[59]   The 1960 Commercial Code of Ethiopia provides that a married person may carry on a trade as though he were unmarried and debts contracted by the trading spouse are debts of the marriage which may be recovered from the personal estate of each spouse and from common property: Arts 16 and 19.

[60]   RFC, Art 70(1).

[61]   RFC, Art 70(2) and (1).

[62]   Civ C, Arts 1896, 1891 and 1988. In accordance with these provisions, co-debtors are jointly and severally liable to their creditors. The latter may require all the debtors or any one of them to discharge the obligation in whole or in part and the liability of each debtor shall continue until the obligation is fully discharged.

[63]   It is worth noting that some effects of marriage subsist after dissolution. Prohibition of marriage is one such effect. A person's duty to supply maintenance to his relatives by affinity where the marriage is dissolved by death is another.

[64]   Civ C, Arts 664–682 and 690–695.

(2)   Procedures for granting divorce by mutual agreement are also quite cumbersome.

(3)   All applications for divorce must be submitted to and decided by family arbitrators.

(4)   The cause(s) of divorce are, as a rule, required to be identified.

(5)   Causes are further classified into serious and non-serious. The former are statutory while the latter are not. Adultery, desertion, absence and confinement in a mental health care institution are the only serious causes to the exclusion of all others.

(6)   Family arbitrators are duty bound to attempt to reconcile the spouses where the causes are not statutory and this usually takes years.

(7)   Divorce is mainly fault-based in the sense that the party responsible for adultery and desertion in serious causes and, in all non-serious causes, the party filing an application for divorce is subjected to unequal treatment when division of common property takes place.

(8)   Unequal treatment implies awarding a greater portion or the whole of community property to the party not at fault and there is even the possibility of arbitrators awarding up to one-third of the personal property of the responsible party to the other.

Although statistics of court cases are not properly maintained, nor are there systems of case reporting in the country, the years through which the Code has been in force have undoubtedly proved that it is women who have been victimised by operation of these irksome rules. This may be attributed to the social and economic position of women, to the inefficiency of the machinery of justice, to the bias of family arbitrators and other law enforcement organs as well as to a host of other factors.

That is the reason why the RFC in many respects adopted a different approach to the adjudication of matrimonial disputes. Although the number of people in the country who may not share this view is considerable, the relevance of the institution of family arbitration was questioned for years. Some people even went to so far as to brand it as too anachronistic to be preserved. Even during the early days of the Code, it was a source of concern to many.[65] The reasons were, and still are, manifold. As opposed to the traditional practice of voluntary submission of disputes to a panel of elders, family arbitration is compulsory.[66] Nor does it conform to the trial procedure of an ordinary court of law. Arbitrators are usually lay people but, nevertheless, they are expected to apply the complex written rules of substance and procedure.[67] Problems of enforcement of rulings and awards should also not be overlooked since family arbitration councils are informal and ad hoc institutions of adjudication. As sitting on a family arbitration council is a voluntary social responsibility, arbitrators also have the right to refuse to continue serving in this capacity at any time during the course of the proceedings.

---

[65]   See, for example, Aklilu Wold Ammanuel, 'The Fallacies of Family Arbitration in Ethiopia', *Journal of Ethiopia Law*, 8.2, 1972.

[66]   Civ C, Arts 665, 666, 723, 725–728, 731 and 738. See also provisions of the Civil Code on Arbitral Submission (Arts 3325–3345) and those of the 1965 Code of Civil Procedure (Arts 315–320 and 350–357).

[67]   Civ C, Arts 723, 725, 727, 728, 731 and 732.

Under the new law, the role of arbitrators is only that of reconciliation.[68] The notion of fault-based divorce has been reduced to a position of insignificance. In fact, spouses are not even obliged to state the reasons for their divorce. Unlike the practice under the Civil Code, only when justice requires it may a court award damages to the innocent spouse where the other spouse is found responsible for the divorce.[69] Although the distinction between divorce by mutual consent (Arts 77–80) and divorce by petition (Arts 81–84) is not clear enough, the stringent conditions of the Civil Code have been liberalized to a considerable degree. Where a petition for divorce is presented before it in whatever form, the court is required to discuss with the spouses, separately or jointly, and counsel them to renounce their intention to divorce provided, however, that spouses whose marriage has lasted for less than six months are not permitted to file such an application.[70] If this does not work out where the application is for divorce by mutual consent, the court gives the parties a cooling period of not more than three months after which it may approve the agreement. But the court is also duty bound to see to it that the divorce request presented before it is the genuine expression of the will of the spouses.[71] Where it is presented with a divorce by petition, the court may direct the spouses to make a choice of their own arbitrators who will attempt to settle the dispute amicably. If this again fails, the court gives the spouses an additional cooling period of not more than three months after which it may pronounce the divorce. Upon the request of the court, or on their own motion, the spouses may agree on the consequences of their divorce before or after its pronouncement.[72] The RFC in addition carries detailed rules of procedure on the settlement of disputes leading to divorce and other forms of matrimonial disputes.[73]

E   Cohabitation without marriage

It is not an overstatement to say that the practice of *concubinatus* is as old as Ethiopian society itself. Even in the predominantly Christian areas of highland Ethiopia, the practice was so obvious that is was not uncommon for kings and the nobility to take their concubines on long expeditions, and even to battle fronts, while leaving their wives at home. This was in sheer disregard of clearly spelt out provisions in the *Fetha Nagast* (the law of the Kings),[74] not to mention the strict precepts in the scriptures of the Monophysite Church. As the law of the modern

---

[68]   RFC, Arts 80(1) and 82(4).

[69]   RFC, Art 84.

[70]   RFC, Art 77(3).

[71]   RFC, Arts 78 and 80(1).

[72]   RFC, Arts 82 and 83.

[73]   RFC, Arts 108–122.

[74]   The *Fetha Nagast* was the official written law of the Christian population in Ethiopia for several centuries though seldom adhered to by ordinary people with the exception of some parts of the clergy. On concubinage, it is stated under Chapter 25 that 'having a concubine is forbidden in [the] saintly law ... since it is contrary to lawful marriage ... [that] it is continuous fornication ... [that] no man shall be permitted to live with a concubine in his house ... [that] if he wishes to live with her, he must marry her according to the requirement of a lawful marriage ...'. The *Fetha Nagast*, translated from *Geez* by Aba Paulos Tsadeua, Faculty of Law, Haile Selassie I University, 1968.

era, the Civil Code, on the other hand, has provisions that recognize this institution as a state of fact in which a man and a woman live together as husband and wife and accords it some degree of protection.[75] It, however, draws distinctions between cohabitation without marriage and other forms of *concubinatus*. For the relationship to be valid, partners should live together and should not be bound by marriage with another person since this would amount to adultery, an offence punishable under the law.[76] Article 709 of the Civil Code places a strong emphasis on the element of living together and says:

> 'The mere fact that a man and a woman keep up sexual relations between them, *even if repeatedly and notoriously*, is not sufficient by itself to constitute an irregular union between such a man and a woman.'[77]

This was one of the areas which were subjected to heated debates during the many public discussions conducted in different fora over an earlier draft by the Federal Ministry of Justice.[78] Some argued for it not to be given any place in the law, others for even better protection and still others to carry it over from the Civil Code, no improvements having been made. It is the position of the second group that found its way into the law.

Not only is cohabitation without marriage recognized under the RFC, but it was also made to give rise to community property between the cohabitants provided the relationship lasts for three years or more and without prejudice to whatever the couple may have agreed concerning their property.[79] Such a union does not create community property under the Civil Code. Upon termination of the relationship, it is only where equity requires (whatever this may mean to the individual judge) that the man may be ordered to pay to the woman an indemnity corresponding to not more than three months' allowance.[80]

Other effects of cohabitation without marriage in the RFC are the presumption of paternity, duty of contribution to common expenses and prohibition of marriage with each other's relatives just as though the parties were married. The relationship may be terminated at the wish of the partners at any time.

V   PARENTAGE

Maternal filiation is the basis upon which a person's paternal filiation is established. In other words, a person whose mother is unknown cannot possibly have a father in the eyes of the law.[81] While the rule *mater semper certa est* (the biological fact of childbirth) is employed to determine the former, paternal

---

[75]   Civ C, Arts 708–718.

[76]   *Penal Code of the Empire of Ethiopia*, Art 618, *Negarit Gazetta* Extraordinary Issue No 1, 1957.

[77]   Emphasis added. Note, however, that both laws refer to cohabitation without marriage as 'irregular union'.

[78]   No other draft Bill in the recent history of the country attracted more public attention and secured wider participation than this draft. See the report cited at note 15 *supra*.

[79]   RFC, Art 102.

[80]   Civ C, Arts 712 and 717(2).

[81]   RFC, Art 125.

filiation is mainly established by the application of the probability of begetting principle. The law attaches paternity to situations or facts that may be considered to be highly consistent with the true physical act of begetting – the answer to the question who of all men is most likely to have caused the pregnancy of the mother.[82] Since the premise of the law is the conventional difficulty of ascertaining paternity, modern advances in forensic genetics, in DNA and in reproductive technology seem to have little or no impact on the law-making process.[83] Artificial insemination (AI), in vitro fertilization (IVF) and issues of surrogacy,[84] which have revolutionized the age-old assumption of parentage as a factual genetic relationship, do not seem to have been heeded.

In view of this fact, the following are the only avenues that lead to the determination of paternity in the RFC.

(1)   Where there is a relation provided for by the law between the mother and a certain man.
(2)   Where a certain man acknowledges the child as his.
(3)   Where a court declares a certain man to be the father.[85]

The only relationships provided for by law in the RFC are marriage and cohabitation without marriage. If a child is born of a woman engaged in either of these two relationships, the law presumes paternity of the man living with her in line with the old rule *pater est querm nuptiae demonstrant*. The child must, however, be born 180 days after the commencement, or within 300 days following the termination, of the relationship. This is a forceful presumption which may only be rebutted by the presumed father in the most stringent of circumstances.[86] Under the RFC, an action for disavowal may succeed only when the man decisively shows that he could not have had sexual relations with the mother of the child during the supposed period of conception, or when he proves that it was absolutely impossible for him to father the child. Such petition is required to be made within 180 days following the day he knew, or he should have known, of the

---

[82]   For early discussions on the law of filiation in the Ethiopian context, see George Krzeczunowicz, 'The Ethiopian Law of Filiation', *Journal of Ethiopian Law*, 3.1, 1966; and a subsequent work by the same author, 'The Ethiopian Law of Filiation Revisited', *Journal of Ethiopian Law*, 11, 1980.

[83]   In Sweden, for example, out of some 100,000 child births every year, about 2000 paternity matters are registered for investigation by the Forensic Genetics Institute. Åke Saldeen, 'Sweden: Paternity and Custody', *The International Survey of Family Law (2000 Edition)*, ed Andrew Bainham (Family Law, 2000), p 351.

[84]   On the legal implications of recent developments in this area, see, for example: Marsha Garrison, 'Law Making for Baby Making: An Interpretive Approach to the Determination of Legal Parentage', *Harvard Law Review*, 113.4, 2000; Efie Kounougeri-Manoledaki, 'Sperm, Ovum and Fertilized Ovum Outside the Human Body: Their Legal Status and Treatment in Modern Greek Civil Law', *The International Survey of Family Law (2000 Edition)*, ed Andrew Bainham, (Family Law, 2000); Peter Lodrup, 'The 1997 Revision of the Norwegian Children Act 1981', *The International Survey of Family Law 1995*, ed Andrew Bainham (Martinus Nijhoff Publishers, 1997); Rhona Schuz, 'Israel: The Right to Parenthood: Surrogacy and Frozen Embryos', *The International Survey of Family Law 1994*, ed Andrew Bainham (Martinus Nijhoff Publishers, 1996); and Kenneth Mck Norrie, 'Reproductive Technology, Transsexualism and Homosexuality: New Problems for International Private Law', *International and Comparative Law Quarterly*, 44.4, 1994.

[85]   RFC, Art 125; Civ C, Art 740.

[86]   RFC, Arts 126–130; Civ C, Arts 741–745.

birth of the child. Furthermore neither the mother, nor the child himself, nor the man who claims to be the father may bring an action for contestation of paternity.[87]

A child's paternal filiation is determined by means of acknowledgement where he is born out of marital wedlock or *mutatis mutandis* in a relationship that does not amount to cohabitation without marriage. It may further be agreed that a child who has been disowned by his presumed father in accordance with the rules of disavowal may be acknowledged. In all other cases, his juridical bond will remain only with the mother for it is stated in the law that other forms of relationship between a man and a woman do not have any effect sustainable under the law. The acknowledgement may be made before an officer of civil status, by a written will or by any other document attested by a competent authority.[88]

The law also provides that an act of acknowledgement cannot be valid if the mother openly declares that it is not well founded or if it is not accepted by the child himself in the event it is made after the latter has attained the age of majority at eighteen.

A valid acknowledgement determines the child's status, after which the law does not discriminate on the basis of illegitimacy. Gone are the days of the old biblical verse 'the inequity of the father is visited upon the child'.[89]

Once the acknowledgment is made, there is little or no room for repudiating acknowledgment since the grounds for repudiation cannot be easily met. If a person was a minor at the time he made the acknowledgement, he may revoke it so long as he is still a minor or within a year following the cessation of his incapacity provided, however, that revocation is impossible where the guardian had consented to the act. Acknowledgment may also be revoked on the ground of violence but not on grounds of error or fraud. A man who claims that he was deceived by his unfaithful mistress does not succeed in his actions in the ordinary course of events.[90]

While the first two approaches provide for paternity by operation of the law (presumption *pater vero*) and paternity by the free will of the man, in the third case it is the judge who determines the father. The rape and abduction of the mother, seduction accompanied by abuse of authority or by a promise of marriage, written statements by the alleged father, and his participation in the care, maintenance and education of the child are all facts that can give rise to a judicial declaration of paternity. The man against whom the action is brought may disclaim responsibility by showing that the mother had relations with another man at the time of conception, or by proving that he was absent during this period, or through blood testing and other reliable medical evidence.[91]

---

[87]   RFC, Arts 167–179; Civ C, Art 782–795.

[88]   RFC, Arts 107, 131–142; Civ C, Arts 721, 746–757.

[89]   Article 836 of the Civil Code, for example, specifies that 'the legitimacy or illegitimacy of the deceased or of his heir shall not affect the ascertainment of the heirs or the value of the portion of each of them'. Likewise, Art 6 of the Constitution has this to say: 'Children born out of wedlock shall have the same rights as children born in wedlock'.

[90]   RFC, Arts 140–141.

[91]   RFC, Arts 143–144. Note, however, that Art 758 of the Civil Code considers only rape and abduction as facts that may constitute grounds for judicial declaration of paternity.

VI ADOPTION

Often as a remedy for saving a childless marriage, adoption is an institution that has been practised for centuries in many parts of Ethiopia. What modern laws have done is just to fine tune it. Both the Civil Code and the RFC provide for adoption to be established by an agreement mainly between members of the adoptive family and those of the child's family of origin. The immediate consequence of the agreement is to assimilate the child into the adoptive family for all intents and purposes. Ascendants and collateral relatives of the adopter may, however, expressly object to this move by filing their protest in a court registry, in which case the adoption produces no effect with regard to them.[92]

Any person who is not less than 25 years old may adopt a child under the age of 18. An unborn child may also be adopted on the condition that the agreement for adoption may be revoked by the mother within six months following the birth of the child. If the adoption is made by spouses, it is sufficient for one of them to meet the age requirement, but in all cases of adoption by married persons, the agreement of both spouses is required unless the child to be adopted is the offspring of the other.[93] The law provides that the adopted child, his spouse and his descendants retain their bonds with the family of origin. Yet, when a conflict arises between the two families in all matters affecting the adopted child, the family of adoption prevails.[94] As may reasonably be expected, this rule may sometimes operate to the detriment of the adopted person since, in practice, courts do not usually entertain petitions of adopted persons for intestate succession when a parent in the family of origin dies leaving other children.

It is mandatory for an agreement for adoption to be approved by a court and, in so doing, the paramount consideration is the best interest of the child[95] as is enshrined under Art 3 of the United Nations Convention on the Rights of the Child and reiterated by the provisions of Art 36(2) of the Constitution. Thus, prior to approving an agreement of adoption, the court is obliged to take into account the opinion of the child where possible, the ability of the prospective adopter, as well as the effects of the agreement on the welfare of other children of the latter. In the event of adoption by a person who is not an Ethiopian, and this obviously includes intercountry adoptions, further conditions are laid down. First, the adoption may not be approved unless it is shown that there are no opportunities for the child to be raised in his own country. The court is also required to take into consideration 'the availability of information that will enable it to know that the adopter will handle the adopted child as his own and will not abuse him'. To this effect, the court is further bound to order the relevant government organ to undertake special measures of investigation with regard to the social and economic position of the adopter.[96]

---

[92] RFC, Arts 180–183.

[93] RFC, Arts 184–187. Note also that the age of the adopter in the Civil Code is required to be 18 while no mention is made regarding the age of the person to be adopted. See Civ C, Art 797.

[94] RFC, Art 183.

[95] See also Civ C, Art 805. For a discussion of the notion of the best interest of the child in the Ethiopian context, see Tilahun Teshome, 'The Child and the Law in Ethiopia: the Case of the UN Convention on the Rights of the Child', *Journal of Ethiopian Law*, 18, 1997.

[96] RFC, Art 193.

The law also accords private and government orphanage institutions the right to hand over children under their custody to adopters in much the same way as do families of origin. In approving an adoption agreement to which any such institution is a party, the court is expected to see to it that sufficient information on the identity of the child and of the adopter is supplied to the government organ entrusted with the responsibility of following up the welfare of children.[97]

A child may not be adopted by several persons unless they are spouses, but upon the death of the adopter, or where one of the spouses who have adopted him dies, he may be adopted by another person or, in the latter case, by the new spouse of the surviving adopter.[98] The adopter cannot revoke the adoption, but a court may, upon application by the relevant organ or any interested person, do so where it is shown that the adopter does not treat the child as his own, or mistreats him under conditions similar to slavery, engages him in immoral acts or handles him in any other manner that is detrimental to his welfare and personality development.[99]

VII CONCLUSION

Although there are still areas to be further considered by the Ethiopian legislator in the light of the realities in the country and global developments, it does not amount to an overstatement if one concludes that the new law is a step on the right track. The difficulty of addressing all important problems of a law such as the RFC, with over 300 Articles on the different aspects of family law, in a brief discussion like this one, I presume, is understandable. As someone who has personally witnessed many of the discussions on the draft law, I can only make a modest attempt to highlight areas that were subjected to divergent opinions and heated debates. There are still areas such as the rights of minors, duties and responsibilities of the guardianship authority, procedures on dispute settlement, proof, and the obligation to supply maintenance which, were it not for the scope of this article, would deserve equal consideration.

---

[97]   RFC, Art 192.
[98]   RFC, Art 189.
[99]   RFC, Art 195.

GERMANY

THE REGISTERED PARTNERSHIP ACT OF 2001

Nina Dethloff [*]

By far the most important issue in German family law during the last year has been the introduction of a registered partnership for same-sex couples. In Germany homosexuals have long been discriminated against both socially and legally. Up until 1969 German law punished 'indecency' between men with a custodial sentence. It was not until 1994 that homosexuals were for the first time given fully equal treatment in the area of criminal law. Since then, the legal issues surrounding cohabitation of same-sex partners have increasingly become the centre of interest.[1] Same-sex partners were constrained to settle their personal and property-right relations by way of a contract or will. Family status was, however, denied to them. A number of rights thus remained the exclusive domain of married couples. After the Federal Constitutional Court denied same-sex partners access to marriage in 1993,[2] the legislator was increasingly called upon to provide same-sex partners with a legal framework for their relationship.[3]

I   THE NEW REGISTERED PARTNERSHIP

After heated discussions the German Parliament (*Bundestag*) recently decided to enact the new Registered Partnership Act of 2001 (LPartG), which entered into force on 1 August 2001.[4] This Act governs the establishment, the legal effects and the dissolution of registered partnerships. It is contained in Article 1 of the Act Aimed at Terminating Discrimination against Same-sex Partnerships which also

---

[*]   Prof Dr LLM, Chair in Civil Law, Private International Law, Comparative Law and Private European Law at Rheinische Friedrich-Wilhelms Universität Bonn.

[1]   In detail: Schimmel, 'Eheschließungen gleichgeschlechtlicher Paare?' (Berlin, 1996); Verschraegen, 'Gleichgeschlechtliche "Ehen"' (Vienna, 1994).

[2]   Judgment of the BVerfG of 4 October 1993, *Neue Juristische Wochenschrift* 1993, pp 3058–3059.

[3]   Cf Diederichsen, 'Homosexuelle – von Gesetzes wegen?', *Neue Juristische Wochenschrift* 2000, pp 1841–1844; Schwab, 'Eingetragene Lebenspartnerschaft: Ein Überblick', *Zeitschrift für das gesamte Familienrecht* 2001, pp 385–398; Battes, '"Ehe" für Homosexuelle?', *Renovatio* 2001; see also Strick, 'Gleichgeschlechtliche Partnerschaft: Vom Straftatbestand zum Status?', *Deutsches und Europäisches FamilienRecht* 2000, pp 82–94; from a constitutional point of view Krings, 'Die "eingetragene Lebenspartnerschaft" für gleichgeschlechtliche Paare', *Der Gesetzgeber zwischen Schutzabstandsgebot und Gleichheitssatz, Zeitschrift für Rechtspolitik* 2000, pp 409–415; Scholz/Uhle, 'Eingetragene Lebenspartnerschaft und Grundgestz', *Neue Juristische Wochenschrift* 2001, pp 393–400.

[4]   Gesetz zur Beendigung der Diskriminierung gleichgeschlechtlicher Gemeinschaften: Lebenspartnerschaften, BGBl.2001 I 266.

provides for effects of registered partnerships in other areas of the law.[5] The LPartG governs (1) the establishment, (2) the legal effects, and (3) the dissolution of registered partnerships. The legal framework for registered partnerships is in many ways comparable to matrimonial law, although in certain areas the Registered Partnership Act contains rules which deviate considerably from those governing marriage. The following overview will point out where, in light of the differences as well as the similarities between same-sex couples and spouses, the provisions of the new legal regime for registered partners adequately regulate the respective matters.

1   Establishment of the registered partnership

The initial prerequisite for the establishment of a registered partnership is that the partners are of the same sex. Thus, the reference point for the Act, in line with the principle of protection of a person's private life, is the gender rather than the sexual orientation of the partners, as is the case with marriage. Although registered partnerships will, in reality, generally be established by homosexually oriented partners – the discrimination against whom the legislator primarily sought to eliminate – a registered partnership can also be entered into by two heterosexual partners of the same sex, eg by two close friends. Unlike the French *Pacte Civil de Solidarité* (*PACS*), however, the registered partnership is not open to all unmarried persons regardless of their sex.

A registered partnership can only be established between *two*, not between *several* persons. As with marriage, registered partnerships are therefore based on the principle of monogamy. Even though it cannot be ruled out that in individual cases more than two persons may be joined in a relationship that is meant to be lasting – as is the case in other cultures where partners of different genders live in polygamy – the social reality, at least for the moment, is that a close community based on mutual responsibility such as that envisaged by the law generally exists only between two people. The Act takes cognisance of this fact by limiting the number of partners to two.

The provisions governing the declaration of intent to enter into a registered partnership are fundamentally the same as those governing marriage. The partners must, while present in person, declare to each other their mutual intent to enter a partnership for life. The declarations cannot be made subject to a time limitation or dependent upon conditions.[6] While the draft required that the declarations be made, as with a marriage, before a registrar, the Act itself merely provides for the declaration to be made before a proper authority.[7] For reasons of legal competence, it therefore falls to the individual *Länder* (Federal States) to determine who these authorities are. Due to their competence in these matters and for the sake of legal clarity, the majority of the *Länder* have given this

---

[5]   The second part of the reform, in a separate Act, is aimed at improving the legal status of same-sex couples especially in the area of social security law and tax law. The *Bundesrat* has refused to consent to this Supplementary Act (Lebenspartnerschaftsgesetzergänzungsgesetz), BT-Dr 14/4878; BR-Dr 838/00.

[6]   § 1 I, 1 and 2 LPartG.

[7]   § 1 I, 3 LPartG.

responsibility to the registrars, who generally maintain public records concerning personal status.

The establishment of a registered partnership is prohibited where one of the partners is a minor.[8] This requirement cannot – as it can in the case of marriage[9] – be waived. Furthermore, a registered partnership can be established only by someone who is not already married or living in a registered partnership with someone else.[10] This restriction is an expression of the principle of monogamy. Surprisingly, in the converse situation, the existence of a registered partnership does not constitute an impediment to marriage: the law concerning legal impediments to marriage has remained unchanged. § 1306 BGB provides only that marriage may not be entered into while another marriage exists, not if a registered partnership exists. According to the wording of this provision, the registrar cannot refuse his or her participation in the marriage ceremony if a spouse is already in a registered partnership. Nor does the existence of a registered partnership constitute a reason to dissolve a marriage. There is, furthermore, no legal bias for *ipso iure* dissolution of such a registered partnership upon the conclusion of a marriage.[11] The result is that a partner can live both in a legally valid registered partnership and in a legally valid marriage.

Both registered partnership and marriage are, however, based upon the principle of monogamy. Their legal effects are geared towards an exclusive relationship. If both a registered partnership and a marriage are allowed to exist alongside each other, the personal and property rights and obligations of the two relationships may collide. Moreover, it is not apparent what justifies this curious situation wherein one cannot establish a registered partnership while married, but can contract a lawful marriage in spite of the existence of a registered partnership. It must be asked whether the legislator's failure to include registered partnerships in the list of legal impediments to marriage in § 1306 BGB is not, in fact, an astonishing oversight. Since this omission results in a gap in the law that was presumably not envisaged, an extension by analogy of the impediment of bigamy aimed at spouses to partners seems justified. A registrar called upon to preside over such a ceremony would then be constrained to refuse his or her participation in the marriage if a spouse was already in a registered partnership. A marriage contracted while a registered partnership still exists could then be dissolved. In the interests of the need for legal certainty one hopes that the legislator will clarify this point.

Furthermore, a registered partnership cannot be established between persons the closeness of whose relationship falls within the prohibited degrees of consanguinity, ie between parents or grandparents and children, and between full and half siblings.[12] Finally, a registered partnership cannot be validly established if there is no common intent on the part of both partners to assume the obligations of mutual care and support, of a communal arrangement of life and of the taking

---

[8]   § 1 II no 1 LPartG.

[9]   § 1303 II BGB.

[10]   § 1 II no 1 LPartG.

[11]   This is considered by Schwab, 'Eingetragene Lebenspartnerschaft: Ein Überblick', *Zeitschrift für das gesamte Familienrecht* 2001, pp 385–398 at 389.

[12]   § 1 II no 2 LPartG.

on of responsibility for each other.[13] This provision, which was not included in the draft of the LPartG, as in the case of the corresponding rule in § 1314 II no 5 BGB, precludes the establishment of sham partnerships which are obviously geared to other purposes, for example to obtain a residence permit.

Remarkably, the LPartG does not contain any provisions which set out grounds for nullity. Unlike matrimonial law, LPartG does not lay down a court procedure whereby the dissolution of a registered partnership may be demanded on the basis of the existence of irregularities present at its establishment, with effect for the future. If a partnership was entered into in the absence of the relevant prerequisites or with the existence of an impediment to its establishment, the registered partnership will generally be rendered ineffective, provided that not only directory provisions were breached. The absence of any provisions governing erroneous declarations of intent to enter into a registered partnership, such as § 1314 II BGB for marriages, gives rise to the question whether there remains room for the application of the general provisions governing erroneous expression of intention. Since in that event fraud, as well as errors about any relevant aspects, would lead to retroactive nullity even though the partnership may in fact have been lived out, it seems preferable to apply the provisions on the dissolution of partnerships.

2   Legal effects of the registered partnership

(A)   PERSONAL LEGAL EFFECTS

The LPartG has designed the registered partnership as a relationship of communal rights and responsibilities. The principle of solidarity between the partners is given form in the personal area through the provision contained in § 2, which creates the obligations for registered partners of mutual care and support, the communal arrangement of life and the acceptance of responsibility for one another. Prevailing legal opinion derives from the duty to a conjugal life imposed upon spouses, a duty to a common household and to cohabitation.[14] In LPartG, the legislator included an obligation to establish *a communal arrangement of life*, which phrase was inserted at a late stage by the Committee on Legal Affairs. The legislator thus distanced himself from the formulation given concerning the duties of conjugal life and has thereby rightly refrained from a misguided importation of such legal obligations from matrimonial law.

The rules concerning names are comparable to those pertaining to spouses.[15] Registered partners may therefore, as an expression of their bond, choose a common partnership name or keep the name that they currently hold. A registered partner whose birth name does not become the joint partnership name may also add his or her name to the partnership name. The only thing that LPartG has not done is to lay down a directory provision governing the selection of a joint name, such as that provided by matrimonial law in § 1355 I, 1 BGB, a remnant of the formerly mandatory joint name now held to be unconstitutional.

---

[13]   § 1 II no 4 LPartG.

[14]   Brudermüller, in Palandt, *Bürgerliches Gesetzbuch*, 60th edn (München 2001), § 1353, para 7.

[15]   § 3 LPartG.

(B) GENERAL FINANCIAL CONSEQUENCES

In the financial area, the obligation of solidarity finds its most significant expression in the partners' obligation to provide each other with appropriate financial support.[16] This means that both partners must contribute through their work and assets. It goes without saying that registered partners, just like spouses – as is expressly provided for spouses in § 1356 BGB – may divide tasks between themselves by mutual consent. In line with this division of tasks, partners may fulfil their obligation to contribute to the upkeep either by housework or by making available the economic means gained through employment. The maintenance due comprises the partners' subsistence, ie household costs and the personal needs of each partner. The entitlement to maintenance does not, however, extend to the children of a registered partner, even if they live in the common household.

Beyond the obligation towards maintenance, the LPartG provides for certain further general financial consequences. They include primarily the so-called *Schlüsselgewalt*, ie the joint entitlement and joint obligation arising from contracts concluded by one partner; this provision applies also in matrimonial law. It entitles each partner to conduct any business aimed at ensuring the partners' adequate subsistence on behalf of both partners. Such contracts generally bind and benefit both partners.[17] The other partner can therefore be held liable for any contracts entered into by the other, for example to procure food and clothing, furniture or a vehicle intended for personal use, provided that the transaction is not disproportionate to the partners' financial circumstances and standard of living.

This means that the other party to contracts of this kind gains an additional debtor irrespective of the division of tasks within the registered partnership, the additional debtor possibly being unknown to the creditor. Such creditor protection seems reasonable only if relationships are generally characterised by a differentiated division of tasks (ie each partner tends to assume separate areas of responsibility) and only the partners' joint liability enables the partner who is not gainfully employed to carry out his or her tasks independently. As far as the writer of this article is aware, there seems to be a lack of detailed socio-economic studies dealing with the question of how same-sex partners in Germany divide their tasks. One may assume, however, that a differentiated division of tasks is much rarer in same-sex partnerships than it is in marriages. One reason for this is that there are – at least at the moment – far fewer children in same-sex partnerships than there are in marriages,[18] a fact that is also, however, a consequence of the prohibition of joint adoptions.[19] In Germany, taking care of children still frequently results in a division of labour due to prevailing working conditions as well as the lack of child-care facilities. Secondly, same-sex partnerships lack the continuing effect of a traditional role model. Thus, the strong protection afforded to creditors in LPartG seems questionable.

---

[16] § 5 LPartG.

[17] § 8 II, 2 LPartG in connection with § 1357 II, 2 BGB.

[18] Dannecker, 'Sexualwissenschaftliches Gutachten zur Homosexualität', in Jürgen Basedow, Klaus J Hopt, Hein Kötz and Peter Dopffel (eds), *Die Rechtsstellung gleichgeschlechtlicher Lebensgemeinschaften* (Tübingen 2000), pp 333–350, at pp 345–347.

[19] See below.

As in the case of the matrimonial provision in § 1362 BGB, it is assumed for the benefit of the creditors of a registered partner that the movable goods in the possession of either partner belong to the debtor.[20] This provision takes into account the fact that the issue of ownership is often unclear in a life partnership and removes the burden of proof from the creditor. Finally, there are important limits to the freedom of contract arising from the establishment of a registered partnership. A partner requires the consent of the other partner to dispose of household goods in his or her possession or of his or her assets as a whole.[21] Contrary to the corresponding provisions of matrimonial law, which apply only in the matrimonial property regime of accrued gains, the freedom of contract of partners in a registered partnership is limited irrespective of the partners' property regime. The same is true regarding the substitution rule, according to which household goods acquired to replace lost or useless goods become the property of the partner who was owner of the goods that were substituted.[22]

(C)   CONSEQUENCES IN PROPERTY LAW

Unlike spouses, registered partners are required to make a declaration concerning the property regime at the establishment of the registered partnership.[23] The partners have the option to choose either the property regime of *Ausgleichsgemeinschaft*, which is an equivalent to the matrimonial property regime of accrued gains, or to settle their financial position by means of a notarised partnership contract; in this contract they can either modify the property regime of accrued gains or choose between the two optional types of property regime available to married couples, that of separation of property or that of communal property. If registered partnerships do not, in fact, generally show the division of tasks typical of marriages, then there is no need for a legally mandated property regime which secures a share of the accrued gains for the partner who is not gainfully employed. Rather, the obligation to choose a property regime adequate to the relationship in question seems an appropriate solution. The fact that the LPartG does not offer a similar option concerning the *Versorgungsausgleich*, whereby the spouse participates in the partner's entitlements, expectancies or the mere prospect of drawing old age benefits (§ 1587 BGB), but rather neglects to regulate the *Versorgungsausgleich* between registered partners entirely is, however, inconsistent.

(D)   PARENTAL CARE AND CUSTODY

LPartG does not allow the joint adoption of a child by registered partners, or the adoption of a child of the other partner, with the consequence that both partners become his or her legal parents. It does, however, take into account the possible presence of minors in registered partnerships and has therefore established the so-called *kleines Sorgerecht* (minor custody right).[24] Accordingly, the registered

---

[20]   § 8 I LPartG.

[21]   § 8 II LPartG in connection with §§ 1369, 1365 BGB.

[22]   § 8 II LPartG in connection with § 1370 BGB.

[23]   § 1 I, 4 in connection with § 6 I LPartG.

[24]   § 9 LPartG.

partner who is not a parent of the child may have certain parental rights and duties, in the same way as the law now provides for the new spouse of a parent.[25]

First of all, the registered partner is given the right to decide, with the parent who has the care and custody of the child, on matters concerning daily life. This right entails factual obligations of care for the child, but includes also the authority to represent the child in relevant legal transactions jointly with the other partner. Family courts have the power to curtail or exclude these rights if this is necessary for the welfare of the child. Secondly, in the event of imminent danger, the registered partner of a parent is entitled to perform any legal acts which may be required for the benefit of the child. However, these parental rights and duties exist only if the parent who lives in a registered partnership is the sole person having the care and custody of the child, but not if that partner shares care and custody with the other parent. In the event of the dissolution of the registered partnership, the partner of the parent has the right of access to any children, provided that the partner has lived in the same household as the children over an extended period of time.[26] This right to access exists regardless of whether the parent in the registered partnership is the sole person having the care and custody of the child, or if he or she shares it with the other parent. Furthermore, the protection afforded to the stepfamily following the fundamental reform of child and parent law now also extends to the registered partner. The registered partner of a parent, who has lived with the parent and the child in the same household over an extended period of time, is entitled to refuse a demand by the other parent to surrender the child if and for as long as the welfare of the child would be endangered by the surrender.[27]

While the new 'minor custody right' helps to alleviate specific problems concerning stepchildren who are the offspring of a former marriage or other relationship of one of the partners, LPartG does not adequately deal with cases in which the child is not the issue of an earlier relationship of one of the partners, but is the product of a joint decision by the partners to be parents. Thus, two female registered partners could raise a child born to one through artificial insemination, although German law at present does not allow this. Furthermore, it would also be possible for one registered partner, male or female, to adopt a child on his or her own, which would subsequently be raised by both registered partners. In these cases, a factual parent–child relationship would come into being with the non-adopting partner as well. Since the child has a legal relationship with only one parent in cases such as these, it would be in the child's best interest if its relationship to the other partner could be secured through adoption. It would thus acquire an additional alimony debtor. Such a provision would be of particular importance if the biological parent or the parent by adoption were to become financially insolvent or die. Moreover, the law ought to make provision for the care and custody of such children which is in the best interest of the child in the event of dissolution of a registered partnership. The current mere right to access is not able to accommodate cases in which the child has predominantly or exclusively been cared for by the other registered partner, while the biological

---

[25] § 1687 b BGB.
[26] § 1685 II BGB.
[27] § 1682, 2 BGB as amended.

parent or parent through adoption pursued gainful employment. Therefore, registered partners ought also to be given the opportunity jointly to adopt a child or to adopt the child of the other registered partner.

(E) RIGHTS OF THE SURVIVING PARTNER

The surviving registered partner is treated, for the purposes of the law of inheritance, essentially the same as a spouse. In relation to statutory heirs of the first class, ie the children, the registered partner is entitled to a statutory portion of one-quarter of the deceased's estate; in relation to statutory heirs of the second class, ie the parents or siblings, or in relation to grandparents, the registered partner is entitled to a statutory portion of one half of the deceased's estate. If there are no statutory heirs of the first or second classes nor grandparents, the surviving registered partner inherits the entire estate. Thus the LPartG resolves the tension between partners' and relatives' right to a share in the deceased's estate in the same way as in matrimonial law, by stipulating that the partner's share in the deceased's estate is governed by the surviving relatives' degree of relationship to the deceased. The registered partner, as a continuing effect of community, is also entitled to the items forming part of the partnership household and to the gifts received when the registered partnership was established. Furthermore, registered partners can now draw up a joint will, as spouses can. If the deceased has excluded the registered partner from the inheritance by means of a disposition by will, the surviving partner is entitled to demand from the heirs half the statutory portion of the deceased's estate as his or her compulsory portion. The provision contained in the draft of LPartG, according equal tax status with spouses to registered partners in terms of inheritance tax, did not become law because it failed to secure a majority in the *Bundesrat*. Finally, of great importance is the surviving partner's right to become a tenant of the home of joint residence where the dead partner was the sole tenant.[28]

3   Dissolution of the registered partnership

(A)   PREREQUISITES OF *AUFHEBUNG*

A registered partnership, like a marriage, is dissolved by death or court judgment. The *Aufhebung* of the registered partnership, the term used by the Act to refer to the dissolution of a registered partnership by judicial decree, is comparable to the divorce of spouses in a marriage. The governing rules differ significantly, however. A registered partnership can be dissolved if one of the following three criteria is met:[29]

(1)   if both registered partners have declared that they do not wish to continue the registered partnership, the court then dissolves the registered partnership 12 months after the declaration;

---

[28]   § 569 I BGB. See Löhnig, 'Veränderungen im Recht der Wohnraummiete durch das Lebenspartnerschaftsgesetz', *Zeitschrift für das gesamte Familienrecht* 2001, pp 891–895.

[29]   § 15 LPartG.

(2)   if only one registered partner has made a declaration to the same effect, dissolution will take place after 36 months;

(3)   if its continuation would impose an unacceptable hardship on the partner who files for dissolution, for reasons relating to the person of the other registered partner.

When one of these criteria is present, it is safe to assume that the registered partnership no longer has any chance of continuing; therefore LPartG is, in the final analysis, founded on the principle of irretrievable breakdown. Unlike matrimonial law, however, LPartG does not specifically provide for an irrefutable presumption of breakdown if one or both partners declare that they want to divorce and have lived separately during the relevant period, but rather clearly delineates these facts as grounds for dissolution. Thus, contrary to matrimonial law, the statute openly allows for a consensual divorce, provided that the requisite waiting period has been fulfilled.[30] LPartG has erected a significantly higher barrier to the dissolution of a registered partnership than matrimonial law does by omitting a provision for breakdown as a general ground for divorce. Consequently, a registered partnership can only be dissolved against the will of one partner before the expiration of the waiting period of 36 months, if its continuation would impose an unacceptable hardship on the partner who files for dissolution, for reasons relating to the person of the other registered partner. The absence of such a general ground for divorce will presumably lead to a fairly large number of petitions for dissolution based on the hardship clause.

LPartG differs materially from the law of divorce in that dissolution does not require a period of separation, but the completion of a waiting period equalling the periods of separation in divorce law in extent. In practice, registered partnerships will therefore be considerably harder to dissolve than marriages. Whereas spouses who have separated are free to decide to file for a divorce even towards the end of their separation, registered partners have to declare their intent to discontinue their partnership at the beginning of the period. Moreover, it is easily ascertained whether such waiting periods have been completed, as the requisite declarations are of necessity publicly registered. On the other hand, it is difficult for a court to establish whether legal separation, which – to protect the financially weaker party – may occur inside the conjugal home,[31] has actually been in effect for the required amount of time. There is no reason for such differential treatment. If the legislator deems the prerequisite of living apart as unsuitable due to the danger of circumvention, he should consider the introduction of waiting periods in general.

(B)   CONSEQUENCES OF DISSOLUTION

After the dissolution of a registered partnership, the effects of the obligation to support and care continue in the guise of an entitlement to post-partnership maintenance.[32] A partner is entitled to financial support from the other if the partner so demanding cannot care for himself or herself because he or she cannot be expected to take up gainful employment particularly on account of old age,

---

[30]   Cf Dethloff, *Die einverständliche Scheidung*, 1994, p 101f.

[31]   § 1567 I, 2 BGB.

[32]   § 16 LPartG.

sickness or disability. Finally, on dissolution of a registered partnership, a court judgment may be issued concerning the partners' joint home and the household goods.[33] The law makes corresponding provisions for partners living apart.[34]

II   CONCLUSION

The new registered partnership substantially contributes to the reduction of discrimination against same-sex partnerships. Couples of the same sex are offered the chance to express their close bond through the acceptance of legal responsibility. As a consequence of the legal recognition of the registered partnership as a community based on mutual responsibility, provisions in matrimonial law that, like maintenance obligations, are an expression of this obligation to care and support are applied to registered partnerships. The fact that LPartG in other areas has created provisions which deviate from matrimonial law does not amount to discrimination where the matrimonial provisions – such as the matrimonial property regime of accrued gains and the *Versorgungsausgleich* – are intended to counteract the effects of a mostly differentiated division of tasks, which generally comes about with the existence of children.

---

[33]   § 17 and 18 LPartG.
[34]   § 12–14 LPartG.

HONG KONG

HONG KONG FAMILY LAW: MOVING FORWARD WITH ITS PLURAL HERITAGE

Bart Rwezaura[*] *and Rebecca Ho*[**]

I INTRODUCTION

The last *Survey* contribution on Hong Kong family law, covering the years 1994 to 1997, reported on the quickening pace of statutory reforms in various areas of family law. It was noted then that the imminent transfer of sovereignty from Britain to the People's Republic of China (PRC), and the extension to Hong Kong of a series of international human rights treaties, had provided the necessary impetus for those reforms. Four years down the road it seems the right moment to consider and report on the way judges have understood such reforms as revealed in court decisions. Therefore, although statutory changes enacted since the last report, including certain proposed reforms, are examined, the primary focus of this survey is on the decisions of superior courts and the role of judges in the development of Hong Kong family law during the last four years.

A significant feature of Hong Kong family law is its plural heritage. From the early British colonial period until 1971, Hong Kong had two systems of family law operating alongside one another. The main object of the 1971 reforms was to achieve a gradual integration of the Chinese system of family law with the received English common law system, but with the latter occupying a more dominant position in this process. The process of 'meshing' the two systems of law, or better still, of modernisation of Hong Kong family law, continues to this day, albeit now taking place primarily in the courts. Thus, courts have had to deal with intricate questions involving the applicability of Chinese customary law as it was practised in Hong Kong and mainland China during the last century.

Moreover, due to the geographical and cultural proximity of Hong Kong and mainland China, there has historically been a continuous flow of people between the two jurisdictions. Inter-marriages and *de facto* unions have resulted between Hong Kong people and mainland Chinese that have generated particular problems for family law. Perhaps the most intractable and enduring is the question of immigration law and policy involving family members on either side of the border. But there is also the more recent problem of the so-called mainland mistresses of Hong Kong married men and their children.

[*]   Associate Professor of Law, University of Hong Kong.
[**] Faculty of Law, University of Hong Kong.
      The authors wish to acknowledge the assistance of Sarah Cheng, Faculty of Law, University of Hong Kong, and Sharon Melloy, who read through this *Survey* contribution and made valuable suggestions.

On the other hand, international human rights law and its emerging jurisprudence have also exerted some influence on the development of the law. Although still in its formative stages, human rights jurisprudence appears to cut across the two underlying systems of family law providing an indirect push towards the integration of the Chinese family law system with the more dominant received English common law system. Hong Kong's thriving market economy, on the other hand, has also generated its own share of family law litigation particularly in the area of matrimonial property. This survey explores the above themes showing, wherever possible, the direction of Hong Kong family law in the coming years.

II   THE LONG SHADOW OF CHINESE CUSTOMARY LAW

In 1999 a High Court judge prefaced his judgement with these revealing remarks:

> 'Concubines are a relic of China's imperial past. Their survival well into the twentieth century is an anachronism, inconsistent with modern thinking about monogamy, female emancipation and equality of treatment for women. The legal status of concubines now comes before the Court again – this time in the latest episode in the saga relating to the estate of a woman who was taken in concubinage in Nationalist China in 1945.'[1]

Few would dispute that the institution of concubinage is out of step with the values deeply held by many Hong Kong people. It is also true that judges steeped in the ways of the English common law, whether local Chinese or expatriates, have limited understanding of and interest in Chinese customary law.[2] Not surprisingly, Hong Kong courts have traditionally relied on precedent as well as expert opinion, the latter often hired at considerable cost to the litigants.[3]

Ironically, the difficulties and high costs of proving the existence of a Chinese customary law in the Hong Kong courts were among the reasons why the Marriage Reform Ordinance (MRO, Cap 178) was enacted in 1971.[4] The MRO, besides putting an end to Chinese customary marriages, including concubinage, also specifically provided for a system of voluntary registration of existing Chinese customary marriages.[5] Furthermore, the MRO also enacted an

---

[1]   See Keith JA in *Chan Chiu Lam & Others v Yau Yee Ping (No 2)* [1999] 3 HKLRD 502 at 503.

[2]   See Su Yigong, 'The Application of Chinese Law and Custom in Hong Kong' 29 (1999) HKLR 267 at 292.

[3]   Experts on Chinese customary law continue to be called especially in probate cases involving issues of personal status. As noted by Deputy Judge Chu in *Ng Kuk Mui v Yu Bik Fong* [HCA 2/97] 'the general rule is for expert evidence to be adduced, either by way of testimony or, with leave of the court, by affidavit'. The Deputy Judge in this case criticised Counsel for the plaintiff for choosing not to call an expert witness in order to save costs for his client. But as will be noted in this article (see **IV** below) legal fees in Hong Kong are a worrying aspect of civil litigation.

[4]   See the 1967 White Paper on Chinese Marriages in Hong Kong (Hong Kong Government Printer, Hong Kong), 1967, p 6.

[5]   Section 4 (MRO) states that all marriages contracted on or after 7 October 1971 shall be monogamous and shall be contracted only in accordance with the Marriage Ordinance (Cap 181). Section 5 (MRO) states that no man may take a concubine and no woman may acquire the status

authoritative definition of a Chinese customary marriage to guide courts and the registrar of marriages in this modernisation process.[6] A new form of marriage known as the Chinese *modern marriage*, which had also emerged in Hong Kong following the enactment in 1930 of the Chinese Civil Code, was also validated and accorded retrospective recognition. Despite its popularity, especially among the urban working class, the Chinese *modern marriage* was not legally recognised in Hong Kong as the Civil Code itself was not part of Hong Kong law.[7]

As the cases below show, the 1971 reforms achieved the modernisation of Hong Kong family law by defining its future development. But the reforms did not and could not instantly eliminate all the features of the Chinese traditional system. Therefore, as long as people who had contracted marriage under Chinese customary law remain alive, courts have to hear disputes involving such family relationships whenever and however they arise. Indeed, it is more often on the death of a wealthy Chinese patriarch that his or her children and widows find themselves locked in a court battle over who has an interest in the deceased's estate. And the larger the estate, the more intense and costly will be the fight. These disputes invariably lead to questions of personal status, such as whether the applicant is a child of the marriage or whether the applicant's claimed status of a widow is sustainable under the old Chinese customary law. Some of these disputes involve parties who contracted their marriages in mainland China and this invariably calls for proof of what the law was in mainland China at the time of the marriage.

All this is not surprising given that a large number of Hong Kong people emigrated from mainland China and many had married there before migrating to Hong Kong. In short, so long as some of Hong Kong's population still trace their cultural identity back to what Keith J called the 'relic of China's imperial past', Hong Kong courts will have to adjudicate their family disputes. As Leonard Pegg aptly noted in 1994, '[i]t is not yet time to consign these kinds of marriage to the history books'.[8]

---

of concubine after 7 October 1971, provided the status of concubines shall not be affected by the new law. Moreover, the legal status of children born of existing unions whether born before or after the appointed date shall not be affected.

[6] Under s 7 (MRO), a marriage shall constitute a customary marriage 'if it was or is celebrated in Hong Kong before [7 October 1971] in accordance with the traditional Chinese law and custom'. And a marriage shall be deemed to accord with Chinese law and custom 'if it was celebrated or is celebrated before [7 October 1971] in Hong Kong in accordance with the traditional Chinese customs accepted at the time of the marriage as appropriate for the celebration of marriage either— (a) in the part of Hong Kong where the marriage took place; or (b) in the place recognised by the family of another party to the marriage as their family place of origin'. See also *Chan Chung-hing v Wong Kim-wah* [1986] 2 HKLR 715.

[7] Section 8 (MRO) provided for retrospective recognition of the *modern marriage* as well as its definition. A *modern marriage* was defined by s 8 of the MRO as being a marriage celebrated in Hong Kong before 7 October 1971 between 'a man and woman each of whom, at the time of the marriage, was not less than 16 years of age and was not married to any other person'. Such a marriage was valid notwithstanding the fact that its celebration did not comply with the Marriage Ordinance or the personal or religious law of the parties, including Chinese customary law.

[8] See Leonard Pegg, *Family Law in Hong Kong* (Butterworths Asia, 3rd edn, 1994), at p v.

A   Who may inherit the estate: the widow or the concubine?

In *Ng Kuk Mui v Yu Bik Fong Rebecca*[9] the plaintiff, Madam Ng Kuk Mui applied on 3 March 1997 to the High Court seeking grant of the letters of administration of the estate of her late husband Mr Yu Kau Sun. The said letters of administration had previously been granted to the defendant, Yu Bik Fong on 31 October 1995 on her application as the surviving child of the union between the deceased, Yu Kau Sun, and her mother Madam Mok Wei Wan. The first issue before the court was whether the plaintiff was the lawful *kit fat* wife of the deceased under Chinese customary law.[10] If so, then she had a prior right to the grant of the letters of administration, as the lawful surviving spouse, irrespective of whether the defendant was the lawful and natural daughter of the deceased. The second issue was whether Madam Mok (the defendant's mother, now also deceased) was lawfully married to the deceased in Hong Kong under Chinese customary law.

Deputy Judge Chu held, granting the application, that the plaintiff had successfully proved that she was a lawful *kit fat* wife of the deceased. The court also held that the relationship between the defendant's mother, Madam Mok, and the deceased was not a lawful marriage under Chinese customary law. This followed from the fact that the deceased was already married in China in 1945 before coming to Hong Kong in 1956 when he began to cohabit with Madam Mok. Moreover, his first marriage with the plaintiff had not been dissolved.[11] It should be noted that Hong Kong courts have always held that the burden of proving the existence of an alleged customary marriage between the plaintiff and the deceased lay upon the plaintiff. Not only that, the burden of proving that the alleged ceremony amounted to a valid Chinese customary marriage is also placed upon the plaintiff.[12] Hence, considering that there was no legal requirement to register such customary marriages and, furthermore, given that in this case the alleged marriage was celebrated 56 years ago, the plaintiff was fortunate to have been able to put together acceptable evidence to prove such a marriage.

It appears also that the deceased husband had told Madam Mok, his Hong Kong 'wife', that he was unmarried and had no children. Madam Mok must have believed this story especially considering that her husband never returned to his homeland China until 1977 – a period of 21 years. And while in Hong Kong, he

---

[9]   HCAP 2/97.

[10]   The term *kit fat* refers to the first marriage between a bachelor and a spinster. According to custom a Chinese man refers to his first wife as 'kit fat' wife. Before the abolition of concubinage in 1971, a Hong Kong Chinese male could add to the first marriage any number of concubines but he could not legally marry more than one principal wife, ie *kit fat*. See Athena Liu, *Family Law for the HKSAR* (Hong Kong University Press, Hong Kong, 2000), p 31.

[11]   The court was unable to decide, due to lack of evidence, whether Madam Mok could be regarded as a concubine of the deceased by virtue of her cohabitation with him. In the absence of vital evidence, the legal status of Madam Mok was deemed to be similar to that of a mistress. But this finding was not fatal because the defendant was held to be entitled to a share in her late father's estate even as an illegitimate child. This is because Hong Kong amended the law in 1993 to enable an illegitimate child to inherit from the intestate estate of his or her father. See s 2 of the Intestate's Estate Ordinance, Cap 73. For details on the effect of the Parent and Child Ordinance of 1993, see B Rwezaura, 'Birth in or out of Wedlock: Does it matter any more? The Parent and Child Ordinance' in R Glofcheski (ed), *Law Lectures for Practitioners 1994* (Hong Kong Law Journal Ltd, Hong Kong, 1994), pp 264–295.

[12]   See L Pegg (1994), at pp 9–10.

had made representations to Government officials that he was married to Madam Mok. He had also taken Madam Mok with him on his subsequent visits to his home county in the Guangdong Province of China. Perhaps no one will ever know whether the deceased believed that his first marriage had ended and that his second union was a valid marriage. As Deputy Judge Chu aptly noted:

> '[Madam Mok] might have been told by the deceased that he was married to the plaintiff or she might have suspected it. Equally, it is possible that the deceased had kept the truth from her and assured her that he had never undergone any ceremony with the plaintiff, in much the same way as he had assured the plaintiff [that he was not married to Madam Mok].'

This case represents what might be described as a pattern whereby the migration of Chinese men from mainland China into Hong Kong involved, to a certain extent, their separation from their families in China and, subsequently, their founding of new family units in Hong Kong.[13] Some might argue that as long as the men remained culturally and economically dominant, their women were in no position to ask too many questions about the men's past. As in this case, the litigation was in fact between the children born of these two women, the potential beneficiaries of the estate, rather than the women themselves, one of whom had in fact died shortly before the dispute began.

B   Of concubine *de jure* and concubine *de facto*

The case of *Chan Chiu Lam & Ors v Yau Yee Ping*,[14] like *Ng Kuk Mui* above, also came before the courts to determine whether the surviving children had a right to inherit the estate of their late father's concubine. The right to inherit from a stepmother or a father's concubine is provided under s 4(5) of the Intestate's Estate Ordinance (Cap 73) which states in effect that if the intestate leaves issue but no husband or wife, the residuary estate shall belong to the issue of the intestate. Section 2(2)(b) of the same Ordinance states that where the intestate is a female, reference to a child or issue of any person shall mean 'a child of a valid marriage to which her last husband and another female were parties'. A child of the union of concubinage is also under this Ordinance deemed to be the child of a valid marriage.

The relevant issue to be determined in this case was whether the plaintiffs were the children of a valid marriage to which the deceased's last husband and another female were parties. The trial court held that they were such children; but on appeal, the Court of Appeal found that the union of concubinage to which the last husband of the intestate and another female were parties, and of which the plaintiffs were the issue, was not a valid marriage. The plaintiffs were, therefore, not entitled to inherit the estate of their late father's concubine. In coming to this conclusion the Court of Appeal agreed with Keith J, the trial judge, that there was an important distinction between concubine *de facto* and concubine *de jure*. A

---

[13]   For details on the history of Hong Kong law and policy towards Chinese immigrants into Hong Kong, see Albert Chen, 'Immigration Law in Hong Kong' 33 (1988) *McGill Law Journal* 632.

[14]   [1998] 2 HKC 569.

concubine *de facto* was a union which, although formed in accordance with Chinese customary law, was not recognised by the 1931 Civil Code of the Republic of China. In the words of Rogers JA, a concubine *de facto* was no more than a mistress and it did not matter that the law subsequently accorded such a mistress certain rights including the right to maintenance. Therefore, in view of the fact that the plaintiffs were the issue of a union not legally recognised by the law of the parties' domicile, ie the Republic of China at the time, Hong Kong courts, applying the common law principles of private international law, were bound to hold that the plaintiffs did not qualify to inherit the estate of Madam Chu Lee, the intestate. The Court of Appeal further noted that the rules of private international law applied in Hong Kong, recognised the efficacy of legislation which removed the capacity to contract a polygamous marriage previously enjoyed under the personal law of the parties. The same principle would apply where there had been a foreign law, as in this case the Chinese Civil Code, abolishing the institution of concubinage.

Here again the dispute was between the children of Chinese parents who had migrated to Hong Kong as adults having been previously married in Mainland China. Their legal status as children of a valid union, and therefore, their inheritance rights, fell to be determined by legal principles of Chinese state law. The Court of Appeal held that although the Chinese Civil Code (1931) made no mention of concubines as such, the omission was a deliberate policy decision to abolish such unions.[15] This decision is also notable for drawing a clear distinction between the law governing capacity to marry (ie the law of domicile) and the law relating to formal validity of the marriage (ie the law of the place of celebration). After reviewing past decisions of Hong Kong courts, Ribeiro JA concluded that once a person's law of domicile is established, the common law rules of conflict of law must be applied rather than Hong Kong law simply because the person in question, and despite his/her foreign domicile, was of Chinese ethnicity and resident in Hong Kong.

C   The sovereignty of monogamy

As in most former British colonies, the law and those responsible for its administration assumed that the monogamous form of marriage was superior to all others. One illustration of the supremacy of monogamy is the received statutory laws found in most British territories that were designed to enable the local population to 'convert' their potentially polygamous marriages into a Christian or civil form of marriage. This facility, however, may seem like a ploy because once the potentially polygamous marriage was converted into a monogamous marriage, the couple permanently lost their right to revert to their original status by changing their law of domicile or religion. Even today the assumed cultural superiority of

---

[15]   See Su Yigong, 'The Application of Chinese Law and Custom in Hong Kong' 29 (1999) HKLJ 267 for a careful and informed analysis of the impact of English common law on Chinese customary law in Hong Kong, showing how Hong Kong judges are barely able to scratch below the surface of Chinese customary law. The court also relied on *Tang Lai Sau-kiu v Tang Loi* [1987] 1 HKLR 85 that held that the Chinese Civil Code (1931) had abolished the status of concubinage.

the monogamous form of marriage appears clearly in the law as is demonstrated by two recent decisions.

The first decision is *Re Estate of Wong Wong*.[16] Here, the deceased husband Mr Wong had married Madam Au in China in 1944 and their marriage was registered as a monogamous marriage under the laws of the Republic of China. Subsequently, the couple emigrated to Hong Kong where they acquired a new domicile of choice. In 1958 Wong entered into a union of concubinage with Madam Lee which union was valid according to Chinese law and custom. On Wong's demise, his two widows jointly applied for letters of administration in relation to his estate. Although no dispute existed between the two women, the probate registry queried the status of Madam Lee on the ground that the late Mr Wong may have lacked the legal capacity to enter into a union of concubinage. The registry's doubt was based on the fact that Wong's marriage contracted in 1944 was monogamous and the law in the Republic of China at that time permitted only monogamy. Following this query, the two widows applied to the High Court for a decision on the merits. The High Court rejected Madam Lee's application holding, first, that the right to take a concubine existed only when the man's first marriage was polygamous; and secondly, that change of domicile did not operate to turn a marriage that was monogamous at its inception into a potentially polygamous marriage. Hong Kong courts, therefore, will treat a monogamous marriage contracted in China or any other jurisdiction as a monogamous marriage for all purposes. The judge rejected the suggestion that change of domicile should operate both ways by converting, as in *Ali v Ali*,[17] a potentially polygamous marriage into a monogamous marriage, and on the reverse side, by converting a monogamous marriage into a potentially polygamous marriage if the parties changed their religion or law of domicile.[18]

The second decision is *Leung May Ling v Leung Sai Lun Robert*[19] which went all the way to the Court of Final Appeal. The only issue before the courts was whether a subsequent marriage between the same parties at the Registry had triggered s 13 of the Wills Ordinance thereby revoking an existing testament. Section 13(1) of the Wills Ordinance simply states that a will shall be revoked 'by the subsequent marriage of the testator' except a will expressed to be made in contemplation of that marriage. The facts of the case show that the testator was first married in 1951 but his wife died in 1963. The first marriage produced four children. In 1966 the testator went through a Chinese customary marriage with Madam Leung (the first respondent) and again in 1985 he went through another ceremony of marriage under s 38 of the Marriage Ordinance (Cap 181) with the same wife, Madam Leung.[20] This marriage produced three children. The testator

---

16   [1998] 3 HKC 405.

17   *Ali v Ali* [1966] 1 All ER 664.

18   The same conclusion is reached by L Pegg, *Family Law in Hong Kong* (Butterworths, Singapore, 2nd edn, 1986) at pp 28–30.

19   [1997] HKLRD 712, [1998] 1 HKLRD 208 and FACV No 5/198 decided on 29 January 1999.

20   Section 38 of the Marriage Ordinance states that 'parties to any non-Christian customary marriage duly celebrated according to the personal law and religion of the parties before the appointed date under the Marriage Reform Ordinance (Cap 178) may unless the husband has any other wife, contract with each other a marriage under this Ordinance; and such marriage shall not invalidate the previous customary marriage'.

died in 1996 whereupon his children by the first marriage produced a will, which had been executed by the testator in 1967, naming them his executors and the only beneficiaries of his estate. There was no other testamentary document and all parties agreed that the said will was authentic. Madam Leung and her three children challenged this will arguing that it had been revoked by the 1985 marriage, in accordance with s 13(1) of the Wills Ordinance.

The trial judge held that the marriage contracted between the testator and Madam Leung in 1985 pursuant to s 38 of the Marriage Ordinance was a valid marriage and its effect was to revoke the 1967 will. On further appeal by the appellants, both the Court of Appeal and the Court of Final Appeal upheld the decision of the trial court. The Court of Final Appeal agreed with the two courts below noting that the real issue before the court was one of statutory interpretation of the phrase: 'the subsequent marriage' in s 13(1) of the Wills Ordinance. Consequently, a marriage under s 38 of the Marriage Ordinance has the effect of revoking a will made before the celebration of that marriage.

This case demonstrates yet again the dominance of the monogamous form of marriage. First, it may be asked why the testator went through a second marriage ceremony with the same wife, particularly after the enactment of the Marriage Reform Ordinance 1971? Secondly, what was the original object of s 38 of the Marriage Ordinance, which seemingly beckons to those who are already married to marry again? As Litton PJ noted, '[i]n logic it is anomalous that parties to a valid marriage, including a customary marriage, should be able to go through a second Registry marriage when the first is still extant' (p 5). But it seems that the logic lies in the fact that the second ceremony has the effect of converting the Chinese customary marriage (widely regarded as polygamous)[21] into a monogamous marriage carrying a higher status in the eyes of the law. For example, such a conversion has the effect of raising the status of the wife. In her new status the wife would access some of the statutory remedies available to parties married monogamously under the Marriage Ordinance (Cap 181). These remedies include the right to petition for divorce under the general law and to apply for orders for the division of family assets, custody of children and maintenance. These remedies were not available to a wife under Chinese customary law until 1979 following an amendment to the Matrimonial Causes Ordinance (Cap 179) which empowered the courts to grant such remedies. Even then, this special dispensation was available only to parties married under Chinese customary law who had also registered their marriages under Part IV of the

---

[21]   Much of the controversy as to whether a Chinese customary marriage is monogamous or polygamous has hinged heavily on the fact that it is not a union of one man and one woman to the exclusion of all others. Carol Tan has argued, for example, that the Chinese customary marriage is neither monogamous nor polygamous, while Tungtsu Chu has described it as 'a system of one wife among many concubines'. Su Yigong argues that the term 'monogamy' in traditional Chinese does not mean the same thing as this term is used under English common law. Chinese customary law did not forbid a man to marry more than one woman, 'but only one was entitled to be called "wife" while all others had to be given other titles to show their distinction from the primary wife'. He concludes that if one were to disregard the notion of personal status 'it may not be wrong to label the traditional Chinese marriage as polygamous'. See Su Yigong, 'The Application of Chinese Law and Custom in Hong Kong' 29 (1999) HKLR 267, at 276. Chu Tung-tsu, *Law and Society in Traditional China* (Zhong Hua Shu Ju, Beijing, 1981 (reprinted in 1996)) at 130, and Carol Tan, 'The Twilight of Chinese Customary Law Relating to Marriage in Malaysia' 42 *International and Comparative Law Quarterly* 147, at 149.

Marriage Reform Ordinance.[22] All this suggests that parties married under Chinese customary law, especially the wife, would be better off converting their marriage under s 38 of the Marriage Ordinance. In this case there is no indication that the testator and his wife, Madam Leung, were aware that the second marriage ceremony would trigger the revocation of the 1967 testament.

D   The *bao ernai* or mainland mistresses

The opening up of mainland China for trade, particularly the establishment of special economic zones in southern China, has generated new economic opportunities for Hong Kong people who now travel regularly to southern China on business. Indeed, some Hong Kong companies have established factories in China where the cost per unit of production is much lower than in Hong Kong. Some Hong Kong men have also established relationships with mainland women in what are now widely characterised as 'second homes', and their partners are known as *bao ernai* or mistresses. The impact of these affairs has been considerable as gathered from the press and from commentators on social issues. In 1995 for example, one legislator stated that, 'mainland mistresses pose a new social problem in the territory, with dozens of heart broken wives seeking help from local social welfare organisations every month'.[23] He suggested that 'anyone living with a woman who is not his wife for two years, who financially supports her, or who has a child by her, will be liable for prosecution. [A]nd cheating husbands would be fined under the new law, but could also be sent to jail if they failed to pay up'.[24]

Not surprisingly, this proposal was quickly rejected for being either too difficult to enforce or in conflict with fundamental liberal values. According to Robin Macleish, the Principal Assistant Secretary for Home Affairs, the proposal concerning the two years' cohabitation could be easily evaded by men returning briefly to Hong Kong before the two years had elapsed and then going back to the Mainland to begin cohabitation all over again. Robin Macleish also thought it would be difficult to gather sufficient evidence to sustain a criminal conviction. Most legislators and other government officials thought it was more realistic to increase public awareness on the importance of family life and the detrimental effect of extramarital affairs on families. The social welfare department pledged to provide moral as well as material support to families adversely affected while also pushing for a more rigorous enforcement of alimony and child support obligations.

More controversial, however, was the suggestion by one academic that mainland mistresses should instead be legalised in order to protect both families. According to Dr Ng, a Reader in psychology at the University of Hong Kong, although Hong Kong had abolished concubinage as a feudal Chinese custom in

---

[22]   See s 9 of the Matrimonial Causes Ordinance Cap 179 (as amended by Ordinance No 63 of 1979, s 4).

[23]   See Eric Li Ka-Cheung, 'Protect victims of "bigamy affairs"' *Sunday Morning Post*, 29 January 1995, at p 13.

[24]   See Quinton Chan, 'Proposal to jail men who keep concubines' *Sunday Morning Post*, 29 January 1995, at p 4.

1971, this custom had in fact not died down. In Ng's opinion, it was better to recognise *bao ernai* than criminalizing it. Such recognition would give official status and legal protection to mistresses and their children born out of wedlock while also removing the social stigma attaching to these mainland families. It would also protect 'the children of these unions in disputes over inheritance and residence in the Territory'.[25]

It is now over five years since the debate began and neither the law to prohibit nor the law to legalise these unions has been enacted. What is certain, however, is that the numbers of Hong Kong men establishing a 'second home' in mainland China have increased rather than dwindled. Although no accurate figures exist, the numbers of children born in these unions have also soared.[26] As one academic has recently noted, '[s]everal villages in Southern China have now become known as the "lover's nest" where most of the women are mistresses to Hong Kong men. Included among the Hong Kong men are not only businessmen and professionals but also those from the lower socio-economic stratum including truck drivers and workers'.[27] The question whether the mainland mistress is indeed a concubine or merely a by-product of the burgeoning market economy of China is presumably of little significance to those families directly affected. At present the problem of mainland mistresses remains unresolved, posing a challenge to the Hong Kong government, its social welfare system, and its immigration department. More importantly, with the substantial removal of the legal consequences of illegitimacy, the children of these unions are lawful children of their Hong Kong fathers like other children of the marriage.[28] This is not only consistent with international human rights law but also with Chinese customary law, which draws no distinction between children, whether their mother is a wife or a concubine.

---

[25] See Apple Wan, 'Legal status call for mistresses' *The Standard*, 30 January 1995, and So Lai-Fun, 'Plea on Concubines' *South China Morning Post*, 30 January 1995.

[26] It is reported that most of the mainland mistresses are aged between 30 and 39 years and have an average of three children, most of them under the age of 12 years. See Wong Chi-shing, 'Action urged on infidelity' *Eastern Express*, 21 January 1995.

[27] See Khun Eng Kuah-Pearce, 'The Cultural Politics of Mainland Chinese Migration to Hong Kong', paper presented at the Conference on Immigration Law and Policies, University of Hong Kong on 24 February 2001 at pp 16–17. It should not be supposed, however, that only Hong Kong men are guilty of keeping mistresses in China. There is a larger number of Chinese and Taiwanese men who are also keeping mistresses in mainland China. Until early this year there was intense debate in China calling on the government to change the law to make extramarital affairs a criminal offence. On 28 April 2001, the National People's Congress amended its marriage law but did not go as far as some women's groups had wanted. Under the amended Marriage Law, bigamy remains a criminal offence but cohabitation, although unlawful, is only a ground for divorce. The new law now entitles the aggrieved spouse to sue his or her former spouse's cohabitant for compensation after divorce.

See 'Legislating Love ...' *South China Morning Post*, 30 April 2001 and 'Scorned wives see way out of concubine culture' *South China Morning Post*, 20 July 2000, p 9.

[28] B Rwezaura, 'Birth in or out of Wedlock: Does it matter any more? The Parent and Child Ordinance' in R Glofcheski ed, *Law Lectures for Practitioners 1994* (Hong Kong Law Journal Ltd, Hong Kong, 1994), pp 264–295.

III ISSUES OF IMMIGRATION AND SPLIT FAMILIES

Since the resumption of sovereignty by the People's Republic of China in July 1997, Hong Kong's immigration law and policy has been largely driven by the desire to control the entry into Hong Kong of immigrants from mainland China. In order to achieve a fair and orderly mechanism of entry into Hong Kong, a system of exit permits was set up during the early 1980s whereby applicants wishing to enter Hong Kong as visitors are granted a two-way permit and those permitted to settle here under the existing daily quota system are granted a one-way permit. Priority is often given to applicants seeking family reunification, which includes children and spouses (mainly wives) whose parent or husband resides in Hong Kong.[29]

In the years immediately preceding the change of sovereignty, illegal immigration into Hong Kong increased considerably, thereby creating pressure on the government to tighten its control on immigration from mainland China. This included people claiming the right of abode under Art 24 of the Basic Law (BL). Article 24 of the BL grants the right of abode to Chinese citizens born in Hong Kong before or after the establishment of the Hong Kong Special Administrative Region. The same right is conferred on a person of Chinese nationality born outside Hong Kong, as to those Hong Kong residents who have a right of abode in Hong Kong under Art 24(1) and 24(2) of the BL. It is believed that many people who entered Hong Kong illegally before July 1997 expected to be automatically granted the right of abode. This group included pregnant women who 'sneaked' into Hong Kong to deliver their babies, expecting their children to become Hong Kong permanent residents.[30] Consequently, tight control of entry into Hong Kong by immigrants from mainland China became the major policy concern of the government.[31] It is against this background that we must locate recent decisions of the courts touching on the rights of children and more generally, on the right to family union.

One of the ways the government sought to check the possible influx of immigrants was the enactment on 21 June 1997 of the Immigration (Amendment)

---

[29] In 1993 the daily quota of one-way permit holders from mainland China was raised from 75 to 105 persons and then again to 150 in 1995. It is estimated that an annual total of 54,750 persons are admitted into Hong Kong under this system. Moreover, an estimated total of 197,600 persons are reported to have entered Hong Kong since July 1997. This number includes 85,412 children and at least 80,600 separated spouses. See Timothy Tong, Deputy Secretary for Security, 'Hong Kong's Immigration Policy on Persons from the Mainland of China', paper presented at the Conference on Immigration Law and Policies, University of Hong Kong, 24 February 2001, at p 4.

[30] See *Chong Fung Yuen v Director of Immigration* [2000] 3 HKLRD 661 where the Court of Appeal held that Art 24(2)(1) of the BL gives Chinese citizens born in Hong Kong at any time the right to become permanent residents without any further requirement that the parent of such a child should be a permanent resident of Hong Kong. An appeal by the Director of Immigration to the Court of Final Appeal against this decision was dismissed on 20 July 2001 with no order as to costs. See *Director of Immigration v Chong Fung-Yuen (an Infant)* FACV No 26 of 2000.

[31] Sham marriages have also been used by mainland Chinese immigrants to evade immigration regulations. In a recent case, 23 people have been arrested by the Hong Kong Independent Commission Against Corruption (ICAC) on suspicion of operating a 'fake marriage racket'. See Stella Lee, '23 Arrested over fake marriages racket' SCMP, 5 October 2001, at p 4. See also Marcal Joanilho, 'Marriage racket smashed, says ICAC', where the ICAC is reported to have 'smashed a bogus marriage scam matching Hong Kong people with mainlanders seeking SAR residence', SCMP, 20 February 2002, at p 6.

(No 3) Ordinance (No 124 of 1997). The Ordinance stated in effect that in order to enter Hong Kong, children claiming a right of abode under Art 24(3) of the BL must have a 'certificate of entitlement' issued by the Immigration Department. The new ordinance was to operate retrospectively to 1 July 1997 in order to claw back all the children who had entered Hong Kong without such certificates. Moreover, those who were already present in Hong Kong and not in possession of the 'certificate of entitlement' would be immediately sent back to the mainland. The 'Amendment No 3' set off a series of court challenges going all the way to the Court of Final Appeal. In what may be called 'Round One' in this legal battle, all the courts held that 'Amendment No 3' was in contravention of Art 24 of the BL and could not stand. The courts ruled that the imposition of the 'certificate of entitlement' was a restriction on the express right granted by Art 24 of the BL. They also held that a child of a permanent resident acquired the right of abode under Art 24(3) of the BL even if neither of his or her parents was a Hong Kong permanent resident at the time of that child's birth.[32]

At first the government promised to comply with the court's decision but later successfully sought a new interpretation of Art 24 of the BL from the National People's Congress in June 1999. By this time, the dispute between the government and the right of abode seekers had transformed into what came to be known as Hong Kong's constitutional debate.[33] Other changes in the law were also made about the same time to restrict the entry of mainland children into Hong Kong. Under s 5 of the Immigration (Amendment) (No 2) Ordinance (No 122 of 1997) the government sought to exclude children born out of wedlock from the ambit of Art 24(3) of the BL. This provision was successfully challenged in court. According to Justice Keith, 'Ordinance No 2 plainly violated Art 24(3) of the BL because children of Hong Kong permanent residents are no less their children simply because they may have been born out of wedlock'.[34] The government's appeal to the Court of Appeal and later to the Court of Final Appeal was dismissed in both courts.[35]

In 1999, the government made another attempt to exclude adopted children from the ambit of Art 24(3) of the BL. In the Court of First Instance, Keith J ruled that adopted children were not excluded as children born outside Hong Kong 'of those residents listed in categories (1) and (2)'.[36] The Director of Immigration successfully appealed to the Court of Appeal where it was unanimously held that adopted children were not the children 'that the resident gave birth' (per Leong JA) and, therefore, such children did not satisfy the criteria laid down in Art 24(2), (3) of the BL (per Mayo V-P). The court also rejected the argument that the protection of 'family life' and the 'family unit' under various human rights treaties required the inclusion of an adopted child within the scope of Art 24(2),

---

[32]   See *Ng Ka Ling & others v Director of Immigration* (1999) 2 HKCFAR 141.

[33]   See Johannes MM Chan, H L Fu and Yash Ghai (eds) *Hong Kong Constitutional Debate: Conflict over Interpretation* (Hong Kong University Press, 2000).

[34]   See *Cheung Lai Wah (An Infant) v Director of Immigration* [1997] 3 HKC 64 at 91.

[35]   See *Cheung Lai Wah (An Infant) & Ors v Director of Immigration* [1998] 1 HKC 617 and *Ng Ka Ling & Ors v Director of Immigration* [1999] 1 HKLRD 58.

[36]   See *Xie Xiaoyi & Ors v Director of Immigration* [1999] 2 HKLRD 505.

(3) of the BL. The Court of Final Appeal dismissed an appeal against this decision on 20 July 2001.[37]

Earlier in 1998, the government also succeeded in excluding stepchildren as a category of persons qualifying under Art 24(3) of the BL.[38] In this case, the court placed emphasis on the importance of natural 'birth' adding that a stepchild was not 'born of' a Hong Kong permanent resident as envisaged by Art 24(3) of the BL. This interpretation was affirmed by the Court of Appeal in *Xie Xiaoyi*, the adoption case cited above. All the above cases show a determined effort by the Hong Kong government to ensure the success of its restrictive immigration policy.

Apart from the challenges based on Art 24, there have been others directed primarily at the discretionary powers of the Director of Immigration. Following previous decisions, courts have consistently refused to interfere, holding that the Director has a very wide discretion under s 13 of the Immigration Ordinance (Cap 115) and it is not for the courts to say how that discretion should be exercised. In the words of Godfrey JA, courts do not wish to impose 'unrealistic standards on the Hong Kong Government's attempt to resolve the difficult and intransigent problems'.[39] More recently, the Court of Final Appeal has also added its voice, holding that the Director of Immigration 'has no duty to consider humanitarian grounds in considering the making of a removal order against [an illegal immigrant]. But he can take such grounds into account if he thinks it appropriate in the case in question'.[40]

Hong Kong's immigration policy continues to be strongly attacked by human rights activists and other liberal elements in the community for its insensitivity and rigidity.[41] On the other hand, there are others who argue that unless the influx of immigrants into Hong Kong is strictly controlled, there will be undue pressure on the social infrastructure, especially upon housing, health and education. It remains to be seen whether the major economic changes now taking place in mainland China will slow down or better still, reverse the flow of immigrants into Hong Kong. It is perhaps too early to expect that Hong Kong people might one day wish to emigrate to mainland China, not only to conduct business and to establish second homes, but also to reside there permanently.

IV THE RISING COST OF DIVORCE: IS IT A DETERRENT?

Hong Kong is widely known for its astronomical legal fees. It has been said that it is far cheaper to hire a London silk and maintain him or her in a five-star hotel

---

[37] See *Tam Nga Yin, Chan Wai Wah, Xie Xiao Yi v Director of Immigration* FACV Nos 20 and 21 of 2000 (CFA).

[38] See *Lui Sheung-kwan & Ngan Sau-ying v The Director of Immigration* [1998] 1 HKLRD 265.

[39] Per Godfrey JA, *In re Hai Ho-tak & Cheng Chun-heung v A-G & Director of Immigration* [1994] 2 HKLR 202 at 210.

[40] *Lau Kong Yung & Others v Director of Immigration* [1999] 3 HKLRD 805 at 806.

[41] See Philip Dykes SC, 'Discretion and Immigration Control', paper presented at the Conference on Immigration Law and Policies, University of Hong Kong, 24 February 2001; Paul Harris, 'Due Process and Aliens', paper presented at the Conference on Immigration Law and Policies, University of Hong Kong, 24 February 2001; and Bart Rwezaura, 'The Duty to Consider Best Interests in the Administration of Hong Kong Immigration Law' paper presented at the Conference on Immigration Law and Policies, University of Hong Kong, 24 February 2001.

than to hire a Hong Kong barrister.[42] This is true whether one is dealing with a complex commercial case or highly contentious litigation over child custody or division of matrimonial property.[43] Unless legally aided, litigation can wreck the lives of litigants, turning them into penniless paupers. Complex court procedures where lawyers tend to have a free hand have left judges lamenting but still helpless to assist the litigant who ultimately must foot the bill.[44] Those caught in this web include a wife in *Y v Y*[45], who unsuccessfully applied for a court order to release a capital sum from the family assets to finance her continued litigation against her husband. The court held that there was no statutory provision or common law principle that entitled either party in matrimonial proceedings to seek a release of capital for the purpose of financing legal costs. According to Hartmann J, the common law of England, as applied to Hong Kong via Art 8 of the Basic Law, did not sanction such an application. The court also held that Roman-Dutch law, relied upon by the wife, was not part of Hong Kong law. In *Yip Ku v Kwan Kuk Lin*,[46] the husband failed in his application to the High Court for an interim lump sum payment of HK$6 million to enable him to continue with the hearing of his ancillary relief application. Consequently, he decided to represent himself throughout the remaining portion of the proceedings.

The financial burden on the parties to a divorce can never be underestimated. Where the parties are legally aided, it appears their financial burden may be relieved.[47] In such cases, the litigation costs are then passed on to the taxpayer. For example, during the year 2000, the Legal Aid Department received a total of 21,736 applications for assistance in civil cases, out of which 47% were matrimonial cases. And of all the successful applications, 60% of the certificates

---

[42] Ronny Tong, former Chair to the Hong Kong Bar Association, was quoted as saying that top barristers charge about US$750 an hour 'for consultation work and up to HK$80,000 (ie US$10,230) a day in court'. See Cris Prystay, 'Price of Justice?' *The Asian Wall Street Journal*, 22–28 February 1999. One experienced solicitor believes that these figures are lower than her past experience indicates. She remembers cases where top barristers have been paid HK$150,000 for a day in court (Sharon Melloy, personal communication).

[43] A 1999 survey found those Associates in Hong Kong charge between US$275 to US$400 an hour. 'That is 25% to 45% more than their peers in Japan, who charge US$150 to US$300 an hour. Associates in London charge US$250 to US$350 an hour, while those in New York charge US$150 to US$350.' See Cris Prystay, 'Price of Justice?' *The Asian Wall Street Journal*, 22–28 February 1999. For a detailed and up-to-date analysis of this issue, including 'hard' evidence of actual fees paid out in recent years, see *Interim Report and Consultative Paper of Chief Justice Working Party on Civil Justice Reform*, Hong Kong SAR (2002), at pp 17–36. Also available at *http://www.civiljustice.gov.hk*.

[44] The court's power to secure the 'just, expeditious and economical disposal' of a case was highlighted by Justice Henry Litton NPJ in an article where he argues that lawyers should bear responsibility over wasted costs. He notes that the court has power under the Rules of the High Court to ask the parties' representatives to estimate the costs involved before the court makes any interlocutory order. He also called upon the judges to be more proactive in ensuring that trials are not unduly prolonged. See Henry Litton, 'Old Wine in New Bottles: Civil Justice Reform in Hong Kong' (2000) 30 *Hong Kong Law Journal* 351. More recently, another judge has also strongly criticised personal injury litigation lawyers and called for an overhaul of the system. See Conrad Seagroatt, 'Reform and Reformation: A Personal Critical View of Personal Injury Litigation' (2002) 31 *Hong Kong Law Journal* 351. These and other related issues are now under consideration by the Chief Justice Working Party on Civil Justice Reform cited above at note 43.

[45] [1997] 3 HKC 43.

[46] [1997] 1 HKC 484.

[47] In appropriate cases, the Legal Aid Department recovers its costs from the amount awarded to the other spouse who is mainly the wife.

were granted to applicants in matrimonial cases.[48] Furthermore, between 1999 and 2000, the expenditure for civil cases by the Legal Aid Department on civil cases was about HK$489 million and 38% of the total expenditure (ie about HK$186 million) was on matrimonial cases.[49] It can be inferred from these figures, therefore, that where a large number of people caught up in matrimonial proceedings are also in need of legal aid, it is in the end the taxpayer who pays at least the larger portion of the bill.[50] Thus, in what might be regarded as a form of 'damage control', the Legal Aid Department has now introduced a system of fixed costs in matrimonial proceedings whereby solicitors are encouraged to elect in advance for a fixed rate fee.[51] It is also being mooted that the introduction of a system of contingent fees might somewhat ease the legal aid bill as well as assist unrepresented litigants.[52]

In the meantime, some 'do-it-yourself' divorce kits costing as little as HK$340 are being proffered, and at least one law firm has advertised a fixed fee of only HK$1,997 for simpler matrimonial cases.[53] And couples intending to divorce can now obtain application forms from the Family Court Registry at a fee of HK$685,[54] and may represent themselves, especially where the divorce is uncontested. As numbers of unrepresented litigants in civil proceedings keep rising, the adversarial system has predictably come under increasing strain, often leading to the slowing down of the entire judicial process.[55]

The cost of litigation is also aggravated by the use of civil procedural tools not primarily intended for matrimonial litigation. A good example is the use of *Anton Piller* orders[56] and *Mareva* injunctions[57] in matrimonial proceedings. In

---

[48] See *http://www.info.gov.hk/lad/eng/ginfo/statistics.htm*. A total of 5,445 matrimonial cases applications were successful.

[49] See *http://www.info.gov.hk/lad/eng/pub/report.htm*. In 1998–1999, the Legal Aid Department spent HK$138.9 million on matrimonial cases, 34% of the total expenditure of HK$408.5 million.

[50] '[F]or every two couples getting married, another gets divorced. Census and Statistical Department figures show 39,474 people were married for the first time in 1990. That figure dropped to 27,040 in 1999. During the same period, the number of divorces increased significantly to 13,408 from 5,551.' See Ella Lee, 'Family Crisis: Divorce rates are increasing, more people are having affairs and domestic violence on the rise' *Sunday Morning Post*, 19 August 2001, at p 9.

[51] See also the District Court (Fixed Costs in Matrimonial Causes) (Amendment) Rules 2000, LN 52 of 2000. These rules provide for fixed costs payable for a wide range of matrimonial work done by solicitors in the District Court. However, until last year when the Legal Aid Department became interested in the fixed costs option, few solicitors were opting for it. Under the current arrangement, solicitors instructed by the Legal Aid Department are encouraged to opt for fixed costs in all matrimonial matters and it seems that many are now taking this option.

[52] See Jane Moir, 'Law Officials to study "no win, no fee" system' SCMP, 21 February 2002, p 1.

[53] Kym Leo, 'Splitting the costs', *South China Morning Post*, 22 October 2000, p 4. The exchange rate for the Hong Kong dollar is approximately US$1 to HK$7.74.

[54] See Matrimonial Causes (Fees) (Amendment) Rules 2000.

[55] Recent statistics show that unrepresented litigants in the High Court account for slightly more than 40% of the total. See the Report of the Chief Justice's Working Party on Civil Justice Reform, at pp 54–70 (op cit at note 43). An early response by the Chief Justice is the establishment of a resource centre for unrepresented litigants in the High Court and District Court to assist such litigants in the preparation of their cases. See Chief Justice's Address at the Opening of the Legal Year, 15 January 2002, para 19.

[56] Named after the English Court of Appeal decision in *Anton Piller KG v Manufacturing Processes Ltd* [1976] Ch 55. See also D B Casson and I H Dennis, *Odgers' Principles of Pleading and Practice in Civil Actions in the High Court of Justice* (Stevens & Sons, 22nd edn, 1981) at 63–65.

Overholt v Overholt,[58] it had been informally agreed between the parties that the wife could keep all the family photographs while the husband could have access to them for purposes of copying and would return them to the wife within three months of receipt. The husband, however, suspected that the wife had not delivered all the photographs to him for copying. He applied successfully for an ex parte *Anton Piller* order to search the wife's home for the missing photographs. The search was done and a total of 8,000 articles were seized but the husband was still not satisfied. He wanted to conduct another *Anton Piller* raid, which the wife strongly opposed and applied for the discharge of the original order. In discharging the order, Sakhrani J expressed the view that an *Anton Piller* order was a rare weapon to be used only in 'extreme and exceptional cases', and least of all, in family proceedings.[59] In *Tan Li Hui Cheng v Tan Kian Chee*,[60] Le Pichon J expressed the view that an ordinary *Mareva* injunction was different from an injunction obtained under s 17 (MPPO) or under the court's inherent jurisdiction. For example, in matrimonial proceedings it was not necessary, unless the court demanded it, for the petitioner to give an undertaking in damages.[61] Nor is there a requirement that an applicant put all facts material to the substantive application before the court because that would defeat the purpose intended to be served.[62] In short, the use of certain tools in civil practice might impose constraints or burdens on the applicant when such difficulties could be avoided by making the appropriate application.[63] It has also been noted that lawyers who are experienced in general civil litigation are more likely to invoke such procedural tools than matrimonial lawyers.[64]

Judges have also adversely commented on extensive forms of discovery in ancillary relief proceedings as being oppressive to the other party and sometimes amounting to an invasion of personal privacy. Thus, in *Y v C*,[65] the Court of

---

[57]   Named after *Mareva Compania Naviera SA v International Bulkcarriers SA* [1975] 2 Lloyd's Rep 509, [1980] 1 All ER 213, CA, where Lord Denning granted an injunction to restrain the charterer from disposing of its money held in a London bank until the court had ruled on a claim made against it by a ship owner. For more details on the use of *Mareva* injunctions, see D B Casson and I H Dennis, *Odgers' Principles of Pleading and Practice in Civil Actions in the High Court of Justice* (Stevens & Sons, 22nd edn, 1981) at 59–63.

[58]   [1999] 2 HKLRD 445.

[59]   Much of what has been said by experienced judges about *Anton Piller* orders suggests that it is a rare weapon in the court's armoury that ought to be used very sparingly indeed. And when a party seeks to use it in matrimonial litigation, the court should be suspicious and should not grant it unless it is absolutely necessary and where no other court process can achieve the ends of justice. There must also be adequate safeguards to ensure the absence of humiliation and distress that such invasion of privacy entails. See *Tamco Electrical & Electronics (Hong Kong) Ltd v Stephen Ng Chun fai* [1994] 1 HKLR 178 and *Lock International Plc v Beswick* [1989] 1 WLR 1268.

[60]   [1997] 4 HKC 95.

[61]   Relying on *Will v Will* [1993] 2 HKLR 398, at 405.

[62]   At p 106B.

[63]   In the words of Le Pichon J, 'In deciding whether to exercise its inherent jurisdiction, the court is not required to have regard to many restrictions and safeguards surrounding the use of worldwide *Mareva* injunctions and to assimilate the use of and procedure for injunctions in the Family Division to those in commercial law. In *Shipman* [*v Shipman* [1991] 1 FLR 250] the learned judge held that the matrimonial field called for a different approach. I respectfully agree.' See *Tan Li Hui Cheng v Tan Kian Chee* [1997] 4 HKC 94 at 104C–D.

[64]   Sharon Melloy, personal communication.

[65]   CACV No 254 of 2000.

Appeal referred to the 'breathtaking' degree of disclosure, adding that it was a waste of time, a waste of expense, and a waste of paper.[66] The Court of Appeal has also commented on the length and costs incurred in ancillary proceedings, noting that discovery had often been unjustifiably lengthy, detailed, complicated and expensive.[67] Therefore, although it is not disputed that a lawyer must put the interests of his or her client first, there seem to be cases where the adversarial system seems to run wild leaving the judges helplessly watching and seemingly unable to stop the train.[68] This phenomenon is perhaps best summed up by Mortimer V-P's critical remarks in *K v K*,[69] where he stated that:

> '[I]t is well known that ancillary proceedings take too long and are expensive. Often too great a detail is gone into. Too much time and expense is involved. This Court has said as much on previous occasions.'[70]

One of the measures taken recently and widely viewed as a more concrete response, and one that will hopefully have long-term impact, is the introduction of a court-annexed mediation. At the initiative of the Chief Justice Andrew Li, a three-year pilot scheme on family mediation began in the year 2000 and has been running well under the careful monitoring of the judiciary and the legal profession. Also a program for the training of family mediators is under way. If successful, court-annexed mediation will become a new feature of Hong Kong family law. It is expected that mediation will not only alleviate some of the problems associated with high costs of litigation but will also address other shortcomings that are widely blamed on the adversarial system in family litigation.[71] Furthermore, in February 2000 a Working Party on Civil Justice Reform, established by the Chief Justice 'to review the civil rules and procedures of the High Court and to recommend changes thereto with a view to ensuring and

---

[66] At p 6 of judgment.

[67] *K v K*, Court of Appeal Civil Case Nos 253 and 277 of 1998 (decided on 23 February 1999).

[68] In *Y v C* (CACV No 254 of 2000) the Court of Appeal noted that in the 'Court below the cross-examination of the respondent appears to have been both exhaustive and exhausting. At the end of the fourth day of the cross-examination, the judge had to remind Counsel that he should not be repetitive. The judge warned Mr Lam that it might be necessary to curtail his cross-examination. Such warning appears to have been amply justified and, if we might say so as a matter of encouragement and not criticism of a judge who was obviously bending over backward to be fair throughout, somewhat overdue. Despite that cross-examination continued, in total there were 5 days of cross-examination in a case where the relevant facts could surely have been brought to light far more quickly' (at pp 6–7 of judgment). In 1989 the Law Reform Commission recommended that 'procedures at the Family Court be streamlined and that there be continuous monitoring of the system by effective case management'. See Sub-Committee on Guardianship and Custody Consultation Paper, The Law Reform Commission of Hong Kong, December 1998, para 15.89 at 339. A recent amendment to the Matrimonial Causes (Amendment) Rules 2001 seeks to reduce costs by simplifying procedures and reducing the time spent on hearing undefended divorces and judicial separation which previously could not be entered in the special procedure list.

[69] [1998] 1 HKLRD 32.

[70] Ibid, at p 3 of judgment. But then, some would argue that in the absence of tight case management the lawyer has to strike a balance between avoiding wasted costs and being sued by the client on account of leaving some stones unturned.

[71] Ibid. For comment on the background leading to the introduction of the family mediation pilot scheme, see B Rwezaura, 'Hong Kong Family Law in the Last Decade of British Rule' in R Wacks (ed), *The New Legal Order in Hong Kong* (1999), 563–594, at 591.

improving access to justice at reasonable cost and speed was established'.[72] It is expected that the Working Party will begin public consultations in September 2001.

V   SHARING THE FAMILY CAKE: THE ROLE OF THE COURTS

It is now widely agreed that the liberalization of divorce in many jurisdictions, including Hong Kong, has shifted the focus of litigation away from a fight over who gets the divorce to a battle over who gets the property and the children. In the words of Lord Nicholls of Birkenhead, divorce always raises the question as to 'how the property of the husband and wife should be divided and whether one of them should continue to support the other'.[73] In Hong Kong, as in many other jurisdictions, this important question is reserved for the courts to decide, applying s 7 of the Matrimonial Proceedings and Property Ordinance (MPPO) (Cap 192).[74] Although s 7 (MPPO) provides a list of guidelines to assist the court in allocating family assets, courts still have wide discretion. Therefore, the most important question examined in this section is how courts have exercised their statutory power during the last four years.

In *Kam Leung Kit Yee v Kam Ying Fai*,[75] the Court of Appeal upheld the decision of the family court ordering the former wife to transfer to her former husband her 50% interest in the flat constituting the matrimonial home. In addition the husband was ordered to pay to the wife a lump sum of HK$90,000. The wife's main ground of appeal was that the family court had erred in failing to recognise and to put into account the potential rise in the value of the flat when the non-alienation restriction under the Home Ownership Scheme expired six months after the hearing.[76] It was argued for the wife that the court ought to have adjourned the ancillary relief proceedings for at least six months at which time the market value of the flat would be established. The Court of Appeal unanimously held, dismissing the appeal, that the family court judge had meticulously balanced the interests of both parties in a fair and equitable manner. It was also held that the judge was entitled to rely on all the relevant information put by the parties before the court. Moreover, given that both parties had agreed to the valuation of the flat and no application for adjournment had been made, it was not open to the appellant wife to challenge the way the court had exercised its discretion. The Court of Appeal also took the view that parties had the duty to provide to the court all relevant information concerning all the circumstances of the case including any matters specified in the claim.[77] In the absence of such information, the court

---

[72]   See the Chief Justice's Address at the Opening of the Legal Year, 15 January 2001, para 19, also at p 1 of the Working Party's Interim Report and Consultative Paper (cited at note 41).

[73]   *White v White* [2000] 2 FLR 981 at 983, per Lord Nicholls of Birkenhead.

[74]   Based on s 25 of the English Matrimonial Causes Act 1973.

[75]   [1997] 1 HKC 385.

[76]   Families may purchase a flat for residential purposes under the Home Ownership Scheme at a subsidised price from the Housing Authority. This is on condition that the flat may not be sold or alienated before the expiry of 10 years. After 10 years, the restriction is removed and this usually has the effect of raising the market value of the property.

[77]   Relying on *Jenkins v Livesey* [1985] 1 AC 424 at 436H–437A per Lord Brandon of Oakbrook.

would be entitled to base its discretion on the material available before it. There is no hard and fast rule on how the court should exercise its discretion under s 7 (MPPO). The court has the power to decide on a case-by-case basis to achieve fairness between parties and in this case the family judge had exercised his discretion correctly.[78]

This decision underscores the principle that an appellate court will rarely interfere with the discretionary powers of a lower court unless its decision is irrational or plainly wrong. The Court of Appeal stressed that the seven factors in s 7 (MPPO) are part of the overall circumstances the judge has to take into account in distributing family assets and these factors are merely the judge's 'tools but not his masters'.[79] This case also stresses the principle of civil procedure that 'whoever alleges must prove'. It is also bad news for those claimants, as noted above, who are forced to represent themselves for lack of money.[80] Such litigants are unlikely to know precisely what evidence to bring to the court in order to achieve a favourable outcome.

The Court of Appeal decision in *Y v C*[81] sheds additional light on the application of s 7 (MPPO) and the importance of 'conduct of parties' as one of the factors the court has to consider. The wife in this case applied for variation of a consent order made in 1984 awarding her nominal maintenance in the sum of HK$1 per annum. At the time of divorce in 1984, the incomes of both parties were relatively the same. In 1984, at the age of 53 years, and in relatively good health, the wife decided to retire and was paid HK$1.2 million from the provident fund. She gave away most of her pension money to her relatives who in turn lost it in their own business ventures. The husband also retired later in 1987 at the age of 57 and was paid HK$600,000 which he invested in what later became a successful business. As the court noted, the husband started his business ventures 7 years after the parties separated and 3 years after their divorce. It is in the light of this background that the wife applied for a lump sum of HK$1.8 million and in the alternative, maintenance at a monthly rate of HK$10,000 until her death.

Although the family court rejected the wife's application for a lump sum payment, it made an order in her favour for maintenance at HK$10,000 per month for two years. This order was approved by the Court of Appeal, which dismissed the wife's appeal, holding that the family judge had correctly exercised his discretion. The factors put into account by the judge include the fact that:

(i) the husband had paid his former wife a total sum of HK$252,000 in compliance with the court's interim maintenance order;

---

[78] The court considered the fact that the husband had been living in that flat for ten years and needed a roof over his head. The wife was already living with another man with whom she had jointly bought a flat worth HK$1.4 million and whom she planned to marry. The view taken by the family judge was that it would be unfair to take away the husband's accommodation or to deny him the benefit of a rising property market when the wife already had a home in which she owned a 50% interest and which was also liable to appreciate in value. The wife also ran a magazine business with a loan from her close relatives and this, in the court's view, provided her with a steady income.

[79] Per Liu JA at p 390E–F.

[80] See *Yip Ku v Kwan Kuk Lin* [1997] 1 HKC 484.

[81] CACV No 254 of 2000.

(ii)   the wife had been imprudent and incompetent in the way she managed her provident fund payment of HK$1.2 million;

(iii)   the wife had lived on her own for 16 years after the marriage in circumstances where it might be reasonably supposed that she could maintain herself;

(iv)   the wife was in reasonably in good health and, as a retired teacher, she could continue to support herself by working part time. Moreover, had she not made a choice to retire early instead of working, she could have boosted her provident fund payment; and

(v)   the husband's newly acquired wealth had been made entirely after the divorce and the former wife had not played any role in its acquisition.

This decision sheds further light on the application of s 7 (MPPO). First, the appellate court will not interfere with the exercise of discretion under s 7 (MPPO) even if the appellate court would have come to a different decision. It will interfere only where the exercise of discretion exceeds the generous ambit within which reasonable disagreement is possible between reasonable people; or where the decision is plainly wrong.[82] Secondly, the decision places due weight on the 'conduct' of the two parties. In this connection, the judge thought it was not fair to order the husband to pay money to a former wife who had been imprudent with her own money. Moreover, this was a former husband who had continued working until he was 57 years old and whose own provident fund money was a mere 50% of what the wife had been paid. Furthermore, the husband had cared for the two sons of the marriage without any help from his former wife. Indeed, as the Court of Appeal reasoned, the trial judge had been too generous to the wife in awarding her monthly maintenance of HK$10,000 for two years. Even then the Court of Appeal did not disturb this order. One might argue that this was an appropriate case for ordering a 'clean break' in 1984 at the time when the marriage was dissolved.

In the meantime, news of the House of Lords decision in *White v White*[83] has reached Hong Kong, with one family court judge confirming that the decision should be followed in Hong Kong.[84] A 'big money' case currently pending in the High Court and reported to involve over HK$5 billion is set to test the waters as well as the extent to which *White v White* will be followed in Hong Kong.[85] Furthermore, preparations for the launching, in July 2002, of a pilot scheme on financial dispute resolution (FDR) is underway. The pilot scheme follows closely a similar scheme introduced in England by the Family Proceedings (Amendment No 2) Rules 1999.[86]

---

[82]   Relying on Lord Justice Asquith's dictum in *Bellenden (formerly Satterthwaite) v Satterthwaite* [1948] 1 All ER 343, at 345 and quoted in *G v G (Minors: Custody Appeal)* [1985] 1 WLR 647, at 651–652.

[83]   [2000] 2 FLR 981.

[84]   See HH Judge Saunders, 'The Impact of *White v White*', paper presented at Continuing Professional Development Course (CPD), Law Society of Hong Kong, 12 November 2001, at p 6.

[85]   See Sherry Lee, 'Do you take this contract?', SCMP, 19 February 2002, at (Features) p 1.

[86]   See Report of the Working Group to consider the reform of ancillary relief procedures. For a comment on the English scheme, see District Judge M Gerlis, 'Ancillary Relief – Progress or Decline?' [2001] Fam Law 891.

VI   THE RIGHT TO WASH ONE'S DIRTY LINEN IN OPEN COURT

The right to wash one's dirty linen in open court was the subject of an application to the High Court in 1999. The petitioner, a husband, applied to the court for a public hearing of his application for ancillary relief.[87] This was a complex case estimated to take eight weeks of hearing. The petitioner, who was previously represented by counsel, was now appearing in person as he had run out of money and his application for advance payment from his share of the family assets had been denied.[88] Waung J allowed the application for an open court hearing on two grounds. First, no regulations had been made under the MPPO directing the court to hear the trial of ancillary relief in chambers. Secondly, even if the rules exist, the trial judge had discretion under rule 81(2) of the Matrimonial Proceedings Rules (MPR) (Cap 179, Sub Leg) to hear ancillary relief either in chambers or in open court.

In exercising his discretion, Waung J also paid attention to Art 10 of the Bill of Rights Ordinance (Cap 383) which makes provision for the public hearing of cases.[89] He rejected argument by Counsel for the wife who strongly opposed the application, arguing that it was unprecedented for ancillary relief applications to be heard in open court. Counsel also revealed that the hearing would introduce evidence dealing with intensely personal and private issues that should not be revealed in open court.[90] In rejecting Counsel's submission, the trial judge commented that 'the matrimonial jurisdiction of Hong Kong has lived far too long in a world which is not in accordance with the fundamental principle of open and public justice and it [was] time for major changes to take place.'[91]

On appeal by the wife, the Court of Appeal disagreed with the trial court holding that regulations did exist under the MPPO directing the court to conduct the trial of ancillary relief in chambers with discretion to hold an open court hearing where appropriate. In the words of Rogers JA, 'there can be no doubt ... that rule 81 (MPR) must also derive its authority from the MPPO'. Concerning whether the trial judge had correctly exercised his discretion under rule 81(2) of the MPR not to hear ancillary relief in chambers, the Court of Appeal also held that the trial judge had wrongly exercised his discretion. According to Mortimer V-P, the trial judge had based his decision on irrelevant considerations. He had gone beyond the particular case before him. He had failed to put into account the strong submission of Counsel for the wife. And there 'were no features of it sufficiently relevant and unusual upon which he could rely'.[92] Rogers JA also expressed the view that:

---

87 See *Y v K* [1999] 3 HKLRD 650.

88 See *Yip Ku v Kwan Kuk Lin* [1997] 1 HKC 484.

89 Based on Art 14(1) of the International Covenant on Civil and Political Rights (ICCPR).

90 The evidence included 'the petitioner's black market activities in China, the parties' humble start in Hong Kong, the gambling activities of the parties, the adultery of the petitioner and the incident with a Filipina maid, the allegations of forgery, the question of tax evasion and tax investigation, matters relating to the trusts and allegations against third parties in connection with the trust and many other factors which should point to the wisdom of holding the trial in chambers' at p 656.

91 At p 656.

92 At p 565.

'the need for the applications for ancillary relief to be heard in chambers far outweighs any of the other considerations which have been aired and have been put to us by the petitioner. The factors which the petitioner has put before us today do not show that there is any public interest in having the parties' private affairs ventilated in public. Justice is far more likely to be achieved if the proceedings are in chambers.'[93]

The boundaries of open justice in ancillary proceedings have also been recently tested at the European Court of Human Rights.[94] In an action filed by two fathers against the United Kingdom, the European Court held that 'the denial of a hearing and pronouncement of judgment in public in child custody proceedings did not violate the right to a fair trial as guaranteed by Article 6 of the European Convention of Human Rights'.[95] The European Court, in language resonating that of the Hong Kong Court of Appeal, stated that custody proceedings were prime examples of cases where the exclusion of the press and public might be justified in order to protect the privacy of the child and parties and to avoid prejudicing the interests of justice. The court stressed that 'it was essential that the parents and other witnesses felt able to express themselves candidly on highly personal issues without fear of public curiosity or comment'.[96] Putting aside the question of open justice, it should be noted also that accessibility of court judgments in matrimonial proceedings continues to be a problem in Hong Kong. Only those judgments that are considered worthy of reporting by individual judges and with the consent of the parties involved are accessible to the public for inspection and possible photocopying at the High Court Library. This means that a large number of matrimonial decisions are inaccessible to the public, the legal profession and the academics. It remains to be seen whether the English Court of Appeal decision in *Clibbery v Allan* will generate sufficient interest to trigger any changes in this area of the law.

VII RECENT AND PROPOSED LEGISLATION

Recent statutory changes and proposed legislation could be grouped roughly into three main categories. The first relates to reform proposals to the law of child

---

[93]   At p 659.

[94]   See *B v United Kingdom & P v United Kingdom* (Application Nos 36337/97 and 35974/97) (2001) *The Times*, May 15.

[95]   At p 565. Article 6 states in effect that everyone is entitled to a fair and public hearing in all cases, civil and criminal, and that the court's judgements shall be pronounced publicly. Restriction of this right is permitted 'in the interests of morals, public order or national security in a democratic society, where the interests of juveniles or the protection of the private life of the parties so require, or to the extent strictly necessary in the opinion of the court in special circumstances where publicity would prejudice the interests of justice'.

[96]   At p 4. Yet the question of confidentiality in matrimonial proceedings (except where children are involved) has been thrown into doubt in a recent decision of the English High Court Family Division, in *Clibbery v Allan & Anor* [2001] All ER (D) 182. More recently, an appeal against this decision to the Court of Appeal ([2001] EWCA Civ 45, [2002] 1 FLR 565) has been dismissed, with the court holding that 'there should no longer be an automatic presumption that information disclosed in divorce related wrangles should remain a secret'. See 'Judge supports right of lover to reveal her story' (2002) *The Times*, 31 January. For a comment on *Clibbery,* see Peter Watson-Lee, 'When clients spill the beans' *Gazette* 98/28, 12 July 2001, at 16, and David Burrows, 'Confidentiality of Family Proceedings' *Gazette* 98/28, 12 July 2001.

custody, guardianship, adoption and child protection. The second seeks to make it clear that a husband may be guilty of an offence of rape against his wife. The third is an amendment to the existing system of attachment of income orders. Finally, the recent establishment of the Women's Commission may be seen as further indication that women's rights issues continue to attract interest in the community.

A Reform of child law

In December 1998, the Law Reform Commission Sub-Committee on Guardianship and Custody published a Consultation Paper outlining proposals for reform of the law of child custody and guardianship. The proposals are intended to bring the law up to date and to comply with certain provisions of the United Nations Convention on the Rights of the Child (CRC) to which Hong Kong became a party in 1994. The term 'custody' is to be replaced with terminology comparable to s 8 orders under the English Children Act 1989. It is also proposed that a 'checklist' should be enacted to give guidance to the courts in allocating parental responsibility over minor children.

The voice of the child is to be heard in all proceedings concerning children and the term 'best interest' is to replace 'welfare' of the child, on the ground that the former terminology is more appropriate for Hong Kong conditions and also mirrors Art 3 of the CRC. The common law principle that a father is a natural guardian of his legitimate children is to be abolished and the term 'guardian' is now to be confined to persons other than the parents appointed to discharge parental responsibility. The term 'parental responsibility' is also preferred and recommended as being consistent with the proposed concept of best interests of the child. These recommendations together with a few proposed changes in the law of child adoption are still under consideration and will be the subject of a future *Survey* article after their enactment.[97]

Other proposed legislation is the Prevention of Child Pornography Bill (2000) which seeks to prohibit the production, possession and proliferation of child pornography. The term 'child pornography' is defined to mean a film, photograph, publication, computer-generated image, or picture that indecently depicts a person who is, or looks like, a person under the age of 16 and includes data stored on a computer disc or by other electronic means which is capable of conversion into such a film, photograph, publication, image or picture. It is an offence for any person to print, make, produce, reproduce, copy, publish or import, distribute or show any child pornography. Anyone who employs a person under the age of 16 for the purposes of making child pornography also commits an offence under this law.[98]

The Law Reform Commission has also recommended the raising of the age of criminal responsibility from the current age of 7 years to 10 years. This follows

---

[97] At which time recent court decisions on the law of the child, not covered in this edition of the *Survey*, will also be discussed.

[98] *http://legco.gov.hk/yr98-99/english/bills/c176_e.htm*. This will amend s 21 of the Control of Obscene and Indecent Articles Act, Cap 390. Penalties for offences under this law range from a fine of HK$2 million and 8 years' imprisonment (on conviction upon indictment) to HK$.0.5 million and 2 years' imprisonment (on summary conviction).

persistent calls from children's rights groups and others that Hong Kong's age of criminal responsibility is very low in comparison to other jurisdictions. Furthermore, it has been recommended that the presumption of *doli incapax* should be retained, except that this presumption should reflect the revised minimum age of criminal responsibility and be applied to children between the ages of 10 and 14 years.[99]

B   Criminal liability for marital rape

In 1999 and again in 2000 the United Nations Committee on the Elimination of Discrimination Against Women expressed concern that marital rape was not considered an offence in Hong Kong. Similar concerns have been voiced within the Hong Kong community.[100] It is now proposed to amend the Crimes Ordinance (Cap 200) to make it abundantly clear that a husband is liable to commit the offence of rape if he has sexual intercourse with his wife without her consent. The proposed change follows a landmark decision of the House of Lords in *R v R (Rape: Marital Exemption)*[101] and the subsequent repeal of s 1(1) of the English Sexual Offences (Amendment) Act 1976 by the Criminal Justice and Public Order Act 1994. Further ancillary amendments are to be made to s 124(2) of the Crimes Ordinance to make it clear that the defence under the latter section does not apply to non-consensual intercourse. Under s 124(2) it is a defence for a man to have unlawful sexual intercourse with a girl under 16 years if he has reasonable ground to believe that the woman is his wife notwithstanding the invalidity of the marriage. Section 146(3) of the Crimes Ordinance will also be amended to make it plain that the defence under this section does not apply to non-consensual acts of gross indecency with or towards a child under 16 years even if the person charged reasonably believed that he or she was married to that child.[102]

C   Attachment of income orders

In June 1997 three pieces of legislation were amended to empower the court to order attachment of income orders (AIOs) against maintenance payment defaulters.[103] The court had jurisdiction to order attachment of income if satisfied

---

[99] In accordance with the presumption of *doli incapax*, the law presumes that a child between the ages of 7 and 14 years is incapable of committing a crime, unless the prosecution proves beyond reasonable doubt that, at the time of the offence, the child was well aware that his or her act was seriously wrong, and not merely naughty or mischievous.

[100] See B Rwezaura, 'Hong Kong Family Law in the Last Decade of British Rule' in R Wacks (ed), *The New Legal Order in Hong Kong* (1999), 563–594, at p 568.

[101] [1991] 3 WLR 767.

[102] See *Discussion Paper on Proposed amendment to the Crimes Ordinance (Cap 200) Marital Rape and related sexual offences*, Department of Justice, 21 March 2001, p 8. For a detailed comment on this proposal, see Robyn Emerton 'Marital Rape and Related Sexual Offences: A Review of the Proposed Amendments to Part XII of the Crimes Ordinance' (2002) 31 *Hong Kong Law Journal* 415.

[103] See s 20 of the Guardianship of Minors Ordinance (Cap 13); s 28 of the Matrimonial Proceedings and Property Ordinance (Cap 192); and s 9A of the Separation and Maintenance Orders Ordinance (Cap 16). As amended by ss 6,14, and 30 of the Marriage and Children (Miscellaneous Amendment) Ordinance 1997, No 69 of 1997.

that the payer had failed to pay 'without reasonable excuse'.[104] It was then hoped that such a change in the law would ease the problems of enforcing maintenance orders faced mainly by former wives and their children. Unfortunately, the new system did not become popular as originally anticipated. Parties and their solicitors remained attracted to the more expensive system of collecting maintenance by judgment summons.[105] The new Bill now seeks to relax restrictions imposed upon the 1997 AIO scheme by giving the court flexibility in applying the relevant legal procedures. Under the proposed AIO scheme, the court may make an AIO upon the agreement of the parties. Alternatively, the court may also make a pre-emptive attachment of income order if it has reasonable grounds to believe that the maintenance payer will not make full and punctual payment in compliance with a maintenance order.[106]

D   The new Women's Commission

The year 2001 began with the formation of the 21 member Women's Commission charged with the 'mission' of assisting Hong Kong women to 'fully realise their due status, rights and opportunities in all aspects of life'.[107] Among its tasks, the Commission is to advise the Government on the development of a long-term vision and strategies related to the development and advancement of women; on the integration of policies and initiatives which are of concern to women, which fall under the purview of different Policy Bureaux; to keep under review, in the light of women's needs, services delivered within and outside the Government and to identify priority areas for action, and monitor the development of new or improved services; to initiate and undertake independent surveys and research studies on women's issues and organise educational and promotional activities; and to develop and maintain contact with local and international women's groups and service agencies with a view to sharing experiences and improving communication and understanding.[108] Although it is too early to make any meaningful evaluation of the Commission's work, it should be noted that its creation appears to have generated considerable enthusiasm in the Hong Kong community, especially among women's groups. It is very much hoped, therefore, that the Government under whose umbrella the Commission now operates, will give it full support as well as a high degree of autonomy so that it can effectively and vigorously perform its tasks.

---

[104]   See B Rwezaura, 'Hong Kong: Hong Kong Family Law and the 1997 Countdown', in A Bainham (ed), *The International Survey of Family Law 1996* (Martinus Nijhoff Publishers, 1998), 186–213, at pp 204–205.

[105]   See *Gray v Gray* [2001] 1 HKC 148.

[106]   See Attachment of Income Orders (Amendment) Ordinance, No 20 of 2001.

[107]   See 'Women's Commission to hold Public Forum on Future Direction of Work', Press Release, 10 May 2001.

[108]   Summary of Mission Statement from the website of the Women's Commission, at *http://www.women.gov.hk/women/eng/about.htm.*

VIII CONCLUSION

This survey has highlighted some of the major developments of Hong Kong family law during the last four years. The plural heritage of the law has been stressed showing the continuing influence and dominance of English common law and its interaction with Chinese culture and Chinese customary law. Hong Kong's proximity to the motherland has continued to play an important role in the development of Hong Kong family law. Cross-border issues relating to split families and the impact of the so-called 'mainland mistresses' and their children on Hong Kong society remain unresolved. They will continue to generate pressure on public policy with some making their way into the court system.

Hong Kong liberalized its divorce law in 1995 making it relatively easy for couples to obtain a decree of divorce. However, it is now apparent that litigation has shifted to post-divorce adjustment, especially issues of family property and maintenance. Hence, what lawyers habitually call *ancillary relief* is truly the central feature of family litigation today.[109] Such family litigation continues to claim a lion's share of family savings as well as carving out a large share of the legal aid fund. It is now widely agreed that the high cost of litigation is closely related to the archaic system of civil justice whose reform is now under consideration. Until then some remedial measures being taken include better case management, an option for fixed costs, and persistent calls and lamentation from the bench urging counsel to be more cost-conscious and to save trees. It is very much hoped that the family mediation project, now under way, will ease some of the problems noted above. Finally, international human rights standards have continued to provide the ethical framework as well as the stimulus for the development of Hong Kong family law.[110] Today Hong Kong law reform draws inspiration, not only from Britain, the former colonial power, but also from some of its neighbours, including the older common law jurisdictions of Australia, Canada and New Zealand. This trend is also set to continue in the coming years.

---

[109] The term is defined under Rule 2 of the Matrimonial Causes Rules, Cap 179, to cover a range of orders mainly dealing with financial provisions after the granting of the decrees of separation, nullity of marriage or divorce.

[110] See B Rwezaura, 'Recent Developments in Hong Kong Family Law: The Impact of Human Rights Treaties' in Alice Lee (ed) *1998 Law Lectures for Practitioners* (Hong Kong Law Journal Ltd, Hong Kong, 1998), pp 141–165.

ITALY

RECENT CHANGES IN THE JUDGE-MADE LAW OF SEPARATION AND DIVORCE AND PERSPECTIVES ON LAW REFORM

*Leonardo Lenti**

I   THE ITALIAN DIVORCE SYSTEM

The Italian divorce system differs from the majority of systems in place in Europe in a few respects. The Italian system includes both the personal separation of husband and wife, and divorce: the first does not dissolve the marriage and does not therefore permit the spouses to re-marry, whilst the second dissolves the marriage definitively, leaving the spouses free to re-marry.

Separation, according to Italian law, originates from the *separatio quoad thorum et mensam* of canon law. For a long period of time, separation represented the 'divorce of Catholics', as commonly asserted by Italian and French jurists in the nineteenth century, and it was the only legal solution that enabled husband and wife to break off conjugal cohabitation without clashing with the Catholic principle of the indissolubility of marriage.[1]

With the introduction of divorce into Italian law in 1970, separation took on a very different role: from the 'divorce of Catholics' to becoming the first stage of the divorce procedure.

According to statute no 898, which was passed in 1970, divorce can be granted for a number of causes, amongst which is legal separation, which must be ruled upon by a judge and last for at least three consecutive years, without any interruption. A glance at judicial statistics shows the importance of separation. In fact, separation is the single statistically relevant cause for divorce: more than 98% of divorces are granted on the basis of an uninterrupted 3-year separation.[2] All other grounds for divorce account for just over 1% of all cases.[3] This legal system has resulted in separation becoming not only the first stage of the divorce procedure, but in nearly all cases it has become *an almost unavoidable step* in obtaining the divorce ruling.

---

[*]   Professor of Private Law, Faculty of Law, University of Turin.

[1]   On a strictly formal level, this principle was not affected by the rules governing the invalidity of marriage, applied by ecclesiastical courts.

[2]   Istat, *Statistiche giudiziarie civili*, year 1992 and year 1993, table 4.15; year 1994, table 4.16; year 1995 and year 1996, table 4.17.

[3]   The other main grounds for divorce are the invalidity of a marriage obtained in a foreign country by a spouse with foreign citizenship, and one of the spouses having been convicted of a criminal offence with a particularly long sentence, or of criminal offences which are detrimental to family relationships.

Therefore, in nearly all cases, the dissolution of the marriage comes at the end of a lengthy legal procedure consisting of two separate stages: the stage of legal separation and the stage of divorce.

(a)   *Legal separation*: Legal separation can be ruled upon by a judge with the mutual consent of both spouses or at the request of one spouse only, notwithstanding opposition from the other, if cohabitation has become intolerable. In this second case, responsibility can be attributed to a spouse, if his or her conduct was in breach of conjugal duties. The imputation of responsibility has unfavourable consequences in relation to financial issues.

(b)   *Divorce*: After at least three consecutive years of separation, during which time the couple were not reconciled, the marriage can be dissolved, ie the divorce itself can be granted, leaving both partners free of conjugal bonds. The decree is granted by the judge on the request of both spouses by mutual consent, or on the request of either of the spouses, even that spouse who is found responsible for the separation,[4] and notwithstanding opposition from the other spouse.

Both stages of the legal procedure, the separation and the divorce itself, begin with a special hearing in which the judge attempts to reconcile the parties, meaning that the judge attempts to convince the parties to resume cohabitation.[5]

Italian legislators have therefore chosen to discourage divorce by means of procedural obstacles rather than substantive limits.[6]

In Italy, separation is of fundamental importance in dissolution of a marriage, and not just because it is during the legal proceedings for separation that an eventual dispute is most bitter and more psychologically traumatic.

In fact, in most cases and unless there are substantial changes in the circumstances, the legal provisions of the separation play a decisive role in the final decision regarding the future structure of the life of the divorcees. In particular, the decisions taken at the time of separation regarding custody of children and the right to live in the family home often remain unchanged and are therefore of a substantially definitive nature.

The decisions taken by the courts regarding the imputation of responsibility for separation represent an irreplaceable source of knowledge of living law regarding conjugal duties, a knowledge that cannot be found in divorce decrees. It is from the separation decrees that we can see how, during the past 30 years, the judge-made law has incorporated the changes that have occurred in socially accepted customs and values in terms of conjugal ethics.

---

[4]   On this point, see Court of Cassation, 10 June 1992, no 7148. The full text of all the judgments ruled by the Court of Cassation from 1986 onwards is available on the CD-Rom *Juris Data, Sentenze della Cassazione civile*, Giuffré, Milan and is updated annually. I will therefore avoid giving the place of publication of judgments referred to herein if they are reported in the above-mentioned CD-Rom.

[5]   In this sense, the attempt to reconcile the couple is a mere formality, particularly during proceedings for divorce. Although an attempt at judicial reconciliation does effectively take place during the procedure, its real aim is to encourage the parties to reach an agreement concerning the conditions for the separation or divorce.

[6]   Abortion was regulated in 1978 in a similar way: by procedural obstacles rather than substantive limits. The *Code Napoléon* of 1804 used the same system when regulating divorce by mutual consent.

For these reasons, separation is the most discussed, most studied and most problematic stage of the proceeding and is therefore the most interesting and significant moment of the legal procedure leading to divorce.

II   THE INTOLERABILITY OF COHABITATION

Article 151, para 1 of the civil code states the intolerability of cohabitation and serious damage to the children's upbringing as bases for separation. However, in the living law, that is judge-made law, the only real cause for separation is the intolerability of cohabitation, that is, the irretrievable breakdown of marriage.

Damage to the children's upbringing originates directly from canon law and is not present in the law of other European countries. It has no direct influence on judge-made law: I know of no judicial precedents in which a separation was recognised for this cause alone, in the declared absence of intolerability of cohabitation. In fact, the law offers other and far more effective means for safeguarding children against parental abuse, such as the provisions in Arts 330 and 333 of the civil code.

One can therefore state that the cause of separation is the intolerability of cohabitation, as results from the unanimous declaration by both parties or, failing this, as ascertained by the court.

The precise definition of 'intolerability of cohabitation' is the object of a distinct interpretative attitude both in the precedents in court and in scholarly debates.

The general and abstract interpretative issue under discussion is whether the intolerability of cohabitation should be assessed in *subjective* or *objective* terms.

According to the majority of scholars, the intolerability of cohabitation should be seen in an entirely *objective* light; its existence should therefore be assessed by an external and impartial authority, the judge, using an objective standard for reference. This standard should be based mainly on the rules given in a sort of ethical code of marriage duties, more or less faithfully taken from the tradition of Catholic marriage doctrine.

These statements are backed up by the abstract declamations of principle which appeared for many years in the courts' judgments and which are still seen today, especially in the judgments ruled by the Court of Cassation.[7] According to that declamation, repeated an infinite number of times with very few variations,[8] this ground for separation should consist of a number of factors or objective

---

[7]   Such abstract declamations are frequently found in the headnotes which for many scholars are the sole source of information concerning judgments by the courts. During the last 30 years, however, a considerable segment of scholars, culturally more qualified but still a minority, has developed a contrasting attitude taking more consideration of the judgment rather than the headnote.

   In Italy, the length of headnotes varies from 50 to 300 words. They are not written by the judge but are drafted by a special office of the Court of Cassation (for judgments ruled by this court), or by the editor of the legal journal that publishes the judgment. The headnotes are extremely important from a practical point of view since they represent the instrument used to trace the judgment in both paper and electronic archives. A judicial precedent for which the headnote was badly handled is very difficult to trace and requires extensive and time-consuming research which is rarely carried out.

[8]   By way of example, out of the many available, see Court of Cassation, 10 January 1986, no 67.

circumstances, which make it possible to discern judicially the existence of a situation which, due to its gravity, makes cohabitation objectively difficult, and therefore unsustainable without heroic gestures which cannot reasonably be expected. It is often highlighted that the standard required should be fairly strict: in particular, the simple fact that one or both spouses claim that cohabitation has become intolerable should not in itself be considered as proof of the existence of such a situation.

A logically necessary consequence of an 'objective' interpretation is that the judge should refuse the separation request each time the situation submitted for his/her decision does not, in his/her opinion, appear to represent an objective intolerability. Furthermore, the stricter the objective criteria used by the law, the more frequently requests should be refused on the grounds that the condition does not exist.

According to a minority of scholars, intolerability should be considered in a *subjective* sense. This view is supported by the observation that one of the most typical characteristics of marriage today is mutual consent, that is the reciprocal desire to live together as a couple. Married life in this day and age is based on a loving relationship that binds two people together to form a couple: it is therefore deeply rooted in their subjectivity and in the individual dynamics of their relationship, in the peculiarity of the agreement on which they founded their marriage and that is continuously adapted and readjusted. Any reference to objective parameters defined by a general and abstract code of ethics, and with which the couple may not even be in agreement, would be seen as an unacceptable imposition and as damaging to the independence of their choices.

The 'subjective' interpretation implicitly but inevitably debases the judges' control over the intolerability factor. It can be observed that the unwillingness to continue cohabitation by even one of the spouses is not something that can easily be judged by a third person, especially when the third person has the cultural standing and functions of a judge and not those of a family counsellor or a psychologist specialised in family matters. The firm intention of one spouse to leave the other, to start legal separation proceedings and to carry them through, having refused reconciliation during the hearing in court, is in itself a clear and unmistakable sign that any possibility of continuing life as a couple can be excluded, marriage has broken down and therefore cohabitation has become intolerable. It is hardly worth reminding the reader of the obvious: living together cannot be imposed by the authorities.

As far as opinions are concerned, it appears to me that the arguments used to support the 'subjective' interpretation are convincing.[9] However, it is not opinions

---

[9]   Limited here to the two strictly legal arguments. First, as already mentioned, the courts now agree unanimously that legal separation can be found even if the intolerability of cohabitation appears to be founded on facts that are linked directly to the conduct of the spouse presenting the request and is therefore caused by his/her actions alone; that is even if these actions are inconsistent with the duties arising from marriage. This attitude appears to me to be ethically and logically compatible only with a 'subjective' interpretation of intolerability.

   Secondly, in the case of divorce, the courts, in line with the majority of scholars, have for some time interpreted Arts 1 and 2 of the divorce statute (1970, no 898), which state that the judge is required to ascertain the impossibility of continuing or resuming cohabitation, coherently with a 'subjective' interpretation which is clearly in contrast with the 'objective' theory: in fact the

that I wish to discuss here. There are other far more important factors to consider, decisive factors of a quantitative nature, unmistakably suggesting that in reality the courts favour the 'subjective' interpretation, even if the opposite is often declared. Therefore the 'subjective' interpretation represents the living judge-made law.

Article 151 of the civil code has been in practice for more than two decades during which thousands of judgments published by legal journals upheld the intolerability of cohabitation, whilst a very small number of judgments considered cohabitation as not intolerable.[10]

Furthermore, legal statistics highlight an even more significant factor: in 1993 (the last year in which the tables of statistics give this information independently) the intolerability of cohabitation was accepted in 99.3% of cases and rejected in 0.7% of cases.[11] In the results of a survey which goes back further and was carried out on the cases held in a large tribunal, the number of accepted cases of intolerability was even smaller.[12]

The fact that requests for legal separation are almost never refused is of fundamental importance and cannot be dismissed as mere statistics: it indicates the real attitude of the courts in assessing the intolerability of cohabitation. Since it does not make sense to assume that all the cases brought before a judge are objectively serious enough to make cohabitation excessively distressing, we can conclude that the courts make a 'subjective' assessment of the intolerability of cohabitation.

Cohabitation can legitimately cease even on the basis that one spouse is no longer able to offer the other what he or she expects or demands from the relationship as long as this point of view is expressed in these terms and upheld for the entire duration of the legal proceedings, notwithstanding opposition or declarations to the contrary by the other spouse.

It is hardly worth noting that this is the logical consequence of a well-known fact that is common in all countries of European culture, ie that married life in the present day and age is based on and bound by a loving relationship, solidarity and a free exchange of give and take rather than the binding force of the legal tie.

In conclusion, the Italian system that regulates the separation of a married couple is based on a fundamental principle, although often not admittedly so, that each spouse retains the right to free himself or herself of the marriage bond unilaterally should he or she so wish, even if this is against the wish of the other

---

failure to reconcile the parties before the judge is in itself judged as sure evidence that cohabitation cannot be continued or resumed, without any further elements being required.

10 See Court of Appeal, Genoa, 17 May 1977 and Court of Cassation, 8 November 1979, no 5752, both unpublished but analysed by G Nocera and A Sodo, *L'intollerabilità della prosecuzione della convivenza ai fini della separazione giudiziale tra coniugi* (*Rassegna di diritto civile*, 1982, p 171); Tribunal of Genoa, 16 June 1980 (*Diritto di famiglia e delle persone*, 1981, p 778); Court of Appeal, Genoa, 18 August 1987 (*Nuova giurisprudenza civile commentata*, 1988, I, p 245); Tribunal of Terni, 29 September 1992 (*Rassegna giuridica umbra*, 1993, p 42).

11 Istat, *Statistiche giudiziarie civili*, year 1993, table 4.1; this data has been completely ignored as of 1995. The statistics are not considered as entirely reliable and cannot therefore explain whether these figures are based on substantial motivations (cohabitation judged as being not intolerable) or on procedural motivations (which is more likely).

12 See research carried out by S Runfola Testini on the Tribunal of Bari (*Rassegna di diritto civile*, 1980, p 181).

spouse and independently of any objective situations specifically or analytically governed by law.

This principle is very similar to that of the majority of the countries in Europe and North America.

III NEW ATTITUDES OF THE COURTS CONCERNING CONJUGAL DUTIES DURING THE PAST DECADE

Over the last 10 years, the law governing separation has not been subject to any consistent statutory modifications. Despite this there have been radical changes compared to the past due to profound modifications in the judge-made law.

During the past ten years, the Court of Cassation in particular has started to follow the same type of attitude in interpreting the intolerability of cohabitation that was already widely used by the first degree and the appellate jurisdictions, and has moved away from an attitude based on the principle of the indissolubility of marriage, which continued to influence decisions until approximately ten years ago, despite the fact that this no longer reflected the contents of the law in place since 1970.

This continuing attitude in favour of the indissolubility of marriage resulted in divorce being considered for a long time as a sort of 'foreign body', furtively introduced into the Italian legal system, that needed to be interpreted as a solution of an almost exceptional nature. Despite evidence to the contrary provided by statistical data and by public opinion, for many years the Court of Cassation considered separation as differing from divorce on the grounds that its sole aim was to reconcile the couple.

The Court of Cassation interpreted and applied the law relating to separation and divorce as if each had a different and opposing aim. Therefore any interpretation that compared the two was systematically refused, and any overlap between the two also denied. The denial of a link between them had important consequences on the interpretation of the separation rules.

The majority of the first degree and appellate jurisdictions had for some time taken a different attitude: an awareness of the fact that the principle of the dissolubility of marriage had full right to a place in the Italian legal system, and closer attention to the political principles of the law concerning marriage and upheld by the legislator that passed the 1975 reform, despite the fact that the regulations that were intended to express this view were not always coherent or technically adequate.

The most important aspects of the turnaround of the Court of Cassation's interpretation during the past ten years are:

(a)   the imputation of responsibility for the separation, especially concerning the negotiation of conjugal duties and the effective relationship between the infringement of these duties and the breakdown of the marriage; and

(b)   the issue concerning the existence of personal duties between husband and wife after separation.

IV   DECISIONS CONCERNING THE IMPUTATION OF RESPONSIBILITY FOR LEGAL SEPARATION

Article 151, para 2, of the civil code foresees that if the intolerability of cohabitation derives from the conduct of one spouse, if the spouse in question is aware of such conduct,[13] and if such conduct is a breach of conjugal duties, then the other spouse can require the responsibility for the separation to be attributed to the former. Both spouses can also be held responsible for the separation, if both have behaved in breach of conjugal duties and the conduct of both has contributed to the intolerability of cohabitation.

Responsibility for the separation constitutes the main penalty that can be imposed on the spouse who has infringed his/her duties (Arts 143 and 144 of the civil code): the consequences affect the financial side of the separation only, more precisely alimony and inheritance.

The judge-made law governing conjugal duties, which is found almost exclusively in separation decrees, underwent a turbulent phase of evolution from the beginning of the 1990s. This represents the logical, although not always suitably explicit, starting point for the re-writing of the judge-made law on this subject by the Court of Cassation.

During the last ten years the Court of Cassation has finally started to put into practice the ideas and principles expressed by the 1975 reform, but virtually ignored for a long time. I refer here to the idea that the relationship between spouses should be a loving relationship with solidarity, governed by the principle that decisions concerning family life should be made and agreed to by both spouses according to their personal values: an idea that is common to all European societies today.[14] This is exactly the opposite of the old idea of a monolithic family, based on the overriding authority of the husband–father, on the coercive force of the legal bond between spouses, and on the application of conjugal duties and ethical values defined by the Catholic tradition.

Today, the judge having to assess responsibility takes ever more consideration of the particular and specific issue of the married life of the spouses and not just the social conditions in which they live. The way they organised their life as a couple, their particular values, their culture and, in general terms, their overall personality have become fundamental issues in the assessment. However, notwithstanding this process of relativity and personalisation, as long as an assessment of responsibility is required, the courts cannot avoid a system that defines the minimum requirements for conjugal duties and that must be applied to all couples irrespective of their values, based on the fundamental and typical characteristics of conjugal life in today's society which distinguish this relationship from other social relationships.

It is on this basis, although not unanimously, that intolerability of cohabitation is increasingly *identified with the irretrievable breakdown of the marriage, the*

---

[13]   The awareness that the conduct in question is contrary to conjugal duties is indispensable for responsibility to be allocated; failing this, the separation can still be found to exist but without attribution of responsibility.

[14]   It is becoming increasingly difficult to find a code of conjugal duties that is generally accepted and at the same time based on strong, influential values widely acceptable for their intrinsic and unquestionable justness.

break-up of the substantive unit formed by the couple, ie the failure of the reasons that caused the formation of the family unit and life together in the first place.

The judge – as repeatedly mentioned – must take into consideration the overall relationship between the spouses and attempt to understand the dynamics of the actions and reactions, which are often very complicated, that led to the breakdown of the marriage. The two most common problems that the judge comes up against, which are co-related, are, first the *causal relationship* between intolerability and individual acts of conduct in breach of conjugal duties, and secondly, the *mutual wrongs* endured by the spouses. On this subject, the judge must assess which actions can be justified as a reaction to the conduct of the other spouse, and which cannot be justified whatever the conduct of the other; it is these unjustified actions that are taken into consideration when assessing responsibility.

Since the first judgments in which the 1975 reform was applied, the courts have continued to indicate the causal relationship between intolerability and conduct as an indispensable prerequisite in attributing responsibility. In practice, however, according to the attitude of the Court of Cassation until the beginning of the 1990s, any relevant violation of the traditional ethical code of marriage, for example adultery, represented cause for intolerability and, as a consequence, for responsibility, irrespective of how the fact actually affected the dynamics of the conjugal relationship and the balance between action and reaction.

This system also resulted in relevant consequences on the subject of mutual wrongdoing. The courts constantly applied the rule whereby violation of conjugal duties by one spouse in reaction to that of the other spouse was only accepted if the reaction was proportional to the action committed and was just aimed at avoiding, as far as possible, the unacceptable situation created by the wrongdoings of the other spouse. Therefore, violation of conjugal duties was reduced almost exclusively to neglect, the lack of mutual affection and solidarity which are at the basis of married life, as justification for the extreme remedy of moving out of the family home. On the other hand, any action considered as a relevant violation of conjugal duties, even in the case of a reaction to a much more serious wrongdoing by the other spouse, was considered cause for attributing responsibility.

Since the beginning of the 1990s, a new attitude has become widespread in the Court of Cassation's judgments although still with a degree of uncertainty: when assessing responsibility, only those violations of conjugal duties which occurred before the breakdown in the relationship can be taken into consideration. Any violation occurring after this time, no matter how objectively serious, cannot be taken into consideration. It is argued, in fact, that violations occurring when the cohabitation was intolerable cannot be considered as the *cause* of the intolerability, since the substantive unit formed by the couple had already broken down. On the basis of this attitude taken by the courts, the judge is required to look further into the dynamics of the couple to determine as precisely as possible the moment and the causes of the break-up, ie when and why cohabitation became intolerable, in order to identify and distinguish those violations of conjugal duties which actually caused the break-up.[15]

---

[15]   The factors leading to the conclusion that had cohabitation become intolerable, before conduct representing a violation of conjugal duties occurred, must emerge in the motivation clearly and unmistakably from the judgment in question: see Court of Cassation, 7 September 1999, no 9472.

Based on this new attitude, the Court of Cassation has considered there to be no case for responsibility when:

–   adultery by one of the spouses occurred after the breakdown in the conjugal relationship: in one case, this breakdown was confirmed by a separation agreement that was later revoked;[16] in other cases it was evident from the lack of commitment between the couple due to the long-term lack of a substantial relationship[17] or insuperable differences in age, culture and way of life;[18]
–   the husband failed to accept the return of the mentally incapacitated wife to the family home after she had left the home for a period of time by mutual consent;[19]
–   the husband inflicted blows on the wife after she admitted having an extra-marital relationship and that she did not wish to resume cohabitation after a period of consensual separation;[20]
–   the wife had refused the husband's invitation to live with him, years after the parties had mutually agreed not to live together except during the weekend for reasons related to the jobs of both and which continued to exist.[21]

Based on this attitude developed by the courts, the above rule concerning mutual wrongdoing must be revised: conduct that can be considered as a reaction following the actual breakdown in the relationship cannot be cause for responsibility, even if such conduct represents an action contrary to conjugal duties.

Acceptance of this new attitude by the Court of Cassation presents a few uncertainties. There have been cases where the court, whilst declaring its acceptance of this view, has limited its innovative capacity to a large degree: in one case, the matrimonial crisis was distinguished from the intolerability of cohabitation which represented the final outcome;[22] in another two cases, the court affirmed that the failure of the violation of conjugal duties to influence the intolerability of cohabitation 'must be deemed exceptional and must be scrupulously and accurately demonstrated', with proof that cohabitation was already reduced to a 'purely formal' fact.[23]

---

[16]   See Court of Cassation, 18 September 1997, no 9287.
[17]   See Court of Cassation, 18 March 1999, no 2444.
[18]   See Court of Cassation, 22 February 1996, no 1394.
[19]   See Court of Cassation, 20 December 1995, no 13021.
[20]   See Court of Cassation, 12 November 1996, no 9909.
[21]   See Court of Cassation, 11 April 2000, no 4558.
[22]   See Court of Cassation, 26 June 1996, no 5916, handed down by the same judge who also issued the decree referred to below.
[23]   See Court of Cassation, 27 June 1997, no 5762 and 14 August 1997, no 7630, handed down by the same judge.

V   DO THE PERSONAL DUTIES BETWEEN HUSBAND AND WIFE STILL EXIST AFTER SEPARATION?

In Italian textbooks on private law it is still customary to find it stated that separation does not cancel conjugal duties, it merely weakens their importance. Up until 1974 this statement represented precisely the juridical norm of the times: the spouses remained obliged to respect all conjugal duties which were not incompatible with the separation (Art 156, para 1, of the civil code as it appeared at the time). Although not obliged to live together, the spouses were required to remain faithful and to offer each other moral and material assistance; this last duty, material assistance, which almost always fell on the husband, differed after separation in that it was fulfilled by means of monetary payments (alimony).

Each serious violation of these duties could be penalised by modifying the type of separation, from separation for mutual consent to fault separation, according to the attitude developed by the courts during the last few decades of the 1800s.[24] To be more precise, a separation already determined to be consensual could, on request of one spouse, be newly determined to be fault separation, the responsibility being attributed to the other spouse who had violated conjugal duties.

The important consequences deriving from this newly attributed responsibility were the loss of maintenance rights for the spouse accused of violating conjugal duties and the loss of status as legitimate heir and as forced heir. The modification of the type of separation was used mainly to penalise the infidelity of the separated wife: it is worth noting that bringing this issue to court was obviously in the financial interest of the husband, as pointed out above.

The first change came in 1974. The Constitutional Court declared that the duty to remain faithful in the case of separation was against the constitution, judging it blatantly irrational, contrary to the principle of equality, for legally separated spouses to be compared in this respect to spouses living together.[25]

In 1975, the reform in family law cancelled (from Art 156 of the civil code) the norm concerning the continuance of those conjugal duties incompatible with living apart.

Despite this, the Court of Cassation soon reaffirmed that the type of separation could still be modified, although for different reasons. Based on the claim that the aim of separation is to reconcile the couple, the court affirmed that any type of conduct which reduced the possibility of a reconciliation was to be attributed to the spouse in question. In this way, the separation could be newly adjudicated with responsibility attributed to that spouse, who therefore lost the right to alimony.[26] The first degree and the appellate jurisdictions disagreed on this point: some followed the example of the Court of Cassation, whilst others regarded modification of the type of separation as no longer admissible after 1974–1975.

---

[24]   The fist example of such a judgment came from the Court of Appeal, Casale, 31 December 1874, *Annali*, 1875, II, p 264.

[25]   See Constitutional Court, 30 April 1974, no 99, *Diritto di famiglia e delle persone*, 1974, p 938.

[26]   See Court of Cassation, 10 January 1977, no 69, *Foro italiano*, 1977, I, p 62; Court of Cassation, 9 May 1977, no 1785, *Foro italiano*, 1977, I, p 1363.

At the beginning of the 1990s, the attitude of the Court of Cassation underwent a sea change on matters concerning conjugal relationships which resulted in a radical change: as of 1994, the Court of Cassation abandoned its previously consistent attitude to embrace the opposing theory, which denies the possibility of modifying the type of separation.[27] The Court of Cassation fully acknowledged the introduction of the principle of the dissolubility of marriage, which has been in place for some time now, and has drawn from it an interpretation that is logically necessary as well as fundamental: separation is the preliminary for divorce.

The main reasons behind this new attitude taken by the Court of Cassation are the following:

– no duties of a personal nature can continue to exist between separated spouses;
– ascertaining intolerability in a cohabitation that has already been legally dissolved is a contradiction in terms since the sole cause for separation is that cohabitation has become intolerable and attributing responsibility is a secondary element in separation decrees.

These motivations are also supported by what was previously stated concerning the imputation of responsibility: the attitude now established and accepted even by the Court of Cassation excludes the imputation of responsibility for conduct found to have occurred after the break-up of the relationship, ie after cohabitation had become intolerable. This implies that the imputation of responsibility cannot be based on violations of conjugal duties occurring after the separation request was presented in court, and certainly not after the legal separation was adjudicated.

In conclusion, we can now say that, according to the law applied by the courts, legally separated spouses are not bound by mutual conjugal duties. The only exception to this is the obligation that one of the spouses is under to pay the other, should the circumstances arise, sums of money on a regular basis in consideration of their economic conditions (alimony).

VI PERSPECTIVES ON LAW REFORM

Taken together, the innovations introduced by the judge-made law, described in the preceding paragraphs, indicate that the time is ripe for Italian society to review the entire legal system governing the dissolution of marriage. This review should be aimed at rationalising laws as well as adapting them to the new values and needs that have clearly emerged in society and in judicial practice.

The main principle governing the matter will remain unvaried,[28] that is that each spouse retains the right, should he or she so wish, unilaterally to free himself or herself from the marriage bond, even against the will of the other spouse and

---

[27] See Court of Cassation, 7 December 1994, no 10512; Court of Cassation, 17 March 1995, no 3098; Court of Cassation, 17 July 1997, no 6566; Court of Cassation, 19 September 1997, no 9317.

[28] See end of Section **II** above.

independently of any objective situations specifically and analytically governed by law. This should, however, become transparent and should not be disguised as moral declamations which do not correspond either to the operational rules actually in use in the courts or ethical attitudes widely accepted by society.

The fact that civil society is ripe for this review of the law does not, unfortunately, mean that the political world is ready for such a change.

During 1997 and 1998, the Italian Parliament prepared a Bill of reform for the law governing separation and divorce which was clearly oriented as previously described. The Bill was prepared by a special committee taken from the Justice Commission of the Chamber of Deputies, with representatives from all the political parties represented in Parliament. Despite this extensive convergence of opinions, the Bill was 'forgotten' for more than two years and the Parliament completed its 5-year term in May 2001 without even reaching the final debate.

The reason for this can probably be found in the unusual situation in which the Italian political system has been for some years.

For foreign readers, a brief introduction may be helpful in understanding the situation: the numerous, small Catholic-inspired parties that have sprung up following the break-up of the Christian Democratic party, which had been in power for more than 50 years, are in competition with each other (and unsuccessfully so) in a bid to monopolise the part of the electorate that is faithful to the pronouncements of the hierarchy of the Catholic church, an electorate that no longer coincides with the so-called Catholic world. Each party tries to appear the most faithful in embracing the doctrines of the Catholic hierarchy.

Any statute that reforms the law of separation and divorce cannot help having a significant impact on the ethics of marriage: for this reason, the hierarchy of the Catholic church has always taken an interventionist position on the subject with the aim of preventing the approval of statutes inspired by legal principles which diverge from the principles of the Catholic tradition that they defend.[29] What to them appears unacceptable in the Bill mentioned above is the uniformity of the regulations concerning the consequences of separation and divorce (with the exception of the effective dissolution of the bond, which is reserved to the divorce decree) and the removal of juridical responsibility for the separation, which results in removing the legal enforceability of conjugal duties.

In any case, it would appear that the political principles of the regulations contained in the Bill of reform correspond reasonably well to the customs of today's society. It is very unlikely, in my opinion, that future legislators will be able to deviate from this to any significant degree, even if they do find the political backing to intervene on the subject.

The main points contained in the Bill of reform referring to the topics discussed in this paper are the following.

(a)   The regulations governing divorce itself will be included in the civil code, whereas they are currently separate from the civil code. This fact has had a

---

[29]   It is well known that the approval of the divorce law (1970) and the law on abortion (1978) caused strong reactions from the hierarchy, resulting in the proposal to hold abrogating referenda: the outcome was that these statutes, in favour of which the large majority of electors had voted, remained in place.

strong symbolic value: divorce will no longer appear as being foreign to Italian marriage law.

(b)   Article 151, para 2, of the civil code, which envisages responsibility for the separation will be repealed, meaning that the violation of conjugal duties will no longer be subject to penalties.[30]

(c)   It will no longer be necessary to obtain a separation decree before being able to obtain a divorce: having begun the legal separation procedure and appeared at the initial hearing to attempt a reconciliation would be sufficient; the divorce could be granted after three years of uninterrupted separation from the date of the hearing. It would appear from the wording of the proposed statute that the final judgement of separation would no longer be required, with the desired result of reducing separation suits. I am not fully convinced however that the wording of the Bill of reform reflects the real intentions of the legislator: it may simply be a technical error.

(d)   The consequences of separation and of divorce in terms of alimony, which are currently unreasonably different, will be unified.

(e)   The rules governing separation and divorce proceedings, which are currently unreasonably different, will also be unified.

---

[30]   Unless, obviously, such violations are criminal offences such as the violation of the duty to provide family assistance (Art 570, Criminal Code), the abuse of corrective measures (Art 571, Criminal Code), maltreatments within the family (Art 572, Criminal Code).

JAPAN

FAMILY LAW IN JAPAN DURING 2000

Satoshi Minamikata[*] *and Teiko Tamaki*[**]

I INTRODUCTION

In 2000, we witnessed a number of developments in Japanese family law. In particular, the introduction of the Prevention of Child Abuse Act 2000 (the 'PCA Act') led to the development of issues relating to child abuse.

We will examine:

(1)   the PCA Act and a number of related issues;
(2)   judgments declared by the Japanese courts on other family law issues; and
(3)   research trends and interests of Japanese family law academics.

We note in passing that the Guardianship of Adults Act 1999 (including the revision of part of the Civil Code) became effective in April 2000, in order to provide for enduring powers of attorney for vulnerable people, particularly the elderly. However, we do not deal with this Act here because as yet there is a lack of sufficient information concerning the implementation of this.[1]

II THE PCA ACT AND CHILD ABUSE – RELATED ISSUES

The PCA Act took effect on 17 May 2000. The PCA Act aims to provide more efficient and appropriate protection for victims of child abuse. Prior to the PCA Act, protection and remedies for victims were afforded by provisions of the Criminal Code, the Civil Code and the Welfare of Children Act 1947.[2] However,

---

[*]   Professor of Law, Faculty of Law, Niigata University.

[**]   Research Assistant, Faculty of Law, Niigata University.

    The authors gratefully acknowledge the editorial assistance of Mr Andrew Sulston.

[1]   The Guardianship of Adults Act, 1999 provides, *inter alia*, that: (1) an adult person is entitled to appoint his/her personal representative (guardian) by contract before she/he loses legal capacity; (2) the previous protection scheme for an incompetent person is revised and four measures are, instead, stipulated to protect the interests of an incompetent person according to the degree of his/her legal capacity; and (3) a deaf person is eligible to make a will through a notary public with the assistance of an interpreter using sign language. See more details in Y Matsushima 'What has made family law reform go astray?' in *The International Survey of Family Law 1997*, ed A Bainham (Martinus Nijihoff Publishers, 1999) and K Niijima 'Guardianship for Adults' in *The International Survey of Family Law (2001 Edition)*, ed A Bainham (Family Law, 2001).

[2]   Since 1947, the Welfare of Children Act 1947 was partially revised several times in order to protect children involved in child abuse cases.

these provisions and related provisions were sometimes inadequate, insufficient and slow in protecting the welfare of children involved.

A   PCA Act provisions

The PCA Act contains the following sections to provide for intervention in child abuse cases. In s 2, four categories of child abuse cases are legally defined as is the precise nature of child abuse. Section 4 then defines the roles of central government and local authorities in providing various measures for dealing with child abuse cases. The PCA Act also provides that a certain group of officials in charge of child welfare and education must take responsibility for uncovering child abuse cases, as far as possible, at an early stage and any person who suspects child abuse should inform the welfare authorities promptly (ss 5, 6 and 7). Those sections allocate specific responsibilities in child abuse cases. Elsewhere, the PCA Act provides for specific action to be taken when a child abuse case is discovered, in particular emphasising the need for immediate response and intervention (s 8) and providing that the welfare authorities are entitled to enter private premises in order to investigate a child abuse case, with the assistance of the police if necessary (ss 9 and 10). By these provisions, it is hoped that the welfare authorities will be able to discover child abuse cases at an earlier stage and tackle these cases more appropriately and efficiently than under previous provisions. In addition, publicity and education about child abuse cases is recommended for ordinary citizens (s 4).

B   Application of the PCA Act

While the provisions in the PCA Act are only intended to provide basic and fundamental guidelines for resolving child abuse cases, the PCA Act is seen as more useful in terms of protecting the victims of child abuse cases with the simultaneous application of the Welfare of Children Act 1947. For the purpose of protecting child abuse victims, the courts will increasingly admit the victims to child protection institutions. Some professionals engaged in the task of protecting child abuse victims claim that the PCA Act is insufficient in some respects in providing remedies for these victims. In part, this is due to the fact that there was a disagreement among legislators in understanding the needs of child abuse victims and agreeing on individual measures to be laid down in the PCA Act. For instance, the range of people responsible for reporting a suspected child abuse case to the authorities is restricted, and it is not clear how far the authorities are entitled to proceed with entering and inspecting private premises where child abuse cases are suspected. It is also said that a tougher approach should have been taken to removing parental rights and duties.[3] An additional difficulty is said to be a lack of sufficient staff in the child welfare divisions of local authorities where staff have heavy case loads often making it difficult to provide a prompt and

---

[3]   M Ishikawa, 'Legal Policy and Issues on Child Abuse', *Jurist* No 1188, pp 6–9; T Yoshida, 'Removal and Suspension of Parental Rights and Duties in Child Abuse Cases', *Jurist* No 1188, p 15.

adequate response to a child abuse incident.[4] For these reasons, the PCA Act should be examined and revised in order to provide more efficient protection for the victims of child abuse.[5]

C   The wider context and recent trends

The implementation of the PCA Act can be said to reflect the recent social movement in Japan on issues of child welfare, such as the ratification of the UN Convention on the Rights of the Child in 1994 and the enactment of the Protection of Children and Punishment of Perpetrators in Child Prostitution and Pornography Act 1999, following the discovery of serious cases of violence and abuse involving children. The number of reported child abuse cases in law reports has recently increased.[6]

III   RECENT COURT CASES IN FAMILY LAW

The courts decided a number of family law cases and provided new interpretations of a number of family law issues during 2000. The cases discussed below include both Supreme Court and lower court decisions. It should be remembered that lower court decisions might be dismissed or revised on reaching the higher courts.[7]

A   Gender identity disorder

Japanese courts have traditionally decided applications for determination of a person's sex by reference to the applicant's chromosomal sex determined on a scientific basis. This approach was questioned in the Determination of the Tsuchiura Branchi of the Mito Family Court, 22 July 1999 in *Kateisaibangeppo* Vol 51 No 12 p 40, where an applicant registered in the Family Registration Book as 'female' made an application to the family court to amend the registration to 'male'. The registration as 'female' had been made because of the deformation of 'her outer lip' (sexual organ) at birth, although the applicant regarded 'herself' as

---

4   When the PCA Act was passed in the Lower House of the Parliament, the Committee for Legal Affairs of the Lower House made the supplementary resolution declaring that central and local governments should take appropriate and substantial measures to develop staff and facilities for protecting child abuse victims and promotion of the welfare of those victims.

5   PCA Act, Appendix, s 2.

6   For recent examples, see: (1) on child sexual abuse, the Determination of the Sasebo Branch of the Nagasaki Family Court, 23 February 2000 (*Kateisaibangeppo* Vol 52 No 8 p 55); (2) on child battery and injury, the Determination of the Yokohama Family Court, 11 May 2000 (*Kagetsu* Vol 52 No 11 p 57); (3) on child physical and mental abuse, the Determination of the Aki Branch of the Kochi Family Court, 1 March 2000 (*Kagetsu* Vol 52 No 9 p 103) and the Determination of the Yokosuka Branch of Yokohama Family Court, 19 May 2000 (*Kagetsu* Vol 52 No 11 p 65); and (4) on child neglect, the Determination of the Kishiwada Branch of the Osaka Family Court, 12 November 1999 (*Kagetsu* Vol 52 No 4 p 36).

7   The court decree on gender identity disorder discussed below, for example, was overturned in December 1999. Some cases cited here were decided in 1999 but were reported in the 2000 edition of the relevant law reports.

'male'. The court created a precedent in granting the application by considering not only the applicant's sex chromosome but also other factors such as how 'she' recognised 'her own sex'.

On the other hand, courts have been hesitant to accept applications for changes of sex to be registered in Family Registration Books[8] where the applicant has voluntarily undergone a surgical operation to alter genital organs. In 1997, the Ad hoc Committee of the Psycho-Neurology Society of Japan on Gender Identity Disorder set out a number of well-considered procedures for sex organ operations in its *Report and Recommendations on Gender Identity Disorder*. In 1998, the first such operation was performed in Japan.[9] Prior to this incident, a Japanese 'man' who had suffered from gender identity disorder went to Australia to have a genital operation in 1997. 'He' then applied to the family court to change 'his' registration in the Family Registration Book from male to female. The family court and the high court dismissed 'his' application stating that sex should be judged on the basis of an applicant's sex chromosome. Although the courts admitted that gender identity disorder is a serious social issue, a genital operation has yet to be regarded as legitimate medical treatment for such disorder (Order of the Tokyo High Court, 9 February 2000, *Hanreijiho*, Vol 1718, p 2). It is likely on the basis of these decisions, that the courts will entertain applications for amendment of sex registration for hermaphrodites, but it is less likely that the courts will entertain applications based on gender identity disorder because of which a person has had sex organ operations.

B Application of section 768 of the Civil Code: dissolution of cohabitation on the death of a cohabitant

Courts have applied most of the provisions relating to marriage to disputes between cohabitants based on the principle that cohabitation should be treated on a similar basis to marriage. In fact, cohabitation has been dealt with differently in only two respects, which are that a cohabitant is not entitled to take the partner's family name and the cohabitant does not have the right to succeed to the partner's property on death. Accordingly, s 768 of the Civil Code – governing division of matrimonial property – is applied to a breakdown of cohabitation in the same way as to a breakdown of marriage. It is commonly observed that a male cohabitant must divide his property with his female cohabitant at the end of their relationship. In this respect, a cohabitant can enjoy legal protection notwithstanding the absence of a legal marriage. However, if a cohabitant dies intestate, his/her surviving cohabitant has no right to claim the property of the deceased cohabitant. It is argued that s 768 of the Civil Code should be applied to such a case by drawing an analogy with marriage in order to protect the surviving cohabitant, but the Supreme Court has rejected this on the basis that it may cause confusion (Decree of the Supreme Court, 10 March 2000, *Kagetsu*, Vol 52 No 10 p 81). A

---

[8] See more details on family registration in S Minamikata et al *International Encyclopaedia of Laws – Family Law Japan* (Kluwer Law International, 1999).

[9] In the first case, a 'female' changed her sex to 'male', and in the second case, a 'male' changed his sex to 'female' and was only allowed to change his first name to a female one when he applied for amendment of sex registration (*Mainichi News Paper*, 26 June 1999).

male cohabitant had died intestate after 26 years of cohabitation and his surviving female cohabitant asked the legal beneficiaries to allocate to her a certain portion in consideration of her services to the deceased, especially in the final period of his life. The Supreme Court's rejection of her application has been criticised for its potential to encourage unfair behaviour. For instance, a cohabitant can obtain certain property from the other by dissolving their cohabitation immediately after the other has become ill, but she/he would not be given any property if they continue to live together and she/he takes care of the other cohabitant until her/his death. In this respect, cohabitation and marriage are different in terms of financial protection.

C   Dividing the matrimonial property on marriage breakdown: pension rights and retirement pay[10]

Recent cases on s 768 of the Civil Code and the division of matrimonial property at the time of divorce have turned on the point of whether a pension and retirement pay are included in matrimonial property and should be divided between a married couple. Concerning retirement pay, the Tokyo District Court declared in 1999 that a court can estimate a wife's portion of the matrimonial property at the time of divorce taking the husband's retirement pay into consideration if the timing of their divorce was within six years of his retirement (Decree of the Tokyo District Court, 3 September 1999, *Hanreijiho* No 1700 p 79).

With regard to pension rights, while the courts generally reject a claim to divide the pension rights at the time of divorce, in a recent case a court ordered a husband to make a periodical payment to his ex-wife until her death as a part of the matrimonial property where the pension had already started to be paid (Decree of the Sagamihara Branch of the Yokohama District Court, 30 July 1999, *Hanreijiho* No 1708 p 142).[11]

D   Mother–child relationships and DNA tests

It has become common for courts to use DNA fingerprinting tests to determine a father–child blood relationship. The Tokyo High Court, however, in a rare case, recently used a DNA fingerprinting test to determine a mother–child relationship where the mother had applied to the court to deny her mother–child relationship with a deceased woman who was registered as her legal daughter in the Family Registration Book (Decree of the Tokyo High Court, 26 August 2000, *Hanreitaimuzu* No 1025 p 266).

---

[10] Retirement pay is a lump sum, non-contributory allowance paid once at the time of one's retirement in Japan. The amount of retirement pay is calculated according to the number of years of service and the reason for retirement. A pension scheme provides a certain amount of money monthly when people reach their full pension entitlement age at around 60–65 depending on each pension scheme. These pension funds are furnished by contributions from employees, employers and the government.

[11] In this case, the court ordered the defendant husband to pay a lump sum to his ex-wife instead of dividing his pension rights.

E   Child custody criteria

It is not uncommon for parents to disagree as to which parent should act as a child's custodian after breakdown of marital life. In this situation, a custodian has the rights and duties connected with caring for the child or children on a day-to-day basis (Civil Code, s 766). A parent or any other appropriate person can be appointed as a custodian with the parents' agreement or pursuant to a family court determination. A court will determine an application for custodianship having regard to the child's welfare and all relevant circumstances, particularly how the child has been cared for by the parent with whom the child currently lives. If a parent has taken the child from the other parent by force, she/he will be ordered by the court to return the child to the other by reason of justice and fairness (Determination of the Tokyo High Court, 20 September 1999, *Kagetsu*, Vol 52 No 2 p 163). Meanwhile, Kyoto Family Court appointed a father as a custodian who was given the parental rights and duties for sons of 15 and 13 and a daughter of eight years old. The court examined all the circumstances including the father–child relationship after the divorce, his capacity for domestic chores and his income, and stated that maintaining his relationship with his children would be in the best interests of the children (20 August 1999, *Kagetsu*, Vol 51 No 1 p 98). This decision suggests that to some extent the court can adopt a gender-neutral view in such disputes rather than their traditional pro-mother approach.

IV   FAMILY LAW RESEARCH TRENDS

Judging from publications of family law academics in Japan, the following themes received particular attention in 2000.

First, many academics discussed issues arising from the Guardianship of Adults Act 2000, child abuse and domestic violence.[12] Secondly, the Family Lawyers Conference (an associate society of the International Society of Family Law in Japan) chose as a subject the Japanese approach to mediation in family disputes where lawyers argued the pros and cons of this in comparison with the western theory and practice of ADR or alternative dispute resolution. Thirdly, some academics wrote on gender identity disorder and its complicated implications for the family registration scheme as discussed above. Finally, with the rapid development of medical technology, DNA fingerprinting tests raised the issue of whether a parent–child relationship should be determined only by genetic factors or also by social factors such as the welfare principle and the parties' intentions. Since the rule for determining the parent–child relationship is based on both factors in current law, controversy among lawyers remains.

---

[12]   The Prevention of Domestic Violence and Protection of Victims Act was enacted in May 2001. The Act indicates that society has now begun to be aware of the violence caused to vulnerable family members resulting in physical, emotional and financial difficulties in everyday life.

V   CONCLUSION

In 2000, lawyers in Japan continued to conduct research on legal issues which were discussed during the 1990s, but with the added complication that many such legal issues have become more difficult and complex because of the diversity of values in society. Many issues are emotive and have been discussed in a new and challenging way.

One good example of this is the issue of gender identity disorder and sex organ operations. The 'suffering' from gender identity disorder and desire to have sex organ operations gained a high profile in Japanese society. This is because of both the rapid development in medical technology, which means that those people's needs may be met, and also the changes in people's attitudes and views concerning such matters. 'Patients' with gender identity disorder, who often kept silent for a long time, are now encouraged to be more positive and forthright in making appeals that they may change their sex in order to confirm or obtain their gender identity. In one case, a female claimed in public that she wanted to become 'male' by an operation. In the past, many cases were reported where a male became 'female' through a sex organ operation (although he was still regarded as a male in point of law), but the reverse situation has been less obvious. Bringing these factors together, sexual equality for both sexes may be close to being fulfilled in this area. It can also be pointed out that new developments in medical technology including sex change operations and DNA fingerprinting are gradually changing the nature of family relationships.

In contrast to these developments, the issue of pension rights of cohabitants reflects the uncertainty in terms of legal protection and rights surrounding cohabitation. In an ageing society where people can expect little from the State in terms of financial support, the division of rights for cohabitants is especially crucial by comparison with married couples. In this connection, an ageing society is likely to cast a shadow over many legal issues relating to the family.

Child abuse and parent–child relationships were an important topic in 2000. In the case of child abuse, the general public at large, rather than a specialist minority, began to focus on child abuse.[13] It is claimed that the number of child abuse cases has more than doubled in a decade. The number of cases in which specialist child abuse advice was sought was 1,101 in 1991 and 11,631 in 1999. As a measure of recent change, the number in 1997 was only 5,352, obviously showing the rapid increase in these three years.[14]

It is, however, unclear whether the cases increased substantially or the cases to be reported increased during that period. In point of fact, applications to the family court to admit child abuse victims into a child welfare institution were 49 (36) in 1997, 39 (22) in 1998 and 88 (48) in 1999.[15] These numbers are very small compared with child abuse cases where advice was sought from specialists. Furthermore, the numbers of cases in which the family court was requested to

---

[13]   For instance, 93 articles on child abuse matters were reported in *Asahi Shimbun* (one of Japan's large newspapers) in 2000. Subscribers may therefore read an article on child abuse approximately once every three days.

[14]   See the Ministry of Health and Welfare, *Child Welfare Cases reported to the Ministry of Health and Welfare*, 1999 edition, website: *http://www.mhlw.go.jp*.

[15]   Figures in brackets indicate the number of approved cases.

remove parental rights and duties on the ground that those rights and duties had been abused were 3 (1), 9 (2) and 6 (1) in 1997, 1998 and 1999 respectively. Also, the numbers of children who are admitted to stay at child welfare institutions are not substantially increasing (26,759 in 1998 and 27,195 in 1999).

It has been said repeatedly that the particular concern about child abuse and its victims has grown in society. This concern may not be reflected directly in the actual number of child abuse cases detected but perhaps, with people beginning to regard child abuse as a serious infringement upon the rights and interests of a child victim, child abuse may have become a social problem to be tackled by society as a whole.

KENYA

'SITTING ON HER HUSBAND'S BACK WITH HER HANDS IN HIS POCKETS': COMMENTARY ON JUDICIAL DECISION-MAKING IN MARITAL PROPERTY CASES IN KENYA

Celestine Nyamu-Musembi[*]

I   INTRODUCTION

The current state of the law on marital property in Kenya has developed exclusively through judicial interpretation and innovation. The Kenyan parliament has not enacted a statute explicitly addressing division of assets between spouses on divorce or separation. The basis for determining disputes over marital property in Kenya is an English statute – the Married Women's Property Act (MWPA) 1882. The purpose of the statute was to recognize a married woman's legal capacity to hold property in her own right and to transact in it. Prior to the MWPA 1870, a predecessor of the 1882 statute, the English common law applied the doctrine of coverture, under which the wife's legal identity was subsumed into her husband's. Upon marriage the husband became seised of all freehold lands held by the wife both prior to marriage and in the course of the marriage. He was entitled to collect rents and profits from them. The wife had no power to dispose of the property during the marriage. The husband could dispose of it to the extent of his share, or the entire estate with her consent.[1] The MWPA changed all this by recognizing a wife's separate legal interest in property, thus replacing her total incapacity under common law with a rigid doctrine of separate property.[2]

This nineteenth-century English statute is applied to Kenya by virtue of section 3 of the Judicature Act, which spells out the sources of law that should guide Kenyan courts. In addition to the Constitution, statutes enacted by the Kenyan parliament, Islamic and Hindu law and the various African customary laws, the courts are also to apply 'the substance of the common law, the doctrines of equity, and the statutes of general application in force in England on 12 August 1897 … so far only as the circumstances of Kenya and its inhabitants permit …'.[3] This is known as the 'reception clause', since it permits the reception of English law. The clause exists in the laws of all former British colonies. The date, 12 August 1897, refers to the date when Kenya became a colony. Legal

---

[*]   LLB (Nairobi); LLM, SJD (Harvard); Advocate of the Supreme Court of Kenya; Research Fellow, Institute of Development Studies, University of Sussex. The author would like to thank Wanza Kioko for help in collecting unreported cases.

[1]   NV Lowe and G Douglas, *Bromley's Family Law* (Butterworths, 1998) at 106–107.

[2]   Ibid at 111–112.

[3]   Section 3, Judicature Act, Chapter 8 of the Laws of Kenya.

developments in England subsequent to that date do not have binding authority on Kenyan courts. The rationale for this cut-off date, which varies in each former British colony, was that it was expected that each colony would adapt the English common law to suit its specific circumstances, and therefore the English common law would develop in different directions in different places.

I v I, a 1970 High Court case, was the first case to establish that the MWPA did apply to marriages solemnized in Kenya. The respondent wife had sought a declaration under s 17 of the MWPA claiming a half share in the proceeds of the sale of a house that the parties held in joint registration. The applicant husband objected to the application of the MWPA in determining the parties' respective interests in the proceeds. He relied on the qualifier in the reception clause which states that English law shall apply only in so far as the circumstances of Kenya and its inhabitants permit. The court responded to this objection by observing that 'the circumstances of Kenya and its inhabitants do not generally require that a woman should not be able to own property'.[4]

This article traces the path of the Kenyan judiciary's interpretation and application of the MWPA for the 27-year period between this first case in which the statute was invoked in Kenyan courts and a key 1997 decision. The article describes and evaluates the shape that marital property law has taken in that period by examining six cases that are regarded as milestones in the path of marital property law in Kenya. The cases show that there has been a guarded expansion of the scope of judicial discretion under the MWPA. Kenyan judges have, in specific cases, rejected a narrow interpretation of the court's power to adjust property interests between the parties. Also commendable is the judges' rejection of any suggestion that a statute that recognizes married women's capacity to hold property is alien to Kenya's cultural context. In this spirit, Kenyan courts have held the MWPA to be applicable in property disputes involving parties married under African customary law and under Islamic law.

However, rigid adherence to a title-based separate property system tends to produce absurd and unjust results. In a context where 95% of the registered land nationally is held individually in men's names, a rigid title-based approach predetermines the outcome in marital property disputes. Even co-ownership of the matrimonial home is a rarity. In addition, even though courts have gradually looked beyond monetary contribution in assessing a non-title holding spouse's beneficial interest, there is still a bias in favour of monetary contribution, thus devaluing activities such as home-making and childcare. From a gender equality perspective, marital property cases in Kenya portray women (wives) as unproductive dependants unless the contrary is proved, which contradicts the reality of women's central roles in managing families.

II   APPLYING MWPA IN A PLURAL FAMILY LAW SYSTEM: *KARANJA* AND *ESSA*

Kenya has a plural family law system that draws from both statutory national laws and the various cultural and religious normative orders represented in the country.

---

[4]   Trevelyan J in *I v I* (1971) *East Africa Law Reports* 278 at 281.

People may choose to marry under statute, either under the Marriage Act (chapter 150) or the African Christian Marriage and Divorce Act (chapter 151). Kenyan Muslims may marry in accordance with Islamic law, which is provided for under the Mohammedan Marriage and Divorce Act (chapter 156). Similarly, Kenyan Hindus may marry in accordance with Hindu religious practice, which is provided for under the Hindu Marriage and Divorce Act (chapter 157). Kenyan law also recognizes marriages created in accordance with any of the various African customary law systems. Such marriages are not registered under any statute.

In *I v I* the court had dealt with a marriage solemnized under statute. Could the MWPA be applied to marriages solemnized under the non-statutory regimes? The courts were faced with this issue in two cases. The first, *Karanja v Karanja*,[5] dealt with application of the MWPA to a marriage solemnized under Kikuyu customary law. The second, *Essa v Essa*,[6] dealt with application of the MWPA to resolve a marital property dispute between a Muslim couple.

In *Karanja* the parties had been married for 20 years. The property in dispute included six pieces of real estate within the city of Nairobi, all registered in the name of the husband. The wife sought a declaration of joint ownership over five of the six properties on the basis of direct or indirect contribution to their purchase. With respect to the sixth property, she sought a declaration of full ownership on the basis that it was purchased with her earnings from salaried employment.

The husband objected to the application of the MWPA, as well as to the application of English cases based on the MWPA, which had established that where only one spouse had title to property in which the other spouse claimed an interest, the court could infer a trust in favour of the non-title holding spouse to the extent of his/her share.[7] He argued that these cases were 'inapplicable to the African way of life where no intention to share land with his wife could be attributed to a husband'.[8] He called two 'expert' witnesses on Kikuyu customary law to testify on married women's (lack of) capacity to own land. One witness was adamant in maintaining that married women had no entitlement whatsoever to land and other forms of property: 'All property belongs to the husband because the wife should be under him'.[9]

The other witness conceded that circumstances had changed quite considerably and that women, married or unmarried, could own property in their own names. The court relied on the evidence of this witness as a more honest and fair statement of Kikuyu customary law.[10] The court observed that, even if it were

---

5   [1976] *Kenya Law Reports* 307.

6   *Fathiya Essa v Mohamed Essa* (unreported) Civil Appeal No 101 of 1995 (Nairobi).

7   The cases cited were *Chapman v Chapman* [1969] 3 All ER 476; *Gissing v Gissing* [1970] 2 All ER 780; *Falconer v Falconer* [1970] 3 All ER 449; *Hazell v Hazell* [1972] 1 All ER 923.

8   *Karanja* at 310.

9   The witness also maintained that a wife cannot report to the police if her husband beats her: *Karanja* at 310.

10   This view also found support in a monograph compiled by Eugene Cotran on marriage and divorce under the various customary law systems, which stated with respect to Kikuyu customary law: 'In the event of a dissolution of the marriage, the wife is entitled to take all her property, whether acquired before or after the marriage. Property obtained through the joint efforts of the

to accept the version of customary law presented by the first witness, the court
would have been bound to reject it since it contradicted a written law, the MWPA.
Section 3 of the Judicature Act sets out criteria for the application of customary
law, one of which is that customary law shall apply only if it does not contradict a
written law on the specific subject matter in dispute.[11] The court concluded that a
presumptive trust in favour of a wife with respect to property registered only in
the husband's name does apply 'where an African husband and wife in Kenya are
both in salaried employment and both [contributed] to the household expenses and
education of the children'.[12] The court awarded her one-third of the property.

In *Essa*, the parties had been married under Islamic law for 16 years. One year
after marriage, the wife had resigned a relatively well-paying job in Nairobi and
started working in a Mombassa business owned by her husband and his parents for
no pay. The parties later set up a dress business in partnership, which the wife ran
single-handedly. In the course of the marriage, they acquired three pieces of real
estate in prime areas of Mombassa town. Two of these were registered in the
husband's name. The third was the matrimonial home which was registered in
their joint names. At the time of the proceedings, the home was occupied by the
husband. The wife sought a half share of the notional market rent for the home
and a declaration of joint ownership 'or ownership thereof that may be just' with
respect to the other two properties.

Over objections to the application of the MWPA to a Muslim marriage, the
court reiterated the ruling in *I v I* regarding the status of the MWPA as a statute of
general application, adding that the Act 'applies equally to Muslims as it does to
non-Muslims in Kenya'. The court awarded the wife a half-share in one of the
properties, a rental commercial building, based upon evidence that she made
payments from her business toward the purchase of the property. Her claim for a
notional rent on the matrimonial home was denied since the home was occupied
by the husband and occasionally by the children of the marriage. The third
property had been registered in the joint names of the husband and the children of
the marriage, in accordance with an order of the High Court.

Essa and *Karanja* are significant because, by applying the MWPA across the
board to Kenyan marriages irrespective of the specific normative systems, the
courts have accomplished what the legislature has not been able to do.[13] They

---

husband and wife is divided between them.' See Eugene Cotran, *The Law of Marriage and
Divorce* (Sweet & Maxwell, 1968).

[11]   This proviso is arguably subject to the exemption clause in s 82(4) of the Constitution. Section 82
       prohibits discrimination. Subsection 4, para 'b' provides that the prohibition of discrimination
       will not apply with respect to the application of personal laws (eg African customary law and
       Islamic law) to matters relating to marriage, divorce, adoption, burial, devolution of property on
       death, or any other matter of personal law. See Kenya Const. See also Zimbabwe Const,
       Art 23(3)(a) and (b) (rev 1996); Zambia Const, Art 25(4)(c) and (d). What would happen if a
       court refused to apply a certain norm of customary law on grounds that it contradicts a written
       law, then the court's ruling is challenged on the basis of this constitutional exemption? So far no
       Kenyan case has dealt with this scenario.

[12]   *Karanja* at 311.

[13]   There have been various legislative attempts at harmonizing the various family law systems in
       Kenya. A Presidential Commission was set up in 1967 to review and propose reforms to the law
       of marriage and divorce. The Commission's draft legislation was presented to Parliament in 1979
       and again in 1985 but on both occasions it encountered immense hostility and failed to pass. See
       Republic of Kenya, *Report of the Commission on the Law of Marriage and Divorce* (1968);
       Kenya National Assembly Reports, 1979 and 1985.

have established a minimum national standard that guarantees spouses a fair (though not always equal) division of marital property. The reality of the plurality in family law systems means that substantive rights of spouses are determined by the respective normative systems. There are wide variations between and within the various African customary systems, and between these African customary systems, Islamic and Hindu systems and the statutory systems. *Essa* and *Karanja* open up an avenue of redress for people dissatisfied with what their respective normative systems offer them.

III   EXPANDING THE SCOPE OF JUDICIAL ENQUIRY: WHICH PROPERTY, HOW MUCH DISCRETION?

There has been a measure of progress in Kenyan courts' expansion of the categories of property covered under the MWPA. The Act does not limit its application to particular types of property. However, prior to the *Karanja* case, the statute had only been applied with respect to the matrimonial home in the Kenyan context. Indeed, all the English cases cited in *Karanja* dealt with the matrimonial home and its contents. The court in *Karanja* stated explicitly that the MWPA is not limited in its application to the matrimonial home and its contents. Since then the court has applied the MWPA to commercial rental property, bank accounts and income from businesses operated jointly by the spouses. The criterion seems to be any property that was acquired as part of a joint venture, whether both partners made direct financial contribution or indirect non-monetary contribution, although the latter is given less weight.

Less tangible forms of property such as pension funds and 'career assets' (expected future earnings resulting from professional qualifications) have not yet been dealt with in Kenyan courts.

The nature and extent of judicial discretion under the MWPA has been a subject of discussion, both in England and in Kenya. In *Karanja*, counsel for the husband argued for a very narrow construction of the court's discretion under the MWPA, relying on the English case *Pettitt v Pettitt*.[14] In *Pettitt*, the House of Lords had ruled that the MWPA is merely a procedural rather than a substantive statute, and therefore it did not give the court authority to pass property rights from one spouse to the other. The court has no more power to vary title or to create property rights in marital proceedings than it has in any other type of case dealing with property.

'The procedure was devised as a means of resolving a dispute or a question as to title rather than as a means of giving some title not previously existing ... In a question as to the title to property the question for the court was – "Whose is this", and not – "To whom shall this be given".'[15]

The court rejected the ruling in *Pettitt* as too narrow a view of the powers of the court. The judge ruled that, notwithstanding the statement of the law in *Pettitt*,

---

[14]   [1969] 2 All ER 385.

[15]   *Karanja* at 308–309 (quoting Lord Morris in *Pettitt v Pettitt*).

nothing precludes a judge, based upon the evidence presented, from granting a declaration of ownership or joint ownership, or from making an order for the sale of property registered in the name of one spouse and payment of part of the proceeds to the other spouse. The fact that one spouse holds title does not tie the court's hands with respect to the application of equitable doctrines which enable it to recognize the other spouse's beneficial interest.

IV   EXPANDING THE SCOPE OF JUDICIAL ENQUIRY: WHAT COUNTS AS CONTRIBUTION?

Kenyan courts insist upon strict proof of contribution before they can make a finding of a beneficial interest in favour of a non-title holding spouse. There has been a gradual expansion in the range of factors that a court will take into account in assessing contribution. However, as discussion of the cases will reveal, this expansion has not gone far enough.

A   By the work of her hands: *Kivuitu* and non-monetary contributions

In *Karanja*, the tone of the court emphasized a wife's ability either to make direct contribution toward the family's investments, or to use her income from employment to meet household expenses, thus freeing up her husband's income and enabling him to invest in acquisition of property. The decision did not therefore deal with non-financial contributions such as housework, farm work and childcare. The first case in which the court addressed the issue of non-financial contributions was the 1991 case of *Kivuitu v Kivuitu*.[16] The property in dispute was the matrimonial home which was registered jointly in the names of the spouses. It had been purchased mainly with funds sent home by the husband while he was on a three-month trip abroad. The wife identified the house and negotiated and finalized the purchase and formal transfer. There was scant evidence of a direct financial contribution toward the purchase by the wife, but there was evidence that she had earned some income, on and off, from employment and some business ventures, which she had spent on family expenses. The High Court judge had awarded her a one-quarter share in the property as reflective of her contribution, despite the fact that she was registered jointly as title-holder with the husband. She appealed, seeking a declaration that she was entitled to an equal share.

The Court of Appeal judges decided that financial contribution alone was too narrow a basis on which to determine the parties' interests. Therefore a court needed to examine non-monetary contributions as well. Justice Omollo posed two hypothetical scenarios. The first, an urban housewife who spends her time preparing meals, maintaining the home, ensuring 'that the children are in a position to go to school in clean uniforms and that the husband also goes to work in clean clothes …'.[17] The second, a wife in the rural home who tills the land, takes care of the children, and generally keeps the home running. He concludes

---

[16]   [1991] 2 *Kenyan Appeal Reports* 241.

[17]   *Kivuitu* at 248.

that these women do definitely contribute to the acquisition of property even though their contribution is not quantified in monetary terms. Limiting the definition of contribution to monetary contribution 'would clearly work an injustice to a large number of women in our country where the reality of the situation is that paid employment is very hard to come by'.[18] Thus, even in the absence of evidence of any financial contribution, a wife's contribution in this capacity would be considered.

Kivuitu was acclaimed as a landmark case and it was relied upon in several subsequent applications under the MWPA. Most notably, the case of *Omar Said Jaiz v Naame Ali*[19] took *Kivuitu* one step further to rule that, even without clear evidence of the extent of actual contribution made by both spouses, since the property was acquired through a joint venture it would be considered joint property.

B   Pushing proof of contribution to its limits: *Kimani*

Kivuitu seems to suggest that the *fact* of contribution could be presumed by virtue of a wife's participation in managing the family's affairs. Therefore, in a dispute over property registered only in the name of the husband, the starting point would be the *extent* of the wife's contribution and what value to attach to it, not whether she contributed at all. The optimism that *Kivuitu* generated was dampened by a 1995 High Court decision, *Beatrice Wanjiru Kimani v Evanson Kimani Njoroge.*[20]

The parties had been married under statute for 16 years, with some periods of intermittent separation in between. The wife was a high school teacher, while the husband had a better paying job as a US embassy staff member. The property in dispute included five pieces of land and a house, all registered in the name of the husband, as well as a business dealing in auto parts and hardware. The wife alleged that she partly financed the purchase of these properties by taking out loans from Mwalimu Savings and Co-operative Society on four occasions, and on this basis she sought a half-share in the property.

The husband denied that the wife made any contribution toward the purchases, adding that two of them were made at a time when their relationship was strained and marked by repeated separations, and therefore she had not collaborated with him in any way toward acquisition of the property. He alleged that, other than paying the housemaid's salary, the wife made no contribution toward household expenses and the children's welfare.

At the High Court level, the judge accepted the husband's argument and ruled that the wife had no interest whatsoever in the property, as the parties were unlikely to have co-operated in acquiring property together, in view of the strained relationship. That she had custody and care of the children during the periods of separation was not regarded as a contribution at all, since the husband had sent money for their schooling. I find it difficult to accept that in 16 years a salaried wife made zero contribution to assets acquired in the course of the marriage. The judge ruled that a wife's contribution cannot be presumed:

---

[18]   *Kivuitu* at 248.

[19]   High Court Civil Case No 5147 of 1987 (Bosire J, 1994).

[20]   High Court Civil Case No 1610 of 1995 (Kuloba J, 1997).

'Contribution of whatever form must be proved on evidence unless it is admitted. There is no presumption that every wife is an automatic asset ... A wife, whether she be a working woman or a housewife must be considered on the basis of her individual worth.'[21]

This insistence on strict proof of contribution is echoed in the most recent of the six cases discussed here, the *Nderitu* case:

'[A wife must prove] that she contributed directly or indirectly to the acquisition of the assets. It is not enough for her [to] simply show that during the period under review she was sitting on the husband's back with her hands in his pockets. She has to bring evidence to show that she made a contribution towards the acquisition of the properties.'[22]

In the absence of strict proof of contribution, there is no basis for awarding a spouse a beneficial interest in property held by the other spouse.

On appeal, the Court of Appeal agreed with Justice Kuloba's statement of the law on the subject, but remitted the case for retrial before a different High Court judge, on grounds of bias. The judge had made additional comments which constituted an 'off-course discourse on women bordering on bias against the female gender ...'.[23]

There is a basis for arguing that once it is established that a couple was married for a certain period, say ten years, there should be a presumption in favour of equal ownership, at least of the matrimonial home and its contents. The burden of proof should shift to the party claiming that the non-title holding spouse has no entitlement to the family's assets.

C   Reproductive labour as contribution? *Nderitu* (1997)[24]

The parties in this case had been married for 24 years under Kikuyu customary law. The property in dispute included nine pieces of land, a wholesale business, a bank account and several motor vehicles, all of which were registered in the husband's name. All of the property was acquired after marriage from profits earned in informal businesses selling second-hand clothes (*mitumba*). The informal business was managed jointly by the couple, as was the wholesale business established subsequently. The wife worked full time in the businesses. She claimed a half-share in the property. The High Court judge awarded her 30% in all the properties except the marital home in which she was awarded a 50% share. The refusal to award her 50% in all the property was based on the judge's acceptance of the husband's argument that, since three of their five children were delivered through Caesarean operations, the wife had been incapacitated at those times and therefore her contribution to the family's businesses was diminished.

---

[21]   Kuloba J in *Beatrice Kimani v Evanson Kimani Njoroge*, HCCC No 1610 of 1995.

[22]   Kwach JA in *Tabitha Wangeci Nderitu v Simon Nderitu Kariuki*, Civil Appeal No 203 of 1997 (Nairobi).

[23]   Civil Appeal No 79 of 1997 (Nairobi).

[24]   *Tabitha Wangeci Nderitu v Simon Nderitu Kariuki*, Civil Appeal No 203 of 1997 (Nairobi).

The Court of Appeal reversed that part of the judgment, awarding her 50% across the board. The Justices observed that no medical evidence was produced to prove her incapacitation. In my view that is simply beside the point; it is outrageous that a husband would cite his wife's pregnancy and childbirth as a basis for penalizing her. More importantly, the Court of Appeal ruled for the first time that childbearing counts as a contribution to family welfare and therefore creates an entitlement to marital assets. As Justice Kwach put it, '… the wife was putting her life at risk to augment the numerical strength of the family, and I cannot think of a greater contribution than bearing children'.

An important question to ask is whether the court would be willing to push this argument to its logical conclusion: that in all cases where a marriage has resulted in children there is a presumption that a wife, by virtue of such child-bearing, has established a claim to property registered solely in the name of the husband, and all that the court needs to do is establish the extent of her claim. In the *Nderitu* case, there was strong evidence of the wife's intense involvement in running the family businesses, as well as the fact that she was paying for college tuition for the couple's youngest daughter. In the absence of such evidence of financial contribution, would the court still have ruled that she was entitled to 50% or any share of the property on the basis of her childbearing role? Or would the court have been more inclined to view her, as (in Justice Kwach's words) 'sitting on her husband's back with her hands in his pockets'?

V   OVERVIEW OF KEY SHORTCOMINGS OF THE MWPA AND ITS APPLICATION IN KENYAN COURTS

A   The absurdity of separate property

The High Court judge in *Kimani* reiterated that Kenyan law on marital property is founded on the principle of separate property. Each spouse retains whatever he or she owned before marriage, as well as what he or she acquired during marriage. Marriage alone does not confer a proprietary interest, and there is no such concept as 'family property' or 'matrimonial property' since the 'family' is not a legal entity in Kenyan law.

From a comparative perspective, does a common law-based separate property regime necessarily dictate a conclusion that there is no such thing as marital property or family property? Most US jurisdictions that have common-law based separate property regimes have managed, by statute, to establish a practice whereby a couple's assets are categorised into marital and non-marital (separate), and the former is then divided up between the spouses. Assets commonly regarded as marital are the matrimonial home and its contents.[25] Where the marriage is of

---

[25]   Leslie J Harris and Lee E Teitelbaum, *Family Law* (2nd edn, Aspen Publishers, 2000) 445. I do not mean to suggest that the US system is without problems. Empirical research has exposed several problems. For example, a study conducted after New York enacted its equitable distribution statute found that, on average, women receive half, but over 90% of the cases are settled, rather than litigated. In the settled cases, only about one-fifth divided the property equally. Teitelbaum and Harris (above) at 452 (citing Marsha Garrison, 'Good Intentions Gone Awry: The

seven to ten years' duration, there is a strong presumption in favour of a 50:50 division between the spouses. The parties are presumed to have intended such assets for the benefit of the marriage or family. Such a practice does not depend on establishing that the family is a legal entity.

In England, as in Kenya, the courts place emphasis on separate property as the guiding principle. The starting point is to establish legal ownership. Then the court will enquire into any claim of beneficial ownership in favour of the non-title holding spouse. Beneficial ownership may be based on either a written declaration of trust or a resulting, implied or constructive trust, if the court has grounds for inferring a common intention to share the property.[26] With respect to the matrimonial home, the 1978 Law Commission had recommended that spouses should be statutory co-owners, subject to any agreement to the contrary, or unless one party owned the house prior to marriage and wished to exclude it from co-ownership. This recommendation was not implemented.[27]

Viewed against the history of coverture, the MWPA's recognition of separate property for married women had a progressive liberal agenda: the person who acquires property owns it and has the power to transact in it, regardless of gender and marital status. The MWPA is rooted in formal equality.[28] There are three main problems with this approach. First, the approach is clearly inappropriate for assets that are, by definition, intended for common use, such as the matrimonial home and its contents. In the case of Kenya's rural subsistence economy, this would apply to land devoted to the family's food production as well. Most of the Kenyan cases deal with property in land, since land is the main asset in Kenya's socio-economic context. Applying a strict separate property regime in such cases has produced injustice for the non-title holding spouse. This injustice is made sharper by prevailing social norms that tacitly and subtly dictate that the husband is the one who has the socially legitimate authority to exercise control over family resources. Formal law and practice, for example on formal registration of land, reinforce these norms by registering family land predominantly in the names of men on the basis that they are 'male heads of households'.[29]

Impact of New York's Equitable Distribution Law on Divorce Outcomes', (1991) 57 *Brooklyn Law Review* 621, at 673–674.

[26] Nigel Lowe and Gillian Douglas, *Bromley's Family Law* (Butterworths, 1998) at 134–151.

[27] Ibid at 113–114; Alison Diduck and Felicity Kaganas, *Family Law, Gender and the State: Text, Cases and Materials* (Hart Publishing, 1999) at 206.

[28] Alison Diduck and Felicity Kaganas, *Family Law, Gender and the State: Text, Cases and Materials* (Hart Publishing, 1999) at 195 (pointing out that the MWPA and other reforms of the nineteenth and twentieth century were consistent with the liberal politics of the day, which brought about other changes such as abolition of the slave trade and the extension of the right to vote to women and the non-propertied classes).

[29] For a critique of the use of the 'male head of household' concept in formal registration of land in Kenya, see Achola O Pala, 'Women's Access to Land and Their Role in Agriculture and Decision-Making on the Farm: Experiences of the Joluo of Kenya', (1983) 13 *Journal of Eastern African Research and Development* 69; Jean Davison, 'Who Owns What? Land Registration and Tensions in Gender Relations of Production in Kenya', in *Agriculture, Women and Land: The African Experience*, ed Jean Davision (1988), 157. For critiques of the use of the concept in other contexts, see Bina Agarwal, *A Field of One's Own: Gender and Land Rights in South Asia* (1994); Gillian Hart, 'Imagined Unities: Constructions of "the Household" in Economic Theory', in *Understanding Economic Process* (Monographs in Economic Anthropology, No 10), eds Sutti Ortiz and Susan Lees (1992), 111.

It is common practice for land to be registered only in the husband's name. This is the case both with respect to land acquired through purchase (even when purchased through joint efforts) and with respect to inherited land that is understood to be for the benefit of the family and not the exclusive property of the individual who is officially registered as its owner. Statistics show that only 5% of the registered land nationally is held by women. The incidence of joint registration is very low; joint registration between spouses almost non-existent. In a context where the pattern of formal registration of land has already predetermined that the husband will be the title-holding spouse, a strictly title-oriented separate property approach to marital property disputes reinforces gender hierarchy.

The second problem with a separate property approach is that, as is the case with formal equality generally, this approach to acquisition and allocation of property within the family masks substantive structural inequalities. Men and women do not have equal access to the resources and income necessary for the acquisition of property. In the cases discussed, the female partners either earned no income at all (for instance, in *Essa* and *Nderitu* where they worked in the family business without remuneration) or earned substantially less than their husbands (as in *Kimani*, *Karanja* and *Kivuitu*). Nor do men and women enjoy the same status in the family-based networks that determine and facilitate access to property through means such as inheritance. In fact, while men as a group have a higher literacy rate than women and therefore have better access to cash to purchase land, they are also generally better positioned than women as a group to secure their entitlements to family land.

Thirdly, from a policy perspective, what values are promoted by a strict separate property system? It is simply not reflective of the nature of marriage. While marriage is seen and spoken of as a sphere of altruistic behaviour, where people make personal sacrifices for the sake of the relationship, the law of marital property in fact penalizes such self-sacrificial behaviour. The strict separate property regime projects the image of atomistic and disconnected individuals. Some commentators on US family law have criticized the individualistic entitlement-based approach that characterizes strict separate property regimes for engendering expectations that are at cross-purposes with the values of stability, mutual dependency and co-operation in marital relationships.[30]

B Bias against non-monetary contribution

Despite the fact that what the judges take into account in assessing contribution has expanded gradually in the last 27 years, there is still a tendency to equate contribution with financial contribution. Thus, the more the activity undertaken by the non-title holding spouse resembles financial contribution (ie the more amenable it is to monetary quantification) the more likely it is that a court will

---

[30] Susan Prager, 'Sharing Principles and the Future of Marital Property', (1981) 25 *UCLA Law Review* 1. See also Deborah Rhode and Martha Minow, 'Reforming the Questions, Questioning the Reforms: Feminist Perspectives on Divorce Law', in *Divorce Reform at the Crossroads*, ed Stephen Sugarman and Herma Hill Kay (1991).

view it as contribution entitling her to a share of the assets.[31] Certainly the court will be more likely to award her an equal share in such a case. In *Essa*, for instance, the award of a 50% share to the wife was based on evidence that she was actively involved in collecting the rent, managing the commercial property in dispute and advancing money from her business from time to time. In *Nderitu*, the wife had managed the business almost single-handedly, with the husband merely playing an overseeing role and receiving the money from her and banking it.

It is necessary to establish a firm principle recognizing that non-monetary contribution, for example through homemaking and childbearing and childcare, establishes an interest in assets acquired during the marriage. The starting point in a dispute should not be whether the non-title holding spouse is entitled at all, but the extent of her/his entitlement.

C   The larger picture: images of women as dependent and unproductive

When three Court of Appeal judges[32] decided to order a retrial in the *Kimani* case on grounds of bias based on the High Court judge's prejudicial comments against women in general, the judges implicitly acknowledged that questions of gender identity and equality are centrally implicated in decisions on marital property. The issue extends beyond gender relations in the domestic sphere to the perception of women in the broader social, economic and political context.

From a gender equality perspective, the state of the law, as developed by the Kenyan judiciary thus far, projects an image of women as unproductive dependants, rather than equal partners in a marriage relationship. Regardless of the duration of a marriage, a wife must strictly prove her contribution to the assets acquired during the marriage. The attitude that a wife is an unproductive dependant unless there is strict proof to the contrary is captured in Justice Kwach's statement in the *Nderitu* case: that she must prove that she was not simply 'sitting on her husband's back with her hands in his pockets'.

VI   CONCLUSION

The MWPA, a nineteenth-century English statute that prior to 1971 had never been applied to Kenya, has been turned into a resource for Kenyan women, albeit only for those who have access to knowledge about it and the legal services needed to pursue claims under the statute. Perhaps the credit for the developments noted goes to the litigants' lawyers, but the judges too are to be commended for creating room for the MWPA's progressive development in the course of its application in the Kenyan context. With no legislative intervention in sight, the judicial role continues to be crucial. With this comes the need for clearly spelled out guidelines for judges exercising the discretion that s 17 of the MWPA vests in the court. What are the relevant criteria to be taken into account in deciding

---

[31]   This is the trend in England too. Nigel Lowe and Gillian Douglas, *Bromley's Family Law* (Butterworths, 1998) at 142 (noting that it is doubtful that the court will make a finding of a beneficial interest unless the contribution is in the form of money or money's worth).

[32]   Justices Gicheru, Lakha and Omollo.

marital property cases? What weight is to be placed on factors such as duration of the marriage, income-earning capacity of the spouses, monetary and non-monetary contribution, and fault (since Kenya's divorce law is still fault-based)?

The Kenyan courts have not erred on the side of exceeding the discretion that the MWPA permits. Rather, they have engaged in self-policing and have not therefore gone far enough, even within the scope that the MWPA would allow. For instance, there is nothing to prevent the courts from establishing a firm presumption in favour of a non-title holding spouse's beneficial interest in cases involving marriages of long duration, rather than starting from the premise that such an interest must be proved strictly. The courts could do more.

Finally, the procedure for filing claims under the MWPA raises issues of access to justice. The claims are filed by way of an Originating Summons before a High Court judge. Litigation before the High Court is costly and due to its relatively complicated procedure, people without legal representation will rarely file suit in the High Court. Legal fees are beyond the means of a majority of Kenyans. In addition, legal services, including legal aid services, are concentrated in urban areas, leaving rural areas with little or no access to legal services. In resolving intra-familial disputes, people tend to rely more on informal dispute resolution or on the mediating function that is sometimes played by local administrative agencies. The MWPA procedure could be amended to confer jurisdiction on magistrates' courts as well, so as to create more options for people who may choose to invoke the formal legal system in resolving marital disputes.

KOREA

VIOLATION OF THE CONSTITUTION IN KOREAN FAMILY LAW

*Mi-Kyung Cho**

I INTRODUCTION

This paper deals with three decisions of the Korean Constitutional Court,[1] wherein two provisions of the Korean Civil Code and one of the Tax Act were judged to be in violation of the Korean Constitution. Although the Tax Act decision is not, strictly speaking, a family law ruling, it is connected to the provision of the Korean Civil Code[2] which deals with the division of property on divorce.[3]

I will be talking about all three decisions, but will concentrate more on the one regarding the Prohibition of Marriage Clause as the issue has not been resolved and is still the subject of much heated debate while that section of the Korean Civil Code has yet to be amended.

The following are the three decisions which, interestingly, were all adjudicated in 1997:

(1) The Decision of July 16 1997,[4] 95 HunKa 6, etc: On Art 809 of the Korean Civil Code (Prohibition of Marriage between Persons with Same Surname and Same Ancestral Line).

(2) The Decision of March 27 1997,[5] 95 HunKa 14, etc: On the Limitation Period of Art 847 of the Korean Civil Code (Action for Denial of Paternity).

(3) The Decision of October 30, 1997,[6] 96 HunBa 14: On Art 29-2(1)(i) of the Inheritance Tax Act (Old Version, Gift Tax on Matrimonial Property Distribution following a Divorce).

---

*   Professor of Family Law, Director, Division of Law, Ajou University, Suwon.

1   As of 31 July 1998, in nearly 10 years, the Court has adjudicated 3,469 cases. Of the total number, 251 cases, including 182 Constitutionality of Laws cases, have been decided unconstitutional. These figures show that the Court has been very active in safeguarding our Constitution: see *http://www.ccourt.go.kr*.

2   Korean Civil Code (hereinafter KCC): Law No 471, 22 February 1958, effective 1 January 1960 Art 839-2.

3   Mi-Kyung Cho, 'The claim of division of property on divorce', in *The International Survey of Family Law 1995*, ed A Bainham (Martinus Nijhoff Publishers, 1997), pp 321–323; Mi-Kyung Cho, 'The Relationship between Social Change and Family Law in Korea', *The Changing Family, Family Forms & Family Law* (Hart Publishing, 1998), pp 103–113.

4   See *http://www.ccourt.go.kr*. Case No 51: The Decision of 16 July 1997, 95 HunKa 6, etc. On Art 809 of the Korean Civil Code (Prohibition of Marriage between Persons with Same Surname and Same Ancestral Line) 9-2 *Korean Constitutional Court Report* (hereinafter KCCR), pp 1–31.

5   The Decision of March 27 1997, 95 HunKa 14, etc: On the Limitation Period of Art 847 of the Korean Civil Code (Action of Denial of Paternity): 9-1 KCCR, pp 193–218.

Let us first look at the decision regarding the incompatibility of the Prohibition of Marriage Clause.

II   DECISION OF INCOMPATIBILITY WITH THE KOREAN CONSTITUTION ON PROHIBITION OF MARRIAGE

The Decision of July 16 1997,[7] 95 HunKa 6, etc: On Art 809 of the Korean Civil Code: Prohibition of Marriage between Persons with Same Surname and Same Ancestral Line.

Article 809 of the Korean Civil Code reads as follows:

> 'Article 809 [Prohibition of Marriage between Parties Whose Surname and Origin of which are Common] (1) : A marriage may not be allowed between the blood relatives, *if both surname and the origin of which are common to the parties.*'

The Constitutional Court ruled that this Article violates the fundamental human right to the pursuit of happiness and freedom of choice in marriage as outlined in Arts 10,[8] 11(1),[9] 36(1)[10] and 37(2)[11] of the Korean Constitution.

In Korea a child takes his or her father's surname[12] and the country has about 275 surnames[13] in total. As surnames are derived from a specific blood ancestor some people with the same surname do not share the same ancestor. There are 282 specific Kim[14] blood ancestors and this is the surname that is borne by the largest number of Koreans[15] (about 9 million out of a total population of 40 million). For example, there are about 4 million Kims who originated in

---

[6]   See *http://www.ccourt.go.kr*. Case No 55: The Decision of October 30 1997, 96 HunBa 14: On Art 29-2(1)(i) of the Inheritance Tax Act (Gift Tax on Matrimonial Property Distribution under a Divorce: Old version, Law No 4283, 31 December 1990) 9-2 KCCR, pp 454–477.

[7]   See *http://www.ccourt.go.kr*. Case No 51; note 4 (above).

[8]   Article 10 Korean Constitution: All citizens shall be assured of human dignity and worth and have the *right to pursue happiness*. It shall be the duty of the State to confirm and guarantee the fundamental and inviolable human rights of individuals.

[9]   Article 11(1) Korean Constitution: All citizens shall be *equal before the law*, and there shall be *no discrimination* in political, economic, social or cultural life on account of *sex*, religion or social status.

[10] Article 36(1) Korean Constitution: Marriage and family life shall be entered into and sustained on the basis of individual dignity and *equality of the sexes,* and the State shall do everything in its power to achieve that goal.

[11] Article 37(2) Korean Constitution: The *freedoms and rights* of citizens may be restricted by Act only when necessary for national security, the maintenance of law and order or for public welfare. Even when such restriction is imposed no essential aspect of the freedom or right shall be violated.

[12] Article 781 KCC [Entry into Family Register of Surname and Origin of Surname of Child] (1) A child shall assume its father's surname and the origin of surname and shall have its name entered in its father's family register.

[13] National Bureau of Statistics, Economic Planning Board, *Report on the Korean Surname and Its Origin* (1988) Vol 1, p 3.

[14] *Ibid*, pp 12–228.

[15] *Ibid*, p 12.

Kimhae and about 1.5 million who are from Kyungju.[16] As these two Kim clans descend from different blood ancestors, a Kimhae Kim and a Kyungju Kim can marry. But, until the Constitutional Court's decision in 1997, none of the approximately 4 million Kimhae Kims could marry each other, despite the absence of any close blood relationship, even if their relationship was 100 times removed.

The second largest surname is Lee, and Lees amount to about 6 million people.[17] The third largest group is the Parks at 3.5 million.[18] Similarly to the Kims, the Lees and Parks are divided into many ancestral groups. Pie Charts 1 and 2 below set out the distribution of surnames in South Korea.

Although, according to Art 809 of the Korean Civil Code, none of the Kimhae Kims could marry one another, many men and women with the same surname and sharing the same ancestral line chose to live together as husband and wife. However, the relationship was not recognized as a legal marriage. On three separate occasions, the National Assembly passed provisional legislation, with a time-limit of one year (in 1977,[19] 1987[20] and 1995[21]), allowing these factual marriages to be given the status of a legal marriage. With 4,577 in 1978, 12,443 in 1988, and 27,807 in 1996, a total of 44,827 same name/common ancestor couples became legally married.[22]

Article 809 of the Korean Civil Code has been criticized on the ground that it infringed the freedom of choice in marriage. Many family lawyers as well as the Law Association have been asking for the abrogation of this Article. At the same time, many Confucian-oriented conservatives urged its preservation. However, in 1997 the Constitutional Court at last declared that Art 809 of the Korean Civil Code is incompatible with the Constitution.

The following is a summary of this decision.[23]

THE FACTS

Article 809(1) of the Korean Civil Code prohibits marriage between two persons having the same family name with the same ancestral line ('Dongsungdongbon'). This prohibition is based on a long-practised tradition which can be traced back at least to the late Yi Dynasty.[24] People with the same family name of the same origin were regarded as members of the same 'family'. In recent times, however, the number of people in one such 'family' has so multiplied that some 'families' came to have over two million members. However, the prohibition has persisted.

---

[16] *Ibid.*

[17] Economic Planning Board, *Report on the Korean Surname and Its Origin* (1988) vol 1, p 228.

[18] *Ibid*, p 444.

[19] Law No 3052, 31 December 1977.

[20] Law No 3971, 28 November 1987.

[21] Law No 5013, 6 December 1995.

[22] 9-2 KCCR p 15.

[23] See *http://www.ccourt.go.kr*. Case No. 51; note 4 (above).

[24] 1392–1910 AD.

PIE CHART 1 – DISTRIBUTION OF SURNAMES
population: 40,419,652 (all surnames 275)

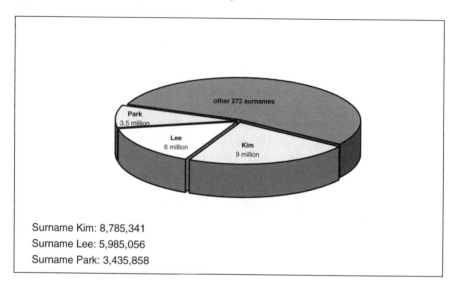

Surname Kim: 8,785,341
Surname Lee: 5,985,056
Surname Park: 3,435,858

PIE CHART 2 – DISTRIBUTION OF ANCESTRAL LINES OF SURNAME KIM
(all ancestral lines of surname Kim: 282)

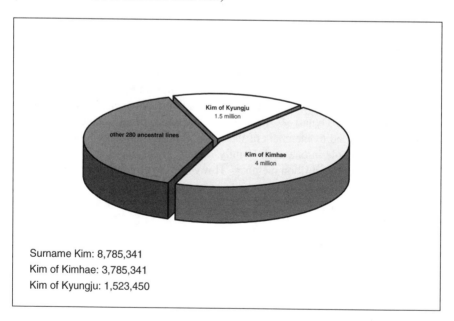

Surname Kim: 8,785,341
Kim of Kimhae: 3,785,341
Kim of Kyungju: 1,523,450

National Bureau of Statistics, Economic Planning Board, *Report on the Korean Surname and Its Origin* (Republic of Korea, 1988) Vol 1, pp 2–1343.

EXPLANATION OF DISTRIBUTION PIE CHARTS

Pie Chart 1 is the distribution pie of surnames.

40 million Koreans have 275 surnames. Among them 9 million are Kims, 6 million are Lees and 3.5 million are Parks.

According to an old Korean joke, if you were to throw a stone from the top of any mountain, it would hit a Kim, Lee or Park.

Pie Chart 2 shows the ancestral line of 9 million people with the Kim surname.

The Kims have 282 ancestral lines in total. Among them 4 million people are Kimhae Kims and 1.5 million are Kyungju Kims. According to Art 809 of the Korean Civil Code, the 4 million Kimhae Kims could not marry each other before the 1997 Korean Constitutional Court decision.

Couples who married despite the prohibition have been ostracized by their families and have usually lived with a sense of guilt. Their de facto marriages can not be registered and can be annulled under the Civil Code. Many times this prohibition was severely criticized in and out of the National Assembly, yet it continued to survive.

Six couples, whose marriage registrations were rejected, appealed to the Seoul Family Court. The Seoul Family Court, after accepting the plaintiffs' complaints, suspended the case and referred the constitutionality issue to the Constitutional Court on 29 May 1995.

THE ISSUE

The issue was whether Art 809(1) of the Korean Civil Code ('Marriage Prohibition Clause') which prohibits marriage between two persons of the same family name from the same origin was constitutional.

DECISION

In a 7–2 decision, the court held that Art 809(1) of the Korean Civil Code was incompatible with the Constitution, and that, if the National Assembly did not amend it by 31 December 1998, it would become null and void, commencing on 1 January 1999. Until the National Assembly amended the Marriage Prohibition Clause, other courts and government agencies, including local governments, should not apply the clause.

REASONING

The legislative purpose of the Marriage Prohibition Clause did not fall under the permissible category of restricting individual human rights for 'social order' or 'public welfare' prescribed in Art 37(2)[25] of the Korean Constitution. Such prohibition also violated the equal protection clause of the Constitution by *discriminating against gender, because it applied only to surnames from the same patrilineal blood*. Also, the Marriage Prohibition Clause infringed the pursuit of happiness, which includes the freedom to choose one's spouse, and was inconsistent with the right to marry guaranteed by Art 36(1)[26] of the Constitution.

Article 809(1) of the Korean Civil Code lost its validity as a result of the Constitutional Court's decision and the Korean Supreme Court, respecting the decision, amended the Rules of the Supreme Court on the Registration of Family Relations.[27] According to these amended Arts 2 and 3, a de facto marriage between a man and woman with the same surname who share a common original ancestor more than eight times removed[28] can be registered in the Family Register and transformed into a legal marriage.

For the past 30 years, feminist and family law academics have waged a nation-wide campaign to have the provision annulled.[29] The majority of family lawyers, as well as the Ministry of Justice, think that reform of the family law rules is urgently needed since these rules do not reflect modern life and, by giving husbands and fathers predominant powers, are rooted in anachronistic paternalism and *sexual discrimination*. Nevertheless, the abrogation of Art 809 of the Korean Civil Code is encountering the desperate resistance of conservative supporters of Confucianism, among others. The Ministry of Justice presented a Reform Bill to the National Assembly but Art 809 was *excluded* from it by the Legislation and Judiciary Committee, which moved a resolution in December 1999 *not to repeal it*,[30] in spite of the Korean Constitutional Court's 1997 decision.

However, many members of National Assembly hesitated to vote for the Reform Bill, chiefly because the resistance is so fierce that they feared angering both feminist and conservative electors. They chose to postpone any decision on the resolution despite the 31 December 1998 deadline imposed by the Constitutional Court. As the term of the former 15th National Assembly ended in May 2000 (following the April Parliamentary elections) the Reform Bill automatically died. The Ministry of Justice is planning to re-introduce its Reform Bill and already has made a public notice of the Reform Bill of the Korean Civil

---

[25]   Note 11 (above).

[26]   Note 10 (above).

[27]   Rules of the Supreme Court on the Registration of Family Relations No 535, 30 July 1997.

[28]   Besides the prohibition of marriage in Art 809, there is Art 815 of the Korean Civil Code which makes invalid a marriage between blood relatives within the eighth degree. Their marriage is null and void:

   Article 815 KCC [Nullity of Marriage]. A marriage is null and void if it falls under any of the following Subparagraphs: (1) Where there is no common consent to marry between the parties; (2) Where there exists or existed between the parties the relationship of lineal blood relative, collateral blood *relative within the eighth degree* of relationship and spouse to one of such relatives.

[29]   Mi-Kyung Cho, 'The Family Law Reform and the Improvement of the Status of Women', *University of Louisville Journal of Family Law* (*Annual Survey of Family Law*) (The International Society of Family Law, 1995) Vol 33/2, p 437.

[30]   Ministry of Justice, Reform Bill of the Korean Civil Code, proposed in 13 November 1998; Legislation and Judiciary Committee records No 208/16, 17 December 1999, 15. National Assembly; see *http://www.assembly.go.kr*.

Code in June 2000,[31] which is a prerequisite necessary to submit a Bill to the National Assembly. And the 16th National Assembly, which took office in June 2000, is expected to pass it. The debate, however, will not end there.

The Ministry of Justice's Reform Bill,[32] which includes Art 809 of the Korean Civil Code, reads as follows:

'Reform Bill of Art 809: [The Scope of Prohibition of Marriage]

(1) Marriage is not allowed between paternal or maternal blood relatives within the eighth degree of relationship (including blood relatives before adoption).

(2) Marriage is not allowed between the parties if either of them is or was the spouse of a blood relative within the sixth degree of relationship, or the blood relative of the spouse within the sixth degree of relationship, or if either of them is or was the spouse of the blood relatives by affinity within the fourth degree of relationship of the spouse.

(3) A marriage is not allowed between parties who were blood relatives within the sixth degree of relationship of the adoptive father or adoptive mother or relatives by affinity within the fourth degree of relationship of the adoptive father or mother.'

In many countries, the prohibited degrees of marriage are very narrow[33] and even a union between a same sex couple can be recognized as a legal partnership.[34] Compared to this world-wide trend, Art 809 of the Korean Civil Code appears very odd and anachronistic as well as lacking any rational basis. It must be reformed.

---

[31] See *http://www.assembly.go.kr*: Period of Public Notice: 13 June 2000–3 July 2000 (21 days). A Reform Bill of the Korean Civil Code of the Ministry of Justice was proposed on 16 October 2000 (Legislation and Judiciary Committee No 160214). This included a reform proposal relating to Art 809 KCC. A further Reform Bill of the Korean Civil Code was proposed by Mr Young-Hee Choi and 19 other members of the National Assembly on 28 November 2000 (Legislation and Judiciary Committee No 160419) which also included a reform proposal relating to Art 809 KCC.

[32] Note 30 (above).

[33] Germany: §1307 BGB (Burgerliches Gesetzbuch); England: Nigel Lowe and Gillian Douglas, *Bromley's Family Law* (9th edn, 1998) pp 31ff; United States: Uniform Marriage and Divorce Act § 207, HD Krause, *Family Law* (3rd edn, 1990) pp 49ff.

[34] Åke Saldeen, 'Family Counselling, the Tortious Liability of Parents and Homosexual Partnership', *University of Louisville Journal of Family Law* (1995) Vol 33/2, p 519; Lynn D Wardle, 'Same-sex Marriage and the Limits of Legal Pluralism', *The Changing Family (Family Forms & Family Law)* (Hart Publishing, 1998) pp 381–396; Ingrid Lund-Anderson, 'Cohabitation and Registered Partnership in Scandinavia – The Legal Position of Homosexuals', *The Changing Family (Family Forms & Family Law)* (Hart Publishing, 1998) pp 397–404; Elsa Steyn, 'From Closet to Constitution: The South African Gay Family Rights Odyssey', *The Changing Family (Family Forms & Family Law)* (Hart Publishing, 1998) pp 405–431; Nicholas Bala and Martha Bailey, 'Controversies about Same-Sex Couples and Children', *The International Survey of Family Law 1997*, ed A Bainham (Martinus Nijhoff Publishers, 1999) pp 79–103, etc.

III DECISION OF INCOMPATIBILITY WITH THE KOREAN CONSTITUTION ON LIMITATION PERIOD OF DENIAL OF PATERNITY ACTION

The Decision of March 27 1997,[35] 95 HunKa 14, etc. On the Limitation Period of Article 847 of the Korean Civil Code: Action for Denial of Paternity

In this case, the court held that the Limitation Period of Art 847 (Action for Denial of Paternity) of the Korean Civil Code is incompatible with the Korean Constitution on the ground that the *one-year limitation period* for the action for denial of paternity was too short and infringed a fundamental human right, ie the dignity of the person, the husband's right to pursue happiness in his family life as guaranteed by Arts 10,[36] 36(1)[37] of the Korean Constitution.

Article 847 of the Korean Civil Code reads as follows:

> 'Article 847 [Action for Denial of Paternity] (1) An action for denial shall be brought against the child or the mother with parental authority *within one year from the day on which the husband became aware of the child's birth.*'

The following is a summary of the decision.[38]

THE FACTS

Two district courts had requested a ruling from the Constitutional Court on the compatibility of the Limitation Period of Art 847 with the Constitution. A husband brought an action for denial of his paternity to the Seoul Family Court and, at the same time, requested a ruling on the constitutionality of the one-year limitation period. Another husband had brought a similar action in the Chungju District Court. After accepting the plaintiffs' complaints, both courts suspended the proceedings and referred the issue to the Constitutional Court on 11 July 1995 (Seoul Family Court) and on 2 March 1996 (Chungju District Court).

THE ISSUES

At issue was whether Art 847(1) of the Korean Civil Code (Action for Denial of Paternity) which prescribes that an action of denial shall be brought ... *within one year from the day on which the husband became aware of the child's birth,* is compatible with the Korean Constitution or not.

The Constitutional Court had to decide whether or not the *one-year limitation period for action for denial of paternity* was too short a time to protect the legitimate interests of the husband who is not a child's genetic father.

---

[35] 9-1 KCCR pp 193–218.

[36] Note 8 (above).

[37] Note 10 (above).

[38] Note 35 (above).

DECISION

The Constitutional Court held that Art 847(1) of the Korean Civil Code is incompatible with the Constitution, and ordered that until the National Assembly amended the Limitation Period of the Denial of Paternity clause, other courts and government agencies, including local governments, should not apply the clause.

REASONING

(1) The National Assembly may decide the limitation period for an action for the denial of paternity at its discretion. However, in so doing, the National Assembly must take into account the social conditions, the traditions, interests of parties, and the constitutional aspects of marriage and family life. If the limitation period allowed is so short or unreasonable that the period would elapse before the father could ensure that the child is his, or makes it impossible to initiate a denial of paternity action, then the lawmakers' decision cannot be considered reasonable.

(2) It is usual for a husband to believe that a child born to his wife is his daughter or son.[39] Article 847(1) of the Korean Civil Code provides that the husband cannot proceed with an action for denial of paternity if one year has elapsed since the day on which he became aware of the child's birth, rather than when he realized the child was not his genetic son or daughter. Moreover, it corresponds neither to today's social realities nor to the tradition that views blood relationships as being very serious and important. The one-year limitation period is too short to be reasonable and, in an unjust and extreme manner, removes from the husband any real chance to deny his paternity. For this reason Art 847(1) of the Korean Civil Code violates the right to the pursuit of happiness, the dignity of the person and the fundamental marital rights of the husband guaranteed by Arts 10[40] and 36(1)[41] of the Korean Constitution.

Following the decision, the Ministry of Justice drafted the Reform Bill of Art 847 of the Korean Civil Code. It reads as follows:

'Reform Bill of Art 847 [Action for Denial of Paternity]

(1) An action for denial of paternity shall be brought against the child or the mother with parental authority within *one year from the day on which the husband became aware of the fact that the child was not his own child* or within *five years* from the day on which the husband became aware of the *child's birth.*'

The Ministry of Justice's Bill to reform Arts 809 and 847 of the Korean Civil Code is expected, as mentioned earlier, to be passed by the 16th National Assembly which began in June 2000.

---

[39] Article 844 KCC [Presumption as Husband's Child] (1) A child conceived by a wife during the subsistence of the marriage shall be presumed to be the child of the wife's husband.

[40] Note 8 (above).

[41] Note 10 (above).

I have so far reviewed two decisions regarding the Korean Civil Code. I would now like to talk about the Korean Constitutional Court's decision regarding a provision of the Tax Act.

IV DECISION THAT A GIFT TAX ON MATRIMONIAL PROPERTY DISTRIBUTION FOLLOWING DIVORCE IS UNCONSTITUTIONAL

The Decision of October 30 1997,[42] 96 HunBa 14 on Art 29-2(1)(i) of the Inheritance Tax Act (old version, Law No 4283, 31 December 1990)

The revenue office considered the property a divorced woman received in a divorce settlement to be a gift from her husband and therefore imposed a gift tax on it. The Korean Constitutional Court ruled that the property acquired by the divorced wife according to Art 839-2[43] of the Korean Civil Code to be her own property rather than a gift and that, therefore, the imposition of a gift tax was unjust and *unconstitutional* according to Arts 11(1),[44] 38[45] and 59[46] of the Korean Constitution.

Although this decision is not directly related to the family law rules of the Korean Civil Code it did take Art 839-2 of the Korean Civil Code into account. One can therefore say that this decision is indirectly based on the Korean Civil Code.

The following is a summary of the decision.[47]

THE FACTS

Under Art 839-2 of the Korean Civil Code, a divorced party may request that the former spouse distribute matrimonial property. Art 29-2 of the Inheritance Tax Act provides that a gift tax shall be imposed on the person who receives property exceeding the amount of a matrimonial estate stipulated by the same Act. The petitioner, divorced and charged with a gift tax on her share of property, challenged the constitutionality of Art 29-2 in the course of a trial seeking

---

[42] Note 30 above.

[43] Article 839-2 KCC [The Claim of Division of Property]

(1) One of the parties who has been divorced by agreement may claim a division of property against the other party.

(2) If no agreement is made for a division of property as referred to in paragraph (1), or if it is impossible to reach an agreement, the Family Court shall, upon the request of the parties, determine the amount and the method of division, taking into consideration the amount of property realized by the cooperation of both parties as well as other circumstances.

(3) The claim for division of property of paragraph (1) lapses when two years has passed from the date of divorce.

See also note 2 (above).

[44] Note 9 (above).

[45] Article 38 Korean Constitution: All citizens shall have the duty to pay taxes under the conditions as prescribed by Act.

[46] Article 59 Korean Constitution: Types and rates of taxes shall be determined by Act.

[47] Note 6 (above); p 43.

annulment of the tax in the Pusan High Court. When the court dismissed her motion to refer the case to the Constitutional Court, she filed a constitutional complaint with this court.

THE ISSUE

The issue was whether the imposition of a gift tax on distributed matrimonial property contravened the principles of legal taxation and equal taxation.

DECISION

By an 8–1 decision, this Court held that Art 29-2(1)(i) of the Inheritance Tax Act was unconstitutional.

REASONING

Basically, the system of property distribution in connection with a divorce is characterised as a settlement of common property made by mutual efforts in marriage, although it also has the function of supporting the economically vulnerable party.

Therefore, it is deemed unnecessary to impose a gift tax resulting from the gratuitous acquisition of property. If tax policy requires that property distributed under a bogus divorce perpetrated for tax evasion purposes be treated as a gift, then more detailed legislation would be needed so that a true distribution of property can be distinguished from a bogus one. Consequently, a gift tax in this case without legislative clarification transgressed the appropriate proportionality between the legislative objective and its means, and represented an undemocratic view of taxation. The imposition of a gift tax on the amount in excess, without any rationale, contravenes the principle of legal taxation since it is incompatible with the constitutionally guaranteed property right.

The main legislative objective lies in maintaining a balance between the imposition of a gift tax on property distributed under a divorce and the imposition of inheritance tax on property inherited following the death of a spouse. However, divorce and the death of a spouse have several differences concerning property and status relations, although both of them have in common the termination of marital relations. Hence, it conflicts with the principle of equal taxation to treat the function of a gift tax as complementary to inheritance tax. Such treatment resulted in unfavorable discrimination against the person in question, who received her own part of the common property.

This Tax Act provision had fortunately already been abrogated in 1998.[48]

V   CONCLUSION

I have presented three decisions of the Korean Constitutional Court related to Korean Family Law.

---

[48]   Inheritance Tax and Gift Tax Act, Law No 5193, 30 December 1996 (partial amendment of Law No 5582, 28 December 1998); the decision of the Korean Constitutional Court was about old version, Law No 4283, 31 December 1990.

(1)   Article 809 (Prohibition of Marriage between Persons with Same Surname and Same Ancestral Line) of the Korean Civil Code is incompatible with the Korean Constitution since it violates the fundamental human rights to the pursuit of happiness and freedom of marriage as provided in Arts 10, 11(1), 36(1) and 37(2) of the Korean Constitution.
(2)   Article 847 (limitation period of Action for Denial of Paternity) of the Korean Civil Code is incompatible with the Korean Constitution in that too short a limitation period violates the fundamental human right to pursue happiness as defined in Arts 10 and 36(1) of the Korean Constitution.
(3)   Article 29-2(1)(i) of the Inheritance Tax Act was unconstitutional on the grounds that the imposition of a gift tax on the divorced wife who had obtained property acquired during the marriage is unjust and unconstitutional according to Arts 11(1), 38 and 59 of the Korean Constitution.

This Tax Act Rule had already been amended, but including the above-mentioned two decisions, the reform of Korean family law is expected to be passed some time in 2000 by the current National Assembly which began in June 2000.

NAMIBIA

FAMILY LAW REFORM IN NAMIBIA: WORK IN PROGRESS

Dianne Hubbard [*] *and Elizabeth Cassidy* [**]

I   INTRODUCTION

Namibia is a small country which is short on human and material resources. This fact hampers progress in a number of fields. To give a concrete example, the 2001 population of some 1.8 million includes only about 270 lawyers. The same small base of expertise is evident in other fields. This means that key organisations and individuals are stretched very thin, both inside and outside government, especially in the field of gender.

Namibia, which is sometimes referred to as Africa's last colony, was a German colony which came under South African control after World War I. After a liberation struggle which spanned more than 20 years, Namibia became independent from South African rule on 21 March 1990. This event heralded a period of legal and social change which has provided favourable opportunities for gender developments.

The Namibian Constitution and key international commitments relating to family law were detailed in Namibia's previous contribution to the *Survey*.[1] In brief, the Namibian Constitution provides a strong backdrop for sexual equality. It is one of the few constitutions in the world that uses gender-neutral language throughout, and it explicitly forbids discrimination on the basis of sex. It explicitly provides for equality in all aspects of marriage, and gives special emphasis to women in the provision which authorises affirmative action. Furthermore, it explicitly states that customary law survives only to the extent that it does not conflict with the Constitution, meaning that customary law may not entail any form of sex discrimination. The Constitution also puts men and women in an identical position with respect to citizenship, including the acquisition of citizenship by marriage.

---

[*]   Dianne Hubbard has served since 1993 as the Co-ordinator of the Gender Research & Advocacy Project of the Legal Assistance Centre, a non-governmental organisation engaged in research, education, litigation, legal advice and lobbying in a range of areas. The Gender Research & Advocacy Project has worked closely with the government on a number of gender-related law reforms. Ms Hubbard also lectures on the topic of Gender and the Law at the University of Namibia.

[**]   Elizabeth Cassidy is a lecturer in Constitutional Law at the University of Namibia and has worked as a consultant to the Gender Research & Advocacy Project of the Legal Assistance Centre on several projects since 1998.

[1]   Fareda Banda, 'Family Law Reform in Namibia' in A Bainham (ed), *The International Survey of Family Law 1996* (Martinus Nijhoff Publishers, 1998), 265–278, at 267–274.

As previously noted, Namibia is a signatory to the UN Convention on the Elimination of All Forms of Discrimination Against Women (CEDAW) and the UN Convention on the Rights of the Child. However, it is deserving of emphasis that Namibia is amongst the few nations in the world to have signed these Conventions with no reservations. Namibia was the first country in the world to ratify the Optional Protocol to CEDAW, which gives individuals and groups the right to complain directly to the UN about violations of the Convention, as well as giving investigative powers to the committee which monitors CEDAW in instances of grave or systematic abuse of women's human rights.[2] However, the provision of the Constitution which makes these Conventions part of Namibia's domestic law remains untested.[3]

Namibia is also a party to many other international Conventions, including the following:

- the International Covenant on Economic, Social and Cultural Rights;[4]
- the International Covenant on Civil and Political Rights;[5]
- the International Convention on the Elimination of All Forms of Racial Discrimination;[6]
- the Convention on the Rights of the Child;[7]
- the African Charter on Human and People's Rights.[8]

Namibia is also a signatory to the non-binding SADC Declaration on Gender and Development (1997) and the accompanying Addendum on Prevention and Eradication of Violence against Women (1998).

Namibia's Parliament currently comprises 20% women.[9] However, only three out of nineteen Ministers are women, plus the Director-General of the National Planning Commission.[10] Furthermore, none of the five Standing Committees in

---

[2] Namibia ratified the Optional Protocol to CEDAW on 26 May 2000. It came into force on 22 December 2000, after being ratified by the required minimum of 10 countries.

[3] Article 144 of the Namibian Constitution states that 'unless otherwise provided by this Constitution or Act of Parliament, ... international agreements binding upon Namibia ... shall form part of the law of Namibia'. But the import of this statement has not yet been explored in any actual case.

[4] Accession on 28 November 1994.

[5] Accession on 28 November 1994. Namibia also acceded to the Optional Protocol and the Second Optional Protocol (aiming at the Abolition of the Death Penalty) to this Covenant on the same date.

[6] Accession on 11 November 1982.

[7] Ratification on 30 September 1990, without reservations. Namibia's Parliament debated the Optional Protocol to the Convention on the Rights of the Child on the Involvement of Children in Armed Conflict in April 2001, but the ratification process is not yet complete.

[8] Accession on 16 September 1992.

[9] The National Assembly includes 25% women (18 women amongst 72 elected and 6 appointed members). There are only two women amongst the 26 members of the National Council, elected from the 13 Regional Councils (7.7%). This means that Parliament as a whole includes just over 20% women. This exceeds the world average of 13.7% considerably, although it is still far from the ideal of a perfect balance. (Sweden comes closest, with a Parliament that is 42.7% female.) Statistics from Inter-Parliamentary Union (*www.ipu.org/*) (June 2001).

[10] In addition to the 19 Ministers, there are three other positions which are at Cabinet level: the Director-General of the National Planning Commission (currently female), the Head of National Intelligence and the Speaker of the National Assembly (both currently male).

the National Assembly or the four Standing Committees in the National Council which deal with legislation of a general nature is currently chaired by a woman.[11]

The last local government elections, held in 1998, resulted in local councils comprising 41% women, as a result of an affirmative action provision which required that a minimum number of women be placed on all party lists. In contrast, only some 3% of regional councillors are women, as no affirmative action provision applied at this level of government.

The law which provides a procedure for official recognition of traditional authorities requires that they 'promote affirmative action amongst the members of that community', particularly 'by promoting women to positions of leadership' – but contains no specific monitoring or enforcement mechanisms.[12]

Women or men who believe that they have experienced discrimination on the grounds of sex can bring a court challenge under the Constitution, but the only person to take this route so far in Namibia is a white German male.[13] The majority of the public is apparently content to let Government take responsibility for implementing the constitutional principle of non-discrimination.

Furthermore, there are many areas where law reform is needed on gender grounds, not because of formal inequality, but because the present laws are simply inadequate to serve gender needs effectively. One of the key examples here is Namibia's law on maintenance, which is completely gender-neutral but nevertheless unsatisfactory to serve the needs of the single mothers who are its primary users. Another dramatic example is domestic violence, where the current criminal and civil law do not meet the needs of the women who are most often injured or killed at the hands of their 'loved ones'. For these reasons, law reform on gender issues is crucial to the advancement of equity between women and men in Namibia.

Shortly after Independence, the government established a Department of Women Affairs (DWA) in the Office of the President, which played a co-ordinating and facilitating role on gender issues as well as having responsibility for monitoring Namibia's implementation of CEDAW and the Beijing Platform for Action. In consultation with a range of government bodies and NGOs, the Department of Women Affairs drafted a National Gender Policy and Plan of Action which was approved by Cabinet in 1997, but the Gender Commission which is supposed to function as the monitoring body for these policies has not yet been put into place.

The National Gender Plan of Action (1998–2003) contains the following list of areas where law reform must take place in the section on 'Gender and Legal Affairs': maintenance; rape and other sexual offences; customary law on marriages and inheritance; children's rights, including protection from abuse and

---

[11] There are a total of nine Standing Committees in the National Assembly, only one of which is chaired by a woman. The Vice Chair of the Standing Committee on Human Resources, Equality and Gender Development is a woman. There are a total of seven Standing Committees in the National Council, none of which is chaired by a woman. However, since the Standing Committees are drawn from Parliamentary backbenchers, there are a limited number of women in the pool.

[12] Traditional Authorities Act 17 of 1995.

[13] There are several pending cases involving potential legal challenges to various laws on the ground of sex discrimination, but none of these have progressed to court at the time of writing. These cases are outlined in the text below.

neglect and the status of children born outside marriage; divorce; domestic violence; affirmative action; and abortion. As of mid-2001, the only item from this list to be addressed through law reform is rape and other sexual offences.

The Department of Women Affairs was made into a full-fledged Ministry of Women Affairs and Child Welfare in March 2000. Whilst this move is perceived as a signal of government commitment to gender issues, the Ministry itself has not up to now played a leading role in pushing for law reform on family law or other gender issues.

The Law Reform and Development Commission is a statutory body with responsibility for conducting research and making recommendations for legal change. The majority of its members have other full-time duties, and it has only a very small staff. This body has initiated most of the family law reforms which have moved forward to date, although such reforms can also be originated directly by appropriate line ministries as well.

II   CASE-LAW DEVELOPMENTS

As mentioned above, the Namibian Constitution contains several provisions that are relevant to family law. Article 10 guarantees equality before the law and freedom from discrimination on various grounds, including sex. Article 14 protects the family, granting men and women of full age the right to marry and establish a family, and requiring that men and women have equal rights relating to marriage.[14] Article 15 provides for children's rights. Since 1996, a handful of court decisions, discussed below, have considered Articles 10 and 14. Article 15 has not yet been interpreted by the Namibian courts.[15]

A   Gender equality generally and in marriage

Article 10 of the Constitution provides: '(1) All persons shall be equal before the law', and '(2) No persons may be discriminated against on the grounds of sex, race, colour, ethnic origin, religion, creed, or social or economic status'.[16] Article 14(1) provides, in relevant part, that 'men and women ... shall be entitled to equal rights as to marriage, during marriage, and at its dissolution'.

The Namibian courts have developed the following analysis for Article 10 questions: a differentiation based on one of the grounds enumerated in Article 10(2) will violate that sub-article if it constitutes 'unfair discrimination',

---

[14]   Furthermore, unlike the situation in some countries, the Constitution's provisions concerning citizenship provide that a child born to a Namibian father or mother is eligible for Namibian citizenship, as is a foreigner married to a Namibian man or woman. See Chapter 2 of the Namibian Constitution.

[15]   Article 15 grants children the right to a name, to acquire a nationality, and, as long as it is in their best interests, to be cared for by their parents. It also forbids the economic exploitation of children and the preventative detention of children under 16.

[16]   Sexual orientation is not included as a prohibited ground for discrimination. In *Chairperson of the Immigration Selection Board v Frank and Another*, Case No SA 8/99 (SC 5 March 2001), which is discussed more fully below, the Supreme Court found that Namibian immigration law's failure to treat same-sex life partners in the same way it treats spouses for purposes of granting permanent residence permits did not violate Article 10(2).

which is determined primarily by considering the effect of the discrimination on the dignity of the victim or victims,[17] while a differentiation on any other ground will violate Article 10(1) if it is unreasonable and not rationally connected to a legitimate object.[18]

The Namibian Supreme Court's Article 10 cases include two involving differentiations based on sex. In the first of these cases, a man sought, but was denied, the same right as a woman to a change of name upon marriage. In the other, a married woman tried, but failed, to avoid a lawsuit through the application of the common law rule that treated her as a minor who could not enter into contracts or sue or be sued.

In *Muller v President of the Republic of Namibia and Another*, a man who wanted to take his wife's surname challenged the law that required him to comply with certain formalities to do so but did not require any formalities for a woman to take her husband's name. The court agreed with Mr Muller that the law in question differentiated on the basis of sex, but found that the differentiation was not unfair discrimination. The court reasoned as follows.[19] First, it believed that the differentiation did not impair the dignity of Mr Muller, who, as a white male who came to Namibia after Independence, was not part of a prior disadvantaged group.[20] The court further found that the purpose of the differentiation was not to disadvantage or impair the dignity of males but rather to regulate changes of surnames, which was in the public interest. The court also felt that the differentiation 'gave effect to a tradition of long standing in the Namibian community that the wife normally assumes the surname of the husband'. Finally, the court noted that Mr Muller was not without a remedy – he could change his surname by following the procedure prescribed in the Act.[21]

The court's reasoning in *Muller* is somewhat puzzling. While it is undoubtedly true that regulation of name changes is in the public interest, Mr Muller was not arguing that name changes could not or should not be regulated. He simply was contending that the exemption from the name change formalities for women taking their husbands' names upon marriage be extended to include men taking their wives' names in the same circumstances. The exception would still be limited to marriage, only it would apply to both spouses. This would seem to be a fair and reasonable way to eliminate the sex-based differentiation while protecting the state's interest in controlling changes of name.[22] The court,

---

[17]   In this, the Namibian Supreme Court followed the approach of the South African Constitutional Court.

[18]   See *Muller v President of the Republic of Namibia and Another*, 2000 (6) BCLR 655 (NmS); *Mwellie v Minister of Works, Transport and Communication and Another*, 1995 (9) BCLR 1119 (NmH).

[19]   *Muller*, 2000 (6) BCLR at 668A-H.

[20]   This, however, should not be taken to mean that only historically disadvantaged Namibians can suffer unfair discrimination, as Article 10 by its terms protects all persons in Namibia.

[21]   This, of course, begs the question presented in the case, which was whether the fact that different procedures exist for men and women is unfairly discriminatory.

[22]   Alternatively, it has been suggested that both men and women should be required to go through formalities to change their names upon marriage. See E Bonthys 'Deny Thy Father and Refuse Thy Name: Namibian Equality Jurisprudence and Married Women's Surnames' 117 SALJ 464 (2000). Bonthys makes a compelling argument that a regime that makes it easy for women to take their husbands' surnames upon marriage discriminates against women. This raises the question

however, preferred to uphold the differentiation. Yet, the court offered no reason why it is not necessary to regulate women changing their names upon marriage but it is necessary to regulate men doing so. Unfortunately, it seems that the court may have viewed the case as presenting only a trivial or insignificant problem: it emphasized the tradition of Namibian women taking their husbands' names, and noted that the Permanent Secretary of Home Affairs had testified that he was not aware of any husband in Namibia other than Mr Muller who wanted to change his name to his wife's. Tradition, however, does not equal constitutionality, especially in terms of a Constitution that was intended to make a sharp break from Namibia's past.[23]

In *Myburgh v Commercial Bank of Namibia*,[24] a bank brought an action against a woman who failed to make payments on a loan. Mrs Myburgh argued in defence that under the common law she lacked capacity to be sued, as she was a woman married in community of property. The court, however, refused to allow her to hide behind this discriminatory rule, holding that the legal disabilities imposed on women married in community of property by the common law violated both Article 10(2) and Article 14(1) of the Constitution. With respect to Article 10(2) and the question of unfair discrimination, the court found that the differentiation – which was 'based on stereotyping which does not take cognizance of the equal worth of women but reduces them, in the eyes of the law, to minors who cannot act independently, but need the assistance of their husbands' and which 'takes no cognizance of the fact that in many marriages in community of property the intelligence, training, qualifications or natural ability or aptitude of the woman may render her a far better administrator of the common estate than the husband' – impaired the dignity of women as a class and individually.[25] With respect to Article 14(1), the court found that subjecting a wife to the guardianship of the husband did not afford the parties equal rights during marriage.

The court in *Myburgh* also found, based on Article 66(1) (which provides that '[b]oth the customary and the common law of Namibia in force on the date of Independence shall remain valid to the extent to which such customary or common law does not conflict with this Constitution ...'), that the common law disabilities imposed on married women became invalid when the Constitution took effect at Independence (on 21 March 1990). The statutory law in force at the time of Independence, by contrast, remains valid until repealed or amended by Parliament or declared unconstitutional by a court. [26]

The Namibian courts have not yet specifically addressed the question of the effect of Article 10's guarantee of gender equality or Article 14's guarantee of equal rights between men and women as to marriage on customary law that treats women and men differently. However, in light of *Myburgh*, aspects of the

---

whether the result in the *Muller* case might have been different if both the husband and wife had been the plaintiffs, rather than only the husband.

[23]   It was, for example, a longstanding tradition in many Namibian communities that corporal punishment could be imposed as a sanction by traditional tribunals, yet the High Court nevertheless found such punishment to be unconstitutional: *State v Sipula*, 1994 NR 4 (HC).

[24]   Unreported, Sup Ct Case No SA 2/2000 (8 December 2000).

[25]   Slip opinion at 17.

[26]   Article 140(1); *Myburgh*, slip op at 8–14.

customary law which have not been given statutory recognition and which violate Article 10 or 14 became invalid upon Independence.

B   Equality in marital property regimes and inheritance

The general law in force in Namibia still includes parts of the Native Administration Proclamation of 1928.[27] As a result, the default marital property regime applicable to a marriage in Namibia today depends on the race of the couple and where the marriage occurred. Specifically, marriages between 'natives' in northern Namibia are deemed to be out of community of property, unless the couple agrees otherwise beforehand, while the reverse is true for all other marriages (they are automatically in community of property unless the couple agrees otherwise in advance). Intestate estates are also treated differently depending on the race of the deceased: the estates of 'natives' who die without a will are divided according to 'native law and custom', whereas the estates of whites or coloured people who likewise die intestate devolve under the general Namibian law of intestacy.

These statutory racial differentiations seem patently inconsistent with Article 10, and they are being challenged as such in two cases currently before the Namibian High Court.[28] In addition, one of the cases also seeks the invalidation, under Article 10, of the common law rule that illegitimate children do not inherit from their father if he dies intestate, as legitimate children do. Should the court find these provisions to be unconstitutional, in terms of the *Myburgh* case the common law rule will be considered to have become invalid upon Independence,[29] while the aspects of the Native Administration Proclamation would only be invalid from the time they are declared so by the court.

C   Family

In its entirety, Article 14 provides as follows.

(1)   Men and women of full age, without any limitation due to race, colour, ethnic origin, nationality, religion, creed or social or economic status, shall have the right to marry and to found a family. They shall be entitled to equal rights as to marriage, during marriage, and at its dissolution.

(2)   Marriage shall be entered into only with the free and full consent of the intending spouses.

(3)   The family is the natural and fundamental group unit of society and is entitled to protection by society and the State.[30]

---

[27]   No 15 of 1928.

[28]   *Ashikoto v the Kwanyama Traditional Authority and Others; Kauapirura v the Herero Traditional Authority and Others.*

[29]   This raises a significant practical question: Does this mean that all of the estates in which this common law rule was applied since Independence could be subject to being reopened by any illegitimate children who were excluded from inheritance by the rule?

[30]   Article 14 is virtually identical to Article 16 of the Universal Declaration of Human Rights. The only difference is that Article 16(1) of the Universal Declaration only prohibits limitations on the right to marry and found a family based on race, nationality or religion.

In the only case to date interpreting Article 14, the Supreme Court took a limited view of the provision, holding that it protects only heterosexual marriages and families based on such marriages, and not homosexual relationships, not even where a same-sex couple is raising a child together.

In *Chairperson of the Immigration Selection Board v Frank and Another*,[31] two women – a German citizen who had resided in Namibia since 1990 (Ms Frank) and her long-time lesbian partner (Ms Khaxas, a Namibian citizen) – challenged the denial of Ms Frank's application for a permanent residence permit. A majority of two judges ordered the Board to reconsider Ms Frank's application, as they found that the Board had not complied with the constitutional requirement of administrative justice.[32] With respect to the women's claims that the denial of the permit violated their rights to equality, non-discrimination, family, privacy and freedom of movement, however, the majority found no constitutional violations.[33]

In terms of the right to a family, the majority found that the references to marriage and spouses in Article 14(1) and (2) and Article 4(3) (which relates to citizenship by marriage) refer only to heterosexual marriages. Because the Constitution does not mention homosexual relationships, despite the fact that their existence must have been known to its framers, the majority concluded that 'it was never contemplated or intended to place a homosexual relationship on an equal basis with a heterosexual marital relationship'. [34]

The majority also found Article 14(3) to be limited to families based on heterosexual marriages. The majority relied on Article 14(3)'s reference to the family as the 'natural and fundamental group unit of society', and concluded that it 'was clearly not contemplated that a homosexual relationship' could be such a unit.[35] The majority also believed that that Article 14(1) and (2) support the conclusion that what is meant by 'family' in Article 14(3) is a family founded on a marriage between a man and a woman. It believed that 'Article 14 clearly does not create a new type of family'. The protection extended is to the 'natural and fundamental group unit of society as known at the time as an institution of Namibian society'.[36]

Although the two women for years had been raising Ms Khaxas' son together, the majority not only dismissed the idea that they constituted a family, but suggested that their situation could be harmful to the child, stating:

'The claimed benefits to the son ... may even be diminished by the confusion created by a son, born from a heterosexual relationship, forced to adapt to and grow up in a homosexual "family" where he would possibly not be certain who takes the role of father and who of mother; who is the "spouse" and how do the "spouses" give effect to their sexual relationship in regard to sexual satisfaction. ... Insofar as it is suggested that to grant a permanent residence permit to first respondent is in the interests also of the child of second respondent, the following marks may be apposite. The Namibian

---

[31]   Unreported, Sup Ct Case No SA 8/99 (5 March 2001).
[32]   Article 18. The Chief Justice agreed that the Board failed to comply with the administrative justice requirements but would have ordered the Board to grant the permit.
[33]   Chief Justice Strydom's minority opinion did not address any of these issues.
[34]   Majority opinion at 71–72.
[35]   *Ibid* at 72–73.
[36]   *Ibid* at 73.

Constitution in its Article 15, the African Charter in its Article 18(3), the International Covenant on Civil and Political Rights in its Article 14, all require measures by the State for the protection of the child. Whether or not the interest of the minor child of Khaxas is protected by being raised within this lesbian partnership, is a debatable and controversial issue which was not debated before this Court and need not be decided in this case. What is clear, however, is that the "family" unit relied upon by respondents is not the "natural and fundamental group unit" referred to in Article 14(3) of the Namibian Constitution.'[37]

In sum, the *Frank* majority concluded that

> '[t]he "family institution" of the African Charter, the United Nations Universal Declaration of Human Rights, the International Covenant on Civil and Political Rights and the Namibian Constitution, envisages a formal relationship between male and female, where sexual intercourse between them in the family context is the method to procreate offspring and thus ensure the perpetuation and survival of the nation and the human race.'[38]

This view, however, does not necessarily accord with the realities of Namibian society today, in which, for example, many children are being raised by single mothers (or, more rarely, fathers), by unmarried heterosexual couples, or by grandparents or other relatives. Does the *Frank* decision mean that none of these very common family groupings are entitled to constitutional protection? To be sure, on its facts *Frank* involved only the question whether a grouping based on a homosexual relationship constituted a family. However, the court's language defining a family in terms of a formal heterosexual relationship and the procreation of children calls into question Article 14(3)'s applicability to a variety of situations in which many Namibians live today.

III LEGISLATIVE REFORMS AND REFORMS IN PROGRESS

Although there have been many significant law reforms concerning gender in the 11 years since Namibia became independent, family law and customary law issues have received relatively low priority. Action in the area of the 'public' sphere of political participation and formal employment has taken precedence over action concerning the more 'private' spheres of household economy and family relationships.

This terminology is used purely for analytical purposes, without any intent to deny that 'the personal is political'. As Beth Goldblatt points out in a recent article on law reform in South Africa, an assumed dichotomy between public and private

---

[37]   *Ibid* at 76–77.

[38]   *Ibid* at 77. However, the Supreme Court's limited interpretation of the International Covenant on Civil and Political Rights seems inconsistent with the *Toonen* case, where the Human Rights Committee held that the reference to 'sex' in the Covenant's anti-discrimination provision encompasses sexual orientation. *Toonen v Australia*, Communication No 488/1992, UN Doc CCPR/C/50/D/488/1992 (1994).

has been used by liberal thinkers as a justification for 'lack of state interference in the family where men control women and children, often with violence'.[39]

There has been some recognition of the interaction between 'public' and 'private' spheres of existence, in the form of some recognition of family responsibilities in the laws relating to formal employment. The Labour Act prohibits discrimination in any aspect of employment on the basis of sex, marital status, family responsibilities and sexual orientation (amongst other things), as well as forbidding harassment on the same grounds. It also provides for three months of maternity leave for any woman who has been employed for at least one year by the same employer.[40] This provision has been supplemented by the Social Security Act, which provides maternity benefits (80% of full pay for 12 weeks, up to a wage ceiling of N$3000) through a mandatory combined scheme for sickness, maternity and death benefits financed by matching employer and employee contributions.[41]

These reforms will obviously have significance primarily for the minority of Namibian women who are in formal employment – only about one-third of all women who are of an employable age, according to the 1991 Census.[42] And even some women in the most vulnerable forms of formal employment are excluded from full coverage. The Labour Act defines employees broadly to give full coverage to domestic workers, who were excluded from pre-independence labour legislation, but the Social Security Act covers only employees who work more than two days a week for the same employer – thus excluding women who do domestic work in different households on different days of the week.[43]

The more exclusively 'private' area of family relations has received little attention since Independence, with the exception of developments relating to violence in the family.

A   The Married Persons Equality Act

The only law enacted since Independence in the area of family law is the Married Persons Equality Act, which was discussed in some detail in the previous contribution to the *Survey*.[44] This law eliminates the discriminatory Roman–Dutch

---

[39]   Beth Goldblatt, 'A Feminist Perspective on the Law Reform Process: An Evaluation of Attempts to Establish a Family Court in South Africa', 13 SAJHR 373 (1997) at 376, referring to K O'Donovan, *Sexual Divisions in Law* (1985).

[40]   Labour Act 6 of 1992. See sections 45 and 107 on discrimination and section 41 on maternity leave.

[41]   Social Security Act 34 of 1994. Neither Act makes any provision for paternity leave or parental leave, which reinforces the notion that women bear the primary responsibility for child care. Additional funds planned under the Act to set up a national medical aid scheme and pension plan have never materialised.

[42]   According to the 1991 Census, of the 517,082 women aged 10 years and older, only 173,032 are formally employed whilst 215,008 are 'economically active'.

[43]   See the definition of 'employee' in section 1 of the Social Security Act 34 of 1994, compared to the definition of 'employee' in section 1 of the Labour Act 6 of 1992.

[44]   Fareda Banda, 'Family Law Reform in Namibia' in A Bainham (ed), *The International Survey of Family Law 1996* (Martinus Nijhoff, 1998), 265–278, at 275ff. What may not be entirely clear from this previous discussion is that the Married Persons Equality Act does not affect the default marital property regimes, but only the exercise of power by husband and wife over joint or separate property.

law concept of marital power which previously applied to civil marriages. Couples married in community of property must now consult each other on all major transactions (with husbands and wives being subject to identical powers and restraints), whereas couples married out of community of property have the right to deal with their separate property independently. However, enforcement of this consent requirement is effected primarily through applications to the High Court (which sits only in the nation's capital), making the procedure too costly and inconvenient to benefit most Namibians.

The gender-based inequalities in customary marriage, which stem from a different source, were not addressed by this law. However, it did give husbands and wives in both civil and customary marriages equal powers of guardianship in respect of children of the marriage. It also makes a wife's domicile independent of that of her husband in both civil and customary marriages, and provides that the domicile of children of the marriage will be the place with which they are most closely connected.[45]

The symbolic import of this Act is probably even more important than its practical provisions, as it sends out a clear message that the law will no longer recognise husbands in civil marriages as 'heads of household' – an aspect of the law which generated much controversy both inside and outside Parliament.

While the Married Persons Equality Act has been a positive first step, it does not sufficiently address discrimination in the family, as the United Nations CEDAW Committee noted in its response to Namibia's first report under this Convention in 1997.[46]

B   Violence against women in the family

Violence against women is a particular problem in Namibia and has been a mobilising force for women's organisations in many communities. Following on from years of lobbying from a broad range of groups, a progressive Combating of Rape Act was passed by Parliament in 2000, coming into force in June of that year. Of relevance to the topic of family law is the fact that this new law provides that 'No marriage or other relationship shall constitute a defence to a charge of rape under this Act'.[47] This is a significant change from the previous legal position, which made it impossible for the crime of rape to occur within a marriage.

Law reform on domestic violence is also under way, with a draft Bill on the table. Domestic violence has been widely recognised as a serious problem in Namibia. Although there are no national statistics on the problem, in a 1999 survey medical practitioners estimated that one half of all the women and children they treat have been victims of domestic violence.[48] Another indicator is the fact

---

[45]   These aspects of the law, although praiseworthy, will be of practical relevance to few Namibians.

[46]   Convention on the Elimination of All Forms of Discrimination against Women, CEDAW/C/1997/II/L1/Add 2, 14 July 1997, paras 37 and 59.

[47]   Combating of Rape Act 8 of 2000, section 2(3).

[48]   Debie LeBeau, *The Nature, Extent and Causes of Domestic Violence against Women and Children in Namibia* (1997). The Law Reform and Development Commission commissioned this study, which draws on information from doctors, nurses, social workers, police officers, community leaders and victims of domestic violence.

that social workers report that 400–500 children are removed from their homes each year in terms of Namibia's Children's Act because of various forms of abuse and neglect.

A study of police dockets opened during a sample of three months in 1994 indicated that one-fifth of all violent crimes reported to the police occur in the context of domestic relationships.[49] The current proportion would probably be even higher, as domestic violence has been more openly spoken about in recent years. More information about the incidence of domestic violence will probably be known in future, as Namibia is currently participating in a WHO Multi-Country Study on the health consequences of domestic violence, which will involve extensive survey samples in two of Namibia's 13 regions.

A preliminary draft Domestic Violence Bill was published by the Law Reform and Development Commission in December 2000, drawing heavily on research by the Legal Assistance Centre. This draft proposes a broad definition of 'domestic violence' which would include physical abuse, sexual abuse, economic abuse, intimidation, harassment and serious emotional, verbal or psychological abuse in domestic relationships. It also proposes a broad definition of 'domestic relationship', which would cover spouses under civil or customary law, cohabitating partners, family members and persons in other forms of intimate relationships. The draft Bill suggests a two-pronged approach to domestic violence, including civil and criminal components.

The civil prong of the proposed system would entail a simple procedure for obtaining 'protection orders' from magistrates' courts. Protection orders are court orders that prohibit the perpetrator from engaging in further violence or threats of violence. They could in appropriate cases place restrictions on future contact with the victim, or order the perpetrator to leave a residence which he or she shares with the victim. Violation of a protection order would be a criminal offence. Complainants would be able to obtain protection on an urgent basis by means of an interim protection order issued in the perpetrator's absence. The perpetrator would be given an opportunity to state his or her side of the case before the order was made final.

On the criminal side, the draft Bill would make it easier for the law to take into account the special complexities of crimes which occur within domestic relationships. For example, one possibility is to establish diversion programmes for cases involving first offenders where there is no serious injury. Instead of proceeding to trial, the accused could participate in an appropriate treatment or counselling programme. The availability of this option would depend on the circumstances of the case, taking the victim's wishes into account. The goal would be to emphasise rehabilitation in appropriate cases, such as those where the victim of the violence would like to maintain the relationship. The Bill also proposes special bail procedures, and protection for the privacy of the victim which would not be available in normal criminal cases.

The draft Bill also suggests that the new law should give the police a specific duty to respond to all domestic violence cases. Police would be expected to give

---

[49] Law Reform and Development Commission and Legal Assistance Centre, *Domestic Violence Cases Reported to the Namibian Police: Case Characteristics and Police Response* (LRDC 9, 2000).

the complainant a brief, standard explanation of the criminal and civil options available, in simple language. Where necessary, police would also be expected to escort the victim to the home to collect personal belongings and to provide transport to a hospital or clinic, shelter or other safe place.[50]

Public demand for the passage of this law is high, fuelled by regular reports of grisly incidents of domestic violence. Some observers expect it to be introduced into Parliament before the end of 2001. The proposed Bill is currently with the Ministry of Justice, undergoing some revision.

Persons who have experienced family violence will also benefit from the anticipated Vulnerable Witnesses Bill, which will implement mechanisms to reduce the trauma of court testimony in sensitive cases, such as testimony behind screens or by means of closed-circuit television and procedures to prevent badgering of witnesses in the guise of cross-examination. This draft Bill is currently under discussion in the Ministry of Justice.

C   Allocation of communal land

In general, law reforms in the area of customary law have been slow to come, probably because of the potential political ramifications of imposing change in this area.[51] Customary family law remains virtually untouched.[52]

The major development in the field of customary law is the Communal Land Reform Bill. However, the process of communal land reform, in contrast with commercial land reform, has been very slow. The Government aimed at passing legislation concerning communal land by the end of 1995, but has been struggling for some time now to come up with a land management programme for communal

---

[50]   Law Reform and Development Commission, *Report on Domestic Violence* (LRDC 10, 2000). The UN Special Rapporteur praised the general approach which is being contemplated in a March 1999 report, noting that the proposed strategy is based on the United Nations Framework for Model Domestic Violence Legislation:

'Namibia: The Special Rapporteur is encouraged to note that positive steps are being taken to remedy the Government's reported failure to provide adequate remedies and support in cases of domestic violence. She notes with interest a discussion document published in November 1998 which contains proposals based on the United Nations Framework for Model Domestic Violence Legislation. The Special Rapporteur encourages the Government to take all steps to ensure the document assists the process of policy development and reform.'

(*Integration of the Human Rights of Women and the Gender Perspective: Violence Against Women (Violence against women in the family),* E/CN4/1999/68, para 220.)

[51]   For example, the Act establishing the Council of Traditional Leaders mandated by Article 102(5) of the Constitution came into force some eight years after Independence. The Council of Traditional Leaders Act 13 of 1997 came into force on 31 March 1998 – GN 64/1998, GG 1828 – following on the heels of the Traditional Authorities Act 17 of 1995, which also came into action fully only with the first designation of traditional leaders in terms of its provisions in March 1998.

[52]   The only exceptions are the provisions of the Married Persons Equality Act discussed above. There have also been a few statutes which have defined terms such as 'marriage', 'spouse' and 'dependant' to include customary marriages for particular purposes. Examples include the Namibian Citizenship Act 14 of 1990, the Regional Councils Act 22 of 1992 and the Local Authorities Act 23 of 1992 (for the purposes of disclosures of conflicts of interest), the Employees Compensation Act 30 of 1941 (as amended by Act 5 of 1995) and the Arms and Ammunition Act 7 of 1996 (concerning possession of a firearm by a 'spouse'). The Combating of Rape Act 8 of 2000 (for purposes of removing the marital rape exemption) specifies that 'no marriage or other relationship' shall constitute a defence to a charge of rape, thus being worded broadly enough to cover both civil and customary marriage.

areas that accommodates different interest groups, and to identify an appropriate role for traditional leaders who presently have responsibility for the allocation of communal land. Desires to maintain communal lands as 'communal' clash with the ambitions of many wealthier farmers who see private tenure as a first step towards greater commercialisation and profit. The National Assembly passed the Communal Land Reform Bill in February 2000, but it was rejected by the second house of Parliament, the National Council, which cited concerns that the proposed new option of acquiring leasehold rights might benefit wealthy farmers at the expense of others.[53]

Access to land is an issue of overriding concern in the rural areas where the majority of Namibia's population lives. Historically, women's access to land has often been through male relatives. This has meant that the fruits of a woman's labour on the land do not always belong to her or fall under her control. This has affected women's ability to provide an adequate standard of living for all of the members of the household and their access to disposable income (as opposed to mere subsistence). It also means that changes in marital status can be catastrophic for a woman – a woman may, for example, endure violence at the hands of an abusive husband rather than risk losing access to land as the result of a divorce. Insecure tenure can also discourage women from investing in long-term agricultural strategies which might be better for the environment – such as planting trees or taking steps to improve the fertility of the soil.[54]

In terms of the current version of the Bill, men and women are equally eligible for rights to customary land, and the treatment of widows and widowers is identical. This will alter the current practice in some areas, whereby a widow can be dispossessed of the communal land she occupies upon her husband's death, or forced to pay an additional occupation fee. While the system of individual land rights which is proposed is gender-neutral in all aspects, it remains to be seen whether or not such neutrality will be sufficient to alter long-standing traditions of allocating land to male family members and male control over many of the major decisions concerning the land.

The Communal Land Reform Bill is expected to receive further attention from Parliament during 2001, although any firm predictions about this controversial Bill would be foolhardy.

D   Recognition of customary marriage

Customary marriage was never legally recognised as 'marriage' during the colonial period, primarily because of its potentially polygynous nature. The term 'customary union' was used in laws and other official contexts to differentiate unrecognised customary marriages from civil marriages. Many post-independence laws have explicitly included customary marriage in general provisions

---

[53]   'NC explains its rejection of Communal Land Bill', *The Namibian*, 19 May 2000; see *www.namibian.com.na/*.

[54]   For a further discussion of these issues, see Louise Fortmann, 'Why Women's Property Rights Matter'. The CEDAW Committee expressed concern in its report that women in rural areas were still unable to own land and encouraged legal change in this area. Convention on the Elimination of All Forms of Discrimination against Women, CEDAW/C/1997/II/L1/Add 2, 14 July 1997, paras 34 and 55.

concerning marriage, but the treatment of customary marriage remains inconsistent.[55] The Married Persons Equality Act equalised the age at which boys and girls may enter into civil marriage without special State permission at 18, but set no minimum age for customary marriage.[56] The need to develop a system for formal legal recognition of customary marriages was emphasised by the United Nations CEDAW Committee in response to Namibia's first country report presented in 1997.[57]

A subcommittee of the Law Reform and Development Commission has considered the question of recognition of customary marriage, and has made a report on this topic to the full Commission. The subcommittee's recommendations are not available to the public, but a member of this subcommittee has indicated that the continuation of a dual system has been recommended. The subcommittee has proposed, in general, that registration of customary marriage will be encouraged for purposes of proof of marriage, but not required as a condition of recognition. Traditional leaders will act as marriage officers, but the test of whether a customary marriage has taken place will depend on the customs of the community. It is proposed that the default property regime for customary marriage will be in community of property, as in South Africa, and that divorce will be in terms of a separate procedure governed by customary law.[58] There is, as yet, no draft Bill on this issue on the table.[59]

E   Maintenance

Maintenance emerged as a priority concern shortly after Independence. Many women complained about the difficulty of securing maintenance for their children, and about the inefficient operation of the maintenance courts, which fall under legislation inherited from South Africa and dating from 1963.[60] In 1993, the Legal Assistance Centre began carrying out extensive research into the operation of Namibia's maintenance courts, in consultation with the Law Reform and Development Commission. The Legal Assistance Centre's research findings,

---

[55]   For example, the Employees Compensation Act 30 of 1941 (as amended by Act 5 of 1995) makes explicit provision for customary marriage, by stating that 'surviving spouse' (for purposes of the section on payment of compensation in the event of death from a work-related accident) includes 'a surviving partner in a marriage by customary law'.

On the other hand, the Medical Aid Funds Act 23 of 1995 defines 'dependant' in relation to a registered medical aid scheme as including the 'spouse' of a member and the child of a member (including a step-child or an adopted child), but it does not define 'spouse' or make any reference to customary marriage.

[56]   Before this Act was in place, boys could enter civil marriage at 18 while girls could enter civil marriage at 15. Minors (persons under the age of 21) also need the permission of both of their parents to marry.

[57]   Convention on the Elimination of All Forms of Discrimination against Women, CEDAW/C/1997/II/L1/Add 2, 14 July 1997, paras 43 and 57. The Committee was also very concerned about the existence of polygyny. See paras 43 and 56.

[58]   Comments of Professor Manfred O Hinz at a workshop of the Southern African Legal Assistance Network in Windhoek, March 2001.

[59]   Recommendations for law reform on this issue were made by the Legal Assistance Centre in *Proposals for Law Reform on the Recognition of Customary Marriages* (1999). This document is also available in full on the Legal Assistance Centre's website at *www.lac.org.na*.

[60]   Maintenance Act 23 of 1963.

which included draft legislation, were published in September 1995.[61] This research was considered by a subcommittee appointed by the Law Reform and Development Commission specifically for this purpose. This subcommittee submitted a report on maintenance to the full Law Reform and Development Commission about one year later, in August 1996. Another year passed. In September 1997, the Law Reform and Development Commission published a report based on the subcommittee's recommendations. It contained recommendations for law reform, but no draft Bill.[62]

Now, almost four more years have gone by. The draft maintenance legislation got all the way to Cabinet at one stage, but was sent back for more work. It still sits somewhere inside the Ministry of Justice. Meanwhile the South African law which Namibia inherited has already been discarded by South Africa, which enacted a new law on maintenance in early 1998.[63]

The slow progress here is particularly significant because maintenance is a matter which is central to so many other areas of concern. The research conducted by the Legal Assistance Centre showed that women in both rural and urban areas use the maintenance courts and are concerned about more effective mechanisms for securing maintenance, and that many women find traditional approaches to maintenance under customary law increasingly inadequate.[64] Remittances such as maintenance payments and pensions can be crucial sources of income for survival in any household, and maintenance can be particularly significant in the 38% of all Namibian households which are headed by women, 71% of which are in rural areas.[65] Fear of not being able to support children independently can keep a woman in a violent relationship.[66] The lack of maintenance to pay school fees or other school expenses can hamper the ability of the next generation to get an education – which is in turn a factor associated with crimes by young offenders.[67] Thus, ensuring access to secure and reliable maintenance payments should be amongst the nation's highest priorities.

There is a complementary system of State maintenance grants for children, but law reform in this area is part of a package of children's legislation which has been stalled somewhere in the reform process since the first draft Bill on this topic was put forward by the Ministry of Health and Social Services in 1994. The

---

[61]   Legal Assistance Centre, *Maintenance: A Study of the Operation of Namibia's Maintenance Courts* (1995).

[62]   Law Reform and Development Commission, *Report on Maintenance* (LRDC 5, September 1997). The reason given for not including draft legislation in the report was that the proposed amendments to the existing Maintenance Act should be consolidated for re-enactment to produce a clearer law (at 1).

[63]   Maintenance Act 99 of 1998.

[64]   The existing Maintenance Act mechanisms are available to anyone with responsibility for a child, and the Act treats civil and customary marriages in the same way for the purposes of maintenance. See section 5(6).

[65]   Statistics from 1993/94 National Household Income and Expenditure Survey.

[66]   The United Nations CEDAW Committee, reacting to Namibia's first report, stressed the importance of women's economic empowerment to reduce dependency on men which can create increased vulnerability to domestic violence. Convention on the Elimination of All Forms of Discrimination against Women, CEDAW/C/1997/II/L1/Add 2, 14 July 1997, para 52.

[67]   Data collected on 100 young offenders screened by the Legal Assistance Centre's Juvenile Justice Project in Windhoek between January and May 2000 showed that almost 18% of them left school because of financial problems.

existing system of State grants, which falls under the Children's Act 33 of 1960, was once administered by the second-tier governments established under the apartheid regime. For six years following Independence, this grant system had the ignoble distinction of being one of the last vestiges of direct racial discrimination, with grant criteria and amounts being different for different 'population groups'. This distinction was eliminated in 1996, with 'family allowances' now standing at N$100 for the mother and N$100 each for up to three children in cases where the mother earns less than N$500/month and the father is dead, imprisoned or otherwise unable to provide support.[68] With the increase in the number of children orphaned by AIDS – the care of whom falls disproportionately on female family members – this system of State back-ups is likely to become even more important and so is in urgent need of re-examination.[69]

F   Children's rights

Children who are in need of care or protection are currently dealt with in terms of the Children's Act 33 of 1960, an outdated law inherited from South Africa at Independence. This law covers adoption and the removal of children from the family home in cases of abuse or neglect, as well as a number of related topics. The Ministry of Health and Social Services commissioned a draft Child Care and Protection Bill to replace the Children's Act in 1994, after convening a national workshop on the topic in June of that year. However, this legislation has reportedly been with the legal drafters in the Ministry of Justice since then.

Children who are born outside marriage still experience discrimination under both civil and customary law on the issue of inheritance. Under the current civil law, these children can inherit from their fathers only in terms of a written will – even if paternity is formally acknowledged on the birth certificate. They are also generally disinherited under customary law systems of inheritance. As noted above, a court case challenging this basis for discrimination is scheduled for later in 2001, and may bring about reform in this area by invalidating the common law on this point from the date of Independence.[70]

The current civil law also discriminates against the fathers of children born outside marriage, by giving all custodial and guardianship powers to the single mother – who can even give up the child for adoption without notifying or obtaining the consent of the father. This would appear to be a violation of the constitutional promise that children have a right, subject to legislation enacted in

---

[68] Fathers with custody of children can theoretically claim this allowance if they are disabled or of pensionable age, but (not surprisingly) this affects few men in practice. Information obtained by telephone from Ministry of Health and Social Services by Willem Odendaal, Legal Assistance Centre.

[69] A report published in 1998 estimated that well over 120,000 Namibian children would lose their mothers to AIDS during the next 10 years, with an equal (and largely overlapping) number losing their fathers as well. Ministry of Health and Social Services/UNICEF, *More Than the Loss of a Parent; Namibia's First Study of Orphan Children*, at 1.
This has already proved to be an underestimate, with a recent UNAIDS report stating that AIDS has already left behind 67,000 orphans as well as 6,600 children living with HIV: 'AIDS set to decimate Namibia', *The Namibian*, 28 June 2000.

[70] See the discussion of the *Myburgh* case at **II.A** above. The case in question is *Kauapirura v the Herero Traditional Authority and Others*.

the best interests of children, 'to know and be cared for by their parents' (Article 15(1)) as well as the provision on sexual equality and equality before the law (Article 10). Irresponsible fathers sometimes cite this inequity as an excuse for not honouring their obligations to pay maintenance. A case challenging the discriminatory treatment of single fathers is currently pending.[71] A draft Children's Status Bill was commissioned by the Ministry of Health and Social Services in 1994 as a companion to the proposed Child Care and Protection Bill, but this piece of legislation appears to be similarly stalled.

G   Inheritance

The issue of inheritance is an extremely urgent one, particularly under customary law where some systems of inheritance discriminate against women as well as children born outside marriage. While the Communal Land Reform Bill as it currently stands will prevent women from being thrown off their land upon the death of their husbands, it does not address other sexual inequalities in traditional systems of inheritance, nor does it ensure that a widow remaining on a piece of land will be able to retain any resources with which to utilise the land. The general topic of inheritance has been investigated by a special subcommittee of the Law Reform and Development Commission, but no proposal for reform has yet been made public.

IV   AREAS IN NEED OF ATTENTION

There are a number of other family law issues which are in need of reform.

A   Divorce

Namibia's divorce rate, by world standards, is not high. About one out of every 15 civil marriages ends in divorce, while the 1991 census figures, which take into account both customary and civil marriages and divorces plus informal separations, indicate that about one out of every 10 marriages in Namibia break down.[72] However, Namibia's law on civil divorce still follows an antiquated system based on 'guilt' and 'innocence' which is not adequate to meet the needs of either men or women. Divorces of civil marriages can now be granted only by the High Court in Windhoek, and the only grounds for divorce which are generally available are adultery and malicious desertion.[73] These grounds are

---

[71]   In the case of *Karl-Heinz Beukes v Jana Nel*, the Legal Assistance Centre is representing a single father who is challenging the constitutionality of the common law principle that denies fathers of children born out of wedlock any legal right of access to children, primarily on the basis that this position violates Article 10 of the Namibian Constitution.

[72]   Legal Assistance Centre, *Proposals for Divorce Law Reform in Namibia* (2000), Chapter 2. This report is available in full at *www.lac.org.na*.

[73]   These two grounds originate in Roman–Dutch common law. An additional two grounds were added by the Divorce Laws Amendment Ordinance 18 of 1935, in an effort to mitigate some of the hardships of the narrow common-law grounds: the imprisonment for at least five years of a

based on the principle of fault – the idea that one spouse must be guilty of committing some type of wrong against the other spouse. Unlike the law of most countries today, Namibian law does not allow a divorce to be granted simply because the couple's marriage has irretrievably broken down.

B   Marital property

The default property regimes for civil and customary marriage are also in need of re-examination. At present, old apartheid legislation sets different default regimes for blacks who enter civil marriage in certain parts of the country.[74] This system has been the subject of several court challenges on constitutional grounds, but at the time of writing there has been no definitive ruling on this point.[75] In the area of customary law, there is a need for a closer examination of the relative rights of husbands and wives to own and control property.[76]

C   Cohabitation

Reform in the area of marital property regimes should be coupled with an examination of the property consequences of cohabitation, to ensure adequate protection for women and children in informal marriage-type relationships which seem to be occurring in increasing numbers.

D   Sexual orientation

A particularly controversial topic in the realm of family law is the question of gay and lesbian rights. Strong condemnations of homosexuality have been made in Parliament. The Minister of Home Affairs publicly called for the 'elimination' of gays and lesbians, and the President went so far as to order police to arrest, imprison and deport gays and lesbians. As a result of such official statements, security forces reportedly ordered men to remove their earrings or to have them forcibly ripped off, apparently interpreting earrings on men as a badge of homosexuality.[77]

The Combating of Rape Act has now expanded the definition of rape to include forcible sodomy, but the common law on sodomy which criminalises the

---

spouse who has been declared a habitual criminal; or the incurable insanity of a spouse which has lasted for at least seven years.

[74] This stems from the fact that portions of sections 17 and 18 of the Native Administration Proclamation 15 of 1928, which deal with marriage and succession, were brought into force in the area north of the Police Zone *only*, with effect from 1 August 1950, and remain in force at present.

[75] See footnote 28 and accompanying text above.

[76] It is relevant to note in this regard that the CEDAW Committee recommended that the government ensure that research is done to identify the customary laws that contravene 'the letter and spirit' of sexual equality and make attempts to replace those laws: Convention on the Elimination of All Forms of Discrimination against Women, CEDAW/C/1997/II/L1/Add 2, 14 July 1997, para 50.

[77] See, for example, 'President urges "Gay purge"', *The Namibian*, 20 March 2001; 'SFF launch earring "purge"', *The Namibian*, 2 May 2001.

act between consenting adults remains on the books.[78] Consensual sexual contact between lesbians is not similarly criminalised.

Gay and lesbian couples are not currently recognised in Namibia as being analogous to marriage relationships for any legal purposes, as the *Frank* case discussed above indicates, and progressive law reform in this area is highly unlikely given the current political and jurisprudential climate.[79]

The *Frank* case itself emphasised that it is not a licence for discrimination against gays and lesbians, stating that: '*Nothing in this judgement justifies discrimination against homosexuals as individuals, or deprives them of the protection of other provisions of the Namibian Constitution.*'[80] However, it may be necessary in future for gays and lesbians to resort to international forums to assert their rights to full protection against discrimination.[81]

V   CONCLUSION

In the area of family law, Namibia's progress has been fairly slow and conservative, particularly in the area of customary law where there is a tension between gender equality and a commitment to 'African traditions', despite the fact that customary law in its current form was strongly influenced by the colonial authorities.[82]

Another source of conservatism has been the influence of the Christian churches, given the fact that Namibia is predominately Christian (with perhaps as much as 95% of the population being Christian). Indeed, parliamentary debate on the Married Persons Equality Act centred around perceived contradictions between provisions advancing gender equality and Biblical dictates on the husband as the head of the household.

Another factor has been the reluctance of people in Namibia to challenge unconstitutional laws in court – probably attributable to a mixture of lack of knowledge and access, distrust of the legal system as a hold-over from Namibia's colonial past, and trust that the government will take care of these matters in its own time – with the result that even laws setting different rules for 'natives' remain on Namibia's books almost 12 years after Independence.

The conservatism in the area of family law is particularly striking if viewed in contrast to the progressive legal developments in the area of violence against women in the years since Independence. However, the second decade in

---

[78]   The government has cited this law as a basis for refusing to make condoms available to prisoners to reduce the chances of HIV infection.

[79]   The Labour Act 6 of 1992 prohibits discrimination on the basis of sexual orientation, but 'gay-bashing' by members of the public and some members of government has increased in visibility and intensity since that law was passed.

[80]   Unreported, Sup Ct Case No SA 8/99 (5 March 2001).

[81]   As noted above, Namibia ratified the International Covenant on Civil and Political Rights on 28 November 1994, and the Committee which monitors this Convention stated in 1994 in the *Toonen* case that 'sex' in the Covenant's provisions on discrimination includes 'sexual orientation': *Toonen v Australia*, Communication No 488/1992, UN Doc CCPR/C/50/D/488/1992 (1994).

[82]   On this point, see Heike Becker, *Namibia Women's Movement 1980–1992, From Anticolonial Resistance to Reconstruction* (1995) at 84–91.

Namibia's independent existence is likely to be crucial in family law developments, as the various legal developments 'in progress' are brought to fruition.

THE NETHERLANDS

REFORMS IN DUTCH FAMILY LAW DURING THE COURSE OF 2001: INCREASED PLURIFORMITY AND COMPLEXITY

Wendy Schrama[*]

I INTRODUCTION

In 2001 family law has changed again in many respects. Not only have child protection measures (including a Bill aimed at the penalisation of virtual child pornography) been proposed, but also the Bill on the Storage and Disclosure of Information Relating to Gamete Donors has been accepted by the Second Chamber.[1] Further, the Act of 31 May 2001 to Simplify the Rights and Duties of Spouses has been accepted by both the Second and the First Chamber and entered into force on 22 June 2001.[2] Although these developments are of great importance for family law, this review concentrates primarily on two other important milestones: the Act of 21 December 2000 to open marriage to same-sex couples and the Act of 21 December 2000 to make the adoption of Dutch children available to same-sex couples.[3] In the last report, these Bills were discussed with respect to the debates in the Second Chamber of Parliament.[4] Both Acts entered into force on 1 April 2001. Just after midnight on 1 April 2001, the first marriages between same-sex partners were concluded by the Mayor of Amsterdam, who in his former capacity as State Secretary of Justice had been advocating the Act in Parliament. The media from all over the world converged on Amsterdam, while in the meantime the Dutch people themselves did not seem to be very impressed.

Same-sex marriages raise some specific questions which will be considered after some general remarks concerning the new legislation have been made (section **IIA**); especially, the relationship between registered partnerships and marriages requires further consideration (section **IIB**). The legal position of civil status registrars who refuse to conclude same-sex marriages on the grounds of personal conscience is another issue which will be examined (section **IIC**).

---

[*] Lecturer in Law, Molengraaff Institute for Private Law, Faculty of Law, Utrecht University.

[1] Second Chamber, 2000–2001, 46–3548 and 3549. The Bill is currently being discussed in the First Chamber: First Chamber, 2000–2001, 23 207, no 3a.

[2] This Bill was extensively discussed in the previous Dutch report: C Forder, 'To Marry or Not To Marry: That is the Question', *The International Survey of Family Law (2001 Edition)*, ed A Bainham (Family Law, 2001), p 301ff. The Bill concerning the system of balancing debts and credits between spouses is currently being discussed in the Second Chamber (Second Chamber, 2000–2001, 27 754, A–B and nos 1–4). Government proposals to introduce an amended property system have not yet resulted in a concrete Bill to that effect.

[3] Acts of 21 December 2000, Staatsblad 2001, nos 9 and 10.

[4] Dutch report, C Forder, 'To Marry or Not To Marry: That is the Question', *The International Survey of Family Law (2001 Edition)*, ed A Bainham (Family Law, 2001), p 301ff.

Secondly, this new legislation makes it necessary to take a closer look at the position of children born and/or raised in same-sex relationships. First, some general remarks concerning recent developments will be discussed (section **IIIA**). Thereafter, attention will be paid to the latest developments with respect to shared custody under Art 1:253t Civil Code (section **IIIB**) and automatic shared custody by marriage and registered partnership (section **IIIC**). The debates in the First Chamber of Parliament on the legislation making the adoption of Dutch children available for same-sex couples are reported in section **IIID**. The review then continues with a brief comparison of the different regulations with respect to parenthood, custody, maintenance and family name which apply to five different situations in which a child might be raised (section **IIIE**). In this way, the practical consequences of the new legislation may be best illustrated. Finally, the last section deals with some critical remarks (section **IV**).

II   THE ACT OPENING MARRIAGE TO SAME-SEX COUPLES

A   General remarks

The Act to open marriage to couples of the same sex consists of five Articles only. The most important of these provisions is Article I, which contains the amendments to the existing family law in order to make possible the introduction of same-sex marriages. Article 1:30 of the Civil Code, which used to determine that a marriage could only be concluded between a man and a woman, has been changed. It now states in its first section that a marriage may be concluded by two persons of the opposite sex or two persons of the same sex. The new legislation introduces a very simple procedure to convert a marriage into a registered partnership and vice versa (Art 1:77a Civil Code and Art 1:80g Civil Code). A simple deed of conversion drawn up by the civil status registrar suffices for a conversion. The marriage or registered partnership ends when the deed of conversion has been entered in the relevant register. A conversion does not affect the existence or non-existence of legal ties between the partners and children born before the conversion.

A marriage brings about far-reaching consequences: if the spouses do not otherwise agree, a community of property applies, specific maintenance duties apply between spouses during and after marriage, the spouses are *inter se* liable for the costs of running the household and under certain conditions a joint liability *vis-à-vis* third persons applies for each other's household debts. Apart from this, a marriage has important legal effects in inheritance law, for the family name and nationality of the spouses and their children, and with respect to revenue law, pension rights and social security.

Although in principle there are no differences between a same-sex marriage and a marriage between a heterosexual couple, there is one exception with respect to the right to enter into a same-sex marriage: the king or queen (or a potential successor to the throne) has no right to marry a partner of the same sex. In the view of the Government they should be excluded, since the nature of an hereditary monarchy cannot be reconciled with a same-sex marriage, which can never lead to the birth of children to the spouses.[5] Thus, 'marriage' in Art 28 of the Constitution, which concerns a marriage of the king (or queen), should be interpreted as referring exclusively to a marriage between a man and a woman. How these different interpretations of the concept of marriage in the Constitution and in the Civil Code (and all other legislation) have to be reconciled with each other is unclear. Several factions in the First Chamber have heavily criticised the approach adopted by the Government.[6]

Another important difference between a same-sex marriage and a marriage between a heterosexual couple concerns the status of a same-sex marriage at the international level. This status is unclear and the Permanent Committee on Private International Law, which has been requested by the Government to draft an advice on the international aspects of the Act, has not yet reported.

In order to give some idea of the number of people who have shown an interest in same-sex marriage it is useful to provide some statistical data.[7] However, these are only based on the first six months after the Act entered into force, so they are perhaps not a reliable predictor of future developments. The number of same-sex couples who married in the first six months amounted to 1900. This is 3.6 percent of the total number of all marriages performed in the first six months of 2001. In almost 600 of these same-sex marriages, one or both of the partners had been married before with a partner of the opposite sex. Of all same-sex marriages, 55 percent are male couples and 45 percent are female couples.

As the debates in the Second Chamber were discussed in last year's report, this review will now deal only with the arguments put forward in the First Chamber of Parliament. In general, the relations between the factions reflect the attitudes of the parties in the Second Chamber. As expected, the factions were split along religious lines into a pro- and contra- division, both being very pronounced in their (ideological) position. The debates between the religious parties and the Government have been characterised as 'a discussion between two deaf persons', which suggests that the gulf between the political parties *inter se* and the parties and the Government was actually too great for any really meaningful discussion. In the end, all parties voted in favour of the Bill, except for the strict Protestant parties (RPF, GPV, SGP) and the Christian Democratic Party (CDA).

The CDA faction expressed doubts relating to the basis of the decision to make marriage available to same-sex couples, since a registered partnership has largely the same legal effects as a marriage.[8] It has to be admitted that the Government's reasoning raises questions in this respect. The far-reaching decision to open marriage to same-sex couples is, according to the Government, based on the principle of equality, although at the same time the Government sticks to the view that the equality principle laid down in Art 1 of the Constitution, in international treaties and in the case-law of the Dutch Supreme Court (*Hoge Raad*) does not require marriage to be made available to same-sex couples. Article 1 of the Constitution and the treaties serve only as 'a source of inspiration' for the law.[9] The Government also referred to the symbolic nature of a marriage

---

[5] First Chamber 15–659 and 15–671, 19-12-2000.
[6] Eg First Chamber 15–670, 19-12-2000.
[7] Provisional data of the Statistics Netherlands (Centraal Bureau voor de Statistiek).
[8] First Chamber 14–600, 18-12-2000.
[9] First Chamber 15–652 and 15–672, 19-12-2000.

which is lacking in a registered partnership. The CDA faction, however, rejected this justification and considered that it was not a sufficient reason for such a far-reaching decision.[10]

The attitude of the strict Protestant factions in the First Chamber was one of absolute rejection. For them the concept of marriage is exclusively a union of one man and one woman. This follows from the nature of things as created by God. They considered the proposed change to be inconsistent with this view.

The Green-Left party was in favour of the Bill, although it stressed that it would be more satisfied if family law would allow people a free choice with respect to the form of their affective relationship. The State should interfere as little as possible.[11] Finally, the Liberal-Left (VVD) and Labour (PvdA) were both in favour of the law.

B   The future of the Registered Partnership Act

An important issue raised by the opening of marriage for same-sex couples concerns the relationship between registered partnership and marriage.[12] Should both institutions be preserved, although they are similar to a large extent? This question has become – unwittingly – more complicated with the possibility for heterosexual couples to register a partnership. The decision to make the registered partnership available to heterosexual couples is based on the presumed need of heterosexual couples to opt for a regulation which contains a lesser degree of symbolism than marriage. However, with this decision the Government rather tried to reduce the (symbolic and emotional) differences between the registered partnership and marriage which might be felt in society. The Government hoped that it would be sufficient to overcome allegations of discrimination against homosexuals.

It was one decision to make the registered partnership available for heterosexual couples, but quite another not to reconsider the status of the institution of registered partnership now that marriage for same-sex couples has been made available. The goal of the Registered Partnership Act – equality for same-sex partners – has been achieved and in this respect there is no use in preserving the registered partnership. However, given the availability of the registered partnership for heterosexual couples, it has become somewhat more complicated. The Government decided to postpone any definite decision on the future of the institution of registered partnership until 2006 when the Act opening marriage to same-sex couples will be evaluated. In the meantime, the registered partnership will be preserved. This decision is contrary to the advice of the Council of State concerning the Act to open marriage to same-sex couples which leaves no room for doubt: the Government should abolish one of the two institutions.[13] The single argument put forward by the Government in order to justify its different decision is the number of heterosexual couples who have taken up a registered partnership. This demonstrates, in the view of the Government, the need for the registered partnership. A total of 4433 heterosexual couples chose to

---

[10]   First Chamber, 15–672, 19-12-2001.

[11]   First Chamber 14–609, 18-12-2000.

[12]   See also section **IIIC** below.

[13]   Second Chamber, 1998–1999, 26672, no B.

register their partnership in the period from 1 January 1998 until 1 January 2001. This number is not impressive considering that 267,418 marriages were registered in the same period. It is less than 2 percent of the total number of heterosexual couples who formalised their relationship in the same period.

The Government's reasoning creates the risk that the decision to preserve both the registered partnership and marriage for the time being might have a great impact on the future development of family law. For it might be presumed that there will still be a certain need among heterosexuals for the registration of their partnership in 2006. This would probably lead the Government to the conclusion that there are sufficient grounds not to abolish the registered partnership. There are, however, many questions which have to answered before any definite decision on the future of the registered partnership can be taken. What is the role of the State with respect to the regulation of relationships based on affection? Is there a model for regulating relationships based on affection which should be preferred? What does family law offer to the group of 1.3 million unmarried cohabitants? Should marriage be abolished?[14] With the course of events as described there is a risk that the legislator will again avoid answering questions such as these without just cause.

During the debates in the Second Chamber of Parliament, the CDA and the strict Protestant parties had already questioned the need for the existence of the registered partnership alongside marriage. The CDA faction had opposed the availability of the registered partnership for homosexual couples, since these couples could now marry. The children born to married couples would have a better legal position than those of registered partners. With the availability of marriage, the registered partnership should be abolished, they argued.[15] In the debates in the First Chamber, the Labour party also touched upon this subject. In its view, either marriage or registered partnership should be abolished, but given the fact that there was a certain need among heterosexual couples to register a partnership, Labour could accept the decision of the Government to preserve both institutions.[16]

C   The legal position of civil status registrars with religious objections to same-sex marriages

Is a civil status registrar excused from having to register a marriage between two persons of the same sex on grounds of personal conscience? This question has received quite a lot of attention, for it was not only an important issue during the parliamentary debates, it also attracted a great deal of publicity in the media. The Government succeeded in reaching a compromise between the parties which were concerned about the position of the civil status registrars and the parties for whom the non-discrimination against same-sex couples was the guiding principle. On the one hand, a legal right for the civil status registrars to be excused from having to register such marriages was not recognised. Such a legal right was strongly favoured by the Christian parties.[17] On the other hand, the conscientious

---

[14]   Cf First Chamber 15–665, 19-12-2000.

[15]   Second Chamber, 58–4211, 20-3-2001.

[16]   First Chamber, 14–601, 18-12-2000.

[17]   First Chamber 14-599, 18-12-2000; First Chamber 14–605, 18-12-2000; First Chamber 15–664, 19-12-2000.

objections of civil status registrars should be considered with respect. The Government decided not to provide for any statutory provisions, but to leave it to the discretion of the individual city councils to find a pragmatic solution. If a civil status registrar was not willing to register a same-sex marriage, the city council could for example employ a different working schedule or it could arrange for the temporary replacement of the civil status registrar. In the end, a solution should be readily available, because there are at least two civil status registrars in each city and, in addition, a civil status registrar from another city council could be asked to register the same-sex marriage.[18] Notwithstanding this respect for such objections on the grounds of personal conscience, the right of same-sex couples to marry in any given city or town is decisive. In the opinion of the Government, the objections of civil status registrars who are contracted after the Act entered into force will also have to be considered with respect. The Green-Left party strongly opposed this, for in its view new registrars should be compelled to conclude same-sex marriages, since they know that this a part of their legal duty.[19]

The Christian parties feared that this proposed solution, not based upon an Act or other formal regulation, would not work very well in practice. The Government promised to keep a close eye on the functioning of the compromise and to take appropriate measures if this turned out to be necessary.[20] Up until now it does not seem to be working perfectly: during the debates in Parliament, the chairman of the council in Amsterdam already stated that civil status registrars would not be excused from having to register a same-sex marriage in Amsterdam. Further, the city council of Leeuwarden decided not to renew the contract of a civil status registrar who twice refused to register a gay marriage. Despite these signals of malfunction in the system, the Government has as yet not proposed any new measures.

III   PROTECTION OF CHILDREN BORN IN SAME-SEX MARRIAGES AND REGISTERED PARTNERSHIPS

A   General remarks

With the availability of marriage for same-sex couples, the traditional connection between marriage and descent belongs partially to the past, for it is no longer self-evident that marriage creates legal parenthood. Whereas the husband of the mother is presumed to be the father of a child born to her, this rule does not apply to same-sex spouses. In the opinion of the legislator such a step would be too far from biological reality, since the same-sex spouse could never be the biological parent of the child. It was not necessary to amend the existing law in this respect, since the text of the relevant provisions ('the husband', 'the father') already excludes same-sex partners from the presumption of paternity.

This means that there is no legal relationship whatsoever between the 'social parent' (ie the same-sex spouse of the biological parent) and the child. However,

---

[18]   Second Chamber 2000–2001, 26 672, no 12 (Letter by the State Secretary to the Second Chamber of Parliament) and First Chamber 15–658, 19-12-2000.

[19]   First Chamber 14–609, 18-12-2000.

[20]   First Chamber, 15–672, 19-12-2000.

the Government and Parliament shared the opinion that it would be in the best interests of the child to protect the relationship between the social parent and the child who is brought up in a same-sex marriage, although it was not evident which kind of protection should be chosen.

A similar question had actually already been raised when the Act on registered partnership was introduced. Then two options had been taken into consideration: on the one hand, adoption for same-sex couples and, on the other, shared custody and guardianship. Both suggestions had been proposed by the Kortmann Commission.[21] Protection by means of adoption was at this stage rejected by the Government. It argued that the nature of adoption as a measure of child protection would be contrary to the use of adoption as a way of establishing parenthood. The Government preferred to introduce the Shared Custody and Guardianship Act, which entered into force on 1 January 1998. Although this Act has already been discussed in previous reviews, in the next section further attention will be paid to the Act. It will thus be possible to put the developments in a broader perspective and to deal in some detail with the similarities and differences between the different custody regulations. In addition, new developments in the case-law and the legal literature will be examined.

B   Shared custody under Art 1:253t Civil Code

On the basis of Art 1:253t Civil Code, inserted in the Civil Code by the Shared Custody and Guardianship Act, 'a person who has a close personal relationship to the child' may apply, together with the legal parent, to the court for a shared custody order.[22] This request is granted only if the legal parent is the sole holder of custody rights. Extra requirements have to be met in situations in which the child has another legal parent who has no custody rights. The legal parent and the social parent must have taken care of the child during an uninterrupted period of at least one year before the request has been submitted to the court. Further, the parent who applies for shared custody should have had sole custody for at least three uninterrupted years. The court has to reject the request if there is a substantial reason to believe that the interests of the child will be neglected if the request is granted. If the court grants shared custody, the legal provisions regulating shared parental custody will apply, subject to any legislative provision to the contrary.[23]

In the legal literature, the position of the child in the procedure has been criticised. A child of 12 years and older (or younger if the child is sufficiently mature) has a right to be heard by the judge,[24] but his/her consent is not required.[25]

---

[21]   Report by the Kortmann Commission to investigate whether marriage should be made available to same-sex partners, The Hague, October 1997, discussed in *The International Survey of Family Law 1997*, ed A Bainham (Martinus Nijhoff Publishers, 1999), pp 264–268.

[22]   Shared guardianship is exercised by two social parents. Shared guardianship is governed by provisions which are similar to those in the case of shared custody. This paragraph deals only with shared custody.

[23]   Article 1:245, s 5 Civil Code.

[24]   Art 809 Code of Civil Procedure.

[25]   It is argued in the legal literature that although adoption and shared custody resemble each other as to their legal effects, the position of the child differs considerably, as adoption requires the consent of the child. See for example P van Teeffelen, 'Sociaal en biologisch ouderschap, Enige kritische opmerkingen over Art 1:253t Civil Code', in *Tijdschrift voor Familie- en Jeugdrecht 2001*, p 134.

One of the consequences of shared custody is that the social parent has a duty to maintain the child during the period in which he/she is its custodian. Even after the child has reached the age of 18 years and the custody has been terminated as a result, the partner is still under a duty to maintain the child until he/she is 21 years old. If the shared custody is terminated by means of a court order and the social partner no longer has custody, his/her maintenance duty continues for a period which is equivalent to the duration of the period during which the social parent has shared custody with the legal parent. In special cases, the court may determine a longer period at the request of the legal or social parent.[26]

Further, a special provision allows the legal parent and the social parent to apply together for an order changing the family name of the child to the family name of the legal parent or that of the social partner.[27] A child of 12 years or older has to consent to the proposed change.[28] Further, the request can be granted only if the order for shared custody has been granted and if such an order is not contrary to the best interests of the child. This regulation seems to be inconsistent with the general principle of the law on surnames in that caution has to be exercised with respect to a change of family name of children.[29]

In three recently published decisions, the requests for a change of the family name of the child to the family name of the partner were rejected.[30] The Court of Appeal of The Hague stressed the importance of the family name as part of someone's identity. Since it is possible that at a given moment one of the legal parents will again be entitled to custody rights, the change of the family name to that of the social parent should be considered with reservations. The Court of Appeal of Arnhem deemed that it was not in the best interests of the child to allow a change of the child's name to that of the social parent, since there would be a risk that the relationship with the father, whose name the child had, would seriously be damaged. Such an order could affirm the father's fears that this would harm the relationship with his child. In another decision, the Court of Appeal of Arnhem also rejected a request to change the child's surname. The mother of the child argued that it would be in the best interests of her daughter if she could acquire the same family name as the step-brother, which in the mother's view view justified a change into the name of her new spouse.[31] The court decided that the interests of the daughter to preserve her relationship with her father by continuing to bear his family name, taking into consideration the young age of the girl and the fragile relationship with her father, outweighed the other interests.

A breakdown of the relationship of the legal and the social parent does not in itself alter the shared custody. If the parents no longer want to share custody, they have to file an application to the court for the termination of the shared custody. The non-custodian legal parent has no right to file an application for the

---

[26]   Article 1:253w Civil Code.

[27]   Article 1:253t(5) and Article 1:282 (7) Civil Code.

[28]   A child younger than 12 years old may be heard: Art 809, s 1 Code of Civil Procedure. The other legal parent must be heard: Art 800, s 1 in conjunction with Art 798, s 1 Code of Civil Procedure.

[29]   In other situations, more stringent norms have to be met before a change of name will be allowed. Cf P van Teeffelen, 'Sociaal en biologisch ouderschap, Enige kritische opmerkingen over art 1:253t Civil Code', in *Tijdschrift voor Familie- en Jeugdrecht 2001*, p 136.

[30]   Court of Appeal of The Hague, 19 April 2000, *Tijdschrift voor Familie en Jeugdrecht 2000*, pp 151–152 and Court of Appeal of Arnhem, 2 May 2000, *Tijdschrift voor Familie- en Jeugdrecht 2000*, pp 238–239.

[31]   Court of Appeal of Arnhem, 11 April 2000, *Rechtspraak van de Week 2001*, no 130.

termination of the shared custody. The court determines whether a request for termination will be granted and who will have custody rights.[32] Custody might be given to one of the legal parents, to both legal parents together, or to the social parent.[33] The criterion which the judge has to apply in determining whether termination of the shared custody should be ordered is whether there has been a change in circumstances. According to the Government, this criterion should thus be interpreted that shared custody should in principle continue to exist, unless it would be detrimental to the child's interests.[34] In determining future custody, the court has to consider what is in the best interests of the child. The court is free to consider the circumstances of the case, since the law does not assign a preference for the legal parents over the social parent. If the legal and the social parent do not apply for any order after their separation, they will continue to have shared custody.

If the legal parent dies, the social parent automatically becomes solely entitled to custody rights.[35] The non-custodian legal parent is always allowed to apply for sole custody on the basis of a change of circumstances, but the law does not lay down any principle of preference as far as he/she is concerned.[36] A court may even consider that a change in the place of residence might be detrimental to the child, which might result in an actual preference for the social parent.

The practical impact of the law should not be underestimated. It is only since 1998 that after a divorce the ex-spouses as a matter of law continue to exercise parental custody together. Before that time, the court in most cases granted custody rights to one of the ex-spouses, usually the mother. As a result, the situation in which a parent has sole custody rights occurs relatively often. Consequently, the potential of the law – which requires sole custody as a prerequisite – is quite broad. Once the legal parent has had sole custody for three years, it will be very difficult for the other legal parent to prevent the granting of an order awarding shared custody to the legal parent along with the social parent. For, as stated above, the judge may refuse the request only if, taking into consideration the interests of the other legal parent, there are serious indications that the interests of the child will be neglected if shared custody is given. This only gives the judge a fairly narrow discretion to weigh the interests of the persons involved.

The case-law seems to indicate that the interests of the other biological parent do not carry much weight. In a decision of July 2001, the Dutch Supreme Court (*Hoge Raad*) held that the interests of the legal parent should be taken into consideration in determining whether a shared custody order should be granted. However, the interests of the child were paramount.[37] The father of the child had argued that it would not be in the interests of his daughter to lose contact with him completely. Further, he referred to the fact that the parental access agreement had not been adhered to by the mother which made it more difficult for him to develop

---

[32] Art 1:253v, s 3 Civil Code and Art 1:253n Civil Code. The court should give the non-custodian legal parent the opportunity to apply for a sole or shared parental custody order.

[33] If the court grants custody to the social parent, both legal parents may always request sole or shared parental custody on the basis of a change of circumstances: Art 1:253v, s 4 Civil Code.

[34] First Chamber, 2000–2001, 27 047, no 249b, p 6.

[35] Art 1:253x, s 1 Civil Code.

[36] Art 1:253x, s 2 Civil Code.

[37] Dutch Supreme Court (*Hoge Raad*), 13 July 2001, *Rechtspraak van de Week 2001*, no 130 and also published in *Nederlands JuristenBlad 2001*, p 1378.

the still tentative relationship with his daughter. In his view, the Court of Appeal should reject the application for shared custody on the basis of the arguments put forward by him. The Supreme Court determined that the sole fact that there is no parental access agreement, or that such an agreement does not work in practice, in itself does not constitute a sufficient reason to reject the application for shared custody.

This narrow interpretation of the interests of the other legal parent in the case-law is only one aspect which shows the weak legal position of the non-custodian legal parent. His/her position is also not well safeguarded in another respect: as stated above, after the death of the legal parent having custody, it is the social parent, not the other legal parent, who will automatically acquire sole custody. Taken together with the fact that the non-custodian parent has no right to request the termination of shared custody and that the child might bear the family name of the social parent, the law leaves the non-custodian legal parent in a weak position. The position of the legal parent with custody is not much better. As stated above, after a breakdown of the relationship of the legal and the social parent, the court is free to assess the custody regulation, without being bound by a legal preference for the legal parent. The lack of consideration for the position of legal parents has been criticised in the legal literature, especially for being inconsistent with one of the leading principles of the legislation on custody: the preference for legal parents over and above social parents.[38]

C   Automatic shared custody by dint of marriage or registered partnership

According to the Shared Custody and Guardianship Act, partners would first have to apply to the court for a shared custody order if a child were to be born during their registered partnership or same-sex marriage. Thus, there might be children in respect of whom the legal parent would be sole holder of custody rights, as not all couples would resort to the courts. This could result in a so-called 'custody vacuum' if that parent should die or lose his/her custody rights. In order to overcome this problem, a Bill[39] has been drafted which seeks to introduce automatic shared custody when a child is born to partners who have registered a partnership or who have entered into a same-sex marriage. Attention has already been paid to this Bill in last year's report.[40]

Although the title of the Bill seems to suggest that this regulation is only applicable to registered partners, it applies to same-sex marriages as well. The Act has no effect with respect to heterosexual married couples, for there is already a legal provision providing them with automatic shared custody.[41]

Two men who have registered a partnership or who have married one another, do not qualify for automatic shared custody, for a child can not be born to them during the registered partnership or marriage. Since the situation in which two

---

[38]   P van Teeffelen, 'Sociaal en biologisch ouderschap, Enige kritische opmerkingen over Art 1:253t Civil Code', in *Tijdschrift voor Familie- en Jeugdrecht 2001*, p 133ff.

[39]   Amendment to Book 1 of the Civil Code in connection with automatic shared custody in the event of a birth during a registered partnership, Second Chamber, 1999–2000, 27 047 and First Chamber, 2000–2001, 27 047.

[40]   Dutch report, C Forder, 'To Marry or Not To Marry: That Is The Question', *The International Survey of Family Law (2001 Edition)*, ed A Bainham (Family Law, 2001), at pp 315–319.

[41]   Art 1:251, s 1 Civil Code.

men raise a child together does occur in practice, it has been the subject of discussion in Parliament. Labour and Green-Left introduced an amendment[42] according to which the custody rights would pass to the father and his partner by means of a simple registration with the county court registrar in the event that the mother dies or her custody rights are terminated.[43] This registration procedure, which is the same procedure which unmarried heterosexual couples follow to acquire shared custody, is very simple. The registrar has a limited competence and he may not determine whether shared custody will be in the best interests of the child.

Green-Left[44] was in favour of this amendment and initially the Liberal Left party also supported the amendment.[45] The Christian parties opposed the extension of this possibility to two male partners.[46] The Government advised against accepting the amendment by Labour and Green-Left. The interests of the deceased mother or the interests of a mother whose custody rights have been terminated require intervention by the courts. Even more important, in the view of the Government, is that this simple registration procedure would be detrimental to the interests of the child, because there is no opportunity to take into account the child's interests and its opinion.[47] Therefore, in these complex situations, a court procedure with the necessary competence to weigh all the interests involved, including those of the mother, her family and the child, is to be preferred to an informal registration procedure with the county court registrar with few safeguards. The amendment was only supported by the factions of the Labour party, Green-Left and the Socialist party and thus it did not obtain the required majority.[48]

Although the Bill is not as controversial as the Bills mentioned before, the parties in the Second and First Chamber had very different opinions concerning the Bill. The strict Protestant parties and the CDA greeted the Bill with disappointment, for they deemed this measure to be excessive, whereas the Labour party and Liberal Left, both in favour of the Bill,[49] insisted on even more far-reaching measures than those provided in the Bill.

The CDA stressed that it is not the task of the State to prevent a custody vacuum from arising. Heterosexual couples should marry each other if they want to prevent a custody vacuum. The parents are primarily responsible for the well-being of their children and the State should not take over this responsibility. Marriage provides the best protection for children, and parents should not be discouraged from marrying. Further, this faction stated that the distinctiveness of the registered partnership and marriage is very important for the CDA. In its opinion a clear policy on the rationale of registered partnerships is lacking, and it rejected the argument of the Government[50] that the different emotional

---

[42]   Amendment by the Members of Parliament Santi and Rabbae, Second Chamber, 2000–2001, 27 047, no 9.

[43]   For example, because the child has been mistreated or neglected. The amendment resembles the advice of the Kortmann Commission (footnote 21 above).

[44]   Second Chamber, 58–4214, 20-3-2001.

[45]   Second Chamber, 58–4211, 20-3-2001.

[46]   Second Chamber, 58–4215, 20-3-2001.

[47]   Second Chamber, 2000–2001, 27047, no 12 and Second Chamber, 58–4216, 20-3-2001.

[48]   Second Chamber 61–4279, 27-3-2001.

[49]   First Chamber 2000–2001, 27047, no 249a, p 2–3.

[50]   Second Chamber, 58–4219ff, 20-3-2001.

appreciation of marriage and the registered partnership is, together with the still existing differences between both institutions, a sufficient ground to allow registered partnership to subsist alongside marriage.[51] In the legal literature, similar doubts have been expressed.[52] In addition, the CDA stressed the inconsistent policy of the Government in this respect. The Bill erodes the essential difference between a marriage and a registered partnership, namely that a registered partnership has no effects on the relationship with children. At the moment there are still differences between a marriage and a registered partnership with regard to maintenance, inheritance law and nationality, but according to the CDA it is difficult to understand why these differences should be preserved if this is not in the interests of the child. Thus, the crucial differences between a registered partnership and a marriage might even disappear completely in the future.[53]

Another criticism, expressed by all the Christian parties, is whether this law is really necessary: is the very small risk of a custody vacuum a sufficient reason for creating such a far-reaching legal provision? Moreover, in practice no problems have been reported concerning such a custody vacuum.[54] With respect to these exceptional situations, less far-reaching measures should have been taken into consideration, for example temporary automatic transfer of custody rights to the partner of the deceased parent until the court comes to a definite decision. Such a regulation would leave unaffected the nature of the registered partnership as an institution which was only meant to deal with the relationship between the partners *inter se* and not to touch upon the relationship with the children.[55] The Government admitted that there are other means to achieve the desired result and that the lack of any provision appears not to result in any great problems in practice. The Government responded with the question of who could object to promoting the interests of the child, especially if this could occur in this relatively simple way.[56]

The Liberal-Left party proposed a more fundamental change to the Bill in the sense that they suggested that a female partner of the mother of the child should have the right to recognise the child. The child would then be integrated into two families and would be placed in a situation which would resemble the situation of children of a couple of the opposite sex as far as possible.[57]

The Bill met with approval from the Green-Left, but this party proposed to apply the regulation also to situations in which more than two persons are involved, for example two legal parents and two step-parents. The Government considered this idea not to be in the best interests of the child.[58]

---

[51] Second Chamber, 58–4211 and 58–4219, 20-3-2001 and First Chamber 2000–2001, 27 047, no 249a, p 1–2. The SGP faction shares this view: Second Chamber, 58—214 and 58–4220, 20-3-2001.

[52] JH de Graaf, Personen- familie- en jeugdrecht, *Ars Aequi* 50 (2001) katern 80, p 4198.

[53] First Chamber, 2–40, 2-10-2001.

[54] First Chamber, 2000–2001, 27 047, no 249a, p 3.

[55] Second Chamber, 58–4213, 20-3-2001 and First Chamber 2–39–40, 2-10-2001 and First Chamber, 2–42, 2-10-2001.

[56] First Chamber, 2–43, 2-10-2001.

[57] Second Chamber, 58–4211, 20-3-2001.

[58] Second Chamber, 58–4221, 20-3-2001.

The Labour party in the First Chamber favoured the general principle of the Bill, but was critical as to some specific aspects.[59] For example, it raised the question of why the procedure to terminate automatic shared custody after a dissolution of a registered partnership or same-sex marriage differs from the procedure after the dissolution of a marriage between a heterosexual couple.[60] Interesting is the remark of this faction that family law is becoming increasingly more complex as a result of the adaptation of the law to different social changes. However, the question should be raised whether it is not now time to reconsider and evaluate the outcomes of this process of adaptation. Is the proposed regulation consistent and is it an appropriate solution; should the differences between custody and guardianship for instance not be abolished, etc?[61] The Government implicitly shared the view that the recent reforms of the family have resulted in patchwork solutions. It also admitted that the developments have followed each other in rapid succession as a result of which they have influenced each other in a way which could not have been imagined in advance.[62] According to the Government, many objections exist as a matter of principle to this course of events, but from a pragmatic point of view the result of the reforms is acceptable, since it meets social needs. Further, the Government stressed that there are no negative aspects of the legislation reported and it promised to evaluate the reforms in a few years time.[63]

In the end, the Bill was accepted by the First Chamber on 2 October 2001; only the Christian parties were against it.[64] It is not yet known when the Act will enter into force.

D Adoption of Dutch children by same-sex couples

After an initial rejection of the recommendation of the second Kortmann Commission to make the adoption of Dutch children available to same-sex couples, the legislator changed its plans and introduced a Bill to Allow the Adoption of Dutch Children by Partners of the Same Sex. This Act, which was

---

[59] There is no opportunity to request a provisional measure with respect to children on the basis of Art 822 of the Code of Civil Procedure, which there should be. Furthermore, Art 1:80d Civil Code on the termination of a registered partnership by mutual consent has not been adequately amended.

[60] According to Art 1:251a Civil Code, a child of 12 years and older may on his/her own initiative request the court to grant custody to one of his/her parents, if a marriage between a heterosexual couple has been terminated. If a registered partnership or a same-sex marriage is terminated, the child has no such right. Labour opposed this different treatment. Also critical is JE Doek, 'Het gezag over minderjarigen, Iets over een doolhof en het zoeken van (rode?) draden', in *Tijdschrijft voor Familie- en Jeugdrecht 2000*, pp 219 and 225. Further, Labour noted a difference as to the criterion for the termination of shared custody used in Art 1:253n Civil Code and in Art 1:251 Civil Code. However, the Government explained that these criteria lead to the same result: shared custody should principally continue, unless this would be detrimental to the child's interests: First Chamber, 2000–2001, 27 047, no 249b, p 6.

[61] First Chamber, 2–41, 2-10-2001. See also: J Doek, 'Het gezag over minderjarigen, Iets over een doolhof en het zoeken van (rode?) draden', in *Tijdschrijft voor Familie- en Jeugdrecht 2000*, p 225.

[62] First Chamber, 2–46, 2-10-2001.

[63] First Chamber, 2–44, 2-10-2001.

[64] First Chamber, 2–46, 2-10-2001.

considered in Parliament together with the Bill opening marriage to homosexuals, entered into force on 1 April 2001.

This reform did not receive a great deal of attention, although it fundamentally changes the nature of adoption. The Government explicitly admitted that this fundamental change did not go hand in hand with a serious reconsideration of adoption.[65] In 1956 adoption was introduced as a means of protecting the best interests of children. Ever since, adoption could only be granted by a judge, who had to consider carefully whether adoption would be in the best interests of the child. Adoption terminates the legal relationship with the legal parent and it creates a new legal relationship with the adoptive parent. Thus, adoption is an exceptional measure, requiring several conditions to be met. The question has been raised in both Chambers of Parliament and in the legal literature whether this Act is not rather a means to create parenthood, which is primarily in the interest of same-sex couples.[66] The best interests of the child seem to be only of minor importance. With this legislation, the link between biological and legal descent belongs to the past and the borders between descent and adoption are fading. It has been suggested in the legal literature that the legal relationship between a same-sex couple and the child should be regulated in a separate title of the Dutch Civil Code (not being descent or adoption).[67]

The route of the Bill up to the Second Chamber has already been described in the previous *Survey*,[68] so that here only the second round of debates, in the First Chamber, will be considered. Again there was discussion about the scope of the law. The political parties and the Government held different views on whether inter-country adoptions should be subject to different provisions (and thus not be available to same-sex partners). The Government, however, adhered to its initial rejection of the extension of the regulation to inter-country adoptions, since, as it explained to the First Chamber, other countries will not allow children to be adopted by partners of the same sex.[69]

All the Christian parties in the First Chamber disapproved of the Bill. They deemed it not to be in the best interests of the child to be brought up in families with two same-sex parents. These children would be in an exceptional position in society, which would be contrary to their best interests.[70] All these parties stressed their feelings that the interests of the same-sex partners appear to be the motive for this legislation rather than a real concern for the children involved. According to these parties, sufficient protection is already provided by means of shared custody and the registered partnership. Further, the CDA invited the Government to consider whether it is really necessary to terminate completely the legal relationship with the parents.[71]

Green-Left would rather prefer a regulation creating legal links by means of the legal recognition of social parenthood. It is not the biological descent which

---

[65]   First Chamber 15–672, 19-12-2000.

[66]   JH de Graaf, Personen- familie- en jeugdrecht, *Ars Aequi* 50 (2001) katern 79, p 4113.

[67]   S Wortmann, 'Kroniek van het personen- en familierecht', *Nederlands JuristenBlad 2001*, pp 1542–1543.

[68]   Dutch report, C Forder, 'To Marry or Not To Marry: That Is The Question', *The International Survey of Family Law (2001 Edition)*, ed A Bainham (Family Law, 2001), at pp 312–315.

[69]   First Chamber 15–660, 19-12-2000. The number of adoptions within the Netherlands is between 50 to 100 a year.

[70]   First Chamber 14–606 at p 608, 18-12-2000.

[71]   First Chamber 14–600, 18-12-2000.

should be the decisive factor, but the care and love given to a child.[72] In reaction thereto the Government expressed the opinion that the choice of a solution by means of adoption instead of the law of descent, is very well considered. The law of descent concerns relationships which are the result of a biological link between the parent and the child. With respect to adoption it is the relationship based upon care, without the existence of such a biological link, which justifies legal recognition. It is a form of 'artificial descent' and it is therefore appropriate, according to the Government, to use adoption instead of the law of descent.[73] Attention was also paid to the question of whether a form of adoption which does not result in the termination of all legal ties between the child and its legal parents would provide a more adequate solution. However, the Government responded that the introduction of such an adoption would not have much meaning for the Dutch system, since in the Netherlands only minors can be adopted. Shared custody to a great extent resembles such an adoption and thus there was no need for such a reform of the law on adoption.[74]

The Bill passed through the First Chamber with ease: only the factions of the CDA, the strict Protestant parties and two members of the Liberal Left faction voted against the Bill, the remainder of the parties supported it.

E   Different families, different outcomes

The new legislation on (automatic) shared custody, registered partnership and same-sex marriage makes it rather difficult to obtain an overall picture of the different rules which determine the legal relationship between (social) parents and children. Therefore, it is useful to elaborate upon this rather complex part of family law.

The situation in which a child is brought up determines this. There are two decisive aspects in determining this. First, it is important to distinguish between whether the partners who raise the child have or have not formalised their relationship. If they have done so, a subdivision should be made between married couples and those who have registered a partnership. A second criterion is whether two partners of the same sex or partners of the opposite sex are concerned. As a result, five situations have to be dealt with depending on whether the child is being raised by:

(1)   married partners of the opposite sex;
(2)   registered partners of the opposite sex;
(3)   partners of the opposite sex who have not formalised their relationship;
(4)   married or registered partners of the same sex (for these two groups, the same rules apply); or
(5)   same-sex partners who have not formalised their relationship.

The resulting sets of rules determine whether parenthood exists, which custody regulation applies and the child's position with respect to maintenance, the law relating to surnames, the child's inheritance rights and nationality. In this

---

[72]   First Chamber 14–612, 18-12-2000.
[73]   First Chamber 15–662, 19-12-2000.
[74]   First Chamber 15–663, 19-12-2000.

section, attention will only be paid to parenthood, custody rights, maintenance and the family name. Inheritance rights and nationality will not generally be discussed.[75] The five following subsections deal with these regulations for each distinct situation. In E6, some concluding remarks will be discussed. In order to understand fully the complex results thereof the different regulations will also be presented in a table (in E7).

E1   OPPOSITE-SEX PARTNERS WHO HAVE MARRIED

The position of the mother does not depend on whether she is married, has registered a partnership or lives in a non-formalised relationship, since the legal mother is the woman who gives birth to the child.[76] If a child is born during the marriage between a man and a woman, the husband is presumed to be the father of the child.[77] Legal parenthood brings about far-reaching legal effects: the child becomes part of the families of his/her two parents,[78] the parents are under a duty to maintain the child[79] and the child has inheritance rights[80] with respect to the estates of both parents.

Both parents have shared custody as a matter of law.[81] In the event that the parents divorce they continue to have shared custody, unless an application by one of the parents for sole custody has been granted by the court.[82] The judge will have to consider whether it is in the best interests of the child to grant custody to one of the parents.

Both parents are under a duty to maintain the child until he/she is 18 years old (with respect to care and upbringing) or 21 years old (with respect to education and maintenance).[83] A divorce does not affect maintenance duties.

The parents may choose the family name (of either the father or the mother) of the child at its birth; if they do not make a choice the child will automatically have the family name of the father.[84]

E2   OPPOSITE-SEX PARTNERS WHO HAVE REGISTERED A PARTNERSHIP

The position of the mother is similar to a married opposite-sex woman. However, the status of the male registered partner is very different from a married opposite-sex partner, since a registered partnership does not establish parenthood between the male partner and the child born during the registered partnership. This difference has far-reaching consequences, since the male partner has to recognise the child if he wishes to become the legal father. Recognition may take place before or after the birth of the child.

---

[75]   Moreover, the consequences of the different situations for social security law and tax law also fall outside the scope of this contribution.

[76]   Art 1:198 Civil Code.

[77]   Art 1:199, sub a Civil Code.

[78]   Art 1:197 Civil Code.

[79]   Art 1:392 Civil Code.

[80]   A child who is the legal child of a parent has a right to inherit a certain share of the estate of his/her deceased parent, of which he/she cannot be deprived.

[81]   Art 1:251, s 1 Civil Code. If the parents marry after the birth of the child, they acquire shared custody as a matter of law as well.

[82]   Art 1:251, s 2 Civil Code.

[83]   Art 1:392 Civil Code and Art 1:395a Civil Code.

[84]   Art 1:5, s 4 and 5 Civil Code.

If the male partner recognises the child, he is under a duty to maintain the child until he/she is 18 or 21 years old[85] and the child has a legal right to inherit a portion of his estate. The parents may choose the family name of the father for the child, but if they do not choose the father's name at the moment of recognition, the child will retain his/her mother's family name.[86]

Recognition alone, however, does not have any automatic effects with respect to custody rights. Thus, only the mother has custody.[87] If the parents want to have shared custody, they would – if the parents have not registered a partnership – have to register as having shared custody with the county court registrar (see E3 below). However, if the parents have registered a partnership *and* if the recognition has taken place before the child's birth, the father acquires automatic shared custody with the mother. This is because Art 1:253aa Civil Code (implemented by the Act on Shared Custody) determines that the *parents* have automatic shared custody with respect to a child born *during* a registered partnership. This implies that both registered partners have to be the legal parents of the child at the moment of its birth. If the male registered partner recognises the child after its birth, only the mother will be the custodian.[88] The parents will have to follow the registration procedure at the county court in order to obtain shared custody.[89]

If the male registered partner does not recognise the child, he is obliged to maintain the child as long as the registered partnership continues and the child is to be considered as a child of the family[90]. This duty is based on Art 1:395 Civil Code on step-parents and finds its basis in the registered partnership.[91] If the registered partnership is dissolved, this duty is terminated. It is important to notice that the regulation of maintenance is thus independent from the question whether the partners share custody.[92] Only the mother has custody, but the partners may apply for shared custody on the basis of Art 1:253t Civil Code.[93] The child has no inheritance rights with respect to the male partner's estate and the family name of the mother is the child's family name.[94]

A dissolution of the registered partnership does not alter the custody rights.[95] If the parents have had (automatic) shared custody, they will continue to have it after the dissolution of the registered partnership. Either parent may request sole custody; the court has to consider whether a change of circumstances justifies the

---

[85] Art 1:392 Civil Code and Art 1:395a Civil Code.

[86] Art 1:5, s 2 Civil Code.

[87] Art 1:253b s 1 Civil Code.

[88] Art 1:253b s 2 Civil Code.

[89] Art 1:252 Civil Code.

[90] This concept has to be broadly interpreted: First Chamber 2000–2001, 27 047, no 249b, p 2.

[91] First Chamber 2000–2001, 27 047, no 249b, p 2.

[92] The relationship between, on the one hand, Art 1:395 Civil Code and, on the other, Art 1:253w Civil Code, which regulates maintenance duties for shared custody cases, both of which seem to be applicable in certain situations, has not yet been clarified. To complicate this even further, the male registered partner who is the begetter of the child may be under a maintenance duty as if he were a parent of the child on the basis of Art 1:394 Civil Code.

[93] See, with respect to the consequences of shared custody under Art 1:253t Civil Code, E4 below.

[94] Art 5, s 1 Civil Code.

[95] It is not relevant whether the registered partnership is dissolved on the basis of mutual consent or by a court order.

granting of such an order.[96] As the Government explained, this criterion should be interpreted in the sense that shared custody should principally continue, unless this would be detrimental for the child's interests.[97] Further, the judge has to consider to which parent the sole custody should – in the best interests of the child – be granted.

A dissolution of the registered partnership affects the maintenance duty of the registered partner who is not a legal parent, since he/she is only under a maintenance duty as long as the registered partnership continues.[98]

Compared to married parents of the opposite sex an important difference is that the spouse of the mother is presumed to be the father of the child, whereas the male registered partner is not. A comparison with an opposite-sex couple who have not formalised their relationship reveals that registered partners may acquire automatic shared custody (if the male partner has recognised the child before its birth), whereas the other couple have to register shared custody with the registrar of the county court. Another difference between registered partners and a couple who have not formalised their relationship is that the male registered partner, who is not the legal parent[99] of the child, is under a duty to maintain the child during the registered partnership, whereas the male partner, who is not the legal parent[100] of the child, has to maintain a child with respect to whom he shares/shared custody with its mother.

E3   PARTNERS OF THE OPPOSITE SEX WHO HAVE NOT FORMALISED THEIR RELATIONSHIP

This situation concerns parents who have not registered a marriage or a partnership with one another. Whether they are cohabiting or not is in principle not relevant. The mother of the child is, by right of birth, recognised as the legal parent,[101] she is under a duty to maintain the child[102] and the child has inheritance rights in its mother's estate. She will have sole custody.[103] The child will have his/her mother's family name.[104]

In order to become a legal parent, the male partner has to recognise the child. He might do so before or after the birth of the child and from the moment of recognition onwards he is the legal parent with all the rights and duties as mentioned above with respect to maintenance, inheritance rights and the law relating to surnames (see subsection E2 above).

After the recognition of the child, the father has no custody rights and in order to acquire shared custody with the mother, the parents have to register together with the county court registrar as having shared custody.[105] This is a simple procedure which requires no court intervention. The registrar has a limited

---

[96]   Art 1:253n Civil Code.
[97]   First Chamber, 2000–2001, 27 047, no 249b, p 6. See footnote 60 above.
[98]   Art 1:395 Civil Code.
[99]   Nor the begetter.
[100] Nor the begetter.
[101] Art 1:198 Civil Code.
[102] Art 1:392 Civil Code.
[103] Art 1:253b, s 1 Civil Code.
[104] Art 1:5, s 1 Civil Code.
[105] Art 1:252, Civil Code.

competence and he may not determine whether shared custody will be in the best interests of the child.

If the male partner has not recognised the child, he is not under a duty to maintain the child,[106] the child has no inheritance rights in the man's estate and the child has his/her mother's surname.[107] The mother has sole custody, but the partners may file an application to the court for shared custody on the basis of Art 1:253t Civil Code.[108]

The breakdown of the relationship does not affect the custody arrangement, nor the maintenance duties. If the parents have had shared custody, they will continue to do so after the dissolution of their relationship. Either parent may request sole custody; the court has to consider whether a change of circumstances justifies the granting of such an order and which custody regulation is in the best interests of the child.[109]

E4   SAME-SEX PARTNERS WHO HAVE CONCLUDED A MARRIAGE OR ENTERED INTO A REGISTERED PARTNERSHIP

In the event that a child is born during a registered partnership or marriage between same-sex partners, only one of the partners can be the legal parent. The same-sex partner of the parent is not a legal parent, since there is, despite their marriage or registered partnership, no presumption of parenthood. Further, there is no possibility for the partner to recognise the child, since only the biological father of a child may do so. If the necessary preconditions are met, the partner may adopt the child, in which case the partner acquires the status of a legal parent. This situation will not be discussed any further.

The fact that there is no parenthood relationship between the social parent and the child does not mean that there is no legal recognition at all of the social parenthood. According to Art 1:253sa Civil Code, both registered and married same-sex partners will, as a matter of law, have shared custody with respect to a child born *during* their registered partnership or marriage.[110] However, there is an important exception to this rule: if the child has another legal parent, the registered partners/spouses will not acquire automatic shared custody. Since a child cannot be born to two male registered partners or spouses, in practice automatic shared custody can only be acquired by same-sex couples comprising two women, without there being a legal father. An example is the situation in which the child is conceived by an anonymous sperm donor.

A duty to maintain a child exists for the same-sex partner of the parent of the child as long as the registered partnership or marriage continues and the child is to be considered as a child of the family.[111] This duty is based on Art 1:395 Civil

---

[106]   Unless he is the begetter of the child: Art 1:394 Civil Code.

[107]   Art 1:5, s 1 Civil Code.

[108]   See, with respect to the consequences of shared custody on the basis of Art 1:253t Civil Code, E4 below.

[109]   Art 1:253n Civil Code. See E2 above.

[110]   This means that there is a difference between a same-sex marriage and a marriage between partners of the opposite sex. For the first category, the registration of a marriage after the child's birth does not result in automatic shared custody by the parent and his/her partner, whereas a marriage between spouses of the opposite sex would do so.

[111]   This concept has to be broadly interpreted: First Chamber 2000–2001, 27 047, no 249b, p 2.

Code on step-parents and finds its basis in the registered partnership or marriage.[112]

Article 1:253sa, s 3 Civil Code declares that Art 1:5, s 4 Civil Code, which lays down the right to choose the child's family name, is applicable. The partners may together express a preference for either the family name of the parent or the family name of the partner.[113] If such a choice has not been made when the child's birth is registered, the child will have the mother's family name.

After the dissolution of the same-sex marriage or registered partnership, the shared custody continues, unless one of the partners applies to the court for sole custody. The same regulation (Art 1:253n Civil Code) applies as explained under subsection E2 above. If the marriage or registered partnership is dissolved, the same-sex spouse or registered partner is no longer under a duty to maintain the child on the basis of Art 1:394 Civil Code.

If a couple consisting of two men raise a child, they may apply for shared custody under Art 1:253t Civil Code (if one of them is the legal father of the child) or Art 1:282 Civil Code (if neither of them is a legal parent). Several requirements have to be met in such situations, mostly aimed at the protection of the interests of the other legal parent who has no custody rights. If there is another legal parent, the legal parent and the social parent in the same-sex marriage or registered partnership must have taken care of the child during an uninterrupted period of at least one year before the request is submitted to the court. Further, the parent who applies for shared custody should have had sole custody for at least three uninterrupted years. The court has to reject the request if there is a substantial reason to believe that the interests of the child will be neglected if the request is granted.

A duty to maintain a child exists for the same-sex partner of the parent of the child as long as the registered partnership or marriage continues and the child is to be considered as a child of the family (Art 1:395 Civil Code). In addition, there is a duty for the partner who has shared custody to maintain the child until he/she is 18 or 21 years old. If the shared custody is terminated before then, the duty to maintain the child continues for a period which is equivalent to the period in which the custody has been exercised by the partner together with the legal parent.[114] How these different maintenance duties relate to each other has not yet been clarified.[115]

If the request for shared custody has been granted the partners may apply together for an order changing the family name of the child into the family name of the legal or the social parent. The court may grant the order if it is not contrary to the child's best interests, and, if the child is 12 years or older, he/she has not objected to this.[116]

A child has no inheritance rights in relation to the partner of the parent. A Bill introducing a limited inheritance right for children who are subject to shared

---

[112] First Chamber 2000–2001, 27 047, no 249b, p 2.

[113] Art 1: 253sa, s 3 Civil Code in conjunction with Art 1:5, s 4, 5 and 7 Civil Code.

[114] Art 1:253w Civil Code.

[115] See footnote 92 above.

[116] Art 1:253t, s 5 Civil Code. See **IIIB** above..

custody and who are not legal children of the deceased, has not yet been prepared.[117]

The dissolution of the registered partnership or marriage is, as such, irrelevant for the custody arrangement. The partners/spouses continue to have shared custody and have to apply to the court if they want an order granting sole custody to one of them.[118] This regulation has already been described in E2 above. If the marriage or registered partnership is dissolved, the same-sex spouse or registered partner is no longer under a duty to maintain the child on the basis of Art 1:394 Civil Code.[119]

E5 SAME-SEX PARTNERS WHO HAVE NOT FORMALISED THEIR RELATIONSHIP

When the child is being raised by same-sex partners who have not formalised their relationship, only one of these partners may have the status of a legal parent. The other partner is not legally related to the child who is being brought up by both partners together. Therefore, for the parent, the same regulations apply as to any legal parent (maintenance, inheritance rights, surname) and with respect to the same-sex partner no such specific regulations apply. The partner has no possibility of recognising the child.

The parent and the partner cannot acquire automatic shared custody. If the partners wish to have shared custody or shared guardianship (if neither of them is the child's legal parent) they will have to apply for such a measure to the court on the basis of Art 1:253t Civil Code. The regulation as mentioned in E4 above will apply.

With respect to the duty to maintain the child and the surname of the child, the same regulations apply as described in E4 above.

E6 CONCLUSION

In conclusion, there are important differences between the different situations dealt with above. First, it is very important whether a partner is a legal parent or not. Secondly, there are important differences between shared custody on the basis of Art 1:253t Civil Code and automatic shared custody on the basis of Arts 1:253aa and 253sa Civil Code. Shared custody has to be awarded by a court, which has to take into consideration several specific requirements. Automatic shared custody comes into being as a matter of law if a child is born during a registered partnership or same-sex marriage and if there is no other legal parent.

The duty to maintain the child in the five situations described has a different legal basis, which results in different duties. A parent is always under a duty to maintain the child until he/she has reached the age of 18 or 21 years old. A partner (not being a legal parent) who has shared custody on the basis of Art 1:253t Civil

---

[117] Second Chamber 1999–2000, 22 700, no 31: a letter from the Minister of Justice to Parliament. In this letter it has been argued that it is too great a step to create intestate inheritance rights, since without further research it is not obvious that this is in accordance with the will of the person having custody who is not the parent. Therefore, further research has to be carried out before new legislation can be drawn up. See also C Forder, 'To Marry or Not To Marry: That Is The Question', *The International Survey of Family Law (2001 Edition)*, ed A Bainham (Family Law, 2001), p 301ff.

[118] Article 1:253v, s 3 Civil Code in conjunction with Art 1:253n Civil Code.

[119] But he/she might be under such a duty on the basis of Art 1:253w Civil Code.

Code is obliged to maintain the child until he/she is 18 or 21 years old or, if the shared custody has been terminated before this and has not been awarded to the partner, for a period equivalent to the duration of the shared custody. A registered partner or same-sex married partner is under a maintenance obligation only as long as the registered partnership or marriage subsists. After the marriage or registered partnership has been terminated this duty ends. The relationship between the different maintenance duties, which seem all to be applicable in certain situations, has not yet been clarified.

Further, there are different regulations with respect to the name of the child. Where there are two legal parents, the parents may choose the family name of either of them at the moment of registration of the birth or the recognition. Where the partners (not being both the legal parents) have automatic shared custody it is possible to give the child the family name of the partner. There are no extra requirements; if no choice is made, the child will have his/her mother's name. If the partners share custody on the basis of a court order under Art 1:253t Civil Code they will have to file an application to the court for a change of name. Such a change may not be contrary to the best interests of the child, and the child of 12 years and older has to consent to the change. The case-law seems to indicate little willingness to grant orders for changing the name of the child into that of a social parent.

In the end, the conclusion seems to be justified that the current system is rather complex. The question is whether this is really necessary or whether it will be possible to simplify the regulations when the reforms are evaluated in due course. In addition, the question should be raised whether all the differences between the five situations are always justifiable, especially from the point of view of the child's interests.[120] For the moment, finding one's way through the labyrinth of different sets of regulations is not easy for lawyers, let alone for the rest of the Dutch population.

E7   TABLE

See the table set out on the following pages.

---

[120]   Cf J Doek, 'Het gezag over minderjarigen, Iets over een doolhof en het zoeken van (rode?) draden', *Tijdschrijft voor Familie- en Jeugdrecht 2000*, at p 217ff.

	Opposite-sex partners who have married	Opposite-sex partners who have registered a partnership	Opposite-sex partners who have not formalised their relationship	Same-sex parents who have registered a partnership or married	Same-sex partners who have not formalised their relationship
Parenthood	Woman: Legal status of mother. Man: Legal status of father.[121]	Woman: Legal status of mother. Man: Status of father, but only after recognition.	Woman: Legal status of mother. Man: Status of father, but only after recognition.	Partner 1: Legal status of parent. Partner 2: No status of parent (recognition not possible).	Partner 1: Legal status of parent. Partner 2: No status of parent (recognition not possible).
Custody					
Conditions and legal basis of custody	Parents have automatic shared custody under Art 1:251 CC.[121]	If the child is recognised before its birth, both parents have automatic shared custody under Art 1:253aa CC. If the child is recognised after its birth, the parents may register as having shared custody with the county court registrar under Art 1:252 CC. If the child is not recognised, only the mother has automatic custody. The partners may apply for	After recognition of the child the parents may register as having shared custody with the county court registrar under Art 1:252 s 1 CC. If the child is not recognised, only the mother has automatic custody. The partners may apply for shared custody under Art 1:253t CC.[123]	If the child is born during the marriage or registered partnership and if there is no other legal parent, the partners acquire automatic shared custody under Art 1:253sa CC. If there is another legal parent, the partners have to apply for shared custody under Art 1:253t CC.[124]	Under Art 1:253t CC the parent and his/her partner may acquire shared custody if, where there is no other legal parent: (1) the parent has sole custody; (2) the partner has a close personal relationship with the child. If there is another legal parent; (3) where there has been one year's actual care of the child by the parent and partner; and

---

121 'CC' is the abbreviation of 'Civil Code'.

	Opposite-sex partners who have married	Opposite-sex partners who have registered a partnership	Opposite-sex partners who have not formalised their relationship	Same-sex parents who have registered a partnership or married	Same-sex partners who have not formalised their relationship
		shared custody under Art 1:253t CC.[122]			(4) the parent must have had sole custody for 3 years. The court determines whether there are substantial indications that the interests of the child will be neglected if the order is granted.
End of shared custody[125]	After a divorce, shared custody continues. Under Art 1:251, s 2 both parents may request sole custody. The criterion is the best interests of the child.	After termination of the registered partnership, shared custody continues. Under Art 1:253n CC both parents may request sole custody. The criterion is whether the circumstances have changed and which custody regulation is in the best interests of the child.	After the breakdown of the relationship, shared custody continues. Under Art 1:253n CC both parents may request sole custody. The criterion is whether the circumstances have changed and which custody regulation is in the best interests of the child.	After the dissolution of the marriage or registered partnership, shared custody continues. Under Art 1:253v, s 1 in conjunction with Art 1:253n CC both parents may request sole custody. The criterion is whether the circumstances have changed and which custody regulation is in the best interests of the child.	After the breakdown of the relationship, shared custody continues. The other legal parent may request sole custody under Art 1:253v, s 3 CC. If sole custody is granted to the partner, both parents may always request sole or shared custody under Art 1:253v, s 4 CC. The criterion is whether the circumstances have changed and which custody regulation is in the best interests of the child.

122   See with respect to shared custody under Art 1:253t Civil Code the last column of the table.
123   See footnote 122 above.
124   See footnote 122 above.
125   Custody always ends when the child is 18 years old.

	Opposite-sex partners who have married	Opposite-sex partners who have registered a partnership	Opposite-sex partners who have not formalised their relationship	Same-sex parents who have registered a partnership or married	Same-sex partners who have not formalised their relationship
Maintenance	Both parents have a duty to maintain the child until he/she is 18 or 21 years old (Art 1:392 CC and 1:395a CC).	Both parents have a duty to maintain the child until he/she is 18 or 21 years old (Art 1:392 CC and 1:395a CC). If the man has not recognised the child, he is under a duty to maintain the child *during* the registered partnership (Art 1:395 CC).[126] If the begetter has not recognised the child, he is under a duty to maintain the child as if he were a parent under Art 1:394 CC.[127]	Both parents have a duty to maintain the child until he/she is 18 or 21 years old (Art 1:392 CC and 1:395a CC). If the begetter has not recognised the child, he is under a duty to maintain the child as if he were a parent under Art 1:394 CC.	The parent has a duty to maintain the child until he/she is 18 or 21 years old (Art 1:392 CC and 1:395a CC). The partner is, under Art 1:395 CC, obliged to maintain the child *during* the marriage or registered partnership. After termination thereof he/she is no longer under such a duty.[128]	The parent has a duty to maintain the child until he/she is 18 or 21 years old (Art 1:392 CC and 1:395a CC). The partner is, under Art 1:253w CC, obliged to maintain the child until he/she is 18 or 21 years old, or after the termination of shared custody, for a period equivalent to the period of shared custody. In special cases, the court may determine a longer period.
Surname	The parents may choose the family name of either parent. If they do not make a choice when they register the child's	The parents may choose the family name of either parent. If they do not choose the father's name at the moment of recognition, the child will	The parents may choose the family name of either parent. If they do not choose the father's name at the moment of recognition, the child will	The parents may choose the family name of either parent. If they do not make a choice when they register the child's birth, the child will have the	The partners may apply to the court for an order changing the name of the child into the name of the parent or the name of the partner (Art 1:253t, s 5 CC). The

126 If the mother and the male registered partner share custody on the basis of Art 1:253t Civil Code, the situation as mentioned in footnote 92 above applies: both Art 1:395 Civil Code and Art 1:253w Civil Code seem to be applicable and their relationship has not yet been clarified.

127 In this situation, there might even apply three different maintenance regulations: Art 1:394 Civil Code, Art 1:395 Civil Code and Art1:253w Civil Code. See footnote 122 above.

128 In this situation, the maintenance regulations of Art 1:253w Civil Code and Art 1:394 Civil Code both seem to be applicable. See footnote 122 above.

Wendy Schrama

Opposite-sex partners who have married	Opposite-sex partners who have registered a partnership	Opposite-sex partners who have not formalised their relationship	Same-sex parents who have registered a partnership or married	Same-sex partners who have not formalised their relationship
birth, the child will have the father's name (Art 5, s 4 CC).	continue to have the mother's name under Art 1:5, s 2 CC. If the man does not recognise the child, the child has his/her mother's name (Art 1:5, s 1 CC).	continue to have the mother's name under Art 1:5, s 2 CC. If the man does not recognise the child, the child has his/her mother's name (Art 1:5, s 1 CC).	mother's name (Art 1:253sa, s 3 CC and Art 5, s 4 CC).	court has to reject the request if a child of 12 years or older does not consent, if the request for shared custody has been rejected or if it is contrary to the interests of the child. The case-law seems to indicate a reserved approach.

IV CRITICAL REMARKS

The social developments in recent years have demonstrated their profound impact on family law. Family law used to be designed for the standard situations which most often prevailed. The social developments have resulted in increased pluriformity in the ways in which people provide shape to their lives. As a result, family law has become more complex and there is no longer one default regulation. Instead, family law resembles a patchwork of regulations, with some main principles for the situations which occur most often and a whole body of regulations with only a limited scope of application designed for specific situations. Although the law should certainly take social developments into account, it is a pity that the process of reform has taken place without looking at the overall picture of family law. Too much attention has been paid to the reforms in isolation from other developments and without looking into the future, as a result of which the coherence between several parts of family law has been overlooked. Despite these negative remarks, there is hope for the future, since the Government itself has recognised these problems. It is to be hoped that the proposed evaluation of the new legislation will offer the opportunity for improvement.

NEW ZEALAND

A YEAR OF REPORTS

Bill Atkin[*]

I   INTRODUCTION

Continuing consternation about the handling of child protection cases is reflected in two major reports written in New Zealand in 2000. While this issue is in no way unique to New Zealand, New Zealand has its own stories to tell. One report is a distressing story of a boy who died shortly before his fifth birthday at the hands of his mother's partner.[1] The other report is a highly critical examination of the department responsible for child abuse cases.[2] Media attention paid to these reports and other cases (one where a grandmother given the care of her grandchild was so unable to cope that the child was left permanently brain damaged) has highlighted the question for the general public. The notion is dawning that policies of fiscal constraint and constant departmental restructuring have their costs in the lives of children.

The law relating to children has featured in other reports produced in 2000. The Law Commission has been working for some time on the law of adoption, and its final report recommends that adoption law, currently isolated in an old piece of legislation passed in the 1950s, be located in a new and widely encompassing Care of Children Act.[3]

Shortly beforehand, a rather brief discussion paper was released by the Ministries of Justice and Social Policy.[4] It raises questions about the law on guardianship, custody and access. Links can be made between these matters and adoption.

The year 2000 therefore represented a time of new ideas, investigations and recommendations for law change. While Parliament continued to consider a major overhaul of the law relating to the division of married and de facto couples' property (reforms were first introduced in 1998, and not enacted until 2001[5]), generally speaking, things were quiet on the legislative front. At the same time,

---

[*]   Reader in Law, Victoria University of Wellington.

[1]   Office of the Commissioner for Children, *Final Report on the Investigation into the Death of James Whakaruru* (Wellington, 2000).

[2]   Michael Brown, *Care and protection is about adult behaviour: The Ministerial Review of the Department of Child, Youth and Family Services* (Report to the Minister of Social Services and Employment, Wellington, December 2000). The report was released to the public in March 2001.

[3]   Law Commission, *Adoption and Its Alternatives: A Different Approach and A New Framework* (Report 65, Wellington, September 2000).

[4]   Ministry of Justice and Ministry of Social Policy, Responsibilities for Children especially when parents part: The Laws about Guardianship, Custody and Access (Wellington, August 2000).

[5]   Therefore to be discussed in a future survey.

little of dramatic impact happened in the courts. The year was more one of reports than of law-making.

II   THE DEATH OF JAMES WHAKARURU

The story of James Whakaruru was one of several tragedies involving children which hit the media headlines. He was born in 1994. Although not the first assault, in July 1996 James ended up in hospital with serious injuries. His mother's partner, Ben Haerewa, was convicted and imprisoned. The boy was again injured and taken to hospital early in 1997. Shortly afterwards Haerewa was released from prison. At that point, counsel for the child obtained a protection order against Haerewa under the Domestic Violence Act 1995. A protection order is designed to prevent contact between the protected person and the respondent and most commonly is sought by adult victims of abuse. Despite the order, in May 1998 and March 1999, James suffered further injuries, emergency surgery being required for the first of them. Then in April 1999 James was again brought to the hospital with extensive internal injuries and tissue damage suggesting prolonged beatings. He died shortly after arrival. Haerewa was subsequently sentenced to 12 years' imprisonment for manslaughter and James' mother received a two years' suspended sentence for her part in the death.

The agency with primary responsibility for dealing with a child in such situations is the Department of Child, Youth, and Family Services (carved off during a bout of restructuring from the former Department of Social Welfare). The procedures for dealing with a child abuse case are set out in the Children, Young Persons, and Their Families Act 1989. The 1989 Act sets in place some essential procedures when a report of child abuse is made. The report is to be investigated, the local care and protection resource panel is to be consulted (this is a group of professional and community people knowledgeable in child care matters), and, if the investigating social worker reasonably believes that the child is in need of care and protection, a family group conference must be convened. The latter brings together the key people in the child's life, especially family members or, to use the Maori term, members of the whanau.

One of the reasons why James died was because the statutory steps were not followed. Instead, the social worker encouraged an application for custody to be made to the Family Court under the Guardianship Act 1968. This Act is not geared to child abuse but more to disputes between parents when relationships break down. After some months, the Court granted the mother custody with additional guardianship and access to the maternal grandmother. The Court asked the department to monitor the situation but this was not done. Two reports from departmental social workers to the Court contradicted themselves. One expressed concern for the boy, the other denied any concern.

This story could of course happen anywhere. Sadly, it is not unique. But the report of the Commissioner for Children, whose office is in part designed to investigate these situations, highlights several disturbing features of the system in New Zealand. One of the underlying systemic reasons for the tragedy was that, although the risks to James were known to several agencies in the community, at no stage were the pieces properly put together. He had come before social workers, police, the court, the hospital and other health professionals. He had for instance been seen 40 times by people in the health sector. Yet, the right inter-agency links were not made. The report noted 'strong anecdotal evidence of inadequate resources' but more chilling is the following:[6]

'Co-ordinated work takes time, money and effort. The fragmentation of services and narrow focus on single agency outputs in the last fifteen years has worked to the detriment of child protection.'

What this means is that the thinning down of the State and the competitive, accountancy model for the public service which has been politically fashionable accounts in part for James' death. Individual blame can be placed at the feet of particular players, but this must not detract from more basic issues about how the machinery of the State operates.

The Commissioner for Children set out three main factors for a strong care and protection system:[7]

'There ought to be strong working relationships between all agencies involved with children, both government and non government, so that crucial information is shared.

There ought to be high levels of community and professional knowledge about care and protection so that child abuse and neglect is recognised and reported appropriately.

There ought to be fundamental and operational adherence to the care and protection legislation and clear, strong links between the policies and practices of other jurisdictions, so that in all matters the best interests of the child are of paramount concern.'

The case of James Whakaruru shows how New Zealand legislation is not harmonious, nor is it being followed properly. Three statutes entered into the picture: the Children, Young Persons, and Their Families Act 1989; the Guardianship Act 1968; and the Domestic Violence Act 1995. The first of these is the governing statute on child abuse, yet as James' story reveals, the other two can also be used to determine questions of custody and to obtain protection orders, thus diverting the focus from the 1989 Act. The themes of the incoherence of child law and the weakness of the arms of State responsible for the protection of children are picked up in other reports.

III REVIEW OF THE DEPARTMENT

Controversy over child and protection issues has raged for some time in New Zealand. During 2000 Judge Michael Brown, a former Principal Youth Court Judge, conducted a ministerial review of the system. The primary focus was inevitably on the operations of the Department of Child, Youth, and Families

---

[6] Office of the Commissioner for Children, *Final Report on the Investigation into the Death of James Whakaruru* (Wellington, 2000) at 5.

[7] Ibid, at 25.

Services. The report mentions disturbing complaints of under-resourcing, a demoralised workforce which is inadequately trained and supervised, 'seemingly bizarre management decisions' and 'appalling communication'.[8] The report itself has curious features including pages of quotations from other sources and somewhat vague recommendations such as suggesting a review of the 'operationalisation' of the Children, Young Persons, and Their Families Act 1989. Nevertheless, it sends a clear message that the community must do a lot better for its children.

The review's criticisms reach several different levels. At the highest level, it is pointed out that the department is faced with contradictory legislative obligations. On the one hand, there are duties to protect children. On the other, there are requirements under the Public Finance Act 1989 relating to financial accountability, the emphasis being on efficiencies, outputs, purchase agreements and other such terminology. The report states:[9]

> 'I am reliably informed that the department has received legal advice that where the Chief Executive is unable to meet statutory expenditure obligations she may be in breach of her statutory duty but that the duties under the Public Finance Act are paramount in any conflict between her statutory responsibilities.'

Put a little more graphically, Judge Brown said that 'the much vaunted notions of accountability and transparency can themselves become illusory if those public monies become shrouded in a cloak of fatuous outputs and nonsensical outcomes' and, even more telling, 'Viewed cynically this would appear to be the paramountcy of the dollar instead of the child'.[10]

At another level, the report notes that social workers are under-resourced and overworked. They tended to stay in the job for only two years, which means that, not surprisingly, the quality of work is low. Although the government had promised, in response to an earlier review in 1992, that 90% of staff would be professionally qualified, by 2000 the reality was that only 44% of frontline staff and 55% of recruits had such qualifications. Low pay and the stressful nature of the work did not help in retaining staff. One of the report's recommendations for dealing with this is to advance the development of social work as a profession and require staff exercising statutory powers to be registered professionally.

New Zealand has a voluntary rather than mandatory system of reporting child abuse (although the issue of mandatory reporting has been the subject of considerable debate over the years). When a notification of child abuse is made, there is a statutory obligation to investigate it. The department categorises notifications into critical, very urgent, urgent and low urgency. According to the report, on 31 October 2000, 3379 notifications, mostly in the urgent or low urgency categories, had not been allocated to a social worker for investigation. Judge Brown described this as 'deplorable' and not surprisingly recommended that sufficient funding be made available to reduce the number of unallocated

---

[8] Michael Brown, *Care and protection is about adult behaviour: The Ministerial Review of the Department of Child, Youth and Family Services* (Report to the Minister of Social Services and Employment, Wellington, December 2000) at 7–8.

[9] Ibid, at 24–25.

[10] Ibid, at 31–32.

cases to zero within six months and to keep it there.[11] To assist in this, the report also recommended that the department contract some of its work out to non-governmental agencies. Where there is a statutory duty this would still have to be discharged by the department, but this need not be so in other situations such as follow-up work.

One of the hallmarks of the Children, Young Persons, and Their Families Act 1989 is the emphasis on placing a child wherever possible with kin. This is especially important for Maori, Maori children making up 45% of the department's caseload (Maori form just under 15% of the population). Although not exploring the issues in any great length, Judge Brown suggested that the relationship between the department and Maori would be better if there was a stop to 'maladroit posturing and talking in stereotypical generalisations' and also recommended that 'the practice concerning the placement of children with family and whanau be reviewed, to ensure that all placements are made in the best interests of the child'.[12] The implication, supported by the James Whakaruru story, is that many placements with family have not been good for the child.

IV REVIEW OF CUSTODY AND ACCESS

The Government released a discussion paper in 2000 in which it invited the public to address various questions about the law relating to guardianship, custody and access. The law on this was passed over 30 years ago and, although there have been amendments to deal with child abduction and the effect on children of allegations of violence against a party in custody and access cases, a full review of the law is well overdue. However, the current discussion paper was prompted largely by the attempted introduction into Parliament of a Bill on joint custody. An opposition Member of Parliament from one of the smaller right wing parties was motivated by fathers' interest groups to prepare a Bill enacting a presumption in favour of shared parenting or joint custody.[13] The Bill was voted out at the first stage, with the Government promising a review of the law.

The subsequent discussion paper contains little analysis or argumentation. It raises issues about the appropriateness of the present language, children's rights and parental rights and responsibilities. Little attempt is made to unpack these. For instance, children have few rights under New Zealand law to bring proceedings or really affect proceedings about their well-being. A classic example of this from outside the guardianship arena was an attempt by a 17-year-old student to obtain child support from her parents.[14] Under the Child Support Act 1991 only a custodian can apply for child support. With some ingenuity, the girl argued that, as she had left home, she was her own custodian and should therefore be able to apply. The Judge rejected this argument because it strained the language of the

---

[11] Ibid, at 70.

[12] Ibid, at 85 and 76. These comments are all the more pertinent as Judge Brown is Maori.

[13] Shared Parenting Bill in the name of Muriel Newman MP. Under the Bill, priority would have been given to 'shared parenting to both parents', meaning 'joint custody split equally (50:50) between the parents'.

[14] *Hyde v CIR* [2000] NZFLR 385.

legislation too much. The case illustrates how the law can fail to take children's rights seriously and the Government's discussion paper is no exception.

The paper raises the question of the role of people other than parents in a child's life. This is important especially for Maori who place greater weight on people's relationship to their whanau than to their parents. The rights of wider kin to apply for orders, or be involved in custody and access disputes, are limited under the current law. These rules may be easily relaxed if that is thought desirable from a policy point of view, but more controversial would be any idea of borrowing the family group conference procedure from child abuse cases. From some points of view, this may ensure a less intense confrontation between the two parents and allow for input and influence from less emotionally involved members of the family. On the other hand, the breakdown of the relationship between two adults has traditionally been treated as a matter for those two people to resolve. To impose other family members on a separating couple may create more tension than the reverse.

Three cases decided in 2000 add to the debate about the role of people other than the natural parents. In *Re T (Custody and Guardianship),*[15] a non-Maori couple living in Sydney, Australia, sought custody and guardianship orders with respect to a young Maori boy whom the natural parents had informally placed in their care. The couple had already adopted an older child born to the same parents. A family group conference held shortly before the proceedings effectively endorsed the arrangement and accepted that the couple would be involved with the Maori community in Sydney (which is large), thus ensuring that the boy would grow up aware of his culture. The only opposition came from the Department of Child, Youth, and Family Services which insisted throughout that the boy should be with the mother. This was against the mother's strong wish, backed up by the father. The Judge decided to grant the orders. The case is instructive because it shows the need for flexible approaches. As the psychologist who prepared a report in this case said, the position of the department was replacing one form of paternalism with another.

The second case concerned the position of a testamentary guardian. Under s 7 of the Guardianship Act 1968, a parent may write in his or her will the name of a person to be the child's testamentary guardian in the event of the parent's death. In *P v C*[16] the children lived with their mother after the parents' separation but when she was diagnosed with cancer an aunt moved into the house and helped care for the family. The mother appointed the aunt a testamentary guardian. After the mother's death, the children went to live with their father, who had remarried. The father and his new wife sought to adopt the children but the aunt refused to give her consent because the adoption would be contrary to the mother's wishes expressed in her will. A testamentary guardian has a veto over an adoption unless the court dispenses with the need for the consent. The principal grounds for dispensation are that the parent or guardian has abandoned, neglected, persistently failed to maintain or persistently ill-treated the child, or failed to exercise the normal duty and care of parenthood.[17] On the facts, two years had slipped by since

---

[15]   [2000] NZFLR 594.
[16]   [2001] NZFLR 193.
[17]   Section 8, Adoption Act 1955.

the mother's death and the aunt and the children had become estranged. The drive for the adoption came from the step-mother who was now playing an important part in the children's lives. Although the case-law requires the test for dispensation to be considered over the whole of a child's life,[18] the Judge found that the aunt no longer had a close and nurturing relationship with the boys and was therefore unable to exercise the normal duty and care of parenthood. He held therefore that there were grounds for dispensation and added that he did not believe that 'it is appropriate to allow the issue [of whether there should be an adoption] to be decided by the aunt'.[19]

This decision has some worrying features which ought to be taken into account when reviewing the guardianship law. As the Judge himself pointed out, the role of testamentary guardian is different from that of a parent who is a guardian. If the testamentary guardian is to fulfil the office properly, then roles such as consenting to adoption should not lightly be stripped away. It appears that the Judge (and presumably the father and his new wife) did not fully appreciate that the law has deliberately created the office of testamentary guardian so that a deceased parent can have an ongoing role in the upbringing and welfare of the child. It is impossible to know how many people provide for testamentary guardians in their wills but anecdotally the number is probably quite significant. Fortunately most parents survive beyond the time when their children reach adulthood. The government's discussion paper raises no questions about testamentary guardians, which is something of a gap in the report. But in so far as it hints at greater participation by kin and others in a child's life, then there is some justification for maintaining the role of the testamentary guardian, and, so long as it is in the best interests of the individual child, treating that role seriously.

The third case is *Application by B (Adoption)*.[20] As in the previous case, the applicants for an adoption were a natural parent, here the mother, and her new husband, who was the brother of her first husband, the natural father. Since the separation, the father had had little to do with the children, now aged 7 and 10, and the new husband had been a social parent for nearly seven years. The father had taken no part in the adoption proceedings. The Judge held that the father's consent could be dispensed with because he had failed to exercise the duty and care of parenthood, thus forfeiting his right to veto an adoption. However, when it came to the question of whether an adoption order should be granted, the Judge refused on the basis that such an order would distort the children's family relationships. Instead, he made the new husband an additional guardian and granted a custody order in favour of the mother and husband. Step-parent adoptions are still frequently made in New Zealand, but the case just discussed typifies a contrary approach. This leads us to the Law Commission's report on adoption.

---

18 Especially the Court of Appeal decision in *Director-General of Social Welfare v L* [1989] 2 NZLR 314.

19 [2001] NZFLR 193, at 200.

20 [2000] NZFLR 673.

V   REVIEW OF ADOPTION

The report of the Law Commission setting out a new framework for the law of adoption follows an earlier paper which invited public submissions.[21] As a result of this process, a final set of recommendations was reached.

At the heart of the report is a recommendation that there be a new 'Care of Children Act' which would bring together the varying pieces of New Zealand law which deal with children – the Adoption Act, the Children, Young Persons, and Their Families Act and the Guardianship Act. The new Act would also define who is a parent, although the report does not explicitly state that the current law on paternity (found primarily in the Status of Children Act 1969 and the Family Proceedings Act 1980) would be incorporated. The proposal, which may not sound remarkable at first, is actually very ambitious because the existing law does not operate on a consistent set of principles. The Guardianship Act assumes that a child's parents will be the central legal figures; the Children, Young Persons, and Their Families Act vests this role in the family and family group, and the Adoption Act makes the birth mother, the father to a much lesser extent, and the Family Court the key decision-makers. Into this mix we must also put additional and testamentary guardians, and other caregivers.

The Law Commission is only partly successful in finding a way through this confusion. For example, it defines 'guardianship' in terms of parental power, which ostensibly excludes other guardians. Yet, the report makes it clear that the latter would continue. The report also sets out a list of parental responsibilities and rights, adapted from the Children (Scotland) Act 1995. It is again not clear where other guardians fit into this picture, nor fathers who under the present law are not automatically guardians.[22] Rather more successful is a recommendation to regard adoption as the permanent transfer of parental responsibilities and rights, thus avoiding the fiction in the present law which treats the adoptive parents as if they were the birth parents.[23]

The Law Commission would also have a 'parenting plan' accompanying an adoption order. The idea presupposes that adoption will be 'open adoption' and the main purpose of the plan would be to set out how the various parties would carry this into effect. The report says that '[a] challenging issue is the status that the law should confer upon open adoption arrangements'.[24] The difficulty is that it is hard to force contact between people who do not desire it. If, for example, adoptive parents made it difficult for a birth parent to keep in touch, what sanction could the law seriously contemplate imposing? For largely pragmatic reasons therefore, the report suggests that there should be no resort to the courts to enforce open adoption but that mediation services should be available when disputes arise. With the incorporation of the Children, Young Persons, and Their Families Act

---

[21]   Law Commission, *Adoption: Options for Reform: A Discussion Paper* (NZLC PP38, Wellington, 1999).

[22]   Under s 6 of the Guardianship Act 1968, an unmarried father who was not cohabiting with the mother at the time of the birth is not a guardian of the child. He can apply to the court to be appointed a guardian.

[23]   Section 16, Adoption Act 1955.

[24]   Law Commission, *Adoption and Its Alternatives: A Different Approach and A New Framework* (Report 65, Wellington, September 2000) para 112.

into the proposed Care of Children Act, it might be expected that a family group conference would be a pre-requisite before an adoption can take place. The Law Commission backs away, however, from this idea, no doubt because it would seriously undermine the position of the parents, especially the birth mother, in determining whether to consent to adoption.[25] Meetings of families are simply to be encouraged, but not mandated.

One of the novel aspects of the report is the recommendation for an extra kind of adult/child relationship, to be called 'enduring guardianship'.[26] The hallmarks of enduring guardianship are that it would create a legal relationship lasting throughout life, which could be removed only under very narrow circumstances, and would give the child a right to inherit in the event of an intestacy. As with ordinary guardians appointed by the court, an enduring guardian would be an additional guardian, not, as in adoption, replacing the birth parents. The report considers that this new concept could be especially suitable for step-parent and relative adoptions and would have symbolic value.[27]

The importance of enduring guardianship lies less in its legal significance than in the moral and social benefit of providing explicit recognition of the social importance of the extra parent in the child's life. Enduring guardianship provides a means by which a child's security and sense of familial belonging can be incrementally strengthened.

We can but speculate on how popular enduring guardianship would be. It has the advantage of being more durable than regular guardianship and it does not destroy the blood links as does adoption. On the other hand, these may be seen as disadvantages by some when they realise that it falls short of adoption (it would not be recognised internationally and the enduring guardians would not have exclusive parental authority) and yet is life-lasting like adoption, even if circumstances change dramatically. In the public's mind, adoption gives a seal of approval to a new family structure. Will enduring guardianship be perceived the same way?

The Law Commission considers that there should be 'a high threshold' before a step-parent adoption is granted.[28] The report recommends that a judge must consider the following three matters:[29]

–   the degree of contact that a child has with the other birth parent and that birth parent's extended family, and the effect that granting the adoption order might have on these relationships and degree of contact;
–   whether enduring guardianship or guardianship would be a more appropriate option than adoption to regulate the status of the child in relation to a step-parent; and
–   whether the step-parent has lived with the child for not less than three years preceding the adoption application.

---

25   Ibid, at para 219.
26   Ibid, at paras 117-125.
27   Ibid, at para 125.
28   Ibid, at para 373.
29   Ibid, at para 375.

The Law Commission's proposals properly reflect some anxiety about step-parent adoptions but do not make them impossible. While the judge has to consider the matters set out above, they are not conditions which must always be satisfied. For instance, there may be situations where three years have not elapsed and yet for other reasons an adoption should proceed. The recommendations appear therefore to retain flexibility in the system, while focusing attention on the other legal avenues available to the parties.

The report makes many other detailed recommendations, only one of which will be mentioned. The Law Commission recommends that de facto couples and same-sex couples ought to be eligible to adopt. The inclusion of same-sex couples will doubtless invite opposition from certain circles, but it has the merit of being consistent with New Zealand's human rights laws. It was the issue which attracted the second largest response from people making submissions on the Law Commission's earlier discussion paper. Forty-six supported adoption by same-sex couples, twenty-eight objected. The Law Commission thought that same-sex applicants should be assessed on their merits, although '[t]he way in which the couple intend to involve opposite gender role models in the life of the child is a matter requiring investigation by the social worker'.[30] In the Commission's view, the test of the child's best interests in each case (whether same-sex applicants or not) should be the essential question.

VI   ENDURING POWERS OF ATTORNEY

This survey has concentrated on various reports relating to children and the law. One report which may have more impact at the opposite end of life is the Law Commission's discussion paper on enduring powers of attorney.[31] Enduring powers, that is ones which are effective despite the onset of the donor's incapacity, were introduced into New Zealand law in 1988.[32] In New Zealand, enduring powers can relate to both property and personal matters, but unlike Britain there is no system of registration. The Commission pointed to a lack of safeguards in the New Zealand scheme and the opportunity therefore for the aged to be exploited. It referred to a study of 130 cases of elder abuse carried out by a support group for the elderly and this found that 40 cases were attributable to misuse of enduring powers.[33]

The point is reinforced by one of the rare cases on enduring powers to reach the courts.[34] The attorney was a granddaughter of the woman in question. By the time of the litigation, the woman had died. Another granddaughter challenged the attorney's actions which depleted the grandmother's estate from $86,000 to $30,000. The attorney spent money on renovating her house, ostensibly to make it more habitable for the grandmother, and on a car. The judge, whose task was

---

30   Ibid, at para 359.
31   Law Commission, *Misuse of Enduring Powers of Attorney* (NZLC PP40, Wellington, 2000).
32   Sections 94–108, Protection of Personal and Property Rights Act 1988.
33   Law Commission, *Misuse of Enduring Powers of Attorney* (NZLC PP40, Wellington, 2000) para 18.
34   Re Tindall [2000] NZFLR 373.

essentially to see whether the case should proceed, was not unsympathetic to the expenditure on the house but had sufficient doubts about the car to set the attorney's actions down for review.

The Law Commission floated several ideas to tighten up on the present scheme. It suggested that notice of the donor's mental incapacity be given to near relatives, and that the grant of an enduring power should be witnessed by a solicitor and supported by medical evidence that the donor was capable of making the grant. The Commission rejected the idea of a system of registration.

The feedback received by the Commission on its discussion paper confirmed that there was a need for further safeguards to curb abuse of enduring powers.[35] On the other hand, there was a desire not to complicate what for many people is a simple and effective method of providing for their future circumstances. Evidence indicated that many people of all ages sign an enduring power at the same time as a will. The Commission's revised recommendations therefore step back a bit from what was suggested in the discussion paper. In particular, the need for a solicitor to witness the grant of the power would not apply where the attorney was to be the donor's spouse or de facto partner or where the donor was aged under 68 and was not a patient in any hospital, home or institution.

---

[35]   Law Commission, *Misuse of Enduring Powers of Attorney* (NZLC R71, Wellington, 2001).

PAKISTAN

TESTING THE LIMITS OF FAMILY LAW REFORM IN PAKISTAN: A CRITICAL ANALYSIS OF THE MUSLIM FAMILY LAWS ORDINANCE 1961

*Shaheen Sardar Ali**

I   INTRODUCTION

Caught in the grip of competing and unresolved normative conflicts, legally pluralistic jurisdictions find themselves in a hybrid legal system fraught with contradictions, duality and compromise. Nowhere is this conflict more apparent than Pakistan where Islamic law, English secular legal principles and customary norms interact to produce an amoebic, boundary-less set of regulatory norms. Which set of rules will dominate varies from time to time and on a case by case basis. Thus 'secular', statutory law is more likely to govern the 'public' sphere including matters of State, inter-State relations as well as relations with international institutions, administrative matters and financial regulations. As opposed to this, a separate 'private' sphere has emerged for which the term 'Muslim personal law' has been coined by jurists because it pertains to issues governing marriage, dower, divorce, inheritance, polygamy, custody and guardianship; in short, all matters relating to family law. Interestingly, and by design, one might add, all laws affecting the status of Muslim women have historically been relegated to Muslim personal law.

The purpose of this article is to highlight the limits of legal reform in the area of family law (or personal law, as it is more commonly referred to), with particular reference to the position of women in Pakistan. Using some provisions of the Muslim Family Laws Ordinance 1961, and examples of its application through case-law, it will be argued that, in an environment of legal pluralism such as that prevalent in Pakistan, formulations of statutory law are seldom the sole determinants of women's rights, even if these profess to be based on religious injunctions. In the zealously guarded 'protected' sphere, application of Islamic family law is achieved after undergoing a subtle, almost imperceptible process of filtration through a maze of cultural norms and prevailing political and economic compulsions. Therefore, efforts at empowering women through black letter legal reform, to the exclusion of societal perceptions of their rights, tend to have little acceptability and ownership amongst the people.

*   Reader, School of Law, University of Warwick, UK and Professor of Law, University of Peshawar, Pakistan. Formerly Minister and Chair NCSW.

II   HIERARCHICAL CATEGORIES OF ENTITLEMENTS AND THE ISLAMIC LEGAL TRADITION: IMPLICATIONS FOR WOMEN IN FAMILY LAW

The Islamic legal tradition, on which family law in Pakistan is based, emanates from its main sources, ie the *Quran*,[1] *Hadith*,[2] *Ijma*[3] and *Qiyas*.[4] Yet, the body of principles informing Islamic law, collectively known as the *Sharia'* do not form a homogenous entity as these depend on interpretations of the sources, particularly the *Quran* and *Hadith*, influenced by cultural and ethnic differences, historical contexts, colonial pasts, the sect or school of jurisprudence (*madhab*) that a particular community subscribes to, as well as political and economic policy of Muslim States.

It has been argued that the basic tone and complexion of Islam is reformative, enjoining upon people equity and justice for all.[5] The ethical voice of the *Quran* is said to be egalitarian and non-discriminatory.[6] At the same time, it concedes to resourceful, adult Muslim men, as the privileged members of society, responsibility to care for (and exercise authority over), women, children, orphans, and the needy. The *Quran* therefore also contains verses validating the creation and reinforcement of hierarchies based on gender and resources. These verses, not exceeding 6 out of a total of 6666 that make up the text of the *Quran*, appear largely in the area of family law and are always punctuated by exhortations of justice, equity and kindness to women. Yet, legislation based on these verses fails to capture these provisos, and the position of women in Islam appears to be determined solely by rules derived from a literal and restrictive reading of these few verses.[7]

---

[1]   The religious text in Islam, believed by Muslims to be the word of God and the primary source of Islamic law.

[2]   The traditions of the Prophet Muhammad, records of his actions and sayings. The second source of Islamic law.

[3]   Consensus of opinion. It has been defined as agreement among the Muslim jurists in a particular age on a question of law.

[4]   Analogical deduction. As a source of law it comes into operation in matters not covered by a text of the *Quran* or *Hadith*, nor determined by *Ijma*.

[5]   For this line of argumentation, see generally: F Rahman, 'Status of Women in the Quran' in G Nashat (ed) *Women and Revolution in Iran* (Westview Press, 1983); JL Esposito, *Women in Muslim Family Law* (Syracuse University Press, 1982); A al-Hibri, 'A Study of Islamic Herstory: Or how did we ever get into this mess?' (1982) 5 WSIF; B Utas (ed), *Women in Islamic Societies* (London, 1983); F Hussain (ed), *Muslim Women* (St Martin's Press, 1984); F Mernissi, *Beyond the Veil* (Indiana University Press, 1987); F Mernissi, *Women and Islam*, translated by Mary Jo Lakeland, (Basil Blackwell, 1991); L Ahmed, *Women and Gender in Islam: Historical Roots of a Modern Debate* (Yale University Press, 1992); AA An-Naim, *Toward an Islamic Reformation* (Syracuse University Press, 1990) and R Hassan, 'An Islamic Perspective' in J Belcher (ed), *Women, Religion and Sexuality* (WCC Publications, 1990).

[6]   *Ibid.*

[7]   These *Quranic* verses include the following: 2:221; 2:228; 2:282; 24:30; 4:3; 4:34.

III *IBADAAT* AND *MUAMALAAT*: ESPOSITO'S HIERARCHICAL NOTION OF RIGHTS IN THE ISLAMIC TRADITION

An hierarchical notion of rights has been developed by John Esposito. He states that through Muslim exegesis, a systematic study of the value system of the *Quran* and the hierarchisation of its ethico-religious values has evolved.[8] This method provides a context within which one can understand the value of specific *Quranic* regulations by shifting the emphasis beyond the specific regulations to its intent, to the value it sought to uphold.[9] Thus the *Quranic* prescription has two levels of importance – the specific injunction or command, details of which may be relative to its space and time context, and the ideal or *Quranic* value, realisation of which the specific regulation intends to fulfil. Since the task of the Muslim community is the realisation of these *Quranic* values, the goals of jurists is to ensure that *fiqh* regulations embody these *Sharia'* values as fully and perfectly as possible.

Verses from the *Quran* have been used both to support a woman's subservience to a man and to defend her rights to equality. This seeming contradiction can be resolved by an analysis of the relevant *Quranic* verses through a system of 'hierarchization of *Quranic* values' used by John Esposito to deal with rights of women in Islam. This method, it is stated, is reminiscent of the process by which *Quranic* values were first applied to newly encountered social situations in the formative period of Islam by differentiating between the socio-economic and the ethic-religious categories in *Quranic* legislation.[10] While women's status is inferior to men in the former, they are full equals in the latter as to the spiritual and moral obligations imposed upon them, in their relationship to their Creator, and in the compensation prepared for them in the Hereafter.[11] The status difference of men and women in the socio-economic sphere belongs to the category of *Muamalaat* (social relations), which are subject to change; their moral and religious equality belongs to the category of *Ibadaat* (religious duties towards God), which duties are immutable.[12] By applying the principle of 'hierarchization' of *Quranic* values, the Muslim reformers argue that the moral and religious equality of men and women 'represents the highest expression of the value of equality'[13] and therefore constitutes the most important aspect of the *Quranic* paradigm on the issue. The position of women in family law would fall into the category of *Muamalaat*, an area where men have a perceived advantage. Women on the other hand, are perceived as a class of persons in need of protective rather than equal rights with men.[14] The Muslim male is accorded more rights than Muslim women, although strictly in co-relation to the responsibilities imposed on them regarding women and children in their charge. An inference that Muslim

---

[8]   IR al-Faruqi, 'Towards a New Methodology of Quranic Exegesis' *Islamic Studies* (1962) 35.

[9]   Esposito, *op cit* n 5 at p 107.

[10]   *Ibid.*

[11]   For example, as stated in *Quranic* verses 33:35; 9:71; 40:40; 9:72; 48:5; 57:12; 3:195; and others.

[12]   Esposito, *op cit* n 5 at p 108.

[13]   *Ibid.*

[14]   For instance, the husband is charged with the responsibility of 'providing' for his wife and children; a husband is obligated to lay down a sum of money or other property as dower for his wife in the contract of marriage, inheritance laws of Islam provide the female heir a minimum of half share compared to a male heir in similar relationships, and so on.

feminists have drawn from this framework is that, where men do not or cannot shoulder the responsibility of being providers and protectors of women and children, they will not be entitled to that more privileged position.

Despite these popular beliefs regarding women as being of a lesser status than men, jurists and students of Islamic law do acknowledge that there exists sufficient ambiguity and vagueness in the principles of Islamic law to justify exploration of alternative views favourable to women, and on a basis of equality with men.[15] Family law reform in the twentieth century in many parts of the Muslim world have followed this route and codified interpretations according a more equitable position to Muslim women.

IV   AN OVERVIEW OF LEGISLATION AFFECTING FAMILY LAW IN PAKISTAN[16]

Laws affecting women's rights and position in the family are derived from a variety of sources. Family law in Pakistan is a mixture of codified law and customary practices based on religious norms and administered in a secular, procedural framework of a modern-day dispute resolution forum – the judiciary.[17] It has been stated that statutory laws are not the only determinants in the final resolution of conflicts, particularly in multi-faceted societies such as Pakistan. Cultural norms and religious rules are just as potent a force, if not more, as legislative enactments. The judiciary cannot be expected to operate in a vacuum; neither can it steer clear of societal norms and political pressures. Nowhere is this trend more visible than in judgments handed down in family law cases reflecting the status of women both in the eyes of the law as well as society. A distinctive feature of the legal system in Pakistan is that since a combination of Muslim

---

[15]   Some alternative and progressive interpretations have indeed been employed in a number of Muslim jurisdictions where family law reform has been undertaken. In Pakistan these 'reformed' laws include the Child Marriages Restraint Act, 1929, the Dissolution of Muslim Marriages Act, 1939 and the Muslim Family Laws Ordinance, 1961, the focus of the present paper.

[16]   This section draws on research conducted for Working Papers commissioned by Shirkatgah, Lahore for the Women and Law (Pakistan) Country Project, Shirkatgah, Lahore, 1992–93. These include: SS Ali and N Azam, 'Trends of the Superior Courts of Pakistan in Guardianship and Custody cases (1947–92): An Analysis' (Ali and Azam, Custody and Guardianship); SS Ali and R Naz, 'An Analysis of the Trends of the Superior Courts in Pakistan in Cases relating to Marriage, Dower and Divorce' (Ali and Naz, Marriage, Dower, Divorce); and K Arif and SS Ali, 'Trends of the Superior Courts Regarding Succession and Inheritance Rights of Women'. A compilation of these papers is presented in C Balchin (ed) *A Handbook on Family Law in Pakistan* (Shirkatgah, 1994). For this section, see the Introduction of the Handbook. For a very detailed discussion on the subject, see K Arif, 'The Evolution and Development of Muslim Family Law in Colonial India', unpublished paper.

[17]   Some of the laws regulating family issues in Pakistan include: the Majority Act, 1875; the Guardians and Wards Act, 1890; the Child Marriages Restraint Act, 1929; the Muslim Personal Law (Shariat) Application Act, 1937; the Muslim Personal Law (Shariat) Application Act, 1962; the Muslim Personal Law (Shariat) Application (Removal of Difficulties) Act, 1975; the Muslim Personal Law (Shariat) Application (Removal of Doubt) Ordinance, 1972; the Dissolution of Muslim Marriages Act, 1939; the Muslim Family Laws Ordinance, 1961; the West Pakistan Rules under the Muslim Family Laws Ordinance, 1961; the West Pakistan Family Courts Act, 1964; the West Pakistan Family Court Rules, 1965; the Dowry and Bridal Gifts (Restriction) Act, 1976; the Dowry and Bridal Gifts (Restriction) Rules, 1981.

personal law (both codified and uncodified with all its variations)[18] and statutory law is applied by courts in adjudicating such cases, judges have more discretion to put their own construction on existing principles. The legacy of colonialism, which moulded general trends in courts and guided codification of family law, is still evident in statutory law of post-independence Pakistan.[19]

The politics of personal law both during the colonial era and leading up to the present time has had an important bearing on family law reform and its implications for women. For instance, the promulgation of the Shariat Applications Acts[20] was ostensibly to accede to the longstanding demand of the Muslim community to be governed by their own religious laws. Islamic law recognises women as heirs. Yet, these very laws, as enacted, excluded inheritance from the purview of the Shariat Acts in order to please the Muslim landed gentry of India. This trend of excluding women from inheritance continued well into the post-independence era and it was only in 1962 that amendments to the Muslim Personal (Shariat) Application Act conceded this right to women.[21] Also, in the interest of political expediency, un-Islamic customary practices denying Muslim women their rights were ignored when 'Islamising' other laws.[22]

A   Child Marriages Restraint Act 1929 (CMRA)[23]

Another piece of colonial legislation in the area of family law was the CMRA. This law, aimed at restraining the solemnisation of child marriages[24] is one that can truly be placed in the category of standard-setting legal norms rather than laws one would expect to have immediate and widespread use. It provides for punishment of persons (parents or guardians) who contracted their minor children in marriage.[25] But keeping in view the prevalent social norms and in the interest of the minors themselves, marriages contracted in contravention of the CMRA were not made invalid.

---

[18]   Some provisions of Muslim personal law have been incorporated in statutes, but there is no one consolidated code covering all areas of personal law. Neither would it be possible to have one uniform code, primarily due to divergent views of the various schools of juristic thought in Islam.

[19]   See generally, MR Anderson, 'Islamic Law and the Colonial Encounter in British India' in C Mallat and J Connors (eds), *Islamic Family Law* (Graham and Trotman, 1990). Also see *BZ Kaikaus v President of Pakistan* PLD 1980 SC 160 for a brief history of the administration of Muslim law in India.

[20]   NWFP Muslim Personal Law (Shariat) Application Act, 1935; Muslim Personal Law (Shariat) Application Act (XXVI of 1937).

[21]   In the province of the Punjab, the Muslim Personal Law (Shariat) Application Act, 1948 was only passed by the Punjab Assembly when women demonstrated outside the Assembly building urging members to vote in favour of the Bill. The reluctance of members stemmed from the fact that the majority belonged to the landed class and were not prepared to give away immovable property to female heirs.

[22]   For example, see s 26, Regulation IV of 1827 which says: 'the law to be observed in the trial of suits shall be Acts of Parliament and Regulations of Government applicable to the case: in the absence of such Acts and Regulations, the usages of the country in which the suit arose; if none such appears, the law of the defendant, and in the absence of specific law and usage, justice, equity and good conscience alone'.

[23]   Act XIX of 1929.

[24]   *Ibid*, Preamble.

[25]   *Ibid*, ss 4, 5, 6 and 7.

B   The Dissolution of Muslim Marriages Act, 1939 (DMMA)[26]

This is one of the most important pieces of legislation promulgated in the area of Islamic family law in the subcontinent. The preamble states that its purpose is to:

> 'consolidate and clarify the provisions of Muslim law relating to suits for dissolution of marriage by women married under Muslim law and to remove doubts as to the effect of the renunciation of Islam by a married Muslim woman on her marriage tie.'

The DMMA codifies and regulates, to that extent, the grounds on which a woman married under Muslim law may obtain a judicial decree of dissolution of marriage from the courts. Section 2 of this Act enumerates these grounds that include, *inter alia*: the husband's whereabouts being unknown for 4 years, failure by a husband to maintain his wife for 2 years, failure to perform marital obligations for 3 years, the husband's impotence, insanity or suffering from leprosy or a virulent venereal disease. Cruelty and abuse, whether physical or mental, and emotional distress inflicted by the husband is also a ground for dissolution of the marriage. The wife may also seek divorce if the husband interferes in how she manages her property, or obstructs her in the performance of her religious profession or practice. Section 2(vii) of the DMMA extends the option of puberty (*khiyar-ul-bulugh*), available to a Muslim girl to repudiate her marriage if brought about while she was a minor, to include a marriage contracted on her behalf by her father or grandfather. An important provision of the DMMA is s 5, which states that dissolution of the marriage contract under this Act will not affect the wife's right to dower.

The DMMA was amended twice by the Muslim Family Laws Ordinance 1961 (MFLO). These amendments provided the added ground for dissolution where the husband took an additional wife in contravention of the procedure laid down in the MFLO. It also allowed women to repudiate marriages contracted by their guardians before they attained the age of 16 (as opposed to 15 set out originally in the Act).

C   The Muslim Family Laws Ordinance, 1961 (MFLO)

After the independence of Pakistan in 1947, consistent pressure from women's groups led to the setting up of a Commission on Marriage and Family Laws (also known as the Rashid Commission)[27] in June 1955. This body was briefed with

---

[26]   Act VIII of 1939.

[27]   The Commission on Marriage and Family Laws was appointed by the Government of Pakistan, Ministry of Law Resolution No F 17(24)/55-Leg, dated 4 August 1955. The report of this Commission was published in the *Gazette of Pakistan Extraordinary* on 20 June 1956 under notification no F9(4)/56-Leg. A number of other committees have followed. Thus in 1975 the Pakistan Women's Rights Committee was set up. The report of this Committee chaired by Mr Yahya Bakhtiar, then Attorney General of Pakistan, was submitted in 1976. Nothing came out of this exercise as the report came out at a time when the government of the day was caught up in a political crisis that eventually brought it down. In 1985, the third report, known as the Report of the Commission on the Status of Women, 1985, chaired by Begum Zari Sarfaraz, also made some useful recommendations. But the government declared the report as a classified document as it was only when a new government came into power in 1988 that the report was made available to the people of Pakistan. The latest in the series of reports is the report of the Commission of Inquiry for Women submitted in 1997.

exploring ways of restricting polygamy and giving women more rights of divorce than had been granted to them under the DMMA. The Commission presented its report in July 1958, but it was not until 1961 that some of its recommendations took the form of the Muslim Family Laws Ordinance, 1961.[28] Amongst its major recommendations included the one on abolishing polygamy. But, as has consistently been the case in Pakistan, elected governments find themselves unable to legislate and implement meaningful reform due to popular pressure. It took an army general, Mohammad Ayub Khan, to promulgate the MFLO and that too only limited/inhibited[29] polygamy rather than abolishing it outright.

The MFLO contained some very important provisions that were advantageous to women. The unilateral right to terminate the marriage contract, technically known as *talaq* belongs to the husband under Islamic law and he has to pay the wife the dower on pronouncement of this form of divorce. For the first time in the history of the subcontinent, the right to triple *talaq*[30] or instantaneous, irrevocable divorce by the Muslim husband was curtailed and the principles of *talaq-i-ahsan* and *talaq-i-hasan* were incorporated into the law, thus regulating and formalising the process of divorce.[31] *Khula*,[32] as well as the delegated right to divorce (*talaq-i-tafwid*) for women, was also recognised in statute, the latter being incorporated as an option in the standard marriage contract (*nikahnama*). Polygamy was restricted in that a husband desirous of a subsequent marriage had to submit an application to the Arbitration Council besides seeking the permission of the existing wives.[33] In the event of the husband contracting such a marriage, the MFLO made him immediately liable to payment of the dower of the existing wife/wives.[34] The Ordinance under its s 4 also provided security for children of predeceased issue of a propositus. In addition to this, the MFLO amended the CMRA, by raising the legal age of marriage for females from 14 to 16 years and for males from 18 to 21.[35]

1   IMPLEMENTING THE PROCEDURAL FRAMEWORK FOR MARRIAGE AND DIVORCE UNDER THE MFLO: LESSONS FROM THE FIELD

The focal point of Islamic family law is the institution of marriage from which flow rights and obligations of all parties concerned. In the Islamic legal tradition,

---

[28]   VIII of 1961.

[29]   Albeit rather half-heartedly.

[30]   There are three modes of pronouncing *talaq*: *talaq-i-ahsan, talaq-i-hasan* and *talaq-ul-biddat*. The first two offer some scope for reconciliation as the divorce does not become irrevocable for some time. The time afforded before the divorce becomes irrevocable is the first kind of waiting period. Then there is the period of *iddat*, which is a period during which a woman whose marriage has been terminated either by death or divorce may not remarry. *Talaq-ul-biddat* (the third mode) is an irrevocable divorce as soon as it is pronounced and there is no chance of reconciliation. This mode is not the one sanctioned by the Prophet Mohammed, and hence is rejected by some Muslims.

[31]   Section 7 of the MFLO, 1961.

[32]   The concept of the wife being able to 'buy' her freedom by returning her dower is technically known as *khula* which affords a woman the right to get out of an undesirable union.

[33]   Section 6 of the MFLO, 1961.

[34]   *Ibid.*

[35]   *Ibid*, ss 10 and 12. But s 12 now stands omitted by Federal Laws (Revision and Declaration) Ordinance (XXVII of 1981).

marriage is a civil contract between a consenting adult Muslim male and female for the procreation and legalising of children. Proposal and acceptance of the marriage contract must be in the presence and hearing of two male, or one male and two female, witnesses. Dower, or *mahr*, consisting of money, jewellery or other property, stipulated to be paid by the husband to the wife, is an integral component of the contract. Interestingly enough, the initial premise of entering into this contract is one of complete equality where either party may, subject to agreement from the other, make stipulations including the amount and mode of payment of dower, dissolution of marriage, and so on. However, once the contract is made, inequality between the contracting parties emerges. For instance, under the 'protective' right of dower as 'consideration' for the marriage contract, the husband becomes the protector and the wife, the protected. She retains the dower (or the right over it if not paid already), so long as she remains the wife or the husband dissolves the marriage tie by *talaq*. But if the wife is desirous of terminating the contract by invoking *khula*, then this protection of dower money or property must be returned to the husband to 'ransom herself from her husband'.[36] The MFLO attempted to lay down procedures for formalising some key elements of family law as applicable to Muslims in Pakistan.

2   REGISTRATION OF MARRIAGES UNDER THE MFLO

Islamic jurisprudence does not require a formal instrument as evidence of a valid marriage contract and evidence of an oral ceremony will suffice. Despite centuries of a 'written' legal documentation culture, many parts of the Muslim world continue to practise the oral tradition. Lack of documentary evidence of marriage, however, led to a number of difficulties particularly for women. Since a Muslim male can contract up to four wives at a time in the institution of marriage and not document these, husbands could contract subsequent marriages without the knowledge or consent of the existing wife/wives. The result, often seen, was widows desperately seeking recognition as the widow of the dead husband and heir to his property. Section 5 of the MFLO tried to address this issue and provides for registration of all marriages solemnised under Muslim law, whether by the Nikah Registrar (marriage registrar) or any other person. This provision of the law was considered a significant victory for women on a number of counts. It was in the interest of women to have marriages registered and recorded and available as public documents, enabling them to secure their right to inherit from deceased husbands.

Application of s 5, however, led to very different results on the ground. To begin with, practice of registration of marriages remained confined to large cities and urban centres of the country. Rural communities and the tribal areas of Pakistan, for the most part, continued with the practice of oral ceremonies (the only written evidence of the marriage, if at all, would be the document outlining the amount and nature of *mahr* agreed upon by the family of the bride and groom).[37] The consequences struck me personally when my husband and daughter accompanied me to the British Embassy in Belgium for an endorsement of their

---

[36]   The *Quran*, verse 2:229.

[37]   The author, a Professor of Law, belongs to Swat in the north west frontier province of Pakistan and has no documentary proof of her marriage of 27 years standing!

visas as my dependants to enter the UK. The Visa Officer refused to acknowledge them as my family because I had no proof of marriage. I insisted that I came from a community where we follow an oral legal tradition (I did not believe in 'cooking up' a marriage certificate when I had none), but this was brushed aside as a fairy tale of a bygone era!

Lack of awareness among people as to the value of documentation is perhaps to be primarily blamed for failure to implement the registration of marriages clause of the MFLO. Coupled with this is the imperceptible disregard, almost contempt of the written law, in matters as 'private' as marriage, births and deaths. Stricter enforcement of s 5(3), (4) and enhancing the punishment for its violation is an option that has been suggested. Clauses (3) and (4) make it incumbent upon whoever conducts a marriage ceremony (if it is a person other than the Nikah Registrar himself), to inform the Nikah Registrar of the event. Presently, contravention of this provision entails simple imprisonment for a term of up to 3 months and a fine of up to one thousand rupees, or both.

There also appears, arguably, a discreet contradiction between ss 3 and 5 of the MFLO. Section 3 declares in unequivocal terms that:

'The provisions of this Ordinance shall have effect notwithstanding any law, custom or usage, and the registration of Muslim marriages shall take place only in accordance with those provisions.'

Yet, s 5 fails to take contravention of its regulatory procedures to its logical conclusion, and unregistered and oral marriages are not considered void. Case-law too has adopted this view as well as stating that there is no need for any formal instrument of marriage.[38] In order to protect parties who may be adversely affected by non-registration of marriage, courts have insisted on deciding each case on its own merits. Thus, rather than regard non-registration as conclusive proof of non-existence of a marriage, other circumstances have also been given due weight.[39] These examples reflect the obstacles in the way of effective enforcement of laws in a society in transition and subject to parallel legal norms and, where in the interest of the parties, a lenient view of its application has to be adopted.

3 THE MFLO AND THE OFFENCE OF ZINA (ENFORCEMENT OF HUDOOD) ORDINANCE, 1979: 'UNHOLY' ALLIANCE OF THE 'SECULAR' AND 'RELIGIOUS'?

Until the decade of the 1980s there appears little case-law on the validity or otherwise of an unregistered marriage. This, however, became one of the most litigated sections of the MFLO (along with the section on notice of divorce) due to its interaction with the Offence of Zina (Enforcement of Hudood) Ordinance, 1979. In the context in which the so-called 'Islamisation' of laws took place in Pakistan, it is important to understand why non-registration of marriages and divorce became such a crucial issue for human rights lawyers. In 1979, General Zia-ul-Haq gave the country his flavour of 'Islamisation' by promulgating

---

[38]   *Habib v The State* PLD 1980 Lah 791; *Abdul Kalam v The State* 1987 MLD 1637;

[39]   *Muhammad Akram v Farman Bi* PLD 1989 Lah 200.

the Hudood Ordinances, 1979; the Qanoon-i-Shahadat Act, 1984; and the Qisas and Diyat Ordinances. *Zina*, or sexual intercourse outside of marriage, was declared a criminal offence against the State and an unbailable offence.

The MFLO required all marriages to be registered. Where a marriage has not been registered as laid down by s 5 of the MFLO, a complaint may be filed against the parties accusing them of *zina*. This provision of the law, therefore, which was originally intended to protect women and their rights thus became a tool in the hands of vindictive family members or other foes. These cases arose where marriages were contracted without the knowledge or consent of the families of the parties.

4   REGULATION OR ISLAMISING DIVORCE? A CRITIQUE OF SECTION 7 OF THE MFLO IN THE LIGHT OF CASE-LAW

In Islamic family law, dissolution of marriage may take one of the following routes: at the instance and initiative of the husband, known as *talaq*; at the instance and initiative of the wife known as *khula*; by mutual consent of both parties known as *mubarat*. The *Quranic* injunctions on the subject, outlined in chapter 4 (*An-Nisa*), contrary to popular perceptions, fall short of according the Muslim male a unilateral right to dissolve the marriage tie (*talaq*) without assigning any cause. In a famous Pakistani case, *Khurshid Bibi v Mohammed Amin*,[40] their Lordships were of the view that *talaq* is not an unfettered right of the husband as the *Quran*, in 4:35, provides for the appointment of arbiters to curtail the unbridled exercise of this right. These fetters, however, have their limits, and if the husband is determined to go ahead with the pronouncement of divorce then no court is competent to stop him from doing so. (The MFLO, in s 7, has attempted to regulate and provide a role for judicial forums to restrain the husband. See discussion below.)

Islamic law confers on a woman the right to seek dissolution of the marriage tie through *khula*. In cases cited from the time of the Prophet Muhammad, the only question asked by him of the woman would be if she was willing to forego her dower. If she agreed the marriage stood dissolved.[41] This right of the woman, in later developments became a qualified right and the woman had to convince the court of her fixed aversion and irretrievable breakdown of the marriage in order to obtain *khula*.[42] Although some leading judgments from the superior courts of Pakistan have tried to equate the right to pronounce *talaq* by the husband with the right of *khula* available to the woman,[43] it is submitted that there are major differences between these two modes of dissolution of marriage. No matter what obstacles one places in the husband's right to give *talaq*, at the end of the day, by its very definition, *talaq* may be pronounced with or without the intervention of a court of law. On the other hand, if a woman fails to convince the judge of the genuineness of her case for *khula*, she cannot unilaterally terminate the marriage

---

[40]   PLD 1967 SC 97.

[41]   The oft-quoted case of Jamila, who sought dissolution of marriage on the basis that she did not like her husband's looks and considered him ugly.

[42]   PLD 1967 SC 97.

[43]   For example in *Safia Begum v Khadim Hussain* 1985 CLC 1869 and *Syed Mohammed Rizwan v Mst Samina Khatoon* 1989 SMCR 25.

contract.[44] Social construction of the content of a woman's right to *khula* thus overrides her right within Islamic law.

A further right as regards dissolution of marriage, is *talaq-i-tafwid*, or delegated right of divorce given to the wife in the contract of marriage. Muslim women may take advantage of the fact that marriage is a civil contract and stipulations limiting or even prohibiting the husband from dissolving the marriage tie can be incorporated in it. An effort at achieving some measure of equality may thus be successful.[45] Section 7 of the MFLO has incorporated this as a valid mechanism for dissolution of marriage as has the contract of marriage drawn up under the Rules implementing the MFLO.

It may be argued that s 7 of the MFLO attempted to 'Islamise' the procedure for dissolution of marriage. As indicated earlier, the popularly practised mode of *talaq* was for the husband to pronounce the triple *talaq* (*talaq-ul-biddat*), resulting in immediate termination of the marriage and eviction of the wife from the marital home. The basic protection that section 7 provides is requiring the husband to follow a certain laid-down procedure for *talaq* involving the local authorities. This procedure, without stating so explicitly, incorporates the *talaq-i-ahsan* (most preferred) mode in s 7(3) that reads thus:

'Save as provided in sub-section (5), *talaq* unless revoked earlier, expressly or otherwise, shall not be effective until the expiration of 90 days from the day on which notice under sub-section (1) is delivered to the Chairman.'

The 90-day period is coterminous with a compulsory waiting period (*iddat*) during which the marriage is suspended, but not terminated. By holding the husband to this period, after which the divorce becomes irrevocable, the unilateral right of divorce allowed to men (and not to women), is toned down and chances for reconciliation kept alive until the period of waiting expires.[46] Section 7(4) further requires the parties to appear before an Arbitration Council to attempt reconciliation. Section 7(6) minimises the requirement of an intervening marriage by the woman (*halala*) in cases where former spouses wish to remarry. It states that:

'Nothing shall debar a wife whose marriage has been terminated by *talaq* effective under this section from remarrying the same husband, without an intervening marriage with a third person, unless such termination is for the third time effective.'

Muslim women through the centuries have been the subject of this practice (*halala*) resulting from hasty pronouncement of the triple *talaq*. The repentant husband was told that his wife now had to marry another man, consummate the

---

[44] For instance, see *Aali v Additional District Judge I, Quetta* 1987 CLC 27, *Raisa Begum v Mohammed Hussain* 1986 MLD 1418 and many others.

[45] Here a note of caution as regards these stipulations favourable to women. Societal pressure strongly discourages use of these rights afforded to women. For details, see SS Ali, 'An Analysis of the Trends of the Superior Courts of Pakistan in matters relating to Marriage, Dower, Divorce' (1993), Working Paper for the Women and Law Project, Women Living Under Muslim Laws.

[46] Section 7 of the MFLO seeks to ensure a 90-day gap between the pronouncement of divorce and its taking effect. By so doing the section codifies the spirit of *talaq-i-ahsan*.

marriage and remarry after that man divorced her. The MFLO, by providing a 90-day 'breathing space', resulted in some respite to women from the humiliation of marrying another man simply to remarry the husband who had so summarily divorced her.

The most explosive provision of the MFLO however is s 7(1). This seeks to ensure a written notice of *talaq* to the Chairman of the Union Council with a copy to the wife, making the fact of termination of marriage clear and unequivocal. Contravention of this procedure makes the husband liable to simple imprisonment for one year and/or a fine extending up to rupees 5000. This supposedly straightforward procedural requirement became the cause of some of the gravest miscarriages of justice when the MFLO interacted with the *zina* provisions of the criminal law since 1979 and gave rise to a large body of case-law.

Prior to the Prohibition of Zina (Enforcement of Hudood) Ordinance, 1979, in most cases relating to non-registration of *talaq*, courts held that the woman was still married. Courts acted on the belief that the objective of the MFLO was to protect women from the ill-effects of arbitrary divorce and the subsequent waiting period of 90 days was held to place some limitation and restraint upon the husband's unilateral and arbitrary right to divorce. This safety net was extended considering the social structure of Pakistan, where a divorced woman is akin to a pariah, with little support or respect both within her family and the wider social circle.

However, with the promulgation of the Hudood laws, the insistence of the provisions of the MFLO that only *talaq*, duly written and notified, would be effective became a disadvantage to women. Vindictive former husbands who had failed to send written notices to the Union Council, alleged that their former wife, who after being divorced had remarried, was guilty of adultery and liable to be charged for *zina*. This offence, if proved, was punishable with lashes and/or stoning to death.[47] The courts finally declared that failure to notify did not invalidate the *talaq* itself. In a landmark judgment, Naseem Hassan Shah CJ held that:

> 'where a wife bona fide believing that her previous marriage with her former husband stands dissolved on the basis of a talaqnama although the husband has not got it registered with the Union Council enters into a second marriage, neither the second marriage nor the fact of her living with the second husband will amount to Zina because of her bona fide belief that her first marriage stood dissolved.'[48]

Judgments including the above are 'damage containment' responses by courts to the interaction of the MFLO and the Hudood laws. While these have saved women from the disastrous consequences of being found guilty of adultery, they have almost nullified provisions of the MFLO to offer some relief to women against arbitrary and unregistered *talaq*.

Legal pluralism has also played an incisive role by playing up provisions of codified family law, primarily the MFLO, against literalist, inflexible

---

[47] Some leading cases include: *Shera v The State* PLD 1982 FSC 229; *Muhammad Siddique v The State* PLD 1983 FSC 173; *Mirza Qamar Raza v Mst Tahira Begum* PLD 1988 Kar 169; *Muhammad Sarwar Mst Shahida Parveen v The State* PLD 1988 FSC 42.

[48] *Bashiran v Muhammad Hussain* PLD 1988 SC 186.

interpretations of Islamic law. The outcome is case-law consisting of contradictory rulings some declaring the MFLO un-Islamic; others upholding the Islamic nature of the statute. Section 7, requiring registration of *talaq*, has alternately been found 'Islamic'[49] and 'un-Islamic'![50]

5   SECTION 6 OF THE MFLO – RESTRICTING POLYGAMY? A VIEW FROM WITHIN

Islamic family law permits a Muslim male to marry lawfully up to four wives at the same time. Polygamy thus stands permitted in Islam although the *Quranic* verse on the subject states it with clear provisos:

> 'And if you fear that you cannot act equitably towards orphans, then marry such women as seem good to you, two, three or four, but if you fear that you shall not be able to deal justly (with them) then only one.'[51]

The debate around polygamy raises a number of questions. Does, for instance, the *Quranic* verse create an obligation for all male Muslims to emulate the practice or is it a qualified 'right' to be exercised under certain 'controlled' circumstances set out in the verse above?[52] Al-Hibri, is of the opinion that the mere fact that the Prophet Mohammed was polygamous in his later life is no evidence of a 'right' of Muslim men also to be polygamous. She argues on the basis of the *Quranic* verses that state quite clearly that neither the Prophet nor his wives are like other men and women.[53] Secondly, the passage in the *Quran* which has been used to justify polygamy also attaches a condition for such action, ie requiring the man to make an undertaking to deal justly with all his wives. Reinforcing this condition is the *Quranic* statement (verse 4:129) that 'Ye are never able to be fair and just among women even if you tried hard'. 'Modernist' Muslim scholars are of the opinion that for evolving a rule of law relating to polygamy these two *Quranic* verses must

---

[49]   *Kaniz Fatima v Wali Muhammad* PLD 1989 Lah 490; *Ayaz Aslam v Chairman Arbitration Council* 1990 ALD 702.

[50]   *Mirza Qamar Raza v Mst Tahira Begum* PLD 1988 Kar 169; *Allahdad v Mukhtar* 1992 SCMR 1273.

[51]   The *Quran*, verse 4:3.

[52]   ARI Doi, in his book entitled *Shariah: The Islamic Law* (Ta Ha Publishers, 1984) at p 146 outlines the various circumstances for which he considers polygamy to be the 'best solution'. These situations include the wife suffering from a serious disease; where the wife is barren or is of unsound mind; where the wife is old and infirm; where the wife is of 'bad character' and cannot be reformed; where the wife moves away from her husband's place of residence, is disobedient and difficult to live with; as a result of many men dying during war leaving behind a large number of widows. The final reason that Doi advances is that if the husband feels that he simply cannot do without another wife and is capable of providing equal support to the existing wife (wives), then he is justified in doing so. Doi has in effect provided a carte blanche to the man to marry if he feels like it. This hardly appears in consonance with the contextual rationale behind the *Quranic* verse.

[53]   The *Quran*, verse 33:32, 50. For example, while the Prophet encouraged widows and divorcees to remarry, his own wives were not to be remarried after his death. They were considered 'the mothers of all believers', and no believer may marry his mother. However, as the Prophet grew older he gave his wives the choice to leave and marry another male more fulfilling perhaps of husbandly duties. All but one wife refused to leave him. See, al-Hibri, *op cit*, n 5 at p 216 (citing J Al-Afghani (1945) at p 79).

be read and interpreted together.[54] The implication of the combined passages in the opinion of Al-Hibri would be as follows:

(a)   if you can be just and fair among women, then you can marry four wives;
(b)   if you cannot be just and fair among women, then you may marry only one;
(c)   you cannot be just and fair among women; from which follows that you may marry only one wife. Furthermore, given (c), the condition for (a) is never satisfied, so that we can never conclude: You may marry four wives.[55]

In response to the above argument, it has to be said that some Muslim thinkers claim that the words 'justly' and 'just', occurring in the two *Quranic* passages above, have two different meanings; hence the view that these cannot be combined to draw an inference.[56] Abdur Rahman Doi also challenges the view of the modernists who consider verse 4:129 as a legal condition attached to polygamous unions.[57] Citing Shaikh Mohammed bin Sirin and Shaikh Abubakr bin al-Arabi, he makes the point that the inability to do justice between women referred to in the *Quran* is in respect of love and sexual intercourse only which is beyond the control of the man. Justice required of man is, in the opinion of these scholars, confined to matters of providing equality in residence, food, clothes to co-wives. So long as a man can provide these, he is seen as being just between women.[58]

The Rashid Commission had drawn on 'reformist' interpretation of religious text in Islam and sought inspiration from family laws of other Muslim states where polygamy stood abolished.[59] The strong dissenting note of Maulana Ihtesham-ul-haq Thanvi, a member of the Commission, and fear of adverse public opinion led to a 'watered down' version, regulating, rather than abolishing polygamy altogether. Section 6 of the MFLO thus qualifies a husband's right to contract subsequent marriages by requiring him to apply to the Chairman of the Arbitration Council stating reasons for the proposed marriage. He also has to state whether consent of the existing wife/wives has been obtained. The Chairman then convenes a meeting of the parties or their representatives to satisfy himself that the proposed marriage is 'necessary'.[60] Refusal to grant consent to the proposed marriage by the wife does not prevent the husband from remarrying. Neither does failure to obtain permission from the Arbitration Council invalidate the subsequent marriage. The only reprisal for non-compliance is laid out in s 6(5) which states that in the event of failure to obtain permission by the husband, he is liable to:

---

[54]   al-Hibri, *ibid*, at p 216; Rahman, *op cit*, n 5 at pp 45–49. Law reform in Muslim jurisdictions in the twentieth century has relied upon this interpretation.

[55]   al-Hibri, *op cit*, n 5 at p 216. Taha's arguments follow a similar line. He states that polygamy is not an original precept in Islam and a combined reading of verses 4:3 and 4:129 leads to an implied prohibition of polygamy.

[56]   al-Hibri, *ibid*, and accompanying footnotes.

[57]   Doi, *op cit*, n 53, chapter 8, especially pp 147–150.

[58]   *Ibid.*

[59]   Tunisia and Morocco are examples. Turkey has a secular legal system that prohibits polygamy.

[60]   The wife's infertility, insanity or incapacity to perform marital obligations have been considered as 'acceptable' reasons for remarriage.

'pay immediately the entire amount of the dower, whether prompt or deferred, due to the existing wife/wives, which amount, if not so paid, shall be recoverable as arrears of land revenue; and on conviction upon complaint be punishable with simple imprisonment which may extend to one year, or with fine which may extend to Rs 5000, or with both.'

A review of family law cases since coming into force of the MFLO reveals that very few have been filed invoking contravention of s 6. In three reported cases on the subject, where the husband was said to have entered into a subsequent marriage without seeking prior permission of his existing wife, a plea was advanced for declaring the subsequent marriage void and illegal.[61] Likewise, one appellant argued that since her husband's second marriage had neither been registered as required by s 5, nor had she granted him permission as required under s 6 of the MFLO, it should be declared illegal.[62] The court however, in all these cases held that, although in contravention of s 6, polygamous marriages of this nature were valid.

V BEYOND LAW REFORM AND LEGAL PLURALISM: THE 'LIVING' LAW

This paper has attempted to highlight the rhetoric and reality of Islamic family law as enunciated in some substantive provisions of the MFLO. A number of interesting patterns are revealed in how the written law tends to be undermined by varying interpretations of religious law as perceived through the lens of custom, tradition and socio-economic and political positioning on the subject. These views are summarised below.

(1)   Courts appear to reflect public opinion, societal trends and attitudes towards the family and domestic relations. For instance, it is generally accepted that what transpires between the spouses is solely a 'private' matter and must be resolved within the private sphere, ie the familial circle rather than through application of statute law in the courts. Therefore, no matter how advantageous the written law is to women in family law, its application will be in the light of a woman's position within that sphere. Since women are clearly at a disadvantage in this area, it follows that constitutional provisions of equality before law and equal protection of the law become irrelevant in a family dispute. It is interesting that, in family cases, the equality provisions of the constitution of Pakistan are seldom invoked or applied.[63] On the other hand, in matters pertaining to the 'public sphere' of

---

61   *Abdul Basit v Union Council, Ward no 3*, Peshawar Cantt 1970 SCMR 753; *Inayat Khan v District Magistrate*, Sialkot 1986 PCrLJ 2023; *Mst Ghulam Fatima v Mst Anwar* 1981 CLC 1651.
62   *Mst Ghulam Fatima v Mst Anwar* 1981 CLC 1651.
63   *Abdul Waheed v Asma Jehangir* PLD 1997 Lah 301.

life including entry to professional institutions[64] or eligibility for jobs,[65] article 25 of the Constitution[66] is prominently used.[67]

(2)   An important point that needs to be flagged here is the fact that, in a society sceptical of the efficacy of law and wary of state institutions such as police and judiciary, law reform cannot be an effective vehicle for positive change. People, by and large, are hesitant to use formal judicial forums (courts) for dispute resolution and would prefer out-of-court settlements. Courts, largely male-dominated establishments, inhibit women not used to operating in the public sphere hence limiting their access to justice. Knowledge of family laws may enable women to negotiate within the family sphere but if these 'formal' laws lack legitimacy then this power too is limited.

(3)   The most prominent issue, however, is the problem of a heterogeneous legal system with completely divergent normative bases. Thus, certain aspects of family law, such as marriage, dower, divorce etc, are regarded as having their base in religious law and are hence immutable. Reform, even one purporting to be based on a more enlightened version of religion, can be controversial and stand rejected. Further, legislation in family law has often amounted to piecemeal efforts at 'slipping in' progressive ideas in the form of legislative measures on the one hand and balancing political expediency and the dictates of justice on the other. As an example, the case of the MFLO attempt at restricting polygamy may be mentioned. Few people in the Muslim world would deny its permissibility in the Islamic legal tradition. Fewer, however, would be able to uphold it as a practice that they would wish to inflict upon their own daughters. It would not be an exaggeration to state that polygamy today stands as one of the most abhorrent practices in the Muslim world. Most societies have evolved societal norms in an attempt to undermine and resist it. Thus, the sub-continent (Indo-Pakistan) has developed customs of stipulating exhorbitant dower in the marriage contract discouraging the husband from subsequent marriage/s.

(4)   Laws, whether religious, societal or statutory are accepted and used only selectively. A number of judgments have been handed down by courts challenging the 'Islamic' nature or otherwise of a particular statute and paving the way for its subsequent disregard. The MFLO and the DMMA have met with this fate on a number of occasions. Can it be inferred on the basis of relevant case-law, therefore, that the bench itself does not regard statute law as the 'settled' law of the land and believe that it can be thrown up for debate? (see discussion above). In other words, that statute law is not necessarily the 'living' law?

---

[64]   *Shrin Munir v Government of Punjab* PLD 1990 SC 295.

[65]   *Naseem Firdous v Punjab Small Industries Corporation* PLD 1995 Lah 584.

[66]   Article 25 of the Constitution is the main constitutional provision affording equality before law and equal protection of the law, and states thus:

'(1)   All citizens are equal before law and are entitled to equal protection of law.

(2)   There shall be no discrimination on the basis of sex alone.

(3)   Nothing in this article shall prevent the State from making any special provision for the protection of women and children.'

[67]   Women are provided complete equality under the Constitution of Pakistan and this norm of non-discrimination is reiterated in many of its provisions both in the chapter on Fundamental Rights as well as in that on Principles of Policy.

(5)   Application of the MFLO and levels of compliance with its provisions also brings to light another interesting finding. A study conducted in the Women's Study Centre, University of Peshawar reveals that only 57% of the sample population performed marriages in accordance with the provisions of the MFLO and 43% continued to have oral ceremonies. More than 50% of the respondents had never seen a copy of the form used for the marriage contract, neither their own nor anybody else's. While this disregard for the law may be seen as a tedious procedural requirement worth ignoring, even the established (non-controversial) norm of delegated right to divorce of a Muslim woman stated in clause 18 of the marriage contract is not known to most men and women. Why is it that, despite having legitimacy in religion as well as in statute law (the MFLO), *talaq-i-tafwid* has not gained currency among the people?

(6)   If family law reform can result in unsavoury outcomes for women, such as the interaction of the MFLO and the Hudood laws, as well as the issues raised in the preceding paragraphs, is it the favourable option for achieving women's empowerment? Pakistan, among other countries, is one where family law debates are raised in the political arena. Liberal leaders have been known to align themselves with conservative clerics to undermine progressive legislation in this field. Efforts to reform family law nevertheless do offer women some useful fragments of hope. What is required is working towards acceptance of these reforms among the public and evolving more effective implementation mechanisms.

VI   THE WAY FORWARD: SOME PROPOSALS FOR FURTHER REFORM[68]

Forty years have elapsed since the MFLO was promulgated. It was no doubt a courageous effort on behalf of the Rashid Commission and the government of the time to bring some of the important recommendations within the ambit of the statute. As illustrated in the preceding sections, a number of provisions designed to protect women from injustices meted out by husbands and family back-fired due to the juxtaposition of the Hudood Ordinance. Although courts have rectified some of the most glaring loopholes through judgments, these are *ad hoc* measures and very much dependent upon the personal views of the judge. At the same time, the reality is evident that, by virtue of these judgments, a number of substantive clauses of the MFLO have been made redundant and ineffective. Time therefore is now ripe for charting the way forward in family law reform in Pakistan.

The Pakistan Law Commission has been engaged in proposing modifications to the MFLO and its implementing statute, the Family Courts Act, 1964 with a view to addressing these very problems.

Based on wide consultations, the following suggestions have been put forward to the Ministry of Law, Justice and Parliamentary Affairs.

---

[68]   This section draws upon the author's personal experiences as Minister for Health, Population and Women Development in the north-west frontier province of Pakistan and Chair, National Commission on the Status of Women.

(1)   A wife seeking dissolution of marriage shall also claim in the plaint, her dower, dowry, personal property, maintenance, custody of children and right of visitation to meet children to avoid multiplicity of suits.

When the Pakistan Law Commission shared the draft amendments in the law, this particular one came under strong criticism from some women's NGOs. The Pakistan Women Lawyers Association sent their viewpoint arguing that they had serious apprehensions to the effect that joinder of claims/suits in family disputes would lead to delays in trial. They lobbied with the PLC, the Ministry of Law, Justice and Parliamentary Affairs, and the National Commission on the Status of Women. The Secretary of the PLC, however, responding to these concerns, argued in favour of adopting the amendment stating that:

> 'It was indeed with a view to saving spouses from hassle, technicalities and unnecessary expenses that the Commission recommended that all claims/suits among spouses be joined and decided in a single suit, rather than being disposed of separately, one after the other, or by several family courts. That is why the Commission also recommended minor criminal complaints, within the family, to be decided by the same family court rather than the ordinary criminal court. The family court is the most suitable forum to deal with and decide family disputes because it also resorts to conciliation proceedings for reaching an out-of-court settlement. It is only when conciliation proceedings fail that the court would initiate trial. Furthermore, the Commission's recommendations obligate the family court to dispose of all family suits within a period of four months. The family courts will have exclusive jurisdiction to dispose of family cases on a day-to-day basis, otherwise the objective of quick dispensation of justice may not be realised.'[69]

(2)   A family court may pass an interim order to grant maintenance or to preserve and protect any property to secure the enforcement of a decree and no appeal or revision shall lie against it.

(3)   An appeal against a decree of maintenance by the family court is exempted from payment of court fee.

(4)   A family court shall have all powers of a judicial magistrate of the first class to try minor criminal offences where one of the spouses is the victim of an offence committed by the other.

(5)   Where the wife seeks dissolution on the basis of *khula*, the court is required simply to pass an order to that effect on return of the dower to the husband. This particular amendment, too, has been criticised as going back on the gains achieved through case-law. It is a fact that courts in Pakistan have handed down judgments questioning payment to the husband of the entire dower sum as being against the spirit of Islam and an injustice to the wife. In *M Saqlain Zaheer v Zaibun Nisa*,[70] for instance, the court refined and

---

[69]   Faqir Hussain, Secretary, Pakistan Law Commission, letter No F 14(170)/2000/PLC-A.1 dated 10 July 2001 addressed to Mrs Rashida Mohammad Hussain Patel, President, PAWLA, and copied to the author in her capacity as Chairperson, National Commission on the Status of Women, Pakistan.

[70]   1988 MLD 427.

clarified the concept of *zar-i-khula*,[71] in a manner that has benefited women. The court insisted that reciprocal benefits received by the husband should be taken into account, continuous living together, bearing and rearing children, housekeeping etc, could also be counted as benefits, thereby offsetting the benefits that the wife had to return.

Some important issues fail to find mention in the draft proposals for amending the MFLO and related legislation. These include post-divorce maintenance for a former wife and incorporating an adult's right to consent to marriage in statute. *Quranic* injunctions on the mechanism to be adopted during divorce proceedings and the kindness that must be shown to the woman has not found a place in statute law (chapter 4 of the *Quran*). Jurists have argued that, since a divorce implies a termination of reciprocal rights and obligations between the spouses, and both can remarry, the matter of post-divorce maintenance for the wife contradicts this principle. Yet, it is a well-known reality that very few women, whether married, divorced or single, have independent means to spend on their upkeep. Yet, family law reform in Muslim countries, has ignored this pressing need of women to be maintained after dissolution of their marriage. The Indian case of *Shahbano*, ruling for the right of a Muslim woman to post-divorce maintenance, threw the country into political turmoil and Parliament had to intervene to pacify the Muslim minority.

Likewise, the now famous case of *Saima Waheed*,[72] the 19-year-old girl who entered into a contract of marriage without the knowledge and consent of her parents caused confusion and havoc in what was considered a settled area of *Hanafi* Muslim jurisprudence. Incorporating this right may help clarify the position of an adult Muslim woman to enter into marriage of her own volition.

In summation it may be argued that the way forward for legal reform in family law must be used as part of a hybrid approach if the purpose of social engineering is to be achieved. Civil society has to debate these issues and accept ownership for any sustainable and positive change. The written, black-letter law, is at best a standard-setting exercise in an environment where two-thirds of the population is barely literate and where many women have never ventured out of their native village. Implementation mechanisms and access to justice must be strengthened along with developing credibility of institutions responsible for dispute resolution and protection of rights.

---

[71] Amount of valuables to be returned to the husband for the wife's release.

[72] PLD 1997 Lah 301.

PORTUGAL

DE FACTO RELATIONSHIPS AND SAME-SEX RELATIONSHIPS IN PORTUGAL

Sofia Oliveira Pais[*]

I INTRODUCTION: CONCEPT, CHARACTERISTICS AND REASONS TO ENTER A DE FACTO RELATIONSHIP

It has been widely discussed in Portugal, especially in recent years, whether there should be enlargement of the protection of the partners in a de facto relationship and the eventual recognition of rights for same-sex couples.

The concept of de facto relationships has been traditionally understood as the union between a man and a woman living like husband and wife as in the institution of formal marriage. The essential characteristic of a de facto relationship is its free dissolution,[1] as opposed to formal marriage where divorce is usually necessary. In addition, it should be pointed out that in Portugal, while formal marriage is a legal union recognised by law (Art 1576 Civil Code), de facto relationships have been regulated by the legislator only in certain aspects and have not been considered a family law relationship.[2]

There are several reasons that induce individuals to choose to enter a de facto relationship, namely financial difficulty in paying the expenses of a wedding; the existence of legal impediments, for example the impossibility of getting a divorce for those who previously chose an indissoluble Catholic marriage;[3] the rejection of the bureaucracy and State interventionism of formal marriage; the avoidance of formal marriage as an institution that means dominance, hierarchy and the loss of individual identity; the loss of fiscal or other social benefits and the desire to experience living together before a formal marriage.

---

[*] Faculdade de Direito, Universidade Católica Portuguesa, Centro Regional do Porto.

[1] However, the creation of a de facto relationship is no longer unrestricted. In fact, several European laws establish different impediments to its creation, such as consanguinity or the continuing existence of a previous marriage.

[2] Article 1576: 'The sources of relationships in family law are marriage, consanguinity, affinity and adoption'. According to the dominant doctrine, this Article is exhaustive and not illustrative. Therefore, even if the legislator gives to the partner in a de facto relationship certain rights, it should not be considered a relationship having all the effects of family law in general. See FM Pereira Coelho, *Temas de Direito da Família*, Almedina, Coimbra, p 9; Antunes Varela, *Direito da Família*, 1º vol, 5th edn, Livraria Petrony, Lda, Lisbon, p 31; Heinrich Ewald Hörster, 'Does Portugal need to legislate on de facto unions?' *International Journal of Law, Policy and the Family*, 13, 1999, p 274.

[3] In Portugal, because of the Treaty concluded in 1940 between the Portuguese State and the Holy See, couples married by the Catholic Church after that year had to give up the right to divorce. As these partners were not permitted to remarry, and since the only alternative was judicial separation of persons and property, one could predict that the rate of de facto relationships would increase. The truth is that the traditional family structure made those situations rare.

II   THE PORTUGUESE SOCIAL REALITY

In Portugal there are few statistics or sociological studies about this subject. The last reliable figures presented by the National Institute of Statistics, which have come to my knowledge, date from 1991[4] and show that, in a population of around 10 million, more than 194,000 Portuguese live in de facto relationships against 4.8 million Portuguese who are married.[5]

It is also worth mentioning two recent surveys of young people about family lifestyle choices. One of them in 1996 (Torres, pp 50–51) maintains that de facto relationships are not as popular in Portugal as in Central and Northern Europe, and reveals the following information: a survey made in 1996 of the youth in a certain region of Portugal (Loures-Lisbon) shows that 17.2% were married and only 1.6% lived in a de facto relationship; among the singles, 43.2% intended to marry in the future while only 7.7% would choose to live together without marrying. Three years later, another survey appears to confirm the tendency to choose marriage as a lifestyle. In fact a survey made in 1999 of young people (1624 surveyed), aged between 15 and 29 years old, showed that 80% to 90% intended to marry.[6]

These figures have been explained first by the fact that, unlike certain countries where young couples consider de facto relationships as an experience before formal marriage, which occurs generally with the birth of the first child, in Portugal cohabitation generally begins with marriage, especially Catholic marriage. Indeed, Catholic marriage is twice as prevalent as civil marriage, justified particularly by reasons of tradition and social rituals and not so much because of religious convictions (Torres, p 52). This can be seen clearly from the comparison between the numbers of Catholic marriages celebrated in 1996, 1997 and 1998, which were respectively 42,322, 44,457 and 44,644 and those of civil marriages celebrated in the same period, which amounted respectively to 21,350, 21,313, and 21,954.[7] It is also curious to note that, according to the figures of the National Institute of Statistics, contrary to the previous tendency between 1975 and 1995,[8] which produced a decrease in the number of marriages, in recent years the number of marriages in Portugal has increased, even if in a very gradual way.

Secondly, in Portugal, at the present time, there are no particular difficulties in celebrating a formal marriage, nor is it difficult to get divorced. In fact, Portuguese family law has witnessed an enormous evolution and the divorce system has been increasingly liberalised. For instance, since 1975 Catholic couples have been allowed to divorce, and the divorce system has evolved not

---

[4]   Note that new figures will soon be presented by the National Institute of Statistics (see *www.ine.pt*), based on the census of the Portuguese population taken this year (2001). Nevertheless, at this moment there is no further information available on the evolution of de facto relationships in Portugal.

[5]   Cf *http://www.parlamentopt/legisl/inic.legisl/19971006.07.03.0414.0.07* and *http://www.expresso.pt/ed1385/r0461.asp*. To complete the matrimonial statistics for Portugal in 1991, 635,000 were widows, 119,000 were separated and 97,000 were divorced.

[6]   Survey carried out by the Institute of Social Sciences of the University of Lisbon. Cf *http://www.expresso.pt/ed1385/r0461.asp*.

[7]   See *http://www.ine-pt/prodserv/area04/casam.html*.

[8]   In fact the number of marriages has been decreasing consistently since 1970, with 81,461 marriages in that year to 66,003 marriages in 1994. See Torres, p 210. However, this trend seems to be slowing down.

only by the admission of no-fault divorce but also because divorce by mutual consent has been simplified and even stimulated. This change is largely confirmed by the increase in the figures for divorce since 1975, the date on which the possibility of divorce was recognised for those who had a Catholic marriage, which were the majority.[9]

As nowadays there are no particular difficulties, either legal or bureaucratic, in Portugal in celebrating or dissolving a formal marriage, the gulf between formal marriages and de facto relationships is reduced. Besides, as it has been noted (Mary Ann Glendon, pp 492–493), the boundaries become even more subtle with the present tendency, both in Portugal and in many other countries all around the world, towards deregulation of marriage, as well as the recognition of more legal effects of a de facto relationship.

Nevertheless, legal differences between them should be maintained as marriage and de facto relationships intend to accommodate different family lifestyle choices. Therefore, in my opinion, which is consistent with most of the Portuguese authors who have written about this subject (Pereira Coelho, *Temas*, p 19; HE Hörster, pp 275–279; Sofia Pais/António F Sousa, p 702), de facto relationships should not be assimilated to marriage, otherwise there will be a clear violation of the respect due to the individual freedom of choosing one's life. This does not mean obviously that the legislator nowadays should or could ignore the visible social reality of cohabitation. Reasons of equity, like the protection of the children of de facto relationships or the weaker partner in that union, justify, in Portugal and in other countries, the recognition of several legal effects of de facto relationships.

III PORTUGUESE LEGISLATION – THE CONSTITUTION, CIVIL LAW, SOCIAL SECURITY LAW AND LABOUR LAW – PROTECTS THE PARTNERS IN A DE FACTO RELATIONSHIP EXTENSIVELY AND INTENSIVELY

Focusing especially on the Portuguese context, we can say that de facto relationships – traditionally concerning only heterosexual couples – have been protected by law, in specific aspects, at least since the 1970s. Invoking the need to avoid discrimination and social injustice, the Portuguese legislator enacted extensive provisions protecting directly the partners in a de facto relationship. The following are the most relevant ones.

In the Constitution of the Portuguese Republic, Art 36, clause 1 grants to all persons the right to establish a family and to get married, and clause 4 of the same Article prohibits discrimination against children born out of marriage. This provision has been interpreted as conferring the fundamental right to establish a family, which can arise not only from marriage but also from other relationships such as those involving children born within a de facto relationship or adopted by a single parent (Pereira Coelho, p 8; HE Hörster, p 278).[10]

---

[9]   For instance, in 1970, 2% of marriages ended in divorce, while in 1994, the percentage was 21% (this corresponded to 13,582 divorces), see Torres, pp 22–23, 210.

[10] There is no consensus in Portuguese scholarship on the question of whether the ambiguous reference to 'a family' made in Art 36, clause 1 of the Portuguese Constitution should or should

Concerning the Civil Code's protection of de facto relationships, reference should be made to Art 495(3), which confers on a partner in a de facto relationship the right to claim compensation if a third person injures the other partner and causes his death;[11] Art 1871(1)(c), which establishes a presumption of paternity when, during the period of legal conception, the partners lived in a stable relationship as husband and wife; Art 1911(3), which allows the joint exercise of parental power (in other words, joint custody) when the parents live like husband and wife; and Art 2020, which allows the payment of alimony to the survivor of a de facto relationship dissolved by death. Further, Art 85 of the House-Rent Law – Decree 321-B/90, 15/10 – also allows, in the case of death of one of the partners, the transfer of tenancy to the other partner on condition that they had lived as husband and wife at least for two years.

Social security law and labour law extend these benefits.[12] Without being exhaustive, it is worth mentioning the concession to the partner in a de facto relationship of the right to a survivor's pension, by Decree 142/73, 31/3, modified by Decree 71/97, 3/4; the partner in a de facto relationship also benefits from holidays, absenteeism for hospital treatment of the other partner or in the case of death of a relative, according to social security law concerning public offices, namely Decree 497/88, 30/12 modified by Decree 178/95, 26/7 and Decree 101-A/96, 26/7; and in a situation of internal competition for the civil service, the partner in a de facto relationship is preferred for the job all other things being equal – according to Decree 498/88, 30/12 modified by Decree 215/95, 3/8. Civil service law (Decree 24/84, 16/1, Art 52 and Decree 413/93, 23/12, Art 6) also prohibits employees from participating in decisions in the workplace related to their partners in a de facto relationship, because no one can be expected to be sufficiently objective where one's own partner is involved.

In the context of labour law, the situation of the partners in a de facto relationship is also taken into account to establish the period of holidays or the possibility of absence in the case of death of one of the partners – Arts 8 and 24, Decree 874/76, 28/12, modified by Decree 397/91, 16/10, and the right to a pension in the case of death of one's partner because of a work accident according to Arts 20 and 22, Decree 100/97, 13/9.

---

not imply the constitutional recognition of de facto relationships. See Pereira Coelho, Temas, p 8; Geraldo da Cruz Almeida, p 184.

[11] In other words, if a third person injures a partner in a de facto relationship and causes his death, depriving the other partner of care, the partner can sue the perpetrator and claim compensation.

[12] Even if this is not the place to study the consequences attached to a de facto relationship by the criminal law, I would like to make three short observations on the subject, because of their importance in practice: it is important to mention Art 68 of the Penal Code which allows the person with whom the plaintiff lives in conditions similar to a married couple to become 'assistant' in the criminal procedure; Art 207 of the same Code establishes that criminal procedure depends on private accusation when the aggressor and the victim live together as husband and wife; and Decree 61/91, 13/8, Art 15, which is intended to guarantee necessary protection to the women victims of violence, also considers the situation of the partners in a de facto relationship.

IV   LAW NO 135/99 – PURPOSES AND IMPERFECTIONS

It should also be pointed out that in 1999 Law no 135/99, 28/8 was enacted, which was intended to enlarge the protection of heterosexual couples living in a de facto relationship for more than two years, without prejudice to the application of existing legislation concerning de facto relationships. Law no 135/99 began by establishing certain impediments to de facto relationships such as parties not having reached the age requirement of 16, notorious insanity, consanguinity, existing marriage and certain previous criminal convictions in terms very similar to those used in the Civil Code relating to marriage. Then Arts 3 to 5 referred in general terms to the benefits of those living in a de facto relationship: on the death of an owner, the survivor had an option to buy the home and a right to inhabit the home for five years; protection of the right to the transfer of tenancies when a de facto relationship was ended by the death of one of the members; rights to holidays, absenteeism and leave in terms equivalent to those enjoyed by married couples; tax benefits for spouses to apply to de facto relationships, as well as social security pensions in case of death of the beneficiary; the right to adopt according to the general rules; and the right to a service pension for exceptional services given to the country.

In spite of the good intentions of the legislator, this law presented certain problems. A very obvious one related to the fact that the legislator was only concerned with the rights of the partners and paid no attention to the corresponding responsibilities, making the Portuguese law unique in European legislation. Take, for instance, the example of the Catalan law of 30 June 1998,[13] which, in the first chapter concerning heterosexual relationships, allows the partners to regulate their personal and patrimonial relationship, establishing also that the partners in a de facto relationship should contribute to the management of the home and common expenses according to their incomes or property. In addition, Catalan law establishes joint liability to third persons for debts arising from the normal expenses of family life. These rules found no equivalent in the Portuguese law, where the legislator was apparently only concerned with conferring benefits on the partners in a de facto relationship and considering just their individual advantages. However, in other relationships, such as formal marriage, the interests of third persons, such as creditors, are also taken into consideration by the Portuguese legislator, establishing, for instance, the joint responsibility of the married couple for debts arising from family expenses.[14] Therefore, on a first analysis of the Portuguese law, it could almost appear that the deep concern of the legislator to avoid discrimination against those in de facto relationships might lead to an undesirable result, discrimination against marriage, when the Portuguese social reality shows that de facto relationships are a rare phenomenon and Portugal has one of the highest marriage rates in the European Union.[15]

---

[13]   Llei sobre unions estables de parella –30 juny de 1998 – see
http://www.biblioteca.udg.es/fd/jornades/PLRdc.httm.

[14]   Article 1691, no 1, Civil Code. Some authors – Pereira Coelho, *Temas*, p 16 – argue that this Article, which establishes joint responsibility of the spouses for debts arising from normal family life, should also be applied by analogy to de facto relationships.

[15]   See Torres, p 50.

Furthermore, it must be pointed out that the Portuguese law on de facto relationships has not been applied, since it has not been brought into force. However, the extensive legislation existing in Portugal at the moment assures a high degree of protection to heterosexual de facto relationships. In fact, as we have already stated (Sofia Pais/António F Sousa, p 706), the protection given by the Portuguese legislature to the de facto relationship is so great that it is perhaps larger or equal to the protection given by those systems that consider the de facto relationship as a secondary kind of marriage.

V BILLS PRESENTED BEFORE THE PORTUGUESE PARLIAMENT CONCENING SAME-SEX RELATIONSHIPS AND DOMESTIC PARTNERSHIPS

In this context it is important to bear in mind that the protection mentioned above relates only to heterosexual de facto relationships and that no reference has been made to same-sex relationships. However, in recent years, four Bills have been presented in the Portuguese Parliament with the purpose of recognising homosexual rights: the Socialist Bill, the Communist Bill, the Green Party Bill, and the Bill from the left of centre party.[16]

All these Bills had common features and purposes. All of them were aimed at extending the existing regime applying to de facto relationships to same-sex couples despite using different language and other minor differences. All of them invoked the need to avoid discrimination against individuals because of their sexual orientation, which extended to homosexuals and led to restrictions of their rights, as well as indefensible differences and injustices. However, not one of the Portuguese Bills recognised, at that time, the possibility of adoption by couples of the same sex,[17] arguing that this was a subject about which there was no consensus as yet.

There were differences in the terminology used and in the scope of application of the law. On the one hand, while the majority of Bills would apply to the legal situation of two persons, independently of their sex, living in a de facto relationship for more than two years, the Socialist Bill used the expression 'domestic partnership' (*vida em economia comum*), which was defined as the 'situation of two persons who publicly and notoriously live in a community of table and home for more than two years'. The use of this expression, similar to those in other laws, (for instance, the French law employs the phrase 'Pacte civil de solidarité'[18]), was justified by the proponents with the following arguments:

---

[16] Socialist Bill – Projecto de Lei no 105/VIII, 23/2/2000; Communist Bill – Projecto de Lei no 115/VIII, 29/2/2000; Bill by the Green Party – Projecto de Lei no 6/VIII (PEV), 29/10/1999; Bill by the left of centre party – Projecto de Lei no 45/VIII(BE), 16/12/1999 – see *http://www.parlamento.pt/legis/inic.legis.*

[17] Nevertheless, note that the left of centre party does not reject the possibility of adoption by homosexual couples. In other words, it argues that existing Portuguese law concerning adoption should be modified; however, the Bill concerning de facto relationships is not the proper place in which to introduce the necessary changes.

[18] The civil solidarity pact enacted in France, in December 1998, is an agreement between two persons whatever their sex to organise their common life – see Loi AN no 118 of 14/10/1998 published in *Juris Classeur Périodique – La Semaine Juridique Notariale et Immobilière*, no 43,

'the absolute indifference towards the sexual orientation of those to whom is conferred legal protection'; the need to achieve the goal of avoiding discrimination against homosexual couples and the concern of the legislator in respecting the privacy of individuals, therefore 'not imposing or impeding the revelation of the sexual orientation of the partners'; to enjoy legal protection it was enough to prove a life in common as long as it was not created by contract.

On the other hand, the Bill of the left of centre party was the most complete one. In contrast to the others, it considered that Law no 135/99 was incomplete and that the protection of a de facto relationship in terms equivalent to those of married couples should be conferred on issues like: access to the hospital of the partner in a de facto relationship when that partner was ill; for the purpose of a request for residence or work permit with a view to joining the family; for conferring political asylum, as well as for the recognition of de facto relationships constituted abroad as long as the partners had a residence in Portugal. In addition, this Bill intended to create the possibility for the registration of de facto relationships.

Finally, it is worth mentioning that only the Communist and the left of centre parties considered the issue of the dissolution of a de facto relationship; according to the left of centre party, dissolution should occur at the will of one of the partners, declared to the register services, while the Communist Bill established dissolution by death or marriage of one of the partners or the cessation of cohabitation.

The issue of extending the protection of heterosexual de facto relationships to homosexual couples was debated among Portuguese authors long before the presentation of these four Bills in Parliament, revealing different conceptions of the family and especially of marriage, as well as their social and juridical value.[19] Some authors are clearly opposed to the protection of homosexual unions in general, emphasising the fact that in the Portuguese context mere cohabitation in reality is of little relevance[20] and that mere cohabitation does not justify the right to receive social benefits except when there are children involved. It was also argued that extending the existing law on de facto relationships to homosexual couples is only the first step towards allowing in the future same-sex marriage, which would destroy the institution of marriage which is necessarily based on sexual difference.[21] Other authors argue that, in conformity with the current Portuguese Constitution, homosexual de facto relationships should not be excluded from the benefits conferred by the law on heterosexual de facto relationships.[22]

---

23 October 1998, at 1521. On this issue see also Jacqueline Rubellin-Devichi, 'How matters stand now in relation to family law reform', in *The International Survey of Family Law 2000*, ed Andrew Bainham (Family Law, 2000), pp 161–164.

[19] In fact, in opposition to the traditional notion of marriage, characterised by the principal purpose of the procreation and raising of children, there is today a dominant conception of marriage as a relationship of companionship and affection. See D Coester Waltjen/M Coester, pp 50–51.

[20] There are no statistics in Portugal, to my knowledge, concerning the relevance of homosexual relationships in Portuguese society. However, in the United States, some authors (Posner: at 1581) argue that 'three percent is the highest responsible estimate of the percentage of the sexually mature population that has predominantly homosexual orientation'.

[21] See Cruz de Almeida, p 102.

[22] See João Coelho, p 119.

VI THE NEW LAWS: LAW NO 6/2001 AND LAW NO 7/2001

New developments occurred in 2001 with the discussion of the Bills mentioned above before the Portuguese Parliament. After a long debate, the official journal[23] finally published on 11 May 2001, laws governing the legal status of the domestic partnership and of the de facto relationship.

Law no 6/2001 establishes some measures to protect persons in a domestic partnership. This new institution, based on social solidarity, is defined as a situation in which two or more persons, one of whom is at least 18 years old, live in a community of table and home for more than two years, helping each other and sharing resources (Art 2). The law then creates certain impediments to domestic partnerships: the existence of a contract which implies living in the same house, or a working relationship, or the existence of a domestic partnership for temporary and specific purposes; or when one of the persons in a domestic partnership is under physical or psychological coercion (Art 3). Finally, Arts 4–9 refer to the benefits of those living in that situation: rights to holidays, absenteeism and leave, both in public and private employment, in terms equivalent to those enjoyed by married couples; preference for a job in the civil service in terms equivalent to married couples; tax benefits for spouses to apply to the situation of two persons living in a domestic partnership, with proper adjustments; on the death of the owner, an option for the survivor to buy the home and to inhabit it for five years,[24] as well as the right to the transfer of tenancies.

Law no 7/2001 revokes Law no 135/99 and replaces the existing regime governing heterosexual de facto relationships with a more comprehensive one. According to the new law, a de facto relationship is defined as the legal situation of two persons, independently of sex, living together for more than two years (Art 1). In other words, with this qualification, same-sex relationships are also protected by law, meaning that the new law re-establishes the regime established by the previous law but extending it to homosexual couples.

Just as in Law no 135/99, certain situations are excluded from the scope of application of Law no 7/2001, such as relationships involving persons aged less than 16 years old, persons of notorious insanity, those related by consanguinity, persons party to a previous subsisting marriage and those having certain previous criminal convictions (Art 2).

Concerning the rights conferred on the partners in a de facto relationship, Law no 7/2001 also confirms the benefits established by the previous law: on the death of an owner the survivor has an option to buy the home and a right to inhabit it for five years (Art 4);[25] protection of the right to the transfer of tenancies when a de facto relationship ceases on the death of one of the partners (Art 5); rights to holidays, absenteeism and leave, both in the civil service and in private

---

[23]   Diário da República – I Série – A, no 109, 11-05-2001, pp 2796–2798.

[24]   Except where there are ascendants or descendants, who had lived with the deceased for at least one year and intend to continue inhabiting the house, or if there is a will providing for a different solution (Art 5).

[25]   There are certain exceptions to this solution. For instance, if there is a will providing for a different solution; and in the cases mentioned in Art 4, the descendents of the deceased may inhabit the home.

employment, in terms equivalent to those enjoyed by married couples; preference for a job in the civil service in terms equivalent to those enjoyed by the married couples; tax benefits for spouses to apply to de facto relationships, as well as social security pensions on the death of the beneficiary; and the right to a service pension for exceptional services given to the country (Art 3).

In addition, the new law clarifies two issues: creation and dissolution of a de facto relationship. Under Art 7 of Law no 7/2001, the partners in a de facto relationship have the right to adopt according to the general law, meaning that only couples of different sex, living in a de facto relationship, can adopt in terms similar to those of married couples established by Art 1979 of the Civil Code, without prejudice to the legal rules concerning adoption by single persons. Article 8 of the same law, following the views urged by the left of centre party and Communist Bills, determines that the dissolution of a de facto relationship occurs by the will, death or marriage of one of the partners.

In conclusion, both laws are particularly important in the Portuguese context because of their innovative character. However, it must be pointed out that they cannot yet be applied, since they have not been implemented. As we have already noted, the existing Portuguese legislation apparently assures a high degree of protection to de facto relationships, but actually, so far, only heterosexual relationships have been protected. The situation may change in the near future.

REFERENCES

Almeida, Geraldo da Cruz, *Da união de facto, convivência more uxorio em direito internacional privado* (Pedro Ferreira ed, Lisbon, 1999)

Coelho, FM Pereira, 'Casamento e família no direito português', in *Temas de Direito da Família* (Almedina ed, Coimbra, 1986), 3–29

Coelho, João PT, 'A Família: perspectiva evolutiva do conceito tradicional', in (1993) *Revista do Ministério Público*, no 54 (Lisbon), 113–123

Coester-Waltjen, D and Coester, M, *International Encyclopedia of Comparative Law*, vol IV, 'Persons and Family', Chap 3, 'Formation of marriage' (Mohr Siebeck, Tübingen, 1997)

Glendon, Mary Ann, 'Patterns of contemporary legal response to the social phenomenon of the facto marriage', in *Konflikt und Ordnung, Festschrift für Murad Ferid zum 70. Geburtstag* (CH Beck, München, 1978)

Hörster, Heinrich Ewald, 'Does Portugal need to legislate on de facto unions?', in (1999) *International Journal of Law, Policy and the Family* 13, at 274–279

Pais, Sofia and Sousa, António F, 'A União de Facto e as Uniões Registadas de pessoas do mesmo sexo', in (1999) *Revista da Ordem dos Advogados*, no 59 (Lisbon), 692–752

Posner, Richard A, 'Should there be homosexual marriage? And if so, who should decide?', in *Michigan Law Review*, Vol 95 no 6, 1578–1587

Rubellin-Devichi, Jacqueline, 'How matters stand now in relation to family law reform', in *The International Survey of Family Law (2000 Edition)*, ed A Bainham (Family Law, 2000), pp 143–164

Torres, Anália Cardoso, *Divórcio em Portugal, ditos e interditos* (Celta ed, Oeiras, 1996)

RUSSIA

FIVE YEARS OF THE RUSSIAN FAMILY CODE: THE FIRST RESULTS

Olga A Khazova[*]

I   INTRODUCTION

It is now more than five years since the Russian Family Code came into force.[1] How far do the new Code's provisions correspond to the current situation in Russia? What are the main shortcomings of the Family Code? Are there any gaps in it? What are the main problems the judges face when applying the Code's provisions to real life situations? What corrections and amendments, if any, ought to be made to the Code? These and other similar questions inevitably arise when one tries to estimate the results of applying a new law. The limits of this paper do not allow me to go into a detailed analysis of the whole Code.[2] Therefore, I will discuss several provisions chosen from different parts of the Code in order to give the reader some ideas of the mistakes that were made in the Code, to show the outcomes of some of our not very successful attempts to introduce new rules and some of the weak points of the new law.

The Family Code 1995, being part of a 'comprehensive revision of Russian private law',[3] was adopted in a period of radical economic, social, and political changes. It was necessary to bring Russian family law into line with the current situation in the country, with the new RF Constitution 1993, the new Civil Code 1994, and the UN Convention on the Rights of the Child, and to secure the ideas of freedom and those values which were brought into being by *Perestroika* and by the reforms of the 1990s as applied to family law. The significant changes that were introduced into Russian family law by the Code were undoubtedly a good reason for its strong reception.[4]

However, the Code was not planned to be as radical as might have been expected, taking into account the period of its formulation. The initial 'directive' was to be a bit more conservative when compared with the revision of the civil

---

[*]   Institute of State and Law (Russian Academy of Sciences), Moscow. The draft of this paper was presented to the 10th World Conference of the International Society of Family Law (Brisbane, Australia, 9–13 July 2000).

[1]   The RF Family Code was adopted on 25 December 1995 and came into force on 1 March 1996.

[2]   For more details on the new Russian Family Code, see O Khazova, 'The New Family Code' and 'Three Years After the Adoption of the New Russian Family Code', in *The International Survey of Family Law 1996*, ed A Bainham (Martinus Nijhoff Publishers, 1998) at 371, and *The International Survey of Family Law (2000 Edition)*, ed A Bainham (Family Law, 2000) at 323 (respectively).

[3]   M Antokolskaya, 'The 1995 Russian Family Code: A New Approach to the Regulation of Family relations', in (1996) *Review of Central and East European Law* No 6, at 635.

[4]   See, for example, *ibid* at 660.

legislation and specifically the new Civil Code, which aimed to be the legal basis for 'the economic revolution in Russia'.[5] It was necessary to preserve those positive family law provisions which were accumulated during the Soviet era[6] and to adjust them to the new realities, without changing family law completely. Although fulfilment of this task had inevitably required a full revision of all the provisions of the previous legislation[7] from the perspective of their 'fitness' for the new situation in the country, in the opinion of one of the commentators on the Family Code, in the post-Soviet era, family law underwent 'surprisingly few changes'.[8] Another wrote some time ago: 'Bearing in mind the complexity and delicacy of family relations, the legislator has treated the building up of new legal constructions with care. The Family Code, luckily, cannot be called a revolutionary document'.[9] Therefore, in contrast with the new Civil Code, the compromise character of the Family Code 1995 was predetermined from the very beginning; and I must confess that this conservatism in the Code explains some of its main drawbacks.

Thus, looking at the Code critically today, we do not seem to be as enthusiastic about it as we were at the time of its adoption. Now we can see the principal shortcomings of the Code more clearly, and the provisions where the wording might be better or should have been entirely different. To a certain extent, this is explained by numerous gaps, inaccuracies, or even errors, which were the result of the haste with which the Code had been drafted and which themselves do not promote the Code's success. However, there are also the shortcomings which can be explained not by this rush, but by the above-mentioned initial conservatism of the Code. I will risk arguing that now, just five years later, in some respects, the Code is already outdated. It is true that, on the whole we are witnessing great changes in the family and in family law. Also there are significant changes in Russia itself and it is very difficult to create a 'perfect' document that will correspond to the reality in full and will work properly for a long period of time, when a country is in transition. However, I am sorry to say that this is a poor excuse; 'a limited success' for the Code was inherent in it from the very beginning and the causes of this lie in the initial compromise approach and the lack of consistency in some of those solutions which were promoted by the Code.[10]

---

[5]   AL Makovsky, 'Preface to the English Translation of the Civil Code', in P Maggs with A Zhiltsov (ed and transl), *The Civil Code of the Russian Federation. Parts 1 and 2* (International Centre for Financial and Economic Development, Moscow, 1997) at 53.

[6]   Russian family law is, perhaps, one of the few areas where liberal rules were established long before they were in the West: equality of spouses, equality of children born in and out of lawful wedlock, and no-fault divorce were all introduced into Russian law as far back as 1917–1918.

[7]   The RSFSR Code on Marriage and the Family 1969.

[8]   WE Butler, 'The Russian Family Code', in *Russian Family Law* (Simmonds & Hill Publ. Ltd, London, 1998) p xxiii.

[9]   PV Krasheninnikov, 'Introductory', in *Family Code of the Russian Federation with Clause-By-Clause Comments* (in Russian) (Spark, Moscow, 1996) at 5.

[10] See, for example, rules on maintenance between spouses (below).

II TRYING TO REFORM DIVORCE PROCEDURE

One of the main tasks of the Code was to give more freedom to the spouses in divorce and to simplify divorce procedure, provided there was mutual consent. At the same time, on the contrary, it was necessary to put child-related matters in divorce proceedings under the strict control of the court. The Code obliged the court, when making a divorce decree, irrespective of the type of divorce procedure (ie whether there was mutual consent to divorce or not), to raise of its own motion questions concerning a child's residence and, what is more important, questions on child maintenance. The idea behind this provision is quite clear: the child's interests must be given proper consideration in every case and the child must get maintenance, independently of whether the child's parents have reached a maintenance agreement or not, whether one of them has filed a maintenance suit or not, or whether they have asked the court to help them to solve this problem or not. The previous law required the court only to be informed formally during the divorce hearing if the spouses had come to an agreement on the custody and upbringing of the children.[11] In practice, the result of this rule was that a lot of children were left without any money at all. The new rule, as it appeared at least initially, improved the situation. But it turns out that this section of the Code, if interpreted literally, continues in fact to work in the old way (or, strictly speaking, does not work at all), because it does not oblige the court to investigate thoroughly the details of a particular case as far as they relate to children issues or to satisfy itself of the presence of a real agreement between the parents. In this section (s 24) the Code says:

'(1)—When dissolving a marriage in a judicial proceeding the spouses *may submit* for consideration of the court an agreement concerning with which of them minor children will reside, payment of children's maintenance ... , the amount of the maintenance ...' (italics added).

'(2)—If there is no agreement between the spouses with regard to questions specified in para (1) of the present section, and also if it is established that the particular agreement violates the interests of children ... , the court shall be obliged to: determine with which of the parents minor children will reside after divorce; determine from which of the parents and in what amount alimony shall be recovered for their children ...'

Being, as everywhere, extremely over-worked, the courts in Russia are reluctant to do what they are not obliged to do by law. The law, in this case the Family Code, says that the parties 'may submit' their agreement for the court's consideration, but they are neither obliged to do it in principle, nor to do it in written form. It means that, in practice, if there is no written agreement or no obvious dispute, the judge will be happy just to hear in the court room that there is consent between the parties with regard to their children. What exists behind this consent, whether there is such a consent in reality, and whether the child will get any maintenance, the court will hardly check. It also means that the Code did not succeed in giving the child's interests proper protection under the law.

---

[11] The RSFSR Code on Marriage and the Family 1969, s 33.

III SURROGATE MOTHERHOOD AND PRESUMPTION OF PATERNITY

Another example of the Code's provisions in which the wording is also far from perfect, concerns the legal rules on surrogate motherhood. The Family Code 1995 is the first legal document in Russia which contains special provisions on surrogacy. In s 51 (para 4, part 2) it is provided that 'a married couple, who have agreed to implantation of an embryo in another woman in order for the gestation of a child, can be registered as the child's parents only if this woman (surrogate mother) gives her consent to such a registration'. This means that, under Russian law, the surrogate has the right to keep the child. Apart from numerous ethical and legal problems in the field of human reproduction which we currently face, and which remain unsolved in the Code, there is a serious gap in the above-mentioned provision at a very basic level. The Code does not require the surrogate to be a single woman, which means that she may be married. But the Code does not say a word about the surrogate's husband and the 'husband-related' consequences of her serving as a surrogate mother. There is no provision in the Code or in any other Russian legislative provision which would require the husband of a woman who is going to become a surrogate to be asked if he wants to have such a baby or not and, strictly speaking, no one in a fertility clinic is obliged to get his consent to the use of assisted reproduction techniques with respect to his wife.

Thus, if a surrogate decides to keep a baby, her husband will be 'automatically' considered the child's father with all the consequences in law attaching to the legal rule on presumption of paternity. In this case there does not seem to be a great ethical dilemma and, in my opinion, the question might be solved quite easily if the law required the informed documentary consent, not only of a prospective surrogate, but also of her husband.[12]

Also in connection with surrogacy it is impossible to pass over the fact that, as follows from the text of the above-mentioned section, Russian family law speaks only about 'a married couple' in this regard. Thus, it is a kind of response to one of the difficult and controversial issues in human reproduction, namely access to ART.[13] However, the validity of this section is rather contentious from a constitutional point of view, and it also contradicts the existing law on citizens' health.[14] The point is that this provision, if interpreted literally, not only restricts the right of those who are not married to get access to a surrogate program (even if they have fertility problems), but it also restricts the right of *de facto* spouses to be registered as the legal parents of their child in the birth registration books, if a child was born as a result of surrogacy (even if there is no dispute). In practice, we have already faced situations where agencies, on registration of civil status,

---

[12] I foresee that it might be argued that this is an intrusion into women's reproductive freedom, but that is a topic for separate discussion.

[13] Concerning legal regulation of access to ART in Russia, see O Khazova, 'Artificial Conception of Human Life and Access to ART: Formulation of a Problem', in Romanovskyi (ed), *Law, Freedom, Person* (a collection of articles in Russian), (Arkhangelsk, 2001) at 127–135.

[14] The Fundamentals of RF Legislation on Citizens' Health 1993 provide for the right of every woman to benefit from assisted reproduction (s 35).

refused to register unmarried couples as the legal parents of children who were born 'for them' by surrogates.[15]

IV MAINTENANCE BETWEEN SPOUSES

A Maintenance agreements

A lot of controversy, both among legal scholars and lawyers, has been caused by the legal rules on maintenance agreements between family members. Aiming to give them more freedom in solving their financial problems, the law stipulates that the members of a family, principally the spouses, may make maintenance agreements. However, it turns out that the respective provisions of the Code do not work in practice in the way in which they were supposed to work. This means there is not much sense in these agreements on the whole, because they add nothing very new to those rules which regulate maintenance by law.

The Code stipulates that 'an agreement concerning the payment of alimony (amount, conditions, and procedure for payment of alimony) is made between *the person obliged to pay alimony* and the recipient thereof ...' (s 99, italics added). On a strict reading of the law, this section concerns only those who are obliged to provide maintenance by law, and does not cover those who maintain their spouse or other family member voluntarily, while not being legally obliged to do so. In accordance with Russian family law, the list of family members who are under such a duty is relatively short and, strange though it may seem, does not include the spouses themselves in the majority of cases.

Although it is stated in s 89(1) of the Code that 'the spouses are obliged to maintain each other', it is mostly their moral duty; to become a legal duty there must be certain grounds stipulated by law. These grounds are listed in part 2 of this section and in s 90 as applied to the spouses and ex-spouses respectively. Leaving aside some details and nuances that are not important in the present context, the list includes: a needy (ex-)spouse, unable to work; an (ex-)wife during pregnancy and three years after the birth of a common child, and a needy (ex-)spouse looking after a common disabled child. In practice it means that in the overwhelming majority of cases, if the spouses do not attain the pension age or are not disabled, if they do not have a disabled child in the family, or the wife is not pregnant etc, if they are young enough and can work (even if they have five common children) to get alimony for a spouse's maintenance by court order is impossible.[16] Therefore, it also means that if a married woman has decided to stay at home and 'devote herself to her family', she will not acquire the right to claim alimony from her husband during the marriage or after its dissolution only because of her status as a wife. She is not entitled to any payments, even on a temporary basis, as compensatory or 'rehabilitative' alimony, which would allow her to adjust to the new financial situation. The maintenance agreement, as it is formulated in the Family Code, will not help her in this regard either. The same is

---

[15] In particular, such a case was considered recently by the Federal Court of St Petersburg.

[16] I do not discuss here the legal duty of parents to maintain their children. That is regulated by law separately and has no connection with maintenance of a spouse.

true in relation to the husband if he fulfils the role of homemaker during the marriage and therefore needs some temporary support after its dissolution.

B   A little history

Thus, generally speaking, there is no legal obligation between the spouses to maintain one another in Russian law, if there are no special justifying circumstances (old age, incapability to work, pregnancy, a disabled child in the family, or some other reason), and the law does not provide any 'maintenance protection' for the 'housewife' who has contributed to the well-being of the family by working in the home.[17] The origin of this rule goes back to the post-revolutionary law and to 'the Soviet family model which knew no "housewife-marriages"'.[18] After the Socialist Revolution of 1917, women were declared equal to men. The new *Bolshevik* legislation on marriage and the family gave the woman equal rights in family relations and made her free from subordination to her husband and dependence on him. It inevitably implied that to become free from economic dependency on her husband, to achieve economic freedom in reality, and not only in theory, the woman had to work herself. The State, being in economic collapse after the Revolution and the civil war, was also interested very much in women's participation in the labour market, and to improve the economy of the country it was necessary to release as many 'human resources' as possible. The female workforce made a great contribution in this respect, and pushing women out of their homes and into the labour market became the family policy of the State. The conception of marriage as a union free from any mercenary spirit and based only on love fitted perfectly into the post-revolutionary mood and ideas of freedom and freedom of love included this new strategy towards the family. According to the new social order, everybody, irrespective of their sex, was supposed to work, and the right of a woman to claim maintenance from her husband only because of her status as a wife was abolished as 'a bourgeois survival of the past'. Alimony was declared to be 'not a charity'. The State could not allow one spouse to be a parasite at the expense of the other[19] – this would be incompatible with the ideology of the proletarian State. This ideology survived through the decades of Soviet power, although very soon it entirely lost its flavor of freedom. It still dominates among the general public, and those involved in the formulation of the new law also appeared to be under its influence.

---

[17]   The situation is different as to the spouses' property relations. The rules concerning the matrimonial regime of community of property, which is in operation in Russian law, provide that 'the right to common property shall also belong to the spouse who during the marriage managed the household, cared for the children, or for other justifiable reasons had no independent means' (s 34, para 3 of the Family Code).

[18]   K Kullerkupp, 'Family Law in Estonia', in *The International Survey of Family Law (2001 Edition)*, ed A Bainham (Family Law, 2001), at 102. The discussed legal rules on spousal maintenance are typical not only for Russia, but for the other independent States which made up the former USSR Republics. Also n 24 below.

[19]   DM Genkin, IB Novitskyi, NV Rabinovitch, *Istoria sovetskogo grazhdaskogo prava (History of Soviet Civil Law – in Russian)* (VIYUN, Moscow, 1949), at 440.

C   New social reality

All the recent changes in Russia affected first of all and most of all women, especially women with children. The last 10 years turned out to be extremely unfair to them. The reality was that, because of high unemployment among women, the collapse of the system of social services, and the high cost of services in the private sector, many women were forced to stay at home (or their incomes were extremely low). At the same time there appeared to be quite a lot of women who did not want to get into the labor market at all, but preferred to stay at home looking after children and fulfilling the traditional duties of a housewife. They were deprived of this right for a long time and we are witnessing today the restoration of the housewife role in Russia – a new trend, which acquired the name 'patriarchal renaissance'. It is a natural reaction to the decades of double-employment and the policy of forced separation of women from the family. However, the result is that a married woman, who has decided to stay at home and who does not have her own financial means and who is, therefore, dependent on her husband in full, may be left literally without a penny in the event of divorce or conflict in her family.

The only way for the law to meet this new social reality, in my opinion, is to restore the institution of spousal maintenance, and it seems to be right that 'a revival of spousal maintenance' not only could, but also should occur.[20] An economically weaker partner, in the event of divorce or separation, needs to have some time to adapt to the new reality (to find a job, to acquire certain skills, etc), and he or she needs certain financial protection during this time. If the State is not in a position to take this responsibility on itself, it must fall on family members, ie in this context the other spouse, who should fulfil this task. To rely on any agreement or contract between the spouses is not enough in this regard; there must be a clear mechanism stipulated by the law that would protect a housewife or one spouse whose income is much lower than the other's: maintenance should be considered 'as a right, expected and earned'.[21]

However, the new Russian family law did not respond to this new social reality; it appeared not to be ready for this 'return of women to the family', independently of the reasons for this phenomenon. Why did it happen? Why did the new law not provide any protection for an economically weaker partner, who is usually, but not necessarily,[22] a woman? Why were these changes not made in the Code on time? These are the questions, the answer to which we may find in our Soviet past.

---

[20]   R Bailey-Harris, 'Equality or Inequality within the Family? Ideology, Reality and the Law's Response', in *The Changing Family. International Perspectives on The Family and Family Law*, ed J Eekelaar and T Nhlapo (1998) at 253.

[21]   'Equality and Support for Spouses', in (1994) *The Modern Law Review* 57 at 681.

[22]   There are also a lot of families where the wives are, on the contrary, the only or the main breadwinners, and, of course, nowadays we speak about these matters on a gender-neutral basis.

D   The principle of sex equality

One of the explanations as to why the Soviet ideas have survived the latest revision of family law is our formal understanding of the principle of sex equality in general and, specifically, equality between the spouses. The result is an underestimation of the so-called 'gender approach' in the regulation of matrimonial and family relations. It may sound strange that the Family Code, adopted in a country which was the first in the world to declare full equality between a man and a woman, to give women equal political and civil rights and to equalize them with their husbands in family relations, 'suffers' from the shortage (or sometimes even lack) of a gender-based approach. One may reasonably ask: 'What's wrong with the gender equality in Russian family law?' The history of sex equality in this country is different from that in the West and it explains a lot about our attitude to the whole issue. For Russians, who were brought up for three or even four generations with the idea of full equality, it is difficult even to imagine that in the middle of the 1960s in many Western countries the husband was still formally recognized by law as 'the head of the family' and that attempts to eradicate this discrimination were met with resistance both by law-makers and by the general public. In the West, women have been struggling for equal rights for a long period of time; they got equality in a piecemeal fashion, step by step, being fully conscious of what they were struggling for; it was their 'achievement' indeed. As a result of this 'quiet women's revolution', women in the West, in certain respects, have got in reality much more equality than women in modern Russia.[23]

In Russia, as a result of our by no means 'quiet' and by no means 'women's' Revolution, the situation was absolutely different. In order not to be misunderstood I need to stress, especially, that it would be completely wrong to deny the importance of the declaration of sex equality in Russia in 1917. Emancipation of women in general and abolition of their subordinate position regarding their husbands in particular, in one of the first post-revolutionary *decrets*,[24] and equalization of their rights with men's rights at the constitutional level a year later, were the greatest events not only for Russia, but, as the future showed, also on a global scale. However, as a result of Revolution of 1917, Russian women got full equality with men at once, to an extent neither society nor women themselves were prepared for both economically and psychologically, 90% of Russian families corresponding to the patriarchal type. The initiative in the very formulation of a 'women's question', as it was called in Russia, did not belong to the women.[25] They did not choose the way, or the methods, as to how this 'women's question' was solved. Emancipation in Russia was in fact brought

---

[23]   Also we have to bear in mind that the sex equality movement in the West took place in a totally different political context and was accompanied by totally different ideas about human rights and freedoms.

[24]   *Decret* of 18 December 1917 'On Civil Marriage, On Children, and On Keeping of Civil Registry Books', SU RSFSR, 1917, no 11, s 160.

[25]   See LV Babaeva, *Zhenshchiny Rossii v uslovijahk social'njgj pereloma: rabota, politika, povsednevnaja zhizn (Women of Russia at the Social Turning Point: Work, Policy, Everyday Life)* (in Russian) (Moscow, 1996) at 15–17.

about 'from above', which made it to a certain extent compulsory.[26] One of its main purposes was to release maximum 'human resources' to improve the economy of the country and this determined the 'artificial' character of Soviet emancipation from the very beginning. Social and economic policy, carried out by the State for several decades afterwards, led to double employment of the overwhelming majority of Soviet women, the impossibility for them to remain at home and to be just housewives, if they would prefer this kind of activity, a chronic state of being over-tired and a 'stable reaction of idiosyncrasy'[27] to the very issue of sex equality and emancipation of women. To overcome this stable negative reflex to 'the women's question', to a significant extent a subconscious negativity to the problem of equality, it was necessary that the severe realities of recent years set Russian women back a long way.[28] Only now, 10 years after the collapse of the Soviet Union, the women's movement in Russia has been revived and approaches its second stage.[29] It is a natural process, but it passes through different time periods and in different forms compared to those in the West.

Seventy years of 'declared equality' did not pass without trace in the gender thinking of the specialists in family law either. Until recently we took it for granted that the problem of sex equality had been solved in this country, without going too much into the question of whether the declared equality corresponded to the reality, and the majority did not see any problems in this regard. It suffices to say that in family law textbooks, even in those that were published recently, in the comments on the Family Code, there was not much space devoted to these issues; usually a few lines or a couple of paragraphs at most. Those who worked on the draft Code were certainly influenced by the stereotype of this already achieved full sex equality, but did not see or did not recognize the new trends in time. This explains some of the Code's major drawbacks.

---

[26] *Ibid.* The part that women had to play in Soviet society was determined more by 'economic necessity than by political ideals'. (See Keniry, 'Proletariat to Pauper: An Analysis of International Law and The Implications of Imperialism for Equality in Post-Communist Russia', in (1996) *American University Journal of International Law and Policy* 11 at 479.) Therefore, feminism, which would reveal quickly the 'just for show' character of 'Soviet equality', was declared as bourgeois and 'a wrecker' movement in the USSR and was in fact forbidden in this country for a long period of time. (See E Kochkina, 'Gendernye raskopki rossiiskoi istorii' ('Gender Excavations of Russian History'), in *V Rossii chto-to proiskhodit ... (Something Is Going On in Russia ...)* (in Russian) (Moscow, 2000) at 123.)

[27] E Kochkina, *op cit.*

[28] It is interesting to note a similarly complicated attitude to gender issues: sceptical – 'not relevant' to the country, 'imported from the West' and, at the same time, negative – closely linked to the Soviet past, within the other post-socialist countries – the former USSR Republics. (See, for example, A Neimanis, *Gender and Human Development in Latvia* (UNDP, Riga, 1999), at 8–9.)

[29] Because of the peculiarities of Russian history in this regard, the Russian movement for sex equality does not fit completely into the Western scheme, where two 'waves' of the women's rights movement are usually distinguished: the first from 1850 until 1920, and the second which began at the end of the 1960s. (See LF Harding, *Family, State, and Social Policy* (Macmillan Press, London, 1996), at 18–19).

SCOTLAND

JUSTICE FOR THE CHILD OFFENDER IN SCOTLAND?

Elaine E Sutherland[*]

I INTRODUCTION

Recent Scottish contributions[1] to the *International Survey* have had two main themes. The first was cautious optimism that the new Scottish Parliament would make a difference, at least in terms of speedier implementation of law reform proposals, and possibly in reflecting the will of the Scottish people, than had been the case prior to devolution. The second involved analysing the impact of the Human Rights Act 1998 which, essentially, incorporated the European Convention on the Protection of Human Rights and Fundamental Freedoms 1950 (hereinafter the 'European Convention') into the legal systems of the United Kingdom. Discussion concentrated on civil, as opposed to criminal, child law. This year, attention will focus on the child in conflict with the criminal law and will continue the previous themes while broadening the second to take account of other relevant international instruments.[2] It might be argued, of course, that this is not 'family law' at all. However, narrow compartmentalisation has often been found to be unhelpful in the family law context.[3] Where, as is the case in Scotland, most children who offend are dealt with through diversion from the criminal courts, and the same forum also deals with children who are in need of protection, the distinction between civil and criminal law is blurred further.

There could not be a better time to examine children in conflict with the criminal law. In Scotland, as elsewhere, there is concern over children offending, with public perception often being fuelled by enthusiastic media reporting of serious or persistent offenders. It seems to make little difference that some of the most sensational reports relate to events outside the country.[4] Virtually all the branches of the legal establishment have been active in the area. In the mid-1990s, the Scottish Office commissioned research into what information was available on youth offending in Scotland with the intention that it should form a base line for

---

[*] Reader, School of Law, University of Glasgow and Professor, Lewis and Clark Law School, Portland, Oregon.

[1] EE Sutherland, 'Consolidation and Anticipation' in *The International Survey of Family Law (2000 Edition)*, ed A Bainham (Family Law, 2000), p 329; EE Sutherland, 'How Children are Faring in the "New Scotland"' in *The International Survey of Family Law (2001 Edition)*, ed A Bainham (Family Law, 2001), p 363.

[2] Passages in this chapter are based upon what the present author wrote in 'The Child in Conflict with the Criminal Law' in *Children's Rights in Scotland*, ed A Cleland and EE Sutherland (W Green, 2001). Thanks go to W Green for permission to use the relevant passages.

[3] For example, the issue of domestic abuse requires consideration of, and coherence between, both criminal and civil law.

[4] Events like the murder of James Bulger, in England, and the series of school shootings, in the USA, have undoubtedly influenced public opinion.

future research.[5] Subsequently, an impressive range of research was commissioned by the Central Research Unit.[6] The Scottish Executive turned its attention to juvenile offending in November 1999 and commissioned a Review of Youth Crime.[7] The Advisory Group[8] set up to conduct the Review produced its First Report[9] in June 2000. The Executive responded[10] and engaged in further consultation. In October 2000, the Scottish Law Commission was invited to consider the age of criminal responsibility and it published a Discussion Paper in July 2001, setting forth its tentative proposals for reform of the law and inviting comment.[11]

Most children and young people who offend in Scotland are dealt with through the children's hearings system, which often diverts them from the criminal courts altogether. The hearings system had already been subject to criticism from the European Court of Human Rights[12] and various reforms, introduced by the Children (Scotland) Act 1995 (hereinafter the '1995 Act') and the corresponding Rules (hereinafter the '1996 Rules'),[13] were designed to meet the criticisms.

The first post-Human Rights Act challenge to the children's hearings system came before the Scottish courts in *S v Miller*.[14] We will return to the case but, briefly, it concerned a 15-year-old boy referred to a children's hearing in respect of his allegedly having committed the offence of assault to severe injury. S was alleged to have assaulted a third party, L, in the course of what appears to have been a fracas involving S, his father, and L, with S's father dying some months

---

[5]   S Asquith, M Buist, N Loughran, C Macaulay and M Montgomery, *Children and Young People Offending in Scotland* (CRU, 1998).

[6]   Reports are usually available on the Central Research Unit's website at *www.scotland.gov.uk/cru* which also provides information on publications pending and research in progress.

[7]   The background to, relevant documents of, and latest news on, the *Youth Crime Review* can be found on the web at *www.scotland.gov.uk/youth/crimereview*.

[8]   The Advisory Group comprised individuals from a wide range of agencies involved in juvenile justice including the judiciary, the children's hearings system, government, social work, education, the police and children offender support and victim support groups. A notable omission from the Working Group was representation of academia, despite the fact that research and commentary on juvenile justice comes, most frequently, from that quarter.

[9]   *Report of Advisory Group on Youth Crime* (2000).

[10] *Scottish Executive Response to the Advisory Group Report on Youth Crime Review* (2000).

[11] *Discussion Paper on the Age of Criminal Responsibility* (Scot Law Com Discussion Paper No 115, 2001). The discussion paper can be found on the web at *http://www.scotlawcom.gov.uk*. Comments are invited by 31 October 2001 and, having considered these, the Scottish Law Commission will produce a report, setting out firm proposals for reform, if such proposals are deemed appropriate. Implementation of any proposals then becomes a matter for the Scottish Parliament.

[12] *McMichael v United Kingdom* (1995) EHRR 205. While this case was concerned with child protection, the European Court was critical of a number of aspects of the hearings system generally, including the fact that, while reports of social workers and others were available to panel members, only the 'substance' of the reports was made known to the child and the family. As a result, the Children's Hearings (Scotland) Rules 1996 now provide for reports being made available to the 'relevant persons' (usually parents, see below), although they are still not given to the child. This was one of the issues addressed in *S v Miller* 2001 SLT 531, discussed below.

[13] The Children's Hearings (Scotland) Rules 1996 (SI 1996/3261) supplement the 1995 Act.

[14] 2001 SLT 531. The case can be accessed on the Scottish Courts website at *www.scotcourts.gov.uk*.

later as a result of injuries sustained during the incident.[15] In many ways, the decision is disappointing. Instead of grasping the opportunity to subject the hearings system to rigorous analysis in the light of the broad range of international standards on juvenile justice, the Inner House of the Court of Session chose to plump for a narrow, somewhat technical, interpretation of the European Convention and concluded that children's hearings were not the 'determination of a criminal charge' and the child was not a person 'charged with a criminal offence'. Neither the United Nations Convention on the Rights of the Child 1989 (hereinafter, the 'UN Convention'), nor a wealth of other international material, was addressed.[16] This is particularly regrettable since it is trite law that the European Convention is a 'living instrument' and the European Court has not been slow to utilise the UN Convention as an aid to construing its own, rather adult-centric provisions.[17] On a more positive note, the case illustrates attempts by both the legislature and the Scottish Children's Reporter Administration to make the hearings system more compliant with the European Convention, albeit cynics might observe that these were simply pre-emptive defensive strikes on matters that should have been addressed long ago.

That the Scottish courts are currently preoccupied with the European Convention is hardly surprising, not least because of the deluge of cases since the Human Rights Act 1998 came into force. However, this does not explain the somewhat schizophrenic attitude of the legal establishment to the UN Convention. On the one hand, when considering how the law on physical punishment of children might be reformed, the Scottish Executive downplayed the Convention stating that 'its provisions do not have the force of law in Scotland'.[18] On the other hand, the importance of the UN Convention has been acknowledged in other law reform proposals[19] and by the courts.[20]

---

[15] The possibility that S may have been attempting to defend his father, thus raising the issue of self-defence, is hinted at: see Lord Penrose at p 562.

[16] Since cases in Scottish courts proceed on an adversarial basis, it might be argued that the judiciary simply decide a given case on the basis of what is argued by counsel. However, judges regularly shake off this passive role and, indeed, in *S v Miller*, Lord Rodger (at p 539) demonstrated his own extensive scholarship on European criminal law.

[17] See, for example, *Keegan v Ireland* (1993) 18 EHRR 342 (Art 7 of UN Convention used in interpreting Art 8 of the European Convention) and *Costello-Roberts v United Kingdom* (1994) 19 EHRR 112 (Art 16 of UN Convention used in interpreting Arts 3 and 8 of the European Convention). In *T v United Kingdom* and *V v United Kingdom* (2000) 30 EHRR 121, it made use of both the Beijing Rules and the UN Convention in finding that the European Convention rights of two 10-year-olds, convicted after trial of the murder of a 2-year-old in England in 1993, had been breached.

[18] Scottish Executive, *The Physical Punishment of Children: A Consultation* (Scottish Executive, 2000), para 3.25. This is not an accurate statement, particularly in the context of law reform. After indefensible delay, the Deputy First Minister indicated, on 6 September 2001, that the Scottish Parliament would soon have the opportunity to consider draft legislation dealing with physical punishment of children. Disappointingly, the proposed legislation will not ban all physical punishment of children and, thus, will fall short of the UN Convention standards. See 'No smacking rule for children under three', Scottish Executive Press Release, SE3050/2001, which can be found on *http://www.scotland.gov.uk/pages/news/2001/09/SE3050.aspx* for a description of the proposed legislation. Public and media reaction to the proposed legislation has been mixed and it remains to be seen what actually emerges from the legislative process.

[19] See, for example, *Report on Family Law* Scot Law Com No 135 (1992) and *Discussion Paper on the Age of Criminal Responsibility* Scot Law Com Discussion Paper No 115 (2001).

II   INTERNATIONAL STANDARDS

What, then, are the international standards in the context of juvenile justice? Drafted, as it was, with the needs of post-World War II Europe in mind, the European Convention is not generally child-specific. However, and stating the obvious, 'children are human beings too' and the human rights guaranteed by the European Convention, including the prohibition on torture (Art 3), the right to liberty and security (Art 5), the right to a fair trial (Art 6) and the right to respect for private and family life (Art 8), apply to children.

The UN Convention, being child-specific, addresses juvenile justice directly in Arts 37 and 40 and, of course, other provisions are relevant. In addition, several other international instruments address juvenile justice issues. The International Covenant on Civil and Political Rights 1966 addresses certain narrow areas of the administration of juvenile justice, requiring: the separation of juveniles and adults; speedy adjudication; and that trial procedures should take account of the age of juveniles and the desirability of promoting their rehabilitation.[21] The United Nations Standard Minimum Rules for the Administration of Juvenile Justice, known as the Beijing Rules and adopted in 1985, address the administration of juvenile justice from the perspectives of the child's rights and child development. While the Beijing Rules predate the UN Convention, a number of the Rules find expression in Art 40, thus making them binding, at least in international law terms. In 1990, the United Nations adopted two further instruments, the United Nations Guidelines for the Prevention of Juvenile Delinquency, known as the Riyadh Guidelines, and the United Nations Rules for the Protection of Juveniles Deprived of their Liberty, known as the JDL Rules. Unless incorporated into the UN Convention, these 'rules' or 'guidelines' are of similar, non-binding, effect.[22] However, the European Court and courts in other jurisdictions[23] have cited them and they should be seen as a part of the general regime of international regulation of juvenile justice, albeit they were not mentioned in *S v Miller*.

That prevention is a primary goal of the juvenile justice system is recognised both specifically, through the Riyadh Guidelines and, more generally, through the UN Convention, when it seeks to promote the welfare and inclusion of children. International regulation has several strands, but fundamental is the importance of recognising the child's age, both in the context of ascribing responsibility and in the conduct of proceedings.[24] Respect for human rights, including the presumption of innocence, information of the charges, decision by an independent and

---

[20]   In *White v White* 2001 SLT 485, at p 494, Lord McCluskey stressed that 'the presumption to be applied when interpreting legislation found to be ambiguous is that Parliament is to be presumed to have legislated in conformity with the [UN] Convention, not in conflict with it'. Of course, this is of no help whatsoever, when domestic law is unambiguously inconsistent with the Convention.

[21]   Arts 10(2)(b) and 14(4).

[22]   For a discussion of the various forms of international regulation and their interaction, see G Van Bueren, *The International Law on the Rights of the Child* (Martinus Nijhoff Publishers, 1995), chapter 7. See also U Kilkelly, *The Child and the European Convention on Human Rights* (Ashgate, 1999), chapter 3.

[23]   See, for example, *McKerry v Teesdale and Wear Valley Justices* (unreported) 7 February 2000, QBD, where reference was made to the Beijing Rules.

[24]   See, for example, UN Convention, Art 40(3) and Beijing Rules, r 14.

impartial body in a fair hearing, and legal or other assistance, is stressed.[25] In addition, the child's well-being is a concern, with continuity of family relationships being an integral part of that well-being.[26] The child's reintegration into society is also viewed as an important goal, and Van Bueren explains the shift in emphasis from 'rehabilitation' to 'reintegration' as reflecting the greater responsibility placed on society, rather than the individual, in the latter.[27] That is not to suggest that the child is absolved of developing a sense of responsibility for his or her actions, although the focus is on helping the child to do so by promoting his or her sense of belonging in society.[28] Having a suitably wide-ranging and effective variety of dispositions is inherent in this process.[29]

Article 37(3) of the UN Convention encourages diversion of children from formal trial, provided that 'human rights and legal safeguards are fully respected'. In the light of this and the fact that the emphasis in the hearings system on the paramountcy of the child's welfare,[30] and on the participation of the child[31] and the family[32] in the process, one might expect that the children's hearings system would be seen as one of the United Kingdom's showpiece institutions. Any such expectation was shown to be illusory when the United Kingdom ratified the UN Convention subject to a specific reservation in respect of the children's hearings system, principally due to the lack of legal representation offered, at least in the early stages of intake into the system.[33] In its *Concluding Observations on the United Kingdom*, the UN Committee on the Rights of the Child identified juvenile justice as one of its 'Principal subjects of concern'. It stated:

'The administration of the juvenile justice system in the State party is a matter of general concern to the Committee. The low age of criminal responsibility and the

---

[25] Art 37(2).

[26] UN Convention, Arts 5 and 9; Beijing Rules, r 19; and JDL Rules, r 59.

[27] *The International Law on the Rights of the Child*, op cit, at pp 172, 173.

[28] Beijing Rules, rr 10 and 11.

[29] UN Convention, Art 40(4).

[30] 1995 Act, s 16(1).

[31] *Ibid*, ss 16(2) and 45(1).

[32] *Ibid*, s 45(8) and 1996 Rules, r 7. The 1995 Act uses the term 'relevant person'. A relevant person is anyone, including a parent, who has parental responsibilities or rights in respect of the child, or who appears ordinarily (other than by reason of employment) to have charge of, or control over, the child: 1995 Act, s 93(2). If the non-marital father has not acquired parental responsibilities or rights and is not caring for the child he is not a relevant person, a position which the European Court found unobjectionable in *McMichael v United Kingdom* (above). He is permitted to attend a hearing if he qualifies as the genetic father, but not on equal terms with relevant persons.

[33] The Reservation was in the following terms: 'In Scotland there are tribunals (known as "children's hearings") which consider the welfare of the child and deal with the majority of offences which a child is alleged to have committed. In some cases, mainly of a welfare nature, the child is temporarily deprived of its liberty for up to seven days prior to attending the hearing. The child and its family are, however, allowed access to a lawyer during this period. Although the decisions of the hearings are subject to appeal to the courts, legal representation is not permitted at the proceedings of the children's hearings themselves. Children's hearings have proved over the years to be a very effective way of dealing with the problems of children in a less formal, non-adversarial manner. Accordingly, the United Kingdom, in respect of Art 37(d), reserves its right to continue the present operation of children's hearings.'

national legislation relating to the administration of juvenile justice seem not to be compatible with the provisions of the Convention, namely Articles 37 and 40.'[34]

Given that the *First Report of the UK to the Committee on the Rights of the Child* focused on the position in England and Wales, with only passing reference to Scotland, it may be that the Committee did not understand the nature and fundamental welfare-based philosophy of the children's hearings system.[35] Nonetheless, we cannot assume that the Committee had no knowledge of the hearings system which, as we shall see, is open to objection on a number of grounds. Due to legislative changes implemented in the Children (Scotland) Act 1995, the United Kingdom Government felt able to withdraw the reservation on 18 April 1997. It may have been premature and over-optimistic in so doing. The United Kingdom's *Second Report* to the UN Committee on the Rights of the Child, which has a separate section devoted to Scotland, is very much more upbeat and confident on the issue of juvenile justice.[36] Whether the carefully crafted account will blind the Committee to some of the system's patent shortcomings will only be known when the Committee's second *Concluding Observations on the United Kingdom* are published.

III THE JUVENILE OFFENDER IN SCOTLAND

Age of criminal responsibility and the fora for decisions

In Scotland, criminal responsibility can attach from the time a child is eight years old[37] and it is far from a matter for pride that Scots law sets one of the lowest such ages in the world.[38] Usually, the child's chronological age at the time of the alleged offence is used in establishing criminal responsibility, but where it can be demonstrated that a child's actual mental capacity is less than the chronological age, the former will govern responsibility.

The UN Convention requires that *an* age of criminal responsibility should be identified, but it does not attempt to specify *what that age should be*.[39] This is a failing of the UN Convention continued from the Beijing Rules. As we have seen,

---

[34] CRC/C/15/Add 34, para 17.

[35] For a discussion of the Anglo-centric nature of the United Kingdom's First Report, see John P Grant, 'Enforcing Children's International Human Rights' in Cleland and Sutherland, *Children's Rights in Scotland, op cit*, chapter 16.

[36] Convention on the Rights of the Child: Second Report to the UN Committee on the Rights of the Child by the United Kingdom 1999, paras 2.9, 2.11 and 2.12. Strictly speaking, this is the First Periodic Report but, since it is the UK's second actual report, that term is used here.

[37] Criminal Procedure (Scotland) Act 1995, s 41. Where a child is below eight years old, he or she has no criminal capacity and cannot commit an offence.

[38] H Johnson, 'Age of Criminal Proceedings in Europe' in *Child Offenders: UK and International Practice* (Howard League for Penal Reform, 1995), p 14 cites the relevant ages provided in a Parliamentary Answer from 27 February 1995. A Lockyer and FH Stone (eds), *Juvenile Justice in Scotland: Twenty-Five Years of the Welfare Approach* (T&T Clark, 1999), at p 245, provides a table of the age of criminal responsibility in other European countries. Both illustrate that most European countries have an age of criminal responsibility considerably higher than 8, with many countries opting for 14, 15 or 16.

[39] Art 40(3)(a).

in its *Concluding Observations on the United Kingdom*,[40] the UN Committee on the Rights of the Child expressed concern over the low age of criminal responsibility in the various parts of the United Kingdom. The European Convention is silent on the issue of age and the lack of international consensus led the European Court to conclude that there had been no violation of Art 3 in *T v United Kingdom* and *V v United Kingdom*.[41]

It is sometimes suggested that the low age of criminal responsibility does not really matter since the vast majority of children who infringe the criminal law in Scotland are dealt with through the children's hearings system, a system which deals also with children in need of protection. The operation of that system and its shortcomings, most notably in human rights terms, will be examined presently. However, it must be remembered that it remains possible for a child as young as eight years old to be prosecuted before an ordinary (adult) criminal court, albeit there is provision for involving the hearings system in advising on disposal.[42] Whether a child under 16 is diverted to the hearings system or tried in a criminal court is, essentially, a matter for prosecutorial discretion. Prosecution of children must be 'at the instance of the Lord Advocate'[43] and successive Lords Advocate have addressed their responsibility by issuing guidelines, the most recent dating from 1996, indicating which offences should be considered for prosecution.[44]

In order to get a sense of what is actually happening, it may be helpful to review the statistics on children's hearings and prosecution. Statistics on children's hearings are readily available and, in 1999/2000, there were 30,598 offence referrals to hearings.[45] Statistics on the prosecution of children under 16 are not readily available, but the Scottish Law Commission reports that, in 1999, only 105 such young people faced criminal proceedings, with the vast majority of them being 14- or 15-year-old males.[46] As the Commission puts it 'only about

---

[40]   CRC/C/15/Add 34.

[41]   (2000) 30 EHRR 121. Despite the provision of legal representation and special arrangements made in the way the court proceedings were conducted, the accused, by virtue of their ages and states of mind, were unable to participate effectively in the proceedings and, thus, had been denied the right to a fair hearing, in breach of Art 6(1), para 89.

[42]   Criminal Procedure (Scotland) Act 1995, s 49.

[43]   *Ibid*, s 42.

[44]   There are three categories of offences covered. First are offences which require prosecution on indictment, including the pleas of the Crown, certain statutory offences, and other serious offences like assault to severe injury and possession of a class A drug with intent to supply. The second category is restricted to persons over the age of 15 years where disqualification from driving is either a mandatory or optional sentence upon conviction, not being a disposal available to a children's hearing. The third category covers children over the age of 16 who are already subject to a supervision requirement from a children's hearing. It should be noted that a reporter's decision not to refer a child to a hearing does not preclude prosecution: *Mackinnon v Dempsey* (unreported) 9 November 1984 (High Court).

[45]   *Statistical Bulletin: Referrals of Children to Reporters and Children's Hearings 1999/2000* (SCRA/MJH2000/24), Table 4. This is an increase of 26.5% on the offence referrals in 1989: p 4. It should be noted that referrals overall increased by 71%, with non-offence referrals increasing by 167%.

[46]   *Discussion Paper on the Age of Criminal Responsibility* Scot Law Com Discussion Paper No 115 (2001), Annex C, at pp 47 and 48. Five males below the age of 14 were prosecuted and all 10 of the females prosecuted were 14 or 15 years old. While the number of children prosecuted has been dropping over the last few years, the reduction between 1998 and 1999 is particularly significant. For previous years, the figures cited by the Commission are: 1994 (246 children prosecuted), 1995 (243), 1996 (203), 1997 (189) and 1998 (179).

0.5%' of children who are accused of offending are dealt with by the criminal courts and the majority of them are referred to a children's hearing for disposal.[47]

The matter of the age of criminal responsibility was referred to the Scottish Law Commission and it has given its tentative views in a Discussion Paper.[48] It addresses the lower age limit only and provides an interesting discussion of two possible meanings of the concept encapsulated in an 'age of criminal responsibility'. First, it can mean the age when a person acquires the capacity to commit a criminal act and, secondly, it can mean the age at which a person may be prosecuted in a criminal court. Concluding that the ages cited by other jurisdictions as their 'age of criminal responsibility' may mean one or other of these, it neatly side-steps the fact that Scotland has a peculiarly low age limit for capacity. It then goes on to conclude that we should abolish the age of criminal responsibility, in the sense of capacity, altogether. Instead, we should consider restricting prosecution on the basis of either an age-based presumption or a statutory rule. If a young person is ineligible for prosecution, the Commission suggests that it should be possible, nonetheless, for him or her to be referred to a children's hearing in respect of the (alleged) conduct. It is certainly arguable that such a system would breach Art 40(3)(a) of the UN Convention, which makes specific reference to 'the establishment of a minimum age below which children shall be presumed not to have the capacity to infringe the penal law'. As the figures cited above illustrate, prosecutorial restraint has been a feature of the system to date. It may be this restraint that led the Commission to contemplate recommendations which, if a presumption rather than a rule on a minimum age for prosecution were adopted, would allow for too much prosecutorial discretion. As experience in the US demonstrates, prosecutors are all too open to fashions and the particular unpopularity of a given offence or offender.[49]

In terms of age and prosecution, it should also be noted that, once a young person reaches 16 years old, he or she will usually be beyond the embrace of the hearings system altogether, despite the fact that the UN Convention applies to all persons below the age of 18.[50] Thus, 16- and 17-year-olds face prosecution in adult criminal courts. The Advisory Group on Youth Crime has suggested that children's hearings might deal with 16- and 17-year-old offenders, although it seems somewhat confused over whether the hearing should continue to be based on the 'welfare' model or should adopt a more 'justice' based approach.[51]

---

[47]   *Ibid*, para 3.11.

[48]   *Discussion Paper on the Age of Criminal Responsibility, op cit.*

[49]   See, for example, L Blumhardt, 'In the Best Interests of the Child: Juvenile Justice or Adult Retribution' (2000) 24 U Haw L Rev 341; SM Davis, 'The Criminalization of Juvenile Justice: Legislative Responses to the "Phantom Menace"' (2000) 70 Miss LJ 1; C Dejong and ES Merill, 'Getting "Tough on Crime": Juvenile Waiver and the Criminal Court' (2001) 27 Ohio NUL Rev 175; EK Klein, 'Dennis the Menace or Billy the Kid: An Analysis of the Role of Transfer to Criminal Court in Juvenile Justice' (1998) 35 Am Crim L Rev 371; T Kole, 'Juvenile Offenders' (2001) 38 Har J Leg 231.

[50]   Art 1 defines a child as being 'below the age of 18 years of age'.

[51]   At one stage it appears to adhere to the welfare approach: Annex C, para 14. However, it also appears to anticipate incorporating elements of a 'justice' model into the hearings system alongside the 'welfare' model: paras 11 and 12.

IV THE CHILDREN'S HEARINGS SYSTEM

Detailed description of the procedure for a children's hearing can be found elsewhere.[52] However, before we examine aspects of the children's hearings system in the light of international standards, it may be helpful to some readers to provide a (very) brief outline of how the system operates in the context of children who are alleged to have committed offences.

Cases come into the system through the Principal Reporter, who has the statutory duty to assess whether a hearing should be convened.[53] In practice, decisions are taken about a particular child by one of the many individual reporters employed throughout Scotland. In assessing the need for a hearing, the reporter must address two issues.[54] First, he or she must be satisfied that there is a *prima facie* case establishing one of the conditions for referral, perhaps better known as the 'grounds for referral'.[55] If no ground of referral applies to the child, then a hearing is incompetent. Secondly, the reporter must believe that compulsory measures of supervision may be necessary. It may frequently be the case that, while a ground of referral exists, the reporter is satisfied that the child's needs can be met by other means or, indeed, that no action is necessary at all.[56] The reporter has enormous discretion in reaching his or her decision and, while the 1995 Act does not make any direction on this point,[57] will be guided by what will serve the child's welfare.

Where the reporter decides that a hearing is necessary,[58] he or she will go on to make the appropriate arrangements.[59] Fundamental to the hearings system are the panel members who sit in groups of three to hear a particular case. Panel members are drawn from the community and trained to discharge their role.[60] The idea is that, once the allegations are accepted or established in court, these lay people will explore not only the allegations but the whole circumstances of the child's life in discussion with the child and the 'relevant persons' (essentially, the child's parents and other persons who look after the child).[61] In order to assist it,

---

[52] See B Kearney, *Children's Hearings and the Sheriff Court* (W Green, 2nd edn, 2000,);
K McK Norrie, *Children's Hearings in Scotland* (W Green, 1997); and EE Sutherland, *Child and Family Law* (T & T Clark, 1999), chapter 9.

[53] 1995 Act, s 56.

[54] *Ibid*, s 52(1).

[55] We are concerned here with the child who is alleged to have committed an offence, and this is one of the grounds. Others include traditional 'child protection' references, like the allegation that the child is suffering due to a lack of parental care or has been the victim of certain offences. Yet others refer to what are known, in other jurisdictions, as 'status offences', like the allegation that the child is beyond parental control, misusing drugs or alcohol or failing to attend school. For a discussion of 'status offences', see section **IV.G** below.

[56] 1995 Act, s 56(4). In 1999/2000, 66% of referrals to reporters resulted in no formal action being taken. Of these, compulsory intervention was deemed unnecessary in 44% of the referrals, while, in a further 13%, the child was already under supervision: *Statistical Bulletin*, Table 9.

[57] While s 16(1) directs the court and the children's hearing to regard the child's welfare throughout childhood as the paramount consideration, no similar direction is given to the reporter.

[58] Where the reporter decides not to arrange a hearing, he or she must inform the child, the relevant persons and the person who brought the matter to his or her attention: 1995 Act, s 56(4)(a).

[59] 1995 Act, s 56(6).

[60] *Ibid*, s 38.

[61] *Ibid*, s 45(8). See footnote 32 for the definition of 'relevant person'.

the hearing will have a variety of reports about the child's background from the local authority's social work department, the child's school and, in some cases, other relevant professionals.

The conduct of the hearing is a matter for the chairman of each hearing and he or she is directed to permit attendance only by persons whose presence is necessary for the proper consideration of the case and to take all reasonable steps to keep the number of persons present to a minimum.[62] However, the child and the relevant persons are entitled, and (usually) obliged, to attend the hearing,[63] subject to possible exclusion of the relevant persons and their representatives.[64] The child and each relevant person may be accompanied by a person to assist them at the hearing[65] and, while the representative may be legally qualified, prior to the decision in *S v Miller*, the absence of legal aid to pay for representation at hearings means that this was not standard practice. The three panel members selected to serve on a particular hearing will be present, as will the reporter, since he or she is obliged to make a record of the hearing. Any safeguarder appointed by the hearing will usually be present.[66] Given the local authority's duty to provide a social background report and to implement decisions of the hearing,[67] a social worker is usually present and is likely to participate in discussions. The right of journalists to be present at a hearing is subject to the hearing's power to exclude them.[68]

The first thing the chairman of the hearing must do, after introducing those present and explaining the purpose of the hearing, is to explain the grounds of referral to the child and the relevant persons, and only where the child and the relevant persons accept the grounds of referral can the hearing proceed.[69] If the child does not understand the grounds of referral, the hearing can either discharge the referral or direct the reporter to apply to a court for a finding as to whether any of the grounds of referral is established.[70] Where the child or any of the relevant persons do not accept the grounds of referral, the hearing can, again, either discharge the referral or direct the reporter to apply to a court for a finding as to whether any of the grounds of referral is established.[71] Where the child or the relevant persons accept only part of the grounds of referral, the hearing can proceed with the hearing in respect of those grounds,[72] or it can discharge the referral, or direct the reporter to apply to a court for a finding as to whether any of the grounds of referral are established.[73] Where the child and the relevant persons accept the grounds of referral as stated, the hearing proceeds to the next stage.[74]

---

[62]   1995 Act, s 41.

[63]   *Ibid*, s 45.

[64]   *Ibid*, s 46.

[65]   1996 Rules, r 11.

[66]   A safeguarder is an independent person appointed by the children's hearing or a sheriff to protect and promote the child's interests; 1995 Act, s 41.

[67]   1995 Act, s 71.

[68]   *Ibid*, s 43(3) and (4).

[69]   *Ibid*, s 64(1).

[70]   *Ibid*, s 65(9).

[71]   *Ibid*, s 65(7)(a).

[72]   *Ibid*, s 65(6).

[73]   *Ibid*, s 67(7)(b).

[74]   *Ibid*, s 65(5).

Where the reporter applies to a court for a finding as to whether the child has committed an offence, proof beyond reasonable doubt is required,[75] with proof in all other cases being on the balance of probabilities. Legal aid has always been available to the child and the relevant person to fund representation at this stage.[76] Where the court finds that none of the grounds of referral have been established, he or she must dismiss the application and discharge the referral.[77] Where the court finds any of the grounds of referral to have been established, it will remit the case back to the reporter to arrange for a hearing to determine the case.[78]

Where the grounds of referral are accepted by the child and the relevant persons or are established in court, the hearing moves on to consider the case. In the case of accepted grounds, the whole process will often be continuous. The hearing considers not only the grounds of referral but also any available reports, including social background reports, and other relevant information.[79] It is of the essence of the hearings system that everyone involved should have the opportunity to participate freely in seeking a positive way forward for the child, and the hearing is directed to discuss the case with the child, the relevant persons, any representative and any safeguarder.

Having considered the case fully, the hearing will then decide on the appropriate disposal of the case. The disposal must be made in the light of the welfare principle,[80] and the following options are open to the hearing: to continue the case; to discharge the referral; to make a supervision requirement.[81] An appeal may be taken to the sheriff court against the decision of a hearing and further appeal on a point of law may be taken to the Sheriff Principal and the Court of Session.[82] In very limited circumstances, there is provision for returning to court where new evidence emerges after a hearing has decided a case.[83] Where a supervision requirement is made, the decision of a hearing must be reviewed by a future hearing within a year and it is possible for the case to be reviewed at an earlier stage.[84] This, then, was the system that was in place when the challenges in *S v Miller* were brought. Below, various aspects of the hearings system are addressed, albeit many of the questions raised were neither asked nor answered in the case.

---

[75] *Ibid*, s 68(3).

[76] *Ibid*, s 68(4).

[77] *Ibid*, s 68(9).

[78] *Ibid*, s 68(10)(a).

[79] *Ibid*, s 69(1).

[80] *Ibid*, s 16(1).

[81] *Ibid*, s 69. 'Supervision' may mean that the child is required to reside in a residential establishment or foster care but, more often, means that the child returns home with social work assistance being provided in some cases.

[82] 1995 Act, s 51.

[83] *Ibid*, s 85.

[84] *Ibid*, s 73.

A   The welfare approach

The children's hearings system is predicated upon treating the child's needs, not punishing his or her deeds.[85] How does this approach measure up to international standards? As we have seen, the UN Convention favours procedures specially designed for children who have fallen foul of the criminal law 'providing that human rights and legal safeguards are fully respected'.[86] It then proceeds to list particular safeguards[87] and these are, not surprisingly, very similar to the fair hearing requirements found in Art 6 of the European Convention. Can these requirements be met in a system premised on the welfare approach? The problem lies, not in the welfare approach itself, but the danger that, in the course of applying it, the hearing can lose sight of the fundamental human rights guarantees. Since the earliest days of the hearings system, warnings have been given that it might not pass muster when subjected to scrutiny in the light of these human rights requirements.[88] Respecting the child's rights to a fair trial does not necessarily mean that juveniles can never be treated differently to adults and, indeed, the limited capacity of juveniles may, itself, mandate different treatment. However, in the name of taking a welfare approach in respect of a juvenile offender, we must not forget that he or she has rights.

Until the decision in *S v Miller*, it was widely assumed that the whole parcel of rights found in Art 6 of the European Convention and Arts 37 and 40 of the UN Convention applied to children's hearings proceedings where the child was referred to the hearing under s 52(2)(i) of the 1995 Act on the basis of his or her alleged commission of an offence. The First Division unanimously rejected that approach when it concluded that, despite a referral under that provision having its roots in an allegation of criminal conduct by the child, the referral did not amount to 'determination of a criminal charge' and the child was not a person 'charged with a criminal offence'.[89] Without wishing to over-simplify the numerous factors which influenced the decision, the *sui generis* nature of hearings[90] and the lack of any penalty being levelled against the child were particularly influential. The court relied on the fact that the child's welfare substantially determines what, if any, compulsory measures of supervision may be ordered in respect of the child. With respect, this approach fails to address the fundamental tension which exists between welfare and rights; a matter on which there is extensive case-law and literature, not least from the US,[91] and in relation to the UN Convention. The

---

[85]   *Report of the Committee on Children and Young Persons* Cmnd 2306 (1964), known as the 'Kilbrandon Report', at para 15. For a discussion of the Kilbrandon philosophy, see Lockyer and Stone, *Juvenile Justice in Scotland: Twenty-Five Years of the Welfare Approach, op cit*, chapters 1 and 2, and EE Sutherland, *Child and Family Law, op cit*, paras 9.5, 9.7.

[86]   Art 40(3)(b).

[87]   Art 40(2).

[88]   See, for example, JP Grant, 'The legal safeguards for the rights of the child and the parents in children's hearings' (1975) JR 209.

[89]   The court considered this issue at length and each of the judgments warrants reading in full; see pp 537–540 (The Lord President), pp 552–557 (Lord Penrose) and pp 568–577 (Lord Macfadyen).

[90]   *McGregor v T* 1975 SLT 76; *Kennedy v O* 1975 SLT 235; *McGregor v D* 1977 SC 330.

[91]   This was the thrust of the reasoning of the US Supreme Court in *In re Gault* 387 US 1 (1967) where it criticised the lack of due process protection afforded to a juvenile in the system operating

decision is all the more regrettable since the court was presented with persuasive examples of the criminal nature of referrals under section 52(2)(i).[92]

It was accepted, however, that the decision of a children's hearing could affect the child's civil rights and obligations, both in respect of his or her liberty and in respect of freedom of family life.[93] The distinction is important since the European Convention affords greater protection to the individual in the context of criminal, as opposed to civil, proceedings. Indeed, it was the court's finding in this respect, combined with eleventh-hour responses by the legislature and the Principal Reporter,[94] that saved the hearings system from the damning criticism it might otherwise have attracted.[95] Assuming that the Inner House decision is not subject to a successful appeal (and none is pending), this means that future challenges to children's hearings proceedings under the European Convention will have to be based on the civil protections offered to an individual, under Art 6(1), rather than the more extensive protection offered by Art 6(2) and (3).

Where does this leave the UN Convention requirements? While some of its provisions refer to a child being deprived of his or her liberty,[96] other provisions regulate the rights of the child 'alleged as or accused of'[97] and, sometimes, 'recognised as',[98] 'having infringed the penal law'. No mention was made of the UN Convention in the course of *S v Miller*, but it is possible that these phrases might be subject to the same narrow interpretation as was Art 6 of the European Convention. Indeed, it might be that the UN Convention's emphasis on the paramountcy of the child's welfare would again be used to distinguish children's hearings proceedings from criminal proceedings. On the other hand, it must be remembered that Art 40(3)(b) of the UN Convention stresses the need to respect the child's 'human rights and legal safeguards' in any special procedures for dealing with children diverted from the criminal justice system. In the light of the European Court's willingness to use the UN Convention to flesh out its own, rather adult-centred, provisions, it is regrettable that this point was not made to the

---

at the time. In the cases which followed *Gault*, the court took the opportunity to explore, in more detail, which rights extended to the juvenile in the criminal process and which did not: see *In re Winship* 397 US 358 (1970), *McKiever v Pennsylvania* 404 US 528 (1971), *Breed v Jones* 421 US 519 (1975), *Schall v Martin* 467 US 253 (1984), *New Jersey v TLO* 469 US 325 (1985). Had the Inner House undertaken a rigorous evaluation of the juvenile justice system and children's rights, it could have drawn on this wealth of material to achieve, at a stroke, what took years to accomplish in the US. It should be remembered that the movement, in the US, away from what was perceived by some as a 'liberal' model of juvenile justice was prompted, at least in part, by a desire for more punitive responses to juvenile offending.

[92] Unlike all the other grounds of referral, the criminal, rather than the civil, standard of proof applies to this ground of referral; the civil rules of evidence in respect of corroboration and hearsay evidence do not; and the Rehabilitation of Offenders Act 1974 applies.

[93] See p 540 (The Lord President), pp 557–558 (Lord Penrose) and pp 576–577 (Lord Macfadyen).

[94] These related to legal aid and documents being made available to children and are discussed below.

[95] In the words of Lord Penrose at p 577, 'Had I been of the opinion that the proceedings were criminal in the relevant sense, there would, in my view, have been a substantial issue whether the system was structurally defective in failing to provide adequate guarantees for the purposes of Art 6'.

[96] Art 37(b) and (d).

[97] Art 40(2)(b).

[98] Art 40(1) and (2)(a).

Inner House. One can only speculate on how the European Court would have treated the matter until it is given the opportunity to do so.

The welfare approach to juvenile justice raises a second issue. In the name of attempting to serve the child's welfare, the legal system may intrude more in the child's life than it would were it simply seeking to punish a wrongdoer. We must examine whether the particular disposal employed actually does anything effective to serve or promote the child's welfare. Perhaps what is really being stressed here is that 'welfare' is more than just good intentions. Essentially, the question is 'Are the measures taken effective?'.

B   Do children's hearings provide a fair and public hearing within a reasonable time before an independent and impartial tribunal?

Article 6(1) of the European Convention requires that, in the determination of civil rights and obligations, an individual is entitled to a 'fair and public hearing within a reasonable time by an independent and impartial tribunal established by law'.[99] That a children's hearing is a tribunal established by law[100] appears uncontentious and the issue of delay is one which the system itself has addressed.[101] The independence of panel members, in terms of their mode of appointment,[102] appears unobjectionable, given that the European Court relies on such factors as 'the existence of guarantees against outside pressures and the question whether the body presents an appearance of independence'.[103] 'Impartiality' denotes a lack of prejudice or bias[104] and requires compliance with both a subjective and an objective test. Harris *et al* find it unsurprising that a breach of the subjective test has never been established before the European Court, since it requires a showing of actual personal bias by the particular judge.[105] Demonstrating a breach of the objective test may be slightly easier to satisfy, since that test requires, essentially, that justice should 'be seen to be done'. Most of the European case-law here relates to trial judges who have been involved in earlier stages of the cases

---

[99]   The right applies also to criminal proceedings and Art 40(2)(b)(iii) of the UN Convention is couched in similar terms.

[100]   A 'tribunal' has been defined by the European Court as 'determining matters within its competence on the basis of rules of law and after proceedings conducted in a prescribed manner': *Belilos v Switzerland* (1988) 10 EHRR 466, para 64. Appeal lies to a court where a children's hearing is not conducted in the prescribed manner, something which recent research has found remains a problem: C Hallett and C Murray with J Jamieson and B Veitch, *The Evaluation of Children's Hearings in Scotland: Volume I: Deciding in Children's Interests* (CRU, 1998).

[101]   *The Blueprint for the Processing of Children's Hearings Cases, Inter-agency Code of Practice and National Standards* (Scottish Office Social Work Services Group, 1999) provides guidance on how cases can be dealt with timeously.

[102]   The fact that they are appointed by the Scottish Ministers, sometimes on the advice of the local Children's Panel Advisory Committee, and can only be dismissed by the Scottish Ministers with the consent of the Lord President, protects against the kind of challenge made successfully to the mode of appointment of temporary sheriffs in *Starrs v Ruxton* 2000 SLT 42.

[103]   *Campbell and Fell v United Kingdom* (1984) 7 EHRR 165, para 78.

[104]   *Piersack v Belgium* (1982) 5 EHRR 169, para 30.

[105]   DJ Harris, M O'Boyle and C Warbrick, *Law of the European Convention on Human Rights* (Butterworths, 1995), p 237.

disposed of by them.[106] The real concern for the hearings system, in terms of independence and impartiality, relates to the role of the reporter in assisting panel members in their deliberation, a matter to which we will return presently.

However, in order to satisfy the European and UN Conventions, it is not enough that the tribunal should be independent and impartial. The individual must also be given a 'fair hearing'. While in civil cases, the right to be present at the hearing is not absolute, it has been supported where the individual's 'personal character and manner of life' are at issue.[107] Provided it is 'established in an unequivocal manner and ... attended by minimum safeguards commensurate to its importance', a person may waive his or her right to be present.[108] The child has both a right and a duty to attend the hearing, albeit he or she can be freed from the obligation to attend, where such presence would be detrimental to his or her interests.[109] It is difficult to imagine circumstances in which it would be detrimental to a child accused of having committed an offence to be present and, in any event, the child cannot be prevented from attending the hearing if he or she wishes to do so.[110]

Yet another aspect of a 'fair hearing' is the concept of 'equality of arms'. This requires that 'each party must be afforded a reasonable opportunity to present his case – including his evidence – under conditions that do not place him at a substantial disadvantage vis-à-vis his opponent'.[111] As we saw in respect of the requirement of an 'independent and impartial tribunal', the notion of justice being seen to be done is important.[112]

What of the 'public' nature of the hearing to which the accused is entitled under both the European and UN Conventions? Article 6(1) of the European Convention contains a whole range of exceptions to the requirement of 'public' justice permitting the exclusion of the public and the press from proceedings. The most significant of these, in the context of children, is the power to exclude 'from all or part of the trial ... where the interests of juveniles or the private lives of the parties so require'. In addition, Art 8(1) guarantees individuals respect for private and family life. The UN Convention requires full respect for the child's privacy

---

[106] See, for example, *Piersack v Belgium* (above) (presiding judge had previously been head of the department of the public prosecutor's office that had investigated the case against the accused: breach of the objective test established). See also *Hauschildt v Denmark* (1989) 12 EHRR 266. Not every involvement of the judge in an earlier stage of the case will give rise to a breach of the objective test: *Sainte Marie v France* (1992) A 253-A (1992) (two members of the appeal court which sentenced the accused had been involved in refusing him bail at an earlier hearing; no breach of Art 6(1)).

[107] *X v Sweden* No 434/58, 2 YB 354 at 370 (1958). In criminal cases, the right to be present at one's own trial is a matter of general principle: *Ekbatani v Sweden* (1988) 13 EHRR 504, para 25.

[108] *Poitrimol v France* (1993) 18 EHRR 130, para 31 (concerning the conviction of the accused for absconding with his children in breach of a custody order).

[109] 1995 Act, s 45(1).

[110] *Ibid*, s 45(2).

[111] *Dombo Beheer v The Netherlands* (1993) 18 EHRR 213, para 33.

[112] A minor, and easily remedied, problem in the children's hearings process can be found in the 'business meeting', to discuss procedural and other matters, which may take place between panel members and the reporter, but without the child or the relevant persons being present: 1995 Act, s 64(1) and 1996 Rules, r 4(1), giving statutory effect to the decision in *Sloan v B* 1991 SLT 530. It is unlikely that the requirements to let the family know that the meeting will take place, for the reporter to make any views they wish to express known, and to report back to them on what happened, will save the practice from successful challenge under Art 6(1).

'at all stages of the proceedings'[113] and does not provide for derogation. Permitting bona fide representatives of the media to be present at hearings, subject to possible exclusion where this is necessary in the child's interests or in order to obtain the child's views or where media presence is causing distress to the child, thus complies with international standards.[114] Similarly, the strict restrictions on what may be reported in respect of children's hearings and related court proceedings would appear to be unobjectionable.[115] However, reporting restrictions may be lifted by the sheriff, the Court of Session in an appeal, or the Scottish Executive 'in the interests of justice'.[116] This may meet the standards of the European Convention. However, it is arguable that it fails to comply with the UN Convention's more exacting standards, given that Convention's emphasis on 'the promotion of the child's sense of dignity and worth', 'the child's reintegration into society', and 'the child's assuming a constructive role in society'.[117]

C   The lack of legal representation

The European Court has interpreted Art 6(1) as meaning that an individual must have a meaningful right of access to a court in respect of civil rights and obligations.[118] While this does not mandate the provision of free legal representation in all cases, a failure to make such provision may constitute a breach of Art 6(1) where the individual would be unable to put forward his or her case effectively without such representation.[119] The UN Convention is rather more explicit in requiring that the child shall have 'legal or other appropriate assistance in the preparation and presentation of his or her defence'[120] and that 'the matter' [guilt or otherwise] shall be determined 'in the presence of legal or other appropriate assistance'.[121] Of course, that brings us back to the question of whether Art 40 applies to proceedings before a children's hearing. In any event, no further guidance is given on what is meant by 'other appropriate assistance', but the obvious inference is that lay assistance is envisaged as being adequate in some cases.

---

[113] Art 40(2)(b)(vii).

[114] 1995 Act, s 43. Where a journalist has been excluded, the chairperson of the hearing may inform him or her of the substance of what has taken place during the period of exclusion but does not appear to be obliged to do so: 1995 Act, s 43(5).

[115] There must be no publication of information which is intended or is likely to identify any child concerned in the proceedings or the address or school of such a child: 1995 Act, s 44(1). The prohibition extends not only to the child accused of the offence but also to any other children involved, including child witnesses. The penalty is a fine up to level 4: 1995 Act, s 44(2). At present, this means that the maximum fine which can be imposed is £2,500, arguably, a sum of no real significance to a major newspaper or television company.

[116] 1995 Act, s 43(5).

[117] Art 40(1). To date, the reporting restrictions have not been lifted in respect of a children's hearing or related court proceedings.

[118] *Golder v United Kingdom* (1975) 1 EHRR 524. While a person accused of an offence must be provided with the essential elements of a 'fair hearing', including the opportunity to defend himself or herself, legal representation need only be provided free of charge 'where the interests of justice so require': Art 6(3)(c).

[119] *Airey v Ireland* (1979) 2 EHRR 305.

[120] Art 40(2)(b)(ii).

[121] Art 40(2)(b)(iii).

Prior to *S v Miller*, the child and the relevant persons could receive a certain amount of legal advice under the Legal Advice and Assistance Scheme,[122] but legal aid was not available to provide the child or the relevant persons with pre-hearing advice nor for representation at hearings. Where did this leave the accused child and his or her family who did not have a legal representative? Aside any assistance they received from friends, spiritual advisers and other lay persons, they were on their own. This created a fundamental problem for the children's hearings system at a variety of stages. When one considers that children were facing decisions about whether to accept the allegation of criminal conduct and what, if any, defences may be available, it cannot be suggested, with the slightest degree of conviction, that they were on an equal footing with the reporter who either is legally qualified or has access to legal advice. In the hearing itself, in the absence of a legal representative, how was the family to judge whether the appropriate procedure had been followed and, thus, whether they had any right to appeal against the hearing's decision? It is hard to see how fundamental fairness could require anything other than full legal representation provided free of charge where the family resources were insufficient to secure such representation. If anything, this position is reinforced by the fact that, assuming the conditions for financial eligibility are met, legal aid was available for court proceedings associated with the hearing, whether in the context of establishing the conditions for referral, the introduction of new evidence, or to appeal against a hearing's decision.[123]

Legal representation was the subject matter of one of the pre-emptive defensive strikes in *S v Miller*, when the court was given a copy of the Convention Rights (Compliance) (Scotland) Bill, which the Minister of Justice has presented to the Scottish Parliament. The Bill is now an Act, and s 6(2) includes children's hearings with the extended list of courts and tribunals for which legal aid is to be made available.[124] Despite the fact that change was in the air, counsel sought to argue that the failure to provide legal aid for representation at hearings was a matter of policy, rather than financial pressure. In the words of the Lord President, 'The view was taken that the introduction of legal representation would detrimentally affect the informal and flexible nature of the proceedings'.[125] The transparency and illogicality of this contention was demolished swiftly by the Lord President, not least because lawyers were not presently prohibited from representing children at hearings.[126] Their Lordships expressed real concerns over the lack of legal aid, due to the range of complexity of proceedings, the fact that panel members are lay persons, the youth and inexperience of many of the children involved, and, in particular, where a child faces deprivation of liberty.[127]

---

[122] Legal Aid (Scotland) Act 1986, Part II.

[123] Legal Aid (Scotland) Act 1986, s 29, as substituted by the Children (Scotland) Act 1995, s 92.

[124] The Convention Rights (Compliance) (Scotland) Bill was passed by the Scottish Parliament on 30 May 2001 and received Royal Assent on 5 July 2001. Ministerial action is required before s 6 becomes operative.

[125] *S v Miller* (above) at p 542.

[126] The Lord President expressed his own view on the flexibility of lawyers in the following terms (at p 543): 'skilled lawyers are chameleons who readily adapt their approach and techniques to the particular tribunal in which they appear'.

[127] See the Lord President at pp 542–546, Lord Penrose at pp 559–563 and Lord Macfadyen at pp 577–579.

The matter was continued to allow for intimation to the Advocate-General and the court concluded that the lack of availability of legal aid would render the system incompatible with the requirements of Art 6(1).[128] In the event, the challenge was rendered moot by eleventh-hour intervention to correct a defect which should have been put right long ago.

D   What information is given to whom?

While the panel members and the relevant persons[129] received copies of a whole range of documents, including a statement of the conditions for referral and any background reports,[130] prior to *S v Miller*, the child was entitled to receive only a copy of the statement of the conditions for referral[131] and not the other documents available to everyone else. Given that the hearing reaches its decision on the basis of the child's welfare, as assessed in the light of all the circumstances of the case, including factors addressed in reports, how could the child exercise his or her rights under Art 6(1) in the absence of knowing what that information is? In addition, how could a child exercise his or her right to express views, as required by Art 12 of the UN Convention and the 1995 Act,[132] since a person can hardly fully express views on a situation in the absence of all the relevant information?

It might be argued, on the basis of Art 3 of the UN Convention, that the child's welfare would not be served by having, sometimes sensitive, information about other family members that is in a particular report disclosed. However, the tension between Arts 3 and 12 is not unique to the hearings system and it falls to the system to find a way to respect the child's rights under both the European and UN Conventions. A further difficulty exists in reconciling the adult family member's right to respect for his or her private and family life, under Art 8 of the European Convention, and the child's rights under Art 6.

This was the subject of the second pre-emptive defensive strike in *S v Miller* since the Principal Reporter presented the court with the guidance he had issued to all reporters requiring that the child would, in future, receive the same documents as the panel members and the relevant persons, save in exceptional circumstances.[133] This, in the court's view, rendered the point moot.[134]

---

[128]   *S v Miller (No 2)* (unreported), 7 August 2001. Since there was a prospect of the court making a declaration of incompatibility between a statute and the Human Rights Act 1998, such intimation to the Advocate General was necessary. In the event, she wisely decided not to attempt to defend the indefensible.

[129]   Prior to the 1995 Act, relevant persons were not given copies of reports and simply had the substance of them disclosed by the hearing chair, a practice the European Court found to be in breach of Art 6(1) in *McMichael v United Kingdom* (above). See also the European Court's decision in *TP and KM v United Kingdom* (unreported), 10 May 2001.

[130]   1996 Rules, r 5(1).

[131]   1996 Rules, r 18(1)(b).

[132]   Section 16(2).

[133]   Lord President at pp 541–542. The exceptions include the situation 'where the information would cause significant harm to the child or any other person or where it would significantly prejudice the prevention or detection of crime or the apprehension or prosecution of an offender'.

[134]   The Lord President did take the opportunity to issue a clear warning that 'a blanket policy that documents should not be supplied to the child' would pose problems under Art 6(1) of the European Convention.

E   The role of the reporter

It has been asserted, on behalf of the Principal Reporter, that reporters 'offer their views to members of the children's hearing on any legal issues that arise'.[135] Remember, the reporter decides whether to convene a hearing, arranges the hearing, and makes a record of the proceedings.[136] At the very least, a reporter who has taken a good faith decision that a child is in need of compulsory measures of supervision can be seen as having a stake in the outcome of the case. It is entirely human to want to be proved right and, to use modern management jargon, it would be all too easy for the reporter to have 'ownership' of his or her original decision. If he or she then plays any significant role in helping the panel members to arrive at their decision, can that decision be regarded as being taken by an independent tribunal? Does the reporter's role offend against the principle of equality of arms? In *Borgers v Belgium*,[137] the Belgian practice of permitting the Procureur General to state his opinion in open court on whether the accused's appeal should be allowed and then to retire with the judges to advise on their opinion, when no such opportunity was afforded to the accused or his legal representative, was found to be in breach of Art 6(1). This suggests that the role of the reporter, in advising the hearing, will have to change in the future and it is regrettable that the point was not explored in *S v Miller*.

F   Secure accommodation

A child can be detained in secure accommodation pending a children's hearing, during continuation or after, once the hearing has reached its final decision.[138] While, in *S v Miller*, it was accepted that this amounts to 'deprivation of liberty' under Art 5(1) of the European Convention, the Inner House simply followed a recent English Court of Appeal decision,[139] in holding that such deprivation of liberty came within the permitted exception under Art 5(1)(d). That allows for deprivation of liberty of a minor 'for the purpose of educational supervision or his lawful detention for the purpose of bringing him before the competent legal authority'. The point does not appear to have been argued with any great rigour and, it must be admitted that the Court of Appeal was itself following a recent European Court decision which gave a very wide interpretation to the term 'educational supervision'.[140] Nonetheless, the criteria for ordering secure accommodation are not limited to the child's education, nor even the child's welfare, since they include the possibility of the child injuring a third party.[141] In addition, once secure accommodation has been authorised, the decision to

---

[135]   In *Miller v Council of the Law Society of Scotland* 2000 SLT 513, at p 516L.

[136]   An argument might be made that the reporter's role as record maker is also in breach of Art 6(1).

[137]   (1991) 15 EHRR 92, effectively reversing *Delcourt v Belgium* (1970) 1 EHRR 355.

[138]   1995 Act, ss 66(10), 68(10), 69(11) and 70(9).

[139]   Cited by the Inner House as *W Borough Council v DK*, 15 November 2000, reported as *Re K (Secure Accommodation: Right to Liberty)* [2001] 1 FLR 526.

[140]   *Koniarska v United Kingdom* (unreported), 12 October 2000.

[141]   1995 Act, s 70(10).

implement the authorisation is highly discretionary.[142] It is likely that the issue of secure accommodation will be revisited in the future.[143]

G   The European Court of Human Rights

The concerns expressed, thus far, are set in the context of the children's hearings system as seen through the lens accepted by the Court of Session; that is, that hearings are not criminal proceedings. It is entirely possible that the European Court would not share this view and it can only be hoped that it is given the opportunity to consider the matter as soon as possible. Were it to differ from the Scottish Court, the accused child would have all the rights spelled out more explicitly in Art 6(2) and (3) of the European Convention. What further issues might then arise?

First, would be protection from self-incrimination,[144] a requirement spelt out explicitly in the UN Convention.[145] Freedom from self-incrimination is also linked to the express right, set out in Art 6(2) of the European Convention and Art 40(2)(b)(i) of the UN Convention, to be presumed innocent in criminal proceedings. While both the Beijing Rules[146] and the UN Convention[147] favour diversion from formal trial, the danger that a child might feel a degree of coercion to 'confess' has long been appreciated and the Beijing Rules suggest that consent to diversion should be subject to review by a competent authority.[148] At the earliest stage of the hearing, whether the child accepts the conditions for referral dictates what will happen next. How many children accept the grounds of referral simply in order 'to get the whole thing over with' or, indeed, for any number of other invalid reasons?

Other jurisdictions recognise 'status offences': that is offences which can only be committed by young people, there being no adult equivalent. A number of other conditions for referral, including the child being 'beyond the control of any relevant person' or 'failing to attend school without a reasonable excuse', look remarkably like status offences. Do status offences pose a problem under either the European or UN Conventions? Failure to attend school without a reasonable excuse can probably be dealt with fairly swiftly, since the European Convention provides that a minor may be deprived of his or her liberty 'by lawful order for the

---

[142]   The child's detention in secure accommodation may be 'during such period as the person in charge of the establishment, with the agreement of the chief social work officer of the relevant local authority, considers necessary': 1995 Act, s 70(9)(b).

[143]   A recent newspaper report suggests that one such challenge will be brought shortly in respect of a 15-year-old boy who was allegedly kept in 'solitary confinement' for 10 days: L McDougall, 'Secure unit "placed teenager in solitary" hit by rights abuse claim', *Scotland on Sunday* 14 October 2001.

[144]   *Funke v France* (1993) 16 EHRR 297; *Sanders v United Kingdom* (1996) 23 EHRR 313. The High Court had the opportunity to consider this requirement in respect of the obligation to give information about who was driving a car at a particular time and the use of that information in prosecuting a person accused of driving after consuming excess alcohol, albeit its decision was overturned by the Privy Council: *Brown v Scott*, 2000 SLT 379 (High Ct); 2001 SLT 59 (PC).

[145]   Art 37(2)(iv).

[146]   Rule 11.1.

[147]   Art 40(3)(b).

[148]   Rule 11.3.

purpose of educational supervision', always providing that the deprivation of liberty is 'in accordance with a procedure prescribed by law'.[149] What of the other grounds? It might be thought that status offences amount to discrimination on the basis of age, but neither the European nor the UN Convention specifies age as one of the prohibited categories of discrimination although each prohibits discrimination on the ground of 'other status'.[150] It could be argued that status offences pass international muster since they indicate a need for protection of the child and, thus, serve the promotion of the child's welfare,[151] or that they serve a preventive function in diverting the child from future, clearly criminal, conduct. On the other hand, status offences may stigmatise a child unnecessarily. The Beijing Rules allow for status offences,[152] the Riyadh Guidelines counsel against penalising children for conduct which would not be considered criminal in an adult,[153] and the UN Convention is silent on the matter. Given the lack of international consensus, it seems unlikely that the European Court would be persuaded that status offences are discrimination *per se*.

One further argument against status offences might be considered. While proof beyond reasonable doubt is required in respect of ordinary offences, these status offences can be established by proof on the balance of probabilities. In respect of failure to attend school, the child faces a 'reverse onus of proof' since it falls on him or her to establish a reasonable excuse. This appears to be a clear violation of the presumption of innocence, albeit a recent sheriff court decision reflects a rather sanguine view of the compatibility with the Human Rights Act 1998 of the parallel offence which a parent can commit.[154]

V CONCLUSIONS

That the new political establishment in Scotland has shown an interest in children and young people in conflict with the criminal law is to be welcomed and the involvement of the various branches of government and the legal system is essential. Looking at different aspects of the juvenile justice system separately is a first step. A considerable body of research has provided hard information about juvenile offending. The Advisory Group on Youth Crime has suggested that children's hearings might deal with 16- and 17-year-old offenders. The Scottish Law Commission has suggested a fresh approach to the age of criminal responsibility, albeit the present author does not support its tentative conclusions and hopes that something very different will emerge in its final Report. While the 'fixes' were conceded at the eleventh hour, somewhat grudgingly, and in response to litigation, *S v Miller* may have resulted in resolving some problems in the

---

[149] Art 5(1)(d). In addition, the importance of education is reinforced in the First Protocol, Art 2. For a full discussion of the child's right to education, see Chap 11.

[150] European Convention, Art 14; UN Convention, Art 2.

[151] UN Convention, Art 3, See also the duty to protect the child from abuse, neglect and exploitation (Art 19), and the obligation to protect the child from sexual exploitation (Art 34).

[152] Rule 3.1.

[153] Guideline 56.

[154] *O'Hagan v Rea* 2001 SLT 30.

system, most notably the scandalous lack of legal representation at children's hearings and the denial of full information to the child.

Certainly, it should not be left to further litigation before other problems with the system, many highlighted by the greater attention being given to human rights, are addressed. At the same time, enthusiasm for devolved government must not result in a rush to implement isolated proposals, since this will result in nothing other than patching here and there.[155] Rather, what must follow is a coherent re-evaluation of the whole system of juvenile justice, drawing on the wealth of available domestic and comparative materials and proposals.[156] This process must not confine itself to a narrow compliance with the European Convention but must embrace the whole panoply of international instruments, including the UN Convention, relevant to the issues.

Without wishing to set the agenda for such a review, several points must be included within it. Not least because it is required by the UN Convention, an age for criminal responsibility must be provided for; an age, one hopes, considerably higher than eight years old. Attention must also be given to the appropriate forum for dealing with children and young people accused of offending and, certainly, the proposal to bring 16- and 17-year-olds within the scope of diversion from the criminal courts must be a part of the discussion. There must be recognition that, whatever the forum and regard for the welfare of the accused in the process, where an individual is being held responsible for his or her criminal conduct, he or she must be accorded the protection recognised internationally as appropriate to criminal proceedings. If the children's hearings system is to remain part of the process – and it is submitted that it should – then further legal safeguards must be built into the system. The role of the reporter in deciding a hearing should be arranged, then acting as clerk and adviser to the hearing, will have to change. Requiring that every children's hearing had a legally qualified chair would remove the need for the reporter to provide advice, at the same time as ensuring that due process requirements were met. In addition, the re-evaluation must not confine itself to the narrow issues of process. There must be firm proposals aimed at both prevention and a range of constructive disposals for those young people who do offend, coupled with adequate funding to make them available. This is the opportunity presented by the spotlight on human rights and it must be seized, with both hands, by the Scottish Executive.

---

155   It may seem ironic that, having complained in the past about undue delay, the plea now is to avoid undue haste. However, this is simply a recognition that neither is desirable.

156   The Scottish Law Commission noted that, when the Law Reform Commission of Hong Kong examined the age of criminal responsibility there, it recommended a general review of the juvenile justice system; *Discussion Paper on the Age of Criminal Responsibility*, para 2.35. While the SLC drew on the work of its counterpart, regrettably, it made no similar recommendation.

SINGAPORE

SUPPORTING MARRIAGE THROUGH DESCRIPTION AS AN EQUAL PARTNERSHIP OF EFFORTS

Wai Kum Leong[*]

I   SUPPORTING MARRIAGE

It is a legitimate expectation that the law should support couples who having chosen to commit to each other in marriage continue this commitment. There are a variety of means available to support marriage both within and outside the law. This article discusses the law in Singapore that optimises legal regulation of the relationship between spouses through a statutory description of marriage as an equal partnership of efforts. The statutory description lacks sanction and is of imperfect obligation. Yet it sets a salutary tone for the law relating to spouses, in particular, whether an interference with their consortium should give rise to relief in damages and the proper exercise of the power to divide matrimonial assets.

While each society searches for its own way to support marriage, it is appropriate to note that there is a proposal in England to support marriage by presenting every couple intending to marry with a clear statement of what their new status means in terms of extra rights and extra responsibilities.[1] It may be that this statement could eventually be incorporated into the marriage statute in England and become the equivalent of the statutory description of marriage in Singapore. It is equally possible that the marriage statute in Singapore may be re-written in such plain English that every couple intending to marry will choose to read the statutory description as part of their preparation for marriage. For the moment, there is only the statutory description in Singapore and its effect appears to be limited to the legal community. Even so, it is worthy of some note that the marriage statute in Singapore, a Common Law country,[2] contains a provision of imperfect obligation in describing marriage.

---

[*]   Associate Professor, National University of Singapore.

[1]   See the consultation document *Supporting Families: A Consultation Document* (England, 2000), available online at *http://www.homeoffice.gov.uk/vcu/suppfam*, issued by the Ministerial Group on the Family. Among its many proposals on how to support marriage is this statement.

[2]   The Common Law, influenced by positivism, generally frowns on a law that falls short of a command backed by sanction.

II   MARRIAGE LAW IN SINGAPORE

The vast majority of Singaporeans[3] who are not Muslims[4] have since 1961 become regulated in the formation of marriage and aspects of their family relationships by the Women's Charter.[5] The Women's Charter was enacted as their common marriage law where previously members of each ethnic or religious community were allowed to marry in the manner of their respective customs or religious rules for celebration of marriage.[6]

Besides the formation of marriage, the Women's Charter also regulates the relationship between spouses including its termination and ancillary applications following such termination and it further regulates some aspects of the relationship between parents and their children. It is the core family statute in Singapore. Of marriage, the original Women's Charter[7] encapsulated one of the then marriage statutes which was closely modelled on the prevailing marriage statute in England. These provisions remain largely as they used to be.[8] A notable difference is the provision that describes the character of marriage which has no equivalent in England.[9] At a time when England, with a much longer legal history than Singapore,[10] is considering whether an extra-legal statement about marriage might serve to support marriage, it may be particularly appropriate to consider how the description has served the smaller, younger Republic.[11]

---

[3]   At the last Census of Population in 1990, there was a 2.7 million resident population of which 78% were Chinese, 14% Malay, 7% Indian and 1% of mixed ethnicity; see *Census of Population 1990: Demographic Characteristics* (Singapore, Dept of Statistics, 1992) at 4 and 5.

[4]   Only 15% of the resident population reported themselves to be Muslim whereas 31% were Buddhist, 22% Taoist, 13% Christian, 4% Hindu and 14% reported they had no religion; see *Census of Population 1990: Religion, Childcare and Leisure Activities* (Singapore, Dept of Statistics, 1994) at 3.

[5]   Cap 353 Statutes of the Republic of Singapore 1997 Revised Edition. For developments towards the enactment of this common marriage and family law for all non-Muslim Singaporeans in 1961, as well as developments since 1961, see Wai Kum Leong, *Family Law Library of Singapore* (CD-ROM) (Singapore, Butterworths, 1999) at P20-61.

[6]   For descriptions of how this diversity came about, see Wai Kum Leong, *Family Law Library of Singapore* at P69-86, and for brief descriptions of what has come to be called local Chinese customary marriage law, local Hindu religious marriage law, local Jewish marriage law and local common law marriage law and the statutory marriage laws, see Wai Kum Leong, *op cit* at P87-112, P112-124, P124-126, P126-130 and P130-148 respectively.

[7]   Ordinance 18/1961 enacted by the Legislative Assembly of the then colony of Singapore.

[8]   The continued substantial similarity of the marriage laws in Singapore and the United Kingdom has been noted in WK Leong, 'Formation of marriage in England and Singapore by contract: Void marriage and non-marriage' (2000) 14 IJLPF 256.

[9]   The author has hailed the enactment of the provision as 'pure creative genius'; see Wai Kum Leong, *Family Law Library of Singapore*, n 5 at C257.

[10]   Singapore became 'founded' as an outpost of the East India Company only in 1819 and its legal system is accepted to have begun only from the Crown document that created its first court in 1826; see a brief description of developments in administration and the legal system in Wai Kum Leong, *Family Law Library of Singapore*, n 3 at P2-4 and P14-20 respectively.

[11]   The independent Republic of Singapore came into being only from 9 August 1965. After gaining a measure of internal independence from Britain, its colonial master since 1819, Singapore was briefly a constituent state of the neighbouring federation of Malaysia from 31 August 1963. It left the federation with some haste and became fully independent in 1965.

III MARRIAGE AS AN EQUAL PARTNERSHIP OF EFFORTS

Section 46(1) of the Women's Charter in Singapore proclaims:

'Upon the solemnization of marriage, the husband and the wife shall be mutually bound to co-operate with each other in safeguarding the interests of the union and in caring and providing for the children.'

This is a classic statutory provision of imperfect obligation as none of its proclamations can be directly enforced. It has been hailed, however, as[12] 'powerful in its proclamation as it is powerless of enforcement.'

The author has argued before that a statement about the character of marriage may be the ideal formulation of law to express the hopes of general society while supporting the subsisting relationship between spouses.[13] The relationship is hopefully of long duration. It is a deep emotional and sexual union, and reasonable people may differ about what each spouse can expect of the other. The parties are adults and entitled to expect their autonomy to continue to be respected. If this intimate relationship is to endure, the partners require the utmost privacy to sort out all manner of rights, obligations, responsibilities and privileges between themselves. Injudicious interference by the law can only cause harm. In this context, the best society can do may be to spell out what the ideal is and leave the parties to achieve this to the best of their abilities.

The author has observed that the provision sets out the ideal in general tones of[14] 'co-operation ... mutuality [and] reasonable expectations'. With this provision, the law in Singapore:[15]

'characterises marriage as an equal co-operative partnership of efforts. [The provision] is powerful in colouring the husband–wife relationship with a tone of mutual respect and reasonable consideration of one another [and] raises the status of the wife to be the equal of her husband. [This] underlines legal regulation of the relationship ... '

While reasonable consideration of the other is expected of a spouse, it is not every failure to meet this expectation that attracts legal consequences. Instead, the law has settled on the trigger for official intervention in the relationship where one spouse has brought legal proceedings against the other. This is, of course, on the assumption that no crime has been committed because the commission of any crime immediately attracts intervention. Unreasonable behaviour of a spouse which violates the expectation in the provision but is short of a crime is not directly condemned until such legal proceedings are pursued. This arises, for example, when a petition for divorce is presented where the marriage has irretrievably broken down. In the petition, the behaviour of one spouse may be

---

12   Wai Kum Leong, *Family Law Library of Singapore*, n 5 at P356.
13   Wai Kum Leong, *Family Law Library of Singapore*, n 5 at P356-357, C257-263, B179 and F165-166.
14   Wai Kum Leong, *Family Law in Singapore: Cases and Commentary on the Women's Charter and Family Law* (Malayan Law Journal, 1990) at 166.
15   Wai Kum Leong, 'The just and equitable division of gains between equal former partners in marriage' [2000] SJLS 208 at 234.

proven to be of such character that the other cannot be expected to continue to cohabit and, on its being proven, the court intervenes in the relationship by granting a decree of divorce. Until legal proceedings are taken, current family law does not do any more than exhort reasonable behaviour. This is the way the law in Singapore balances its dual role to teach married people how to be moral spouses and to support the marriage by giving the relationship the privacy it requires.

The expectations, however, are powerful if only indirectly so. They can support decisions in suits relating to the marital relationship. There is a fairly recent decision of the High Court of Singapore which relied on this view of marriage as an equal co-operative partnership of efforts to dismiss a claim for damages for enticement of his wife brought by the husband against his wife's lover. This view of the relationship also supports the remarkable developments in the law of division of matrimonial assets upon the termination of marriage by the court.

IV   TORT OF ENTICEMENT NOT APPROPRIATE WITHIN A PARTNERSHIP OF EQUALS

The statutory description of marriage influenced the High Court of Singapore's decision in *TPY v DZI.*[16] The husband pursued an action in tort to seek damages from his wife's lover for having enticed her affections from him. Traditionally, enticement was one of the intentional torts[17] developed by the Common Law to compensate for interferences by third parties with the consortium between husband and wife. Being Common Law remedies, these torts would have become part of the basic law of Singapore through the general reception of English law in 1826. Nothing has since been done to the status of the torts, except for criminal conversation. Criminal conversation was abolished with the enactment of the Women's Charter in 1961[18] when it was replaced by the statutory claim for damages which a husband who petitioned for divorce on the ground of his wife's adultery, could seek.[19] In principle, then, the tort of enticement was still subsisting in 1996.

The hearing before Justice Rubin was an appeal from the Registrar's dismissal of the interlocutory application by the defendant to strike out the husband's claim as not disclosing a reasonable cause of action. His Honour began by noting that the tort of enticement appears to embrace the notion of a husband possessing dominion over his wife so that it was incumbent on her forever to please him. He noted the disavowal of this idea by commentators[20] which led eventually to its

---

[16]   [1997] 3 SLR 475.

[17]   The other two intentional torts for injuries to consortium were harbouring and criminal conversation. In addition, the Common Law also allowed the husband to sue for negligent interferences with his consortium. Those torts have all been abolished in England. For discussion of the law in Singapore, see Wai Kum Leong, *Family Law Library of Singapore*, n 5, at P392-399.

[18]   See Women's Charter 1961, section 105.

[19]   Even this statutory claim was abolished by implication when the 1981 revision of the Women's Charter omitted the provision that had hitherto allowed the claim; see this confirmed by the High Court of Singapore in *Tan Kay Poh v Tan Surida & Anor* [1989] 1 MLJ 276.

[20]   *TPY v DZI* [1977] 3 SLR 475 at 477.

abolition in England and Wales by the Law Reform (Miscellaneous Provisions) Act 1970.[21] The judge further noted that this and other torts relating to interferences with consortium have also been critically commented upon in Singapore.[22] This led to his Honour's decision to allow the appeal on the basis that no such suit for enticement is allowed by the law in Singapore today. The actual decision was:[23]

> '[T]he tort ... cannot continue to serve any useful purpose particularly when society no longer subscribes to the view that women are mere chattels and whose existence is only to be in the service of their husbands. Sections [46 and related provisions] of the Women's Charter clearly underscore the aspect that a wife is a person in her own right and not someone who is subordinate to, or a chattel of her husband.'

In other words, marriage being a partnership between equals, this wife disappointed her husband by failing to remain faithful. The law in Singapore does disapprove of her failure to meet its expectations. This disapproval, however, does not go so far as to allow the husband to sue the wife's lover for damages. The Women's Charter sets the ideals but the 'injured' husband will have to cope without the benefit of a legal remedy for her failings.

There is a statutory provision in Singapore which encourages consideration of whether the Common Law, that had been received as basic law here, continues to be suitable today although the High Court in this case did not refer to it. The Application of English Law Act 1993 provides that the Common Law continues to apply[24] 'so far as it is applicable to the circumstances of Singapore and its inhabitants and subject to such modifications as those circumstances may require'. This provision has been regarded as encouraging[25] 'localisation' of rules of the Common Law and equity and as reflecting a 'confident stance of an independent people cognisant of the responsibility of taking the future development of their laws into their own hands'. *TPY v DZI* is one localisation of a common law rule that has lost relevance in modern Singapore. Where marriage is a partnership between equals it is not appropriate to allow a claim for damages that is premised on the proprietary dominion of the husband over his wife's virtue. His interest in her continued virtue needs to be nurtured through a less crude tool than such claim for damages.

V   DIVISION OF MATRIMONIAL ASSETS ACQUIRED BY CO-OPERATIVE EFFORTS

The statutory description of marriage as an equal partnership of efforts assumes dramatic significance in the law of division of matrimonial assets in Singapore. The law in Singapore concerning the effect of marriage on spouses' interests in

---

21   Sections 4 and 5(a), *TPY v DZI* (above) at 478.

22   *TPY v DZI* (above) at 478, citing Cheng Han Tan *Matrimonial Law in Singapore and Malaysia* (Butterworths, 1994).

23   *TPY v DZI* (above) at 479.

24   Cap 7A 1994 Revised Edition of the Statutes of the Republic of Singapore, section 3.

25   See Wai Kum Leong, *Family Law Library of Singapore*, n 5 at P27.

property differs during the subsistence of marriage and upon its unnatural termination by court decree. During marriage, there is minimal effect as the concept of 'separation of property' dictates that a spouse will have no greater interest than a stranger in the same situation. Upon the termination of marriage, however, the court is vested with the power to divide property which is matrimonial assets between the spouses consonant with the concept of 'deferred community of property'. While it may seem a little ironical for the greater effect to arise when the marriage ends, yet the law appears to work well enough at both stages.

The power to divide matrimonial assets was only created in 1981.[26] Although the power to order division of matrimonial assets is of more recent vintage than the power to order the husband to continue to maintain his former wife, even more remarkable is the fact that, despite the power to order maintenance being one-sidedly in favour of wives,[27] it is the power to divide matrimonial assets that is the more often sought and ordered. It has been suggested that the maintenance order of a former wife has probably come to perform a subsidiary role, to supplement the order of division where the family lacks property to make an order of division of reasonable proportions.[28] In the twenty years since the enactment of the power to divide matrimonial assets, the courts in Singapore have interpreted it so that it achieves the general public's expectations of what ought to happen to the family wealth on termination of marriage. The optimal development of the power to divide matrimonial assets in Singapore owes a debt to the statutory description of marriage as an equal partnership of efforts. The description suggests that the wealth of a family is acquired by the spouses' co-operative efforts during the course of their marriage so that, on its termination, each spouse should get a fair proportion of it.

VI LEGISLATIVE DEVELOPMENTS IN DIVISION OF MATRIMONIAL ASSETS

The original provision allowed the court to:[29]

> 'order the division between the parties of any assets acquired by them during the marriage by their joint efforts [or] the sole effort of one party [and even of] assets owned before the marriage by one party which have been substantially improved during the marriage.'

---

[26] Women's Charter (Amendment) Act 26/1980, s 100, which became the famous s 106 in the next revised edition of the statute, viz Women's Charter Cap 353 1985 Ed. For an interesting observation of the likely source of this innovation, see B Crown, 'Property division on dissolution of marriage' (1988) 30 Mal LR 34.

[27] Parliament has not seen fit to extend the obligation of maintenance of a spouse to the wife, both during marriage and after its termination, although calls were made as early as 1987: see Wai Kum Leong, 'The duty to maintain spouse and children during marriage' (1987) 29 Mal LR 56.

[28] See Wai Kum Leong, 'Trends and developments in family law' in *Review of Judicial and Legal Reforms in Singapore between 1990 and 1995* (Butterworths, 1996) 632, at 711.

[29] Women's Charter 1981, s 100.

Among the factors the court was directed to consider in fixing its proportions of division was 'the extent of the contribution made by the other party ... to the welfare of the family by looking after the home or by caring for the family'. The force of this provision was not necessarily appreciated at that time. Singapore, being a Common Law country operating within a 'separation of property' regime, could have interpreted the provision more conservatively. The provision was also clearly internally inconsistent in parts.[30] It could be thought to do no more than allow for a modest adjustment of the interests of the spouses as property law has determined them to be.

The author embraced the enactment from the beginning. Her first article on it described it as innovative, pointing out how it differed from the equivalent power in England (the traditional source of reform of the law in Singapore) which was generally thought only to allow adjustment of spouses' proprietary interests.[31] Of the power in Singapore to divide matrimonial assets, the author suggested that its underlying philosophy should be regarded as the view of the spousal relationship favoured by the Women's Charter:[32]

'Today, it is impossible to deny that both spouses contribute towards whatever is acquired by the family however the spouses choose to distribute the various roles that require to be performed if the family is to function as a unit ... . [W]hether both spouses work and a maid is hired ... or one spouse works while the other takes care of the home on a full-time basis ... both are contributing to the well-being of the unit ... . When, therefore, the spousal relationship ends the two spouses are each entitled to a fair share of what he or she has helped to acquire.'

The original provision of the power to divide matrimonial assets did, however, retain a bias which continued to favour financial contributions over non-financial. Simply by separating property into that acquired by joint efforts and that acquired by sole effort, it suggested that financial contribution remained the dominant consideration so that the non-financial efforts of a spouse might deserve less consideration. Worse still, the provision also contained different directives in relation to the two types of property. While the court should 'incline towards equality of division' of jointly acquired assets, it should ensure in relation to those acquired by the sole effort of one spouse that that spouse should obtain the larger proportion. A literal reading of the provision could have confined it closely to the general principles of property law. Had it been so read, the power would have been exercised more modestly than has fortunately occurred. The author argued that the provision's underlying philosophy should be relied upon to temper this

---

30 B Crown, 'Property division on dissolution of marriage', n 26 at 44–50 observed the difficulties of interpretation of parts of the provision.

31 The provision in the United Kingdom today is Matrimonial Causes Act 1973, s 24(a) which allows the court to 'order that a party to the marriage shall transfer to the other party ... such property as may be so specified, being property to which the first-mentioned party is entitled ...'. This is generally described as allowing for 'property adjustment orders' but see the most recent House of Lords decision in *White v White* [2000] 2 FLR 981, discussed in n 46, which interprets the provision in very bold terms.

32 In Wai Kum Leong, 'Division of matrimonial property upon termination of marriage' [1989] 1 MLJ xiii, at xiii–xiv.

bias. It was suggested that separating matrimonial assets into those jointly acquired from those solely acquired was an 'impracticable' task because:[33]

> 'the very smallest monetary contribution which is in some way referable to the purchase of the asset is critical [so] if this were indeed taken seriously ... the court is required to look into the spousal relationship with an even finer-tooth comb than it would do in an application merely to determine the property rights of the spouses according to property law.'

Further, that the differentiation also 'makes little sense' because:[34]

> 'In directing the court towards 'equality of division' [with] jointly acquired property and that one should get 'a greater proportion' [with] solely acquired property, the section permits the court to make [much] the same order (eg 49% : 51% division)[35] or something close whether it is the one case or the other!'

A few years later, the author was able to observe happily that the power has been interpreted[36] 'with the same bold spirit as prompted its introduction in the Act' and that the courts had generally[37] 'applauded the provision despite its infelicities and worked to overcome most of them'. This allowed the suggestion[38] that the enactment of the power to divide matrimonial assets has brought the law in Singapore on the effect of marriage on the holding of property from the Common Law 'separation of property' model to the hybrid 'deferred community of property' model. In the intervening years between the writings, the courts elaborated on the provision's underlying purpose. One judge said:[39] 'the enactments are meant ... to provide for a just apportionment for the "homemaker" (invariably the wife)'.[40] It was possible then to observe:[41]

> 'Every decision [given was] based upon what was "fair" or "equitable" or "reasonable" in the circumstances. That the terms "fair" and "equitable" are not even in the section itself only emphasises the judges' reading of the purpose of the section

---

[33]　Wai Kum Leong, 'Division of matrimonial property upon termination of marriage' (above), at xv.

[34]　Wai Kum Leong, 'Division of matrimonial property upon termination of marriage' (above), at xv.

[35]　Indeed Chan Sek Keong J, then judge now the Attorney-General, in the High Court of Singapore in *Ong Chin Ngoh v Lam Chih Kian* [1992] 2 SLR 414, observed that the separation of the two groups of assets may be insignificant as his Honour could award 'up to 49% of the matrimonial assets acquired by the sole effort [of one spouse]'.

[36]　Wai Kum Leong, 'Division of matrimonial assets: Recent cases and thoughts for reform' [1993] SJLS 351, at 359.

[37]　Wai Kum Leong, 'Division of matrimonial assets: Recent cases and thoughts for reform' (above) at 360.

[38]　Wai Kum Leong, 'Division of matrimonial assets: Recent cases and thoughts for reform' (above) at 355.

[39]　Rubin J in *Wong Amy v Chua Seng Chuan* [1992] 2 SLR 360, at 370. Another judge, Lai J in the Court of Appeal in Singapore in *Hoong Khai Soon v Cheng Kwee Eng and another appeal* [1993] 3 SLR 34, at 40 said that his Honour would 'make a rough and ready approximation [to avoid a decision which] would be inimical to the concept of a matrimonial partnership'.

[40]　But see *Chan Yeong Keay v Yeo Mei Ling* [1994] 2 SLR 541 and text below corresponding with n 56.

[41]　Wai Kum Leong, 'Division of matrimonial assets: Recent cases and thoughts for reform', n 36, at 360.

to divide matrimonial assets fairly between the spouses upon the termination of their marriage.'

The author could report that decided cases, 12 years after the enactment of the provision, demonstrate that[42] 'the norm appears to range from 35% to 45%' of the matrimonial assets being awarded to the spouse who was full-time homemaker and child carer.[43] This was a remarkable development in a hitherto Common Law 'separation of property' regime. To a great extent, the developments were boosted by the legal description of marriage as a partnership of efforts between equals.

The sheer volume of reported cases on the exercise of the power to divide matrimonial assets soon led to calls for further improvement. The power was reformed in 1996 and substituted by the current provision which reads quite simply:[44] '[t]he court shall have power ... to order the division between the parties of any matrimonial asset ... in such proportions as the court thinks just and equitable'. The most significant change in the current provision from its predecessor is that the current provision no longer separates matrimonial assets into those jointly acquired from those acquired by one spouse only. It, therefore, conveys a more equitable view of property as being all jointly acquired by the partners in marriage. Of this change the author has commented:[45]

'[By abandoning the bias that favoured financial contribution to acquisition] a just and equitable division should, generally, be an equal division.[46] On an equal division, each partner leaves the partnership with half of what he or she helped to gain. An equal division best equalises the economic situations of the spouses ... especially when the marital partnership has continued for a reasonable time so that there has been substantial non-financial contribution to homemaking and child caring.'

The new provision builds on developments under its predecessor so that the established precedents remain relevant today.

---

[42] Wai Kum Leong, 'Division of matrimonial assets: Recent cases and thoughts for reform', n 36, at 388.

[43] In comparison, by 2000, it was observed that the homemaker and child carer who also worked could get 50% of the matrimonial assets; see Wai Kum Leong 'The just and equitable division of gains between equal former partners in marriage', n 15, at 233 and 234.

[44] Women's Charter Cap 353 1997 Revised Edition of the Statutes of the Republic of Singapore section 112.

[45] Wai Kum Leong, *Family Law Library of Singapore*, n 5, at A322.

[46] It is interesting symmetry that the latest House of Lords decision shows similar proclivity towards ordering that the spouses should each obtain about half of the property available for distribution at divorce. In *White v White* [2000] 2 FLR 981 their Lordships would not agree to any 'presumption' of equality of division but Lord Nicholls was prepared to say, at 989: 'Before reaching a firm conclusion ... a judge would always be well-advised to check his tentative views against the yardstick of equality of division. As a general guide, equality should be departed from only if, and to the extent that, there is good reason for doing so.'

VII SIGNIFICANT DECISIONS ON DIVISION OF MATRIMONIAL ASSETS

A review of some significant decisions demonstrates the incremental developments which may be related with the statutory description of marriage as an equal partnership of efforts.

The first major reported case set the norm. The High Court of Singapore in *Shirley Koo v Kenneth Mok Kong Chua*[47] laid down what remained the defining principles of this area of the law. The parties were married some nine years before their marriage fell apart. They had three children. During the marriage, the spouses followed a normal pattern of married life where the husband continued to work and progress in his career while the wife stayed at home and cared for the family. The spouses prospered and by the time of the divorce owned a matrimonial home, an apartment, membership of a country club and cash balances in the husband's bank accounts. The husband argued that only the matrimonial home was a matrimonial asset liable to division. The wife asked for a share of everything. Of what was divisible,[48] Thean J in the High Court decided quite simply that[49] 'all ... assets ... acquired during the marriage' are 'matrimonial asset[s]'.[50] Of the exercise of the power, his Honour decided that it would be impossible to quantify the respective contributions of the spouses with precision so[51] 'I approached the problem in a broad manner'. Of the goal to be pursued, his Honour was in no doubt that the division should be one[52] 'I considered as fair and reasonable'. The former matrimonial home was ordered to be transferred completely to the wife so that she could continue to live there with the three children in her care. The other properties were to remain the husband's in a neat division of their matrimonial assets. In addition, the husband was to pay reasonable monthly maintenance for the former wife and children.

---

[47]   [1989] 2 MLJ 264.

[48]   There was no complete definition of what property fell to be divided under the original power. Indeed, even in 1993, Coomaraswamy J in *Neo Keok Kay v Seah Suan Chock* [1993] 1 SLR 230 at 233, expressed disquiet as to whether it was correct to describe property in Singapore as a 'matrimonial asset' although this did not hinder his Honour from ordering that the former wife, with the agreement his Honour obtained from the husband, should obtain 67% of the limited value of the only property the spouses had at divorce, which was acquired by the sole financial contribution of the husband. Even though his Honour was uncomfortable with terminology, he was completely comfortable with what was the fair outcome. The current provision contains a definition of 'matrimonial assets' in section 112(10).

[49]   *Shirley Koo v Kenneth Mok Kong Chua* [1989] 2 MLJ 264 at 267.

[50]   In the same vein, the Court of Appeal had no difficulty including monies in the Central Provident Fund accounts required compulsorily of employees in Singapore, in place of pension, as matrimonial assets; see *Lam Chih Kian v Ong Chin Ngoh* [1993] 2 SLR 253. The Court of Appeal also included the husband's half-share of a property bought to replace the former matrimonial home despite it being a gift to the husband from his parents before he married; see *Hoong Khai Soon v Cheng Kwee Eng and anor appeal* [1993] 3 SLR 34. Business assets acquired during marriage have been included since the Court of Appeal decision in *Koh Kim Lan Angela v Choong Kian Haw* [1994] 1 SLR 22. And the Court of Appeal demonstrated that it was prepared to scrutinise the family transactions to discover that what appeared to be a gift from his parents to the husband was in fact 22% acquired with the proceeds of sale of a former matrimonial home, which was a matrimonial asset available for division: see *Tan Bee Giok v Loh Kum Yong* [1997] 1 SLR 153.

[51]   *Shirley Koo v Kenneth Mok Kong Chua* (above) at 269.

[52]   *Shirley Koo v Kenneth Mok Kong Chua* (above) at 269.

The High Court demonstrated that, despite its deficiencies, the power could be exercised to achieve fair and reasonable orders of division. It is noteworthy that in this first major case, where the roles in marriage were cleanly separated between the husband and wife, the court had no difficulty giving value to the wife's homemaking and child caring. The decision affirms the description of marriage as an equal partnership of efforts.

The courts have always demonstrated the concern to give proper credit for homemaking and child caring. The author has observed that giving credit for this should not be thought as favouring the wife's contribution (even conceding that it is usually the wife who discharges these roles). Instead:[53]

> 'The judges began by singling out the contributions of the homemaker-wife for special mention. That this was so should be understood not as judicial favouring of the wife ... but simply because the "hang-over" of the "separation of property" required the special mention of the family law concern of giving proper credit to the homemaker's contribution. It was essential to highlight the relevance of non-financial contribution in order to emphasise the purpose of the enactment.'

This is best demonstrated by the Court of Appeal in Singapore decision in *Ng Hwee Keng v Chia Soon Hin William*.[54] The marriage lasted 19 years and a child was adopted. Both husband and wife worked throughout the marriage. The husband had a better paid job than the wife and had even better prospects for the future. The wife had the help of her mother-in-law, who lived with them, in the care of the home. In considering whether the wife should in these circumstances receive any credit for contribution to homemaking and child caring, the Court of Appeal found that despite working[55] 'the wife must have contributed to the welfare of the family by looking after the home and caring for the family. ... [I]t is plain to us that she did make such contribution, notwithstanding that she was working full time'. In the end, the court ordered a division of all the property owned by the couple so that the wife obtained at least 35% of everything.

That credit goes for homemaking and child caring whoever performs it is illustrated by the High Court in Singapore decision in *Chan Yeong Keay v Yeo Mei Ling*.[56] The husband was a pastor. The wife worked as a teacher throughout their 10-year marriage that produced three children. Whenever the husband was in between jobs he stayed at home, and took care of it and the children. Of the jointly owned former matrimonial home, it was clear that the husband contributed only 4.7% towards its purchase. Despite this he was ordered to receive 50% of its proceeds of sale. This case emphasises that the marriage between the parties had been an equal partnership of efforts.

While it should not be thought that all decisions have been consistent with the legal description that equates the contributions of spouses,[57] it is fair to say that

---

[53]   See Wai Kum Leong, 'Trends and developments in family law', n 28, at 703–704 and Wai Kum Leong, *Family Law Library of Singapore*, n 5, at C826.

[54]   [1995] 2 SLR 231.

[55]   *Ibid* at 241, para E.

[56]   [1994] 2 SLR 541.

[57]   A particularly jarring exception is the High Court of Singapore, on appeal, decision in *Lau Loon Seng v Sia Peck Eng* [1999] 4 SLR 408 where, in a marriage that lasted more than 40 years where

the law on division of matrimonial assets has developed in tune with the description. The courts have more often than not interpreted fairness in division within the context of marriage being an equal partnership of efforts. A dramatic challenge was mounted by a statutory board which gave the Court of Appeal the opportunity to re-affirm this. The Court of Appeal in *Central Provident Fund Board v Lau Eng Mui*[58] demonstrated another practical effect of equating the power to order division of matrimonial assets with the character of marriage as a partnership of efforts. The spouses were married many years so that at divorce the husband was only four years away from being able to withdraw his Central Provident Fund (CPF)[59] money. The wife acted as homemaker and brought up three children. Their matrimonial assets consisted only of the money in the husband's CPF account. Justice Chan Sek Keong ordered that $20,000 of this, when it became available, should be paid to the wife as her share.[60] To assure compliance his Honour imposed a charge on the account for this amount so that when the money become available for withdrawal by the husband he would have to pay this amount to his former wife. The Central Provident Fund Board[61] sought to declare the charge unlawful. The High Court rejected the argument[62] whereupon the Board appealed. The Court of Appeal, as befitting the highest judiciary in Singapore, gave a strong judgment upholding the lawfulness of the charge and rejected every argument of the Board that it was against the law. The Board would be hard put to comply with it and the objective of the power to divide matrimonial assets should accede to the more lofty objective of the compulsory savings scheme. Judge of Appeal LP Thean made an uncommon observation thus:[63]

'Before we conclude, we wish to make one observation. A court order ... dividing the CPF moneys of a member between him and his spouse under [the provision on division of matrimonial assets] is not inconsistent with or inimical to the object or the letters and spirit of the CPF Act. Nor is it contrary to the intention of the legislature. The CPF moneys of a member are his savings under a compulsory saving scheme as provided in the CPF Act and these savings are intended for the benefit of the member himself and his family, essentially his spouse, on his retirement. In the unfortunate event that his marriage breaks down irretrievably and it is found by the court that the moneys in his CPF account have been brought about and accumulated through his effort and that of his spouse, direct or indirect, it is only just that a division of such savings between him and his spouse ought to be made on a fair and equitable basis.

---

both spouses contributed to the enhancement of the family business that prospered while the wife also brought up three children, the court reduced the Family Court's order of equal division to one where the wife was to receive 30% of the matrimonial assets. See discussion in Wai Kum Leong, 'The just and equitable division of gains between equal former partners in marriage', n 15.

58   [1995] 3 SLR 109 discussed in Wai Kum Leong, *Family Law Library of Singapore*, n 5, at C703.

59   Every employee in Singapore compulsorily maintains a savings account with the CPF Board into which a fixed proportion of his or her salary is deposited every month. This savings scheme replaces pensions in Singapore which are becoming obsolete.

60   Divorce Petition No 272 of 1991, unreported.

61   The CPF Board administers all the compulsory savings accounts that employees in Singapore must maintain; see n 59 above.

62   *Lau Eng Mui v Ee Chin Kee* [1995] 1 SLR 110.

63   See n 58 above at 121, para I–122, paras A–B.

That is what [the provision] was intended to achieve and that is also what the court seeks to achieve in exercising its power thereunder.'

The court, thus, protected the power from this challenge and powerfully fused it with the view of marriage as the equal partnership of efforts.

There are an increasing number of decisions ordering equal division of matrimonial assets between the spouses. In the latest review, it was observed that where the spouse who was homemaker and child carer also worked and contributed financially to the family, the courts are prepared to give him or her 50% of the value of the matrimonial assets.[64] In *Yah Cheng Huat v Ong Bee Lan*[65] the High Court of Singapore, on appeal, was faced with a marriage that had lasted 21 years before divorce. Both husband and wife worked throughout marriage. The High Court comfortably approved of the Family Court order to divide the parties' former matrimonial home equally. Justice Judith Prakash said:

'When the marriage is good, the parties worked together and accumulated their assets jointly without drawing any distinction between them. There is no way now of determining who earned what share of the assets. ... I consider that the fair division of the home would be to divide it equally between the parties.'

VIII   CONCLUSION

In her latest analysis, the author brings home the connection between the right way to exercise the power to divide matrimonial assets and the legal description of marriage thus:[66]

'Family law must regard the spouse who served as homemaker and child carer as having made equally valuable contribution to the acquisition of property as the other who earned income and paid for property. ... Only then is the character of marriage as a partnership of efforts upheld. Only then does the law hold an even hand in its treatment of the different roles spouses discharge during marriage. Only then does the law treat both spouses fairly in terms of their property holdings.'

A statutory provision to describe marriage, which may appear somewhat powerless, can serve society well in myriad if subtle ways. It is hoped that in time the provision will filter into public consciousness where its lessons may truly teach the general public. A statement of what marriage entails in the way of additional rights, privileges and responsibilities has a role in modern society where information should be more widely available before people become married. A couple intending to assume the awesome responsibilities of marriage are well advised by a statement which describes how the spouses should view the commitment they are about to make to one another.

---

[64]   Wai Kum Leong, 'The just and equitable division of gains between equal former partners in marriage', n 15, at 233 and 234.

[65]   Div Pet 1147/1995, unreported.

[66]   Wai Kum Leong, 'The just and equitable division of gains between equal former partners in marriage', n 15, at 239–240.

SOUTH AFRICA

EBB AND FLOW: THE RETREAT OF THE LEGISLATURE AND THE DEVELOPMENT OF A CONSTITUTIONAL JURISPRUDENCE TO RESHAPE FAMILY LAW

June Sinclair[*]

I   INTRODUCTION

The last chapter in the *Survey* on South Africa[1] covered the years 1997 and 1998. A review of a selection of cases and legislation was offered to demonstrate the efforts of the courts and the legislature to bring the internal rules of private law governing the family into line with the rights enshrined in the Constitution.[2] This enterprise is ongoing. But the tide of legislation is gradually giving way to an increased flow of decisions that are entrenching some, and reshaping other, important assumptions about family relationships.

In keeping with the new approach to the *Survey*, which now reflects the year of publication rather than the annual basis of the contributions, this piece will identify a few themes, some of which had their genesis in legislation and/or cases pre-dating 1999. They span a period of about four years, and are marked by a clutch of important decisions dealing with the implications of the equality (or anti-discrimination) clause in the Constitution, with gender and role stereotyping that pervades our law and persists tenaciously even in the face of valiant attempts to effect substantive rather than formal equality, and with the enormous complexities of pluralism. The majesty of the civil law[3] remains a dominant feature of the legal landscape, as the system tries, not infrequently ineptly, to accommodate the heterogeneity of the South African population, its changing mores, and the diverse sets of customs and beliefs of the African majority.[4] The incongruities of approach to African customary marriage, on the one hand, and Muslim marriages, on the other, also calls for some comment. Not unexpectedly, several of these issues are played out in litigation involving disputes about children and the respective roles of mothers and fathers, married, unmarried and divorced.

---

[*]   Deputy Vice-Chancellor, Honorary Professor of Law, University of Pretoria.

[1]   *The International Survey of Family Law* (*2000 Edition*), ed A Bainham (Family Law, 2000), at 341–350.

[2]   The Constitution of the Republic of South Africa Act 108 of 1996.

[3]   By which term is meant the Roman-Dutch common law, our case-law (which is based on the principle of *stare decisis*), and South African legislation (both pre-dating the demise of apartheid which ended the sovereignty of Parliament and post the advent of a constitutional democracy with a Bill of Rights and the power of judicial review).

[4]   It should not be thought that black Africans have one system of indigenous law. Tribal systems have developed in different ways over time and considerable differences exist between one system and another, making the implications of pluralism much more complex than one might imagine.

II TWO VIGNETTES FROM OUR EQUALITY JURISPRUDENCE

There is already a not insubstantial jurisprudence (and copious academic comment) on the meaning of the equality clause. Some of the cases were decided in terms of the interim Constitution,[5] others in terms of the final Constitution.[6] Two judgments of the Constitutional Court are selected here, not to expound on the difficulties of interpretation of the clause or the varying opinions of judges and authors on the subject, but for the more limited purpose of highlighting the failure of the court, in elucidating the meaning of the admittedly enigmatic concept of equality, to recognize the emergence of new identities and new kinds of relationships and its adherence to outdated notions of role allocations for men and women.

President of the Republic of South Africa v Hugo[7] concerned the exercise by the President of his prerogative to grant remission of sentence to certain categories of prisoners.[8] Imprisoned mothers, with minor children under the age of 12 years on a specified date, were released. Hugo, a male prisoner at the time, and a single parent, challenged the exercise of the presidential prerogative on the ground that it discriminated unfairly against him on the ground of sex/gender and, indirectly, against his appropriately aged son, because the latter's parent was not a woman. The court was, surprisingly to some, open to subjecting the exercise of these special powers to the full scrutiny of the Bill of Rights and to requiring justification. But, having undertaken the task of judicial review, it found that, although the exercise of the powers may have been discriminatory, the discrimination was not unfair and thus did not violate the equality clause.[9]

The court's reasoning was based on an affidavit in which the President argued that the remission of sentences of mothers would serve the interests of small children cared for, in the main by their mothers. Accordingly, the Presidential Act was found to be fair, and to have promoted the best interests of the children concerned. The court made reference to the contextual demands of interpreting the equality clause, requiring the courts to alleviate the disadvantages of past discrimination. Mothers do, but fathers do not, fall into a historically disadvantaged group. Moreover, the court said, the release of male prisoners would not have contributed as significantly to the achievement of the President's purpose as the release of mothers for, generally speaking, mothers are primarily responsible for the care of small children. Indeed, Goldstone J offered the

---

[5] Act 200 of 1993. Section 8 was the equality clause.

[6] Act 108 of 1996. Section 9 is the equality clause.

[7] 1997 (4) SA 1 (CC).

[8] The case was decided in terms of the interim Constitution, and the Presidential powers resided in s 82 of Act 200 of 1993.

[9] The outcome of this case might well have been less disagreeable had the court made more of the difference between the level of scrutiny required for the exercise by the President of special powers conferred by the Constitution and for ordinary legislation, say. The court was not unmindful of the special nature of the prerogative, but elected to subject its exercise to full scrutiny. It should be noted that the power was exercised in favour of a category of prisoners. Had it been exercised in respect of a single prisoner, a constitutional challenge based on discrimination would have been difficult to imagine (Goldstone J at 17). For an approval of the finding of the majority of the court, see Mark S Kende 'Gender Stereotypes in South African and American Constitutional Law: The Advantages of a Pragmatic Approach to Equality and Transformation' (2000) 117 SALJ 745.

observation that, as male prisoners outnumbered female prisoners almost fifty-fold, a public outcry, in a climate of countrywide crime, would almost certainly have resulted from the release of male prisoners who were parents.[10] Continuing in this vein, the court, accepting that the failure to release fathers did constitute a disadvantage, stressed that it did not deny or limit their rights or obligations as fathers in any permanent way. Their incarceration, after all, had resulted not from the Presidential Act under attack, but from their criminal conviction.[11]

This kind of reasoning is unfortunate, and the last-mentioned proposition is startling. Dennis Davis argues that the court at some point permitted principle to give way to pragmatism.[12] In a powerful judgment, dissenting from that of Goldstone J, who delivered the view of the majority, Kriegler J eloquently reminds us of the gender stereotyping that has been fundamental to the disadvantage experienced by women in our society. To regard women (implicitly, all women) as primary caregivers 'is both a result and a cause of prejudice; a societal attitude which relegates women to a subservient, occupationally inferior yet unceasingly onerous role. It is a relic … of the patriarchy which the Constitution so vehemently condemns … Reliance on the generalization that women are the primary care givers is harmful in its tendency to cramp and stunt the efforts of *both men and women to form their identities freely*' (my emphasis).[13] Kriegler J emphasized that the court had been given no data on how many men, who were parents, would have qualified for release, nor any information about a possible public outcry that such a release would have precipitated. The President had not offered any such information, and counsel had not been asked by the court to address the subject. In short, his statement amounts to a view that the court had incorrectly embarked, *mero motu*, on a frolic of speculation to support its finding.

Most disturbing is the fact that the court's admitted generalization about male and female roles will serve to reinforce the widely held and unacceptably simplistic notion that women, regardless of whether single parents or not, regardless of colour, regardless of class, are more responsible for the care of their

---

[10]   At 25.

[11]   At 26.

[12]   At the time of his criticism of this and other judgments, Davis was an academic; he is now a judge of the High Court. See *Democracy and Deliberation* (Juta & Co, 1999), 78 and 'Equality: The Majesty of Legoland Jurisprudence' (1999) 116 SALJ 398 at 404. His writings have excited criticism and contrary views. See the scathing, inordinately lengthy review of the book by Christopher Roederer, 'Dennis the Menace: Post-Structuralist Dabbler or Constructive Interpreter?' (2001) 118 SALJ 177, and Davis's hard-hitting reply, in 'Has Any Author Been Subjected to a "Ruderer" Review? Or Cry the Beloved Academic Halls of Learning' (2001) 118 SALJ 250. The two Davis pieces selected here certainly do not represent the dominant view on our equality jurisprudence. They do, however, grasp the nettle, provoke responses and demand insights that academic commentators all too frequently avoid in favour of bland reproduction of the facts of cases and inevitable accommodation if not wholesale endorsement of the court's findings. Davis's work provides a provocative platform from which to view the stereotyping and failure of the court to accept the emergence of new identities for men and women in South Africa. The critique of his book should be consulted for a different analysis, as should Susie Cowen, 'Can "Dignity" Guide South Africa's Equality Jurisprudence?' (2001) 17 SAJHR 34. This author justifies the foregrounding by the Constitutional Court of dignity in the elucidation of the equality clause. But she does plead for the 'slow' and 'restrained' court (op cit at 54) to develop a comprehensive vision of its role in overcoming subjugation and an appropriate comprehension of the important contexts of disadvantage. The works cited by her are recommended for a fuller picture of the development of our equality jurisprudence.

[13]   At 37, and see Davis (1999) 116 SALJ 398 at 405.

children than fathers are. (The dangers inherent in accepting such a generalization in the South African context will be raised again later.)

The court's conclusion that the male prisoners found themselves denied the right to exercise their rights as fathers not because of the presidential pardon extended to women, but because of their own criminality is astounding. It surely cannot be taken to entail the proposition that the mothers who qualified for release were imprisoned for some reason other than their own criminality?

Clearly 'stung'[14] by the claims about gender scripts and stereotyping made by Kriegler J, O'Regan J, a respected feminist who did not dissent, found it necessary to deliver a separate concurring judgment in which she sought to rebut Kriegler J's view that the presidential pardon violated the constitutional guarantee of equality. She, like Goldstone and Kriegler JJ, relied on the fact that the responsibility borne by mothers is a cause of substantial inequality in our society. To insist on equal treatment of parents, thereby denying to mothers special treatment as members of a structurally disadvantaged group, in her view, would be to take too formalistic a view of equality, would entrench that inequality, and would prevent the ultimate attainment of substantive equality. For as long as the unequal burden in relation to child care rested upon women, she considered, reliance on the generalization about their roles would not cause substantial harm to other women, or to fathers.[15] It should be noted here that Kriegler J did not make any general case against special, compensatory treatment for women. But in his dissent he rejected its justifiability on the facts before him.

The 'trail of confusion'[16] left by the court derives in largest measure from its failure to acknowledge Hugo as a single parent. His child had no opportunity to be nurtured by any female primary caregiver. His wife had died while he was in jail. It is in the denial by the court to afford to single parents who were prisoners and happened to be fathers the benefits that were accorded to single parents who were mothers that the worst aspect of the court's conclusion is revealed. O'Regan J also fell prey to the unsustainable implications of the proposition that the men who were in prison (that is, implicitly, unlike the women who were in prison) were not there because of the particular exercise of the presidential pardon, but because of their criminal convictions. She considered it sufficient that such men could apply at any time, in the ordinary course, for special remission of sentence, if their special circumstances warranted it.

We need to step back now and enquire whether the kind of judgment delivered for the court by Goldstone J in this case, and the attempt by O'Regan J to palliate the full impact of the cogent and stinging criticism of the dissenting Kriegler J, by resorting to the special treatment argument, best serve the women these judges were so anxious to protect. Our equality jurisprudence, it is suggested, was done some substantial harm here, and not only by the result in this case.[17] In the process, 'little was done to contribute to a man's dignity and

---

14   Davis's term, op cit, n 12 above, at 80 and 406, respectively.

15   At 49–50.

16   Again Davis's term, op cit, n 12, at 82 and 407, respectively. Seven of the majority judges concurred in O'Regan's judgment.

17   It is beyond the scope of this piece to enter upon an analysis of the conflation of the right to dignity with that of equality and of several other complex aspects of interpretation of the equality clause that arise from this and other equality cases. These tasks have been undertaken by others,

freedom as a father'[18] nor to encourage fathers to assume the full share of the parenting burden, along with its privileges. The matter goes beyond equality between men and women. Equal treatment of male and female single parents was denied. The majority of the court sanctioned discrimination against single fathers, on the ground that such discrimination was not unfair.

Feminists, among them both academics and judges, have in recent times been notably vociferous in claiming that parenting should be a shared responsibility. Feminists recognize that true equality, especially in the workplace, where the ideal employee is still widely regarded as a man with no childcare responsibilities, will be achieved only when the society reconceives the respective rights and obligations of parents towards their children and of parents towards each other. A judge's view in recent years that '"mothering" is also part of a man's being'[19] is evocative of this trend. The arguments and statements suggest that it will become increasingly difficult for feminists to sustain the refrain that (all) mothers are primary caregivers of their own children and therefore deserve special treatment entrenched in legislation and enforced by the courts in the regulation of parent and child relationships. Put simply, this terrain cannot be represented as uncontested.[20] The extent to which claims for real equality, supported by the call for a change in mindset in society, can reside comfortably alongside claims for special treatment that may ultimately be deeply inimical to the attainment by women of substantive equality, are very hard questions. They demand in each case carefully reasoned answers. And the answers must be situated within the context of a highly complex, very particular society, in which class and race ubiquitously serve to define the roles of mothers towards the nurturing of their children. In substantial sections of our population, mothers are not the primary caregivers of their children. The children of many (white) middle- and upper-class mothers, some of whom work outside the home, are cared for in large measure by black domestic workers. Large numbers of African children are cared for by their grandmothers, within the context of an extended family, in rural areas, and not by their working mothers, who all too often are themselves urban, domestic workers caring for the children of other women. With more and more women employed outside the home, the care of children is being undertaken by persons other than their parents. Increasingly, and encouragingly, in some sections of society, both parents are sharing the childcare responsibility. This is not a generalization. It is the postulation of a mixed and changing set of circumstances which reflect a socio-economic reality and which make the justificatory generalization for special treatment for mothers, relied on so often by courts and academics, more and more

---

notably Davis, op cit, n 12 above, the works of other authors cited here (see especially n 12 above), and the writings cited by those authors.

[18] Davis, *Democracy and Deliberation*, op cit, n 12 above, at 83.

[19] See *Van der Linde v Van der Linde* 1996 (3) SA 509 (O) at 515. The term 'mothering' was an unfortunately gendered choice. 'Parenting' would have been preferable. The sentiment though is abundantly clear, and commendable. The case is discussed along with others involving custody and which demonstrate the acceptance by the courts of the shared parenting role by June Sinclair, 'From Parents' Rights to Children's Rights' in *Children's Rights in a Transitional Society*, ed CJ Davel (Protea Book House, 1999), 62 at 70. Some of the more prominent custody cases received attention in the 2000 edition of the *Survey*.

[20] See, for example, Sinclair, op cit, n 19 above, at 74–75 and the works and cases cited in that piece.

suspect. (This point will be raised again in the context of competing parental claims for custody and the penchant for maternal preference.)

The second vignette offered from the clutch of equality cases has nothing to do with children. Nine judges of the Constitutional Court were confronted with questions about the implications of marriage and the nature of marital status within the context of insolvency. The case raises questions about whether man and wife become 'one' or whether they retain their individuality and deserve to be treated by the law of insolvency as distinct individuals, albeit conjoined in matrimony. The issue in *Harksen v Lane*[21] was the constitutionality of a clause in the Insolvency Act.[22] Section 21 of that Act provides that, upon the sequestration of the separate estate of one spouse, the estate of the other automatically vests in the Master and, upon appointment, in the trustee. The solvent spouse may claim the release of his/her property upon proof of certain circumstances, such as the fact that the property was acquired by the solvent spouse before the marriage, or was the subject of a marriage settlement, or is held with title valid as against the creditors of the insolvent spouse.

The applicant claimed that the statutory provision discriminated unfairly against solvent spouses. Similar burdens are not applicable to other persons with whom the insolvent may have had close commercial dealings, whether they be relatives, such as children, or other persons within the family, or close business associates. Five judges found no breach of the equality clause. There was discrimination, the majority held, but not unfair discrimination against solvent spouses. Solvent spouses, the court also held,[23] do not constitute a vulnerable group adversely affected by discrimination in the past. Even though the provision creates a legal presumption that the property of the solvent spouse was owned by the insolvent, no serious impairment of the dignity of the solvent spouse is entailed.[24] The admitted inconvenience occasioned by the effect of the provision was intended to serve the public interest and to protect the creditors of the insolvent spouse. 'The whole thrust of s 21 is merely to ensure that property which properly belonged to the insolvent ends up in the estate.'[25] Goldstone J, speaking for the majority, concluded that the automatic vesting of the property of the solvent spouse in the trustee 'is the kind of inconvenience and burden that any citizen may face when resort to litigation becomes necessary'.[26] He did not consider the invasive nature of the statutory provision, without which creditors in other jurisdictions manage apparently satisfactorily, to cause harm serious enough to warrant a striking down.

O'Regan J, this time, dissented. And, with her, concurred the other female constitutional court judge, Mokgoro J. Madala J also dissented, as did Sachs J, who delivered his own minority judgment. No harmonious chorus on equality here.

---

[21]   1998 (1) SA 300 (CC). Four of the nine judges dissented.
[22]   Act 24 of 1936.
[23]   At 328.
[24]   At 328 and 329.
[25]   Per Goldstone J at 318.
[26]   At 329.

Does the rule pertaining to insolvency perpetuate or entrench stereotyped role allocations for husbands and wives? Is the only question posed by the case the one so heavily concentrated upon by the judges, namely, whether the provision unfairly discriminates against solvent spouses? Or are there deeper, more insidious manifestations here of stereotyping of the financial interactions between people who live in intimate relationships? Is there nothing to be made of the impact of the provision on and its indirect discrimination against wives, who are certainly members of a vulnerable group that has suffered severe discrimination on account of marital status? Is there no inequality here based on gender that deserved careful attention, but which received almost none?

Goldstone J examined very carefully the nature of the discrimination before him. Although he found it to exist, as against solvent spouses, his view was that the 'inconvenience' occasioned by the provision to solvent spouses was quite within the bounds of reasonableness and not unfair. He did not find fault with the stereotyping of marital relationships entailed in the purpose of the enactment, and he expressed relief that counsel for the applicant had not pursued the point that there was discrimination based on gender here.[27]

It is noteworthy that the judgment of Goldstone J, for the majority, does deal with the historical context within which the provision was originally introduced into our law. It refers specifically, as did O'Regan J, to the passage in the case of *Maudsley's Trustee v Maudsley*,[28] stating that '[o]ne knows that before the amendment of the law in 1926, it was a common practice for traders ... to seek to avoid payment of their debts by putting property in their *wives'* names; on insolvency the burden rested on the trustee to attack the *wife's* title' (my emphasis).[29] Note the gendered explanation for the introduction of the statutory provision. Note the rationale that creditors had to be specially protected against having to launch an attack on the title of wives. Hence the presumption of irregularity on the part of the insolvent and his wife, to justify an automatic vesting of all the wife's property in the trustee of her husband's insolvent estate. The onus rests on her to prove her innocent, valid title.

This provision should also be seen within the context of the rest of the Insolvency Act. There are other provisions in it permitting the setting aside of dispositions without value and transactions which prejudice the rights of creditors.[30] Such provisions are considered adequate in other jurisdictions. The common law also provides a remedy for fraudulent dispositions by an insolvent.

Goldstone J stressed that, at the time the provision was inserted into the Act, there was no doubt that it was directed at the property of women married out of community of property:

'It could hardly have been otherwise, as there were relatively few women at that time who had an independent income. Its purpose was not aimed at disadvantaging or

---

[27]   At 326, note 46.

[28]   1940 TPD 399.

[29]   At 404. A similar provision existed in the predecessor to the 1926 Act – Act 32 of 1916, but the extended definition of 'spouse' was introduced in 1926.

[30]   Notably sections 26, 29, 30 and 31.

prejudicing women as such. Its language was gender neutral and as more women began to have their own income its effect applied more frequently to husbands.'[31]

The judge went on to point to the fact that over the years more and more women have become economically active and have their own property and income. Consequently, he argued, the spouses themselves will find it more difficult to know what belongs to whom:

'Having regard to the close *identity of interests* (my emphasis) between many married couples, they do not always make nice calculations and keep accurate records of their respective contributions to property they acquire.'[32]

Whether the improved position of women and their increased financial independence strengthens Goldstone J's argument for upholding the statutory provision, as he clearly thought it did, is highly debatable. Seen unwaveringly through the spectacles of the creditor it may well do so. And if it is thought that South Africa needs to give creditors more protection than other jurisdictions do, by discriminating against solvent spouses, that case would have to be made. (It did not appeal to O'Regan J, whose dissent is founded on this point.) But had one wished to be sensitive to the protracted and severe discrimination that our law until recently visited upon married women – textbook discussions of their legal status was often, until the eighties, grouped with that of the status of minors and lunatics – one may have thought that the harmful impact of a clause that disproportionately prejudices women married out of community of property (see further below) would have been seen as indirect discrimination, as reinforcing and entrenching oppression and disadvantage of an undoubtedly vulnerable group, and thus to demand striking down.

Marriage out of community of property was until 1984 a matrimonial property regime selected by many white, and several coloured and Asian women in order to avoid falling under the marital power (akin to guardianship) of their husbands, an automatic consequence of marriage in community of property.[33] These women, by antenuptial contract, forfeited the right to a half share in the joint estate built up during the marriage – the essence of community of property – in order to enjoy the full legal status and capacity automatically enjoyed by all men regardless of the marital regime they chose. The choice for women of these race groups was to forfeit financial security in order to enjoy being treated by the law as adults, or retain the right to half of the joint estate, and subject themselves to perpetual tutelage. A fair choice, or an instance of grossly unfair discrimination against women? The position for African women was even worse, and was not remedied until 1988. Until then, their civil marriages always, whether in or out of community of property, entailed the acquisition by their husbands of the marital power.[34] Women were also not taxed separately until recently. Their incomes were

---

[31] At 326 note 46.

[32] At 326.

[33] Men had other sound financial reasons for choosing this popular matrimonial property regime – it avoided automatic sharing of the estate built up during the marriage.

[34] For an exposition of the inequality entailed in and the demise of the marital power, see June Sinclair (assisted by Jacqueline Heaton) *Law of Marriage Vol I* (Juta & Co, 1996), 126–131.

added to the incomes of their husbands, by law, regardless of how they were acquired.[35]

Nowadays, and increasingly, women build up their own estates and enter freely into all manner of business transactions without requiring the consent of their husbands. Does this change, and our newborn dedication to eradicating inequality, not demand that the law respect their separate identity (and indeed that of all married people) as individual businesspersons?

One further observation can be made about the impact of the clause under attack and the argument for indirect discrimination against women married out of community of property. The observation is, not for the want of trying to obtain the required data, based on conjecture.[36] It is similar to the one employed by the court in *Hugo* (regarding the huge number of male parent prisoners who may have benefited from the presidential pardon under attack in that case, which may have caused a public outcry in a country already riddled with crime). It is this: despite the greatly improved legal position of women and the increased financial independence of the better educated, my guess is that by far the most sequestrations of individuals are of the estates of men. This entails that it is the newly acquired financial resources of those women who are achieving their rightful place of independence in our society who disproportionately experience the impact of a clause of the kind under attack in this case. The discrimination therefore is against solvent spouses, but also against a class of women, albeit indirectly. Goldstone J's reliance on the motive and purpose of the 1926 legislation does nothing to palliate its discriminatory impact or rescue it from attack. It is the effect of the provision that is in question here. And it is suggested that it is unfairly discriminatory to spouses, and to women married out of community.

Sachs J came down heavily in favour of demanding that all adults should be entitled to expect from the law respect for their separate identity. Couples in intimate relationships, like other members of a common household, should be entitled to retain their separate identities and not be presumed to have a propensity to collude to prejudice or defraud creditors.

> 'Manifestly patriarchal in origin, s 21 promotes a concept of marriage in which, independently of the living circumstances and careers of the spouses, their estates are merged ... Its underlying premise is that one business mind is at work within the marriage, not two. This stems from and reinforces a stereotypical view of the marriage relationship, which, in the light of the new constitutional values is demeaning to both spouses.'[37]

---

[35]   See Sinclair, op cit, n 34, at 31.

[36]   The office of the Master of the High Court can provide only the number of applications for sequestrations of individuals, not even the number of actual sequestrations. Hence no information on the number of sequestrations of men, as opposed to women, for the years 1996–1999 (the period during which *Harksen*'s case was being litigated) could be obtained. Credit Guarantee, a credit monitoring organization, was able to provide the figures: 2803 sequestrations of individuals for South Africa as a whole for 1996, 3282 for 1997, 4287 for 1998 and 6005 for 1999. No breakdown by gender was available.

[37]   At 346–347.

Interestingly, the word 'patriarchal', the reference to one business mind, that of the husband, and the references to new constitutional values, raise for the reader the promise and the hope that the issue of gender inequality was to receive serious attention, but it was taken no further.

O'Regan's dissenting judgment centres on the impairment of dignity occasioned by the invasive provision, which discriminated, she found, unfairly, on the ground of marital status. This rendered it a violation of the equality clause. Much was made of the seriousness of the invasion and the lack of necessity for the provision in the light of comparative law. The judge actually began to meander down the path of entrenched patterns of discrimination against women within the context of marital status. It is worth recording her words:

> 'Many of the laws governing marriage were based on an assumption that women were primarily responsible for the maintenance of a household and the rearing of children, while men's responsibility lay outside the household. These rules therefore both reflected and entrenched deep patterns of inequality between men and women. Not infrequently women's experience of marriage was ... one of subordination ... In the case before us the discrimination facially affects all spouses ... The applicant did not seek to establish that the provisions under challenge were indirectly discriminatory on the ground of gender. Although I have little doubt that at times provisions discriminating on the grounds of marital status will implicate a pattern of discrimination rooted in one of the patterns established in our past, I cannot conclude that that is the case here.'[38]

This fleeting mention of indirect discrimination against wives, in the form of a disproportionate impact of the clause on certain married women, serves to remind us that the law of husband and wife has been replete with examples of discrimination. But having raised the gender issue, O'Regan abandons it, without a hint of the potential such a claim may have had for the applicant, had she pursued it.

In fairness to the court, it has to be acknowledged that the gender issue was abandoned by the applicant, making it unnecessary for the judges to deal with it. But given the great care and detail that is to be found in the lengthy judgments of Goldstone and O'Regan JJ, and given the emphasis placed by the court on developing step by step our equality jurisprudence, one might have hoped for an assertion from it that, embedded in these facts lay demonstrable manifestations of deeply unfair discrimination against (a class of) married women that had pervaded our law for several centuries and had only recently been eliminated from it.

Dennis Davis's question, 'Quo vadis equality?'[39] is answered by the author in despondent terms. He berates the Constitutional Court's conflation of equality with dignity. He declaims the pragmatism that drove the court in *Hugo* to make an unsustainable distinction between single parent mothers and single parent fathers. He classifies *Harksen*'s case as one concerning identity, not dignity. He laments the fact that, to him, the court has rendered meaningless a fundamental value of

---

[38]   At 338–339.

[39]   Posed within his article at (1999) 116 SALJ 398 at 412–414. For a mild analysis of these cases, and an equanimous acceptance of the conflation of dignity with equality, see Pierre de Vos, 'Equality for All? A Critical Analysis of the Equality Jurisprudence of the Constitutional Court' (2000) 63 THRHR 62. See also, generally, the works cited in n 12 above.

our Constitution and given 'dignity' both a content and a scope that make for a piece of jurisprudential Legoland. For him, equality is too central a concept to be relegated to a secondary meaning. He concludes by urging the court to have the courage to start afresh its search for an equality jurisprudence located within a constitutional vision rather than in formulaic classifications that reduce a core societal value to redundancy. Davis believes that, if that courage is not forthcoming, equality may just as well be deleted from our constitutional text. Harsh and provocative his evaluations may be.[40] For me they serve pointedly to demonstrate how easily the public are duped into believing that an equality clause on a piece of paper will ensure equality, and how easily the majority judgments in the two cases above glossed over the need for South Africans to understand the new identities, new family relationships and new roles for men and women being forged in a formally democratic dispensation governing a society that is struggling to comprehend what is required of it.

III   PARENTS AND CHILDREN

A   Unmarried fathers

In the 2000 edition of the *Survey*[41] the attempts by natural fathers of children born out of wedlock to demand that their consent be obtained before adoption of their children could take place were covered. A provision in the Child Care Act of 1983[42] had provided that the consent of the natural father of such a child was not required for the child's adoption. The provision was struck down as unfairly discriminatory in the case *Fraser v Children's Court, Pretoria North*.[43] The Adoption Matters Amendment Act of 1998[44] demanded that the father's consent to the adoption be obtained, but only provided that he has acknowledged himself in writing to be the father and has made his identity and whereabouts known, as provided for in the Act.[45] The need to obtain the father's consent is dispensed with if the required acknowledgement has not been made, and in certain other situations.[46]

---

[40]   See the works cited in n 12 above and, in particular, Roederer's trenchant criticism of Davis's work. Davis's disquiet about the status afforded to dignity and the consequences for equality are echoed, in mild manner, by Warren Friedman, 'Formal Versus Substantive Equality and the Jurisprudence of the Constitutional Court' (2000) 63 THRHR 314 at 320, in the context of his discussion of a groundbreaking judgment on sexual identity which clearly (and in a unanimous court) repudiates the stereotyping of homosexual relationships as criminal and wrong, and of gay men as felons: *National Coalition for Gay and Lesbian Equality v Minister of Justice* 1999 (1) SA 6 (CC). Further on this case, known as 'the Sodomy case', see Pierre de Vos, 'Sexual Orientation and the Right to Equality in the South African Constitution' (2000) 117 SALJ 17. But de Vos is not deeply concerned about the formulaic constructs entailed in the equality jurisprudence or in the conflation of dignity with equality – see 'Equality for All? A Critical Analysis of the Equality Jurisprudence of the Constitutional Court' (2000) 63 THRHR 62.

[41]   At 341–342.

[42]   Act 74 of 1983, s 18(4)(d).

[43]   1997 (2) SA 261 (CC).

[44]   Act 56 of 1998, which amended the Child Care Act 74 of 1983 – the principal Act.

[45]   Section 4 of the 1998 Act.

[46]   Section 5 of the 1998 Act, which amends s 19 of the principal Act.

Now it is necessary to examine the processes[47] that have been set up for fathers of such children to acknowledge their paternity. They are required, with the consent of the mother of the child, to apply to the Director-General, Home Affairs, for the amendment of the registration of the birth of the child, by recording acknowledgement of paternity and their particulars. Cumbersome, but feasible if, of course, the mother consents.[48] In such a case, the unwed father must within seven days of the consent make the application to amend the birth register and give written notice of and details pertaining to his application to the Commissioner for Child Welfare. If the mother does not consent to this process, the father must apply to the Children's Court for a declaratory order confirming his paternity[49] (which may of course be contested, in which event he will have to prove it). This application has to be made within 14 days of the mother's refusal to grant consent. Within seven days of the granting of the declaratory order by the Children's Court, the father must cause an amendment to be effected to the birth register. Within seven days of making the application to amend the birth register, the father must give notice to the clerk of the children's court that will hear the application for adoption of the child that there is an application pending for the amendment of the birth register and giving details of where such application was made and when. This is 'a hell of a process'. The average man is unlikely to attempt to negotiate this minefield in a normal, increasingly common relationship of cohabitation. Should he discover that the mother wishes to give the child up for adoption (more likely once the relationship breaks down), he is compelled to commence the motion proceedings and administrative process outlined above. This, in order to object to the fact that he has not consented to his child's adoption. The bottom line is that the father has to go through a complex legal process, in a justice system the administration of which has virtually collapsed,[50] in order to obtain a right which the Constitutional Court said he ought in any event to have. Although in theory, therefore, the unconstitutionality has been rectified, the reality is that in practice most men will find it exceedingly difficult to assert, and hence will not assert, the right that the Constitutional Court affirmed is theirs.

My argument has for long been[51] that the law relating to children of parents not married to one another should start with an assumption that accords increasingly with common social practice – an ordinary, marriage-like relationship, but no formal (or legally recognized – as in the case of Muslim marriages – see further below) marriage. In the event of pathology, a speedy and inexpensive family court procedure should entitle the mother, any mother, any parent, in any family situation, to obtain an order deviating from a presumption of

---

[47]   Contained in Regulations promulgated in terms of the 1998 Act. See GN R65 *GG* 19682 of 11 January 1999 (Reg Gaz 6411).

[48]   This is in terms of s 11(4) of the Births and Deaths Registration Act 51 of 1992 and s 19A(8) of the Child Care Act 74 of 1983.

[49]   In terms of s 19A(9) of the Child Care Act 74 of 1983.

[50]   This fact is extraneous to the legal argument being made but cannot be left unstated either. Newspapers are replete with reports of maintenance funds being stolen by court officials, with administrative inefficiencies that deprive old people of their pensions for months on end, and even announcing at one stage that the High Court in Johannesburg could not receive faxes because it had run out of fax paper and had no budget for more.

[51]   See the article referred to in n 19 above, and June Sinclair (assisted by Jacqueline Heaton) *The Law of Marriage Vol I* (Juta & Co, 1996), 120–123.

shared parental responsibility, and rights, and the consequences flowing from such a presumption. (It seems that this may be the direction in which England is moving.[52])

The argument for automatic equal parental rights and responsibilities is not infrequently met with the counter-argument that, because women are primary caregivers, the law should afford them special treatment and continue to prefer them also as parents with legal priority in cases such as the consent to adoption of an extra-marital child. In relation to the constitutionality of the exercise of the presidential pardon releasing female prisoners, in the *Hugo* case,[53] it was argued above that there are serious dangers inherent in this claim for special treatment. The dangers pertain to the achievement of the substantive equality for which women are striving. But they are suspect also because they rely on generalizations about the role of mothers in respect of their own children, and the role of fathers, that are inimical to the encouragement of all parents to share the responsibility of parenting. The maternal preference/primary caregiver argument extends into the realm of custody and access, discussed below, in respect of which similar arguments can be mounted.

Despite what has been put forward as the better position for the law to assume as a starting point, it should not be assumed that there is no force in the argument that absent fathers can make a nuisance of themselves, and that to give them automatic equal rights with mothers of extra-marital children could place a substantial burden on those women who are indeed bearing full responsibility for the upbringing of their children. The point is that a choice between formal equality and special treatment for women has to be made. The choice of equal parental responsibility accords better with a commitment to equality for men, and will, it has been suggested, ultimately advance rather than hinder the project of substantive equality for women. One proviso is always important to stress – the legal system must have in place efficient, speedy and inexpensive remedies to permit the court to intervene in genuine cases of pathology that demand deviation from the rule. South Africa's capacity to meet this requirement is, sadly, lacking.

After several years of not seeking contact with his children, their father sought an order for access in *I v S*.[54] The marriage between the parents had been according to Islamic law and thus not recognized as a valid marriage in South African law, but when the relationship broke down and the marriage dissolved according to Islamic law, the parties had in 1994 entered into an agreement of settlement relating to their property rights and also to the children. The agreement had stipulated the detail for access for the applicant father. He sought, in the application under discussion here, to have the access clause in the agreement made

---

[52] After consultation with the Lord Chancellor's Department – see 1998, Consultation Paper 1: 'Court Procedures for the Determination of Paternity' and Consultation Paper 2: 'The Law on Parental Responsibility for Unmarried Fathers' (Stationery Office) – it was announced on 2 July 1998 (Press Release 201/98) that parental responsibility was to be conferred automatically on unmarried fathers whose names appeared in the birth register. This is aside from the fact that s 4 of the Children Act 1989 permits such fathers to seek an order of court to obtain parental responsibility. The envisaged legislation had not been passed by the time of the 2001 election. But there appears to be widespread support for it that may see it reintroduced. [*Editor's note*: Provision is made to this effect in the Adoption and Children Bill 2001.]

[53] See n 7 above.

[54] 2000 (2) SA 993 (C).

an order of court in terms of the Natural Fathers of Children Born out of Wedlock Act.[55] This statute permits a court to make an order granting a right of access to children born out of wedlock, that is, considered by the civil law to be illegitimate. (That this is the position of children born of marriages celebrated according to the Islamic faith is unacceptable (see further below).)

The applicant had ceased to attempt to exercise his rights of access in terms of the agreement in 1998, and the three children, aged 20, 17 and 14 years were extremely hostile toward their father. They did not want any contact with him and regarded him as an emotionally absent parent whose presence in their lives merely exacerbated acrimony and hostility between him and their mother. The children were considered by a psychologist to be doing fairly well and to be angry at their father's sudden preoccupation with seeing them. Their wishes were respected. The court refused to make the access clause in the agreement an order of court. The question that remains unanswered by the litigation reported is whether the agreement between the parties was enforceable. Certainly as to undischarged obligations relating to property rights it would be.[56] Presumably, as to the access right it would not be, since the court had found it to be not in the best interests of the children that the clause be made an order of the court.

A most unusual case involving a claim for damages by the extra-marital child of a celebrity rugby player and commentator against his father fell to be decided in *Jooste v Botha.*[57] The child, aged 11 years (duly assisted by his mother to bring the action), sued for R450,000 compensation for the fact that the father refused to acknowledge him and give him the love and care that a parent is required, both at common law, and in terms of the Constitution, to give.[58] The father had never failed to maintain the child via regular support payments, but did not wish to have anything to do with him as his father. Not surprisingly, the action failed. But, surprisingly, the judge found it necessary here to distinguish between legitimate and illegitimate children (now known as extra-marital children). He doubted that the equality provision in the Constitution, which expressly outlaws discrimination based on birth, 'put illegitimate children on a par with children born in wedlock ... especially as far as inheritance is concerned'.[59] He found that, despite improvements in the position of the unmarried father and the fact that legislation permitted him to apply for custody and access (which, it was pointed out in the 2000 edition of the *Survey,*[60] the common law entitled such fathers to do anyway), 'he is not a parent within the meaning of the words "parental care"'.[61] These are startling statements and, apart from being erroneous, were not, it is submitted, necessary in order to dispose of the case. The Intestate Succession Act and the

---

[55]   Act 86 of 1997, discussed in the 2000 edition of the *Survey* at 342.

[56]   See *Ryland v Edros* 1997 (2) SA 690 (C) (discussed in the 2000 edition of the *Survey,* at 347–348) and *Amod v Multilateral Motor Vehicle Accidents Fund* 1999 (4) SA 119 (SCA), discussed further below, both of which concerned contractual obligations to maintain.

[57]   2000 (2) SA 199 (T).

[58]   See s 28 generally, and s 28(1)(b) in particular.

[59]   2000 (2) SA 199 (T) at 204.

[60]   At 342.

[61]   2000 (2) SA 199 (T) at 209.

Law of Succession Amendment Act[62] abolished the differences relating to inheritance by illegitimate children that were part of the common law. Illegitimacy no longer affects the capacity of one blood relative to inherit from another.[63]

The judge also dealt with the application of the Constitution – a vexed question – and whether the rights conferred by it are binding not only against the State (vertical application), but also as between private individuals (horizontal application). On the latter issue, he interpreted the provision in the Constitution giving to children a right to 'parental care' as placing an obligation only on the person/s in whose custody the child was – the custodian who, in this case, was the single mother. He could not imagine that the Constitution had intended to create an enforceable right of the kind in issue before him.

No one would quarrel with the result of the case. Indeed it must be questioned what the mother was attempting to achieve in assisting the child to launch the claim, since doing so would not have conduced to a better relationship between father and son, nor could it have been in the child's best interests to bring an action manifestly spurious in law.

The problem with the judgment is that the court could have reached its conclusion without making the incorrect, unacceptable and outmoded statements quoted here. There are certain legal obligations in family law that are hortatory. They lay a foundation for a sound, moral, ordered society. But they are not capable of enforcement through normal legal remedies such as specific performance or damages. The marital wrong of desertion, for example, a ground for divorce prior to 1979, left the innocent spouse only with the very remedy that he or she may have wanted dearly to avert – dissolution of the marriage. No order for specific performance of the duty of spouses to live together and to be faithful to each other has ever existed. Nor has there ever been an action for damages between the spouses for desertion or infidelity. But the obligation to live together and to be faithful is fundamental to the marriage relationship. It is a legal one, and certainly part of our common law. The same is true of the duty of a parent to love and nurture his or her child, whether born in or out of wedlock. There is a host of case-law and legislation dealing with the consequences of a breach of this duty – to deprive the neglectful parent of his or her parental power (responsibility) and place the child in an institution or in foster care, if necessary. Only the economic duty of support to the child is capable of enforcement by judgment and execution; the hortatory part of the parental duty is not. That is that. There can be no doubt that the Constitution did not fundamentally change the common law in this regard.

---

62   Act 81 of 1987, s 1(2), and Act 43 of 1992, s 4 (which inserted s 2D into the Wills Act 7 of 1953), respectively.

63   Prior to the coming into operation of these Acts, an illegitimate child inherited on intestacy from his/her mother but not his/her father. The child was able to inherit under the will of his/her father if the will clearly indicated that he/she should be included. A mere reference to 'my children' was presumed to include only the father's legitimate children, whereas the same expression in a mother's will was presumed to include all her children, for the common law holds that '*een moeder maakt geen bastaard*'.

B   Lesbian partners

Pending at the time of writing is judgment in a case brought by a lesbian judge of the High Court seeking to have certain provisions of the Child Care Act,[64] which regulate adoption, declared unconstitutional. The Act provides for adoption by married couples. The judge, who had some years ago adopted two children, wishes to have the adoption extended to include her lesbian partner as an adoptive parent. From reports in the press it seems that the argument being considered by the court is that the Act discriminates unfairly against same-sex couples and is thus a contravention of the equality clause in the Constitution.[65] In argument for the Ministers of Welfare and Population Development, and of Justice, who are defending the action, it has been pointed out that the Act also does not permit unmarried heterosexual couples to adopt. It will be of great interest to see whether the rights of same-sex couples are extended in this context, and whether the distinction between heterosexual couples who choose not to marry and same-sex couples who are not permitted to marry is clearly made and understood, whether or not it is determinative in this context.[66]

C   Custody

In *Ex parte Critchfield* [67] the maternal preference rule featured prominently in determining the best interests of two young children, a boy aged three years, and a girl aged seven. Several iterations of acrimonious litigation including an urgent application had ensued between the parents. Joint custody had been awarded on divorce, but was described as having been 'an utter disaster'.[68] The parents were before the court as joint applicants in the matter under discussion, seeking a variation of the order made on divorce. The father claimed that he should be awarded custody and the mother awarded liberal access, and the mother made an identical application. The judge's task was to decide how the best interests of these young children could be assured.

Both parents had during the marriage indulged in extra-marital sexual activities, and the husband had had homosexual encounters during the marriage and after its dissolution. Whereas one might have expected the judge to make more of these, he dismissed them as being 'as mild as leaves caressing in the breeze'.[69] He considered the mother's adultery to be more serious transgressions, which exceeded those of the father in number, duration and extent. He dismissed as unimportant the parties' 'unconventional' sex lives and peccadilloes, saying that a court should not be particularly concerned with the sexual predilections of litigants in deciding issues of custody, unless they have posed a threat to the children.[70] It is encouraging to see so clearly the unwillingness of the court

---

[64]   Act 74 of 1983.
[65]   See further section **IV** below, on Marriage and the Constitution.
[66]   See for example *Business Day*, 8 August 2001, p 4.
[67]   1999 (3) SA 132 (W).
[68]   At 135.
[69]   At 139.
[70]   Ibid.

minutely to examine the sexual conduct of warring parties in order to determine the best interests of children. And it is even more encouraging that the homosexual episodes in the father's life were not taken adversely to affect his claim for custody. His case was judged simply on his stable and caring relationship with his children and his suitability compared with the attributes of his less stable former wife.

Psychologists and other witnesses gave protracted evidence. Both parents attempted to convince the court of their suitability to nurture their children. They called as witnesses their respective domestic workers to testify about the children's daily routines. Unwittingly, both parents highlighted the dangers in generalizing about the physical care of children from middle- and upper-class families. The parents both worked, and the children were cared for in the main by female black domestic workers in both households. The mother was no more a primary caregiver than was her husband. Indeed, it seemed to the court that, of the two working parents, the father had arranged flexible working hours to be at home with the children in the afternoons, and seemed to be more concerned about their adjustment to a new lifestyle after the marriage had been dissolved. It is a widespread practice in South Africa that, based mainly on class, many children are cared for substantial periods of their lives by their 'nannies' – black women, with children of their own who, in turn, are cared for in extended families, often in rural areas. This is true in cases where mothers work, but also in cases where they do not. For the children in such households, interaction with their parents is confined to what is dubbed 'quality' time, devoted to intellectual and spiritual development.

As was said in relation to the *Hugo* case, class and race are powerful determinants in defining the roles of mothers in our society. This fact renders reliance on the maternal preference rule in custody matters even more vulnerable to attack than it might be in societies where domestic help is much more rare and much more confined than the holistic, housekeeper–mother role fulfilled by so many black domestic workers in South Africa. Reliance by judges and academics on cases and literature from Anglo-American or European jurisdictions that offer the notion of primary caregiver as a fairer determinant of suitability for custody than the maternal preference rule must therefore also be subjected to careful scrutiny and applied with great circumspection.[71] It is gratifying to see that in the instant case the judge undertook a careful and well-reasoned appraisal of the respective merits of the psychologists' evidence and the factual circumstances of the parents. He was mindful of the maternal preference rule, although he denied its

---

[71] This point is made by Elsje Bonthuys and Tshepo Mosikatsana, the authors of the chapter entitled 'Law of Persons and Family Law' in the 1999 *Annual Survey of South African Law* 119 at 135, where this case is discussed. It is not clear from the discussion of the case what the dispute was or what the court held. But general comments about the issues raised here appear almost randomly peppered within the brief discussion of the case. The authors also discuss the case of *van Rooyen v van Rooyen* 1999 (4) SA 435, in which a father sought custody solely, it seemed, in order to prevent his wife, who had been granted custody on divorce, from removing the children from South Africa and relocating to Australia. The husband had refused permission to the wife to take the children with her. Weighing up the best interests of the children and the reasonableness of the custodian parent's desire to relocate, the court relied on the fact that the mother had been the primary caregiver of the children. As the authors referred to above observe (at 136), there is no fully reasoned judicial pronouncement on the weight to be accorded to the primary caregiver notion here, but the decision does serve as another indication of its legal acceptability.

existence as a 'rule' of South African law, saying only that maternity is a justifiable consideration in determining custody, but should never be elevated into a sole determinant of the question. He also weighed the constitutional claims concerning sex discrimination against fathers in the very common award of custody of small children to mothers. He awarded custody to the father. The order for liberal access for the mother, which both parents wanted, was unduly detailed. But, given the fractious relationship between the parents and the repeated bouts of litigation between them over the children, the detail was probably necessary. The fact therefore that the judge compelled the father to maintain a residence within a 20 kilometre radius of a central point in Sandton, and that he expressly dealt with issues such as a public holiday falling on a Friday and this affecting the length of the access time permitted to the mother, should not attract criticism. Caution against such detailed access orders in the ordinary course should, however, be exercised.

One last aspect of interest in this case is that it included an award of reasonable access for a grandparent – the non-custodian parent's (the mother's) mother.

A case concerning the invocation of the Hague Convention on the Civil Aspects of International Child Abduction Act[72] deserves mention. In *WS v LS*[73] a father of two very young boys brought an application for the return to England of his sons by their mother, who had brought them from England to Cape Town, supposedly for a two-month holiday during a time when there were severe marital difficulties between the spouses. She had refused to hand over the children or to return with them to the United Kingdom, and had instituted divorce proceedings in South Africa. The spouses had engaged in various proceedings stemming from their marital discord. The narrow issue before the court in this case was whether Art 13 of the Hague Convention applied or not. Put shortly, the Article permits a judicial authority not to order the return of a child removed if the person who opposes the return can establish that the person in whose care the child was prior to the removal was not exercising rights of custody at the time of removal, or had consented to the removal, or that there is a grave risk that return would expose the child to harm or otherwise place the child in an intolerable situation. The father of the children had consented to the trip to Cape Town, placing the question of wrongful removal in question. It was held that he had not waived his right to invoke the Hague Convention either by consenting to the holiday, or by not initially pursuing a Hague Convention application while he tried to effect a reconciliation with his wife. The essential issue therefore became the potential harm to the children that an order for return would occasion. In order to situate itself within the context of the 'kidnappings' that the Convention sought to prevent, the court referred to several English cases. It considered the mother to have removed the children lawfully, but to have committed wrongful retention after the elapse of the two-month holiday period. The children had clearly been removed from their habitual residence. The father had offered to pay return airfares to England for his wife and the children. The mother, a South African,

---

[72]   Act 72 of 1996, which incorporated the Hague Convention on the Civil Aspects of International Child Abduction 1980 into South African municipal law as from 1 October 1997.

[73]   2000 (4) SA 104 (C).

argued that returning to England placed her in a precarious position because upon divorce she would have to leave the United Kingdom even were she granted custody of her children, both of whom were born there. She did not have the resources to conduct the divorce litigation in England where, she argued, the parties had temporarily gone to live. Her husband had ancestry rights to remain in England for four years and, after the elapse of a further year, the right to apply for citizenship, which he intended to do. He was involved in an adulterous relationship with another woman, with whom he was living.

The court held that it would be intolerable for a child under the age of one year to be removed from its mother and placed in the care of another woman and that the older child, not yet four years old, would also suffer harm from being separated from his mother and his sibling. On the basis of the age of the children and the role of the mother as primary caregiver, the court dismissed the application for return. The facts appear to justify the finding. But the awkward result is that, by unlawfully removing the children from their habitual home, the mother acquired the right to keep them in another country – precisely what the Convention seeks to prevent.[74]

IV   MARRIAGE AND THE CONSTITUTION

A   Same-sex unions

Marriage in South African private law is defined as a union between one man and one woman, but the question of gay and lesbian unions (and the rights of couples involved in them) is one assuming prominence as a constitutional issue. The Constitution expressly forbids unfair discrimination on the ground of sexual orientation.[75] A High Court judge is in the process, at the time of writing, of suing the Minister of Justice for failing, despite undertakings to do so, to effect changes to the law that determines the remuneration and conditions of service of judges. The Act in issue[76] provides for certain benefits for the spouses of judges. The judge claims that her partner is unfairly discriminated against because she is not eligible for these benefits. The similar treatment of unmarried heterosexual couples has been raised in defence of the Act, since the benefits in question are also not available to them. But such couples have chosen not to marry. Gay and lesbian couples are precluded from doing so. Cases of this kind strengthen the

---

[74]   For a case where return to the habitual residence in the United States was ordered after the child and mother had been (secretly) living in Cape Town for almost two years, and in which the Convention was held not to apply because the removal had taken place prior to South Africa's incorporation of the Convention into its municipal law, see *K v K* (1999) 4 SA 691 (C). The case also deals with the possible conflict between the requirement that return be ordered and the child's best interests, which may not be served by return. See further on this point, MJ Hlophe, 'The Judicial Approach to "Summary Applications for the Child's Return": A Move Away from "Best Interest" Principles?' (1998) 115 SALJ 439.

[75]   Sections 9(3) and 9(4).

[76]   The Judges Remuneration and Conditions of Employment Act 88 of 1989.

arguments of gay and lesbian persons who claim that they have a constitutional right to marry.[77]

Judgment in the above case will undoubtedly be affected by the ruling in *National Coalition for Gay and Lesbian Equality v Minister of Home Affairs*,[78] which dealt with the constitutional validity of a section of the Aliens Control Act that facilitates the granting of immigration permits to spouses of South African citizens or permanent residents.[79] The processes afforded to such spouses are not afforded to same-sex partners of such South Africans (or unmarried couples). On the basis of unfair discrimination on the ground of sexual orientation, the provision was attacked. Central to the court's handling of this matter was determining what constitutes 'family' and 'marriage', for it found that the term 'spouse', as used in the Act, could not be interpreted to include gay and lesbian partners. The court held that a permanent, same-sex relationship could in all respects resemble a marriage and that the family life of couples involved in such a relationship is indistinguishable from that of spouses.[80] It found that the provision in the Act constituted unfair discrimination and an unjustifiable limitation of the right to equality and to dignity of gay and lesbian persons who are in permanent same-sex life partnerships with foreign nationals. This result is not surprising given the empathetic and firm attitude taken by the court in decriminalizing gay sex in the so-called Sodomy case,[81] and in various other cases dealing with the custody rights of gay and lesbian parents.[82] However, the court went much further, and read into the unconstitutional provision in the Alien's Act an additional class of persons entitled to the benefits conferred by it on spouses. It did this because a declaration of invalidity would have done no more than deprive spouses of the benefits, until the legislature intervened to rectify the situation. Such an order would not have extended the benefits in question to the victims of the discrimination. Thus the court concluded that, after the word 'spouse' in the section, the words 'or partner, in a permanent same-sex life partnership' should be read in. The precise meaning of this addition to the section effected, not by the legislature, but by the court,[83] remains to be determined. And the court considered that such an exercise would have to be undertaken 'on the totality of the facts presented'.[84]

---

[77]   See Angelo Pantazis, 'An Argument for the Legal Recognition of Gay and Lesbian Marriages' (1997) 114 SALJ 556, who contends, beyond an argument for equality, that the right to privacy includes the right to marry. See also the 2000 edition of the *Survey*, at 346–347.

[78]   2000 (2) SA 1 (CC), discussed by Ronald Louw, 'Gay and Lesbian Partner Immigration and the Redefining of Family' (2000) 16 SAJHR 313. Indebtedness is acknowledged to this author in the discussion of the case.

[79]   Act 96 of 1991, s 25(5). The Constitutional Court was required to confirm an order of invalidity that had been handed down by the High Court.

[80]   At 32–33.

[81]   See n 40 above.

[82]   See the 2000 edition of the *Survey*, at 342–344.

[83]   To what extent and in what circumstances a court may 'legislate' in this manner is a vexed question. It received considerable attention by the court, but the arguments are beyond the scope of this article.

[84]   At 45. The difficulty of interpreting the words brings to mind the considerable jurisprudence in other jurisdictions relating to unmarried heterosexual cohabitants.

Of interest is the fact that there is no formal recognition of permanent life partnerships of heterosexual couples in South Africa.[85] In other comparable jurisdictions, greater accommodation of the fact that some persons elect not to marry, but live in marriage-like relationships, has been afforded to what are commonly known as cohabitants. Reciprocal financial obligations relating to property and maintenance, and the extension of benefits and special legal protections have featured prominently in the jurisprudence of these jurisdictions. In other words, several of the adjustive, supportive and protective measures of family law have been extended to cohabitants because they live in permanent life partnerships that in all respects mimic the relationships of married persons. The important distinction between homosexual and heterosexual relationships is, of course, that homosexual couples may not marry, whereas heterosexual couples who do not marry have (it is presumed) consciously elected to remain unmarried. This explains why there have been no challenges to legislation on the ground of exclusion of heterosexual unmarried couples who have chosen not to bring themselves within the class 'spouse/s' identified in a particular statute or legal rule. The difficulty inherent in the wording of the provision now rectified by the court in the case under discussion is that the relationship may well qualify for inclusion, but the fundamental justification for the court's intervention may be absent: it is not unlikely that some gay and lesbian couples who live in permanent life partnerships would not wish to marry, even were the law to be altered to afford them the right to do so. They may, for reasons identical to those of heterosexual cohabitants, eschew religious and civil ceremony to make correct and moral, or to 'sanctify' (the *mot juste* in the circumstances), their relationship. As a result of the *National Coalition* case, they would now qualify for the benefits of the judicially 'amended' Act, whereas heterosexual couples in exactly the same circumstances would not.

It is for these kinds of reasons that some writers and activists[86] question the creation in a range of diverse but discrete situations of an institution that is viewed as 'parallel' to marriage for the purpose of avoiding unfair discrimination,[87] but the implicit denial to gays and lesbians of the right to marry. It seems difficult to reconcile the uncontroversial acceptance by the court in the instant case of the proposition that to extend privileges of the kind in the statute to gay and lesbian couples would in no way threaten the institution of marriage,[88] and at the same time the silence of the court on the real issue. The real issue is the right of such couples to marry. It is suggested that to grant them this right would be a tidier and more logical solution, quite apart from a more just one. It would have the result of placing gay and lesbian and heterosexual couples who elect not to marry on the same footing. It would be their choice to bring themselves within the purview of any law governing married persons as persons with a particular status. This is not to say that all difficulties would evanesce. The thorny and as yet not satisfactorily

---

[85] See June Sinclair (assisted by Jacqueline Heaton) *The Law of Marriage Vol I* (Juta & Co, 1996), c 4.

[86] Louw, op cit, n 78 above, is one of these. See also Pantazis n 77 above.

[87] See for another example the decision in *Langemaat v Minister of Safety and Security* 1998 (3) SA 312, discussed in the 2000 edition of the *Survey,* at 346–347.

[88] A proposition that the present writer endorses wholeheartedly – see Sinclair, op cit, n 85 above at 291–292 and 299–300.

addressed question of the extent to which the adjustive, supportive and protective measures of family law should be extended to unmarried couples would remain as complex as ever.[89] At least, however, granting the right to marry to gays and lesbians would manifest an undeniable commitment on the part of South Africans to equality rather than separate but equal treatment, an ugly reminder of our discriminatory past. And it would leave our law uncontaminated by the unjustifiably different treatment that we are creating between unmarried heterosexual and unmarried gay and lesbian couples who live in permanent life partnerships, by choice.

B   Protecting the family, and family life

The Alien's Control Act[90] came in for another drubbing in three similar cases: *Dawood and Another v Minister of Home Affairs, Shalabi and Another v Minister of Home Affairs*, and *Thomas and Another v Minister of Home Affairs*.[91] The cases concerned the circumstances in which foreign spouses of South African citizens and residents are permitted to reside temporarily in South Africa pending the outcome of their applications for immigration permits. The case should be seen against a backdrop of increased xenophobia within the Department of Home Affairs and in the population at large.[92]

The first issue concerned a non-refundable fee that must be paid on application for an immigration permit. It stood at R188 in 1993, and spouses of South Africans applying for permits were exempt from paying this fee. In 1997 it was increased to R7,130 but spouses remained exempt. In 1998 it was set at R7, 750 and the exemption for spouses was abolished. In 1999 it was raised to R10, 020. The High Court had declared the fee regulations to be inconsistent with the Constitution and thus invalid. Although the Department, on behalf of the Minister, argued that the fee was intended to cover administrative and other associated costs, this was rejected by the court, which considered that the fee was unreasonably high and infringed or threatened to infringe the dignity of spouses who could not afford it. The use of such a fee to deter applications and thus increase the likelihood of deportation was regarded as unconstitutional. As this finding related to Regulations promulgated in terms of the Act, the declaration of invalidity did not require confirmation by the Constitutional Court, although that court associated itself with the finding of the High Court.

Also in issue was the constitutionality of a provision in the Act which establishes the general rule that an immigration permit may not be granted unless

---

[89]   See Sinclair, op cit, n 85 above.

[90]   Act 96 of 1991.

[91]   Because of the similarities in the cases they were heard together and reported as one judgment (in two pieces of litigation) in the Cape High Court as 2000 (1) SA 997 (C) and 2000 (1) SA 1074 (C). The judgment of the Constitutional Court, under discussion here, is reported in 2000 (3) SA 936 (CC).

[92]   There is a continuous influx of illegal immigrants into South Africa, particularly from other African countries. Incidents are rife of foreign hawkers being attacked and of foreigners being thrown off moving trains by South Africans who feel that these persons are taking their jobs and wrongly competing with them to earn a livelihood. The unacceptable conditions under which illegal immigrants are kept in detention camps awaiting deportation, unless they can pay the required bribes to corrupt officials, have on several occasions been reported in the press.

the applicant is outside the country at the time the permit is granted and goes on to provide an exception to this rule in relation to spouses, dependent children and aged, infirm or destitute family members who are in possession of a *valid* temporary residence permit.[93] The three applicant spouses had all sought (extensions of) temporary permits pending the outcome of their applications. These had been denied by immigration officers exercising their discretion. The applicants were thus required by the statute to leave the country and return to their countries of origin if they wished to pursue their intentions eventually to reside legally with their South African spouses in South Africa. They challenged the validity of the legislation.

The Constitutional Court was required to confirm the declaration of invalidity of this provision, which had been made by the High Court. O'Regan J delivered the unanimous finding of the Constitutional Court. She explained and accepted the purpose of the legislation as being to regulate and control the entry of foreigners into and their residence in South Africa, and pointed to the fact that, once the temporary permits of foreign spouses expire, the foreign spouses are guilty of a criminal offence if they remain in the country. The essence of the problem before the court lay in the fact that the extension, and granting of temporary permits, which would bring into operation the exception for spouses, is entirely within the discretion of the immigration officer charged with dealing with applications for temporary permits. While the legislation does set out criteria for the granting and/or refusal of immigration permits, that is, on a permanent basis, the precursor – the temporary permit – is either granted or refused in the absence of any legislative guideline enjoining the immigration officer to act in a manner consistent with the principles of the Constitution.

The judge referred both to the justiciable and enforceable right to dignity, entrenched in the Bill of Rights,[94] and to various other clauses in the Constitution that require the nurturing and protection of the fundamental constitutional values of human dignity, equality and freedom.[95] In addition, South Africa's obligations in terms of international covenants to protect the family as a fundamental group unit of society and to enforce the right to marry and raise a family rendered it necessary to evaluate whether the statutory provision constituted a violation or potential violation of those obligations.[96]

It should be noted here that there is no express right to marry and raise a family and no specific protection of the family in the South African Constitution. Whether protection of the family should have been included was the subject of a major debate and considerable contestation during the process of drafting and certification of the Constitution. One reason for not including express protection stemmed from the controversy raging about the definition of 'family'. It is important to note how strongly the court in this case stressed, as did van Heerden AJ in the High Court, that 'South African families are diverse in character and marriages can be contracted under several different legal regimes, including

---

[93] Section 25(9)(b) of the Act.
[94] Section 10 of the Constitution.
[95] See ss 7(1), 36(1) and 39(1), set out at 961 of the judgment.
[96] See Art 23 of the International Covenant on Civil and Political Rights, and Art 18 of the African Charter on Human and Peoples' Rights.

African customary law, Islamic personal law and the civil law'.[97] The judge went on to say that the 'definition of the family also changes as social practices and traditions change. In recognizing the importance of the family, we must take care not to entrench particular forms of family at the expense of other forms'.[98] These words strengthen the court's commitment to recognizing a variety of family forms, including same-sex partnerships, as units that resemble traditional families and deserve legal protection. And yet, as was seen above, in the *National Coalition* case,[99] in relation to the question as to whether such families can encompass what we accept as 'marriage', the court declined to take the final leap. In the case under discussion, two of the couples were married at civil law, but the Dawoods were married according to Islamic law. Their marriage is not recognized in South Africa. This issue and its (unsatisfactory) implications will be addressed further below. At this point, however, it is interesting to note that, for the purpose of deciding whether the provision in the Alien's Control Act was unconstitutional, no differentiation between civil and Islamic marriages was made by the court.

Dignity, the right to dignity, was the peg on which the court hung its decision to declare invalid this provision. It considered that the legislative exception permitting a foreign spouse to apply for an immigration permit from within the borders of South Africa only if he or she is in possession of a valid temporary residence permit constituted an unwarranted and unjustifiable limitation on the right to dignity. Dignity was identified as the constitutional guarantee that protects the family and family life. Compelling the foreign spouse to leave the country, despite considerations of poverty and the possible disruption and even destruction of the relationship that separation of the spouses might induce, was held to be an unacceptable infringement of the right of married persons to cohabit. But it is important to note that this limitation of the right to dignity was carefully analyzed by the court. It was because of the unfettered nature of the discretion to be exercised by the immigration officer to grant or extend a temporary permit, in order to bring the exception into operation in favour of the foreign spouse, and the fact that it was exercised in the absence of any guidelines or criteria to ensure compliance with the right and values in the Constitution, that the provision was regarded as unreasonable and liable to be struck down. The court alluded to a range of circumstances that might have served as guidelines for the exercise of the discretion by the immigration officer, but it declined in this case to legislate itself in order to rescue the provision.[100] The absence of any criteria to guide the exercise of the discretion in question was fatal because it introduced an element of arbitrariness into a decision the outcome of which could potentially forcibly separate the spouses pending the outcome of the application for an immigration permit by the foreign spouse.

Two observations seem apt. The first is to commend the court on its readiness to protect the family and family life, and the acceptance in these circumstances of a wide and liberal interpretation of 'family'. The second is to note the fact that the

---

[97]   At 960.

[98]   Ibid.

[99]   See n 78 above.

[100]   Correctly, it is submitted, and in recognition of the separation of powers. Cf the *National Coalition* case, concerning same-sex partnerships, discussed above.

right to dignity is becoming a wide if not all-embracing catch-all right, used in the view of some writers too liberally and unnecessarily in equality cases, but certainly as a vital tool to fill a possible gap within the context of family law.[101]

C   Muslim marriages and African customary marriages: Grappling with pluralism

Muslim marriages are potentially polygynous, are not recognized as valid, and are not equal in status to those celebrated according to the civil law. Polygyny has been held to be 'contrary to the accepted customs and usages which are regarded as morally binding upon all members of our society'.[102]

Ryland v Edros,[103] decided in 1997, rejected this approach, the court concluding that, while the Muslim marriage was not valid in South African law, contractual obligations flowing from the marriage, including a duty of the husband to maintain his wife, could be enforced (*inter vivos*). The judge stressed, however, that his view was confined to a *de facto* monogamous marriage and should not necessarily be taken to cover the case of a polygynous Muslim marriage.[104]

Flowing directly from this contractual duty of support, a dependant's action was brought against the insurer of a driver who had negligently killed the husband of a woman married according to Islamic rites in *Amod v Multilateral Vehicle Accidents Fund*.[105] The dependant's action in South African law has traditionally been confined to loss of support derived by the plaintiff from a person wrongfully killed and who bore a legal duty of support to the plaintiff, that is, one arising *ex lege*. Contractual obligations of support and those founded upon custom have been considered insufficient to ground the action. This is why, in relation to African customary marriage, prior to its full recognition in 1998, special legislation had to be enacted to give widows married according to customary law a dependant's action.[106] No such legislation has been passed in relation to a claim for loss of support based on a Muslim marriage, or to give legal recognition to such marriages.

The Supreme Court of Appeal in this case considered that the rationale for the dependant's action in our common law is equity, and that the precise scope of the action is unclear from the writings of the Roman-Dutch jurists. What these writers were anxious to protect, in a flexible way, it said, were rights of the *family* of the deceased.[107] For this reason, a divorced wife, receiving maintenance from her former husband, wrongfully killed, was recently afforded a dependant's relief in

---

[101]   See the criticism of the conflation of equality and dignity expressed by Dennis Davis (now a High Court judge) in relation to the two equality cases, *Hugo* and *Harksen*, discussed in section **II**, Two Vignettes from our Equality Jurisprudence, above. The references to the two cases are in n 7 and n 21, respectively.

[102]   *Ismail v Ismail* 1983 (1) SA 1006 (A) at 1026.

[103]   1997 (2) SA 690 (C), discussed and criticised in the 2000 edition of the *Survey* at 347.

[104]   At 709.

[105]   1999 (4) SA 1319 (SCA). The action had failed in the High Court and this discussion is confined to the finding of the Supreme Court of Appeal.

[106]   The legislation is s 31 of the Black Laws Amendment Act 76 of 1963.

[107]   See the judgment of Mahomed CJ at 1324. The implications of the use of the term 'family' and its now very unclear meaning are dealt with below.

Santam Bpk v Henery.[108] It is clear that the courts over time have moved away from the view that the duty of support has to be one *ex lege*, derived from the common law. At common law, the duty of support between spouses terminated on divorce and the courts had to be given statutory powers to prolong it beyond dissolution of the marriage. What now seems to be the criterion is legal enforceability, whether resulting from a court order or a contractual obligation. But the court in *Henery*, and the Chief Justice in *Amod*, held in addition that the right of the person seeking compensation for lost support from the deceased had to be one 'worthy of protection by the law'.[109] Not surprisingly, the court found in this case that the widow married according to Islamic rites was part of a family, had had a legally enforceable right to be maintained by her deceased husband, and that this right deserved recognition and was worthy of the protection of South African law.[110]

Heavily relied upon was the argument that the *boni mores* of the new South African society would find untenable the exclusion of certain persons based on their religion. The ethos of cultural tolerance, pluralism and religious freedom demanded a fresh approach to the marriages of Muslims. But it is most interesting to note that, as in *Ryland v Edros*,[111] the court in this case confined its decision to granting relief in respect of a *de facto* monogamous marriage. Mahomed CJ preferred to leave the issue of polygynous marriages 'entirely open'.[112] In effect, therefore, although the decision echoes the progressive approach taken in *Ryland*, and permits a dependant's action despite the absence of a legally recognized marriage, the relief was granted because the marriage in question did not in fact differ from Christian marriage, the marriage of the civil law. Our tolerance for other faiths and other cultures goes only as far as the 'other' is similar to the traditional. It is a pity that the opportunity was missed for the court to offer a strong opinion on the dissonance of approach in South Africa to Muslim marriages and African customary marriages, both for long denied recognition on the ground of potential polygyny. Polygyny for the African majority, a fundamental part of their culture, is now permitted. For Muslims, only a small minority of the population, it remains an undecided mystery. Given the failure of the legislature to speak on this issue, which is clearly one of discrimination, one would have hoped for a firm, *obiter* pronouncement that no distinction would be made between polygynous and monogamous marriages celebrated according to Islamic rites. The failure of the court to give this assurance creates at least the possibility, if not an inference, that widows in polygynous Islamic marriages will not be protected in the way that their counterparts in African customary law are. How could this possibly be constitutionally justifiable?

Mahomed CJ relied also on the Constitutional injunction to the courts to develop the common law to accord with the spirit of the Constitution.[113] But his

---

[108]   1999 (3) SA 421 (SCA).

[109]   At 427 in *Henery*, and at 1331 in *Amod*.

[110]   At 1327.

[111]   See n 103 above.

[112]   At 1330. The facts of the case did not demand a decision on a polygynous marriage.

[113]   Section 8(3)(a) of the Constitution. See the criticism of the failure by the court fully to develop the common law on Muslim marriages offered by Elsje Bonthuys and Tshepo Mosikatsana 'Law of Persons and Family Law' 1999 *Annual Survey of South African Law* 119 at 145–146.

judgment is narrowly confined to the facts before him. It is based on the proposition that Islamic marriage is undertaken according to well-established rules and is a 'major religion'.[114] Developing the common law to extend the dependant's action to the widow in this case was thus required. What is one to make of the view that it is members of the deceased's *family* that the remedy is intended to protect?[115] This question is an important one in the light of the very generous extended meaning of 'family' espoused in several cases by the Constitutional Court. Same-sex couples are said to enjoy relationships that resemble in all fundamental ways the family relationships of heterosexual couples. Cohabitants surely also fall into this category.[116] Were these persons to enter into contracts creating reciprocal duties of support, would they bring themselves within the purview of the dependant's action? Would it not be discriminatory to say that these relationships are purely consensual, and not based on any recognized, major religion or custom? How far do our new *boni mores* take us down the road to treating marriage and marriage-like relationships equally, if not in all respects, then for limited purposes, including inclusion for the purpose of elucidating the meaning of 'family', and for the purpose of the dependant's action? Progressive judgments we are seeing. The precise implications of the changes in attitude are far from clear.

The Recognition of Customary Marriages Act of 1998,[117] was discussed in the last chapter on South Africa, in the 2000 edition of the *Survey*.[118] The Act came into operation on 1 November 2000.[119] It confers full recognition on African customary marriages and regulates celebration, registration, proprietary consequences and dissolution. It permits polygyny within customary marriage and declares that a customary marriage celebrated prior to its enactment is for all purposes recognized as a valid marriage.[120] It provides further that a customary marriage entered into after the commencement of the Act, and which complies with its requirements, is for all purposes recognized as a valid marriage.[121] The spouses to a customary marriage are placed under a duty to register their marriage,[122] but the Act goes on to state that failure to register a customary marriage does not affect its validity.[123] While spouses married at customary law

---

[114] At 1327.

[115] See n 107 above .

[116] The rights of same-sex couples and the willingness of the courts to extend the meaning of 'family' to them, and the dissonance in treatment created between same-sex couples who would not want to marry even if they could, and cohabiting couples who have presumably elected not to marry, are discussed and in the 2000 edition of the *Survey* at 346. See especially also *Langemaat v Minister of Safety and Security* 1998 (3) SA 312 (T) and my comments on the potential widening of the liability of insurers created by this decision.

[117] Act 120 of 1998.

[118] At 348–350.

[119] See RGN 6909 *GG* 21700 of 1 November 2000.

[120] Section 2(1) of the Act 120 of 1998.

[121] Section 2(2).

[122] Section 4(1).

[123] Section 4(9). On the difficulties of reconciling the provisions of the legislation of the former Transkei (Transkei Marriage Act 21 of 1978), which required registration for validity, and the South African general legislation, and also for the remaining uncertainties regarding the validity of customary marriages, see Elsje Bonthuys, 'Still Unclear: The Validity of Certain Customary Marriages in terms of the Recognition of Customary Marriages Act' (2000) 63 THRHR 616.

may marry one another at civil law, provided that neither is a party to a customary marriage with another person, those who have married at civil law are not competent to enter into any other marriage.[124] The proprietary consequences of a customary marriage concluded after the commencement of the Act mimic the consequences of a civil marriage.

The extent to which the 1998 legislation brings 'into line' customary marriage with civil marriage, the contest between the constitutionally entrenched right to culture and the right to equality,[125] and which aspects of customary law infringe other rights in the Constitution, are some of the issues that have demonstrated the majesty of the civil law, and have excited a veritable flood of academic writing.[126]

Of significant importance to the future of customary law is the Promotion of Equality and Prevention of Unfair Discrimination Act of 2000.[127] This legislation provides for the setting up of equality courts with powers to make a range of orders providing relief to victims of unfair discrimination. Special training and expertise are to be required of persons presiding in these courts. It has been suggested by one writer[128] that the legislation provides a unique opportunity for a move away from legalistic, adversarial methodologies, towards a narrative and less formal mode of adjudicating cases involving alleged discrimination, which will give greater scope for the development of customary law. But a contrary view[129] of the legislation is that it is intended to ensure compliance with the Constitution and also with South Africa's obligations under international law. It will thus lead to an eradication of practices containing discriminatory elements. One of these, patriarchy, is fundamental to African customary law. Marius Pieterse argues that, although cultural representatives claim that the right to culture in the Constitution mandates a degree of tolerance for customary law and

---

[124] Section 10(1) and (4). The language suggests that such a subsequent marriage would be void.

[125] Culture is protected in ss 31 and 211(3). The courts are enjoined to apply indigenous law in so far as it is applicable, but subject to the Constitution. Equality is protected by s 9 of the Constitution.

[126] See, for example, Victoria Bronstein, 'Confronting Custom in the New South African State: An Analysis of the Recognition of Customary Marriages Act 120 of 1998' (2000) 16 SAJHR 558; Chuma Himonga and Craig Bosch, 'The Application of African Customary Law Under the Constitution of South Africa: Problems Solved or Just Beginning?' (2000) 117 SALJ 306 (which deals *inter alia* with the important question of the difference between official and living customary law); IP Maithufi, 'The Recognition of Customary Marriages Act of 1988: A Commentary' (2000) 63 THRHR 509; Wayne van der Meide, 'Gender Equality v Right to Culture: Debunking the Perceived Conflicts Preventing the Reform of the Marital Property Regime of the "Official Version" of Customary Law' (1999) 116 SALJ 100; Barbara Oomen, 'Traditional Woman-to-Woman Marriages, and the Recognition of Customary Marriages Act' (2000) 63 THRHR 274. The most important cases decided on aspects of customary law in recent years are *Mthembu v Letsela* 1997 (2) SA 936 (T) and 1998 (2) SA 675 (T), *Hlophe v Mahlalela* 1998 (1) SA 449 (T), *Mabena v Letsoalo* 1998 (2) SA 1068 (T) and *Zondi v President of the Republic of South Africa* 2000 (2) SA 49 (N).

[127] Act 4 of 2000, which came into force on 1 September 2000: RGN 6875 *GG* 21517 of 1 September 2000. The legislation is demanded by s 9 of the Constitution and lays to rest the question whether discrimination, not only by the State, but also by private persons is impermissible. This was a complex point of interpretation in terms of the vertical and/or horizontal application of the Constitution. The Act of 2000 makes clear that discrimination on any of the grounds outlawed by the Constitution is outlawed also as between private individuals.

[128] Narnia Bohler, 'Equality Courts: Introducing the Possibility of Listening to Different Voices in South Africa?' (2000) 63 THRHR 288. See also GJ van Niekerk, 'Indigenous Law, Public Policy and Narrative in the Courts' (2000) 63 THRHR 403.

[129] See Marius Pieterse, 'The Promotion of Equality and Prevention of Unfair Discrimination Act 4 of 2000: Final Nail in the Customary Law Coffin?' (2000) 117 SALJ 627.

an assurance that 'Western' norms will not be superimposed onto traditional African values, the legislation in effect eradicates outright certain fundamental customary practices. The Act explicitly provides that no person may unfairly discriminate against any person on the ground of gender, and this includes gender-based violence, female genital mutilation, preventing women from inheriting family property (male primogeniture in the law of intestate succession), any practice which impairs the dignity of women, and any policy that limits access of women to land rights, finance or other resources.[130] Lobolo, the paying of a bride price, is seen by some as patriarchal and amounting to a sale of women. Pieterse points out that a decision to outlaw lobolo should not be taken lightly. He also maintains that the list of practices proscribed by the Act appears to wipe out the entire system of customary succession, based as it is on patriarchy.[131]

Pieterse concludes that the statutory alterations effected to customary law by the 2000 Act accord with the spirit of the Constitution as a whole, respect the right to equality, and do not amount to a violation of the right to culture. But he complains that the winds of change have gone way beyond progressive transformation and are likely to brew up a mighty storm. The hasty eradication of fundamental parts of African custom has left a vacuum, he says, which perpetuates the risk of a chasm between the lived customs of people and the official version of their laws. Worse still, this legislation is a clear manifestation of the majesty of the civil law, entrenching the inferior status of customary law that was created by the previous political regime.[132]

---

[130] Section 8.

[131] Op cit, n 129, at 633.

[132] Ibid at 635, and see van Niekerk, op cit, n 128 above, at 416, who pleads for an acknowledgement of the difference between Western legalism and indigenous custom and calls for different considerations of public policy, based also on narrative, to reflect changing societal values.

SWEDEN

ASSISTED REPRODUCTION

*Åke Saldeen**

I   INTRODUCTION

In my report on the development of Swedish family law in 1999 I reported on, inter alia, a proposed investigation by the Ministry of Justice in the form of a Ministerial Memorandum (Ds) with the title 'Joint custody for unmarried parents, together with a linguistic and editorial review of chapter 6 of the Code on Parents, Children and Guardians'.[1] It can now be said only that this proposal has not yet (June 2001) resulted in any legislation. The same applies to another statutory proposal that I reported on in the same report, namely 'New cohabitant rules'.[2]

Not a great deal has happened in the field of family law in Sweden during 2000. However, it can first be mentioned that the Registered Partnership Act (1994:1117), the so-called 'Partnership Act', which entered into force on 1 January 1995, was amended as regards the pre-conditions for registration. Originally, according to the Act, registration was allowed to take place only if at least one of the parties was a Swedish national resident in Sweden. By a statutory amendment in 2000, it has become easier for homosexuals to register a partnership.[3] First, the requirement that at least one of the parties should be a Swedish national has been abolished, as this was considered to create unnecessary impediments for those who wished to become registered partners. Following this amendment, the rule is that registration may take place either (1) if one of the parties has been resident in Sweden for two years, or (2) if one of the parties is a Swedish national resident in Sweden. Furthermore, by this amendment, nationals of Denmark, Iceland, the Netherlands and Norway have been equated with Swedish nationals.

In September 2000, the Ministry for Social Affairs submitted a Ministerial Memorandum containing, inter alia, proposals for so-called egg donation to be allowed in Sweden, something which is at present not the case.[4] A report is provided below regarding part of this statutory proposal. However, I have considered it appropriate not to limit the presentation to the proposal, but to endeavour to provide an outline report on the legal position generally in Sweden as regards assisted fertilisation (assisted reproduction).

---

*   Professor of Private Law, Uppsala University. Translated by James Hurst.
1   Ds 1999:57.
2   Official Government Report SOU 1999:104.
3   Government Bill 1999/2000:77.
4   'Treatment of involuntary childlessness', Ds 2000:51.

II   ASSISTED REPRODUCTION

A   Insemination

Insemination activities have taken place in Sweden for a very long time. There is information, for example, concerning so-called 'spouse insemination' (or 'homologous insemination') being practised as long ago as the 1860s and so-called 'donor insemination' (or 'heterologous insemination') since the 1920s. However, insemination activities were first regulated by statute in 1984. As regards the insemination activities which had already taken place before that Act entered into force, certain principles were applied in practice, such as that insemination could be performed only on a married woman or a woman who lived together with a man in circumstances resembling marriage, and thus not on a single woman. As regards donor insemination, the hospital or clinic generally advised the couple to keep the truth of the child's origin secret. Records kept were, furthermore, intentionally very incomplete, probably among other things because there was then no protection for the donor against claims and applications on the part of the child regarding the determination of legal paternity, inheritance, maintenance, etc.

As stated above, legislation was first introduced in Sweden in 1984. The absence of special legislation in the field in question, together with the removal in 1976 of all limitations under the Code on Parents, Children and Guardians[5] (CPCG) on the right of a lawful husband to bring an action for the revocation of paternity of children born to his wife, resulted in the so-called *Haparanda* case.[6] In this case, which attracted great attention by the media, the Supreme Court felt compelled, on the action of the lawful husband, to make a declaration whereby the child became legally fatherless. As the lawful husband could not be the biological father of the child, as the child was fathered through donor insemination, his action to be declared not to be the father of the child was granted. The issue of whether the lawful husband consented or not to the donor insemination was, on the basis of the law then applicable, of no importance for the outcome of the case. (The donor was anonymous so no paternity action could be directed against him.)

The legislation of 1984, which entered into force on 1 March 1985, included first a special Insemination Act (1984:1140), governing insemination activities as such. It should be emphasised here that, to the extent that insemination activities involve health and medical care, the Health and Medical Services Act (1982:763) and the Professional Practice in the Health and Medical Services Sector Act (1998:531) apply in addition to the Insemination Act. Furthermore, it may be mentioned that the National Board of Health and Welfare has issued regulations and general advice concerning insemination.

As regards the issue of which women should be entitled to undergo insemination, the legislator has considered that, having regard to the interest of the prospective child to grow up in a 'normal' parent–child relationship, insemination should be performed only if the woman is married or cohabits with a man in

---

5   Sometimes now referred to as the Parental Code.
6   Nytt Juridiskt Arkiv – NJA 1983 p 320.

circumstances resembling marriage. Single women – who in accordance with Swedish law are entitled to adopt – are thus not entitled to be allowed to undergo donor insemination. Nor have two persons of the same sex any right to have children through insemination, even if they have entered into a registered partnership (see chapter 3, section 2 of the Registered Partnership Act (1994:1117)). In the report 'Children in homosexual families',[7] which at the time of writing (June 2001) has just undergone the statutory consultative procedure, it is, however, proposed that insemination should be allowed for a lesbian woman with the consent of her registered partner.

The Insemination Act also contains rules, inter alia, about requirements that the lawful husband, or the man with whom the woman cohabits in circumstances resembling marriage, gives written consent to the insemination; rules providing that donor insemination may be performed only at a public hospital[8] (ie publicly funded hospital) and under the supervision of a physician with special competence in gynaecology and obstetrics; that it is an obligation of the physician to consider whether insemination is appropriate having regard to the couple's medical, psychological and social circumstances; and that insemination may be performed only if it can be assumed that the prospective child will grow up in good circumstances.[9] The task of selecting a suitable sperm donor for donor insemination rests with the treating physician. When making this choice, no special requirements concerning the characteristics and qualities of the donor are in principle allowed, eg whether the donor should have a particularly high intelligence quotient. However, requirements or desires that the sperm donor's external appearance should resemble that of the prospective legal/social father, for example as regards height, hair colour and the like, may be prescribed. Information concerning the sperm donor must be noted in a special journal, which must be preserved for at least 70 years (section 3, cf below concerning section 4).

As regards the highly controversial issue of whether a child who has been conceived by donor insemination should be entitled, if he or she so wishes, to obtain information about the donor, ie the genetic or biological father's identity, the Insemination Commission was not unanimous and the opinions received on consultation were divided. However, the Insemination Act ultimately contained the rule (section 4) that a child who has been fathered by donor insemination is entitled, when he or she has attained sufficient maturity, to obtain the information concerning the sperm donor that is noted in the hospital's special journal concerning this. According to the Act, the Social Welfare Committee is under a duty to assist the child upon request to obtain the desired information concerning the donor. In principle, information concerning the sperm donor is otherwise protected by the Secrecy Act (1980:100), chapter 7, section 1. Sweden became the first country in the world to introduce legislation concerning the right of children

---

[7]   Official Government Report 2001:10.

[8]   However, in the Ministerial Memorandum 'Treatment of involuntary childlessness', Ds 2001:51 (see further below), which has not yet resulted in legislation, it is proposed that donor insemination may also be performed, with the permission of the National Board of Health and Welfare, by parties other than publicly funded hospitals.

[9]   If insemination is refused, the couple may request that the issue is considered by the National Board of Health and Welfare. However, there is no appeal from a decision by the National Board of Health and Welfare.

created by donor insemination to obtain information concerning the identity of the donor, legislation that corresponds with Article 7 of the 1989 Convention on the Rights of the Child, which has been ratified by Sweden, wherein it is provided that a child 'shall have ... as far as possible, the right to know and be cared for by his or her parents'. Since then, Austria, among other countries, has also introduced such legislation.

It should also be added that it is indicated by the *travaux préparatoires* to the Insemination Act that parents should normally, when this can be deemed appropriate, inform the child of how he or she was conceived. The Insemination Commission's proposal that information that a child has been conceived by donor insemination, although not the identity of the donor, should be registered with the Population Registration Authority would possibly have facilitated compliance with this duty to provide information. However, the proposal was not implemented, among other things, because virtually all of those consulted distanced themselves from it.

Through a questionnaire survey, the National Board of Health and Welfare has conducted an investigation about whether the intentions of the insemination legislation have been reflected in the same openness concerning the origins of the child on the part of the parents.[10] The questionnaire survey was aimed at all parents who had children, up to and during 1977, following donor insemination at two large university hospitals in Sweden after the Insemination Act was introduced. Of the parents who responded to the questionnaire, approximately 10% stated that they had already told their children that they were conceived through donor insemination and roughly a further 40% said that they intended to tell their children in the future. However, approximately 20% of those parents included in the survey stated that they did not anticipate telling their children how they were conceived and approximately 10% were undecided regarding the issue. (Approximately 20% of the couples chose not to give their views on the issue in question.)

Furthermore, it may be mentioned that the Insemination Act contains a prohibition against importing frozen sperm into Sweden without a licence from the National Board of Health and Welfare, the purpose of which is to prevent commercially operated sperm banks abroad, via mail order or in other ways, supplying such sperm to women in Sweden for self-insemination (section 6).

The insemination legislation from 1984 does not only comprise the Insemination Act discussed here as regards self-insemination activities, but also the introduction of new rules in the CPCG regarding the paternity of children fathered by insemination. According to these rules, the following applies, among other things, when insemination has been performed on a mother with the consent of her lawful husband or cohabitant and when, having regard to all the circumstances, it is probable that the child was fathered by the insemination (CPCG, chapter 1, section 6). If the mother was married at the time of the child's birth, it is presumed that the lawful husband is the father of the child even if the child was fathered by donor insemination, and the lawful husband (and presumably also the child) does not have an opportunity to institute proceedings at

---

[10]   See National Board of Health and Welfare report 'Children born following donor insemination', SoS Report 2000:6.

a court for the revocation of the presumption of paternity. If the mother was not married at the time of the child's birth, paternity must then, for the man who consented to the insemination, be determined either through confirmation or by trial and judgment. In order for an acknowledgement of paternity to be valid, in the manner in which paternity is generally determined as regards children born to an unmarried mother, it is required, among other things, that the Social Welfare Committee approves the acknowledgement. Such approval may according to the Act (CPCG, chapter 1, section 4) be given only if it can be assumed that the man who acknowledged paternity really is the child's biological or genetic father. In this respect, the 1984 legislation now means that the Social Welfare Committee may give its approval even when the child was fathered by donor insemination but the man acknowledging paternity consented to the insemination. If the man refuses to acknowledge paternity, it is the duty of the Social Welfare Committee to institute proceedings at court to have paternity determined. In order to have a determination of paternity granted, it is basically required, according to the so-called legal presumption contained in the Act, that it is established that the defendant and mother had sexual intercourse with one another during the possible period of conception and that, furthermore, having regard to all the circumstances, it is probable that the child was fathered by such sexual intercourse (CPCG, chapter 1, section 5). As regards this issue, the 1984 legislation means that a court, notwithstanding the requirements of the Act for proof of sexual intercourse between the child's mother and the defendant and also that the defendant's paternity should, having regard to all the circumstances, appear probable, may – even if the child has been fathered by donor insemination – declare that the defendant is the father provided he consented to the insemination.

It should be emphasised that in order for the rules reported here to apply, it is not required that insemination is performed in accordance with the rules of the Insemination Act. This means, among other things, that in this particular respect the requirement for consent is satisfied even if it has only been given verbally. However, the consenting man must, of course, have legal capacity.

The rules described here concerning the legal paternity of the lawful husband or cohabitant who consented to insemination do not apply should it transpire that the child was in reality not fathered by insemination but instead by the sexual intercourse of the mother with a man other than the lawful husband or cohabitant respectively. In such a case, the lawful husband, for example, can institute proceedings for the revocation of the presumption of his paternity of the child to whom his wife has given birth.

A situation in which the legal position may be thought debatable and which arose in the so-called *Bollnäs* case, relates to the possibility of legally declaring a donor to be the father of a child who has been fathered by so-called private insemination where the mother is single or where – if the mother is married or living with a man in circumstances resembling marriage – there is no valid consent to the insemination on the part of the lawful husband or cohabitant.

In the so-called *Bollnäs* case, a child born of an unmarried single mother who was fathered by a privately performed donor insemination pursued an action against the donor concerning determination of paternity.[11] The City Court, whose judgment was confirmed by the Court of Appeal, rejected the action and the Supreme Court (HD) did not consider that there was reason to grant leave to appeal. The City Court stated, among other things, the following:

'It is required as an unconditional pre-condition under chapter 1, section 5 of the Code on Parents, Children and Guardians that it is established that the putative father had sexual intercourse with the child's mother during the period when the child could have been fathered. Nothing else has been claimed except that fertilisation took place by artificial means through insemination. However, [the plaintiff] appears to be of the view that the statutory provision contained in chapter 1, section 5 of the Code on Parents, Children and Guardians, is nevertheless applicable. In the *travaux préparatoires* to the Code on Parents, Children and Guardians, the concept of sexual intercourse is not defined but in normal language and in medical terminology this is deemed to mean sexual relations. In the case it must, in order for sexual intercourse to be deemed to have taken place, at least require that the [defendant's] penis was in contact with the sexual parts [of the child's mother]. As this was not the case, the plaintiff's case must be rejected.'

The Court of Appeal added in its judgment that as regards 'children by insemination of unmarried single mothers, the legislator has adopted the standpoint that a paternity action cannot be brought against a sperm donor who is unwilling to acknowledge paternity (see Government Bill 1984/85:2, pages 14 and 20ff and LU 1984/85:10, page 13ff)'.

In my view, there is reason to regret that HD did not consider that there were reasons to grant leave to appeal in this case. As regards the issue of the requirement of sexual intercourse in the said rule contained in chapter 1, section 5, it can actually first be mentioned that HD in one case (NJA 1998 p 184) (relating to the issue of the determination of paternity of a child born of a single mother just a few weeks before the issue of leave to appeal was dealt with in the *Bollnäs* case) considered that paternity can be determined even if sexual intercourse has not been established. This may be so if paternity as such was verified in the case, something which is nowadays possible through the use of DNA technology in connection with medical paternity diagnostics. As regards the statements contained in the *travaux préparatoires* which the court referred to, ie that it should not be possible to institute proceedings against a sperm donor concerning the determination of paternity, it can be concluded that such statements are not usually considered binding. These particular statements furthermore must be said to conflict directly with the above-mentioned Article (Art 7) of the Convention on the Rights of the Child concerning the right of the child to know about his or her

---

[11]   Case number T 445/98 (Svea Court of Appeal Judgment DT 18/92 (T 14237/91)). Cf RH 98:103. See also J Schiratszki, 'Några reflektioner runt de legala konsekvenserna av privat insemination' [Some reflections on the legal consequences of private insemination] *Juridisk Tidskrift* (JT) 1995–96, p 257ff; A Singer, 'Fastställande av faderskap efter "privat" insemination' ['Determination of paternity after private insemination'] JT 1995–96, p 1063ff; A Singer, *Föräldraskap i rättslig belysning* [*Parenthood in Legal Light*] (2000), p 335ff; G Walin, *Föräldrabalken och internationell föräldrarätt* [*The Code on Parents, Children and Guardians and international parent law*] (5th Revised Edition, 1996), p 73; and also Å Saldeen, 'DNA-teknik och faställande av faderskap' ['DNA technology and determination of paternity'] JT 1998–99, p 184.

parents, which has been ratified by Sweden. Having regard to this, I am of the view that the issue in question should as soon as possible be the subject of legislative measures.

B   In vitro fertilisation (IVF)

Activities concerning in vitro fertilisation (IVF), or fertilisation outside the body, have not been practised for as long as insemination activity, and the need for legislation therefore did not exist for long before such legislation was introduced in 1988. In Sweden, the first child conceived by this method was born in 1982.

The activity in question is governed, inter alia, by the Fertilisation Outside the Body Act (1988:711), by various regulations issued by the National Board of Health and Welfare and by rules concerning paternity in the CPCG introduced by the 1988 legislation.

The Fertilisation Outside the Body Act means, inter alia, that such fertilisation for the purpose of fathering children may take place only if the woman is married or cohabiting (cf **II.A** above concerning insemination), the lawful husband or cohabitant gives written consent (cf also **II.A** above concerning insemination) and the egg is the woman's own and the fertilisation takes place with the sperm of the husband or cohabitant. It follows from this, among other things, that so-called 'egg donation' is not allowed according to Swedish law at present. As regards the reasons for donor insemination (see **II.A** above) being allowed but not egg donation, the following can be concluded on the basis of the *travaux préparatoires* to the legislation.[12]

The Government Insemination Commission, which submitted proposals for both the 1984 legislation on insemination (Official Government Report – SOU 1983:42) and the 1988 legislation on fertilisation outside the body (Official Government Report – SOU 1985:5) was indeed of the view in its reports on fertilisation outside the body that such fertilisation with another woman's egg could in several respects be compared with donor insemination, which had already been approved. This implied that one should also accept egg donation. However, there was according to the Commission a great deal that differed between these methods. Donor insemination is a technically simple method which basically could be performed by anyone whosoever. If this method was prohibited, there was therefore a great risk of a 'black market'. The pre-condition for the prospective children of having to grow up in good circumstances was therefore considered better served if the activity was legalised and thereby the subject of control by society. However, egg donation was considered to be such a clinically complicated method that it did not entail the risk of a 'black market' if the method was prohibited. It can also be mentioned that, in the course of the statutory consultative procedure for the proposals of the Insemination Commission, it was stated by, among others, several members of the National Medical Ethical Council (SMER), which at that time did not consider that egg donation should be allowed, that, both in connection with so-called spouse insemination and in the case of so-called donor insemination, the objective is a normal pregnancy. The egg comes

---

[12]   See the immediately following Government Bill 1987/88:160 on Fertilisation Outside the Body.

from the woman who has the pregnancy and delivers the child and half of the genetic characteristics will come from her. In the case of egg donation, however, it is not an issue of a natural, but an artificial, pregnancy where there is no genetic relationship whatsoever between the pregnant woman and the foetus. This was considered to be such a serious deviation from the natural process, probably involving significant psychological consequences for the mother and thereby also for the child, that egg donation could not possibly be compared with donor insemination. It was further stated in the Government Bill[13] by the Minister reporting on the matter:

> '... that fertilisation outside the body with another woman's egg conflicts with the human life process and is to such a great extent in the nature of a technical construction that it is likely to harm the view of humanity. First, fertilisation takes place outside the woman's body, second it is an outside woman's egg that is implanted into another woman. The child's genetic characteristics consequently derive from another woman than the woman who carries the child and delivers the child.'

Egg donation could therefore not ethically be defended or allowed.

In June 1994, the Government assigned SMER (see above) the task of conducting, in conjunction with the medical profession, a review of certain issues related to so-called 'assisted fertilisation', inter alia, the issue of egg donation. In its report submitted in April 1995, 'Assisted fertilisation. Views on certain issues related to fertilisation outside the body', the majority of the Council proposed that egg donation where the egg was fertilised by the husband/cohabitant's sperm should be allowed on medical grounds for women of fertile age. One of the reasons for this change of standpoint was that it was no longer considered proper to make a distinction between men's and women's infertility. The Council also recommended that the same rules as those which applied to donor insemination should apply to egg donation as regards the child's right, when of a mature age, to be able to find out the identity of the donor. SMER also considered that fertilisation outside the body with donated sperm should also now be allowed although still only with the own egg of the involuntarily childless woman. However, the Council considered that fertilisation outside the body with both egg donation and sperm donation should continue to be prohibited in the future, as in such a case there was absolutely no genetic link between the child and the prospective parental couple. However, no amending legislation has been introduced, perhaps partly due to opinions in society being widely divided as regards, for example, the issue of whether egg donation should be allowed or not.[14] However, the Ministry of Health and Social Affairs submitted in September 2000, in a Ministerial Memorandum, a proposal for legislation that is based on the above-mentioned proposal from 1995. The Ministry Proposal has undergone the statutory consultative procedure and a Government Bill with proposals for

---

[13]   See note 12.

[14]   It may be mentioned, for example, that the Office of the Child Ombudsman (BO) considers that egg donation is not an acceptable method having regard to the best interests of the child and the interests of the child in knowing its biological origin. Egg donation should therefore, according to BO, be prohibited until it has been possible to investigate further the risks of harm, etc. See 'Behandling av ofrivillig barnlöshet' ['Treating involuntary childlessness'], Ds 2000:51, p 41.

amended legislation in the field can be expected sometime during the end of the current year (2001). Before explaining here something about this Ministry Proposal, it should be added that, through the 1988 legislation on fertilisation outside the body, rules were also introduced concerning paternity in matters concerning children fathered by fertilisation in this way. These rules (see CPCG, chapter 1, section 7) have the same effect as the rules applicable as regards the paternity of children fathered by insemination (see **II.A** above)

As studies have demonstrated, among other things, that occurrences of deformities of various kinds are more often found among children fathered by fertilisation outside the body than among children fathered in a natural way, and as these deformities are often caused by the multiple-birth frequency in connection with IVF, it was proposed in the Ministerial Memorandum, inter alia, that the National Board of Health and Welfare should issue special rules whereby only one – or, in exceptional cases, two – egg(s) may be introduced into the woman's uterus following fertilisation.

Furthermore, the Ministry Proposal means that IVF treatment may not only be performed with the woman's own egg and the lawful husband's or cohabitant's sperm, as according to current law, but also with the woman's own egg and donated sperm or with a donated egg and the man's sperm. (IVF treatment with both donated eggs and donated sperm would thus continue to be prohibited. Surrogate maternity would, as at present, also be prohibited.) The treated woman's husband or cohabitant would be required to give his written consent. IVF treatment may be provided for a woman who is over 42 years old only if there are extraordinary reasons for so doing, and it is also proposed that this should apply if the egg is the woman's own and has been fertilised by the husband's or cohabitant's sperm. According to the proposal, only women who themselves undertake IVF treatment would be allowed to donate eggs. The egg-donating woman should be of age (ie have attained 18 years) and have given her written consent. According to the proposal, eggs or sperm from deceased women and men may not be used for fertilisation. (It should also be prohibited to use egg rudiments from aborted foetuses for the purpose of creating children.) The child would be entitled to learn how he or she had been conceived and given the opportunity of discovering the identity of his or her genetic mother or father. Furthermore, it may be mentioned that the right to control frozen, fertilised eggs would, according to the proposal, belong only to the prospective parents together.

Finally, it can be noted only that it is proposed that a rule concerning maternity be introduced into the CPCG, whereby the woman who gives birth to a child would be legally deemed to be the mother of the child. To date, there are no special rules concerning maternity in Swedish law. Here instead, as is common elsewhere, the unwritten proposition *mater semper certa est*, because *mater est quam gestatio demonstrant* applies.

UGANDA

FAMILY RELATIONS AND THE LAW IN UGANDA: INSIGHTS INTO CURRENT ISSUES

Lillian Tibatemwa Ekirikubinza[*]

I   INTRODUCTION

This paper sets out to analyse recent developments in various branches of the law which have a direct impact on domestic relations, with a special focus on the husband–wife relationship. Since the main focus is on spousal relations, I have placed my analysis within the Women's Human Rights Discourse and based the critique on the extent to which particular legal provisions are in line with the notion of equality between men and women. I also find it necessary to place the discussion within a gender perspective. The paper is not limited to laws which fall within what is traditionally accepted as family law, such as marriage and divorce laws. It covers the Constitution, the law on succession, land law, and criminal law in so as far as they affect domestic relations and relate to the concept of equality between men and women.

Uganda's 1995 Constitution has been applauded by many as gender sensitive. This among other things is by virtue of the fact that its article on equality between persons specifically outlaws the use of the sex of an individual as a basis for according him/her different treatment.[1] It also states that women shall be accorded full and equal dignity of the person with men.[2] Furthermore, the same Constitution prohibits laws, cultures, customs or traditions that are against the dignity and welfare or interest of women or which undermine their status.[3] Further still, the same Constitution accords men and women equal rights in marriage, during marriage and on its dissolution.[4] Acknowledgement of the need to cater specifically for the rights of women in the new Constitution presents a sharp contrast to the earlier (1967) Constitution whose equality article prohibited discrimination on the ground of race, tribe, place of origin, political opinions, colour and creed but was silent on sex. Furthermore, the 1967 Constitution expressly allowed discriminatory personal laws and cultures to operate in the area of marriage, divorce and devolution of property.[5]

---

[*]   Senior Lecturer and Associate Dean, Faculty of Law, Makerere.

[1]   Article 21(2).

[2]   Article 33(1).

[3]   Article 33(6).

[4]   Article 31(1).

[5]   Article 20(1) stated that no law should make any provision that is discriminatory. The same article, however, exempted the application of its provisions to, among other things, devolution of property or other matters of personal law.

Ugandan women's greatest constitutional achievement is that the principles which entitle them to protection, and promote their equality with men, have been fully institutionalised in the supreme law of the nation. But what is more important is for women to register equality as a practical and meaningful concept. The extent to which this can be achieved depends a lot on women's rights within the family. Emphasis on the family as the most important site of analysis is premised on the recognition that the rights of women in family matters (be it the family of origin or the family of procreation) are central to their rights as individuals. This is because women's societal given roles are centred on and within the family. Consequently, women's lives are affected far more profoundly than are men's by their status in the family, and lack of rights in this area can effectively mean that women cannot exercise any rights they may formally have in other areas. But, the assurance of rights for women in this most personal of spheres is a complex matter, given that most societies value the preservation of the family as much as they purport to value individual freedom.

II   DEVELOPMENTS IN LAND LAW

A   The case for the consent clause

In 1998, a new Land Act was enacted with the aim, among other things, of providing for ownership and management of land. It was recognised by many stakeholders that addressing the inequalities women face in land access and ownership in an agricultural and peasant economy is essential if women are to realise the fundamental human right to equality.

In Uganda the population predominantly depends on subsistence farming for survival. Women make up over 80% of the agricultural labour force but only 7% of the female population own land.[6] A combination of statutory and customary laws have favoured male ownership of property.[7] The customary land tenure system prefers male heirs, and matrimonial property is normally acquired on the husband's inherited land. The man controls a woman's contribution, such as material acquisition or developments on family property. Women's right to land is usually 'access-based' and this is usually through marriage. Consequently, it is common for an irresponsible husband to sell off land which the wife is using to provide food for the family.[8] Furthermore, non-monetary contributions to the land do not automatically give the woman any right to the land. Thus, on divorce, a woman leaves without any property since whatever is on the land belongs to the land.[9] Consequently, under section 40 of the Land Act, it has been provided that a person is prohibited from transferring land without the prior written consent of the

---

[6]   *The 1991 Population and Housing Census*, Ministry of Lands, Housing and Urban Development, Kampala.

[7]   See, for example, section 3 of the Succession Act, which prefers a male to a female relative for purposes of inheritance.

[8]   Tibatemwa-Ekirikubinza, *Women's Violent Crime in Uganda: More Sinned Against than Sinning* (Fountain Publishers, 1999).

[9]   This is the concept originating from English land law and expressed by the Latin maxim – Quicquid Plantatur Solo, Solo Cedit.

spouse. Where any transaction is entered into contrary to this provision, the transfer is null and void. The consent clause was thus a step towards strengthening women's land rights.

B   The ownership clause

During debates on the Land Act, human rights activists lobbied intensively for the inclusion of provisions which would strengthen women's rights to own (as opposed to merely to access) land. As a result, an amendment providing spousal co-ownership of land on which the family resides, or on which the family depends for a living, was introduced and passed by Parliament. The proposed clause was to the effect that a spouse, by virtue of marriage, would acquire a 50% ownership of the matrimonial home. This would be irrespective of the parties' individual monetary contributions to the said property. Consequently, in the case of divorce, the property would be equally shared between the two parties. On the death of a spouse, the surviving partner would be entitled to 50% of the matrimonial home, and this would not constitute part of the estate of the deceased to be divided between other beneficiaries. However, the amendment was 'mysteriously' left out of the final Act and it has become known as the 'lost clause'.

Together with the consent clause, the co-ownership clause would have done a lot in building bridges between the gender equitable provisions of the Constitution and the gender inequalities under customary land tenure.

III   THE LAW ON MARRIAGE AND DIVORCE

In 1994, the Uganda Law Reform Commission embarked on a study of the law on Domestic Relations. The Commission used both primary and secondary data and came up with proposals for a new law.

A   Polygamy

Uganda has a plural legal system in which both monogamy and polygamy are recognised by the law. One of the proposals which proved contentious was the issue of regulation of polygamy. It has been acknowledged by the Commission that 79.5% of the respondents in its study expressed preference for monogamy, and only 18% supported polygamy. The Commission findings also revealed that many people are aware of the negative aspects of the practice and identified polygamy as a contributory factor to many development and health problems such as the prevalence of HIV/Aids, high population growth, low educational standards and poverty. Nevertheless, the Commission proposed that, rather than prohibiting the practice, it should be regulated. The Commission has thus proposed that a man married under a potentially polygamous marriage may marry up to four wives if, among other things, he can satisfy the court that:

(a)   he has financial capacity to maintain his wives and children to the same standard;

(b)   he has capacity to provide a matrimonial home for each wife; and
(c)   he has the ability to provide the same treatment to his wives in terms of
       conjugal rights and all basic needs, and to his children in terms of residence
       and all other basic needs such as education.

It is also provided that the court will not authorise the application unless there is
free consent to any subsequent marriage given by the wife or wives and the
prospective wife declares before the court that she has been informed about the
marital status of the husband.

B   Grounds for divorce

Under the Divorce Act[10] the law is based on the fault principle. It provides for
grounds on which men and women can petition for divorce. The grounds are
discriminatory in that, whereas a husband's proof that his wife has committed
adultery enables him to get a divorce, for a woman, proof of a husband's adultery
is not an adequate ground for a divorce unless the wife proves that, in addition to
the adultery, the husband was also cruel or had deserted her.

The Commission has recommended that the law should provide for no-fault
divorce, or irretrievable breakdown of marriage. Proof of the marriage having
broken down would be enough basis for divorce. Furthermore, either spouse
would have equal rights to bring an application for divorce.

C   Marital rape

In 1997 the Uganda Law Reform Commission undertook a study of sexual
offences with the objective of, among other things, giving effect to the 1995
constitutional provisions and to Uganda's international and regional obligations
arising out of Human Rights Instruments ratified by the country. The Commission
has come up with the Sexual Offences Bill.

Under English common law (which is applicable to Uganda), a husband could
not commit rape on his wife. It has, however, been argued by human rights
activists in the country that, as acknowledged by Lord Robertson 20 years ago:

> 'The whole position of marriage and status of women today is very different from that
> in the past. If a man could be found guilty in whatever way and degree of seriousness
> of violence against his wife, it would be unreasonable not to find him guilty of rape of
> the same wife if the necessary facts (lack of consent) were proved.'[11]

The Commission has, in agreement with other human rights activists,
acknowledged that forced sexual intercourse is a violation of the victim's body,
even if the parties are married. Nevertheless, the Commission 'shied' away from a
full-blown amendment which would remove marital relationship as a defence to
rape. It has thus been recommended that the law should continue to recognise a

---

[10]   Chapter 215, Laws of Uganda.
[11]   In *HM Advocate v Duffy* (1983) SLT 7.

presumption of consent to sexual intercourse between married people provided that:

(1)   where spouses are living in separation, any sexual intercourse in the absence of consent should amount to an offence of marital sexual assault;[12]

(2)   in circumstances where spouses are living together, one of them may refuse sexual intercourse on reasonable grounds, which may include: poor health of the spouse refusing sexual intercourse; reasonable fear that engaging in sexual intercourse would be likely to cause injury or harm to the spouse refusing sexual intercourse; or such other grounds as may be deemed reasonable by the court.

IV   CONCLUDING REMARKS: FROM PATRIARCHY TO GENDER EQUITY

Ugandan policy makers have come to realise that there is a link between gender issues, sustainable development and sustainable livelihood. Since 1995, attempts have been made to come up with laws which reflect the constitutional right to equality between men and women.

It is acknowledged that equal access to and ownership of land is a basic human right. However, the reforms introduced have been only half-hearted. Whereas a move to ensure equitable ownership had been passed by Parliament, once faced with pressure from several other quarters, policy makers succumbed to patriarchy, a clear sign that land issues are ultimately a power struggle.

And, as already mentioned, research by the Uganda Law Reform Commission indicates that society has recognised that inter-familial violence against women is a legitimate concern. However, failure to call marital rape by its name, and failure to criminalise it fully, are an indication that there is a link between familial violence against women on the one hand, and the cultural and social norms which surround gender and other inequities. Women will not be free from violence until there is equality between men and women in the political, social and economic spheres.

It can also be argued that polygamy is the epitome of unequal relations between men and women. Among other things, it allows one spouse (the husband) unilaterally to change fundamentally the quality of the couple's family life. That a country whose Constitution declares equal rights between men and women in marriage is still ready to give legitimacy to polygamy is a clear indication that the fangs of patriarchy are still so deeply embedded in Ugandan society that those in power are not ready to put into operation the equality provision found in the fundamental law of the land.

It is clear that as long as power is still dominated by the male gender, attempts to legislate in favour of women will face constraints.

---

[12] Note that the Commission does not refer to the offence as rape.

THE UNITED STATES

CHANGING FAMILY REALITIES, NON-TRADITIONAL FAMILIES AND RETHINKING THE CORE ASSUMPTIONS OF FAMILY LAW

Nancy E Dowd [*]

Non-traditional family forms continue to vex a family law structure built on status and form, challenging courts to consider relational and contextual analyses that focus on emotion, care, and the content of relationships. In the process, concepts of privacy, equality and liberty are questioned and defended, or recast. The labelling of families as 'non-traditional', or the use of other modifiers, reinforces the implicit norm and definition of a 'real' family. Non-traditional families also frequently generate competing images of decline or creativity, crumbling social foundations or healthy fluidity, and historical consistency versus modern malaise. Much of the challenge to traditional American family law structure has been at State and local level.[1] Less frequently, the United States Supreme Court has considered the implications of current family realities for family and constitutional law.

During the 1999–2000 term, however, the court exercised its discretion to hear *Troxel v Granville*,[2] a case that brought many issues of changing family forms, and the court's view of family and parents, into sharp relief. In *Troxel* the court had to decide whether a Washington State statute that permitted a petition for visitation by third parties was unconstitutional in the context of grandparents seeking visitation with the grandchildren of their deceased son. The court concluded, in a surprisingly splintered opinion, that, *as applied*, the statute constituted an unconstitutional invasion of parental autonomy.[3] While *Troxel* most directly affected grandparent visitation, and more generally third party visitation, in a broader sense the case became an opportunity for an examination of changing family forms. The case is important for what it says about conceptions of family and the ability of courts to accept functional definitions, grounded in emotional and psychological relationships, as opposed to structural, biological, or status-oriented definitions that tend to privilege traditional nuclear, marital, biological, heterosexual families with well-defined gender roles. It is also significant for its discourse about non-traditional families. In Part I of this article, I describe the

---

[*] Chesterfield Smith Professor of Law, University of Florida Levin College of Law. This article was completed with the assistance of the reference librarians at the Northeastern University School of Law and Harold Jones, Northeastern University School of Law, class of 2003, while I was a visiting professor at Northeastern during the spring of 2001.

[1] For example, challenges to marriage statutes on behalf of same-sex couples, the liberalizing of access to adoption records, and permitting adoption by gay and lesbian parents as joint parents or as co-parent adoption are all examples of recent changes in family law at State level.

[2] 530 US 57 (2000).

[3] Ibid at 73 (O'Connor, J, plurality).

Troxel case, including the family stories, the course of the litigation, the arguments raised before the Supreme Court, and the six opinions filed in the court's decision. In Part II, I explore *Troxel*'s significance for visitation by grandparents and other third parties. Because *Troxel* reached a result based on the application of the statute rather than its facial validity, it has done little to resolve many of the issues raised by third party visitation statutes. In Part III, I consider the broader conceptual implications of the case for non-traditional families.

I   THE *TROXEL* DECISION

A   Stories, decisions, arguments

1   THE FAMILY STORIES

Troxel began as three separate visitation petitions that were eventually consolidated in an appeal to the Supreme Court of Washington. Only the Troxel family's petition was appealed to the United States Supreme Court. The three family stories involved in the original stage of the litigation are notable for their intersection with the realities of diverse families and the view they provide of the changing, evolving nature of family life.

The *Troxel* petition involved a request for visitation by paternal grandparents with their two grandchildren.[4] The family story includes the threads of non-marital parenthood, extended family, step-parent adoption, and blended family. The children's father, Brad, never married the mother, Tommie Granville, but they lived together intermittently from 1988 to 1991.[5] Tommie previously had three children with Jeff Granville, and had two children with Brad, their daughters Natalie and Isabelle.[6] The couple separated before Natalie was born, and Brad then lived with his parents, Jennifer and Gary Troxel.[7] The Troxels had been married over 30 years and Gary was a member of the Fleetwoods, a nationally famous band in the 60s. All of the Troxels' four children and their grandchildren lived in Skagit County, Washington.[8] Tommie and Brad agreed to custody and visitation, devised a parenting plan, and filed the plan in 1992 in state court.[9] Under the plan, the girls spent every other weekend with Brad, usually at their grandparents' home.[10]

Brad committed suicide in May 1993.[11] In the period immediately following his death, Brad's brother and sister assisted Tommie in caring for the girls, and frequently the grandparents saw Brad's children during this period at the homes of

---

4   *In re Visitation of Troxel*, 940 P.2d 698, 699 (Wash Ct App 1997).

5   Brief for Petitioner at 2, *Troxel v Granville*, 530 US 57 (no 99-138).

6   Petitioner for Certiorari at 4, *Troxel v Granville*, 530 US 57 (no 99-138).

7   Ibid at 3.

8   Ibid.

9   Brief for Petitioner at 2, *Troxel v Granville*, 530 US 57 (no 99-138).

10 Ibid.

11 Ibid.

their other children.[12] In October 1993, Tommie informed the grandparents that she wanted to limit their contact with the girls to one visit per month, a request with which the grandparents disagreed. The apparent reason for Tommie's request was her relationship with Kelly Wynn, a divorced father of two, and her desire to stabilize their blended family.[13] From October to December the girls did not visit their grandparents at all.[14] In December 1993 the grandparents filed a petition seeking visitation. Regular visits did not resume until April 1994, after a temporary visitation order was obtained by the grandparents.[15]

The trial was held in 1995, nearly a year after the action was filed, when the girls were five and almost three years old. Tommie did not object to visitation, but did not agree with the extent of visitation that Gary and Jennifer requested.[16] The grandparents sought two weekends of visitation each month and two weeks during the summer. In part their rationale was that they would stand in the shoes of their deceased son in relation to his child. Tommie asked for one day of visitation each month but no overnight stays.[17] Tommie's expert also suggested that the Troxels be included in the holiday celebrations of the Wynns. The trial court entered a compromise order, granting the Troxels visitation of one weekend per month, one week in the summer, and four hours on the birthday of each grandparent.[18] Tommie appealed, objecting to overnight visits and the summer vacation visit, and challenged the standing of the grandparents.[19] On appeal, the Court of Appeals agreed that the Troxels lacked standing to file for visitation, since no custody proceeding was pending at the time they requested visitation, and dismissed the petition.[20]

In the course of the litigation, Tommie married Kelly Wynn and had a child with him and Mr Wynn also adopted Natalie and Isabelle in 1996.[21] The controversy regarding visitation was framed, however, as a controversy between Tommie and the Troxels only with respect to Natalie and Isabelle.

The second family story involved the petition of David Clay for visitation in order to maintain a relationship with Justin Wolcott. David's petition was unique because he was not Justin's biological father nor had he ever been married to Justin's mother; his claim for visitation was premised on his status as a

---

[12]   Ibid.

[13]   Ibid. (The timing of the marriage is a bit unclear. The Petitioner's Brief states that Granville married Wynn in 1994, while Justice O'Connor's opinion states that Granville did not marry Wynn until after the visitation trial, which occurred in 1995. *Troxel v Granville*, 530 US 57 at 61 (O'Connor J, plurality).)

[14]   Ibid at 2.

[15]   Ibid at 3.

[16]   Ibid.

[17]   Ibid.

[18]   Ibid at 4–5.

[19]   Ibid 5.

[20]   *In re Visitation of Troxel*, 940 P.2d at 701 (Wash Ct App 1997). In other words, rather than allowing a visitation petition to be brought whenever the parties disagreed, the court reasoned that petitions were limited to changed family circumstances, and specifically to a pending custody dispute. This interpretation would have prevented the Troxels from ever filing a petition, since Tommie was the only surviving parent, so there was no one with whom to have a custody dispute.

[21]   Ibid at 698.

psychological father.[22] Justin was born in 1986 to Lisa Wolcott, who was unmarried at the time. Lisa began a relationship with David, and they lived together from 1988 to 1992. After they separated, David continued to see Justin, whom he regarded as his son.[23] When the relationship between David and Lisa deteriorated, David filed a visitation petition in 1993, and a temporary order gave him visitation every other weekend, which was later reduced to one Saturday per month.[24] In 1994 Lisa sought to terminate visitation. After a trial in October 1995, David's petition was dismissed for lack of standing.[25] The Court of Appeals agreed that David had no standing to seek visitation.[26] Justin was then nine years old. During the litigation Lisa married, and her husband adopted Justin.[27] As in *Troxel*, the threads of non-marital relationship, subsequent marriage, step-parenthood and step-parent adoption are present. The uniqueness of *Wolcott*, on the other hand, is the assertion of fatherhood by a non-biological, non-marital, non-adoptive father who acted as a de facto parent to the child.

The third petition was filed by paternal relatives, including grandparents, an aunt, and an uncle, to maintain their relationships with Sara Stillwell.[28] Sara was conceived during the marriage of Brian Smith and Kelly Stillwell with the assistance of artificial insemination from a donor, and was born in 1992.[29] In 1995 Kelly petitioned for divorce, and both parents sought custody of Sara. In February 1996 Kelly's mother and Brian had a violent altercation over the custody dispute, and both Brian and his mother-in-law died from gunshot wounds.[30] After this family tragedy, Kelly and Brian's relatives could not work out visitation. The Smith relatives then filed a visitation petition. A trial was held in April 1997, when Sara was five years old, and a visitation schedule was established.[31] When Kelly appealed, the appeals court granted a motion to consolidate this case with the pending *Troxel* and *Wolcott* cases.[32] The *Smith* case is a 'true' single parent case with no step-parent or intimate partner in the picture. It also brings together intersections of death, divorce, and families formed within marriage through reproductive technologies.[33]

---

22   *In re Wolcott*, 933 P.2d 1066 (Wash Ct App 1997).

23   Ibid at 1067.

24   Ibid.

25   Ibid.

26   Ibid at 1069.

27   Ibid.

28   *In re Smith et al*, 969 P.2d 21 (Wash 1998).

29   Ibid at 24.

30   Ibid.

31   Ibid.

32   Ibid at 23.

33   Ibid at 24. The *Smith* case is unique for its exposure of the intersections between family realities and legal constructions. It can be characterized as a controversy between a widow and the surviving relatives of the father, or as the nearly ex-wife in a highly contested custody case versus family relatives related to the father who killed the mother's mother (who simultaneously killed her son-in-law). The child is biologically connected to the mother, but legally deemed also the

2   THE STATUTORY SCHEME

The visitation orders in these three family situations were sought under a state law that permitted non-parents to seek visitation.[34] The statute in effect by the time the case reached the Washington Supreme Court provided:

> 'Any person may petition the court for visitation rights at any time including, but not limited to, custody proceedings. The court may order visitation rights for any person when visitation may serve the best interest of the child whether or not there has been any change of circumstances.'[35]

The prior statute (effective until 1996) was quite similar:

> 'The court may order visitation rights for a person other than a parent when visitation may serve the best interest of the child whether or not there has been any change of circumstances.'

> 'A person other than a parent may petition the court for visitation rights at any time.'

> 'The court may modify an order granting or denying visitation rights whenever modification would serve the best interests of the child.'[36]

The context in which these statutes were enacted includes a series of revisions of state law to clarify the rights of non-custodial parents in a dissolution situation with respect to visitation, as well as the creation and clarification of statutes permitting visitation by non-parents independent of any particular circumstances, such as dissolution or a parental death, in the family unit.[37]

The Washington statute reflects similar provisions among all American jurisdictions permitting, to a greater or lesser degree, third party visitation.[38]

---

child of the father by virtue of the operation of the state statute on artificial insemination as well as the marital presumption that any child born during the marriage is the child of the father.

[34]   Wash Rev Code § 26.10.160(3) (2001) and Wash Rev Code § 26.09.240 (amended 1996).

[35]   Wash Rev Code § 26.10.160(3) (2001).

[36]   Wash Rev Code § 26.09.240 (amended 1996).

[37]   See *In re Smith et al* 969 P.2d at 26 (Wash 1998).

[38]   All fifty States have statutes that provide for grandparent visitation in some form: Ala Code § 30-3-4.1; Alaska Stat Ann § 25.20.065 (1998); Ariz Rev Stat Ann § 25-409 (1994); Ark Code Ann § 9-13-103 (1998); Cal Fam Code Ann § 3104 (West 1994); Colo Rev Stat § 19-1-117 (1999); Conn Gen Stat § 46b-59 (1995); Del Code Ann, Tit 10 § 1031(7) (1999); Fla Stat § 752.01 (1997); Ga Code Ann § 19-7-3 (1991); Haw Rev Stat § 571- 46.3 (1999); Idaho Code § 32-719 (1999); Ill Comp Stat, ch 750, § 5/607 (1998); Ind Code § 31-17-5-1 (1999); Iowa Code § 598.35 (1999); Kan Stat Ann § 38-129 (1993); Ky Rev Stat Ann § 405.021 (Baldwin 1990); La Rev Stat Ann § 9:344 (West Supp 2000); La Civ Code Ann, Art 136 (West Supp 2000); Me Rev Stat Ann, Tit 19A, § 1803 (1998); Md Fam Law Code Ann § 9-102 (1999); Mass Gen Laws § 119:39D (1996); Mich Comp Laws Ann § 722.27b (Supp 1999); Minn Stat § 257.022 (1998); Miss Code Ann § 93-16-3 (1994); Mo Rev Stat § 452.402 (Supp 1999); Mont Code Ann § 40-9- 102 (1997); Neb Rev Stat § 43-1802 (1998); Nev Rev Stat § 125C.050 (Supp 1999); NH Rev Stat Ann § 458:17-d (1992); NJ Stat Ann § 9:2-7.1 (West Supp 1999–2000); NM Stat Ann § 40-9-2 (1999); NY Dom Rel Law § 72 (McKinney 1999); NC Gen Stat §§ 50-13.2, 50-13.2A (1999); ND Cent Code § 14-09-05.1 (1997); Ohio Rev Code Ann §§ 3109.051, 3109.11 (Supp 1999); Okla Stat, Tit 10, § 5 (Supp 1999); Ore Rev Stat § 109.121 (1997); 23 Pa Cons Stat §§ 5311-5313 (1991); RI Gen Laws §§ 15-5-24 to 15-5-24.3 (Supp 1999); SC Code Ann § 20-7-420(33) (Supp 1999); SD Codified Laws § 25-4-52 (1999); Tenn Code Ann §§ 36-6-306, 36-6-307 (Supp 1999); Tex Fam Code Ann § 153.433 (Supp 2000); Utah Code Ann § 30-5-2

While some statutes include only grandparents, other statutes more broadly provide for visitation by other third parties as well.[39] Washington's statute was exceptional in that it permitted 'any person' to file for visitation, and also without establishment of a pre-existing relationship or attempted relationship with the child. Some States limit the circumstances under which a petition for visitation can be filed by third parties, such as the dissolution of a marriage or the death of a parent, or a finding of parental unfitness.[40] Washington's statute also was unusual in this respect, since it allowed a petition for visitation to be filed at 'any time'. Finally, like most visitation statutes, Washington's statute determined whether to grant visitation based on the 'best interests' standard. Some States articulate specific factors to be taken into account in applying the standard, and frequently those factors include strong consideration of the objections of the child's parent(s).[41] Washington's statute followed the best interests standard but did not

---

(1998); Vt Stat Ann Tit 15, §§ 1011-1013 (1989); Va Code Ann § 20-124.2 (1995); W Va Code §§ 48-2B-1 to 48-2B-7 (1999); Wis Stat §§ 767.245, 880.155 (1993-1994); Wyo Stat Ann § 20-7-101 (1999).

    For a good description of the movement towards grandparent visitation pre-*Troxel* as well as third party visitation issues more generally, see generally Edward M Burns, 'Grandparent Visitation Rights: Is it Time for the Pendulum to Fall', 25 Fam LQ 59 (1991); Koreen Labrecque, 'Grandparent Visitation after Step-parent Adoption', 6 Conn Prob LJ 61 (1991); Catherine Bostock, 'Does the Expansion of Grandparent Visitation Rights Promote the Best Interests of the Child?: A Survey of Grandparent Visitation Laws in the Fifty States', 27 Colum JL & Soc Probs 319 (1994); Linda D Elrod and Robert G Spector, 'A Review of the Year in Family Law: Century Ends with Unresolved Issues', 33 Fam LQ 865 (2000); Barbara L Shapiro, 'Non-Traditional Families in the Courts: The New Extended Family', 11 J Am Acad Matrim Law 117 (1993); Ruthann Robson, 'Third Parties and the Third Sex: Child Custody and Lesbian Legal Theory', 26 Conn L Rev 1377 (1994); John DeWitt Gregory, 'Blood Ties: A Rationale for Child Visitation by Legal Strangers', 55 Wash & Lee L Rev 351 (1998).

[39] As noted by one amicus, the tendency in visitation statutes has been toward expanding visitation to include extended family and kin:

'Some state custody statutes provide that ... extended family or informal kin, who are neither parents nor grandparents, may petition for visitation. These include great-grandparents, step-parents, siblings, and relatives, or persons who have either maintained a parent–child relationship with the child or who once had physical custody of the child. Only a few states, in addition to Washington, allow any person to join or initiate an action for visitation. In all, at least twenty-one state statutes specifically allow persons in addition to grandparents to petition for visitation. Finally, even in states where there is no statutory grant of standing to other third parties, many courts have exercised their discretion to grant visitation to third parties when it would be in the best interest of the child and/or when the third party has stood in loco parentis to the child.'

(Brief Amicus Curiae Center for Children's Policy Practice Research at the University of Pennsylvania in Support of Respondent, Lexsee 1999 US Briefs 138 (13 December 1999).)

[40] Regarding the circumstances under which a visitation petition could be filed, one amicus brief summarizes the status of the statutes at the time the case was heard:

'Twenty states do not permit grandparents to petition for visitation with grandchildren when the children's parents are married and both parents oppose such visitation. These states specify limited circumstances in which a grandparent may file a petition for visitation, such as a divorce or custody proceeding, the death of a parent, or a child born out-of-wedlock. The other thirty states, including Washington, permit grandparents to petition for visitation regardless of the parent's marital status, even when the parents oppose grandparent visitation. Of these states, four permit the grandparents to petition for visitation when the parents are married only if the child previously resided with the grandparents for a minimum period of three to twelve months. Another eight of these states permit a petition when the parents are married only if the grandparents have been denied visitation with the grandchild.'

(Brief Amici Curiae of AARP and Generations United in Support of Petitioners, Lexsee 1999 US Briefs 138 (12 November 1999).)

[41] 'Twenty-seven States require courts to take into consideration whether the grandparent has already established a substantial relationship with the grandchild in determining whether to award

articulate specific factors to be taken into consideration. A few States make the visitation determination based on a higher showing of harm to the child if visitation is denied, rather than meeting the more affirmative standard of best interests.[42]

Washington's statute was distinctive, then, because it permitted 'any person' to petition for visitation at 'any time' and would grant visitation if it was in the best interests of the child. The petitioner was not required to make a showing of prior relationship in order to file, and no circumstance or change in circumstances were necessary to bring a petition. The breadth of those who could utilize the statute is reflected in the three cases before the court, including biological grandparents, a psychological parent/former boyfriend, and extended family members. Other family scenarios that might have generated a visitation petition include those involving step-parents, non-biological lesbian or gay co-parents, de facto parents, psychological parents, and other extended or kinship or fictive kinship relations. The breadth of the statute's reach to 'any person' would also by its terms include virtual strangers.[43]

---

visitation in an individual case. Eighteen States require the courts to consider the effect of the court-ordered grandparent visitation on the child's relationship with the parent. Thirty-one States explicitly permit grandparents to petition for visitation following adoption by a step-parent.'
(Brief Amici Curiae of AARP and Generations United in Support of Petitioners, Lexsee 1999 US Briefs 138 (12 November 1999).)

For concern over parental objection, see note 40 above. Washington's revised statute required the following factors to be included in a best interests determination: strength of the relationship with the child; the nature of the relationship of the petitioner with the parents or custodian of the child; reasons for objection to granting visitation; effect of visitation on the parental or custodial relationship; the residential time sharing arrangements; good faith of the petitioner, and criminal history or history of abuse or neglect, and any other factor relevant to the child's best interest: Wash Rev Code 26.09.240(6) (1996 Wash Laws ch 177, section 1). The statute was amended in 1996 after the petition for visitation was filed in the *Troxel* case.

[42] See, for example, the revised Washington statute, note 41 above, and the use of procedural standing devices and the application of the best interests standard in effect to apply a 'harm' standard. For an argument on the constitutional requirement of a harm standard, see, eg, Brief of the American Civil Liberties Union and the ACLU of Washington in Support of Respondent, Lexsee 1999 US Briefs 138 (13 December 1999). For the more extreme position that third party visitation per se is an unconstitutional invasion under any standard, see Brief of the Coalition for the Restoration of Parental Rights as Amicus Curiae in Support of Respondent, Lexsee 1999 US Briefs 138 (8 December 1999).

[43] Brief of Northwest Women's Law Center et al, 1999 US Briefs 138 (10 December 1999) (implications of the case for single mothers and lesbian non-biological parents); (Brief Amicus Curiae for Debra Hein in Support of Respondent, 1999 US Briefs 138 (30 December 1999) (mother with adoptive children); Brief of the Domestic Violence Project Inc/Safe House (Michigan) et al, 1999 US Briefs 138 (13 December 1999) (use of visitation statutes by domestic violence perpetrators as a weapon in abuse situations). Several of the briefs bring up the 'stranger' scenario, as do some of the lower court opinions:

'A literal reading of this statute could lead to the sort of absurd result that our canons of statutory construction forbid. Does "any person" have standing to petition "at any time" for visitation with a child? For example, could a member of the state Legislature who has displeased a constituent find herself faced with the considerable expenditure of time, money, and emotional energy to oppose a wholly frivolous petition by that constituent?'
(*In re the Visitation of Troxel*, 940 P.2d 698, 699 (Wash 1997).)

3   THE WASHINGTON SUPREME COURT OPINION[44]

The Washington Supreme Court rejected the statutory construction of the lower courts that a visitation petition could be brought only in the context of a custody proceeding which had been the basis for the finding that the parties lacked standing. The plain language of the statute stated otherwise: a visitation petition could be brought 'at any time'.[45] A majority of the court nevertheless agreed with the Courts of Appeal that the visitation orders were invalid, albeit on the different basis that the statute, in its current or prior form, was unconstitutional under the US Constitution.[46]

The court was closely divided in the case, 5–4, reflecting a strong difference of opinion on the meaning of federal precedents on the rights of parents. The majority opinion of Justice Madsen interpreted federal constitutional protection of family, including the right to non-interference with family privacy to rear one's children, as subject to state interference 'only "if it appears that parental decisions will jeopardize the health or safety of the child, or have a potential for significant social burdens"'.[47] The court found that the State could only exercise its *parens patriae* power to protect the child from harm.[48] Although the State could intervene to protect certain relationships with children, the court construed those instances very narrowly to encompass only situations where a break in the relationship would cause 'severe psychological harm to the child'.[49] The court rejected as a constitutionally compelling interest sufficient for intervention the 'best interests of the child'. 'State intervention to better a child's quality of life through third party visitation is not justified where the child's circumstances are otherwise satisfactory.'[50] In addition, the court viewed the broad language of the statute as dangerous and threatening to 'stable' families who might be required to defend against frivolous or manipulative actions to seek visitation by anyone irrespective of relationship, since the statute did not impose a requirement of a showing of substantial prior relationship as a standing requirement for seeking visitation.[51]

Justice Talmadge, in dissent, strongly disagreed with the majority's interpretation of constitutional precedent as well as its rejection of the best interests standard as constitutionally sufficient. Justice Talmadge argued that parental rights are not absolute, nor is the State prohibited from intervening other than upon a showing of harm to the child.[52] He disagreed with the majority's narrow interpretation of *parens patriae* power both from the perspective of state law and constitutional law.[53] He pointed out that most courts have held grandparent visitation statutes constitutional where they incorporate the best

---

[44]   *In re Custody of Smith*, 969 P.2d 21 (Wash 1998).

[45]   Ibid at 26.

[46]   Ibid. Because the state constitution provided no different or higher standard than the federal constitution, the court evaluated the challenge solely by reference to federal constitutional law.

[47]   Ibid at 29 (citing *Wisconsin v Yoder*, 406 US 205 (1972)).

[48]   Ibid at 30.

[49]   Ibid.

[50]   Ibid.

[51]   Ibid at 30–31.

[52]   Ibid at 32–33 (Talmadge, J, dissenting).

[53]   Ibid at 34 (Talmadge, J, dissenting).

interests of the child standard.[54] Talmadge reasoned that a strong version of parental autonomy is grounded in the assumption that 'family' means an intact traditional family. A less stringent protection for parents is justified by the 'realities of modern living':

> 'The realities of modern living, however, demonstrate that the validity of according almost absolute judicial deference to parental rights has become less compelling as the foundation upon which they are premised, the traditional nuclear family, has eroded ... More and varied and complicated family situations arise ... One of the frequent consequences, for children, of the decline of the traditional nuclear family is the formation of close personal attachments between them and adults outside of their immediate families ... It would be shortsighted indeed, for this court not to recognize the realities and complexities of modern family life, by holding today that a child has no rights, over the objection of a parent, to maintain a close extra-parental relationship which has formed in the absence of a nuclear family.'[55]

Talmadge's opinion reflects a view seemingly more supportive of children's rights but less deferential to the privacy of non-traditional families.

4   THE APPEAL AND DECISION IN THE UNITED STATES SUPREME COURT

On appeal, only the *Troxel* petition for visitation was considered by the United States Supreme Court, rather than all three cases before the Washington Supreme Court. The presence or absence of the other cases arguably was irrelevant, and even the facts of the *Troxel* case were irrelevant, because the Washington Supreme Court had ruled the statute *facially* unconstitutional.[56] Ultimately, however, the facts were important because the United States Supreme Court held the state statute invalid only *as applied*.

The arguments of the parties and amici on appeal included a range of positions on the implications of non-traditional families for constitutional analysis. The basic argument of the grandparents was that the state court had erred in its finding of facial invalidity because the statute was constitutional if the proper level of scrutiny was applied, and, most significantly, if all relevant interests were considered, not solely those of the parents. A balancing analysis should have been used, they argued, including all relevant interests and relationships.[57] Such an analysis would recognize current realities in American families, who represent a wide range of shapes and configurations that often change over time, rather than reflect assumptions tied to the idealized nuclear, marital family.

Advocates for the mother, on the other hand, focused on the importance of parental autonomy and the degree of infringement represented by this broadly worded statute. Emphasizing that this was not simply a grandparent visitation statute, they pointed out that the covered category of persons was limitless. Furthermore, evaluation under the best interests standard was insufficient protection of parental autonomy and family privacy. Because parental status confers constitutional protection, the mother's status as a single mother when the

---

54   Ibid at 37 (Talmadge, J, dissenting).
55   Ibid at 35 (Talmadge, J, dissenting).
56   Ibid at 27.
57   Brief for Petitioner at 7, *Troxel v Granville*, 530 US 57 (no 99-138).

litigation began was irrelevant to her claim of constitutional protection. While some form of third party visitation, particularly grandparent visitation, would be constitutionally permissible, any valid statutory scheme required protection of parental autonomy through standing requirements and evidentiary presumptions that reflected due regard for parental autonomy, all of which were lacking in the Washington statute.[58] Parental status, rather than family structure, was the proper focus.

Interestingly, the amici who presented arguments in the case substantially agreed that parental autonomy is fundamental, extremely important and valued.[59] Disagreement and debate largely focused around the definition and scope of parental autonomy and respect for family relationships and decision-making, and the interrelationship of parent–child relationships with other familial relationships.[60]

---

[58]   Brief for Respondents at 17, *Troxel v Granville*, 530 US 57 (no 99-138).

[59]   Brief of the States of Washington, Arkansas, California, Colorado, Hawaii, Kansas, Missouri, Montana, New Jersey, North Dakota, Ohio, and Tennessee as Amici Curiae in Support of Petitioners, Lexsee 1999 US Briefs 138; Brief of Amicus Curiae of Grandparents United for Children's Rights, Inc (for Petitioner), Lexsee 1999 US Briefs 138 (16 November 1999); Brief of the Amicus Curiae American Academy of Matrimonial Lawyers, 1999 US Briefs 13 (12 November 1999); Brief for the Grandparent Caregiver Law Center of the Brookdale Center on Aging as Amicus Curiae in Support of Petitioners, Lexsee 1999 US Briefs 138; Brief of the National Conference of State Legislatures, Council of State Governments, National Association of Counties, National League of Cities, International City County Management Association, and US Conference of Mayors as Amici Curiae in support of Petitioners, Lexsee 1999 US Briefs 138 (12 November 1999); Brief Amici Curiae of AARP and Generations United in Support of Petitioners, Lexsee 1999 US Briefs 138 (12 November 1999); Brief Amicus Curiae Center for Children's Policy Practice & Research at the University of Pennsylvania in Support of Respondent, Lexsee US Briefs 138 (13 December 1999); Amicus Curiae Brief of Professor Robert C Fellmeth, et al, Lexsee 1999 US Briefs 138 (13 December 1999); Brief of Lambda Legal Defense and Education Fund and Gay and Lesbian Advocates and Defenders as Amici Curiae in Support of Respondent, Lexsee 1999 US Briefs 138 (13 December 1999); Brief of the Domestic Violence Projects Inc/Safe House (Michigan), the Pennsylvania Coalition Against Domestic Violence, inc, the Florida Coalition Against Domestic Violence, the Iowa Coalition Against Domestic Violence, and the Missouri Coalition Against Domestic Violence as Amici Curiae in Support of Respondent, Lexsee 1999 US Briefs 138 (13 December 1999); Brief of the Institute for Justice, Alabama Family Alliance and the Minnesota Family Institute as Amici Curiae in Support of Respondent, Lexsee 1999 US Briefs 138 (13 December 1999); Brief in Amicus Curiae for Debra Hein in Support of Respondent, Lexsee 1999 US Briefs 138 (30 December 1999); Brief Amicus Curiae of the American Civil Liberties Union and the ACLU of Washington in support of Respondent, Lexsee 1999 US Briefs 138 (13 December 1999); Brief Amicus Curiae of the American Center for Law and Justice Supporting Respondent, Lexsee 1999 US Briefs 138 (10 December 1999); Brief of Amicus Curiae in Support of Respondent (Center for the Original intent of the Constitution), Lexsee 1999 US Briefs 138 (13 December 1999); Brief Amici Curiae of Christian Legal Society and the National Association of Evangelicals in Support of Respondent, Lexsee 1999 US Briefs 138 (13 December 1999); Brief of Northwest Women's Law Center, Connecticut Women's Education and Legal Fund, National Center for Lesbian Rights, and the Women's Law Center of Maryland, Inc as Amici Curiae in Support of Respondent, Lexsee 1999 US Briefs 138 (10 December 1999); Brief of the Coalition for the Restoration of Parental Rights as Amicus Curiae in support of Respondent, Lexsee 1999 US Briefs 138 (8 December 1999).

[60]   The amici lined up on either side of the case argued about the standard of review and even the legitimacy of fundamental rights grounded in substantive due process, jurisprudential arguments frequently debated in substantive due process cases. How demanding the standard of review would be varied also depending upon whether one characterized this dispute as one between parents and State, or as intra-familial, between what might be best for the children and what might be best for the parents, and/or between two sets of relevant caretaking adults, parents and grandparents.

Very different views also were presented on the significance of changing family forms and the presence of non-traditional families. Petitioners and their amici most strongly argued that the presence and growth of non-traditional families undercut traditional notions of parental autonomy because the children of such families needed all of the kin and non-kin relationships in their lives that they could get. At the same time, the structure and status of family members in non-traditional families required protection of their relationships.[61] This view of non-traditional families as in need of greater support and therefore as necessitating greater intervention melded with a strong children's rights orientation, emphasizing the needs of children more strongly than the desires of third parties for visitation.[62] Finally, these advocates pressed the argument that parental autonomy has never been recognized as absolute, and in any case is sufficiently protected by the 'best interests' standard.[63]

The irony of the position advocated on behalf of the mother is the combination of making visible a range of family forms while arguing for, or permitting, greater regulation than would have been thinkable for intact, two-parent marital families. Framed within a more progressive definition and supportive recognition of non-traditional families, these advocates argued that these families deserve less support or justify greater intrusion. The affirmative view of this position is greater support for a functional view of family, and therefore the necessity of a standard that reflects actual relationships rather than status or form. The negative view of this position is that it is grounded in the view that anything other than the nuclear, marital heterosexual family is less functional, 'broken', or 'at risk', and therefore deviation from the unstated norm justifies State intervention. A more nuanced view of the greater needs of some families and some children is based on a case-by-case consideration of both relationships and circumstances, with a justifiable concern for greater support (and necessary intervention), when the child is in danger of losing an ongoing loving, caring relationship particularly where the child has special needs or the circumstances are those of family crisis.

---

[61]   'Family units have changed ... The nurturing role of grandparents in raising grandchildren has become more frequent and more direct': Brief of Amicus Curiae of Grandparents United for Children's Rights Inc, Lexsee 1999 US Briefs 138, 13 (16 November 1999); 'Because of the potential for serious psychological harm to children, there no longer is room in our jurisprudence for parents to maintain total hegemony over who may visit their children ... In addition, the present day variations in family arrangements seem boundless. In this fluid diversity of persons with ties to children, the only remaining constant is the children's best interests': Brief of the Grandparent Caregiver Law Center of the Brookdale Center on Aging, Lexsee 1999 US Briefs 138, 2 (12 November 1999); '[C]hild–grandparent relationships have important psychological and social contributions to make toward the healthy development of children': Brief Amici Curiae of AARP and Generations United in Support of Petitioners, Lexsee 1999 US Briefs 138, 12 (12 November 1999). See also Brief of the States of Washington, et al, Lexsee 1999 US Briefs 138 (12 November 1999); Brief of the National Conference of State Legislatures, et al, Lexsee 1999 US Briefs 138 (12 November 1999).

[62]   Brief Amicus Curiae Center for Children's Policy Practice & Research at the University of Pennsylvania in support of Respondent, Lexsee 1999 US Briefs 138, at 15.

[63]   Other amici supporting the grandparents argued that the balance of interests that they saw as constitutionally necessary was not represented in the Washington statute, so that, ironically, while arguing on behalf of the grandparents, they nevertheless supported a statute with more protections for parental autonomy. Some amici also pointed out the other relationships affected by the statute, and therefore the broad range of families affected by a finding of unconstitutionality, including gay and lesbian partners, step-parents, live in partners, psychological parents and de facto parents.

On the other hand, amici supporting the mother's position enfolded all parents, including often stigmatized single parents, gay and lesbian parents, and step-parents, within classic arguments for parental autonomy.[64] Advocates for the mother argued that non-traditional families deserved equal respect and privacy, which could only be accomplished by strong support of parental rights. Support for parents irrespective of the family forms in which they are embedded is linked with a view of parental autonomy historically tied to patriarchal, hierarchical family forms often antagonistic to the non-mainstream parents for whom the arguments were marshalled. Parental autonomy is presented as fixed, set, and strong; as a first principle, established in natural law, pre- or supra-constitutional.[65] According to this view, parental autonomy should be respected either absolutely or more vigorously than was the case under the Washington statute. According to absolutists in this camp, if grandparents need to bring a legal action to establish visitation, harm to the family is inevitable, since the strains of family disagreement are now exacerbated by legal intervention into a private dispute.[66] Most of the amici, however, do not advocate such strong deference to parental authority. They acknowledge a role for relationships other than the parent–child relationship, and the appropriateness of state intervention to protect and support those relationships. But they would argue that other relationships still need to be important enough to merit a hearing, and visitation decisions should accord significant weight to parents' decision-making.[67]

The argument for strong parental rights is also articulated as the constitutional insufficiency of the 'best interests' standard. The critique of the 'best interests' standard as a means to protect parental interests focuses on familiar criticism of the indeterminacy of the standard and the presence of judicial bias.[68] Non-traditional parents in particular need greater protection, not less, according to these amici, to counterbalance the majoritarian, conservative tendencies of judges.[69] Children are best protected, then, by protecting the presumed best judgments of their parents. Even children 'at risk', meaning either those in non-traditional

---

[64]   Brief of the Coalition for the Restoration of Parental Rights as Amicus Curiae in Support of Respondent, Lexsee 1999 US 138 (8 December 1999); Brief Amicus Curiae of the American Civil Liberties Union and the ACLU of Washington, Lexsee 1999 US Briefs 138 (13 December 1999); Brief Amicus Curiae for Debra Hein, 1999 US Briefs 138 (10 December 1999); Brief Amicus Curiae Center for Children's Policy Practice & Research at the University of Pennsylvania, Lexsee 1999 US Briefs 138 (13 December 1999); Brief of the Northwest Women's Law Center, et al, Lexsee 1999 US Briefs 138 (10 December 1999); Brief Amici Curiae of Christian Legal Society and the National Association of Evangelicals, Lexsee 1999 US Briefs 138 (13 December 1999); Brief Amicus Curiae of the American Center for Law and Justice, Lexsee 1999 US Briefs 138 (10 December 1999); Brief of the Domestic Violence Project Inc/Safe House (Michigan), et al, Lexsee 1999 US Briefs 138 (13 December 1999); Brief of the Institute for Justice, et al, 1999 US 138 (13 December 1999); Brief of Lamda Legal Defense and Education Fund and Gay and Lesbian Advocates and Defenders, Lexsee 1999 US Briefs 138 (13 December 1999); Brief of Professor Robert C Fellmeth, et al, Lexsee 1999 US Briefs 138 (13 December 1999); Brief of the Center for the Original Intent of the Constitution, Lexsee 1999 US Briefs 138 (13 December 1999).

[65]   Ibid.

[66]   See, eg, Brief of the Coalition for the Restoration of Parental Rights, Lexsee 1999 US Briefs 138 (8 December 1999).

[67]   See note 64 (above).

[68]   Ibid.

[69]   Ibid.

families generally or a smaller class of children who have suffered highly abusive or traumatic family circumstances, are better protected if the standard ensures that only those who have meaningful, substantial relationships are supported, rather than simply 'any' person.

The differences in these positions touch on core issues of family law, both constitutionally and otherwise.[70] They include the definition of family, the resolution of intra-familial disputes as compared to disputes between families and the State; whether familial determinations should be made on the basis of form or function, and the critique of function as indeterminate. This case also raises questions about how to protect familial privacy and relationships without reinforcing traditional norms; whether to approach family disputes by balancing the rights of all relevant parties rather than preferring particular family decision-makers; and whether differences among families merit differences in legal analysis.

B   The Supreme Court's decision: *Troxel v Granville*[71]

The Supreme Court affirmed the judgment of the Washington Supreme Court 6–3, with six opinions filed in the case.[72] Justice O'Connor's plurality opinion was joined by Chief Justice Rehnquist, Justice Ginsberg, and Justice Breyer. Justices Souter and Thomas concurred separately. The dissenters, each of whom separately filed an opinion, were Justices Stevens, Scalia and Kennedy. All in all, the case produced a very unusual alignment of justices. With so many opinions filed, it also produced considerable confusion as to where a majority of the court stands either on the particular issues of this case or analysis of fundamental constitutional rights of families.

In brief, the plurality opinion of Justice O'Connor reads as if it is a judgment that the statute is facially invalid due to overbreadth, but the opinion avoids that conclusion by finding the statute unconstitutional as applied to the specific dispute between the Troxels and Tommie Granville.[73] Justice O'Connor takes the view that parental power, short of unfitness, should be respected and free from State interference, and constructs the case as an unwarranted power struggle between a parent and a judge.[74] Justice Souter, concurring in the result, would find the statute facially invalid on the basis suggested by the O'Connor opinion.[75] Justice Thomas also agrees that parental autonomy should prevail in this case. His concurrence

---

[70]   One of the interesting patterns in the briefs before the court, nevertheless, is the agreement among opposing advocates on certain propositions. Most advocates did not see the family as turning solely on the parent–child relationship, and recognized the value of kin and non-kin relationships. On the other hand, no party characterized the grandparent–child relationship as involving 'rights' of grandparents. Thirdly, briefs for both parties took the view that a more nuanced statute that limited standing to a narrower category of people based on the nature of their relationship with the child, and perhaps also limited visitation to changed family circumstances would most strongly support the value of non-parental family relationships. They differed only as to whether these qualifications of third party rights were constitutionally required.

[71]   530 US 57 (2000).

[72]   Ibid at 60 (O'Connor, J, plurality).

[73]   Ibid at 73 (O'Connor, J, plurality).

[74]   Ibid at 68–69 (O'Connor, J, plurality).

[75]   Ibid at 79 (Souter, J, concurring).

underscores his view that strict scrutiny should be the standard to evaluate an infringement of fundamental rights, while also reserving the larger issue of whether the entire area of substantive due process merits review.[76]

The dissenters take quite different positions. Justice Stevens argues that the case should not have been reviewed at all, but that once accepted, the grant of review requires that the court address the facial invalidity issues. He concludes that the statute was not facially unconstitutional on either of the grounds that the Washington Supreme Court held that it was. According to Justice Stevens, a finding of harm is not constitutionally necessary in order for the State to exercise its *parens patriae* power because the right of parental autonomy must be balanced against the needs of children. The statute also is not unconstitutionally broad, in his view, because the range of persons and circumstances under which a petition may be filed is limited by the best interests principle.[77] Justice Stevens sees parental power as less absolute, subject to challenge even if unfitness does not exist. He especially would see a basis for a more balanced analysis of contested intra-familial disputes based on children's rights, and in recognition of the fact that many third parties act as de facto parents or have important relationships with children.[78]

In contrast, Justice Scalia focuses on the broader substantive due process issue noted by Justice Thomas, and concludes that parental rights are not constitutional rights. Under Scalia's view, the State is free to structure its statute as it wills without constitutional constraints grounded in the concept of fundamental rights, because no fundamental rights of family or parents are explicit in the text of the Constitution.[79] Finally, Justice Kennedy would vacate and remand the case to the Washington Supreme Court rather than reverse. In his view, one of the grounds for unconstitutionality below, that harm to the child is required before the State can intervene, rests on a misinterpretation of constitutional precedents. Based on his view that the 'best interests' standard is constitutionally sound, Justice Kennedy argues that the court should have reversed and remanded the case for further consideration after clarification of the state court's error in its reading of the constitutional precedents.[80]

What these opinions suggest about how the court defines 'family', and in particular its view of non-traditional families, is especially significant. In several of the opinions, the range of contemporary families, and an acceptance of non-

---

[76]   Ibid at 80 (Thomas, J, concurring).

[77]   Ibid at 84–91 (Stevens, J, dissenting).

[78]   The critique of substantive due process analysis is interesting for family law analysis because it indicates whether the 'constitutionalization' of family law would continue should this analysis become more dominant with a change in the personnel of the court. See, eg, Katherine B Silbaugh, '*Miller v Albright*: Problems of Constitutionalization in Family Law', 79 BUL Rev 1139 (1999); Ann Laquer Estin, 'Family Governance in the Age of Divorce', 1998 Utah L Rev 211; 1994 U Ill L Rev 311; Jill Elaine Hasday, 'Federalism and the Family Reconstructed', 45 UCLA L Rev 1297 (1998); Walter Wadlington, 'Medical Decision Making for and by Children: Tensions Between Parent, State, and Child', 1994 U Ill L Rev 311. The controversy over substantive due process is an area of significant concern for family law and constitutional scholars that will not be addressed in this essay.

[79]   Ibid at 92 (Scalia, J, dissenting).

[80]   Ibid at 94 (Kennedy, J, dissenting).

traditional families, is a strong theme.[81] The nature of parental power with respect to the State and with respect to children, on the other hand, is sharply debated. Before discussing the implications of the opinions, I briefly describe each in greater detail.

1   JUSTICE O'CONNOR'S PLURALITY OPINION

Justice O'Connor's decision reads as if it condemns the Washington statute as unconstitutional because of overbreadth and the failure to accord sufficient, constitutionally required weight to parental decision-making. She describes the Washington third party visitation statute as 'breathtakingly broad' because it permits the filing of a petition by any person at any time.[82] In reaching her conclusion that the decision below should be affirmed, she states that 'we rest our decision on the sweeping breadth [of the statute] and the application of that broad, unlimited power in this case …'.[83] Secondly, she sees as a significant flaw of the statute that it 'contains no requirement that a court accord the parent's decision any presumption of validity or any weight whatsoever'.[84] Citing the court's prior precedents in *Meyer v Nebraska*,[85] *Pierce v Society of Sisters*,[86] and *Prince v Massachusetts*,[87] she describes the rights of parents as a liberty interest that is 'perhaps the oldest of the fundamental liberty interests recognized by this court'.[88] More specifically, she describes it as a 'fundamental right of parents to make decisions concerning the care, custody, and control of their children'.[89] The recognition of this fundamental right is further confirmed by subsequent cases; parental rights as fundamental rights is thus a strong and honored constitutional principle.[90] Deference to parental decision-making is entirely absent in this statutory scheme and, in her view, is glaringly apparent in the application of the statute in this case. Justice O'Connor cites by contrast the provisions in other States' statutes that establish a rebuttable presumption in favor of parental decisions regarding visitation, or make that an explicit and strong factor in reaching a determination under the 'best interests' standard.[91]

Furthermore, in her evaluation of the application of the statute in this case, she suggests additional analysis of facial invalidity. She notes that the mother was a fit parent and had not denied visitation to the grandparents entirely. While she does not see fitness as insulating parental decision-making from challenge, she does see fitness as supporting a presumption that the parent's decision is in the best

---

81   Ibid at 63–64 (O'Connor, J, concurring) and at 101 (Kennedy, J, dissenting).

82   Ibid at 67 (O'Connor, J, plurality).

83   Ibid at 73 (O'Connor, J, plurality).

84   Ibid at 69 (O'Connor, J, plurality).

85   262 US 390 (1923).

86   268 US 510 (1925).

87   321 US 158 (1944).

88   *Troxel v Granville*, 530 US at 65 (O'Connor, J, plurality).

89   Ibid at 60 (O'Connor, J, plurality)

90   Ibid at 66 (O'Connor, J, plurality), (citing *Stanley v Illinois*, 405 US 645 (1972); *Wisconsin v Yoder*, 406 US 205 (1972); *Quillion v Walcott*, 434 US 246 (1978); *Parham v JR*, 442 US 584 (1979); *Stankosky v Kramer*, 455 US 745 (1982); *Washington v Glucksberg*, 521 US 702 (1997).

91   Ibid at 70 (O'Connor, J, plurality).

interests of the child.[92] She expressly declines, however, to address the constitutional validity of the position taken by the state court below that the State could only intervene or order visitation upon a showing of harm to the child.

The significance of the mother in this case not denying *all* visitation was, in her view, that the parent had not cut off the relationship of the grandparents with their grandchildren. Support of the parental decision was therefore appropriate.[93] Justice O'Connor cited approvingly the statutes of States that provide that visitation cannot be ordered unless a parent has denied all visitation as another means to support the primacy of parental decision-making.[94] While she does not expressly support such provisions as constitutionally required, this sign of support provides another example of how a statutory scheme might appropriately give constitutionally required deference to parental decision-making.

Despite this analysis suggesting a conclusion of facial invalidity, Justice O'Connor's plurality opinion rests on the conclusion that the statute was not facially invalid, but rather was constitutionally invalid as applied. The error in the application, according to Justice O'Connor, was multiple: failing to give deference to the judgment of a fit parent, based on the constitutional rule that a fit parent will act in the best interests of the child; giving presumptive weight to the assumption that visitation was in the best interests of the children; allowing a judge to disagree with a parent and have that disagreement enforced through an unbounded best interests analysis; and failing to consider that the mother had not denied visitation entirely. As applied, 'this case involves nothing more than a simple disagreement between the Washington Superior Court and Granville concerning her children's best interests'.[95] This violates the Constitution because 'the Due Process Clause does not permit a State to infringe on the fundamental right of parents to make childrearing decisions simply because a state judge believes a "better" decision could be made'.[96]

Why did the court avoid declaring the statute facially invalid? Justice O'Connor states that this is an area where the court should proceed with great caution, due to both deference to state courts and the intricacies of family scenarios.[97] Finally, the pragmatic consequences for this family would be further litigation, which Justice O'Connor saw as especially burdensome for the mother in this case.[98]

---

[92]   Ibid at 66 (O'Connor, J, plurality) ('Our Jurisprudence historically has reflected Western civilization concepts of the family as a unit with broad parental authority over minor children', quoting *Parham v JR*, 442 US at 602).

[93]   Ibid at 71 (O'Connor, J, plurality).

[94]   See ibid at 71.

[95]   Ibid at 72 (O'Connor, J, plurality).

[96]   Ibid at 72–73 (O'Connor, J, plurality).

[97]   Ibid at 73 (O'Connor, J, plurality).

[98]   Ibid at 75 (O'Connor, J, plurality). But her sense that the litigation would end at this point was apparently inaccurate. After the US Supreme Court rendered its decision, the Troxels asked for the visitation that Tommie Wynn initially had offered. They indicated that if she did not agree to that visitation, they might return to court once again to seek a visitation order. Gordy Holt, 'Grandparents Ready to Settle For Offer Made Early in Dispute', *Seattle Post-Intelligencer*, 6 June 2000, at A5. This continued litigation is entirely appropriate given the court's judgment that the statute was only unconstitutional as applied on the facts of this visitation petition.

Justice O'Connor's reference to the complexity of the issues raised by this case relates back to the context in which Justice O'Connor places this constitutional issue. It is this statement about families, in addition to her articulation of the rights of parents, that is so important in considering the implications of this case. Justice O'Connor acknowledges the diversity of American families, the significance of grandparents in the care of children, the value and necessity of supporting third party relationships, and the challenges all of this creates. She opens her analysis with an acknowledgement of family complexity: 'The demographic changes of the past century make it difficult to speak of an average American family'.[99] She proceeds to focus especially on the prevalence of single parent families, who make up nearly 30 per cent of the families in which children under 18 are raised,[100] and the greater likelihood that children's care and relationships in those families include non-parents, especially grandparents. Third party visitation statutes protect those relationships especially when third parties act as parents.[101] In addition, she recognizes that third party visitation statutes incorporate the view that children's relationships with third parties should be supported, whether those relationships are de facto parental relationships or not.[102] The challenge, as she sees it, of the statutes that spring from these objectives is the potential that they might harm the core parent–child relationship: 'The extension of statutory rights in this area to persons other than a child's parents, however, comes with an obvious cost ... [it] can place a substantial burden on the traditional parent–child relationship.'[103]

2   THE SOUTER AND THOMAS CONCURRENCES

Justice Souter's concurrence in the judgment is grounded in his view that the court should reach the issue of facial invalidity suggested but ultimately avoided by the plurality opinion. He finds the statute constitutionally overbroad, representing an undue infringement on 'a parent's interests in the nurture, upbringing, companionship, care and custody of children'.[104] While declining to set out the boundaries of parental rights, Justice Souter clearly sees the right to select and control a child's associations as crucial to development of the child's character, and therefore in the realm of primary parental decision-making.[105] 'To say the least ... parental choice in such matters is not merely a default rule.'[106] Justice Souter would therefore agree with the implicit facial invalidity analysis of Justice O'Connor concerning the failure to accord due deference to parental

---

[99] Ibid at 63–64 (O'Connor, J, plurality).

[100] Ibid at 64 (O'Connor, J, plurality). See also Nancy E Dowd, 'In Defense of Single Parent Families' (New York University Press, 1997). The most recent demographics indicate continued growth of single parent families based on the 2000 census. The number of households with a single mother as head of the household increased 25% during the 1990s, as compared to an increase of 6% of married couple households. Eric Schmitt, 'For First Time, Nuclear Families Drop Below 25% of Households', *New York Times* 15 May 2001, A1, A18.

[101] Ibid at 64 (O'Connor, J, plurality).

[102] Ibid.

[103] Ibid.

[104] Ibid at 77 (Souter, J, concurring) (citing same cases as O'Connor's plurality opinion).

[105] Ibid at 76 (Souter, J, concurring).

[106] Ibid at 79 (Souter, J, concurring).

decisions. Because that analysis tracks one of the reasons given by the state court to hold its statute unconstitutional, he would decline to consider the validity of the other reason given by the state court (that a finding of harm is required before the State can intervene), and simply affirm the finding of unconstitutionality.[107] He also sees the grant of review, and the basis of the decision below, as purely grounded on facial invalidity, which necessitates reaching the issue.

Justice Thomas' concurrence proceeds from an entirely different perspective. First, Justice Thomas reserves the question of the validity of the court's substantive due process jurisprudence. Secondly, since that issue is not before the court, he clarifies that the appropriate standard of review, in view of the court's prior precedents recognizing a fundamental right of parents to control childrearing, is strict scrutiny. In this case, he concludes that the State's interest is not even legitimate, much less compelling. Framed this way, the State's argument would fail any level of scrutiny. He frames the State's interest as 'second-guessing a fit parent's decision regarding visitation with third parties'.[108] His brief statement suggests that he would support strong protection of parental rights that would limit state intervention to situations to prevent harm to the child.[109]

3   THE STEVENS, SCALIA AND KENNEDY DISSENTS

The dissents in this case are remarkably different. Justice Stevens would find the statute constitutionally valid under the same fundamental rights precedents cited by the justices voting in the majority.[110] He disagrees with the conclusion that this statute is fatally overbroad. If there is a legitimate, constitutional application, he argues, then the overbreadth challenge should fail.[111] An easy example, in his view, of a constitutional application of the visitation statute would be a petition by a prior caretaker of the child.[112] In these circumstances he imagines that an award of visitation would be reasonable and constitutionally sound. Secondly, Justice Stevens critiques the second basis for facial unconstitutionality of the state court, that visitation can only be awarded if there is a showing of harm to the child if it is

---

[107]   Ibid at 79 (Souter, J, concurring).

[108]   Ibid at 80 (Thomas, J, concurring).

[109]   Ibid at 80 (Thomas, J, concurring).

[110]   Ibid at 87. Justice Stevens is quite critical of the grant of certiorari in this case, but argues that once the court took the case, it was bound to decide it by interpreting constitutional principles as facially applied to the statute, since that was the decision of the court below (ibid at 80–81). He agrees, then, with Justice Souter that the court must address the state court's view of constitutional requirements (ibid at 82–83). Justice Kennedy agrees that the court must address the question of whether the analysis below was in error. But Stevens and Kennedy disagree on the appropriate analysis. Justice Stevens is ready to find the statute facially valid, and return the case for the state court to evaluate whether the statute is constitutional as applied (ibid at 85). Justice Kennedy, on the other hand, would prefer to identify the flaws in the analysis and send the case back for the state court to reconsider the facial constitutional challenge (ibid at 94). Kennedy's approach is more deferential to state court construction of its own statutes, although it would require the state court to follow clarified federal interpretation. Justice Souter sees this as a point of difference between him and Justice Kennedy: Souter would permit a more demanding scrutiny by the state court, a higher standard than the federal government, while Kennedy would require the same approach, consistent with the federal standard (ibid at 79 (Souter, J, concurring)).

[111]   Ibid at 85 (Stevens, J, dissenting).

[112]   Ibid.

denied.[113] He finds that view totally without support in the court's precedents. Parental authority is not, he points out, absolute:

> '[W]e have never held that the parent's liberty interest in this relationship is so inflexible as to establish a rigid constitutional shield, protecting every arbitrary parental decision from any challenge absent a threshold finding of harm. The presumption that parental decisions generally serve the best interests of their children is sound, and clearly in the normal case the parent's interest is paramount. But even a fit parent is capable of treating a child like a mere possession.'[114]

As examples of lack of absolute parental authority he cites to the court cases defining the rights of fathers.[115] He particularly notes the court's decision in *Michael H v Gerald D*,[116] where the court had to sort through the claims of a biological father who had established a social relationship with his child in contrast to those of the biological mother and her husband, the legal father of the child since the child was born during the marriage. He cites this case as an example of parental authority that was forced to yield to family interests.[117] Parental rights, in his view, are tied to relationship and family; they are not merely rights in the abstract defined solely by status.[118]

Evaluating the interests at stake in this situation, according to Justice Stevens, is not simply a consideration of the parent versus the State, but must include the interests of the child.[119] Children have liberty interests just as parents do, and must be considered in the analysis.[120] Just as the scope of parents' rights has not been defined, so too the court has not defined the scope of children's liberty interests, and here Justice Stevens again cites *Michael H*. Justice Stevens is careful to suggest that the child's interest is not co-extensive with the parent's, but at the same time he states that the child's interest is not sufficiently protected by a standard that requires a showing of harm before it can be acted upon.[121] The insufficiency of that standard is linked by Justice Stevens to the very diversity of the family situations in which children find themselves:

> '[W]e should recognize that there may be circumstances in which a child has a stronger interest at stake than mere protection from serious harm caused by the termination of visitation by a "person" other than a parent. The almost infinite variety of family relationships that pervade our ever-changing society strongly counsel against the creation by this court of a constitutional rule that treats a biological parent's liberty

---

[113] Ibid at 86 (Stevens, J, dissenting).

[114] Ibid.

[115] Ibid at 87 (Stevens, J, dissenting) (citing *Lehr v Robertson* 463 US 248 (1983); *Michael H v Gerald D* (1989)).

[116] 491 US 110 (1989).

[117] *Troxel v Granville*, 530 US at 88 (Stevens, J, dissenting).

[118] Ibid at 88 (Stevens, J, dissenting). Of course, one might also view *Michael H* as a case that reaffirms the importance of status over relationship, and simply puts parental status in this case below the status of parenthood within marriage.

[119] Ibid at 88.

[120] Ibid at 88 and n 8 (Stevens, J, dissenting).

[121] Ibid at 90 (Stevens, J, dissenting).

interest in the care and supervision of her child as an isolated right that may be exercised arbitrarily.'[122]

The Washington statute, in his view, provides the flexibility to consider the variable situations children find themselves in and protects parents and children through the familiar 'best interests' standard. He also separately notes in a footnote that to suggest that the best interests standard is constitutionally deficient would have broad-ranging consequences, considering its wide use in family law determinations.[123]

Especially notable about Justice Stevens' opinion is his view that the range of family circumstances and non-traditional structures, and the variability in intimate, caring relationships, is critical to a more open consideration and balancing of parental rights with children's rights. Equally important, in his view, is analysis that permits variability rather than rigid rules:

> '[T]he instinct against over-regularizing decisions about personal relations is sustained on firmer ground than mere tradition. It flows in equal part from the premise that people and their intimate associations are complex and particular, and imposing a rigid template upon them all risks severing bonds our society would do well to preserve.'[124]

Justice Scalia's dissent takes an entirely different tack to reach the same conclusion that the Washington statute is constitutional. He would not recognize any *constitutional* limits on the State to legislate with respect to third party visitation because the Constitution does not enumerate parental rights as a protected right. Justice Scalia leaves no doubt that he thinks parental rights are important: he views them as inalienable rights retained by the people under the Ninth Amendment.[125] But those rights are not rights protected by the Constitution.[126] He argues for limiting the reach of prior precedent precisely because the range of views articulated in this 'simple' case indicates the danger of proceeding in this area.[127] Further support for parental rights would require defining 'parent', and 'family', and articulating the interests of others, with the result of federalizing and constitutionalizing family law.

> 'I have no reason to believe that federal judges will be better at this than state legislatures; and state legislatures have the great advantages of doing harm in a more circumscribed area, of being able to correct their mistakes in a flash, and of being removable by the people.'[128]

Having disposed of unenumerated rights, Justice Scalia indicates in a short footnote that the children might claim enumerated rights under First Amendment free exercise or freedom of association protections, a suggestion that would orient

---

[122]   Ibid.
[123]   Ibid at 84, n 5 (Stevens, J, dissenting).
[124]   Ibid at 91, n 10 (Stevens, J, dissenting).
[125]   Ibid at 91 (Scalia, J, dissenting).
[126]   Ibid.
[127]   Ibid at 92 (Scalia, J, dissenting).
[128]   Ibid at 93 (Scalia, J, dissenting).

children's rights in a very different direction than that considered by Justice Stevens.[129]

Finally, Justice Kennedy reaches no conclusion on the validity of the statute because he would remand the case back to the State after correcting the State's error in reading constitutional precedents. Justice Kennedy's dissent is particularly important because more than any other member of the court he considers the implications of an argument that the 'best interests' standard does not satisfy constitutional standards. He criticizes the decision below as incorrectly reading the court's precedents to conclude that the 'best interests' standard is constitutionally insufficient, and erroneously assuming that a showing of harm to the child is constitutionally required.[130] While he would not see the 'best interests' standard as sufficient in all cases to protect parental interests, he nevertheless would not see a 'harm' standard as constitutionally required in visitation statutes.[131]

Justice Kennedy sees the 'best interests' and 'harm' standards as distinctive. He approaches the question of whether either one is constitutionally required by asking whether history or tradition provides an answer.[132] As he notes, because visitation is a twentieth-century phenomenon, history and tradition is of little assistance.[133] Justice Kennedy does not see the consequence of that conclusion as leading to the result that parental authority should be dominant, a view that would support the 'harm' standard. He sees the flaw in such reasoning as its presumption of a nuclear, marital family norm:[134]

'[It is based on the] assumption that the parent or parents who resist visitation have always been the child's caregivers and that the third parties who seek visitation have no legitimate and established relationship with the child. That idea, in turn, appears influenced by the concept that the conventional nuclear family ought to establish the visitation standard for every domestic relations case. As we all know, this is simply not the structure or prevailing condition in many households. For many boys and girls a traditional family with two or even one permanent and caring parent is simply not the reality of their childhood. This may be so whether their childhood has been marked by tragedy or filled with considerable happiness and fulfillment.'[135]

The 'harm' standard might, in his view, preclude recognition of constitutionally significant relationships.[136] By contrast, the 'best interests' standard, a standard well settled in state law, would support recognition of those relationships.[137]

---

[129] Ibid at 93, n 2 (Scalia, J, dissenting).

[130] Ibid at 94 (Kennedy, J, dissenting).

[131] Ibid at 94 (Kennedy, J, dissenting). Because he sees the 'harm' analysis as not merely one of two independent grounds, but rather a 'core' ground in the state court's opinion, he would reverse and remand the case for further proceedings (ibid at 95).

[132] Ibid at 96–97 (Kennedy, J, dissenting).

[133] Ibid at 96 (Kennedy, J, dissenting).

[134] Ibid at 98 (Kennedy, J, dissenting).

[135] Ibid at 98 (Kennedy, J, dissenting) (internal cites omitted). It is significant to note that Justice Kennedy is careful not to assume that the presence or absence of parents may automatically mean a good or bad environment for children. He avoids, therefore, the common myth that two parents are always better than one or that a family with only one parent is by definition is an inferior family structure.

[136] Ibid at 98 (Kennedy, J, dissenting).

[137] Ibid at 95–102 (Kennedy, J, dissenting).

Additional protection of parental interests can be accomplished by other means, including standing, presumptions, and evidentiary requirements.[138] Justice Kennedy is loath to consider the 'best interests' standard as constitutionally deficient, although he leaves the door open to consideration of its insufficiency in certain circumstances. He acknowledges the critique of 'best interests' as indeterminate and the invasiveness of a petition for visitation. If the standard was in fact standardless, it might violate the parent's constitutional rights.[139] But that cannot be known without applying the standard. Thus he concludes there is no constitutional right to a 'harm' standard, and no constitutional defect in the use of 'best interests' in this setting.

II   IMPLICATIONS: *TROXEL* AND THIRD PARTY VISITATION SCHEMES

A   Grandparent visitation

Troxel most directly affects statutes governing grandparent visitation, and more generally third party visitation. Because the court held the Washington statute unconstitutional only as applied, the case invites litigation in visitation controversies regarding whether particular decrees, in the context of specific facts, unconstitutionally invade parental prerogatives or children's interest in ongoing relationships. The court's solicitude for fit parents invites the argument that visitation in the face of parental objection is inappropriate or that the statutory structure facially fails to support appropriately the presumption that parents act in the child's best interest. On the other hand, the court's balancing of parental interests against children's needs lends support to arguments that particular relationships should be supported even in the face of parental objection. Because the decision is limited to the unconstitutionality of the statute as applied, this encourages successive litigation and therefore favors parties with greater resources. This configuration of incentives may exacerbate family tensions because the threshold for overcoming parental decision-making has been raised, while the incentive to downgrade or degrade third party relationships also has increased. On the other hand, the very use of litigation to settle these family matters arguably indicates family relationships are irretrievably broken and a court order will hardly make matters worse.[140]

The array of opinions and range of disagreement among the justices may also generate structural arguments about existing statutes, while not making it entirely clear what structural changes would institutionalize the appropriate balance between the interests of the parents and the interests of the State. Structural arguments most likely will be raised as attacks on the facial validity of visitation

---

[138]   Ibid at 99–100 (Kennedy, J, dissenting).

[139]   Ibid at 101 (Kennedy, J, dissenting).

[140]   As one commentator points out, grandparent visitation cases can often bring into view old family history of the parenting of the parents by the grandparents as relevant to the issue of the value of grandparent visitation with children. Conversely, grandparents may have to critique the fitness of their own children: Stephen A Newman, 'The Dark Side of Grandparent Visitation Rights', *New York Law Journal* 14 June 2000, 2.

statutes, resisting their application early in litigation. The split in the court about evaluating visitation statutes makes it difficult to be clear about whether existing statutes should be amended and, if so, what changes are necessary. A conservative approach would tend to buttress parental decision-making at the expense of children's relationships with third parties, thereby insuring a constitutionally sufficient protection of parental autonomy.

The court's structural disagreements are multiple, and the relationship among the structural issues is unclear. First, there is the issue of whether 'fitness' triggers a strong, even irrebuttable, presumption of parental decision-making as unassailable. Given the high threshold for finding a parent 'unfit', such a presumption would effectively insulate most parental judgments from challenge.[141] The consequence of this view would also merge the 'best interests' determination with 'fitness'; that is, one could not hold that a parent was *not* acting for the child's best interests without finding the parent unfit; or, refusing visitation would have to amount to an act that would establish unfitness. On the other hand, fitness might only create a presumption of good decision-making that would simply shift the burden of showing otherwise to the third party, and would require that the showing be a strong one. The showing necessary, however, would not require painting the parent as unfit; rather, the showing would focus on the affirmative relationship with the child, the importance of ongoing contact, and the ability of the third party to work co-operatively and positively with the parent.

Closely linked to the issue of fitness is the issue of the operation of the 'best interests' standard in this setting. It is unclear whether the 'best interests' standard, as a distinct standard from parental fitness, is constitutionally sufficient to protect parental interests. Furthermore, it is unclear what factors are constitutionally relevant and necessary if the 'best interests' standard is to withstand constitutional scrutiny. On the one hand, the application of best interests according to evolving case-law is one possibility; on the other hand, an articulated set of factors, either exclusive or non-exclusive, might be necessary. It also is questionable what weight should be accorded certain factors, like the parent's objections or difficulties with the visitation request. If this is an evolving standard, then it also might be relevant to consider whether application of best interests in other settings is helpful or distinguishable (eg should the same factors be used as those used in devising parenting plans for parents who have not married or those who have divorced, or are different factors relevant?). Questioning the best interests standard in this framework raises the issue of its sufficiency in other settings, and given the broad use of the standard, the implications beyond visitation statutes are staggering.[142] At the same time, confronting the claims of judicial bias and the

---

[141] On the high standard for determining lack of fitness, see generally Amy Haddix, 'Unseen Victims: Acknowledging the Effects of Domestic Violence on Children Through Statutory Termination of Parental Rights', 84 Calif L Rev 757 (1996); Christina Dugger Sommer, 'Empowering Children: Granting Foster Children the Right to Initiate Parental Rights Termination Proceedings', 79 Cornell L Rev 1200 (1994).

[142] As Justice Stevens noted in his opinion, a search of State custody and visitation laws generated 698 references to the 'best interests' standard: *Troxel v Granville*, 530 US at 84, n 5 (Stevens, J, dissenting).

challenge of applying a discretionary standard in a fair way are critical issues for family law jurisprudence and constitutional due process.[143]

Another structural disagreement among the justices is the strength of parental prerogatives. Some of the justices clearly see the balance as weighing very heavily, nearly conclusively, with parents, while others would see parental rights as one part of a balance of multiple rights-bearers. If parents are conceptualized in opposition to the State, the argument for family privacy is a strong one. On the other hand, if the State acts as a referee between competing interests, balancing and honoring diverse interests is essential. Clearly closely related to this conceptualization of parents' rights, then, is the issue of the scope and content of children's rights.[144] Still a developing concept, the acknowledgement of children and their unique perspective on needs and rights is an area that the court continues to be pressed to address. Efforts to protect parental rights may run foul of this countervailing interest, just as those promoting children's relationships may require fuller articulation of how those relational rights can be balanced against legitimate parental objections. The uncertainly about the scope of parents' and children's rights, and their interrelationship, links them to a final structural issue, that of the appropriate analysis of interfamilial disputes that include many parties with fundamental rights that must be balanced against each other in a familial setting that may require parties who no longer share households or relationships to share and mutually support each other for the welfare of children.

Despite this uncertainty, the opinions nevertheless are suggestive of the kinds of features that members of the court would view favorably in this kind of statute, even if it is unclear whether they are constitutionally necessary. Standing limitations include limiting visitation to those of defined status (such as grandparents) or to those with a significant relationship with the child (such as those who have acted as a de facto parent, for instance a step-parent or godparent). Evidentiary requirements might include not only a strong showing of relationship to establish standing, but also a significant burden of production to substantiate a claim that visitation is in the best interests of the child. In addition, requirements that petitioners for visitation demonstrate their co-operation with parents or a good reason to order visitation in spite of parental objection also appear to be viewed as means to protect parental autonomy while permitting the support of important relationships to children. Finally, articulation of a specific set of factors relevant to a best interests determination seems preferred over an open-ended standard. The range of disagreement among the justices means no template for constitutionality is provided, but drafters of statutes or amendments to existing statutes have indications of the provisions that might insulate a visitation statute against constitutional challenge.

---

[143] For a more extensive discussion of the different biases claimed by mothers and fathers, see Nancy E Dowd, *Redefining Fatherhood* 59–65 (New York: New York University Press 2000). See also Susan Beth Jacobs, 'The Hidden Gender Bias Behind "The Best Interest of the Child" Standard in Custody', 13 Ga St UL Rev 845

[144] For discussion of the concept of children's rights, see generally Barbara Bennett Woodhouse, 'Children's Rights: The Destruction and Promise of Family', 1993 BYUL Rev 497; Barbara Bennett Woodhouse, 'Hatching the Egg: A Child-Centered Perspective on Parents' Rights', 14 Cardozo L Rev 1747 (1993).

B Third party visitation

Many state statutes, like Washington's, are third party visitation statutes rather than grandparent visitation statutes, so the impact of *Troxel* reaches more broadly.[145] Outside grandparent relationships, the issue raised is the difference that other relationships pose for constitutional analysis. Grandparents have a unique connection with at least one parent that may demonstrate the nature of their relationship with their grandchildren and their ability to work with the parent or parents. Grandparents are very common caregivers, both primary and secondary.[146] They characteristically maintain relationships over time.

Non-marital partners and step-parents, in contrast, have relationships with children often derivative of the primary parent. Partners' and step-parents' relationships with children often are not lifelong, if the relationship with the primary parent fails.[147] Some have available legal mechanisms (marriage and adoption) that provide a means to legalize and protect their relationships with children.[148] Homosexual partners, on the other hand, largely lack the ability to legalize their parent–child relationships by use of adoption, and none can formalize them through marriage.[149] Other adults with relationships to children, such as godparents, birth parents, de facto or psychological parents, raise additional questions of whether the particular status and/or relationship is relevant to the analysis or whether the analysis turns not on status but rather on the nature of the relationship of the child to the third party, irrespective of status. In addition, it is not clear how relationships that are important to children but which cannot be characterized as parent–child relationships (such as uncles and aunts or non-kin adults who give care but are not parent figures) will be evaluated.

---

[145] See notes 39 and 40 (above).

[146] According to a survey commissioned by the American Association for Retired Persons, one in ten grandparents are raising grandchildren or regularly providing childcare, and four in ten see their grandchildren every week: Tamar Lewin, 'Grandparents Play Big Part in Grandchildren's Lives, Survey Finds', *New York Times* (6 January 2000, A16).

[147] See, eg, Dowd, *Redefining Fatherhood*, note 144 (above) at 26–31.

[148] Not all step-parents can adopt, but all heterosexual step-parents can marry. On step-parent adoption, see generally Jennifer Wriggins, 'Parental Rights Termination Jurisprudence: Questioning the Framework', 52 SC L Rev 241 (2000); Jennifer Klein Mangnall, 'Comment, Step-parent Custody Rights After Divorce', 26 Sw U L Rev 399 (1997); Mark Strasser, 'Courts, Legislatures, and Second-Parent Adoptions: On Judicial Deference, Specious Reasoning, and the Best Interests of the Child', 66 Tenn L Rev 1019 (1999); Joyce E McConnell, 'Securing the Care of Children in Diverse Families: Building on Trends in Guardianship Reform', 10 Yale JL & Feminism 29 (1998).

[149] No State in the US permits same-sex couples to marry; Vermont permits civil unions. On current marriage issues for same-sex couples, see generally Mary Becker, 'Queer matters: Emerging Issues in Sexual Orientation law: Women, Morality, and Sexual Orientation', 8 UCLA Women's LJ 165 (1998); Nancy Polikoff, 'Why Lesbians and Gay Men Should Read Martha Fineman', 8 Am UJ Gender Soc Pol'y & L 167 (2000); Evan Wolfson, 'Crossing the Threshold: Equal Marriage Rights for Lesbians and Gay Men and the Intra-community Critique', 21 NYU Rev L & Soc Change 567 (1994–95); William N Eskridge, Jr, 'A History of Same-Sex Marriage' 79 Va L Rev 1419 (1993). Same-sex couples are barred by statute from adopting only in Florida, but by custom they are often disqualified from adopting. On same-sex adoption, see generally Jennifer Wriggins, 'Marriage Law and Family Law: Autonomy, Interdependence, and Couples of the Same Gender', 41 BC L Rev 265 (2000); Elizabeth Rover Bailey, 'Note, Three Men and a Baby: Second-Parent Adoptions and Their Implications', May 1997, 38 BCL Rev 569 (1997); Strasser, note 148 (above).

C   Post-*Troxel* Developments

Since *Troxel* was decided there appear to be several patterns of response by state
and federal courts. What I sketch here is by no means intended to be
comprehensive, but rather suggestive of major trends in the first year since *Troxel*
was decided. First, many state courts have simply distinguished their state statute
or the circumstances before them and found *Troxel* inapplicable. Where statutes
include narrower standing requirements or more demanding evidentiary standards
than the 'breathtakingly broad' Washington statute, courts have found that their
statutes sufficiently support parental autonomy and therefore are constitutional.[150]
Alternatively, where the facts have been sufficiently different, the courts have
distinguished *Troxel* on the basis that its holding was limited to the statute's
unconstitutionality as applied.[151] *Troxel* also has been cited for the general
proposition that a parent's right to make decisions regarding the care and welfare
of his or her child is fundamental and constitutionally protected.[152]

In some cases, however, the courts have confronted, rather than avoided, the
implications of *Troxel*. In instances where trial court judges have presumed the
preferability of visitation, and seem merely to have substituted their judgment of
what is best for children, appellate courts have reversed visitation orders that
represented nothing more than, as in *Troxel*, a mere disagreement between a judge
and a parent.[153] The potential to challenge 'best interests' standards in many
settings, not just with respect to visitation, is another predictable use of *Troxel*.[154]

In applying *Troxel* to determine what elements are constitutionally essential in
visitation statutes, however, courts have given the case inconsistent readings. In
New York, for example, courts have held the New York statute both constitutional
and unconstitutional, with little agreement on the reasoning or analysis of *Troxel*.
In *Hertz v Hertz*, the trial court found the state statute unconstitutional because it
contained no requirement that parental decision-making was presumptively valid,
and therefore permitted a judge to impose his or her own view through the 'best
interests' standard.[155] *Hertz* involved a grandfather's petition with respect to
15 grandchildren of his three children. In *Levy v Levy* the judge not only followed
Hertz but carried the reasoning regarding best interests even further, finding that
use of a 'best interests' standard was constitutionally inadequate if it did not link
best interests to a finding of parental unfitness:

> 'Implicit, if not altogether explicit in *Troxel*, is the imposition of a finding of unfitness
> on the part of the parent in order for the grandparent to assert and to successfully

---

[150]   See, eg, *Smolen v Smolen*, 185 Misc 2d 828, 906 (NY Fam Ct 2000); *Lilley v Lilley*, 2001 WL
         359607 (unpublished Tex App 2001); *In re GPC*, 28 SW 3d 357, 363 (Mo App 2000);
         Macaronis, et al v Brown, et al, Lawyers Weekly No 15-001-01 (Ma Fam Ct, 19 February 2001);
         Zeman v Stanford, 2001 Miss Lexis 130 (Miss, 10 May 2001); *Jackson v Tangreen*, 18 P 3d 100
         (Az Ct of App 2000).

[151]   See, eg, *In re GPC*, 28 SW 3d 357, 363 (Mo App 2000); *Scott v Scott*, 19 P 3d 273 (Ok 2001).

[152]   See, eg, *Littlefield v Forney Independent School District*, 108 F Supp 2d 681 (US ND Tex 2000);
         Gruenke v Seip, 225 F 3d 290, 304–307 (3d Cir 2000).

[153]   See, eg, *Punsly v Ho*, 87 Cal App 4th 1099, 105 Cal Rptr 2d 139 (16 March 2001); *Kyle O v
         Donald R* 85 Cal App 4th 848, 102 Cal Rptr 476 (21 December 2000).

[154]   See, eg, *Esch v Esch*, 2001 WL 173198 (Ohio App 2d Dist 2001).

[155]   *Hertz v Hertz*, 186 Misc 2d 222, 717 NYS 2d 497, 500 (Sup Ct Kings County, 26 October 2000).

enforce visitation, absent parental consent. Therefore, a finding of a parent's unfitness appears to be a mandatory condition precedent to a court's ability to exercise its judgment and discretion on the issue of a child's best interest relative to grandparents' visitation ... the presumption that fit parents act in their children's best interest will invariably constitute an impregnable barrier which a court cannot breach or circumvent.'[156]

Levy involved the petition of the paternal grandfather to visit two children when the children's mother terminated visitation about two years after the death of their father in an accident. In contrast, the judge in *In re Frank E Smolen et al* found the New York statute constitutional, on the basis that the statute's limitation of visitation to when 'equity' requires that visitation be granted had been interpreted by New York courts in a manner sufficiently protective of parents' constitutional rights.[157] According to the court, 'equity' had been determined to limit standing to grandparents who could establish the existence of a significant relationship with the child, or serious efforts to establish a relationship. If the grandparent had standing under this requirement, it was then required that the court examine the reason for the parent's denial of visitation, within a context of deference to parents. Because this interpretation of the statute's terms is very protective of parental autonomy, the court reasoned, it is constitutional as interpreted.[158] In *Smolen* both parents were alive but unmarried, and the child and her mother lived with the grandparents until the child was two and a half, and the child spent substantial time with her grandparents until the age of six.

Troxel has also been read as strongly pro-parent while courts find ways to avoid the implications of that position. The Maine Supreme Court read *Troxel* as requiring strong protection of parental rights that would require a showing of harm to the child before a fit parent's decision could be overruled.[159] Yet the court disagreed that this meant that the Maine statute, which did not require such a showing, was constitutionally infirm. In the case before the court, the grandparents had cared for the children of their daughter born when she was a teenager and also after a disastrous first marriage, but then had their relationship with their daughter break down after her second marriage. Because these grandparents had acted *as parents* for their grandchildren for significant portions of the children's lives, the court found an equivalent constitutionally compelling state interest in protecting the substantial pre-existing relationship. The court thus both followed *Troxel* and found a way around the case, by distinguishing the factual scenario from *Troxel* (the long-term, parental relationship of the grandparents with the grandchildren and the parents' refusal of any visitation) and finding the relational difference one that required a de novo consideration of the constitutional analysis of the statute. Because the US Supreme Court had held in *Troxel* that the statute was *unconstitutional as applied*, this gave the Maine Supreme Court the room to hold that its statute, facially far more restrictive than

[156] *Levy v Levy*, 28 *New York Law Journal* (Sup Ct Kings County, 22 March 2001).
[157] *In the Matter of Frank E Smolen et al*, 185 Misc 2d 828, 832, 713 NY S 2d 903 (Fam Ct, Onondaga County, 15 September 2000).
[158] Ibid.
[159] *Rideout v Riendeau*, 761 A 2d 291 (Me 2000).

the statute at issue in *Troxel* in many respects[160] but lacking a harm requirement, nevertheless might be *constitutionally applied* because of the relational characteristics in the case.

Other scenarios similarly seem to tempt courts to find their way out of a strong reading of *Troxel*. An Arizona court interpreted its statute to allow only limited grounds for grandparent visitation, seeming to support parental objection to visitation in accord with *Troxel*. Nevertheless, the court went on to justify the difference in statutory treatment of step-parent adoption to permit grandparent visitation, despite the fact that adoption ordinarily would terminate the standing of grandparents linked through the surrendering parent.[161] A step-parent does not, then, receive the strong deference to a 'parent' that *Troxel* seems to dictate, despite the state court's acknowledgement of a parent's constitutional rights. Similarly, the Mississippi Supreme Court found its statute constitutional as sufficiently protecting parents' rights, although its interpretation of the statute required only that visitation must not deprive parents of their right to rear their children or substantially interfere with that right, a liberal interpretation favoring visitation contrary to the state court's conservative reading of *Troxel*.[162] The Rhode Island Supreme Court also found *Troxel* distinguishable in a case determining the right of a lesbian co-parent to seek visitation over the objection of the biological parent, because the case turned on her claim to be a de facto parent, and therefore entitled to parental rights.[163] Similarly, a New Jersey court found no conflict between the state's recognition of the concept of a psychological parent[164] and *Troxel*'s deference to the decisions of a fit parent.[165]

III IMPLICATIONS: *TROXEL* AND NON-TRADITIONAL FAMILIES

We may ultimately deem the confusion and avoidance generated by *Troxel* for third party visitation statutes unfortunate and tragic, or necessary and creative. The broader significance of *Troxel*, however, may be what it suggests about our view of families and constitutional analysis of family issues. It is particularly important, I would argue, to evaluate the definition of 'parent' and 'family' in *Troxel* from the perspective of non-traditional families. Those traditionally at the margins should be at the center in evaluating what the opinions have to say. The opinions suggest that clearly defined rules cannot capture the variables and intricacies of American families; such rules might ignore critical realities, especially when those realities defy our assumptions about families, family dynamics, and children's

---

[160]   Under the Maine statute only grandparents could apply for visitation, and only in the event of the death of a parent or parents, or the existence of a relationship with the grandchildren, or if an effort had been made to establish a sufficient relationship: *Rideout v Reindeau*, 761 A2d at 298–299.

[161]   *Jackson v Tangreen*, 18 P 3d 100 (Az Ct of App 2000).

[162]   *Zeman v Stanford*, 2001 Miss Lexis 130 (Miss 2001).

[163]   *Rubano v Dicenzo*, 759 A 2d 929 (RI 2000).

[164]   *VC v MJB*, 163 NJ 200, 748 A 2d 539 (2000) ('parent' can include psychological parent, setting forth factors to establish this status that include the voluntary support of such status by the biological or adoptive parent).

[165]   *AF v DLP* 2001 NJ Super LEXIS 164 (Sup Ct, App Div, 20 April 2001) (former lesbian lover and friend could not qualify as psychological parent and therefore had no standing to seek visitation).

perspectives. Rules grounded in status and form are especially problematic in that respect. The quality, strength and importance of relationships is powerfully evident in the situations that give rise to third party visitation requests, irrespective of their fitting our norms, expectations or assumptions. A relational focus, on the other hand, raises problems of indeterminacy and bias. The challenge is to define the relational approach in a way that focuses on the presence of valued connections for children. Finally, a relational approach must interact with form- and status-based approaches, particularly with marriage. In this section I briefly discuss these broad implications of *Troxel*.

First, the court's views of 'parent' and 'family' in the case suggest a more fluid approach to 'family' that recognizes the range of family structures, while their view of 'parent' in the majority of the opinions largely reaffirms traditional deference to parental decision-making.[166] The deference accorded to one with the status of 'parent', therefore, combined with an acknowledgement that families come in a variety of forms and do not necessarily remain stable during a child's minority, may translate into significant protection for non-traditional families when the parent can resist State interference. Single parents, for example, could claim the power of parenthood just as married parents can, thus providing greater protection to their family from state intervention. This is consistent with prior case-law validating extended families as constitutional equals to the married heterosexual nuclear norm.[167] At the same time, the recognition of family diversity seems to suggest an implicit weakening of the rationale to defend the family from state intervention or scrutiny. Several amici argued that a balancing approach that included consideration of more than parents' interests was justified because of the range of different families that deviated from traditional norms, with the implication that distance from the norm justifies intervention.[168] These arguments echoed the dissenting opinion in the Washington Supreme Court, which justified the structure of the statute on the basis of the difference between non-traditional families and the marital, heterosexual norm. Movement away from the presumed norm of the patriarchal family comes with the price of allowing greater intervention. The opinions suggest that because non-traditional families, especially single parents, are less stable and the families are more challenged, visitation to perpetuate loving, significant relationships, even if intrusive, is important to counteract lacunae in these families.[169] Patriarchal norms reassert themselves in paternalistic rationales. Ironically, this may benefit the

---

[166] Those implications may be particularly important as the court during its current term has before it a case involving a non-traditional family in an immigration case involving issues of gender discrimination: *Tuan Anh Nguyen, Joseph Alfred Boulais v INS*, No 98-60418.

[167] See *Moore v City of East Cleveland*, 431 US 494 (1977).

[168] See, eg, Brief Amicus Curiae Center for Children's Policy Practice & Research at the University of Pennsylvania in Support of Respondent, Lexsee 1999 US Briefs 138 (13 December 1999); Brief Amicus Curiae of the American Civil Liberties Union and the ACLU of Washington in Support of Respondent, Lexsee 1999 US Briefs 138 (13 December 1999); Brief of the Amicus Curiae American Academy of Matrimonial Lawyers, Lexsee 1999 US Briefs 138 (12 November 1999).

[169] For an extended discussion of the unfounded myths and stereotypes that underlies the stigmatization of single parent families, see Dowd, *In Defense of Single Parent Families*, note 100 (above), chapter one.

disproportionately female-headed single parent families by reinforcement of parental (and within two-parent, traditionally paternal) authority.

Valuing parents while acknowledging a broader range of families also has implications for step-parents and for gay and lesbian parents. Rather than insulating these families, it has the potential of making them more vulnerable. To the extent that adoption can be used by non-biological gay and lesbian parents, and by step-parents, it arguably affords the opportunity to be a legal parent with the high level of protection that *Troxel* appears to require. On the other hand, limited statutory mechanisms for adoption, and, in the case of gay and lesbian parents, the bar to marriage, means a lack of protection for some parents and no legal structure to remedy the status problem. If the 'family' definition includes step-parents and non-marital partners or both, then the rationale for greater intrusion for non-traditional families deserves questioning on behalf of gay and lesbian families, as well as blended families.

Even if all families should be valued irrespective of form, families nevertheless may vary as to their need for affirmative support, or even for intervention. If support and intervention is tied to status, structure, and a presumed, preferred norm, then the stigmatizing of certain children, because of the families in which they find themselves, will continue. A relational norm would approach the recognition of what constitutes family and the preconditions for support or intervention quite differently than a status-based definition. The critical challenge is how to value and support rather than stigmatize and undermine. Visitation statutes by their nature intervene, although they also support many valued relationships. In order to evaluate whether we are supporting all families, we must bring the marginal families to the center of the analysis, and ask whether they are served by a changing definition.

If nurture is what we mean to support, then nurture must be more carefully defined, and must include positive relationships with other nurturers.[170] The challenges of a relational focus are defining what this means; addressing issues of quality versus quantity; considering the relationship of one caregiver to other caregivers; and clearly understanding children's needs and desires in the circumstances.[171] Avoidance of these tasks because this is difficult privileges status, whether by marriage, birth, or adoption, over relational realities. Articulating more clearly what we mean by nurture, and the interaction of nurture among family members, is an alternative. In other words, we can make the reality and the values more explicit. For example, in my work on redefining fatherhood, I have argued that nurture should include physical, mental, spiritual, emotional, and psychological care, based on the developmental and other needs of children, and the needs generated by specific contexts.[172] Nurture also must include a quantitative component that is significant enough to justify State intervention on behalf of a specific relationship.

Also included in this reorientation of core definitions and visions is the question of the scope of children's rights. 'Rights' in fact may be a problematic

---

[170]   Dowd, *Redefining Fatherhood*, note 144 (above) at 157–180.

[171]   See Martha Minow's classic articulation of the distinction and implications of rules versus standards, in Martha Minow, *Making All the Difference* (1990).

[172]   Dowd, *Redefining Fatherhood*, note 144 (above) at 157.

conception, as it suggests autonomous, independent adults rather than dependent (to a greater or lesser extent) and developing children. It is clear from *Troxel* that the independent perspective of children, rather than their presumed representation either by the State or by their parents, is emerging as a crucial consideration in family law analyses. Just as the implications of any definition of 'family' must be considered from the margin, by putting the margin at the center, so too the resolution of intra-familial disputes over children must recognize children's voices, rather than presuming their representation by someone else.[173]

Troxel's rethinking of family analysis might suggest the need to think whether a relational approach is incompatible with rules focused on status or form, or whether the two can comfortably coexist. For example, a relational approach toward family grounded in changing family realities is contrary to the historical, tradition-oriented analysis of marriage. Greater support for non-traditional families may eventually run into the problem of a constrained view of the right to marry. If marriage provides the best protection against state intrusion, then marriage must remain the strategy for non-traditional families to protect their privacy. But if marriage is in conflict with that broader recognition, then is that an additional argument to orient marriage around the relational inquiry of whether we should value long-term committed relationships between two adults or the traditional norm of heterosexual marriage?

Finally, alongside a more complex, nuanced definition of relationships and nurture must be a heightened concern for bias, given the complaints of both mothers and fathers about different biases in the family law structure. We cannot continue to ignore this complaint about the existing family law structure, nor implement a looser, more complex analysis without attending to this problem. Exploring how to correct for bias might include the articulation of a more complex standard, requiring explicit, detailed factual findings, supporting reports from expert witnesses and guardians ad litem, and monitoring outcomes for patterns of gender or race bias.

IV   CONCLUSION

Troxel provides us with few answers, but many questions. It reflects the diversity of family forms, and the necessity of continued thinking about the function of families, the role of the State, and the resolution of intra-familial disputes. Most significantly, it suggests the dilemmas that face us in supporting all families without stigmatizing some by the manner and reasons for which we intervene. Relational definitions keep us focused on what really matters in a family, while challenging us to articulate more clearly the content and value of those relationships.

---

[173]   See note 145 (above).

ZIMBABWE

BETWEEN A ROCK AND A HARD PLACE: COURTS AND CUSTOMARY LAW IN ZIMBABWE

Fareda Banda[*]

I   INTRODUCTION

'Law making is an inherent and essential part of the judicial process.'[1]

There has been a raft of legislation in post-independence Zimbabwe, not least the overhaul of the law of succession discussed in a previous *Survey*.[2] However, arguably, it is the work of the courts[3] in interpreting customary law and existing legislation to fit into the post-colonial dispensation which have yielded the most interesting points of law. This paper seeks to explore some of those legal developments focusing on court judgments in two broad areas. The first concerns the hierarchy of marriage laws in a plural legal system, which recognizes without specifying the ranking, civil marriage, registered customary marriage and unregistered customary law unions. The second focuses on the issue of property rights of women in unregistered customary law unions and the courts' attempts to ameliorate a seemingly inequitable distribution of property when such unions are terminated by divorce.

II   MARRIAGE LAWS AND INTERNAL CONFLICTS

At the time of writing, Zimbabwe finds itself with three legally recognized forms of marriage. The first is marriage under the Marriage Act[4] which is a civil monogamous union. The second is the registered customary marriage provided for by the Customary Marriages Act.[5] This is a potentially polygynous marriage. Finally there is a marriage by customary rites that is unregistered. Although recognized in customary law as a valid marriage, its validity in general law is in doubt owing to its non-registration.[6] However, an unregistered customary law

---

[*]   Lecturer in Law, School of Oriental and African Studies, University of London.

[1]   Gubbay ACJ in *Zimnat Insurance Co Ltd v Chawanda* 1990 (2) ZLR 143, 154.

[2]   F Banda, 'Inheriting Trouble? Changing the Face of the Law of Succession in Zimbabwe' in *The International Survey of Family Law 1996*, ed A Bainham (Martinus Nijhoff Publishers, 1998).

[3]   The paper focuses on decisions of the High Court and the Supreme Court only.

[4]   Marriage Act [Chapter 5:11].

[5]   Customary Marriages Act [Chapter 5:07], s 3.

[6]   Section 3(1) of the Customary Marriages Act (above) defines a customary marriage as one solemnized in terms of the Act.

union receives limited recognition, with s 3(5) of the Customary Marriages Act providing that it shall be 'regarded as a valid marriage for the purposes of customary law and custom relating to the status, guardianship, custody and rights of succession of the children of such marriage'. It also creates mutual obligations of support during the subsistence of the marriage and at its dissolution, although orders for support are rare in practice.[7] In reality there are also irregular unions which do not fit into any of the legally recognized categories of marriage.[8] The Constitution of Zimbabwe recognizes both general and customary law without setting out a hierarchy between the two.[9]

Although fairly easy to understand, the marriage regime in Zimbabwe is complicated by the ability of parties to contract 'double decker marriages' or to enter into one or more forms of the above marriages simultaneously.[10] Indeed one could envisage a situation where parties have a triple-tier marriage, meaning that they first contract an unregistered customary law union whereby the man pays bridewealth for the woman and a customary union comes into being. They then follow this up by registering their marriage under the Customary Marriages Act before undertaking the final step of converting what would have been a potentially polygynous union into a monogamous one by contracting a marriage under the Marriage Act. Again it is open to one man and one woman to make this marital journey.[11] However, complications arise when the man enters into different unions with different women. Which of the 'marriages' is valid? Does one marriage system carry with it benefits that the others do not? If the two marital regimes are incompatible, can it be inferred that a later marriage cancels out an earlier marriage or that the earlier marriage precludes the contracting of the later marriage rendering the latter null and void? Is it the legal system under which the marriage was contracted which is important in determining validity and hierarchy or is it the timing of the marriage? The position will be explored by looking at the cases. However, it must be noted from the outset that there is a lack of legislative clarity on the matter highlighted by the recent amendment to the Administration of Estates Act which appears to repeal by implication bigamy laws.[12] But more of that later.

The cases in which the above issues have been explored have been to do with property division on divorce or annulment, adultery and also entitlement to pension provision on the death of a man married to two women under different marital regimes.

---

[7]   F Banda, (1993) *Women and Law in Zimbabwe: Access to Justice on Divorce*, unpublished DPhil thesis, University of Oxford, at p 102.

[8]   *Ibid.* Cf W Wa Karanja, '"Outside Wives" and "inside wives": a study of changing perceptions in marriage' in *Transformations of African Marriage*, ed D Parkin and D Nyamwaya (1987) 247.

[9]   Constitution of Zimbabwe, s 23(3)(b) and s 89.

[10] Cf South Africa Recognition of Customary Marriages Act, 1998 (Act No 120, 1998), s 10(1) of which provides: 'A man and a woman between whom a customary marriage subsists are competent to contract a marriage with each other under the Marriage Act, 1961 (Act No 25 of 1961), if neither of them is a spouse in a subsisting customary marriage with any other person'.

[11] Cf *Chikosi v Chikosi* 1975 (1) RLR 140, 143.

[12] F Banda, (1998) at p 543. See also *Chamboko v Chamboko* 1998 (2) ZLR 516, 524.

The case of *Makovah v Makovah*[13] concerned a man who had married a woman under the African Marriages Act[14] without disclosing the fact that he was already married to another woman under the Marriage Act. He appealed a decision of the High Court which, although declaring the second marriage null and void by virtue of being bigamous, had gone on to find that there was a putative marriage between the man and his African Marriages Act wife. He also appealed the awarding of marital property to her arguing that the court a quo did not have the authority to apportion the parties' property, in terms of s 7 of the Matrimonial Causes Act,[15] as it purported to do. The appeal was unsuccessful, with the Supreme Court noting that the man had deliberately misled the marriage officer and African Marriage Act 'wife' as to his marital status.[16] The court was also of the opinion that the court a quo had been right in its use of the Matrimonial Causes Act to apportion marital property, as the said Act made provision for a court to divide marital property on judicial separation, annulment or dissolution of the marriage. The marriage being bigamous had been annulled, but this did not disentitle the second 'wife' from receiving a fair share. However, the Supreme Court did challenge the court a quo's construction of the union as a putative marriage reasoning that the concept, being part of the common law, was alien to African customary law. Any attempt to introduce such a concept into customary law would lead to its distortion. On a sociological note, the court recognized that many people did not realize that contracting a 'church' marriage under the Marriage Act precluded the contracting of other unions.[17] The difficulty was how to deal with the legal consequences of this general ignorance.

The issue has been picked up in other cases, with judges asking that attempts be made to educate or enlighten the populace as to the existence of this bar.[18] Interestingly the legislature has taken note and in the Administration of Estates Amendment Act of 1997[19] it is provided that if a man dies who had been married under the Marriage Act, but had gone on to contract other 'marriages' with different women, those other 'marriages' would not, as in the case just discussed, be declared void.[20] Rather, the estate would be classified as being a polygynous one under customary law. It would thus be governed by the Administration of Estates Amendment Act and not the Deceased Estates Succession Act.[21] The effect of this, as Ncube[22] has noted, is the recognition of legally void marriages. However, it would seem that the prevalence of multiple marriages governed by different regimes would signify a more fluid construct of relationships in the minds of the public at large. The legalities of such arrangements appear not to be of concern. Arguably, a strict reading of the law of bigamy would lead to

---

[13] *Makovah v Makovah* 1998 (2) ZLR 82.

[14] Then Chapter 238 and now the Customary Marriages Act [Chapter 5:07].

[15] Matrimonial Causes Act [Chapter 5:13], s 7(1).

[16] *Makovah v Makovah* (above) at 89. Cf s 6 (1) of the Customary Marriages Act [Chapter 5:07].

[17] *Makovah v Makovah* (above) at 90.

[18] Cf *Chamboko v Chamboko* 1998 (2) ZLR 516.

[19] No 6 of 1997 amending the Administration of Estates Act [Chapter 6:01].

[20] Section 68A(4).

[21] [Chapter 6:02].

[22] W Ncube, 'The White Paper on Marriage and Inheritance in Zimbabwe: An Excuse in Superfluity and Mischief' (1993) *Legal Forum* No 5 vol 4 at 15.

inequitable results for some of the 'wives' which is presumably why the legislature saw fit to make the amendment.

By way of contrast, in South Africa the Recognition of Customary Marriages Act[23] provides that if a person is already married according to customary law he or she cannot then enter a union with another person under a different marital regime. Multiple marriages contracted according to custom are, however, permitted. Issues arising out of the proprietary consequences of such plural marriages will be considered later.

In Zimbabwe, the problems created by a strict adherence to the law of bigamy can be seen in the case of *Makwiramiti v Fidelity Life Assurance of Zimbabwe (Pvt) Ltd & Anor.*[24] Here the appellant, who had been married to the deceased in terms of the Marriage Act, challenged the respondent company with whom her husband had taken out life assurance. On his death she had received all of his pension. However, the respondent company then discovered that the deceased had contracted a second 'marriage' with another woman, the second respondent, under the Customary Marriages Act. The company began paying part of the pension to the second 'wife' thus reducing the Marriage Act wife's entitlement. The first wife sued the pension company. In its defence it pointed to the Pension and Provident Funds Regulations 1991 which defined a 'surviving spouse' as meaning the widow of a deceased member of a pension fund including the widow of a polygynous person. The insurance company decided that the second wife was therefore entitled to benefit.

Showing the wisdom of Solomon, the High Court held that the deceased could not legally have had a Marriage Act marriage as well as a registered customary marriage. However, it decided that the second marriage, although void, was in fact an unregistered customary law union. The second wife was therefore still entitled to benefit from the pension provision as being the widow of a polygynous person.[25] The Marriage Act wife appealed. The appeal was successful, with Gubbay CJ holding that the existence of a marriage under the Marriage Act was an absolute bar to contracting any other marriage. Put simply, the court found that it was '… not possible for a person to be monogamously and polygamously married at one time'.[26] Gubbay CJ's own value system and ranking of the respective marriage laws came through very clearly when he declared:

> 'Indeed, so jealously does the law guard against the profanation of the Christian ceremony of marriage that it criminally punishes bigamy and delictually punishes adultery.'

The question is whether these views are widely held. The matter was revisited in *Chamboko v Chamboko.*[27] Here again a man died leaving two women to whom he had been 'married'. With the first wife he had contracted a registered marriage

---

[23]   Act No 120, 1998, s 3(2).

[24]   1998 (2) ZLR 471.

[25]   Cf *Katiyo v Standard Chartered Zimbabwe Pension Fund* 1994 (1) ZLR 225.

[26]   *Makwiramiti v Fidelity Life Assurance of Zimbabwe (Pvt) Ltd v Anor* 1998 (2) ZLR 471, 474.

[27]   1998 (2) ZLR 516.

under the old African Marriages Act[28] and with the second wife he had purported to contract a civil marriage under the Marriage Act.[29] The second 'wife' had obtained an order entitling her to pension benefits in terms of the pension regulations of the Zimbabwe army by whom the husband had been employed. The plaintiff who was the wife originally married asked, *inter alia*, for an order declaring the second 'marriage' null and void. Was it possible for the deceased to have married someone under the Marriage Act if he had already registered a customary marriage with another person? The court said no. The reason for this was s 16 of the Customary Marriages Act which provides:

> 'No marriage solemnized in terms of this Act or the Marriage Act or registered under the Native Marriages Act (Chapter 79 of 1939) or contracted under customary law before 1 April 1918 shall be dissolved except by order of a court of competent jurisdiction in terms of the Matrimonial Causes Act [Chapter 5:13].'

This means that the deceased would have had to dissolve the first marriage under customary law *before* contracting a civil monogamous union. It could not be assumed that by marrying someone under the Marriage Act, the first marriage contracted according to customary law and registered had been dissolved or superseded. The judge found in essence that the existence of a registered marriage under the Customary Marriage Act regime precluded the registration under the Marriage Act of another marriage with a different person and vice versa.[30] However, one could still upgrade a marriage registered under the Customary Marriages Act to a monogamous one under the Marriage Act provided one was doing so with the same spouse. Clearly then only a spouse in an unregistered customary law union is without protection, a worrying fact when one considers that the vast majority of unions in Zimbabwe fall into this category. However, the judge noted the recent changes wrought by the Administration of Estates Amendment Act 1997 which he described as having 'further confused the position in the interest of convenience'.[31] The court called for legislative intervention to protect 'the proprietary interests of the discarded wife and children'.[32]

Chinhengo J was also of the view that the public needed to be made aware of the provisions of s 16 of the Customary Marriages Act because many of them did not know of the bar to multiple marriages under the different marital regimes once 'registered' with one person,[33] again highlighting the findings of the court in *Makovah v Makovah*.[34]

The paper continues the examination of the problems created by the co-existence of multiple marriage regimes by considering cases dealing with adultery. In *Takadini v Maimba*,[35] it was stated that:

---

[28]   Now the Customary Marriages Act [Chapter 5:07].
[29]   Chapter 5:11.
[30]   *Chamboko v Chamboko* 1998 (2) ZLR 516 at 524.
[31]   *Ibid.*
[32]   *Ibid.*
[33]   *Ibid* at 525.
[34]   1998 (2) ZLR 82.
[35]   *Takadini v Maimba* 1996 (2) ZLR 737.

'The delict of adultery is based on an offence against the institution of marriage in terms of the Marriage Act. So before a woman can be found to have committed adultery, she must be found to have known (on a balance of probabilities) that the person with whom she had a sexual relationship was married *in terms of the Marriage Act.*'[36] (my emphasis)

As a general principle it has been stated that the existence of no fault divorce law means that the courts should be slow to award punitive adultery damages.[37] Also, the mere fact of the adultery will not be enough. The plaintiff will be required to show that *contumelia* or harm was inflicted on the plaintiff and, secondly, that there was a loss of *consortium* or companionship, love and affection. *Takadini v Maimba* was brought on appeal.[38] Mrs Maimba had sued the defendant for adultery damages. The Maimbas had cohabited since 1985 and had registered their marriage under the Marriage Act in 1992. In the same month, her husband commenced a sexual relationship with the defendant. He sued for divorce seven months after registering the marriage. In her defence Takadini said that she had not known that her lover was married to the plaintiff. However, it transpired that two months into her own relationship with the husband of the plaintiff, she was made aware of the existence not only of the fact that Mr Maimba was already married but also that he had a child with his wife. The defendant nevertheless persisted with the relationship and had two children with Mr Maimba. Rejecting her plea, the court decided that she had been 'diligent in ignorance'[39] and had knowingly committed adultery with the plaintiff's husband. However, the court found that the marriage was 'virtually still born'[40] so there 'was virtually no *consortium* to be lost'.[41] The *contumelia* the court found was the fault of Mr Maimba rather than the defendant. With this in mind, the court reduced the adultery damages awarded by the magistrates' court from $10,000 to $1000.

The later case of *Gwatidzo v Gwatidzo*,[42] although accepting the 'knowledge test' propounded in the *Maimba* case, was less sure of the assertion that it was only Marriage Act marriages which enjoyed the protection of adultery laws. In this case a man had entered into an unregistered customary law union with one wife. He then entered into a Marriage Act marriage with a second woman, the plaintiff. He continued to see the first 'wife' with whom he went on to have another child. The plaintiff sued the first customary law union 'wife' for adultery with her husband. The contention was that an unregistered customary law union was not regarded as a valid marriage under s 3 of the Customary Marriages Act. This being the case, the man was free to register a marriage with another woman, something which would not have been permitted under the South African legislation discussed earlier. The defendant did not deny knowing that her husband had entered into a registered marriage with the plaintiff, but being 'traditionally minded' had simply accepted this as his customary 'right'. The

---

[36]   *Ibid* at 741–742.
[37]   *Ibid* at 737.
[38]   *Ibid.*
[39]   *Ibid* at 741.
[40]   *Ibid.*
[41]   *Ibid.*
[42]   HH-232-2000.

judge recognized that, on a formal reading of the facts, the defendant was guilty of committing adultery with the plaintiff's husband, the registered Marriage Act marriage taking precedence over her own. However, he cautioned against taking such an approach, not least because it ranked the general law above the customary law, '... the law, by not outlawing customary marriages whether registered or not, shows no contempt for marriages at customary law'.[43] The judge contended that for many Zimbabweans customary law was the law with which they were most closely associated. Failure to recognize this would 'be patronizing on a large number of people in this country and would constitute the "intolerable affectation of superior virtue ... inherited from the colonial past"'.[44]

The judge considered at some length the complications arising out of a multiple marriage system. He was of the opinion that, although not regarded as valid under the general law by virtue of s 3 of the Customary Marriages Act, unregistered customary law unions remained valid marriages at customary law.[45] The judge had sympathy for the defendant's contention that she had exercised her constitutional right to have customary law applied to her and by implication to her relationship with the shared husband. It was therefore unfair to do what the plaintiff was attempting to do, which was to 'force the application of general law principles upon the defendant who had not chosen that the general law should apply to her'.[46] The issue, therefore, was which of the two marriages the court should privilege? The court decided neither.

> 'I do not think that the law of adultery must be used for the purpose of validating one form of marriage as against another by women who find themselves in the situation of the parties in this case.'[47]

The judge was singularly unsympathetic to the plaintiff's case noting that, as she had found the husband already in a marriage, albeit an unregistered one, it was she who had disrupted the defendant's relationship. Indeed the court found that her insistence that the marriage be registered was borne of her fear of the husband's other relationship and her desire to protect her own position. Moreover, the husband had not made any efforts to terminate the first marriage nor was there evidence that the plaintiff had demanded that he do so before registering her marriage. With this in mind the court found:

> 'She could not possibly have suffered any real injury or *contumelia* and she could not have lost any consortium to talk about. Her claim for adultery damages though technically valid is not such as would warrant an award of damages.'[48]

The case highlights quite clearly the difficulties thrown up by a multiple marriage system that recognizes polygyny and yet still has in existence seemingly

---

[43] *Ibid* at 4–5, quoting Gubbay ACJ in *Zimnat Insurance Co Ltd v Chawanda* 1990 (2) ZLR 435, 437.

[44] *Ibid* at 5.

[45] *Ibid* at 9.

[46] *Ibid* at 10.

[47] *Ibid* at 15.

[48] *Ibid* at 12.

contradictory bigamy and adultery laws. It is difficult to see how this problem can be resolved without privileging one form of marriage over the others and, by implication, one lifestyle choice over another.[49] Also, as the cases reveal, the judge is often faced with validating one woman's rights at the expense of another's. This leads one to consider whether Chanock's[50] suggestion of a unitary legal system should be adopted?[51] However, what would that legal system look like? Would polygyny continue to be recognized or would it be struck down as violating gender discrimination provisions?[52] If polygynous marriages are to be allowed, should non-indigenous men also be allowed to indulge?[53] In a spirit of equality perhaps polyandry should also be allowed. To date, Tanzania is one of the few countries to have one Marriage Act which recognizes marriages[54] contracted according to civil, customary or religious rites.[55]

Staying with marriage, the paper moves on to consider developments (in case-law) on division of property on the dissolution of unregistered law unions. Again, questions have arisen over the limited recognition of customary law unions by the general law. Briefly, the Matrimonial Causes Act[56] makes provision for a court to exercise its discretion in dividing the property of parties who have registered their marriages under the Marriage Act or under the Customary Marriages Act. Ncube[57] has this to say on general law recognition of the proprietary consequences of customary law unions:

> 'Customary law unions, being invalid marriages by virtue of their non-registration, have no proprietary regime. The parties are unmarried in the eyes of the law and therefore their property is treated as the property of unmarried individuals. Upon separation each party takes with him or her the property which he or she acquired and therefore owns. Any joint property is shared in accordance with the shares the parties hold in it.'

Customary law, which governs unregistered customary unions, is notoriously ungenerous in its allocation of property to wives. 'Traditionally' such wives have been granted two categories of property. The first comprises the *mombe ye umai* or motherhood beast which is the cow given to a mother as part of the *lobolo* or bridewealth paid for her daughter. The second category is her *mavoko* or hands

---

[49]   In 1997 the Minister of Justice noted that reform of marriage laws was complicated, and wide consultation was needed. See *Hansard*, 20 March 1997 at col 4363.

[50]   M Chanock, 'Law, State and Culture: Thinking About "Customary Law" After Apartheid' 1981 *Acta Juridica* 52.

[51]   S Coldham, 'Statute Note : Succession Law Reform in Zimbabwe' (1998) 42 JAL 129, 133 also calls for a unified Family Law.

[52]   F Kaganas, and C Murray, 'Law, Women and the Family: The Question of Polygyny in a New South Africa' (1991) *Acta Juridica* 116. See also A Hellum, *Women's Human Rights and Legal Pluralism in Africa* (1999) at p 424.

[53]   Currently they are entitled to marry only one wife at a time, although this does not preclude the taking of *de facto* 'wives'. The latter would not be entitled to any legal protection.

[54]   Section 25(1), Law of Marriage Act 1971.

[55]   Law of Marriage Act 1971. For a discussion of its provisions, see B Rwezaura and U Wanitzek, 'Family Law in Tanzania: A Socio-Legal Report' (1988) 2 IJLFP 1.

[56]   Matrimonial Causes Act [Chapter 5:13], s 7.

[57]   W Ncube, *Family Law in Zimbabwe* (1989) at p 167.

property which is property acquired by the wife as a result of her non-marital[58] labour.[59] By staying silent on unregistered customary law unions, it could be argued that the legislature has not kept pace with the impact of modernization and the growth of the capitalist market economy. The cases which follow are illustrative of the creative ways in which lawyers and courts have tried to close the gap between law and social reality. They also highlight the limitations of judge-led legal change.

The first case to be considered is that of *Mashingaidze v Mashingaidze*[60] which was dismissed on a procedural technicality. Here the applicant was claiming a half share in matrimonial property acquired in the course of an unregistered customary law union. The applicant based her claim on the existence of a tacit universal partnership between the parties.[61] She claimed a half share of the parties' assets. The respondent argued that it was wrong for the applicant to invoke general law principles when they had a customary marriage. The court agreed with this assertion and noted that parties could not invoke a general law concept, namely tacit universal partnership, without establishing why general law should be applied in lieu of customary law. The judge pointed to the choice of law rules in the Customary Law and Local Courts Act[62] and noted that before the general law could be applied, parties had to show that their lifestyle was more in tune with general law than with customary law. However, the judge did go on to note that he had some sympathy for the applicant's cause. He suggested that one way for her to obtain relief would be by establishing that she had contributed 'financially or otherwise during her union with the respondent, particularly so in the case of immovable properties in regard to which general law and not customary law applies'.[63]

In *obiter dicta* Robinson J cited with approval comments made in previous judgments[64] about the need to develop customary law in line with social developments and to mirror changes in society. This last point was picked up by the judge in *Chapendama v Chapendama*.[65]

In the *Chapendama* case, the parties had an unregistered customary law union. An attempt to register the marriage under the Customary Marriages Act

---

[58] One of the effects of a man giving *lobolo* for a woman is to vest her labour value in him or his family. This means that her 'ordinary' work such as ploughing the fields would vest in him but any extra income which she earns as a result of her diligence or other specialist skills which she may have belongs to her personally.

[59] Cf *Jengwa v Jengwa* 1999 (2) ZLR 120, 126.

[60] 1995 (1) ZLR 219.

[61] Two types of universal partnership have been identified in *Chapendama v Chapendama* 1998 (2) ZLR 18, 32. First is the *societas universorum* which is expressly entered into where a marriage or putative marriage exists. The second, which is called a *societas universorum quae ex quaestu veniunt*, is defined as 'one where the parties agree that all they may acquire during its continuance and every kind of commercial venture shall be partnership property'. It is tacit if it can be inferred from the conduct of the parties.

[62] [Chapter 7:05], s 3. In trying to ascertain which law to apply, customary or general, the court has to consider, *inter alia*, the closeness of the parties to general law or customary law, their respective modes of life and the subject matter of the case.

[63] *Mashingaidze v Mashingaidze* 1995 (1) ZLR 219, 223–224.

[64] *Zimnat Insurance Co Ltd v Chawanda* 1990 (2) ZLR 143, 153–154, *Walker v Industrial Equity Ltd* 1995 (1) ZLR 88, *Smith & Anor v Acting Sheriff of Zimbabwe & Anor* 1995 (1) ZLR 158.

[65] 1998 (2) ZLR 18.

was deemed void because the wife's sister had acted as proxy at the marriage ceremony. This meant that s 7(1) of the Matrimonial Causes Act could not be used to distribute the marital property. To get around this problem, the wife claimed that the parties had a tacit universal partnership which entitled her to a 50 per cent share of their assets. They had been together for 30 years and had worked their way up from having very little to having assets of some considerable value. In addition to acquiring property, the husband had also acquired two further wives. The judge identified the issue in the case as trying to ascertain:

> '... what was the true relationship between them for the purposes of a division of the assets. Was it based on a "tacit partnership" as alleged in plaintiff's declaration or was it based on some other relationship such as a customary union or customary marriage?'[66]

Chinengo J accepted the contention of Robinson J in the *Mashingaidze* case to the effect that the court had to be careful about applying general law principles to customary law unions.[67] However, he did acknowledge that a strict adherence to customary law in the division of the parties' property would result in him coming unstuck and perpetrating an injustice.[68] He noted:

> 'However unsatisfactory the application of the general law concept of a tacit universal partnership to an unregistered customary scenario may be, it is the only legal regime available in order to do justice to the parties. And where a basis has been laid for the application of the common law as was stated in *Mashingaidze*'s case *supra*, it is proper to do so.'[69]

Mindful of the choice of law rules, the judge still went through the statutory checklist for the choice of law.[70] He found that the parties were more closely aligned to the general law than to the customary law. The judge then went on to list the two types of universal partnership and concluded that the parties had indeed had a tacit universal partnership. Although calling for a greater recognition of customary law, which was the law governing the majority of relationships in Zimbabwe, the judge highlighted the problems thrown up by the polygynous nature of some customary unions.[71] In the case at hand, the judge had to decide how to divide the assets in the light of the fact that the rights of the other wives were affected. The judge said that had the marriage been monogamous then he would have had no hesitation in granting the wife a half share in the assets.[72] However, in the light of the contributions made by the other wives, he cut her

---

[66]   *Ibid* at 23.

[67]   *Ibid* at 27.

[68]   *Ibid* at 31.

[69]   *Ibid.*

[70]   Contained in s 3 of the Customary Law and Local Courts Act [Chapter 7:05].

[71]   *Ibid* at 32–33. Again the South African legislature has made provision for dealing with such issues. Recognition of Customary Marriages Act, 1998 (Act No 120, 1998), s 7(4)(b), 7(6), 7(7), 7(8) 7(9).

[72]   Cf Recognition of Customary Marriages Act, 1998, s 7(2).

entitlement substantially.[73] Whilst one can see the argument for the need to balance the interests of the other wives, it is contended that the judge treated the plaintiff unduly harshly. He noted that she had been married to the defendant for 24 years before any of the other wives were married, thus suggesting that she had helped to accumulate the bulk of the matrimonial property.[74] For her entitlement to be cut so substantially suggests that she was punished for her husband's acquisition of wives. The loss should have been suffered by the husband who should have been forced to share his half of the property with his remaining wives, rather than asking the first wife to leave the product of her hard work for the benefit of other people. Failure to do this meant that the husband enjoyed a double benefit.

The difficulties of sharing property on the dissolution of one of the unions in a polygynous set-up were again taken up in *Jengwa v Jengwa*.[75] This case highlights the difficulty of achieving an equitable distribution of property where there are many conflicting interests to consider. It also highlights the growing conflict between human rights principles which call for equality between the sexes,[76] together with equal enjoyment and distribution of property[77] and benefits, and the continued existence of polygyny.

In *Jengwa v Jengwa* the appellant and respondent had entered into an unregistered customary law union in 1972 before finally solemnizing the marriage under the Customary Marriages Act in 1987. There had been periods of estrangement between those two dates during which the respondent had taken it upon himself to acquire additional wives. Their precise number could not be easily ascertained by the court although the names of five other women were mentioned in connection with the respondent. He had also registered a marriage under the Customary Marriages Act with one of these wives. The appellant claimed a half share of the matrimonial home which the parties had purchased after the solemnization of the marriage. There were other assets which the respondent did not claim. The registration of the marriage brought the parties within the purview of the Matrimonial Causes Act[78] which left the distribution of marital property to the discretion of the judge. The court noted that the case raised the question 'of the degree of account, if any, to be taken of the claims of other wives, when considering a division of property between a husband and a wife in a polygynous marriage'.[79] The short answer was one third, which was the percentage awarded to the appellant. The judge noted that, given the length of the marriage and the appellant's contribution to the marriage, had she been the only wife, she would

---

[73]   He noted (at 33) that a conservative estimate of the property was $2,500,000. The plaintiff was awarded $300,000.

[74]   Interestingly under the Administration of Estates Amendment Act, 1997, the first wife is given a larger share of the property belonging to a deceased polygynous husband than her co-wives. Of the one third allocated to the wives of the deceased, the first wife is entitled to a third and the remainder is to be shared out by the number of remaining wives: F Banda (1998) at p 540.

[75]   1999 (2) ZLR 121.

[76]   The African Charter on Human and Peoples' Rights, 1981, 21 ILM (1982) Arts 2 and 3.

[77]   Convention on the Elimination of All Forms of Discrimination Against Women, GA Res 34/180, 34 UN GAOR Supp (No 710.46) at 193, UN Doc A/34/46 (1979) Art 16(1)(h).

[78]   Section 7(1).

[79]   1999 (2) ZLR 121 at 125.

have been entitled 'to expect something close to parity with the husband'.[80] Although it had not been necessary to do so in the case at hand[81], the court noted that it was important in cases where there were many wives, including ones in unregistered customary law unions to protect the interests of those wives. The judge said that one of the ways of doing that was to serve notice of any contested property dispute involving a polygynous man on all his other wives.[82] He also noted the difficulty of ascertaining the respective shares of the different wives:

> 'The weight to be attached to such a third party claim must vary from case to case. In some, it may be possible to identify a precise share attributable to a non-litigant spouse. In other cases it might be impracticable to do other than modify the share to a litigant wife, reducing it from that which a wife in monogamy might have expected, in order to protect the interest of the other wives. In some, it might even be proper to disregard the position of other wives on the basis that their rights are insubstantial in the circumstances ... In no case is it proper to fail to consider such a competing interest.'[83]

By way of comparison, the South African statute explicitly provides that where a man has more than one spouse, those other spouses must be joined in the action and the interests of any other third parties be considered.[84] The provision assumes of course that the other wives are known[85] and can be joined in proceedings. The Act further provides that if a man wishes to enter into new marriages subsequent to the passing of the Act, then he will have to present to the court a contract detailing the arrangements made for dealing with the proprietary consequences of his marriages.[86] When presented with such a document, the court has many options open to it[87] which include amending the contract, terminating existing property arrangements or refusing to accept the application if it deems that the proposal does not provide adequately for the interests of any affected parties. Again, in making the application, interested parties have to be joined in the proceedings.[88] If the application is granted, then copies of the order must be given to all interested parties and this would include any other wives.[89] The South African legislature is to be congratulated on the comprehensiveness of its provisions. However, one cannot help but wonder about the practicality of the statute and, in particular, its assumption that wives will be identified and kept in the picture to the extent of being joined in legal proceedings. It is more than likely

---

[80]   *Ibid* at 134.

[81]   This was because the appellant had limited her claim to a half share in the matrimonial home. She had not asked for a share of any of the other assets. See *ibid* at 133.

[82]   *Jengwa v Jengwa* 1999 (2) ZLR 121, 133.

[83]   *Ibid* at 132.

[84]   Recognition of Customary Marriages Act, 1998, s 7(4)(b).

[85]   Although providing for registration of customary marriages, the Act specifically states (s 4(9)) that even if not registered, the marriage remains valid. Without access to documentary evidence, not all wives may know of the existence of co-wives.

[86]   Recognition of Customary Marriages Act, 1998, s 7(6). Cf s 8(4)(b) for provisions for arrangements in the event of dissolution of the marriage.

[87]   *Ibid*, s 7(7).

[88]   *Ibid*, s 7(8).

[89]   *Ibid*, s 7(9).

that, especially in the case of migrant workers, new unions will be formed about which existing wives are not aware and, if aware, that they will not feel able to challenge. Registering an interest may well be seen as such a challenge by the husband and could lead to divorce. Moreover, the statute assumes the existence of property of some value – it would have to be, to justify the complex procedural requirements. It is submitted that for many their property holdings are so small as not to warrant the involvement of the courts.

In light of the increased number of cases[90] in which tacit universal partnership was being claimed, the court in the *Jengwa*[91] case also took the opportunity to consider the rights of women in unregistered customary law union. The judge acknowledged the inequitable distribution of property on the dissolution of an unregistered customary law union.[92] He noted that attempts had been made to circumvent this disability by, for example, extending the protection given to women with unregistered customary law unions by allowing them 'to bring a dependant's action for the death of a breadwinner'.[93] He was less sure about allowing a woman in an unregistered customary law union to bring an action for division of property on the dissolution of an unregistered customary law union. He said that the answer depended upon whether one saw customary law as 'being immutable *mores* discovered by expert evidence'[94] in which case the court could not purport to develop it. However, if one saw customary law as organic and changing to keep up with the times, then 'judicial developments of its principles may be appropriate'.[95] The judge did not indicate which of these two routes he preferred.[96] He later acknowledged the competing forces at play:

'An area of inequality has been encountered by the court and it is striving to address it. It is doing so in a way that might satisfy those wishing to uphold fairness and gender equality but which can be expected to find disfavour with those taking a legalist and conservative view of the law and traditional (dare one say chauvinist?) view of custom.'[97]

Arguably, this is the nub of the problem. It is submitted that the resolution of this dilemma is the greatest challenge facing African women's rights in the twenty-first century. Not surprisingly, this writer favours the approach 'upholding fairness and gender equality' as being consonant with seeing human rights as belonging

---

[90] *Chapendama v Chapendama* (above), *Kuzera v Mudondo* HH-147-98 (unreported), *Chapeyama v Matende and Anor* HH-93-99 (unreported), *Mashingaidze v Mazomba* HH-3-99.

[91] *Jengwa v Jengwa* 1999 (2) ZLR 120.

[92] *Ibid* at 126–127.

[93] *Ibid* at 128. The case cited is *Zimnat Insurance Co Ltd v Chawanda* 1990 (2) ZLR 143.

[94] *Ibid* at 128.

[95] *Ibid* at 128.

[96] Cf L Fishbayn, 'Litigating the Right to Culture: Family Law in the New South Africa' (1999) 13 IJLFP 147.

[97] 1999 (2) ZLR 121 at 129. Cf T Nhlapo, 'African Family Law under an undecided constitution – the challenge for law reform in South Africa' in *The Changing Family: Family Forms and Family Law*, ed J Eekelaar and T Nhlapo (1998), 617.

also to women. The cost of this approach would be to upset the long-term beneficiaries of an inequitable system, but this seems a price worth paying.[98]

The court in *Jengwa* then went on to consider the use of the concept of tacit universal partnership as a way of ameliorating the position of women in unregistered customary law unions and concluded that the courts that had relied on it had perhaps overreached themselves. Specifically, the judge was of the opinion that the decisions of earlier courts had been clouded by their desire to reach an equitable settlement. They had therefore imposed an intention or state of mind on the husbands that they more than likely had not had.[99] He cited as an example of that tendency, the decision in *Chapendama*'s case:[100]

> 'The union there was polygamous. Can it really be thought that the husband in that case voluntarily assented to sharing with the plaintiff, or any or all of his wives, the rights in, rather than the use of, the accumulated property? And if he made the plaintiff his partner, did he not also thus vest his other wives? And if he did so, how could the partnership, involving, as it must, all of them, be dissolved without their being joined?'[101]

Gillespie J put forward as an alternative the notion of unjust enrichment.[102] This would compensate the wife for her contribution to the acquisition of assets. Failure to recognize this contribution would result in her husband being unjustly enriched at her expense:

> 'To permit such an injustice to remain is offensive. It promotes a discrimination against a certain class of woman on the basis of gender. It treats various classes of women differently, denying some women rights in property which others enjoy. It wreaks unfairness between a husband and a wife.'[103]

Building on the non-discrimination principle, the judge went on to cite the accession by Zimbabwe to the Convention on the Elimination of All Forms of Discrimination Against Women, 1979 and, in particular, Art 16(1)(h), which calls for an equal distribution of property, as pointing the court towards an equitable settlement.[104] Controversially he noted:

> 'Indeed a future court might even be persuaded that this rationale compels in all cases a choice of law that declines to apply customary law to marital property rights at all, specifically to avoid discrimination.'[105]

---

[98]   Were the problem reconstructed as being one of race rather than gender, it is submitted that those excluded, both men and women, would claim their rights and demand that the right-holders admit them into the exclusive club. The challenges to the *apartheid* regime and colonialism would bear this out.

[99]   1999 (2) ZLR 121 at 129.

[100] *Chapendama v Chapendama* 1998 (2) ZLR 18.

[101] *Jengwa v Jengwa* 1999 (2) ZLR 121, 129.

[102] *Ibid* at 130.

[103] *Ibid* at 130.

[104] *Ibid* at 131 Cf Nhlapo (1998) at 621.

[105] *Ibid* at 131. Cf CEDAW, Arts 2(f), 5.

Arguably this would have to coincide with the abolition of, or non-recognition of, polygynous unions which may well be seen by some as sacrificing the rights of one's sister for oneself. A flip side of that argument is to say that women should not be competing over men. The judge in *Gwatidzo v Gwatidzo*[106] noted the irony of two women fighting over one man with the one suing the other for adultery:

> 'We have in this tragic-comedy Gwatidzo in the middle. He is not the target of either woman. He is watching the scene from a distance and perhaps rubs his hands gleefully as the drama unfolds and the women who both love him battle it out in the courts. The battle is over him. None dares call him the culprit. None has the pride to tell him off and terminate her relationship with him. She must fight the other woman to the bitter end until she can have Gwatidzo exclusively for herself in the case of the plaintiff or until she can lawfully share him with the other woman in the case of the defendant. Is there not sufficient pride on the part of either woman to terminate her relationship with this man? Perhaps there is, but social realities may impede such action.'[107]

There is, however, increasing pressure to see the formal legal abolition of polygyny in national legal systems. The Committee on the Elimination of All Forms of Discrimination Against Women has declared that polygyny discriminates against women and that it 'ought to be discouraged and prohibited'.[108] However, a defender of customary law could argue that such an approach violates the constitutional recognition of customary law. Additionally, the feasibility of abolishing polygyny has to be considered in the light of women's continued economic dependence on men which makes marriage, and by implication, polygyny a necessary, if not always satisfactory, means of survival.[109] However, there are others who point out that polygyny is bad for children, noting that the acquisition by a man of further wives leads to a diversion of financial support from the first family to the new family to the detriment of the children of the first wife. Similarly, children of the second and subsequent wives arrive in straitened circumstances caused by a diversion of some of the father's funds to look after existing dependants. Polygyny therefore creates a situation whereby all bar the husband/father are the losers.[110] The difficulties thrown up when families are reconstituted and finite resources have to stretch to meet ever-expanding obligations are not unique to Zimbabwe.[111]

The final case to be considered is that of *Nyamwanza v Masiiwa*.[112] The plaintiff sued for a dissolution of the partnership which she said existed between herself and the defendant and claimed a 50 per cent share of the defendant's

---

[106]   HC-H 232-2000.

[107]   *Ibid* at 5.

[108]   CEDAW General Recommendation No 21 UN Doc A/47/38 (1994) at para 14. Cf Draft Protocol to the African Charter on the Rights of Women in Africa (Kigali, 15 November 1999) DOC/OS (XXVII) 159b, Art 7(3) provides: 'Polygamy shall be prohibited'.

[109]   A Armstrong *et al*, 'Uncovering Reality: Excavating Women's Rights in African Family Law' (1993) 7 IJLFP 314, 333–338.

[110]   Cf M Wabile, 'Child Support Rights in Kenya and the UN Convention on the Rights of the Child' in *The International Survey of Family Law (2001 Edition)*, ed A Bainham (Family Law, 2001) 267, at 267 n 2.

[111]   Cf M Maclean and J Eekelaar, *The Parental Obligation* (1997).

[112]   HH-95-2000.

business. It was common cause that the two had enjoyed a sexual relationship since 1989 and had cohabited. Although they had sometimes made out that they were married, no customary formalities were ever completed and the court defined their relationship as having been a non-marital cohabitation arrangement. The plaintiff averred that she had helped the defendant to build up his business contributing part of the start-up costs and allowing her home to be used as the business premises. The defendant denied that the plaintiff had made any meaningful contribution to building up his business and contended that she was not entitled to a share in that business which he said was co-owned with his brother. Preferring the evidence of the plaintiff, the court found that the facts of the case pointed to the existence of a tacit universal partnership between the parties.[113] In considering the parties' respective contributions to the acquisition of assets for the business, the court found that the plaintiff's claim to the business assets ceased after the cohabitation ended and the business was relocated. On that basis Gwaunza J awarded her a 25 per cent share of the partnership assets.

It is interesting to note that, unlike the cases dealing with unregistered customary law unions, in this case the court was able to use the concept of tacit universal partnership to try to reach an equitable solution as between the two competing claims. The court did not have to struggle with the acceptability of applying general law principles to customary law situations as per *Mashingaidze v Mashingaidze*,[114] nor did it have to perform legal gymnastics to find that the parties had lived a general law lifestyle and could therefore enjoy the benefit of tacit universal partnership, as per Chinhengo J in the *Chapendama*[115] case, or indeed consider the possibility of using the concept of unjust enrichment to achieve fairness between the parties as per Gillespie J in the *Jengwa* case.[116] There is some irony in the fact that, unlike other jurisdictions,[117] non-married people are able to access 'justice' more easily than those who are in customary law unions, the most popular form of marriage in Zimbabwe. This points to the need for a radical overhaul in the way that unregistered customary law unions are conceived of in Zimbabwe. A more equitable property sharing arrangement has to be formulated by the legislature. Although not without its difficulties, the South African approach[118] may be a good starting point for this reconceptualization of the property rights of people in unregistered customary law unions in Zimbabwe.

III CONCLUSION

The cases above show quite clearly the conflict and clashes which arise with the development of society in such a way that the social mores conflict with legal

---

[113] *Ibid* at 16, 17.

[114] 1995 (1) ZLR 219. Cf *Nyamwanza v Masiiwa* HH-95-2000 at 15.

[115] *Chapendama v Chapendama* 1998 (2) ZLR 18.

[116] *Jengwa v Jengwa* 1999 (2) ZLR 121.

[117] For example England and Wales, where parties have to prove that there was in existence a constructive or resulting trust or to rely on proprietary estoppel before they can be given a share of the property. The property rights of married people are guaranteed in the Matrimonial Causes Act 1973, as amended.

[118] Discussed earlier.

principles as mitigated by international human rights principles. It is to be hoped that principles of equity and fairness will form the basis of future judicial decision-making.